Communications in Computer and Information Science 887

Commenced Publication in 2007
Founding and Former Series Editors:
Alfredo Cuzzocrea, Xiaoyong Du, Orhun Kara, Ting Liu, Dominik Ślęzak,
and Xiaokang Yang

More information about this series at http://www.springer.com/series/7899

Javier Bajo et al. (Eds.)

Highlights of Practical Applications of Agents, Multi-Agent Systems, and Complexity

The PAAMS Collection

International Workshops of PAAMS 2018
Toledo, Spain, June 20–22, 2018
Proceedings

 Springer

Editors
see next page

ISSN 1865-0929   ISSN 1865-0937 (electronic)
Communications in Computer and Information Science
ISBN 978-3-319-94778-5   ISBN 978-3-319-94779-2   (eBook)
https://doi.org/10.1007/978-3-319-94779-2

Library of Congress Control Number: 2018947368

Printed on acid-free paper

This Springer imprint is published by the registered company Springer International Publishing AG
part of Springer Nature
The registered company address is: Gewerbestrasse 11, 6330 Cham, Switzerland

Volume Editors

Javier Bajo
Universidad Politécnica de Madrid
Madrid
Spain

Juan M. Corchado
Departamento de Informática y Automática
Universidad de Salamanca
Salamanca
Spain

Elena María Navarro Martínez
Departamento de Sistemas Informáticos
University of Castilla-La Mancha
Albacete
Spain

Eneko Osaba Icedo
TECNALIA
Derio, Bizkaia
Spain

Philippe Mathieu
Lille University of Science and Technology
Villeneuve d'Ascq
France

Patrycja Hoffa-Dąbrowska
Poznan University of Technology
Poznan
Poland

Elena del Val
Polytechnic University of Valencia
Valencia
Spain

Sylvain Giroux ⓘ
Faculté des Sciences
Université de Sherbrooke
Sherbrooke, QC
Canada

Antonio J. M. Castro
University of Porto
Porto
Portugal

Nayat Sánchez-Pi
Rio de Janeiro State University
Rio de Janeiro
Brazil

Vicente Julián
Polytechnic University of Valencia
Valencia
Spain

Ricardo Azambuja Silveira
Informatica e Estatistica
Universidade Federal de Santa Catar
Florianopolis, Santa Catarina
Brazil

Alberto Fernández
Universidad Rey Juan Carlos
Móstoles, Madrid
Spain

Rainer Unland
ICB
Universität Duisburg-Essen
Essen
Germany

Rubén Fuentes-Fernández
Facultad de Informática
Universidad Complutense de Madrid
Madrid
Spain

Preface

The PAAMS 18 Workshops complemented the regular program with new or emerging trends of particular interest connected to multi-agent systems. PAAMS, the International Conference on Practical Applications of Agents and Multi-Agent Systems, is an evolution of the International Workshop on Practical Applications of Agents and Multi-Agent Systems. PAAMS is an international yearly tribune for presenting, discussing, and disseminating the latest developments and the most important outcomes related to real-world applications. It provides a unique opportunity to bring multi-disciplinary experts, academics, and practitioners together to exchange their experience in the development of agents and multi-agent systems.

This volume presents the papers that were accepted in the workshops during the 2018 edition of PAAMS: Workshop on Agents and Multi-Agent Systems for AAL and e-Health; Workshop on Agent-Based Applications for Air Transport; Workshop on Agent-Based Artificial Markets Computational Economics; Workshop on Agent-Based Solutions for Manufacturing and Supply Chain; Workshop on MAS for Complex Networks and Social Computation; Workshop on Intelligent Systems and Context Information Fusion; Workshop on Multi-Agent-Based Applications for Energy Markets, Smart Grids, and Sustainable Energy Systems; Workshop on Multi-Agent System-Based Learning Environments; Workshop on Smart Cities and Intelligent Agents; Workshop on Swarm Intelligence and Swarm Robotics; Workshop on Multi-Agent Systems and Simulation. Each paper submitted to PAAMS workshops went through a stringent peer review by three members of the international committee of each workshop. From the 72 submissions received, 47 were selected for presentation at the conference.

We would like to thank all the contributing authors, the members of the Program Committee, the sponsors (IEEE SMC Spain, IBM, AEPIA, AFIA, APPIA, Universidad Politécnica de Madrid, Universidad de Castilla La Mancha – Escuela Superior de Ingeniería Informática, and CNRS), and the Organizing Committee for their hard and highly valuable work. Their work contributed to the success of the PAAMS 2018 event. Thanks for your help – PAAMS 2018 would not exist without your contribution.

This work was supported by the Spanish Ministry of Economy, Industry, and Competitiveness (I+D+i Project Ref. TIN2015-65515-C4-3-R - SURF: Self-organizing sensors and biometrics architecture for dynamic vehicle control in smart cities).

May 2018

Javier Bajo
Elena María Navarro Martínez

Organization

Workshops

W1 – Workshop on Agents and Multi-Agent Systems for AAL and e-Health
W2 – Workshop on Agent-Based Applications for Air Transport
W3 – Workshop on Agent-Based Artificial Markets Computational Economics
W4 – Workshop on Agent-Based Solutions for Manufacturing and Supply Chain
W5 – Workshop on MAS for Complex Networks and Social Computation
W6 – Workshop on Intelligent Systems and Context Information Fusion
W7 – Workshop on Multi-Agent-Based Applications for Energy Markets,
    Smart Grids, and Sustainable Energy Systems
W8 – Workshop on Multi-Agent System-Based Learning Environments
W9 – Workshop on Smart Cities and Intelligent Agents
W10 – Workshop on Swarm Intelligence and Swarm Robotics
W11 – Workshop on Multi-Agent Systems and Simulation

Workshop on Agents and Multi-Agent Systems for AAL and e-Health Committee

Program Committee Chairs

Kasper Hallenborg (Co-chair)	University of Southern Denmark, Denmark
Sylvain Giroux (Co-chair)	University of Sherbrooke, Canada

Program Committee

Juan M. Corchado	University of Salamanca, Spain
Javier Bajo	Technical University of Madrid, Spain
Juan F. De Paz	University of Salamanca, Spain
Sara Rodríguez	University of Salamanca, Spain
Valerie Camps	University Paul Sabatier of Toulouse, France
Cristian I. Pinzón	Technical University of Panama, Panama
Sigeru Omatu	Osaka Institute of Technology, Japan
Paulo Novais	University of Minho, Portugal
Luis F. Castillo	University of Caldas, Colombia
Florentino Fernandez	University of Vigo, Spain
Belén Pérez Lancho	University of Salamanca, Spain
Jesús García Herrero	University Carlos III of Madrid, Spain
Helena Lindgren	University of Umea, Sweden
Goretti Marreiros	Instituto Superior de Engenharia do Porto, Portugal
Gaetano Carmelo La Delfa	University of Catania, Italy
Tiancheng Li	Northwestern Polytechnical University, China

Workshop on Agent-Based Applications for Air Transport

Program Committee Chairs

Ana Paula Rocha   LIACC, University of Porto, Portugal
António Castro   University of Porto and TAP Portugal, Portugal

Program Committee

Alexei Sharpanskykh   Delft University of Technology, The Netherlands
Andrew Cook   University of Westminster, UK
Daniel Silva   University of Porto, Portugal
Elisabete Arsenio   LNEC, Portugal
Henk Blom   Delft University of Technology, The Netherlands
Jan Boril   University of Defence, Czech Republic
Jorge Silva   University of Beira Interior, Portugal
Lorenzo Castelli   University of Trieste, Italy
Rosaldo Rossetti   University of Porto, Portugal
Vladimir Gorodetsky   Russian Academy of Sciences, Russia

Workshop on Agent-Based Artificial Markets Computational Economics Committee

Program Committee Chair

Philippe Mathieu (Co-chair)   Universitè des Sciences et Technologies de Lille, France

Program Committee

Frederic Amblard   University of Toulouse 1, France
Javier Arroyo   University Complutense Madrid, Spain
Hugues Bersini   Université libre de Bruxelles, Belgium
Olivier Brandouy   University of Bordeaux IV, France
Florian Hauser   University of Innsbruck, Austria
Philippe Mathieu   University of Lille, France
Paolo Pellizzari   Ca'Foscari University of Venice, Italy
Ragupathy Venkatachalam   Goldsmiths, University of London, UK
Juan Pavòn   University Complutense Madrid, Spain
Marta Posada   University of Valladolid, Spain
Marco Raberto   University of Genoa, Italy
Roger Waldeck   Telecom Bretagne, France
Murat Yildizoglu   University of Bordeaux IV, France
Freiderike Wall   Alpen-Adria Universität, Austria

Workshop on Agent-Based Solutions for Manufacturing and Supply Chain Committee

Program Committee Chairs

Pawel Pawlewski	Poznan University of Technology, Poland
Patrycja Hoffa	Poznan University of Technology, Poland

Program Committee

Zbigniew J. Pasek	IMSE/University of Windsor, Canada
Paul-Eric Dossou	ICAM Vendee, France
Grzegorz Bocewicz	Koszalin University of Technology, Poland
Paweł Sitek	Kielce University of Technology, Poland
Izabela E. Nielsen	Aalborg University, Denmark
Peter Nielsen	Aalborg University, Denmark
Allen Greenwood	Mississippi State University, USA

Workshop on MAS for Complex Networks and Social Computation

Program Committee Chairs

Vicente Botti	Universitat Politècnica de València, Spain
Miguel Rebollo	Universitat Politècnica de València, Spain
Elena Del Val	Universitat Politècnica de València, Spain

Program Committee

Radosław Michalski	Wrocław University of Science and Technology, Poland
Victor Sanchez Anguix	Coventry University, UK
Jaume Jordán	Universidad Politécnica de Valencia, Spain
Carlos Carrascosa	Universidad Politécnica de Valencia, Spain
Markus Esch	Saarland University of Applied Sciences, Spain
Francisco Grimaldo	Universidad de Valencia, Spain
Alberto Palomares	Universidad Politécnica de Valencia, Spain
Angelo Costa	Universidade do Minho, Portugal
Emilia Lopez Iñesta	Universidad Católica de Valencia, Spain
Miguel Rebollo	Universidad Politécnica de Valencia, Spain

Workshop on Intelligent Systems and Context Information Fusion Committee

Program Committee Chairs

Nayat Sánchez Pi	Rio de Janeiro State University, Brazil
Luis Martí	Fluminense Federal University, Brazil

| José M. Molina | University Carlos III of Madrid, Spain |
| Javier Bajo | Technical University of Madrid, Spain |

Program Committee

José Manuel Molina	University Carlos III of Madrid, Spain
Juan M. Corchado	University of Salamanca, Spain
Nayat Sánchez Pi	Rio de Janeiro State University, Brazil
Luis Martí	Fluminense Federal University, Brazil
Eduardo Segredo	Universidad de La Laguna, Spain
Jesús García Herrero	University Carlos III of Madrid, Spain
Gabriel Villarrubia	University of Salamanca, Spain
Javier Bajo	Technical University of Madrid, Spain
Ana Cristina Bicharra García	Rio de Janeiro Federal University, Brazil
Rosa Maria E. M. da Costa	Rio de Janeiro State University, Brazil
Vera Maria B. Werneck	Rio de Janeiro State University, Brazil
James Llinas	State University of New York at Buffalo, USA
Luiz Satoru Ochi	Fluminense Federal University, Brazil

Workshop on Multi-Agent-Based Applications for Energy Markets, Smart Grids and Sustainable Energy Systems Committee

Program Committee Chairs

Fernando Lopes	LNEG National Research Institute, Portugal
Roozbeh Morsali	Swinburne university - Melbourne, Australia
Rainer Unland	University of Duisburg-Essen and Poznan University of Economics and Business, Germany/Poland

Program Committee

Andreas Symeonidis	University of Thessaloniki, Greece
Anke Weidlich	Albert-Ludwigs-Universität Freiburg, Germany
Bo Nørregaard Jørgensen	Mærsk Mc-Kinney Møller Instituttet, Denmark
Christian Derksen	Universität Duisburg-Essen, Germany
Costin Badica	University of Craiova, Craiova, Romania
David Sislak	Gerstner Laboratory, Czech Republic
Edmund Widl	Austrian Institute of Technology, Austria
Frank Allgöwer	Universität Stuttgart, Germany
Gauthier Picard	ENS Mines Saint-Etienne, France
Georg Frey	Universität des Saarlandes, Germany
Giancarlo Fortino	Università della Calabria, Italy
Hanno Hildmann	NEC Germany, Germany
Hugo Algarvio	LNEG National Research Institute and IST, Portugal
Hugo Morais	EDF – Electricité de France, France
Ingo J. Timm	University of Trier, Germany
Jan Ole Berndt	University of Trier, Germany

Jan Sudeikat	Hamburg Energie GmbH, Germany
Jan Treur	Vrije Universiteit Amsterdam, The Netherlands
Lars Braubach	University of Hamburg, Germany
Lars Mönch	Fernuniversität Hagen, Germany
Marcin Paprzycki	Polish Academy of Sciences, Poland
Maria Ganzha	Warsaw Technical University, Poland
Matthias Klusch	DFKI, Germany
Miguel Ángel López Carmona	University of Alcalá de Henares, Spain
Nir Oren	University of Aberdeen, UK
Olivier Boissier	École Nationale Supérieure des Mines de Saint-Étienne, France
Paolo Petta	Austrian Research Institute for Artificial Intelligence, Austria
Paulo Leitão	Polytechnic Institute of Bragança, Portugal
Paulo Novais	Universidade do Minho, Portugal
René Schumann	University of Applied Sciences, Switzerland
Sascha Ossowski	Universidad Rey Juan Carlos, Spain
Stamatis Karnouskos	SAP, Germany
Steven Guan	Xian Jiatong-Liverpool University, China
Tiago Pinto	Polytechnic Institute of Porto, Portugal
Wolfgang Ketter	Rotterdam School of Management, The Netherlands

Workshop on Multi-Agent System-Based Learning Environments

Program Committee Chairs

Ricardo Azambuja Silveira	Universidade Federal de Santa Catarina, Brazil
Rosa Vicari	Universidade Federal do Rio Grande do Sul – UFRGS, Brazil
Néstor Darío Duque Méndez	Universidad Nacional de Colombia, Colombia

Program Committee

Néstor Darío Duque Méndez	Universidad Nacional de Colombia, Colombia
Ricardo Silveira	UFSC, Brazil
Ana Belén Gil González	University of Salamanca, Spain
Jose Cascalho	Universidade dos Azores, Portugal
Rosa Vicari	UFRGS, Brazil
Demetrio Arturo Ovalle Carranza	Universidad Nacional de Colombia – Sede Medellín, Colombia
Marta Rosecler Bez	UFRGS, Brazil
Ramon Fabregat	Universitat de Girona, Spain
Silvia Margarita Baldiris Navarro	Universitat de Girona, Spain

Tiago Primo	Samsung Research Institute
Martin Llamas-Nistal	University of Vigo, Spain
Fernando De La Prieta	University of Salamanca, Spain
María N. Moreno García	University of Salamanca, Spain
Patricia Jaques	UNISINOS, Brazil
Júlia M. C. Silva	Instituto Federal do Rio Grande do Sul, Brazil
Rosangela Bez	SAMSUNG Research Institute
Fernando Koch	SAMSUNG Research Institute
Vicente Julian Inglada	Universidad Politecnica de Valencia, Spain
Fernando Moreira	Universidad PortoCalense, Portugal
Juan Pavón	Universidad Complutense Madrid, Spain
Angela Cristina Carrillo Ramos	Universidad Javeriana, Colombia

Workshop on Smart Cities and Intelligent Agents Committee

Program Committee Chairs

Vicente Julián	Universitat Politècnica de València, Spain
Adriana Giret	Universitat Politècnica de València, Spain
Juan Manuel Corchado	Universidad de Salamanca, Spain
Alberto Fernández	Universidad Rey Juan Carlos, Spain
Holger Billhardt	Universidad Rey Juan Carlos, Spain
Javier Bajo	Universidad Politécnica de Madrid

Program Committee

Adriana Giret	Universitat Politècnica de València, Spain
Alberto Fernandez	Rey Juan Carlos University, Spain
Angelo Costa	University of Minho, Portugal
Carlos A. Iglesias	Universidad Politécnica de Madrid, Spain
Carlos Carrascosa	GTI-IA DSIC Universidad Politecnica de Valencia, Spain
Gabriel Villarrubia	University of Salamanca, Spain
Holger Billhardt	Rey Juan Carlos University, Spain
Javier Bajo	Universidad Politécnica de Madrid, Spain
Javier Palanca	Universitat Politècnica de València, Spain
José Antonio Castellanos	University of Salamanca, Spain
Juan Francisco De Paz	University of Salamanca, Spain
Juan Manuel Corchado	University of Salamanca, Spain
María Navarro	University of Salamanca, Spain
Marin Lujak	IMT Lille Douai, France
Pablo Chamoso	University of Salamanca, Spain
Ramon Hermoso	University of Zaragoza, Spain
Roberto Centeno	Universidad Nacional de Educacion a Distancia, Spain

Sara Rodríguez	University of Salamanca, Spain
Sascha Ossowski	University Rey Juan Carlos, Spain
Vicente Julian	Universitat Politècnica de València, Spain

Workshop on Swarm Intelligence and Swarm Robotics

Workshop on Smart Cities and Intelligent Agents Committee

Program Committee Chairs

Eneko Osaba	TECNALIA, Zamudio, Spain
Javier Del Ser	University of the Basque Country, Spain
Andres Iglesias	Toho University, Funabashi, Japan and University of Cantabria, Spain
Xin-She Yang	School of Science and Technology, UK

Program Committee

Eneko Osaba	TECNALIA, Zamudio, Spain
Javier Del Ser	University of the Basque Country, Spain
Andres Iglesias	Toho University, Funabashi, Japan and University of Cantabria, Spain
Xin-She Yang	School of Science and Technology, UK

Workshop on Multi-Agent Systems and Simulation

Program Committee Chairs

Rubén Fuentes-Fernández	Universidad Complutense de Madrid, Spain
Frédéric Migeon	Institut de Recherche en Informatique de Toulouse, France
Valeria Seidita	Università degli Studi di Palermo, Italy

Program Committee

Luis Antunes	Universidade de Lisboa, Portugal
Ahmad Taher Azar	Benha University, Egypt
Carole Bernon	Université Paul Sabatier, France
Pietro Cipresso	I.R.C.C.S. Istituto Auxologico Italiano, Italy
Paul Davidsson	Malmö University, Sweden
Alfredo Garro	University of Calabria, Italy
Antonio Guerrieri	University of Calabria, Italy
Ambra Molesini	Università di Bologna, Italy
Paolo Petta	OFAI, Austria
Patrizia Ribino	ICAR-CNR, Italy
Claudio Savaglio	Università della Calabria, Italy
Giuseppe Vizzari	Università di Milano Bicocca, Italy
Kashif Zia	Sohar University, Oman

Organizing Committee

Javier Bajo	Universidad Politécnica de Madrid, Spain
Antonio Fernández Caballero	Universidad de Castilla La Mancha, Spain
Elena Navarro	Universidad de Castilla La Mancha, Spain
Pascual González	Universidad de Castilla La Mancha, Spain
Fernando De la Prieta	Universidad de Salamanca, Spain

PAAMS 2018 Sponsors

Contents

PAAMS Workshop ISCIF

PAAMS Workshop MASGES

PAAMS Workshop SIRS

PAAMS Workshop A-HEALTH

Conceptual Definition of a Platform for the Monitoring of the Subjects with Nephrolithiasis Based on the Energy Expenditure and the Activities of Daily Living Performed

Ivan Miguel Pires[1,2,3(✉)], Tânia Valente[2], Nuno Pombo[1,3,4], and Nuno M. Garcia[1,3,4]

[1] Instituto de Telecomunicações, Universidade da Beira Interior, Covilhã, Portugal
impires@it.ubi.pt, {ngpombo,ngarcia}@di.ubi.pt
[2] Altranportugal, Lisbon, Portugal
tania.ss.valente@gmail.com
[3] ALLab - Assisted Living Computing and Telecommunications Laboratory,
Computing Science Department, Universidade da Beira Interior, Covilhã, Portugal
[4] Universidade Lusófona de Humanidades e Tecnologias, Lisbon, Portugal

Abstract. Nephrolithiasis disease is commonly related with the low activity performance, *i.e.*, the regular performance of physical activity can reduce the risk of kidney stones. Sensors available in off-the-shelf mobile devices may handle the control and recognition of the activities performed, including the energy expenditure and their identification. This paper identifies the common values that should be measured during the treatment of this disease, including water consumption (with regular registration), daily calories intake (defined by a professional) and urinary pH (measured with test strips), which may be combined with the measurement of the energy expenditure and the activities performed. As the treatment and prevention of the Nephrolithiasis disease includes the performance of hard physical activity and the regular trip to the toilet, where this identification provides a control of the evolution of the treatment. The combination of these concepts and the use of the technology may increase the control and speed of the treatment.

Keywords: Activities of daily living · Nephrolithiasis · Water consumption
Calories · Accelerometer · Gyroscope · Magnetometer · Machine learning

1 Introduction

One of the most common problems in the urology clinical area is the Nephrolithiasis disease, popularly known as kidney stones. Kidney stones affect up to 5% of the world population and the lifetime risk of passing a kidney stone is about 8–10% [1]. Increased incidence of kidney stones in the industrialized countries is associated with improved standards of living and also with the race and region of residence [2]. A kidney stone is caused by a disruption in the balance between solubility and precipitation of salts in the kidneys and the urinary tract. A stone forms when urine is in a "supersaturated" state

© Springer International Publishing AG, part of Springer Nature 2018
J. Bajo et al. (Eds.): PAAMS 2018 Workshops, CCIS 887, pp. 3–11, 2018.
https://doi.org/10.1007/978-3-319-94779-2_1

with insoluble crystal-forming substances composed of calcium (Ca), calcium oxalate (CaOx), calcium phosphate (CaP) and uric acid, due to the dehydration or genetic predisposition to over-excrete these ions in the urine [3].

There are several reasons for the occurrence of the Nephrolithiasis disease, including the urine volume being less than 2 L per day, increasing the saturation of calcium oxalate [4] and contributing to the formation of uric acid stones in patients with intestinal disorders [5]. Acid uric stones tend to form in patients with hyperuricosuria and gout diseases. About 15–20% of patients with uric acid stones have a history of gout [6]. With an urinary pH of less than 5.5, uric acid is poorly soluble, but solubility increases with a pH greater than 6.5 [7].

Moderate physical exercise decreases the urinary pH from 6.35 to 5.7 and the total renal excretion of stone forming ions decreases, probably due to extracellular volume contraction (from sweating) and enhanced renal tubular reabsorption [8]. Without an increased fluid intake to compensate for the excessive sweating, it may cause the crystallization of uric acid and calcium oxalate in urine and may enhance the risk of the formation of renal stones composed of these salts [7]. The propensity for spontaneous precipitation of calcium oxalate was higher after exercise, as less soluble oxalate was required to elicit nucleation of calcium oxalate [9].

Mobile devices can handle the easy monitoring and measurement of several important parameters for the treatment of the Nephrolithiasis disease, allowing the registration of several parameters measured by other devices (*e.g.*, measurement of the urinary pH) and parameters inserted by the user, combining them with the recognition of Activities of Daily Living (ADL) [10] and the measurement of the energy expenditure [11–13]. Previous studies have been performed in this field, including the development of a mobile application for the registration of some parameters [14], recognition of ADL using the sensors available in the off-the-shelf mobile devices, *e.g.,* accelerometer, gyroscope, magnetometer, microphone and Global Positioning System (GPS) receiver [15–17], and the measurement of the energy expenditure using the accelerometer sensor [11–13]. The combination of these measurements may increase the speed of the treatment of the Nephrolithiasis disease, because the practice of physical exercise reduces the risk of this disease [18].

The kidney has an important metabolic function and performs a number of oxygen-dependent activities [19]. In spite of having a low physical activity level, the mean estimated daily energy expenditure normalized per body weight is 30.3 ± 4.50 kcal/kg/day. This value is close to the 30–35 kcal/kg/day, previously recommended for patients with Nephrolithiasis disease [20].

There are several studies focused on the measurement of the energy expenditure using the accelerometer sensor [21–24], but we focused our study in the implementation of the method previously proposed and implemented in [11–13], which reports that the energy expenditure per hour is 124.6 kcal for the walking activity, and 149.7 kcal for the running activity.

Based on previous studies available in the literature [18], the performance of intensive physical activity and the low consumption of calories reduces the risk of this disease. When the person does not have the disease, a practice of hard exercise (*e.g.,* walking, running and walking on stairs) should be evaluated, and in other case, the evaluation of drinking and the urinating (or going to the toilet) activities are important for the treatment of this disease. The automatic recognition of the ADL is important for the monitoring of the Nephrolithiasis, the proposed solution will implement a method with accelerometer, magnetometer, gyroscope, GPS receiver and/or microphone, but our purpose will include the use of Artificial Neural networks (ANN), implemented in [25–28] those reported reliable accuracies, as a basis for this research with the inclusion of new activities.

Nevertheless, there are no systems that help in the control of all parameters with automatic measurements in the treatment of this disease. Thus, the main focus of this study consists in the proposal of a multi-sensor mobile system named UrolFit, that may be used to easily control the treatment of the Nephrolithiasis disease, including the daily registration of the values of urinary pH and water consumption, the automatic measurement of the daily energy expenditure with the accelerometer sensors, and the measurement of the ADL using all sensors available in the mobile device, mapping the lifestyle of the subject, based on the concept of a personal digital life coach [29].

This paragraph concludes the introductory section. Section 2 presents the possible methods for each module of the proposed system. The expected results are presented in Sect. 3. Finally, Sect. 4 presents the conclusions of this study.

2 Methods

2.1 Study Design and Participants

Sensors available in off-the-shelf mobile devices can enable the acquisition of several physical and physiological parameters for different measurements, including the amount of calories spent (with the accelerometer sensor), the ADL performed (with the accelerometer, gyroscope, magnetometer, GPS receiver and microphone), the surrounding environment (with microphone) and the geographic location (with GPS receiver). The recognition and control of these parameters is useful for the treatment of the Nephrolithiasis disease. However, it needs the measurement of other parameters, including the urinary pH and water consumption. The solution that is going to be created should be adapted and tested by individuals with different ages and lifestyles for the control of the treatment.

2.2 Non-automatic Measured Parameters Related to the Nephrolithiasis Disease

Nephrolithiasis disease requires the management and registration of the values on a daily basis. These values include the monitoring of daily water consumption and the urinary pH, which should be registered in a mobile application for further combination with the values obtained with the automatic measurement of energy expenditure and recognition of the ADL performed.

Measurement of Urinary pH. A metabolic evaluation starts with a 24-h urinary pH profile, because pH is used to measure urine acidity [8]. A lower urinary pH level increases the risk of the presence of different types of kidney stones, promoting the formation of calcium oxalate (CaOx) and uric acid stones (UA) [8]. The alkalization of the urine is important for the treatment of uric acid stones [8].

Uralyt-U is used in the treatment of acid uric stones, improving the solubility of UA. This medicine prevents the formation of uric acid crystals (stones) and also re-dissolves any crystals that are already present in the urine. The administration method of Uralyt-U includes granules (1 g/dose), that should be taken, 3 times a day and dissolved in a glass of water and then drunk. Uralyt-U has a special indicator paper which consists of 100 yellow paper strips and a color scale within the range of 5.6 to 8. However, Uralyt-U action is based on the fact that it can stabilize the urinary pH within the correct pH range of 6.2 to 6.8.

In the main meals (every morning, and again at midday and in the evening), before taking each dose, the patient should torn off and dip one paper strip into the fresh urine for a few seconds. The color of the strip will alter and should then at once be compared with the color scale (see Fig. 1). After matching the paper strip with the color scale, the patient should insert the value in the mobile application, but, currently, without the mobile application, the user should register their urinary pH level in a traditional table (see Fig. 2).

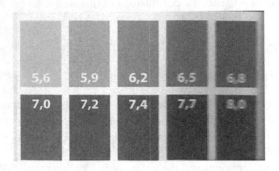

Fig. 1. Example of a Uralyt-U color scale for the measurement of the urinary pH

Water Consumption. The increasing water intake is important to ensure an urinary volume of approximately 2.5 L per day was associated with the reduced urinary supersaturation with CaOx and a significant reduction in stone recurrence [30]. The drink intake as fruit juice is very effective in the reduction of the urinary CaOx saturation and the increasing of urinary citrate excretion [31]. The volume of water consumed should be inserted in the mobile application.

Feeding. An alkaline ash diet is high in citrate, mostly from fruits and vegetables, that can increase urinary pH and citrate excretion [4, 32]. Citrate consumption (through citrate-containing foods, potassium or sodium salt drugs) causes an increase in urinary pH, which results in an increased citrate excretion [4, 32]. A diet rich in animal protein is associated with high urinary excretion of uric acid and a low urinary pH [4, 32]. Uric acid solubility decreases a lot at an urinary pH lower than 5.5, leading to uric acid crystal formation [4, 32]. The calories of the food consumed should be inserted in the mobile application.

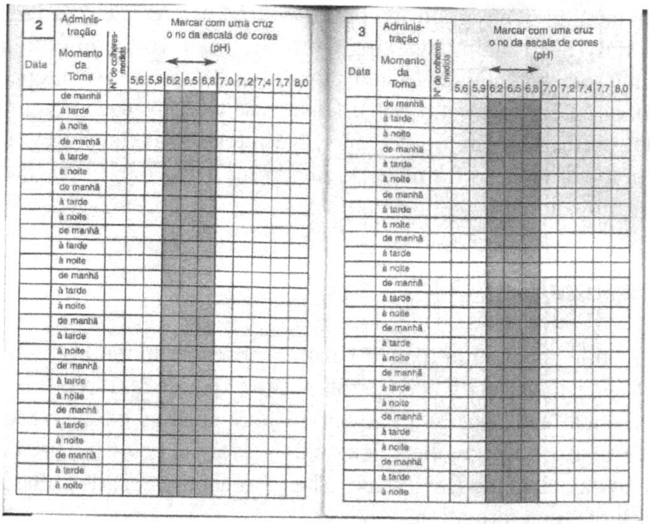

Fig. 2. Example of a Uralyt-U traditional table for the registration of the urinary pH

2.3　Measurement of the Energy Expenditure

The measurement of the energy expenditure can be performed with the accelerometer data as presented in several studies [33–36], but for the development of our study, we will use the model presented in Eq. 1, which was explained in [11–13], for the measurement of the daily energy expenditure (in calories) in order to improve the treatment of the Nephrolithiasis disease.

$$EE\left(\frac{kcal}{s}\right) = \frac{4,83MV + 122,02}{3600}.$$ (1)

where EE is the energy expenditure and MV is the average of the magnitude of vector of the accelerometer data.

　　Based on the accelerometer counts, the model presented in the Eq. 1 is used for the measurement of the energy expenditure. The measurement of the energy expenditure is commonly performed in a time interval, but as the presented model was created for the measurement of energy expenditure in a second, the energy expenditure measured is presented in real time. Based on this model, the amount of energy expenditure is 149.7 kcal/h for running activity, and 124.6 kcal/h for walking activity.

2.4　Recognition of the Activities of Daily Living and Environments

The recognition of ADL and their environments have been studied in the literature [10–15] using the sensors available in the off-the-shelf mobile devices (*e.g.*, accelerometer, magnetometer, gyroscope, microphone and GPS receiver) with data fusion and artificial intelligence methods.

Our implementation is based on the previous studies presented in [25–28], recognizing several ADL (*i.e.,* running, walking, going upstairs, going downstairs, standing, sleeping, driving and watching TV) and environments (*i.e.,* bar, kitchen, bedroom, library, classroom, street, gym and hall). However, with the Deep Neural Networks (DNN) methods used in the previous works, we intend to include new activities and environments in the developed framework, including bathroom, toilet, taking medication, drinking, eating, and others.

3   Expected Results

The proposed mobile application named Urolfit, presented in the Fig. 3, may help the patients to customize their health and personal data experience. It requires the registration of some physical and physiological parameters, such as the age, the gender, the daily goal of energy expenditure, the height and the weight, being the height and weight very important to calculate the BMI value. The increasing the BMI value is associated with an high risk of stone formation.

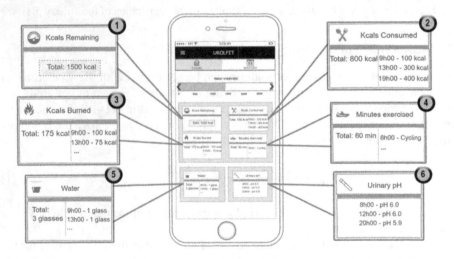

Fig. 3. Mockup of the mobile application proposed

Urolfit will help to set the user daily budget and goals for kidney stones treatment including exercise, hydration and calorie consumption. The features that will be included in the mobile application includes the amount of calories remaining (fig. 3(1)), the amount of calories consumed (fig. 3(2)), the amount of calories burned (fig. 3(3)), the activities performed (fig. 3(4)), the volume of water consumed (fig. 3(5)), and the levels of urinary pH measured (fig. 3(6)).

Firstly, the amount of calories remaining is used to present the difference between the calories consumed and the calories burned.

Secondly, the calories consumed is used to allow the control of the user calorie intake with the registration of the calories consumed with the feeding.

Thirdly, the calories burned will use the automatic method with the accelerometer sensor in order to measure the amount of calories burned during the daily workout.

Fourthly, the activities performed and environments frequented will be presented in order to create a map of the user daily lifestyle.

Fifthly, the user must set the daily water intake goal and log how much he is drinking, and it keeps track. Daily intake tracker and reminder is based on gender, BMI and activity level.

Finally, the measurement of the urinary pH is important to measure, record and calculate the average urinary pH level on a daily, weekly and monthly basis.

4 Conclusions

With the recent technological advancements and the increasing use of mobile devices, there are several ways that it helps to support the user everyday health. The treatment of kidney stones includes the history and a thorough review of diet, water consumption and lifestyle. Urolfit will bring something different to the traditional tables, delivering a well-balanced snapshot of a daily health routine and kidney stones treatment. UrolFit also keeps the patient on track by making it simple, not only to log his drinks and urinary pH measurements, but also to check the progress toward his goal. On the other hand, the tracking of the calories (consumed and burned) and activities performed will help user to meet his treatment and prevention goals related to the Nephrolithiasis disease. By putting together the concept of calorie balance, Urolfit provides an overview of the user overall daily calories consumed and burned, helping the users to achieve a healthier lifestyle. The proposed mobile application will also help in the creation of a personalized daily plan.

Acknowledgements. This work was supported by FCT project **UID/EEA/50008/2013** (*Este trabalho foi suportado pelo projecto FCT UID/EEA/50008/2013*).

The authors would also like to acknowledge the contribution of the COST Action IC1303 – AAPELE – Architectures, Algorithms and Protocols for Enhanced Living Environments.

References

1. Doe, F., Brenner, B.: Nephrolithiasis. In: Harrison's Principles of Internal Medicine, 10th edn., vol. 2, pp. 1672–1678. McGraw-Hill International Book Co., New York (1983)
2. Stamatelou, K.K., et al.: Time trends in reported prevalence of kidney stones in the United States: 1976–1994. Kidney Int. **63**(5), 1817–1823 (2003)
3. Han, H., et al.: Nutritional management of kidney stones (nephrolithiasis). Clin. Nutr. Res. **4**(3), 137–152 (2015)
4. Lemann, J., et al.: Urinary oxalate excretion increases with body size and decreases with increasing dietary calcium intake among healthy adults. Kidney Int. **49**(1), 200–208 (1996)
5. Worcester, E.M.: Stones from bowel disease. Endocrinol. Metab. Clin. North Am. **31**(4), 979–999 (2002)

6. Beara-Lasic, L., Pillinger, M.H., Goldfarb, D.S.: Advances in the management of gout: critical appraisal of febuxostat in the control of hyperuricemia. Int. J. Nephrol. Renovascular Dis. **3**, 1 (2010)
7. Taylor, E.N., Stampfer, M.J., Curhan, G.C.: Dietary factors and the risk of incident kidney stones in men: new insights after 14 years of follow-up. J. Am. Soc. Nephrol. **15**(12), 3225–3232 (2004)
8. Anderson, R.A.: A complementary approach to urolithiasis prevention. World J. Urol. **20**(5), 294–301 (2002)
9. Sakhaee, K., et al.: Assessment of the pathogenetic role of physical exercise in renal stone formation. J. Clin. Endocrinol. Metabol. **65**(5), 974–979 (1987)
10. Foti, D., Koketsu, J.S.: Activities of daily living. In: Pedretti's Occupational Therapy: Practical Skills for Physical Dysfunction, vol. 7, pp. 157–232 (2013)
11. Felizardo, V.D.S.: Validação do acelerómetro xyzPlux para estimação do Gasto Energético com aquisição de diversos parâmetros fisiológicos. In: Departamento de Electromecânica. Universidade da Beira Interior, Covilhã (2010)
12. Felizardo, V., et al.: Acquisition of multiple physiological parameters during physical exercise. Int. J. E-Health Med. Commun. **2**(4), 37–49 (2011)
13. Pires, I.M.S.: Aplicação móvel e plataforma Web para suporte à estimação do gasto energético em atividade física, in Computer Science Department. University of Beira Interior, Covilhã (2012)
14. dos Santos Valente, T.S.: Aplicação móvel para controlo de cálculos renais e consumo de água (2017)
15. Pires, I., et al.: From data acquisition to data fusion: a comprehensive review and a roadmap for the identification of activities of daily living using mobile devices. Sensors **16**(2), 184 (2016)
16. Pires, I.M., Garcia, N.M., Flórez-Revuelta, F.: Multi-sensor data fusion techniques for the identification of activities of daily living using mobile devices. In: Proceedings of the ECMLPKDD 2015 Doctoral Consortium, European Conference on Machine Learning and Principles and Practice of Knowledge Discovery in Databases, Porto, Portugal (2015)
17. Pires, I.M., Garcia, Nuno M., Pombo, N., Flórez-Revuelta, F.: Identification of activities of daily living using sensors available in off-the-shelf mobile devices: research and hypothesis. Ambient Intelligence-Software and Applications – 7th International Symposium on Ambient Intelligence (ISAmI 2016). AISC, vol. 476, pp. 121–130. Springer, Cham (2016). https://doi.org/10.1007/978-3-319-40114-0_14
18. Ferraro, P.M., et al.: Physical activity, energy intake and the risk of incident kidney stones. J. Urol. **193**(3), 864–868 (2015)
19. Silva, P.: Renal fuel utilization, energy requirements, and function. Kidney Int. Suppl. **22**, S9 (1987)
20. Avesani, C.M., et al.: Decreased resting energy expenditure in non-dialysed chronic kidney disease patients. Nephrol. Dial. Transplant. **19**(12), 3091–3097 (2004)
21. Nilsson, A., et al.: Comparison of equations for predicting energy expenditure from accelerometer counts in children. Scand. J. Med. Sci. Sports **18**(5), 643–650 (2008)
22. Garatachea, N., Luque, G.T., Gallego, J.G.: Physical activity and energy expenditure measurements using accelerometers in older adults. Nutr. Hosp. **25**(2), 224–230 (2010)
23. Neville, J., et al.: Accelerometers: an underutilized resource in sports monitoring. In: 2010 Sixth International Conference on Intelligent Sensors, Sensor Networks and Information Processing (ISSNIP). IEEE, Brisbane (2010)

24. Machado-Rodrigues, A.M., et al.: Agreement in activity energy expenditure assessed by accelerometer and self-report in adolescents: variation by sex, age, and weight status. J. Sports Sci. **29**(14), 1503–1514 (2011)
25. Pires, I.M., et al.: User environment detection with acoustic sensors embedded on mobile devices for the recognition of activities of daily living (2017, in Review). arXiv:1711.00124
26. Pires, I.M., et al.: A multiple source framework for the identification of activities of daily living based on mobile device data (2017, in Review). arXiv:1711.00104
27. Pires, I.M., et al.: Pattern recognition techniques for the identification of activities of daily living using mobile device accelerometer (2017, in Review). arXiv:1711.00096
28. Pires, I.M., et al.: Data fusion on motion and magnetic sensors embedded on mobile devices for the identification of activities of daily living (2017, in Review). http://engrxiv.org/x4r5z
29. Garcia, N.M.: A roadmap to the design of a personal digital life coach. In: Loshkovska, S., Koceski, S. (eds.) ICT Innovations 2015. AISC, vol. 399, pp. 21–27. Springer, Cham (2016). https://doi.org/10.1007/978-3-319-25733-4_3
30. Borghi, L., et al.: Urinary volume, water and recurrences in idiopathic calcium nephrolithiasis: a 5-year randomized prospective study. J. Urol. **155**(3), 839–843 (1996)
31. Peters, B.: Beverage use and risk for kidney stones in women. Ann. Emerg. Med. **32**(3), 395 (1998)
32. Asplin, J.R.: Evaluation of the kidney stone patient. In: Seminars in Nephrology. Elsevier (2008)
33. Badawi, H., Eid, M., El Saddik, A.: Diet advisory system for children using biofeedback sensor. In: 2012 IEEE International Symposium on Medical Measurements and Applications Proceedings (MeMeA). IEEE (2012)
34. Carneiro, S., et al.: Accelerometer-based methods for energy expenditure using the smartphone. In: 2015 IEEE International Symposium on Medical Measurements and Applications (MeMeA). IEEE (2015)
35. Lee, M.-W., et al.: A single tri-axial accelerometer-based real-time personal life log system capable of activity classification and exercise information generation. In: 2010 Annual International Conference of the IEEE Engineering in Medicine and Biology Society (EMBC). IEEE (2010)
36. Ryu, N., Kawahawa, Y., Asami, T.: A calorie count application for a mobile phone based on METS value. In: 2008 5th Annual IEEE Communications Society Conference on Sensor, Mesh and Ad Hoc Communications and Networks (2008)

Scheduling of Home Health Care Services Based on Multi-agent Systems

Filipe Alves[1]([✉]), Ana I. Pereira[1,2], José Barbosa[1], and Paulo Leitão[1]

[1] Research Centre in Digitalization and Intelligent Robotics (CeDRI),
Instituto Politécnico de Bragança, Campus de Santa Apolónia,
5300-253 Bragança, Portugal
{filipealves,apereira,jbarbosa,pleitao}@ipb.pt
[2] Algoritmi R&D Centre, University of Minho, Braga, Portugal

Abstract. Home Health Care (HHC) services are growing worldwide and, usually, the home care visits are manually planned, being a time and effort consuming task that leads to a non optimized solution. The use of some optimization techniques can significantly improve the quality of the scheduling solutions, but lacks the achievement of solutions that face the fast reaction to condition changes. In such stochastic and very volatile environments, the fast re-scheduling is crucial to maintain the system in operation. Taking advantage of the inherent distributed and intelligent characteristics of Multi-agent Systems (MAS), this paper introduces a methodology that combines the optimization features provided by centralized scheduling algorithms, e.g. genetic algorithms, with the responsiveness features provided by MAS solutions. The proposed approach was codified in Matlab and NetLogo and applied to a real-world HHC case study. The experimental results showed a significant improvement in the quality of scheduling solutions, as well as in the responsiveness to achieve those solutions.

Keywords: Multi-agent systems · Genetic algorithm
Home Health Care · Optimization

1 Introduction

Over the last decade, Home Health Care (HHC) services have significantly increased [4,10], namely in Portugal. The organization of HHC involves two main issues: medical decisions and organizational decisions. This paper considers the second issue and, more precisely, operational management problems related to human and material resources scheduling and optimization (considering, among others, vehicles and doctors). The scheduling and routing problems in this area are generally performed manually, are complex procedures, essentially because of its mathematical modelling complexity, and most importantly, unexpected events can occur resulting in uncertainty and disruptions requiring

J. Bajo et al. (Eds.): PAAMS 2018 Workshops, CCIS 887, pp. 12–23, 2018.
https://doi.org/10.1007/978-3-319-94779-2_2

real-time actions [15]. Typically, traffic jams, road accidents, and weather conditions should be taken into account when designing a real-world routing problem. In this context, HHC managers need decision support systems capable of solving large real-world situations in reasonable time and providing good solutions in a dynamic environment with numerous time constraints [12].

Multi-agent systems (MAS) [14] offers an alternative way to design and control systems, differing from the conventional approaches due to their inherent capabilities to adapt to emergence or disruptions without external intervention. MAS allow the decentralization of control over distributed structures, providing modularity, robustness and autonomy in systems [11] such as Health Care. On the other hand, Agent-Based Modelling (ABM) platforms are tools that allow the modelling, simulation or interactions of complex adaptive systems by using agents, providing a way to output the simulation results in a graphical manner according to several designed scenarios. These tools provide an easy and powerful simulation capability which enables a fast testing by using MAS [2]. In this context, systems, like HHC, can be viewed as a network of agents, e.g. vehicles or patients, with identifiable attributes, dynamic behaviour, sophistication in autonomous decision-making and alternatives to modify behavioural rules.

This paper addresses the routing problem in HHC, characterized by its dynamic context with uncertainties and random events. The proposed approach combines the optimization features provided by genetic algorithms, with the responsiveness features provided by MAS solutions. The agent-based model was implemented in the NetLogo tool that interact with the centralized genetic algorithm scheduling application codified in Matlab.

The rest of the paper is organized as follows: Sect. 2 describes the problem to be addressed and introduces the system architecture that combines MAS and genetic algorithms to improve the scheduling solutions for HHC services. Section 3 presents the problem formulation in MatLab and a brief description of the genetic algorithm. Section 4 describes the agent-based model, developed in NetLogo, for the dynamic decentralized solutions. Section 5 discusses the simulation results. Finally, Sect. 6 rounds up the paper with the conclusions and points out the future work.

2   Problem Description and System Architecture

This paper considers the problem of assigning tasks outside the Health Care Center of Bragança (HUB), Portugal, in particularly, to find the schedule for home care visits for a certain day. The objective is to minimize the travel time spent by the vehicles during to perform all home visits. In this situation is not considered situations of external disruptions.

More concretely, it was considered the following assumptions, for the patients and vehicles:

– Each patient has his own location, i.e., his home.
– The time matrix of travel between all the localities is known in advance.

- The number of patients who need home care services, and assigned to a working day, is known in advance.
- The list and duration of the treatments are known for each patient.
- Caregivers that perform home care visits are known in advance.
- Each caregiver obtains a list of patients and a planned route from the HHC.
- All trips begin and end up at the Health Care Centre.

In this context, the system architecture for the HHC scheduling system integrates off-line and on-line modules, presented in Fig. 1, which can deal sequentially with the two sub-processes: optimized planning using genetic algorithms and real-time responsiveness solutions using MAS. The two modules are able to exchange information, balancing the decision-making according to the needs.

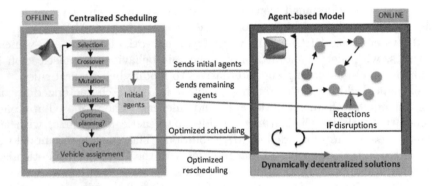

Fig. 1. Developed system architecture.

The left module performs the optimized scheduling for the vehicles routes, running off-line, for a given situation under study. The right module concerns to the dynamic re-scheduling, is response to disruptions or condition changes, e.g. a broken vehicle. In this module, the re-scheduling is obtained by the interaction of individual entities, each one reasoning about its own schedule.

3   Optimization of Centralized Scheduling

This section describes the approach embedded in the off-line module to perform the optimized scheduling.

3.1   Problem Formulation in MatLab

Taking into account all the information, it was considered the follow parameters:

- NP represents the total number of patients that need of home care visits.
- NC is the total number of vehicles used for home care visits in a given day.

Consider the variable $(np; nc) = (np_1, ..., np_{NP}; nc_1, ..., nc_{NP})$, where the patient np_i will be visited by the vehicle nc_i, for $i = 1, ..., NP$, and $np \in \{1, \cdots, NP\}^{NP}$ and $nc \in \{1, \cdots, NC\}^{NP}$.

Then, for a given $(np; nc)$ it is possible to define the route schedule and also the total time needed by each vehicle to finish its work defined in $tt(np; nc)$. So, the objective function is defined as

$$f(np; nc) = \max tt(np; nc) \tag{1}$$

which represents the maximum time spent by the vehicles to perform all visits and treatments by the nurses, including the returning journey to the Health Center. Then the constrained integer optimization problem will be defined as

$$\begin{aligned}
\min \ & f(np; nc) \\
\text{s.t. } & 1 \leq np_i \leq NP, \ i \in \{1, ..., NP\} \\
& 1 \leq nc_j \leq NC, \ j \in \{1, ..., NP\} \\
& np_i \in \{1, ..., NP\} \\
& nc_j \in \{1, ..., NC\}
\end{aligned} \tag{2}$$

where all the patients need to be treated $\cup_{i=1}^{NP} np_i = \{1, ..., NP\}$ and the vehicle nc_i needs to perform all the visits of the patients np_i, for $i = 1, ..., NP$.

3.2 Genetic Algorithm

To solve the minimization problem presented in (2), a Genetic Algorithm was used. The Genetic Algorithm (GA) was proposed by Holland [8]. GA is a stochastic method, whose mechanism is based on simplifications of evolutionary processes observed in nature, namely selection, mutation and crossover [9]. As opposed to many other optimization methods, GA works with a population of solutions instead of one single solution [7]. The Algorithm 1 summarizes GA.

Algorithm 1. Genetic Algorithm

Generates a randomly population of individuals, $\mathcal{P}^0$, with dimension N_{pop}. Set $k = 0$.
while stopping criterion is not met **do**
    Set $k = k + 1$.
    $\mathcal{P}' =$ Apply crossover procedure in population $\mathcal{P}^k$.
    $\mathcal{P}'' =$ Apply mutation procedure in population $\mathcal{P}^k$.
    $\mathcal{P}^{k+1} = NP$ best individuals of $\{\mathcal{P}^k \cup \mathcal{P}' \cup \mathcal{P}''\}$.
end while

The iterative procedure terminates after a maximum number of iterations (number of generations) or after a maximum number of function evaluations [1,3]. The information referred to above concerns centralized decisions, which will allow to calculate the optimized schedule that is passed to the on-line module.

4   Agent-Based Model

The on-line module considers the use of MAS to implement the dynamic and responsive re-scheduling in case of disruption. For this purpose, the agent-based model will be described in this section.

4.1   Behaviour of Agents

The agent-based model considers two types of agents:

– **Patient agent:** These agents represent HUB patients, providing the treatment needs to be performed. They are immobile, totally passive, and do not take the initiative to start the decision process.
– **Vehicle agent:** These agents represent the caregivers (1 caregiver uses 1 vehicle) that move around to provide the health care services at the patient agents location. Vehicles agents only interact with their own patients.

In this paper, only the global behaviour of vehicle agents will be described, since they are the ones that move and interact with the other agents. Figure 2 presents the two main categories of global vehicle behaviour: the passive and autonomous behaviours.

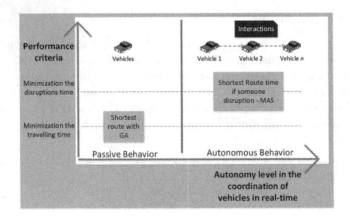

Fig. 2. Dynamic routing vehicle.

In the passive behaviour, the vehicles follow carefully the planned optimized route provided by the off-line module, i.e. using the GA codified in MatLab, without taking into account the disruptions or external problems. In the autonomous behaviour, the vehicle follows the planned route but is able to dynamically adapt the schedule in case of disruptions through the interaction with other vehicles to re-route the visits that were previously allocated to the broken vehicle.

4.2   Interaction Patterns in Autonomous Behaviour

In this work, only the dynamics of autonomous behaviour will be considered. Thus, although, initially, this dynamic involves passive behaviour, since it follows the planned route, it is subject to disruption tests or vehicle failures to evaluate interaction and autonomous cooperation between agents. This dynamic procedure involves decisions that are considered to help a vehicle in the event of disruption (which becomes unavailable) when choosing your help, in other words, the choice of another vehicle (available) that can take the remaining route of patients to visit. Each decision attempts to optimize the following criteria:

– The patients waiting time when a vehicle is interrupted on the route.
– Optimize travel time and its cost.

In this case, the vehicles follow the planned route defined by GA, when occurs a case of disruption in route, the procedure can opportunistically selects other available vehicle in on-line reactive manner (by comparing patients on routes), minimizing the waiting time to solve the problem and the time travelling. As depicted in Fig. 3, the initiator ask for available participants.

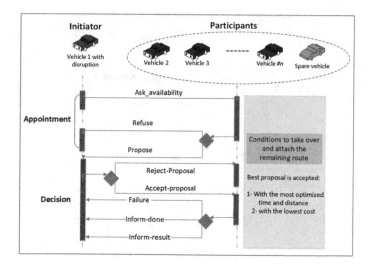

Fig. 3. Interactions and negotiations between vehicles.

The Initiator calls the vehicles until its finds one or more available, in other words, the vehicle must be still on visits and be able until the care task is completed. As shown in the Fig. 3, the initiator scans the agents list and check if there are moving vehicles available to take over the remaining route. For each vehicle available, check time between the current or final patient in its route (depending on the alternative, which will be explained later) with the first patient in remaining route left by the initiator, where the total time for each available participant will be calculated, to visit all the patients. Finally, when the best proposal with the most optimized time is found, the initiator decides and a participant will assume and update their route with the remaining route.

As previously mentioned, the autonomous behaviour includes the interaction with the vehicles and uses as a decision factor the comparison of the shortest distance and time between the remaining route and the next or final patient of the available vehicle route. It should be noted, that the remaining route is already optimized by the GA, so the comparison is done in a global way with the next patient of available vehicle. Therefore, this decision factor switches between the HHC goal (minimize the duration of travel and reduction costs) and the vehicles goal (minimize the time on travel).

For decision factor tests, two alternative methods (as shown in the Fig. 4) were compared:

- Put the remaining route in the final on the available vehicle;
- Put the remaining route in the middle on the available vehicle.

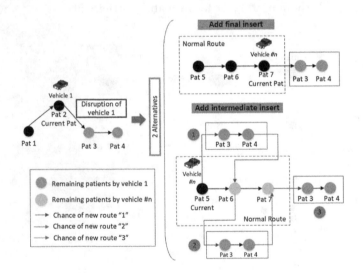

Fig. 4. Alternatives methods for decision factor.

Both alternatives use the decision factor, applied in different forms of comparison with the vehicle available. However the user will have the option to choose the alternative that it wants to show, depending on the needs, that is, may want to test the vehicle available only with the remaining route at the end (the shortest time, assumes the position), or test the remaining route at the various intervals in the route of available vehicle (tries to fit the remaining route in the range with the shortest distance and time). It should be noted that in the two alternatives, the code always look for the total route (vehicle route available

+ remaining route) with the most optimized time. As an example, the Fig. 4 shows that in the intermediate insertion method, the presented case may have three different routes, then the one that is more optimized will be choose.

4.3   Simulation Experiment Protocol

The described agent-based model was implemented in NetLogo [13], which is an agent-based modelling and simulation platform that allows to rapidly instantiate models to observe the behaviour agent-based systems. It provides an intuitive user interface where one can add buttons and control widgets to easily manipulate a model to view different scenarios [6].

Figure 5 presents the NetLogo interface for the implemented agent-based model.

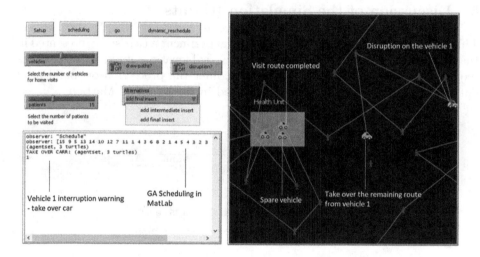

Fig. 5. Screen capture of the NetLogo interface.

As previously described, the agent-based model developed in NetLogo is connected with MatLab to allow the exchange of the optimized scheduling solution. It is often advantageous to implement separate portions of a model in the most appropriate language and to combine the results dynamically. The MatLab-NetLogo extension (MatNet) provides new functions within NetLogo that allow data passing between NetLogo and MatLab, and the calling of any valid, online MatLab commands from within NetLogo. The new tool presented herein facilitates future dynamic integration of these software platforms [5].

In each simulation, two parameters are used to vary the populations of the agents according to the database. For the case study, the simulation protocol involved three crucial steps, it can be applied to many other simulations within the database, thus:

- **Step 1:** The patients are generated from a random selection of the actual health centre database and their coordinates remained unchanged during the experiments. On the other hand, it is possible to select simulation with disruption (tested after certain ticks), or not, and which alternative to test.
- **Step 2:** The scheduling is performed by the user, which is transmitted data simulation and received the overall route of the GA for the vehicles planning (output viewer).
- **Step 3:** It is displayed the vehicle routes sequence and if there is disruption, we can update the dynamic reschedule by agents in their autonomous behaviour in coherence with the chosen alternative.

In conclusion, the trade-off between centralized decisions and dynamic interface provides easy visualization and handling for the independent user.

5   Discussion of the Simulation Results

This simulation tool was applied to test and experiment a case study presented in the data provided by the HUB. However only real locations and treatment times required by patients are used in order to confer the protection of confidential data. The Table 1 shows the parameters used in NetLogo and MatLab.

Table 1. Parameters for the study case

	Value
Number of vehicles agents	5
Number of patients agents	15
Number of localities	12
Number of treatments	5
Duration of treatments	[30,60,75,60,60]
Scene	$50 \ km^2$

For case study, simulations were carried out on a PC Intel(R) Core(TM) i7 CPU 2.2 GHz with 6.0 GB of RAM. The objective of this round of experiments (i.e., alternative #1 and alternative #2) was to highlight the efficiency of the proposed decision factor defined by the ability of the latter to minimize the vehicles travel time and automatically optimize disruptions or failures in vehicles.

GA, had 100% of successful rate since they found a feasible solution in all implementations. Initially the numerical result of the route obtained by the GA

Table 2. Route result of Netlogo output viewer and GA

Vehicles	Patients	Disruptions	Total Time (minutes)
Vehicle 0	{ 11, 7, 3 }		#
Vehicle 1	{ 13, 1 ∼ 14, 10 }	X	#
Vehicle 2	{ 2, 5, 6, 12 }		#
Vehicle 3	{ 15, 8, 9, 4 }		#

in the case study, it is presented in Table 2 with only 4 vehicles, because the fifth is a spare vehicle, that is, it has no assigned route.

It is important to note that the scheduling of the total route obtained by the GA, and that will allow the vehicles agents to identify their own route, is obtained extremely fast, that is, it only took 24 s. From the obtained route, which was tested with disruption, it is possible to verify that vehicle 1 was the one that suffered the stop or failure, leaving to visit the patients 14 and 10, respectively, that is, it will be our remaining route. The total time is not counted because there has been disruption of a vehicle and it is now expected that the autonomous behaviour of the agents can solve the problem. It should be noted again that the remaining route {14, 10} is already optimized by the GA so that it will be included in full and in the same order in another vehicle that may be available. A dynamic reschedule was then applied to each of the alternative methods developed. The Fig. 6 depicts the solutions of the obtained routes by each alternative.

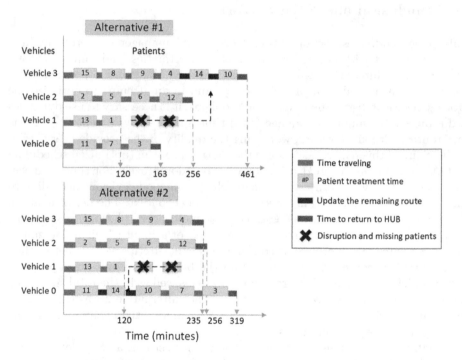

Fig. 6. Route simulation in the proposed alternatives.

Analysing Fig. 6, it is possible to see that the remaining route has been included in different vehicles depending on the alternatives. In Alternative 1, vehicle 3 was available and assumed the remaining route, including it at the end of its route, requiring 461 min to visit all patients and return to the origin point (HUB). In the same alternative, it was found that vehicle 1 only completed the patients before disruption, accounting for only 120 min. The total spent time in minutes by all vehicles in this alternative was 1000 min. On the other hand, in alternative 2, vehicle 0 became available and took the remaining route, including it in its visits interval between patient 11 and patient 7, thus requiring 319 min to visit all patients and return to the HUB. Again, vehicle 1 only visited patients prior to disruption. Consequently, the total spent time in minutes by all vehicles in this alternative was 930 min.

This means that alternative 2 allowed significant reduction of 1 h and 10 min compared to alternative 1, producing an autonomous behaviour more organized and optimized than the first alternative. In this way, the model based on MAS combined with optimization features, allows to perform and visualize the optimum scheduling in a few seconds and still test disruptions in an autonomous and intuitive way for the user. The model also allows a decentralized strategy to support dynamic decision making of a complex problem.

6   Conclusion and Future Work

This paper addresses the operational-level HHC management problem in a dynamic context with numerous constraints, uncertainties, and random events. The system architecture has been proposed to solve the two sub-problems presented in a sequential manner. In this way, and in an attempt to optimize the process in case of disruption or external problems, it is necessary to use dynamics and strategies to minimize damage (such time spent) by each vehicle on home care routes, without, however, worsening the quality of the provided services.

The aim of this paper was to solve the routing problem (optimized scheduling by GA) in a dynamic context using an MAS based approach. For this, we developed and tested two alternatives to help vehicles on good decisions according to their level of autonomy and in a decentralized local context. The performance of these dynamic alternatives was assessed on a multi-agent platform. An experimental study was proposed based on a real case of a Health Unit in Bragança, that represented HHC services. It concludes that the alternative 2, is better than alternative 1, because it allowed to obtain the best time optimization proposal in the vehicle that assumed the remaining route as well as in the total time of all the vehicles in route. Therefore, it is verified that alternative 2 was the alternative that best simulated the dynamic behaviour among the agents, minimizing the response time to external disruptions.

Finally, it was demonstrated the pertinence, robustness, and implementation of distributed approach where the scheduling problem of vehicles was efficiently solved. Moreover, the created connection allowed to obtain a scheduling optimized by a meta-heuristic, in a fast way, with the possibility of interacting in an interface developed in NetLogo. In addition, it allows an independent user to use the platform to simulate multiple cases as well as the dynamic and autonomous interaction of the agents. The main contribution of this paper it was to provide a new way of solving a vehicle routing problem using the vehicles ability to dynamically design his own route in case of external disruptions.

For future work, it is possible to reformulate the problem and take into account a new alternative, which could contemplate a schedule to the remaining route and vehicles available by GA again. Another approach could be to use other meta-heuristics and increase the complexity of the problem.

References

1. Alves, F., Pereira, A.I., Fernandes, F.P., Fernandes, A., Leitão, P., Martins, A.: Optimal schedule of home care visits for a health care center. In: Gervasi, O., et al. (eds.) ICCSA 2017. LNCS, vol. 10406, pp. 135–147. Springer, Cham (2017). https://doi.org/10.1007/978-3-319-62398-6_10
2. Barbosa, J., Leitão, P.: Simulation of multi-agent manufacturing systems using agent-based modelling platforms. In: 9th IEEE International Conference on Industrial Informatics (INDIN), pp. 477–482 (2011)
3. Bento, D., Pinho, D., Pereira, A.I., Lima, R.: Genetic algorithm and particle swarm optimization combined with Powell method. In: AIP Conference Proceedings, vol. 1558, no. 1, pp. 578–581 (2013)
4. Benzarti, E., Sahin, E., Dallery, Y.: Operations management applied to home care services: analysis of the districting problem. Decis. Support Syst. **55**(2), 587–598 (2013)
5. Biggs, M.B., Papin, J.A.: Novel multiscale modeling tool applied to Pseudomonas aeruginosa biofilm formation. PLoS ONE **8**(10), e78011 (2013)
6. Chiacchio, F., Pennisi, M., Russo, G., Motta, S., Pappalardo, F.: Agent-based modeling of the immune system: NetLogo, a promising framework. BioMed Res. Int. (2014). https://doi.org/10.1155/2014/907171
7. Ghaheri, A., Shoar, S., Naderan, M., Hoseini, S.S.: The applications of genetic algorithms in medicine. Oman Med. J. **30**(6), 406 (2015)
8. Holland, J.H.: Adaptation in Natural and Artificial Systems: An Introductory Analysis with Applications to Biology, Control, and Artificial Intelligence. MIT Press, Cambridge (1992)
9. Kumar, M., Husian, M., Upreti, N., Gupta, D.: Genetic algorithm: review and application. Int. J. Inf. Technol. Knowl. Manag. **2**(2), 451–454 (2010)
10. Nickel, S., Schrder, M., Steeg, J.: Mid-term and short-term planning support for home health care services. Eur. J. Oper. Res. **219**(3), 574–587 (2012)
11. Railsback, S.F., Grimm, V.: Agent-Based and Individual-Based Modeling: A Practical Introduction. Princeton University Press, Princeton (2011)
12. Rasmussen, M.S., Justesen, T., Dohn, A., Larsen, J.: The home care crew scheduling problem: preference-based visit clustering and temporal dependencies. Eur. J. Oper. Res. **219**(3), 598–610 (2012)
13. Wilensky, U., Evanston, I.: NetLogo: center for connected learning and computer-based modeling. Northwestern University, Evanston, IL 4952 (1999)
14. Wooldridge, M.: An Introduction to Multiagent Systems. Wiley, Hoboken (2009)
15. Yalçındağ, S., Matta, A., Şahin, E., Shanthikumar, J.G.: A two-stage approach for solving assignment and routing problems in home health care services. In: Matta, A., Li, J., Sahin, E., Lanzarone, E., Fowler, J. (eds.) Proceedings of the International Conference on Health Care Systems Engineering, pp. 47–59. Springer, Cham (2014). https://doi.org/10.1007/978-3-319-01848-5_4

Mood Mirroring with an Embodied Virtual Agent: A Pilot Study on the Relationship Between Personalized Visual Feedback and Adherence

Simon Provoost[1,2(✉)], Jeroen Ruwaard[1,2,3], Koen Neijenhuijs[1,2],
Tibor Bosse[4], and Heleen Riper[1,2,3,5]

[1] Section of Clinical Psychology, Vrije Universiteit Amsterdam,
Amsterdam, Netherlands
{s.j.provoost,j.j.ruwaard,k.i.neijenhuijs,
h.riper}@vu.nl
[2] Amsterdam Public Health, Amsterdam, Netherlands
[3] GGZ inGeest, Amsterdam, Netherlands
[4] Department of Computer Science, Vrije Universiteit Amsterdam,
Amsterdam, Netherlands
t.bosse@vu.nl
[5] University of Southern Denmark, Odense, Denmark

Abstract. Human support is thought to increase adherence to internet-based interventions for common mental health disorders, but can be costly and reduce treatment accessibility. Embodied virtual agents may be used to deliver automated support, but while many solutions have been shown to be feasible, there is still little controlled research that empirically validates their clinical effectiveness in this context. This study uses a controlled and randomized paradigm to investigate whether feedback from an embodied virtual agent can increase adherence. In a three-week ecological momentary assessment smartphone study, 68 participants were asked to report their mood three times a day. An embodied virtual agent could mirror participant-reported mood states when thanking them for their answers. A two-stage randomization into a text and personalized visual feedback group, versus a text-only control group, was applied to control for individual differences (study onset) and feedback history (after two weeks). Results indicate that while personalized visual feedback did not increase adherence, it did manage to keep adherence constant over a three-week period, whereas fluctuations in adherence could be observed in the text-only control group. Although this was a pilot study, and its results should be interpreted with some caution, this paper shows how virtual agent feedback may have a stabilizing effect on adherence, how controlled experiments on the relationship between virtual agent support and clinically relevant measures such as adherence can be conducted, and how results may be analyzed.

Keywords: Ecological momentary assessment · Virtual agent
Feedback · Adherence

© Springer International Publishing AG, part of Springer Nature 2018
J. Bajo et al. (Eds.): PAAMS 2018 Workshops, CCIS 887, pp. 24–35, 2018.
https://doi.org/10.1007/978-3-319-94779-2_3

1   Introduction

Internet-based psychotherapeutic interventions, also referred to as eMental Health interventions, can be effective in the treatment of various mental disorders when compared to face-to-face interventions [1]. Many interventions that target common mental health disorders such as mood, anxiety, and substance use disorders, are based on cognitive behavioral therapy (CBT). Internet-based CBT interventions are either guided, or self-guided, with guidance usually being provided by health professionals or trained volunteers. It has been found that guided interventions are generally more clinically effective, e.g. reductions in symptomatology, than unguided interventions [2]. While the precise contribution of human support remains unclear, a number of working mechanisms have been suggested [3]. One such mechanism is that human support contributes to patients' motivation to complete an intervention, which in turn may increase adherence [4]. Indeed, it has been shown that adherence may be superior when human support is available [5], and that non-optimal exposure or non-adherence to interventions, e.g. not completing exercises or dropping out of interventions early, tends to reduce their clinical effectiveness [6].

The study described in this article is part of a project in which we are looking to bridge the gap between guided and unguided internet-based CBT interventions by automating support through the use of embodied virtual agents. From a literature review of their application in the treatment of common mental health disorders, we concluded that few studies have explored their use in a supportive role to online CBT-based interventions. Although a number of applications seemed feasible and promising, there is still little evidence for their impact on clinically relevant outcomes such as symptom reduction or adherence [7]. Clinical psychology is an applied science, however, which means that there is a strong emphasis on empirical validation when introducing novel technologies. Although from a technological perspective, lots of interesting solutions have been, and are being developed, they cannot be applied in clinical practice without such validation. The present study represents the first in a series of controlled studies in which we aim to discover how and whether virtual agent support can contribute to eMental Health interventions' clinical effectiveness.

Because a detailed study of clinical outcomes in controlled settings, such as symptom severity, requires clinical study populations (ethical implications) and follow-up measurements (long timespan), we chose to study adherence as an outcome measure in this pilot study, on the assumption that it is a potential mediator for clinical effectiveness. We opted for Ecological Momentary Assessment (EMA) as an intervention strategy, also referred to as experience sampling, which refers to the repeated sampling of subjects' current behaviors and experiences in real time, in subjects' natural environments [8]. EMA can be a component of internet-based CBT interventions, for example to measure fluctuations in mood [9]. Additionally, it is a clear measure of adherence, as patients either do or do not respond to EMA requests.

In the remainder of this paper we describe our explorative pilot study, in which we test the hypothesis that virtual agent support can increase adherence to EMA requests. With respect to the virtual agent design, we opted for a simple approach that fulfills the ECA criteria (the agent has an embodiment, communicates with the user, and uses a form of reasoning to simulate agency [10]) in a minimalistic manner. Although frameworks exist for the development of ECAs with their full range of verbal and non-verbal capabilities (e.g. [11, 12]), using them for the development of virtual agents, and their subsequent integration with existing EMA platforms, was considered too time-consuming for this study. Moreover, agents do not necessarily need to be very complicated for motivational purposes, because it has been shown that even the mere presence of an embodied agent can improve user motivation, for example when shown next to a chat dialog box in which instructions and feedback for an interactive game are displayed [13]. A more detailed description of the experiment and the agent's design is provided in the Methods section.

2   Methods

2.1   Design

We conducted an explorative controlled pilot study with a two-stage randomized between-subject design. Participants self-monitored their mood on a smartphone EMA application in which a virtual character could give personalized visual feedback to user responses by mirroring their reported mood state. Approval for the study was obtained from the Research Ethics Committee of the Faculty of Movement and Behavioural Sciences of the Vrije Universiteit Amsterdam (reference number: VCWE-2016-014).

Before study onset, participants were randomly allocated to either a text + personalized visual feedback or a text-only feedback condition, to control for individual differences in initial motivation and other potentially relevant background variables. A known issue with prolonged interaction with virtual agents is that it may become repetitive, leading to a decline in motivation and willingness to interact with a system [14]. Because our agent's design is fairly simplistic we wanted to control for this effect, and therefore, two weeks into the study, participants were randomized again to control for feedback history. Because no changes to the application could be made while the study was ongoing, randomization for the entire study took place before study onset. Participants were assigned to one of four possible groups, each with a different combination of text + personalized visual feedback (F) or text-only feedback (N) during weeks 1–2 and week 3.

2.2   Procedure

Before the study started, participants received an email with an invitation to fill out a digital informed consent form and demographic questionnaire. After giving their consent, participants installed the Android-only EMA application on their mobile devices. The application automatically stopped sending EMA requests once the study was over, after which it could be removed from the participants' smartphones.

2.3   Participants

As part of a research project for a bachelor's degree, students were asked to recruit at least 10 adults from their social network. Inclusion criteria for participation were (1) age 18 years or older, (2) owning an Android smartphone (minimal Android 2.3), and (3) no known severe mental health problems. Participants did not receive financial compensation, and were told that their participation would benefit the education of the student who had approached them.

2.4   Materials

Ecological Momentary Assessment of Mood. To collect self-monitored mood data, we built an Android smartphone application using the movisensXS EMA framework [15]. The app prompted participants to rate their mood on their smartphone at three set time points each day (11:00, 15:00, and 20:00). Mood was assessed through the circumplex model of affect [16], which conceptualizes affective states as two-dimensional constructs comprising different levels of valence and arousal. Previous studies measured valence and arousal through 5-point scales [17]. We decided to tap both dimensions on a 3-point scale scored from −1 to 1 (negative to positive; low to high) (Fig. 1), as this allowed a direct mapping to the visual feedback presented in the next section (Fig. 2).

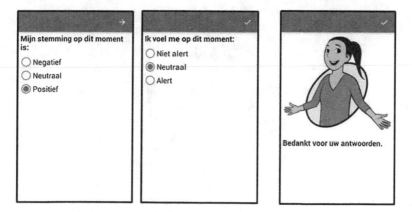

Fig. 1. Screenshots of an EMA response and the system's reply including personalized visual feedback (translated from Dutch): left: "My mood at this moment is [Negative; Neutral; Positive]", middle: "At this moment I feel [Not alert; Neutral; Alert]", right: "Thank you for your answers"

Personalized Visual Feedback With a Virtual Agent. After responding, participants received a message on a third screen, thanking them for their answers. In the personalized visual feedback condition, an embodied virtual agent accompanied this message. It consisted of the female version of the Pick-A-Mood (PAM) model [18] that matched the reported mood. For example, a participant reporting positive valence (+1), and high arousal (+1), was deduced to be in an excited mood (Fig. 2). Our visual feedback can be considered a simple form of empathy, where the system deduces and reflects users' moods based on their response to the EMA requests. With this feedback, we hoped to operationalize two concepts of Dialogue Support from Persuasive System Design [19], the inclusion of which has been found to increase adherence [20]: *social role* ("if a system adopts a social role, users will more likely use it for persuasive purposes") by accompanying the thank you message with the face of a virtual character, and *similarity* ("people are more readily persuaded through systems that remind them of themselves in some meaningful way") by having the character mirror the participant-reported mood.

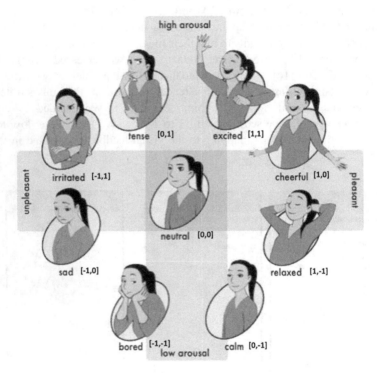

Fig. 2. The Pick-A-Mood model, including an interpretation of mood ratings [Valence, Arousal]. Note that the model had to be tilted slightly clockwise to allow for the interpretation.

2.5   Measures

Adherence. Adherence was represented as a vector of binary values indicating either a response (=1) or no response (=0) to EMA requests on subsequent trials.

Feedback. Feedback was represented as a vector of binary values indicating either text + personalized visual feedback (=1), or text-only feedback (=0), accompanying the 'thank you for your answers' message.

Time. All trials received a sequentially ordered 'time stamp' ranging from the first to the last trial (Range = 1–63). Trials that were missing due to technical issues were added to the dataset, but with *NA* values for adherence, such that all 63 trials were accounted for.

2.6 Statistical Analysis

In our model, we assumed effects of time (people naturally lose interest in EMA after a while [21]), feedback, and individual differences (some people may be more adherent to start with). To analyze the relationship between time and feedback as independent variables, and adherence as dependent variable, we used the *glmer* function from the *lme4* statistical package [22] in the R-environment (version 3.3.2) [23]. For our main hypothesis, we conducted a logistic mixed effects analysis, with a 'feedback (1/0) x time (1–63)' interaction as fixed effect, and adherence (1/0) as the dependent variable. To investigate complex patterns over time, contrasts for the time variable were set to polynomials up to the tenth power. We accounted for individual differences at onset by adding random intercepts for the different participant IDs to our model. The regression model looked as follows in R-syntax:

$$adh \sim feedback * time + (1|id)$$

3 Results

3.1 Participant Flow

A total of 85 participants were recruited and randomized to one of the four groups, with 17 dropping out entirely or failing to install the software on time. From the 68 participants who had started, another 7 dropped out, and 7 were excluded from the analysis as they had experienced technical issues that resulted in either too few EMA requests (e.g. 0 to 2 per day on many different days), or too many (e.g. 4 per day) having been logged in the movisensXS data export files. Our final dataset included 54 participants (see Fig. 3).

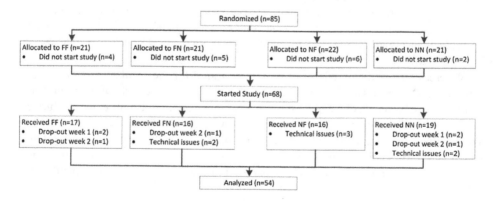

Fig. 3. Participant flow

3.2   Descriptive Statistics

Participants. 49 participants, 24 males and 25 females with mean age of 29.31 (Range = 20–64) filled out the demographic questionnaire, while 5 participants failed to do so.

Adherence. The 54 participants in the final dataset responded to EMA requests in 2004 out of a total of 3080 trials ($M = 37.1$ responses, and $M = 57.0$ trials per participant), resulting in an overall adherence of 65.1%. Note that the total number of trials does not add up to 63 on average (3 measurements per day for 21 days), as some requests were missed, either on the first day (e.g. when a participant started with the 20:00 measurement), or due to technical issues that prevented trials from taking place.

Feedback. The personalized visual feedback group received 1497 (48.6%) requests, and responded to 971 (64.9%). The text-only group received 1583 (51.3%) requests, and responded to 1033 (65.3%). The valence question was answered slightly more positively in the text-only condition, but no large differences existed between the two groups. With respect to the visual feedback provided, *excited* (n = 317 (32.7%)) and *neutral* (n = 241, (24.8%)) were most prominent.

Time. A total of 322 trials were unaccounted for due to technical issues, 183 of which would have contained personalized visual feedback. For our analysis, these trials were added to our dataset with missing values for adherence, giving us a total of 3402 trials. With the ten polynomial contrasts for the time variable our model was able to run, while visual inspection showed that no more than ten polynomials were to be expected.

3.3   The Effect of Feedback

Mixed Effects Logistic Analysis. Summary results of the mixed effects logistic analysis, based on all 3402 trials, are depicted in Table 1 below. Significant effects were found for feedback ($p = .03$), as well as the *feedback * time* interaction for the 3rd ($p = .01$), 7th ($p = .01$), and 9th ($p < .01$) order.

Feedback * Time Interaction. Because of the significant interaction effects, the main effect of feedback cannot be interpreted as such. To further disentangle the model, the analysis was conducted again for both the feedback and no feedback condition, consequently leaving the feedback variable out of the equation. The results of these analyses with regard to the previously significant interaction effects are depicted in Table 2 below.

Whereas no significant effects of time were found for the feedback condition, the significant 3rd ($p = .04$), 7th ($p = .02$), and 9th ($p < .01$) order effects of time remained in the text-only feedback condition. A Chi-square test of the entire model further confirmed the significant *feedback * time* interaction effect ($X^2 (62) = 84.99, p = .03$). To visualize this, Fig. 4 illustrates fluctuations in the no feedback condition (top left), which can be disseminated into separate polynomials of the 3rd (two bends; top right), 7th (6 bends; bottom left), and 9th (8 bends; bottom right) power. Meanwhile, the feedback condition is stable across all trials.

Table 1. Summary of the logistic mixed effects analysis results

Variable	Estimate	Standard error	z-value	P-value
Feedback	0.13	0.06	2.19	0.03*
Time	0.09	0.35	0.27	0.79
Feedback * time	0.07	0.42	0.17	0.86
Feedback * time^2	0.56	0.37	1.49	0.14
Feedback * time^3	0.93	0.37	2.53	0.01*
Feedback * time^4	0.50	0.37	1.35	0.18
Feedback * time^5	−0.42	0.36	−1.18	0.24
Feedback * time^6	0.42	0.35	1.18	0.24
Feedback * time^7	0.91	0.35	2.60	0.01*
Feedback * time^8	−0.08	0.35	−0.23	0.82
Feedback * time^9	−1.21	0.35	−3.45	0.00**
Feedback * time^{10}	−0.01	0.35	−0.02	0.98

*$p < .05$
**$p < .01$

Table 2. Disentanglement of the significant interaction effects from the main analysis

	Variable	Estimate	Standard error	z-value	P-value
Visual feedback	time^3	−0.65	0.52	−1.26	.21
	time^7	−0.74	0.51	−1.45	.15
	time^9	0.69	0.50	1.38	.17
Text-only feedback	time^3	1.05	0.52	2.01	.04*
	time^7	1.13	0.49	2.31	.02*
	time^9	−1.77	0.50	−3.55	.00**

*$p < .05$
**$p < .01$

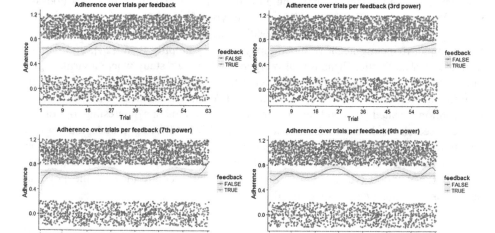

Fig. 4. Visualizations of the overall model (top left), and the three significant polynomial effects, using a smoothed conditional means function

4 Discussion

4.1 Principal Results

Our visual feedback did not manage to increase EMA adherence, but rather kept it stable over time. A cautious interpretation of the results is that personalized visual feedback helped to maintain adherence to EMA in a more predictive manner than when text-only feedback was provided. Notably, as is visualized in Fig. 4, there was no positive or negative linear trend for either condition. This is a surprising result given the assumption that adherence would decrease over time.

4.2 Implications

From a practical point of view, our results are interesting in the sense that from a researcher perspective, a constant flow of information, as provided by participants in the personalized visual feedback condition, may be preferable to the fluctuations observed in the text-only group. Mood, for example, changes relatively slowly over the course of more than one day. From a theoretical point of view, the results are harder to interpret, since the text-only group was at times more, and at times less adherent than the visual feedback group. Since contextual factors (e.g. having time for EMA responses) were controlled for by our randomization, the difference, i.e., fluctuation versus stabilization, can most likely be explained by an effect on participants' motivation. This would require further investigation; a possible future research paradigm to investigate the effect may include a qualitative component, e.g. by asking participants for their reasons to respond or not respond to EMA requests. It could also be interesting to look more closely at the moods that were reported per day as, for example, participants may be less inclined to answer requests when they are having a bad day compared to a good one.

Although personalized visual feedback seemed to have a stabilizing effect on adherence, it failed to increase it. It could be that personalized visual feedback does not matter that much, but it is also possible that the type of visual feedback we presented is not very effective, or cancelled out any positive effects. With regard to mood mirroring, for example, reflecting negative moods may actually amplify them [24], and thereby decrease user motivation. This was also argued following a study where a virtual agent mirrored users' emotional states to motivate them to play a game [25], in which no significant effects on user motivation were found. Within the context of eMental Health interventions related to mood and our current paradigm, one interesting option for future research could be to investigate the effect of mirroring moods that have a negative valence with their equivalents on the positive side of the valence dimension. For example, a reported irritated mood (valence $= -1$, arousal $= 1$) would be mirrored by an excited mood (valence $= 1$, arousal $= 1$), which could alleviate the potential drawbacks of reflecting negative mood states.

4.3   Limitations

The virtual agent was a very simplistic one, which had to do with the technological limitations of the platform that we used to conduct the study. For example, the input for the 'reasoning engine' (Fig. 2) of the embodied virtual agent was limited to the two questions that were answered in the current trial, and the EMA framework offered no options for more advanced animations. Although the agent was hardly impressive from a technological perspective, it did allow us to conduct research on its relationship to EMA adherence, within the limited degrees of freedom for agent design offered by a typical eMental Health framework. Additionally, we did so in a well-controlled paradigm: intervention *with* agent vs. intervention *without* agent.

It could also be questioned whether our specific feedback is the optimal one in this setting. We chose this feedback as it operationalized elements from Persuasive System Design theory (*social role* and *similarity*) known to be beneficial to adherence, and for pragmatic reasons related to the technological limitations of the EMA framework. Although it can be argued that *similarity* often refers more to user characteristics such as age or gender, we considered mood reflection relevant in our case since the task at hand was mood reporting. Some types of feedback that could be equally, if not more, relevant include reminders before EMA requests, targeting feedback only at participants who have been non-adherent for a period of time, or feedback that is specifically designed to uplift participants who report a negative mood.

A last limitation refers to the generalizability of our results. First and foremost, our study was conducted with a convenience sample, whose primary motivation for participation was likely to help out the students by whom they were recruited. Known mental health issues being an exclusion criterion, our study population was most likely quite different from the clinical populations that would typically use eMental Health interventions, and that may instead be motivated by a desire to improve their current situation. Additionally, there is still some debate as to whether EMA can be considered an intervention in itself [26], which means generalizations to our broader context should be made with caution. These limitations are a natural consequence of the exploratory nature of our pilot study, but the methods we used could be applied equally well to contexts with real interventions and patients.

5   Conclusion

The study described in this paper was the first in a series of experiments which we hope will contribute to the empirical validation of the clinical effectiveness of embodied virtual agents in an eMental Health context. We aimed to find out whether feedback, operationalized by an embodied virtual agent, could increase adherence to mood rating requests in a three-week smartphone-based EMA study. While we did not find a significant main effect of feedback on adherence, there was a significant *feedback * time* interaction effect, which became apparent in fluctuations in adherence for the text-only condition, compared to a very consistent pattern in the personalized visual feedback group. To our knowledge, this paper represents one of the first explorative studies that used an embodied virtual agent, in a rigorous randomized and controlled design, to study a clinically relevant outcome measure over a prolonged period of time. Given the explorative nature and the relatively small sample size of this study, the stabilizing effect the virtual agent had on adherence has to be interpreted with some caution. Future studies may include a more sophisticated virtual agent, different feedback, a clinical study population, and a context more resembling CBT interventions.

References

1. Andersson, G., Cuijpers, P., Carlbring, P., Riper, H., Hedman, E.: Guided internet-based vs. face-to-face cognitive behavior therapy for psychiatric and somatic disorders: a systematic review and meta-analysis. World Psychiatry **13**, 288–295 (2014)
2. Richards, D., Richardson, T.: Computer-based psychological treatments for depression: a systematic review and meta-analysis. Clin. Psychol. Rev. **32**, 329–342 (2012)
3. Schueller, S.M., Tomasino, K.N., Mohr, D.C.: Integrating human support into behavioral intervention technologies: the efficiency model of support. Clin. Psychol. Sci. Pract. **24**, 27–45 (2017)
4. Mohr, D.C., Cuijpers, P., Lehman, K.: Supportive accountability: a model for providing human support to enhance adherence to eHealth interventions. J. Med. Internet Res. **13**, e30 (2011)
5. Van Ballegooijen, W., Cuijpers, P., Van Straten, A., Karyotaki, E., Andersson, G., Smit, J. H., Riper, H.: Adherence to internet-based and face-to-face cognitive behavioural therapy for depression: a meta-analysis. PLoS ONE **9**, e100674 (2014)
6. Donkin, L., Christensen, H., Naismith, S.L., Neal, B., Hickie, I.B., Glozier, N.: A systematic review of the impact of adherence on the effectiveness of e-therapies. J. Med. Internet Res. **13**, e52 (2011)
7. Provoost, S., Lau, H.M., Ruwaard, J., Riper, H.: Embodied conversational agents in clinical psychology: a scoping review. J. Med. Internet Res. **19**, e151 (2017)
8. Shiffman, S., Stone, A.A., Hufford, M.R.: Ecological momentary assessment. Annu. Rev. Clin. Psychol. **4**, 1–32 (2008)
9. Wenze, S.J., Miller, I.W.: Use of ecological momentary assessment in mood disorders research. Clin. Psychol. Rev. **30**, 794–804 (2010)
10. Isbister, K., Doyle, P.: The blind men and the elephant revisited. In: Ruttkay, Z., Pelachaud, C. (eds.) From Brows to Trust. HIS, vol. 7, pp. 3–26. Springer, Dordrecht (2004). https://doi.org/10.1007/1-4020-2730-3_1
11. Bickmore, T., Schulman, D., Shaw, G.: DTask and LiteBody: open source, standards-based tools for building web-deployed embodied conversational agents. In: Ruttkay, Z., Kipp, M., Nijholt, A., Vilhjálmsson, H.H. (eds.) IVA 2009. LNCS (LNAI), vol. 5773, pp. 425–431. Springer, Heidelberg (2009). https://doi.org/10.1007/978-3-642-04380-2_46
12. Gratch, J., Hartholt, A.: Virtual humans: a new toolkit for cognitive science research. Proc. Cogn. Sci. Soc. **35**, 41–42 (2013)
13. Mumm, J., Mutlu, B.: Designing motivational agents: the role of praise, social comparison, and embodiment in computer feedback. Comput. Hum. Behav. **27**, 1643–1650 (2011)
14. Bickmore, T., Schulman, D., Sidner, C.L.: Issues in Designing Agents for Long-Term Behavior Change. In: CHI Workshop on Engagement by Design, pp. 1–5 (2009)
15. movisensXS, Version 0.7.4162 (movisens GmbH, Karlsruhe, Germany). https://xs.movisens.com/
16. Russell, J.A.: A circumplex model of affect. J. Pers. Soc. Psychol. **39**, 1161–1178 (1980)

17. Asselbergs, J., Ruwaard, J., Ejdys, M., Schrader, N., Sijbrandij, M., Riper, H.: Mobile phone-based unobtrusive ecological momentary assessment of day-to-day mood: an explorative study. J. Med. Internet Res. **18**, e72 (2016)
18. Desmet, P.M.A., Vastenburg, M.H., Van Bel, D., Romero, N.: Pick-a-mood development and application of a pictorial mood-reporting instrument. In: Proceedings of the 8th International Conference on Design and Emotion, London 2012, Central Saint Martins College, Art and Design, 11–14 September 2012 (2012)
19. Oinas-Kukkonen, H., Harjumaa, M.: Persuasive systems design: key issues, process model, and system features. Commun. Assoc. Inf. Syst. **24**, 485–500 (2009)
20. Kelders, M.S., Kok, N.R., Ossebaard, C.H., Van Gemert-Pijnen, E.W.C.J.: Persuasive system design does matter: a systematic review of adherence to web-based interventions. J Med Internet Res. **14**, e152 (2014)
21. Broderick, J.E., Schwartz, J.E., Shiffman, S., Hufford, M.R., Stone, A.A.: Signaling does not adequately improve diary compliance. Ann. Behav. Med. **26**, 139–148 (2003)
22. Bates, D., Mächler, M., Bolker, B., Walker, S.: Fitting linear mixed-effects models using lme4. J. Stat. Softw. **67**, 1–48 (2015)
23. R Core Team: R: A Language and Environment for Statistical Computing (2016). https://www.r-project.org
24. Pagliari, C., Burton, C., McKinstry, B., Szentatotai, A., David, D., Serrano Blanco, A., Ferrini, L., Albertini, S., Castro, J.C., Estevez, S., Wolters, M.: Psychosocial implications of avatar use in supporting therapy for depression. Stud. Health Technol. Inform. **181**, 329–333 (2012)
25. Burleson, W.: Affective learning companions: strategies for empathetic agents with real-time multimodal affective sensing to foster meta-cognitive and meta-affective approaches to learning, motivation, and perseverance (2006). http://hdl.handle.net/1721.1/37404
26. van Ballegooijen, W., Ruwaard, J., Karyotaki, E., Ebert, D.D., Smit, J.H., Riper, H.: Reactivity to smartphone-based ecological momentary assessment of depressive symptoms (MoodMonitor): protocol of a randomised controlled trial. BMC Psychiatry **16**, 359 (2016)

Multi-agent System for the Recommendation of Electric Bicycle Routes

Daniel H. de la Iglesia[✉], Álvaro Lozano Murciego, Alberto L. Barriuso,
Gabriel Villarrubia, and Juan F. de Paz

BISITE Digital Innovation Hub, University of Salamanca,
Edificio Multiusos I+D+I, 37007 Salamanca, Spain
{danihiglesias,loza,albarriuso,gvg,fcofds}@usal.es

Abstract. Nowadays, recommender systems are a key tool in sectors such as online sales, video playback and music on demand or book recommendation systems. This paper proposes a personalized route recommendation system for users of electric vehicles, specifically for e-bike users. Around the world e-bikes have become a real alternative to other motorized modes of transport and they are used for daily commuting. A multi-agent system is used to manage the information produced by the system, which generates route recommendations for users based on the routes they had travelled previously. Recommendations are provided to users through a smart-phone application, which is in charge of registering the data on the routes users travel.

1 Introduction

In recent years, there has been a great development in the electric bicycle or ebike industry [1]. Electric bicycles are bicycles that can travel longer distances, provide greater mobility and reduce barriers (age, physical limitations, steep terrain, lack of time) compared to conventional bicycles [2]. Electric bikes are standard pedal bicycles that have three main elements: an electric motor, a control system and a rechargeable battery that supplies the motor with power [3]. E-bikes have been recognized as key for increasing the number of bicycle users in the city. For this reason, the biking industry predicts that this will be an important area of sales in the coming years. It is estimated that in the last decade, more than 150 million electric bicycles have been sold [4]. A large part of these sales has been made in China. In 2015, 1.2 million were sold in Europe, and it is estimated that by 2022 the number of sales will triple [5]. The increase in sales is a consequence of the relatively low price of these vehicles (generally, less than € 1,000) and many users opt for e-bikes over scooters [5].

Given this significant increase in ebike users, it is necessary to offer new services that adapt to this type of vehicle [6, 7]. In this case we refer to route recommendation systems for existing bicycle users which do not consider the characteristics of electric bicycles [8]. Therefore, it is necessary to plan new horizons for this type of recommendation systems, which adapt to these new models of bicycles, the ebikes.

© Springer International Publishing AG, part of Springer Nature 2018
J. Bajo et al. (Eds.): PAAMS 2018 Workshops, CCIS 887, pp. 36–43, 2018.
https://doi.org/10.1007/978-3-319-94779-2_4

This paper proposes the use of a multi-agent architecture for the construction of a route recommendation system for electric bicycle users. By means of an application for mobile devices that is able to wirelessly connect to the electric bicycle, it is possible to record all the available data for the routes travelled by users. The combination of route information along with the users' personal data makes it possible to provide e-bike users with personalized recommendations. In order to evaluate the efficiency of the designed system, five of the most active users on the platform were included in a case study where they were recommended with a total of 40 routes for each of them. After an evaluation of the routes that were recommended, users rated between 0 and 10 the recommended routes, thus validating the designed recommendation system. The results showed how the system had recommended 74% of the routes in a correct way for the users.

The paper is organized as follows. In Sect. 2 a review of the current state of the art in recommender systems. Section 3 defines the architecture proposed in this work. Section 4 describes the conducted case study with the objective of validating the system while Sect. 5 analyzes the results and conclusions.

2 Background

Recommender systems are tools and software techniques that suggest items to users according to their preferences [9]. The suggestions aid users in different decision-making processes, such as what items to buy, what music to listen to [10], what news to read [11], what routes to travel, etc.

An *Item* is the term used to denote what the system will recommend to users. Recommendation systems are usually designed for specific domains, that is, they recommend a specific type of article. These recommendations must be completely customized to provide useful information to the user.

Recommendation systems must be able to make personalized recommendations to a community of users within the system. To this end, they store the information found on user profiles which tell the system about the users' preferences and their actions in the system. The system can obtain preferences either implicitly (by monitoring the user's interactions with the system) or explicitly (by means of user assessments in numerical, boolean or other type of ratings). Additional aspects such as context and the reputation of the users/articles in the system, are also considered by present recommendation systems [12].

Current literature contains a large number of recommendation system proposals: based on content, collaborative filtering, reduction of dimensionality and in context.

3 Proposed System

This section describes the multi-agent architecture proposed in the present work. The system will make use of a mobile device application that will record the routes travelled by e-bike users. The system bases its route recommendation on the genuine content provided by users. Figure 1, illustrates the general architecture of the system. The architecture is formed by two large blocks: the lower block contains the JADE platform agents and the upper block the agents in the proposed system.

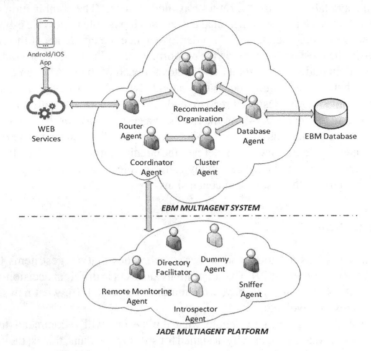

Fig. 1. General diagram of the proposed architecture

Different agents are assigned specific tasks within the system:

Database Agent: It offers services which facilitate access to the database of the platform to the rest of the agents. This agent protects the database form agents who are not granted access to it or are not allowed to modify its contents. To this end, the agent incorporates a module that is in charge of checking agent permissions, services are made accessible only to specified agents.

Coordinator Agent: The proposed virtual organization can be classified as the so-called semi-open companies, since it has a mechanism that controls the admission of agents to societies. Agents have to request entry to this mechanism. The coordinator agent evaluates the proposals of different agent and decides whether they should be allowed to enter a society or not. This agent is in charge of verifying the agents' entry and exit, in and out of the system, as well as the assignment of the roles that the agents will have in the organization.

Cluster Agent: It is in charge of executing the clustering algorithm which obtainins a set of clusters from geographical zones. To this end, the starting and ending points of the routes in the database of the platform are used. Once the clustering process has been completed, this agent will begin a process in which the Coordinator Agent is requested to incorporate a Recommender Agent, for each cluster, into the multi-agent system.

Recommender Agent: This agent is responsible for recommending routes to users on the basis of their previous interactions with the system. There will be a Recommender Agent for each cluster generated by the Cluster Agent, and it will be responsible for recommending the routes that are in the geographical area defined by that cluster. When the user requests a route recommendation the Recommender Agent obtains the data of that user, as well as their geographical position, and will return a set of recommended routes to that user. The recommendation system incorporated by these agents is based on Apache Mahout. The algorithm used falls within the group of collaborative filtering algorithms and it bases its predictions and recommendations on the ratings (ratings) or on the behavior of other users in the system.

Router Agent: It is a reactive agent which receives requests for route recommendations. They arrive to this agent through the web services used by mobile applications. It acts as a router, redirecting these requests to the Recommender Responder which is in charge of executing recommendations from a relevant geographical area.

Mobile App Agent: This is a software agent embedded in Android and IO applications, it is responsible for requesting recommendations to the Router Agent.

Below we describe hoe the agents that make up the Multi-agent recommendation system are deployed. Initially, Route Agent, Coordinator Agent, Cluster Agent and

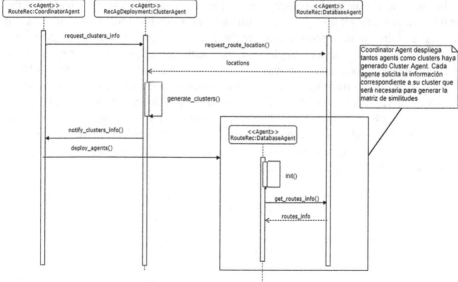

Fig. 2. Recommendation agents deployment

Database Agent are deployed together with the agents the from the JADE platform. Once initialized, the Coordinator Agent performs the periodic process described in Fig. 2.

The Coordinator Agent requests the ClusterAgent to generate clusters from the starting and ending points of the routes in the systems. The ClusterAgent responds by generating a number of clusters and providing information on each route. Once this process is completed, it will deploy an organization of recommendation agents (RecommenderAgent), each one of them will be provided with the information related to their cluster and will have to obtain all the necessary information to generate the recommendations later if this is required.

This process is carried out periodically because routes are continuously generated in the system and new users are registered so the number of deployed agents will change over time as new information is added by the users.

3.1 Route Recommendation Algorithm

The recommendation system has been developed on the basis of the Apache Mahout framework. The system does not evaluate explicit information for recommending routes to users, previous interaction with the system are the only basis for the recommendations. In this case, we have decided to use the routes that users have downloaded.

Once the model is obtained, a collaborative filtering algorithm based on items (item-item collaborative filtering) is used, it uses similarities between article valuation patterns. If two articles tend to have the same positive and negative ratings from users, then they are similar, thus it is assumed that preferences are similar for similar articles. The general structure of this method is therefore similar to content based methods for recommendation and personalization, with the exception that similarity between articles is deduced from the user's valuation patterns instead of extracted article data.

In this case, the Jaccard similarity index (Fig. 3) is used to detect, by means of the similarity metrics that it uses, if there is similarity between two routes. The main reason for the use of this similarity function is that there are no user ratings about the items, but only a record of their activity is registered, that is, the system knows what routes have been downloaded. The Jaccard similarity index (sometimes called the Jaccard similarity coefficient) compares members from two sets in order to see what they have in common and what differentiates them. In this way the similarity of the two data sets is measured, ranging from 0% to 100%. The higher the percentage, the more similar are the two populations. Although it is easy to interpret, it is extremely sensitive to the size of small samples and can give erroneous results, especially when the samples or data sets are very small and have missing observations.

$$jaccard(A, B) = \frac{A \cap B}{A \cup B}$$

Fig. 3. Jaccard similarity index

Recommender systems based on collaborative filtering recommend each item (routes in this case) based on the user's actions. The more users interact with an item, the easier it is to know what elements interest the user and to find similar items. With time the system will be able to offer increasingly precise recommendations. In cases where the algorithm is not capable of recommending any route to the user, the ten most downloaded routes from the user's cluster (position obtained thanks to the geolocation provided by the mobile device) will be suggested. This solutions is a widely used by developers of these recommendation systems.

4   Case Study

The ebikemotion platform for electric bicycles [13] is key for the system developed in this work. This application is compatible with more than 20 electric bicycle brands on the market and has more than 5000 users around the world. The application is intended for the real-time display of all the values of the electric bicycle (state of charge, level of assistance, speed, altitude, etc.). It also registers the values of the routes travelled by the user and recommends calculated by the server.

In order to validate the system, a case study was carried out with the 5 most active platform users. These users completed an average of 200 routes with the application. The case study was intended to evaluate if the routes recommended to these users were suited to their preferences. To this end, each user was asked to rate a total of 40 routes recommended to them by the system. The users viewed the characteristics and location of these routes and rated them, between 0 and 10, according to how interested they would be in travelling these routes. The results of the case study are presented in Table 1, which outlines the ratings of the 5 users.

Table 1.   Evaluation of routes recommended to users

User	Between 0 and 1 point	Between 2 and 3 points	Between 4 and 5 points	Between 6 and 7 points	Between 8 and 10 points
User 1	3	12	1	23	5
User 2	0	1	10	9	20
User 3	9	9	1	15	6
User 4	2	2	3	14	19
User 5	0	0	3	20	17

5   Results and Conclusions

This paper proposes the use of a multi-agent system based on JADE for the recommendation of routes to electric bicycle users. This is done using the ebikemotion platform, which records data on the routes travelled by e-bikes. After analyzing the completed routes, the system generates a set of personalized recommendations for each user based on the routes that were previously travelled.

From the case study results we can see that the majority of the recommendations made to the users were valued positively; the ratings ranged between 6 and 10 points. Only user 3 reported that 19 of his recommendations were not satisfactory and were rated with a score between 0 and 5 points. After an in-depth examination of the routes that had been recommended to this user we discovered that they were located several kilometers away from the routes that this user had normally travelled. This was the reason for which the user gave them a lower rating.

Future lines of work include using more route data distance, average altitude ascended and descended, time, etc.), this will allow to personalize the recommendations further. A future system will also consider the bicycles' current battery charge status in the recommendation of routes.

Acknowledgements. This work has been supported by the GatEBike project: Arquitectura basada en Computación Social para el control Inteligente e Interacción en Bicicletas Eléctricas. RTC-2015-4171-4. Project co-financed with Ministerio de Economía y Competitividad and Fondo Europeo de Desarrollo Regional (FEDER) funds (RETOS-COLABORACIÓN 2015). The research of Daniel Hernández de la Iglesia has been co-financed by the European Social Fund and Junta de Castilla y León (Operational Programme 2014–2020 for Castilla y León, EDU/529/2017 BOCYL). Álvaro Lozano is supported by the pre-doctoral fellowship from the University of Salamanca and Banco Santander. The research of Alberto López Barriuso has been co-financed by the European Social Fund and Junta de Castilla y León (Operational Programme 2014–2020 for Castilla y León, EDU/128/2015 BOCYL).

References

1. AMBE. Asociación de Marcas y Bicicletas de EspañaAMBE | Asociación de Marcas y Bicicletas de España
2. Ling, Z., Cherry, C., MacArthur, J., Weinert, J.: Differences of cycling experiences and perceptions between E-Bike and bicycle users in the united states. Sustainability 9(10), 1662 (2017)
3. Fishman, E., Cherry, C.: E-bikes in the mainstream: reviewing a decade of research. Transp. Rev. 36(1), 72–91 (2016)
4. Citron, R.: Executive summary: electric bicycles Li-Ion and SLA E-bikes: drivetrain, motor, and battery technology trends, competitive landscape, and global market forecasts section 1 (2016)
5. Cherry, C.R., Yang, H., Jones, L.R., He, M.: Dynamics of electric bike ownership and use in Kunming, China. Transp. Policy 45, 127–135 (2016)
6. La Iglesia, D.D., De Paz, J., González, G.V., Barriuso, A., Bajo, J., Corchado, J.: Increasing the intensity over time of an electric-assist bike based on the user and route: the bike becomes the gym. Sensors. 18(1), 220 (2018)
7. De La Iglesia, D., Villarubia, G., De Paz, J., Bajo, J.: Multi-sensor information fusion for optimizing electric bicycle routes using a swarm intelligence algorithm. Sensors 17(11), 2501 (2017)
8. Langford, B.C., Cherry, C.R., Bassett, D.R., Fitzhugh, E.C., Dhakal, N.: Comparing physical activity of pedal-assist electric bikes with walking and conventional bicycles. J. Transp. Heal. 6(July), 463–473 (2017)
9. Resnick, P., Varian, H.R.: Recommender systems. Commun. ACM 40(3), 56–58 (1997)
10. Schedl, M., Knees, P., McFee, B., Bogdanov, D., Kaminskas, M.: Music recommender systems. In: Ricci, F., Rokach, L., Shapira, B. (eds.) Recommender Systems Handbook, pp. 453–492. Springer, Boston, MA (2015). https://doi.org/10.1007/978-1-4899-7637-6_13

11. Barriuso, A.L., de La Prieta, F., Murciego, Á.L., Hernández, D., Herrero, J.R.: An intelligent agent-based journalism platform. In: Bajo, J., Escalona, M.J., Giroux, S., Hoffa-Dąbrowska, P., Julián, V., Novais, P., Sánchez-Pi, N., Unland, R., Azambuja-Silveira, R. (eds.) PAAMS 2016. CCIS, vol. 616, pp. 322–332. Springer, Cham (2016). https://doi.org/10.1007/978-3-319-39387-2_27

12. Abdel-Hafez, A., Xu, Y., Tian, N.: Item reputation-aware recommender systems. In: Proceedings of the 16th International Conference on Information Integration and Web-based Applications & Services - iiWAS 2014, pp. 79–86 (2014)

13. Ebikemotion® – Ebikes Platform

PAAMS Workshop AAAT

Designing Multi-agent Swarm of UAV for Precise Agriculture

Petr Skobelev[1(✉)], Denis Budaev[2], Nikolay Gusev[2], and Georgy Voschuk[2]

[1] Samara State Technical University, Samara, Russia
petr.skobelev@gmail.com
[2] Aeropatrol LLC, Samara, Russia
info@aero-patrol.ru

Abstract. The paper proposes multi-agent technology and a prototype system with together-acting UAVs for joint survey missions. The prototype makes it possible to connect UAVs in a united swarm, proposes coordinated flight plans and adaptively re-configures plans due to disruptive events. The approach to organization of program agents within a prototype subsystem is described. A series of simulation experiments and several flight tests were conducted to evaluate the effectiveness of the distributed scheduling mechanism. The aim of the current and future developments is creation of complex solutions for coordinated management of UAVs for precise agriculture.

Keywords: Unmanned aerial vehicle · UAV · Drone · Swarm
Multi-agent system · Coordinated control · Swarm intelligence · Survey mission
Crops monitoring · Precise agriculture

1 Introduction

More than 10 million acres were mapped by unmanned aerial vehicles (UAVs or drones) in 160 countries on 7 continents in 2016. This generated an estimated $150 million in economic value for the commercial drone industry [1]. Large and small companies are not only integrating commercial drones into day-to-day processes, but also relying on the data from drones. Drone application brings significant time and cost savings over traditional data capture methods.

The main advantages of using drones are achieved when used in time-critical missions or during monitoring of large areas [2]. One of the top drone adoption leader industries is agriculture (see Fig. 1). Drones make it possible to capture on-demand aerial imagery of fields. This means the user can analyze drone map data to understand the health of crops, spot problem areas, and take action quickly to remedy any issues before they spread.

There is a variety of crop management decisions business can make based on drone imagery to help increase the financial potential. Drones are changing agriculture. The insights provided by the average drone and standard camera can prove to be the best investment in season.

© Springer International Publishing AG, part of Springer Nature 2018
J. Bajo et al. (Eds.): PAAMS 2018 Workshops, CCIS 887, pp. 47–59, 2018.
https://doi.org/10.1007/978-3-319-94779-2_5

| Drone Service Providers | Agriculture | Surveying | Constriction | Education | Other |

Fig. 1. Top drone adoption leaders in 2016 by blog.dronedeploy.com.

However, there are some key issues not resolved for drone industry at the moment:

- no real Intelligence Inside UAV;
- difficult to manage several UAVs;
- time consuming if several UAVs;
- no flexibility or rescheduling;
- conflicts and accidents;
- human factor.

For example, there is lack of software to manage a group of UAVs to reassign tasks in case of failure of one UAV, addition of a new area, or addition of a new UAV to the group. Most of the existing software solutions are designed for planning only one UAV mission. On the other hand, drone group management software would use available UAVs resources in the most efficient way (battery or fuel supplies, time resources, hardware/computing resources of UAVs). In addition, quick reallocation of tasks between the drones during mission execution would reduce mission completion time. Thus, the development of such systems of automatic control of drones groups will allow timely receiving detailed information on crops, reduce the costs of plant protection and increase yields.

In this paper, we discuss our work on developing multi-agent technology and proto-type for UAV swarm control. The next section describes some known developments for managing drones groups. The problem statement is described in Sect. 3. The prototype development aspects, high-level description of planning algorithm and criteria are outlined in Sect. 4. Results are presented and discussed in Sect. 5, conclusions and future work in Sect. 6.

2   The Concept of Swarm

Swarms in Nature are societies of simple insects. But at the same time, the phenomenon is that when working together in coordinated manner swarms are able to demonstrate intelligence, flexibility, efficiency, performance, reliability (see Fig. 2).

There are several research projects aimed to propose swarm intelligence in aerial management. For example, DARPA: HART (Heterogeneous Aerial Reconnaissance Team) autonomously manages a large mix of manned and unmanned aircrafts and sensors and distributes streaming video, surveillance and reconnaissance information to warfighters in the field. The system can either dynamically retrieve, in near-real time, the required information from a catalog of geo-registered images or direct manned/unmanned

Fig. 2. Different swarms and behavior

aircraft systems and/or sensors to collect updated intelligence, surveillance and reconnaissance information. The HART system has recently completed testing and is in the final stages of preparation for fielding. Adoption of HART is under active consideration by all military services [3].

Another example is DARPA: CODE (Collaborative Operations in Denied Environment) project. The CODE program seeks to help military's unmanned aircraft systems conduct dynamic, long-distance engagements of highly mobile targets. CODE-equipped UASs would perform their mission by sharing data, negotiating assignments, and synchronizing actions and communications among team members and with the commander. CODE's modular open software architecture on board the UASs would enable multiple CODE-equipped unmanned aircraft to navigate to their destinations and find, track, identify, and engage targets under established rules of engagement. The UASs could also recruit other CODE-equipped UASs from nearby friendly forces to augment their own capabilities and adapt to dynamic situations such as attrition of friendly forces or the emergence of unanticipated threats [4].

In its new projects, DARPA aims to research and develop advanced human-swarm interfaces to enable users to manage potentially hundreds of drones simultaneously in real time. Developed computer programs, such as the Low-Cost UAV Swarming Technology (LOCUST) or Micro-Autonomous Systems Technology (MAST), try to provide a way to control Swarms of unmanned air vehicles (UAVs) and unmanned ground vehicles (UGVs) acting together. The brand new Offensive Swarm Enabled Tactics Program (OFFSET) researches solutions to human-drone swarm communication. As part of drone swarms tactics development DARPA created the Service Academies Swarm Challenge as a collaborative project of the Agency and the three U.S. military Service academies — the U.S. Military Academy, the U.S. Naval Academy, and the U.S. Air Force Academy. The main purpose of the initiative is to encourage students to develop innovative offensive and defensive tactics for drone swarms. In 2017 the initiative held as three-day competition at California Army National Guard post in Camp Roberts and hosted more than 40 Cadets and Midshipmen [5] (see Fig. 3).

Fig. 3. DARPA Service Academies Swarm Challenge, Camp Roberts, California, April 23–25, 2017

Despite a relatively large number of studies of drones for military applications, the authors believe that the use of drones groups is promising for precise agriculture. This is especially true for countries with large areas of crops, as well as lagging in the application of technologies for point spray of fertilizers and plant protection substances. In such a case, regular survey flights by groups of drones can become an indispensable source of operational and more accurate data compared to satellite imagery. However, full automation of the processes of flying over large areas is unthinkable without the development of suitable algorithms and control systems. The authors see this direction as the most promising for the development of this study.

3   Problem Statement

Despite military developments for drone swarm management, there is a lag in the application of UAV groups for civilian industries. We believe that some reasons for this lie in the poorly developed approaches to swarm management for precise domains.

For effective management of resource allocation (incl. drones and their subsystems), it is expedient to use scheduling systems. Nowadays these kinds of systems use the following methods of complex problem solving:

- greedy algorithms, based on heuristic business-rules for specific subject areas;
- traditional methods of optimization and linear programming in the area of mixed real-valued, integral-valued and logical variables, the improvement of precise methods of tasks solving, such as "branch and bound" methods, nonlinear programming methods, methods of constraint programming [6];
- metaheuristics (local search, Tabu Search, GRASP algorithms) [7];
- bio-inspired methods: Ant Colony Optimization (ACO), Artificial Bee Colony (ABC), Bio Inspired and a similar methods, as well Simulated Annealing (SA), Monte-Carlo method and some others [8]:
- artificial intelligence methods, the use of neural networks and fuzzy logic.

Many scheduling systems are based on centralized and deterministic principles. However, distributed coordination in dynamic networks has attracted an interest of numerous researchers in recent years. As shown in [9, 10], the multi-agent technology methods are the most promising and appropriate for the resource allocation algorithm design.

We consider the following problem statement:

1. there is an area for survey mission that is limited in size and may be identified by boundary points coordinates;
2. topography information about the area is known (terrain heights);
3. several different UAVs are available for the joint mission;
4. technical specification of UAVs and equipment is known (ranges of flight, maximum speeds and altitudes, battery capacity, charging time, camera information, etc.) and they could be different for each UAV.

Required functionality:

1. Management system is able to evaluate coordinated flight plans for each UAV in joint group with consideration of their unique characteristics.
2. Management system is not centralized but works by means of communications of all UAVs in a joint group.
3. Each UAV flight plan is proposed by the Smart UAV Agent located on a single-board computer inside a UAV.
4. Each Smart UAV agent is responsible for coordination and validation of flight plan with other UAVs to avoid conflicts and reduce overall mission execution time.
5. Each Smart UAV is able to react on events, plan and re-allocate tasks adaptively, forecast execution time of mission.
6. Each Smart UAV agent is able to choose and change the role dynamically in real time according to the situation and UAV characteristics.
7. Wireless interaction of UAVs is available directly or through a special drone-connector.
8. Interaction with the Command Center is available to meet the objectives.
9. Usage of knowledge base and multi-agent technology is necessary.

The main expected results are reducing the time for problem solving by up to 3–5 times in comparison with individual managing of UAVs by human operators. We believe it is possible due to the ability of UAVs to communicate over the wireless network and coordinate actions.

4   Prototype Development

During the prototype design phase, we have elaborated the following scenario and base scheduling mechanics:

1. Operator sets the initial mission parameters: the boundary points of observation area, selects a mission type, for example, "single flight" or "patrol mission" and determines group members.

2. All UAVs have on board a computer with multi-agent scheduler and are able to share their results wirelessly.
3. Characteristics of the UAVs and their equipment differ and are stored in the knowledge base.
4. For Agents of Regions we introduce Agents of Observation Zones (region is a set of zones).
5. Scheduling is a process of negotiation between Agents of Zones and Agents of UAVs in order to determine the plan of monitoring for the region.
6. If an Agent of UAV decides to take the Zone in plan, it computes the costs and time and shares it with others.
7. If other agents can perform a better plan – the decision is changed.
8. Agents of Zones look for Agents of UAVs in the same manner.
9. After the initial matching each UAV agent and agent of zone are continuing to improve their key performance indicators (KPIs).
10. The scheduling process stops when no agent can improve its KPIs or the time is expired.
11. When a new event occurs – a new task appears or a UAV is unavailable - the process repeats until new balance is found in the schedule.
12. Adaptability is a result of self-organization of UAVs and zones for observation.

A simplified representation of the prototype architecture is shown in Fig. 4.

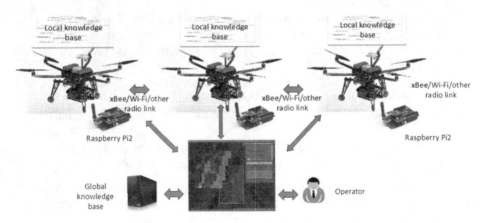

Fig. 4. Prototype high-level architecture

As part of the multi-agent approach, each active entity type within a solved problem is represented by a software agent, which formalizes the logic and needs of that entity.

In addition, each UAV has a separate single-board computer with multi-agent software for distributed mission planning via wireless communications. Scheduling in this case is a process of negotiation between agents in order to determine the compromise resulting plan.

During initial scheduling, the survey area is divided into a finite amount of observation squares with dimensions that correspond to characteristics of the UAVs and their equipment. For example, for the UAV with camera sensor width 4.55 mm, the focal length 3.61 mm, the flight height 119 m, the image width and height 4000 and 3000 pixel respectively, we expect ground sampling distance (GSD) of 3.75 cm/pixel and image footprint on the ground 150 m. Therefore, for the area of 32 × 32 observation squares we expect the total area of 23.04 km². Thus, there is a survey mission with 1024 sub-tasks for the available UAVs (see Fig. 5).

Fig. 5. Observation squares grid with UAV routes

After that, each observation square is associated with its sub-task to perform. Each sub-task has a timestamp of UAV flight in hh:mm:ss. The timestamp renews at the next UAV flight over the observation square. Considering these facts, UAV agents can track how long the square was without supervision. It is important for the patrol mission planning.

When the operator sets mission parameters (boundary points of observation area, mission type, UAVs), all sub-tasks become available for scheduling and are transmitted to UAVs matching mechanism. This mechanism is responsible for the initial distribution of individual sub-tasks (observation squares) between individual UAVs of the group. In fact, the mechanism performs clustering to aggregate observations squares.

Each UAV agent determines its individual area of interest as the corresponding cluster, that is, a set of observations squares, in which the agent has to build a flight path to perform UAV area supervision. Flight plan is also produced by UAV agent onboard a drone's single-board computer. UAV agent analyzes the list of available sub-tasks and evaluates alternatives sets of paths based on the set of planning criteria.

As one of the criteria, the number of possible turns of UAV is considered. As a starting point the algorithm of rapid aerial mapping was considered [11]. Later on this criterion was evaluated into the criterion of total UAVs path distance, which is described further.

During distributed route planning process each UAV agent tries to find possible unvisited and unplanned observation squares (sub-tasks) of specified length (algorithm parameter) from the initial (Home) point. Each alternative set of sub-tasks estimated by a drone agent according to two criteria, described below. The set with the best value is sent for coordination to agents of other drones and to the operators' consoles.

When all the squares in the zone of responsibility of the drones (cluster) are planned, the behavior of the agent of the drone is switched to the optimization of the route. In the process of optimization, the agents of the drones transmit to each other the forecasts of the completion time of the routes. In the event of significant differences in the completion times (the set parameter of the system), agents try to redistribute the observation squares (sub-tasks) among themselves to reduce the delta of the time difference.

This approach allows controlling sub-tasks distribution and balancing in real time, and unlike similar methods of path forming [11–13], it is originally designed to increase the total system performance, resource utilization and reduce mission execution time. Agent key performance indicators (KPI) are applied to evaluate and compare different flight plan trajectories (sub-tasks chains) based on criteria of UAV agent satisfaction.

For prototype, two criteria have been chosen to calculate the agent satisfaction for the considered chain of observation squares. First, the criterion of area observability depends on sub-tasks squares observability. The meaning of this criterion is to enforce agents selecting those observation squares, which were most unexplored in the previous time intervals. UAV agent satisfaction depends on the time during which the square remained without supervision, that is, from the time during which no UAVs of a group were flying over a square for observing (see Fig. 6).

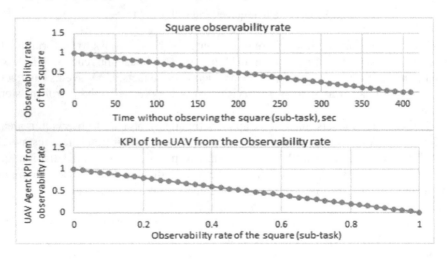

Fig. 6. UAV agent KPI from observability rate of observation square

The second criterion is the total UAVs path distance. The meaning of this criterion is to enforce agents to select a set of squares, which lie along the same line. This provides efficient use of UAVs resources - minimum number of turns on the path and minimum distance without observing a square. UAVs agent KPI are higher when its path contains a set of observations squares lying on a straight line. The attractiveness of the selected squares for the UAV agent is higher, the higher the ratio of path length on observed squares to the total path length (see Fig. 7).

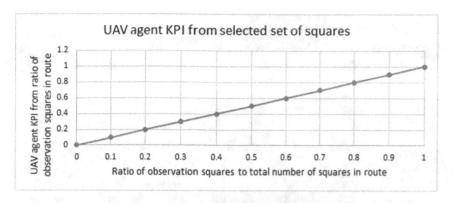

Fig. 7. UAV agent KPI from path distance with observation squares

The overall system satisfaction at a certain step of work is defined as the sum of all UAV agents satisfaction on the criterion of area observability and on the criterion of total UAVs path distance considering criteria weights (the sum of the weights is always equal to 1).

$$KPI_{system} = k_{area\,observ.} * \sum_{i=1}^{N} KPI_{i\,area\,observ.} + k_{path\,dist.} \sum_{i=1}^{N} KPI_{i\,path\,dist.} \qquad (1)$$

During coordination of the flight plan in the group, each UAV provides a set of possible options for changing position. Each of these options is characterized by satisfaction indicators for the UAV (observability and path distance). The overall system satisfaction at a particular planning step is defined as the sum of KPIs of all agents, considering criteria weights. The higher the total KPI of the system, the better the quality of solution in the context of the selected criteria.

Dynamic scheduling mechanism implementation provides adaptive relocating of sub-tasks between UAVs to minimize differences in completion times. During flights UAVs exchange data about execution time forecasts. The UAV detects significant difference between its completion time forecast and the time of another UAV. After that, the UAV agent calculates how many sub-tasks should be transferred from or to the other UAV to reduce the difference between completion times. The UAV agent sends a request to reallocate the calculated number of sub-tasks to other UAVs. Then sub-tasks are reallocated to other UAV(s) or rejection is received (for example, if the UAV has already got some extra sub-tasks and is overloaded in terms of execution time). Thus, adaptive balancing mechanism ensures that the mission is performed in the shortest time even in cases of UAVs various performance and unplanned events.

During the prototype development phase, the General Designer's Stand is implemented to test the proposed multi-agent planning solution. This is the simulation tool for modeling different scenarios of survey and patrol missions with joint UAV group.

General Designer's Stand is represented by 9 separate screens for viewing main indicators and statuses of drones in the group, as well as 4 panels for managing external events, joint group and individual UAVs, knowledge base (see Fig. 8).

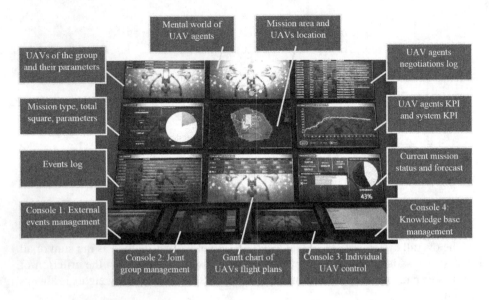

Fig. 8. General Designer's Stand is a simulation tool for UAV group missions modeling

In addition to the stand, there are several computers with single-board computers and installed multi-agent software for distributed planning (Smart UAV Agents onboard UAV). The onboard UAV units are created on the basis of Raspberry Pi 2 and integrated with Pixhawk PX4 flight controller.

5   Experimental Results

A series of experiments was completed during the experimental phase to research the system performance. The input data for every experiment contained the same survey area with 1024 observation squares but a different collection of available UAVs. The main purpose of the experiments was to evaluate effectiveness of distributed scheduling mechanism and assess the formed UAV flight plan with estimation of the time required for preparing flight plans. Other purposes include assessing reaction of the swarm and Smart UAV agents to tasks changing during the scheduling process and even during mission execution in real time.

It should be noted that the logic of drone agents can be performed on a single-board computer (used Raspberry Pi2 connected to Pixhawk PX4 on 3DR IRIS+) directly on the drones or on any compatible computer connected to the system. In the presence of stable communication channels between drones and operator consoles, there was no difference in time between the two variants. However, all the results of the experiments presented below were obtained using directly the single-board computers of the

Table 1. Results of experiments for different numbers of UAVs

Indicator	1 UAV	3 UAVs	4 UAVs	10 UAVs
Time of planning process, sec.	165	62	50	21
Execution time forecast, min.	1205	404	304	145
New area addition time (rescheduling), sec.	6	9	15	13
Overall system KPI (agents satisfaction), %	95	78	79	68

Raspberry P2 and are related to the simulation of the survey mission. Results of experiments are shown in Table 1.

Considering the results, one can make some assumptions and conclusions:

1. The planning process time depends on the number of observation squares in the mission and the number of UAVs involved in scheduling. With the same number of squares, the more devices are involved in distribution process, the faster scheduling works. Alleged explanation is the distributed nature of the planning mechanism, which allows for use of all resources of computing devices in the planning process, which uses all available resources of distributed single-board computers. This reduces the planning time even though there is a need to coordinate routes and search for possible conflicts. However, the need for good communication channels between UAVs should be noted.

2. The bigger the number of UAVs involved in the mission, the less time is required for the survey mission. This is because the entire mission area is divided into separate areas and distributed among several UAVs performing flights in parallel.

3. Thirdly, the system reaction time in cases of disruptive events reduces when a smaller number of UAVs is affected by this change, because coordinating all changes requires negotiation between all agents affected by these changes. For example, when adding a new sub-area of 256 squares for a group of 10 UAVs, only some of the most closely-located UAVs are "diverted" to new tasks. This reduces reallocation time, because not all Smart UAV Agents are distracted by negotiations and approvals.

4. The overall efficiency is characterized by the indicator of system KPI, which is determined by satisfaction of each Smart UAV Agent. Generally, the KPI value for a single-working UAV is higher than the overall KPI for a group of UAVs. This is because UAVs in a group are forced to compete and negotiate to coordinate the final mission plan. They search for a compromise solution, which reduces the individual satisfaction of each Smart UAV agent. Thus, the overall KPI index can be considered only as a signal of plan optimization necessity. And this indicator only can be compared with similar indicators of similar UAVs groups, for example, similar UAV types and number of devices.

5. Multi-agent planning methods provide real-time ability to manage a group of UAVs and monitor and adjust performance of the group through agent key performance indicators and criteria.

In addition to the stand experiments, several test flights of 3DR IRIS+ with onboard multi-agent software were performed. These flights also confirmed the results of simulations.

6   Conclusion

Software systems for management and control of robotic devices and UAV groups are actively developed at the present time. For successful use of such systems, their functionality should allow for adjustment of plans in the changing environment. This includes reaction on unforeseen situations with relocation of tasks between UAVs in a group.

During the project, distributed multi-agent planning prototype was implemented and examined. The planning process is organized through wireless communication between individual Smart UAV Agents on each UAV. Hardware modules for 3DR IRIS UAVs and Pixhawk PX4 flight controller are implemented on the base of single-board Raspberry PI 2.

The developed prototype is developed to plan and coordinate actions of the UAV group, even in real time when some disruptive events occur during mission execution. Therefore, it is possible to fulfill the mission even if several UAVs are excluded from the group. Two criteria have been initially proposed, but this list can be extended and adapted to different domains.

To finalize the prototype and introduce the technology to the market, an industrial partner has been involved. Rassvet JSC in Rostov region has wheat fields with more than 30 000 ha of surface fragmented in smaller areas. The company uses top-level technology and John Deere equipment for wheat production and export sales. Specialists need to monitor all these fields covering large distances on a daily basis (more than 700 km a day).

As the next battle-proven stage in the development, there will be in-field experimental research of a swarm of drones for the industrial client's fields. One of the tasks is to offer not only flight task scheduling algorithms, but a convenient completed end-user toolkit for crop monitoring. The tool should allow to connect to a group different models of drones and automatically manage their work in large areas. It is necessary to consider the applicability for the system of various models of drones available on the market, and not only models with open source flight controller (e.g. PX4 with Mavlink protocol). It is also necessary to investigate the use of heterogeneous groups of drones (rotary and aircraft type, autonomy, payload), as well as the number of necessary operators for different groups of drones and depending on the number of drones in groups.

Acknowledgments. The work was supported by the Ministry of Education and Science of the Russian Federation in the framework of agreement №14.574.21.0183. The unique identification number: RFMEFI57417X0183.

References

1. Commercial Drone Industry Trends. https://blog.dronedeploy.com/commercial-drone-industry-trends-aae2010ff349. Accessed 30 Mar 2017
2. Skobelev, P., Budaev, D., Brankovsky, A., Voschuk. G.: Multi-agent tasks scheduling and control for coordinated actions of unmanned aerial vehicles acting in group. Int. J. Des. Nat. Ecody. **13**(1), 39–45 (2018)
3. Heterogeneous Aerial Reconnaissance Team. https://en.wikipedia.org/wiki/Heterogeneous_Aerial_Reconnaissance_Team. Accessed 3 Nov 2017
4. CODE Takes Next Steps toward More Sophisticated, Resilient, and Collaborative Unmanned Air Systems. http://www.doncio.navy.mil/CHIPS/ArticleDetails.aspx?ID=7908
5. Service Academies Swarm Challenge Recap Teaser. https://www.youtube.com/watch?v=igz2dmDLOZY
6. Pinedo, M.: Scheduling: Theory, Algorithms, and System. Springer, New York (2008). https://doi.org/10.1007/978-1-4614-2361-4
7. Voß, S.: Meta-heuristics: The State of the Art. In: Nareyek, A. (ed.) LSPS 2000. LNCS (LNAI), vol. 2148, pp. 1–23. Springer, Heidelberg (2001). https://doi.org/10.1007/3-540-45612-0_1
8. Binitha, S., Sathya, S.: A survey of bio inspired optimization algorithms. Int. J. Soft Comput. Eng. **2**(2), 2231–2307 (2012)
9. Rzevski, G., Skobelev, P.: Managing Complexity. WIT Press, Boston (2014)
10. Skobelev, P.: Multi-agent systems for real time adaptive resource management. In: Leitão, P., Karnouskos, S. (eds.) Industrial Agents: Emerging Applications of Software Agents in Industry, pp. 207–230. Elsevier (2015)
11. Santamaria, E., Segor, F., Tchouchenkov, I., Schoenbein, R.: Rapid aerial mapping with multiple heterogeneous unmanned vehicles. Int. J. Adv. Syst. Meas. **6**(3–4), 384–393 (2013)
12. Franco, C., Buttazzo, G.: Energy-aware coverage path planning of UAVs. In: Proceedings of Autonomous Robot Systems and Competitions IEEE International Conference (ICARSC), pp. 111–117 (2015)
13. Kamrani, F., Ayani, R.: Using on-line simulation for adaptive path planning of UAVs. In: Proceeding DS-RT 2007 Proceedings of the 11th IEEE International Symposium on Distributed Simulation and Real-Time Applications, pp. 167–174 (2007)

An Electronic Marketplace for Airlines

Luis Reis[1], Ana Paula Rocha[1,2], and Antonio J. M. Castro[2(✉)]

[1] DEI, Faculty of Engineering, University of Porto, Porto, Portugal
[2] LIACC, University of Porto, Porto, Portugal
brochadoluis@gmail.com, {arocha,ajmc}@fe.up.pt

Abstract. In this paper we propose an airline marketplace, modeled as a multi-agent system with an automated negotiation mechanism, where airlines can announce availability of resources (aircraft or aircraft and crew) for lease and other airlines can go there to contract resources to fill gaps in the operation, typically due to disruptions and/or an unexpected increase on the operation. The proposed negotiation occurs in several rounds, where qualitative comments made by the buyer agent on proposals sent by the sellers enables these to learn how to calculate new proposals, using a case-based reasoning methodology.

Keywords: Electronic marketplace · Multi-agent systems · CBR

1 Introduction

According to Kohl et al. [1], "research on the recovery operation to this date only deals with a single airline. Cooperation between airlines is not supported". Nowadays, each airline tries to solve the operations recovery problems with their own resources [2]. If they have an open position for a specific type of crew in a flight, they try to find a suitable one from their own staff. The same happens with aircraft. Sometimes, the airlines have to lease aircraft and crew members when needed (known in the industry as ACMI - Aircraft, Crew, Maintenance and Insurance), but through a direct contact with charter airlines. It is not a usual practice to use only crew members (without being part of the aircraft) from other companies. The electronic marketplace (EM) that we propose in this paper, is a permanently open virtual marketplace where registered airlines (represented by software agents) can meet each other to purchase services and has the possibility to be integrated with systems or tools for airline operations control, like the one we use in this paper. It has the following advantages:

- Airlines that participate in this EM will have more resources available to solve their problems.
- Airlines may take advantage of exceeding resources in specific dates and times and sell services performed by these resources to other airlines.
- Can reduce costs and time for the airline that has a specific problem.

© Springer International Publishing AG, part of Springer Nature 2018
J. Bajo et al. (Eds.): PAAMS 2018 Workshops, CCIS 887, pp. 60–71, 2018.
https://doi.org/10.1007/978-3-319-94779-2_6

When compared with the work of Malucelli et al. [3] we complete the work by proposing a negotiation algorithm for the EM.

Airlines have an Airline Operations Control Center (AOCC) that has the responsibility to ensure that flights meet their planned schedule or, if any problem arises, to find a viable solution that minimizes both the impact in the operational plan and its cost. Research in the air transportation domain has shown that airline companies lose between 2% to 3% of their annual revenue as consequence of disruptions and, that, the impact caused by small disruptions in companies' profits can be reduced by at least 20%, through a better recovery process [4]. Currently, operations management is essentially a manual process, supported by tools, that among other functions include monitoring, event detection and problems resolution and, strongly depends on the tactical knowledge of the AOCC's members [2].

Every time an irregular event that has an impact on the scheduled plan is detected, the AOCC's team has to plan carefully an alternative schedule, to ensure that it minimizes at most the disruption cost. A disruption can be view as composed by four dimensions [2]: aircraft, crew member, passenger and flight. MASDIMA (Multi-Agent System for Disruption Management) [2] addresses the Aircraft, Crew and Passenger recovery problem using an approach that is able to recover all these problem dimensions simultaneously. The present work intends to implement an EM that helps MASDIMA to find the resources (crew and aircraft) needed for its solution.

In Multi-Agent Systems it is required for an agent to interact with other agents whom may not share common goals. This leads to the need to reach agreements [5] through an automated negotiation process. The negotiation decision is a complex process because, most of the times, it does not consider only one attribute but multiple attributes as it is in the case of AOCC. Giving different utility values to the different attributes under negotiation solves the problem of multi-attribute evaluation. Therefore, a multi-attribute negotiation is converted to a single-attribute one, to be made over the evaluation value (examples of this are the work in [6–9]). This is also the approach followed in our work.

The multi-agent system based Electronic Marketplace, presented in this paper, allows companies to negotiate among themselves the missing resources. The negotiation algorithm includes case-based reasoning to learn how to make a counter-proposal. According to Riesbeck and Schank [10], "A case-based reasoner solves problems by using or adapting solutions to old problems.", i.e. case-based reasoning (CBR) focuses on the reuse of knowledge acquired from previous experiences in order to solve new problems. Like humans do, CBR is a problem solving paradigm that uses incremental and sustained learning since new experiences are retained each time a problem is solved making those available for future problems. A negotiation algorithm with a CBR approach has never been considered in the works mentioned.

The rest of this paper is as follows: Sect. 2 is the main section and presents the proposed multi-agent system EM. Section 3 presents the scenarios used in experiments, but only one, as well as the results obtained, is discussed. Finally, Sect. 4 concludes the work presented.

2 The Electronic Marketplace

When a disrupted flight is detected, the AOCC's team should find an alternative trying to minimize both the delay and the disruption cost. The airline electronic market proposed here intends to help the airline company in this disruption management process, by allowing to find external resources, possibly less costly or available sooner than the company's own. In this market there are two types of entities:

- The buyer, that represents an injured airline company. This is the airline company that has a disrupted flight (an unexpected event causing a delay in the flight).
- The seller, that represents a service provider airline company

Being the object under negotiation, a *Need* is identified by the resource(s) needed: a list of crew members and an aircraft fleet as well as relevant information related to the disrupted flight (scheduled departure time, trip time, delay, origin and destination), as depicted in Eq. (1).

$$Need = <Res, STD, TripD, Del, Orig, Dest> \qquad (1)$$

$$\text{with } Res = <CrewList, Aircraft\_Fleet>$$

where: Res is the resource(s) needed, STD is the trip duration; Del is the delay of the disrupted flight; $Orig$ is the airport origin and $Dest$ is the airport destination.

Buyer and sellers will negotiate the resource that buyer identifies as its need. This resource can be a set of crew members, an aircraft or both. When the resource under negotiation is an aircraft, it is required that a crew to handle it should also be provided. For the negotiation to take place, buyers and sellers need to know each other. Sellers should register first, otherwise will be no one in the market to be asked for some resource(s). So, the first step is to have multiple sellers registered and wait for some buyer to register too. When a buyer registers in the market, it retrieves a list containing all registered sellers and starts a negotiation with them. The negotiation is a process where proposals are exchanged between buyer and sellers until an agreement is reached between the buyer and one of the sellers, and the negotiation ends successfully, or no agreement is reached and the negotiation fails.

2.1 The Negotiation Process

The negotiation protocol proposed for the airline EM is based in the FIPA Iterated Contract Net and was chosen because it allows multi-round iterative bidding. This way, it is ensured that a wide space of solutions is subject to discussion and refinement, as it is the case of humans' negotiations. This protocol works with an initiator (buyer in this case) and multiple responders (sellers).

The buyer initiates the negotiation, by sending to all sellers an *Invitation* message, (CFP - Call For Proposals), containing relevant information about the disrupted flight and resource needs (as indicated in (1)). When a seller receives the *Invitation* message, it processes the message verifying if it is able to provide the required resources or not. If yes, the seller replies with a *Proposal* message, containing the price and availability of its proposal (Eq. (3)).

$$Proposal = <\alpha, \rho> \tag{2}$$

$$\text{with } \alpha \in [0, delay\_of\_disrupted\_flight]$$

where: α is the proposed availability and ρ is the proposed price

If the seller is not able to provide the required resources, it replies with a *Refusal* message.

The first round is then concluded and until the end of the negotiation, all rounds are processed the same way, explained as follows.

Airline Company Behavior (Buyer Agent)

Buyer receives one proposal from each interested seller, evaluates all proposals and selects the best one of the current round according to its utility (see Eq. (4)).

$$\mu = \mu_\alpha \times \beta + \mu_\rho \times (1 - \beta) \tag{3}$$

$$\text{with } \beta \in [0, 1]$$

where: μ is the utility of the proposal $[0, 1]$; μ_α is the utility of the availability parameter $[0, 1]$; μ_ρ is the utility of the price parameter $[0, 1]$; β is the importance factor of the availability parameter.

In buyers perspective, the utility of a proposal must measure its availability and price, where it tries to minimize both.

If the best proposal of the current round is better than the best one found in previous rounds (if any), it is considered the new best proposal. If not, the best proposal remains unchanged. Buyer creates then a reply for each received proposal, issuing a qualitative feedback over the availability and price in it, by comparing these values with the ones in the best proposal. This reply or *Feedback* message is send to all sellers that are currently in the negotiation (Eq. (4)).

The qualitative comment included in the *Feedback* message (*QlEv* in Eq. (4)) can assume one of the three options: OK: means there is no need to improve the attribute that received this feedback; LOWER: means the attribute that received this feedback has a high value, should be reduced; MUCH LOWER: means the attribute that received this feedback has a very high value, should be greatly reduced.

$$Feedback = <QlEv_\alpha, QlEv_\rho> \tag{4}$$

where: $QlEv_\alpha$ is the qualitative evaluation of the proposed availability and $QlEv_\rho$ is the qualitative evaluation of the proposed price

Service Provider Behavior (Seller Agent)
When a seller receives the feedback for the proposal sent, it updates its experience history, by recording and reasoning the concerned feedback. Sellers will use its experience history (similar to what humans do) to formulate new proposals during the current and future negotiations, taking also into account its utility (see Eq. (5))

$$\mu = \frac{\rho - \gamma \times \zeta}{(\sigma \times \zeta) - (\gamma \times \zeta)} \tag{5}$$

where: μ is the utility of the proposal $[0, 1]$; ρ is the proposed price; γ is the minimum price multiplier; σ is the maximum price multiplier; ζ is the leasing associated cost.

If a seller does not have any more proposals to propose, it sends a *Refuse* message. This process is explained in more detail in Sect. 2.2.

The negotiation is over when all sellers have sent a refusal message or a deadline is reached. In the last round of the negotiation, buyer sends an *Accept* message to the best proposal's owner, with the accepted proposal data and a *Reject* message to all others. The seller that received the accept message sends back to buyer a *Termination* message with all relevant data about the *Need*. Upon receiving the termination message, buyer unregisters himself from the market as the negotiation is over.

Note that messages exchanged during all the negotiation ensure that agents' (buyers or sellers) information is kept private. Agents never reveal their costs or utility. For instance, if sellers would know the buyer's disruption cost, their strategy would be to ask for a price slightly lower than that cost, making the market an unpractical alternative for buyer.

2.2   Case-Based Reasoning Used in Negotiation

Sellers use CBR (Case-based Reasoning) to decide what to do upon receiving the buyer feedback over the proposal they have sent, consulting a record of previous experiences classified according to its usefulness.

The object that represents an experience, along with its usefulness, is called *case* and is represented by a set of parameters, grouped into three types (*Features*, *Solution* and *Evaluation*), as shown in Fig. 1.

The parameters in *Features* identify the situation of the current case, regarding the feedback buyer gave, the number of sellers in the negotiation and the identification of the resource under negotiation (aircraft or crew). The parameters in *Solution* identify the actions performed (price changing, availability changing) in that specific situation. The parameter in *Evaluation* assigns an evaluation value to the case, that measures its usefulness.

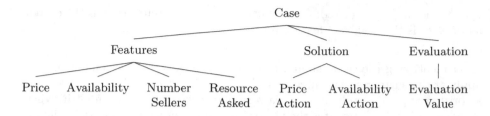

Fig. 1. Case composition

Algorithm 1 expresses the behavior mentioned above and is detailed in the next paragraphs.

Algorithm 1. Formulate New Proposal (using CBR)

Input: Feedback
Output: Proposal
1 SimilarCases := findSimilarCases(Feedback);
2 **if** *SimilarCases.size() > 1* **then**
3   SelectedCase := softmax(SimilarCases);
4   Proposal = processCase(SelectedCase);
5 **else**
6   Proposal = followFeedback(Feedback);
7 **end**
8 updateHistory(PreviousCase,Feedback);

Find Similar Cases

CBR starts by retrieving similar cases to the one received. For this purpose, only parameters identified as *Features* in Fig. 1 are used to compare cases and to identify equal ones. Although all features are used, they do not have the same preponderance on the task, because the feedback over a proposal is more relevant to decide the action to be made than the others parameters. So, to each parameter in *Features* is given a weight. Similar cases are found through the euclidean distance between them, a distance of 0 means that the case is identical, a distance greater than 0 means a different case. To ensure that features' weight has relevance in the distance calculation, the weight was added to the well known euclidean distance formula. So, the distance between two cases is the weighted sum of their features distances, as presented in Eq. (6).

$$d(\kappa, \chi) = \sum_{\eta} \sqrt{(\kappa_\eta - \chi_\eta)^2} \times \varepsilon_\eta \qquad (6)$$

with $\eta \in \{Features\}$

where: κ is the case received; χ is one of the case in the data set; η is the current feature; ε_η is the weight of feature η.

Select a Case

After identifying the set of similar cases, the seller has to select one of them to apply at the current situation, what it does using a softmax algorithm [11]. This algorithm applies a probability to each similar case retrieved from CBR, where a case's probability is greater the higher its evaluation value. The probability of a case being selected is given by Eq. (7).

$$P(k) = \frac{e^{\Upsilon_k}}{\sum_{i=1}^n e^{\Upsilon_i}} \tag{7}$$

where: Υ_i is the evaluation of case i; $P(k)$ is probability of the item k being selected; n is the number of similar cases.

After being assigned a probability to each case, a random value is generated and the first case with cumulative probability greater than that random value is selected. The new proposal to be sent by the seller is generated by applying the actions enumerated in the selected case. If no similar cases exist in the history set, the seller generates a new proposal by following the qualitative comments in the feedback received.

Update History

In order to prevent obsolete cases, every time an experience is reproduced, its evaluation is updated, where the latter the experience, the more important its evaluation is. The evaluation of an experience is updated as Eq. (8) shows.

$$\Upsilon = \Upsilon_{n-1} * (1 - \alpha) + \Upsilon_n * \alpha \tag{8}$$

where: Υ is the updated evaluation value; Υ_{prev} is the evaluation value of an equal experience found in the history set; Υ_{curr} is the evaluation value for the current experience; α is the weight given to the most recent experiment.

If there is no previous experience equal to the current one in the history, the evaluation is simply: $\Upsilon = \Upsilon_{curr}$

Evaluate a Case

The evaluation of the current experience Υ_{curr} is calculated as the difference between the feedback over previous round proposal and the current round proposal, as presented in Eq. (9).

$$\Upsilon_{curr} = \Delta\rho_{feedback} + \Delta\alpha_{feedback} \tag{9}$$

where: $\Delta\rho_{feedback}$ is the price feedback variation; $\Delta\alpha_{feedback}$ is the availability feedback variation.

If the feedback variation is greater than 0, the evaluation is incremented by 0.5 for each attribute. This means that in the worst scenario, where feedback remains unchanged, evaluation is 0. If only one of the feedback values changed, evaluation is set to 0.5 and if both changed, best scenario, evaluation is set to 1.

3   Experiments and Results

To validate our proposal, we have used data provided by a TAP Air Portugal expert in disruption management, regarding disruptions and solutions found for real problems. Each test reflected a disruption and assorted solution possibilities.

The data provided to test the electronic market is composed by 12 disruptions where each disruption contained a considerable amount of fields of which stand out the ID (aircraft tail), delay, cost, disrupted resource, as well as the estimated departure time and number of passengers. The number of crew members of each category (captain, first office, senior cabin crew and flight attendant) was also included.

The metrics used to measure the benefit of the solutions found with the electronic market are the following: Buyer utility, Seller utility, Delay reduction and Price reduction. Three different experiments were executed. The first experiment considered equal weights for the attributes price and availability. The second experiment valued the availability with a weight of 80% and the price with a weight of 20% in the utility calculation. The third and last experiment showed an inversion regarding the values of the second one, i.e. availability with a weight of 20% and the price with a weight of 80% in the utility calculation. In all experiments, disruption number 12 has no results to present because does not exists in seller's data set any resource similar to the one required, so seller gives up the negotiation. Due to paper space limitations, we will only describe the third experiment in Sect. 3.1. In Sect. 4, the results consider the three experiments.

3.1   Experiment 3 (20/80 Experiment)

In this experiment, in order to keep exploring the electronic market evolution to less urgent needs, the weights were distributed 20%–80% between availability and price attributes, respectively. With this change it was expected to find a great cost reduction to the detriment of delay reduction, expecting no delay reduction at all. The chart in Fig. 2 presents the results obtained.

From this experiment it can be concluded that when price is preferred over availability, it is predictable on how the outcome will vary, i.e. for small departure intervals it will be one of the worse possible solutions, but for big departure intervals, it will be the perfect choice. This perspective will be approached later.

The expected is to lease the resources with an availability that tends to delay the flights, which would make the price to be much lower. However, that does not happen, because the departure intervals used for this experiment were small. For this reason, the cost reduction is improved but it is not improved in the same measure as delay reduction, i.e., cost reduction is worsened, having a great range of variation from around 10% to nearly 100%, in the disruptions 5 and 10 respectively. Disruption number 6 has a negative value for buyer's utility and for this reason, it is not a viable solution. The fact that there is no delay reduction or the seller's utility being 0 supports that statement, so this is a case that would never result in a leasing contract. This can be explained by the fact that the minimum price proposed will never be 0 because the seller wants to

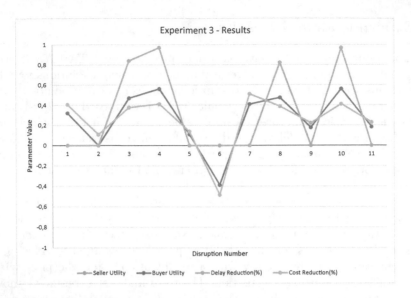

Fig. 2. Experiment 3 results

have some profit from the leasing contract. The average values of the metrics used are presented in Table 1.

Table 1. Experiment 3 - Average values

Seller utility	Buyer utility	Delay reduction (%)	Cost reduction (%)
0.33	0.26	32.73	24.59

In this experiment agents' utilities are close, yet are too low to be considered as a useful scenario for both. There is a mean delay reduction of 32.73% although only four disruptions had their delay minimized, which was not expected, it is explained by the cost-benefit relation. The average cost reduction of 36.72% is too low for what was expected, i.e. as the availability tends to delay it was expected a greater cost reduction than the one obtained.

3.2   Results

The electronic market does not consider any costs unrelated to the disrupted resources. However, in order to choose the most cost-effective solution, passenger related costs must be considered after the market returns its solutions. For instance, the number of passengers that will miss a flight connection due to the delay carries an extra cost to the injured company (passenger cost) and will affect the passenger satisfaction, which also carries an extra cost to the company (passenger goodwill cost). These costs will be added to the aircraft and crew costs, being distributed as follows: (1) Direct Costs: Aircraft cost plus crew cost plus passenger cost; (2) Integrated Solution Costs: Passenger goodwill cost times passenger goodwill weight plus direct costs.

All these costs are considered by the human specialist (at the AOCC) when it must choose a solution to a disruption in its daily operation. This section intends to compare the solutions found by the electronic market to the ones chosen by a human specialist, by presenting the electronic market solutions to the human for him to analyze and validate. The passenger goodwill weight is 5, by default, according to the specialist.

The first step in the comparison between the solutions found by the electronic market and the ones chosen by a human specialist is to see how the three solutions (one of each experiment) obtained in the electronic market impacts in the flight delay and in the number of passengers missing the flight connections.

The second step is to see the disruption and each solution cost and its influence on the passenger and passenger goodwill costs.

The third step is to see the costs without considering the electronic market solutions: original direct costs and original integrated solution cost, i.e. the original integrated solution cost is the sum of aircraft, crew and passenger costs to which is added the result of the multiplication between passengers goodwill cost and its weight, as shown in Eq. (10).

$$IC_{orig} = c_a + c_{cr} + c_{pax} + (c_{paxgw} \times w_{gw}) \tag{10}$$

where: c_a is the aircraft cost; c_{cr} is the crew cost; c_{pax} is the passenger cost; c_{paxgw} is the passenger good will cost; w_{gw} is the weight of good will.

The new integrated costs represent the integrated costs of the electronic market solutions while the original integrated costs represent the company solution integrated costs. The final step is to see if there are savings provided by each one of the electronic market solutions because the specialist always chooses the solution with a higher value of integrated savings. After being introduced the methodology used to calculate the Integrated Savings, the results over all disruptions are presented in Fig. 3.

As shown, the solutions obtained through the electronic market are more cost-effective than the company's solutions, except in the disruption which is identified by **CSTJF** that has no similar resources in the electronic market. When comparing the chosen solution from the electronic market with the disruptive solution, the electronic market solutions present an average delay reduction of 66.85% and an average cost reduction of 63.51%. Disregarding the **CSTJF** disruption, there is at least one solution obtained (considering the three experiments made) in the electronic market that is more cost-effective than the disruptive solution for each disruption, having a total of seven disruptions minimized in each experiment.

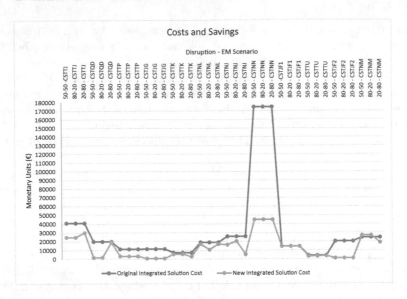

Fig. 3. Costs and savings

4 Conclusions and Future Work

In this paper, it is proposed an electronic marketplace modeled as a multi-agent system to expand a company's solution space regarding disruptions management and enable other airlines to offer their resources to lease. This electronic marketplace provides alternative solutions to companies affected by disruptions, using resources from other companies (and, as such, contributing to increase collaboration between airlines), which is achieved through automated negotiation, where agents negotiate the resource's availability and price for a disrupted flight. Human validation (at the AOCC) is also included to compare the solutions obtained through the EM with the ones obtained with the company's own resources. The Seller agent in the EM uses case-based reasoning to reuse or adapt previous experiences, to the current negotiation, which is also a contribution of our work.

Three different scenarios were tested to validate the concept, as described in Sect. 3. As there were no available resources for only one disruption in the electronic market, the success rate is 91.7% considering the cost reduction parameter and 67.7% considering both cost and delay minimized.

Possible future directions to improve this work, could include firstly, different approaches in the whole process of identifying previous similar experiences (by the seller), like machine learning and q-learning in order to understand how the agent learning process influences the negotiation, either in terms of proposals' price and availability or in terms of utility for each agent. The methodology used (CBR) can also be improved by creating better evaluation scenarios and benefiting the accepted proposal (or the tree of the proposals that lead to the accepted one). Secondly, the usage of heuristics to combine resources instead of doing all possible combinations, would be an interesting feature to include. The usage of clustering algorithms to classify resources (where the parameters would be availability and/or price) in order to have a better and more efficient resource combination is also something to explore. Finally, it would be worthy to use trust models to evaluate the electronic market outcome when considering the relations established between agents and whether that trust measure would influence the agents' behaviour.

References

1. Kohl, N., Larsen, A., Larsen, J., Ross, A., Tiourline, S.: Airline disruption management - perspectives, experiences and outlook. Carmen Research and Technology Report CRTR-0407 (2004)
2. Castro, A.J.M., Rocha, A.P., Oliveira, E.: A New Approach for Disruption Management in Airline Operations Control, vol. 562. Springer, Heidelberg (2014). https://doi.org/10.1007/978-3-662-43373-7
3. Malucelli, A., Castro, A.J.M., Oliveira, E.: Crew and aircraft recovery through a multi-agent electronic market. In: Krishnamurthy, S., Isaias, P. (eds.) Proceeding of IADIS International Conference on e-Commerce 2006, Barcelona Spain, pp. 51–58. IADIS Press, December 2006
4. Chen, X., Chen, X., Zhang, X.: Crew scheduling models in airline disruption management. In: 2010 IEEE 17th International Conference on Industrial Engineering and Engineering Management (IE&EM), pp. 1032–1037. Conference Publications, October 2010
5. Wooldridge, M.: An Introduction to Multiagent Systems, pp. 15–23, 105–111, 129–148. Wiley, Hoboken (2009)
6. Oliveira, E., Fonseca, J.M., Garção, A.S.: Multi-criteria negotiation in multi-agent systems. In: CEEMAS 1999, p. 190 (1999)
7. Vulkan, N., Jennings, N.R.: Efficient mechanisms for the supply of services in multi-agent environments. Decis. Support Syst. 28(1), 5–19 (2000)
8. Matos, N., Sierra, C., Jennings, N.R.: Determining successful negotiation strategies: an evolutionary approach. In: 1998 Proceedings of International Conference on Multi Agent Systems, pp. 182–189. IEEE (1998)
9. Lopes Cardoso, H., Oliveira, E.: A platform for electronic commerce with adaptive agents. In: Dignum, F., Cortés, U. (eds.) AMEC 2000. LNCS (LNAI), vol. 2003, pp. 96–107. Springer, Heidelberg (2001). https://doi.org/10.1007/3-540-44723-7_7
10. Riesbeck, C.K., Schank, R.C.: Inside Case-Based Reasoning. Psychology Press, Hove (2013)
11. Sutton, R.S., Barto, A.G.: Reinforcement Learning: An Introduction, vol. 1. MIT Press, Cambridge (1998)

Artificial Bee Colony Algorithm for Solving the Flight Disruption Problem

Tanja Šarčević[1], Ana Paula Rocha[2], and Antonio J. M. Castro[3(✉)]

[1] Faculty of Informatics, Vienna University of Technology, Vienna, Austria
ta.sarcevic@gmail.com
[2] LIACC, DEI/FEUP, University of Porto, Porto, Portugal
arocha@fe.up.pt
[3] LIACC, University of Porto, Porto, Portugal
ajmc@fe.up.pt

Abstract. This paper presents the optimization algorithm Artificial Bee Colony (ABC) firstly introduced by in 2005 and proposed for optimizing numerical problems. ABC is the swarm-based meta-heuristic algorithm inspired by intelligent behavior of honey bee colonies. In this paper, ABC has been applied on solving the flight disruption problem, by swapping aircraft and/or cancelling/delaying flights, and its performance has been shown through experimentation. The environment and data for experiments are provided by MASDIMA, Multi-Agent System for DIsruption MAnagement developed by LIACC (Laboratory of Artificial Intelligence and Computer Science).

Keywords: Artificial Bee Colony · Swarm intelligence · Optimization
Flight disruption · Air traffic control · Disruption management
Operations Control Center · Multi-agent system

1 Introduction

Artificial Bee Colony (ABC) is one of the most recently defined algorithms by Karaboga in 2005 [1], motivated by the intelligent behavior of honey bees. It is a simple algorithm, and only uses common control parameters such as colony size and maximum cycle number. ABC as an optimization tool provides a population-based search procedure in which individuals called foods positions are modified by the artificial bees over time. The bees' aim is to discover the places of food sources with high nectar amount and finally the one with the highest nectar. In ABC system, artificial bees fly around in a multidimensional search space and some (employed and onlooker bees) choose food sources depending on the experience of themselves and their nest mates, and adjust their positions. Some (scouts) fly and choose the food sources randomly without using experience. If the nectar amount of a new source is higher than that of the previous one in their memory, they memorize the new position and forget the previous one. Thus, ABC system combines local search methods, carried out by employed and onlooker bees, with global search methods, managed by onlookers and scouts, attempting to balance exploration and exploitation processes. A couple of similar approaches to both numerical and combinatorial problems were introduced based on foraging behavior of honey bees. Chong et al. in

© Springer International Publishing AG, part of Springer Nature 2018
J. Bajo et al. (Eds.): PAAMS 2018 Workshops, CCIS 887, pp. 72–81, 2018.
https://doi.org/10.1007/978-3-319-94779-2_7

2006 proposed a bee colony optimization algorithm applied on job shop scheduling [2]. Another example is Pham et al. (2005) with Bees Algorithm for both numerical and combinatorial problems [3]. Lučić and Teodorović in 2001 introduced a Bee System for solving difficult combinatorial optimization problems [4], and numerous others. As ABC was successfully applied to many different problems, it is the aim of this paper to discuss its application to flight disruption problem. The problem is arising in Airline Operations Control Centers (AOCC) in dealing with numerous disruptions that distort the flight operations. By disruptions we are talking about events such as weather, aircraft malfunction, late arrival of incoming aircraft, missing crewmember, that implies a delay in one or more flights. When solving the flight disruption problem, we look for recovery actions such as, swapping aircraft, assign reserve aircraft and/or cancelling/delaying flights, trying that operational costs as well as delays are the lowest possible. Each flight-to-aircraft assignment is causing different operational costs due to distances made by each aircraft, delays, fuel prices, and other costs.

The specific task of efficiently solving the flight disruption problem is just one of the numerous tasks that AOCCs are dealing with. Usually, a disruptive event affects not only one, but three dimensions, – aircraft, crew and passenger, and solutions should be find for all of them. Typically, the Airline Operations Control Center deals with disruptions sequentially, which means solving each of mentioned dimensions individually and one after another respectively. Solutions obtained this way give significant imbalance to the importance of the dimensions in the overall solution, giving aircraft part advantage over the other two dimensions, since aircraft is, usually, the first dimension to be solved in the sequence.

As opposed to sequential approach, the system, MASDIMA (MultiAgent System for DIsruption MAnagement) [5], brings a distributed approach with a Multi-Agent System (MAS) paradigm and delivers integrated solution with all dimensions equally considered. Each of the three dimensions is dealt with by specified agents. The events that cause disruption, like aircraft malfunction, weather and other restrictions, crew problems, passenger and baggage delay, are detected in real-time by the system itself and their impact is then assessed in the operational plan of the aircraft. Figure 1 shows the MASDIMA architecture.

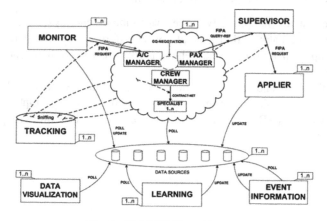

Fig. 1. MASDIMA architecture

The work reported in this paper aims to solve the aircraft dimension problem (flight disruption problem), and the proposed approach will be implemented as a Specialist Agent belonging to the Aircraft Manager agent team of MASDIMA. The rest of this paper is as follows. Section 2 introduces swarm-based paradigm, the Artificial Bee Colony algorithm and its application on solving the flight disruption problem. Furthermore, Sect. 3 describes the experiments done and presents a discussion about the algorithm's performance and impact of different parameters. Finally, Sect. 4 brings the most important conclusions from the experiments done and points out some directions of future work.

2   Solving the Flight Disruption Problem

2.1   Swarm-Based Algorithms

Swarm intelligence is the discipline that deals with natural and artificial systems composed of many individuals that coordinate using decentralized control and self-organization. The discipline focuses on collective behavior of many individuals which results from their local behavior within their neighborhood and their global communication in range of the whole population. In nature, these systems are commonly used to solve problems such as effective foraging for food, prey evading, or colony relocation. Examples of such natural systems are colonies of ants and other insects, bird flocks, schools of fish, etc.

The properties of a swarm intelligence system can be enumerated in the following points:

- multitude - composed of many individuals
- homogeneity - the individuals are relatively homogeneous, i.e. either identical or belonging to a few typologies
- simplicity - individuals have simple behavioral rules by which they exploit only local information
- self-organization - the overall behavior of the system results from the interactions of individuals with each other and with environment

The main characterizing property of the swarm intelligence system is an absence of necessity for a coordinator with a general knowledge of the swarm state. The swarm system come up with a coordinated behavior without a centralized individual controlling the swarm.

Most popular and studied computational systems that are inspired by collective intelligence are Ant Colony Optimization and Particle Swarm Optimization. But Artificial Bee Colony (ABC) optimization also belongs to the same group of swarm-based, nature inspired algorithms.

2.2   ABC Algorithm

The Artificial Bee Colony (ABC) algorithm is a swarm based meta-heuristic algorithm introduced by Karaboga in 2005 [1] for optimizing numerical problems. The algorithm is inspired by intelligent foraging behavior of honey bees. The model for the algorithm was proposed by Tereshko and Loengarov in 2005 [6]. The model consists of three essential components:

1. employed bees
2. unemployed honey bees
3. food sources

The aim of the bee colony is to find rich food sources close to the hive. The model also defines two types of behaviors that are necessary for self-organizing and collective intelligence:

- recruitment of foragers to rich food sources
- abandonment of poor food sources

Bees are continuously changing their environment in the process of their search for food sources, and they are capable of continuously adapting to the new environment.

In ABC, artificial bees are in a search for a good solution of a given problem, i.e. a rich food source. To apply ABC, it is necessary to define the problem that can be converted to the problem of finding the parameter vector that minimizes the objective function. Artificial bees randomly discover initial set of food sources (potential solution vectors), and iteratively evaluate them and improve this set by searching for better food sources in their neighborhood and abandoning poor food sources.

The colony of artificial bees contains three groups of bees: employed bees associated with specific food sources, onlooker bees watching the dance of employed bees within the hive to choose a food source, and scout bees randomly searching for food sources. Both onlookers and scouts are also called unemployed bees. Initially, all food source positions are discovered by scout bees. Thereafter, the nectar of food sources is exploited by employed bees and onlooker bees, and this continual exploitation will ultimately cause them to become exhausted. Then, the employed bee which was exploiting the exhausted food source becomes a scout bee in search of further food sources once again. In other words, the employed bee whose food source has been exhausted becomes a scout bee. In ABC, the position of a food source represents a possible solution to the problem and the nectar amount of a food source corresponds to the quality (fitness) of the associated solution. The number of employed bees is equal to the number of food sources (solutions) since each employed bee is associated with one and only one food source.

The general scheme of the ABC algorithm is as follows:

```
Initialization phase
REPEAT
   Employed Bees Phase
   Onlooker Bees Phase
   Scout Bees Phase
   Memorize the best solution achieved so far
UNTIL (Reached maximum number of cycles)
```

(1) Employed Bees Phase

Employed bees search for new food sources having more nectar within the neighborhood of the food source in their memory. They find a neighbor food source and evaluate its fitness. After finding the new food source, its fitness is calculated and a greedy selection is applied between old and new food source.

(2) Onlooker Bees Phase

Unemployed bees consist of two groups of bees: onlooker bees and scouts bees. Employed bees share their food source information with onlooker bees waiting in the hive, and then onlooker bees probabilistically choose their food sources depending on this information. An onlooker bee chooses a food source depending on the probability value calculated using the fitness values provided by employed bees.

After a food source for an onlooker bee is probabilistically chosen, a neighborhood source is determined in the same way as in the previous phase, and its fitness value is computed. As in the employed bees phase, a greedy selection is applied between the two solutions. Hence, more onlookers are recruited to richer sources and positive feedback behavior appears.

(3) Scout Bees Phase

The unemployed bees that choose their food sources randomly are called scouts. Employed bees whose solutions cannot be improved through a predetermined number of trials, specified by the user of the ABC algorithm and called "limit" or "abandonment criteria", become scouts and their solutions are abandoned. Then, the converted scouts start to search for new solutions, randomly. Hence, those sources which are initially poor or have been made poor by exploitation, are abandoned and negative feedback behavior arises to balance the positive feedback.

2.3 Application in Solving the Flight Disruption Problem

A solution to a disruptive flight, can be achieved by one of the following actions: swapping aircrafts, using reserve aircraft and/or delaying/cancelling a flight. To adapt the ABC algorithm to provide the best solution to disrupted flights, we represent a possible solution as an assignment of aircrafts to all operational flights, including disrupted ones. Aircrafts are initially, and at any point of the algorithm execution, assigned to a flight if and only if the aircraft is not already assigned to some other flight in the same time in the same schedule (i.e., solution). This restriction of the aircraft choice results in all the solutions being feasible, which implies algorithm calculates costs and finds the best one only among the feasible solutions. On the other hand, cancellation of the flight is also possible. If there is such schedule where for some flight the choice of the aircraft is impossible (e.g. because at that time no aircraft is available), then the flight is cancelled and it is penalized with a high number. Penalization for cancellation amounts to approximately 10% of the total calculated cost of a random solution.

After the parameters are set - number of iterations the algorithm will perform *NUMBER_OF_CYCLES*; size of the bee colony *COLONY_SIZE*; number of food sources *FOOD_SOURCES_N* (half the number of *COLONY_SIZE*); and number of trials *TRIALS* -, ABC randomly generates an initial population of food sources – the initial schedules. The initialization phase is followed by the *NUMBER_OF_CYCLES* iterations where Employed Bees Phase, Onlooker Bees Phase and Scout Bees Phase are being performing their tasks.

The first half of the bee population, employed bees, select distinct food sources and explore their neighborhood in search of better food sources. The neighbor of a food source is defined in the following way:

- Choose a random flight in the solution set
- Choose another available aircraft (from reserve or assigned to another flight)
- Change the aircraft of the chosen flight to the new one

If the new solution-plan (flight plus aircraft) obtained in this way has a better fitness value, the new solution-plan is selected and the old one abandoned. This behavior is the optimization part of the algorithm. The fitness of a solution is calculated based on the costs that this choice of solution-plan produces, shown in following formula:

$$fitness_i = (worstScore - objectiveFunction_i) * 100.0/bestScore$$

where worst score and best score are the maximum and minimum value of the objective function among the solution population, respectively, and i is the index of the solution. Objective function of each possible solution is calculated by following formula:

$$objectiveFunction_i = \sum_{aircrafts} (handlingCost_i + fuelCost_i + maitenance_i + ATC_i$$
$$+ takeOffCost_i + landingCost_i + parkingCost_i)$$

As shown, the objective function sums up all the costs related to the choice of the aircraft for the flight, giving them the same weight. As mentioned before, the objective function value can be additionally penalized in case the cancellation of the flight is necessary.

After the better solutions are chosen, onlooker bees start their work. This other half of the bee population selects their food sources based on information about food sources received from employed bees. The information is given by selection probability attribute calculated from the fitness of the solution, according to the following formula:

$$selectionProbability_i = 0.9 * \left(\frac{fitness_i}{maxFitness} \right) + 0.1$$

After all onlookers bees select their food sources, the same technique as in Employed Bees Phase is applied for searching for better sources in the neighborhood.

Every solution contains information of how many times the bee tried to improve it but failed, in a simple counter. If this counter exceeds the predefined parameter TRIALS, the bee who is exploring it becomes a scout bee and finds a new random solution. Due to performance reasons, a solution that exceeds the number of trials is only being abandoned if it is not the best solution found so far. This modification is introduced because of the nature of the problem - the solution space is too big and bees don't manage to improve the already very good solutions which results in abandonment of the best solutions, intuitively undesired behavior.

The pseudo code of the procedure for a flight disruption problem using ABC, that resumes the description given above, is the following:

- Set the parameters *NUMBER_OF_CYCLES*, *COLONY_SIZE* and *TRIALS*
- Set random *COLONY_SIZE/2* schedules
- FOR (each candidate solution-plan)
  - Calculate fitness
  - Calculate selection probability
- END FOR
- Memorize best candidate solution-plan (with best fitness)
- REPEAT
  - FOR (each candidate solution-plan)
    - Find neighbor solution-plan
    - Calculate neighbor's fitness
    - Apply greedy algorithm to choose between current and new candidate solution-plan
    - Calculate better solution's fitness and selection probability
    - Update trial number
  - END FOR
  - REPEAT
    - Use selection probability to choose some of existing solution-plan
    - Find neighbor solution-plan
    - Calculate neighbor's fitness
    - Apply greedy algorithm to choose between current and new solution-plan
    - Calculate better solution's fitness and selection probability
    - Update trial number
  - UNTIL (reached *COLONY_SIZE/2* iterations)
  - Memorize best solution so far

- FOR (each candidate solution-plan)
  - IF (trial > *TRIALS* and this solution-plan is not the best one)
    - Find another random solution and forget the current one
    - Calculate fitness and selection probability
- END FOR
- Memorize best solution so far
- UNTIL (*NUMBER_OF_CYCLES* iterations reached)

3   Experiments and Discussion

3.1   Settings

The implementation of ABC and experiments are done in the environment of MAS-DIMA [5], with real data that contains information about flights and aircrafts from a period of one month.

MASDIMA is a disruption management system based on the Multi-Agent System paradigm (MAS). As shown in Fig. 1, agents in the system are separated in three main layers by their functionality: supervisor, manager agents and specialist agents. Each dimension has its own manager agent whose main task is to negotiate with other dimension manager agents (Passenger Manager, Crew Manager and Aircraft Manager) and the supervisor over a several rounds to find a good integrated solution. Selection of the best candidate solution is done by choosing among the solutions found the one with the lowest cost and delay. Specialist agents are also related to each dimension - Passenger Specialist, Crew Specialist and Aircraft Specialist. Each one of them has a specific expertise that is run by different resolution algorithms. These algorithms are delivering the best candidate solutions from their own perspective, i.e. using costs regarding only their dimension into.

Our proposed ABC algorithm was implemented as a MASDIMA specialist agent working in the Aircraft Manager Agent team. Our proposed ABC algorithm was tested by changing each one of the predefined parameters (the number of cycles, the size of the colony, the trial limit) to see their impact on the performance.

3.2   Influence of the Number of Cycles

This parameter says how long we will let algorithm run. The solution is not likely to reach the global optimum, so it makes sense to stop the algorithm in the phase when the best solution is not improving anymore, or starts to improve very slowly.

Table 1 shows the results obtained by several runs of the algorithm while changing the total number of cycles, and remaining the other two parameters with the same value. In this experiment, colony size is set to 20 bees and limit of trials on 10% of the total cycle number.

The improvement of the solution is noticeably increasing from 400th until 800th cycle, after which we don't see a significant change in the solution improvement.

Table 1. Test results for different number of cycles

Number of cycles	Best solution's cost	Improvement
20	95894891	0.08%
50	95264194	0.31%
100	95139913	0.46%
200	94782343	1.7%
400	94337640	1.82%
600	92263797	3.81%
800	92035075	4.08%
1000	92037320	4.03%

3.3 Influence of the Size of the Colony

The experiment in this case was run on 400 cycles and trial limit of 15 cycles. In Table 2 can be observed that colony size does not influence the result much. It is important to mention that final best result very much depends on the best result from the first population of solutions.

Another note is that increasing the size of the colony, the runtime of the algorithm increases almost linearly. Therefore, it is better option to leave the number of bees reasonably low for the best performance.

Table 2. Results of the experiment over colony size

Colony size	Best solution	Improvement
10	94443398	1.51%
20	95108117	0.95%
44	94153595	1.47%
72	94276091	1.52%

3.4 Influence of the Trial Limit

Trial limit says how fast solutions will get exhausted. Setting this parameter on a high value limits the solution space the bees are exploring. However, setting it to a low value, bees "give up" too fast on trying to improve the solution and the solution search becomes random.

Table 3. Results of the experiment over trial limit

Trial limit	Best solution	Improvement
5	95614998	0.44%
20	94933019	0.81%
50	94383364	1.49%
125	94707546	1.25%
300	95829453	0.39%

The third experiment is testing the impact of the trial limit on the performance result. The experiment has run in 400 cycles and with a population of 20 bees. The results of this experiment are shown in Table 3. The best performance is noticed on medium values which "give space" for solution to be improved, but still restrict the randomness.

4 Conclusions

ABC algorithm has been modified for application on the flight disruption problem and its performance has been analyzed in one month operational flight data. By the results obtained, we can conclude that the ABC algorithm can be successfully used for solving flight disruption optimization problems. Further modifications are welcome on the implemented solution to improve performance. Above all, smart choice of heuristics can contribute in faster reaching of better solutions. Due to the wide solution space, the reduction of random factors in the implementation might be a good idea. For example, strategy for choosing the initial population of solution instead of choosing randomly distributed one, or applying additional methods for smarter choice of neighborhood food sources can be investigated in the future work.

References

1. Karaboga, D.: An idea based on honey bee swarm for numerical optimization. Technical report TR06, Erciyes University, Engineering Faculty, Computer Engineering Department (2005)
2. Chong, C.S., Sivakumar, A.I., Malcolm Low, Y.H., Gay, K.L.: A bee colony optimization algorithm to job shop scheduling. In: Proceedings of the 38th Conference on Winter Simulation WSC 2006, California, pp. 1954–1961 (2006)
3. Pham, D.T., Ghanbarzadeh, A., Koc, E., Otri, S., Rahim, S., Zaidi, M.: The bees algorithm. Technical report, Manufacturing Engineering Centre, Cardiff University, UK (2005)
4. Lucic, P., Teodorovic, D.: Bee system: modeling combinatiorial optimization transportation engineering problems by swarm intelligence (2001)
5. Castro, A.J.M., Rocha, A.P., Oliveira, E.: A New Approach for Disruption Management in Airline Operations Control. Springer, Heidelberg (2014). https://doi.org/10.1007/978-3-662-43373-7
6. Tereshko, V., Loengarov, A.: Collective decision-making in honey bee foraging dynamics. Comput. Inf. Syst. 9(3), 1–7 (2005). University of the West of Scotland, UK

Virtual Environment Mapping Module to Manage Intelligent Flight in an Indoor Drone

Giovanny-Javier Tipantuña-Topanta, Francisco Abad, Ramón Mollá,
Juan-Luis Posadas-Yagüe, and Jose-Luis Poza-Lujan[✉]

University Institute of Control Systems and Industrial Computing (ai2), Universitat Politècnica
de València (UPV), Camino de Vera, s/n, 46022 Valencia, Spain
{giotitoa,fjabad,rmolla,jposadas,jopolu}@ai2.upv.es

Abstract. This paper presents a Virtual Environment Mapping (VEM) module
assembled in an indoor drone in order to be used by creative industries. This
module is in charge of allowing users to capture the environment where the final
recording will take place. Having a virtual representation of the environment
allows both the photography director and the director to test different camera
trajectories, points of view, speeds and camera configuration without the need to
be physically in the recording set. The digitization of the scene will be performed
with a 3D camera on-board of the drone. This paper discusses the overall VEM
architecture, taking into account the requirements it has to fulfil. It will also
present a working demo of the system, with the communication infrastructure in
place and with a proof of concept of the main components of system.

Keywords: Distributed system · Virtual mapping
Intelligent map management

1   Introduction

Creative industries that require controlling a camera require many devices such as
cranes, rails or portable frames in order to obtain interesting shots. These devices often
have many drawbacks: they are complex to mount, handle and dismount. Even so, these
devices have limited movement space. On the other hand, unmanned aerial vehicles,
known as RPAS (Remotely Piloted Aircraft System) or drones obviate the drawbacks.
When recording takes place indoors, like a television or movie set, drones can provide
shots not available to current auxiliary devices because of their stability and precision
[1]. Drone navigation requires knowing the position of the drone at all times. In outdoor
flights, drones can use GPS location systems. When working indoors, GPS has not the
accuracy to allow a safe flight. Therefore, a drone needs an Indoor Positioning System
(IPS). Furthermore, due to smaller spaces and increased risk of damages to property and
people in case of an accident, a much higher accuracy, and safety system, is required.
Typically, the necessary accuracy is in the order of tens of centimetres.

Currently drone indoor navigation is mostly performed using commercial, off-the-
shelf solutions, both for drone control [2] and for trajectory tracking [3]. This latter
aspect is one of the most interesting as far as research is concerned [4].

© Springer International Publishing AG, part of Springer Nature 2018
J. Bajo et al. (Eds.): PAAMS 2018 Workshops, CCIS 887, pp. 82–89, 2018.
https://doi.org/10.1007/978-3-319-94779-2_8

The possibility of having the drone to follow a predefined path allows the director to repeat the shots as many times as required. Therefore, it is necessary to implement a system for enabling the user to edit the paths for designing routes for the drone within the environment. This environment has to be mapped in three dimensions. Drones are the most suitable vehicles to be used for this mapping [5].

Safety is a key factor for both outdoor and indoor flight environments. In most countries, outdoor drone flights on populated areas is very restricted. However, even if indoor flights are not regulated, it is not strange to find elements of value like paintings, sculptures, lamps, furniture and so on. Combined with smaller spaces and the presence of people, indoor drone flights should have higher levels of security than outdoor flights. This aspect therefore determines, largely, all questions relating to the design of both the control architecture and the drone. Consequently, next section describes the system drone architecture, then section three focuses on the map generation system and section four shows the system implemented. Finally, section five summarizes the article.

2 Distributed System Architecture

The system is part of the project Arts indoor RPAS Technology (AiRT). AiRT is a distributed system composed of several devices connected to provide the whole service

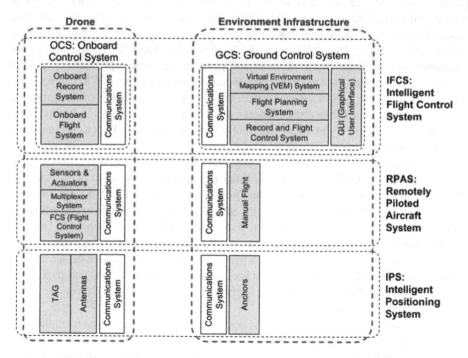

Fig. 1. AiRT distributed system main areas (Drone and Environment Infrastructure) and the three systems involved in each area (IFCS, RPAS, and IPS). In each system, the components must connect to others creating an interesting distributed system.

of recording video or photographs in in-door scenarios using RPAS. Principally, there are two main working areas: Drone and Environment Infrastructure. Each area has common components in the same three systems: Intelligent Flight Control System (IFCS), RPAS system, and IPS system (see Fig. 1).

2.1 Environment Infrastructure

It is the ground system in charge of supporting the drone operability. It is composed of several subsystems: the IPS anchors that give support to Drone indoor positioning, the remote control via radio to control the flight manually, and the Ground Control System (GCS). The GCS is in charge of receiving the whole cloud of points of the scene and surroundings from the Virtual Environment Mapping (VEM) Manager, to generate the flight plan by means of the Flight Planning System. Finally, the Record and Flight Control System control and monitor the Drone flight.

2.2 Drone

In the same way as the Environment Infrastructure, Drone has components, corresponding with the previous presented three subsystems. Concerning the IPS, Drone incorporates four antennas to receive the anchors signal, and one board (caller "tag") that processes the signals and generates the position. Related with the RPAS, Drone includes all sensors like distance or the Inertial Measurement Unit (IMU), a multiplexor system that provides the source that controls the Drone (manually flight or automatic flight), and the Flight Control System (FCS) that is in charge of controlling all the parameters of the flight: drone position and orientation, camera parameters, gimbal parameters. Finally, the third system is the Onboard Control System (OCS) that includes also the VEM manager (synchronized with the GCS). It is in charge of detecting the cloud of points in front of the drone, sending them back to the GCS, receiving the flight plan and transferring it to the FCS, and finally controlling the flight plan according to the operator requirements.

Concerning the record system, there are a Gimbal, a Record Camera, and a VEM Camera, usually a RGBD camera [6]. Gimbal is a specific actuator. It is in charge of orienting the Record Camera to its correct point of interest whatever the position and orientation of the drone is. The Recording Camera (RCam) is in charge of recording the high-resolution video using professional parameters. VEM Camera is a ZCam that provides the drone with the cloud of points of the objects in front of the camera. Both Gimbal and RCam are directly controlled by the FCS using a flight plan or in real time when performing a flight via the OCS that is commanded from the GCS. This paper only focuses on the VEM management both in the OCS and in the GCS during the phase scanning of the environment.

The virtual map of the environment where the drone has to fly is got from the very same drone used for the recording phase. This carries several advantages: there is only one single drone for all the recording operation. There is no need to use different devices for different actions (calibration, scanning, tuning and recording). The size of the equipment to carry, store and move is lower; consequently, the operationally is simplified.

3   Intelligent Virtual Environment Map Generation

3.1   Method to Create the VEM in a Drone

There are many challenges to address for having a proper and reliable implementation of the environment surrounding the area where a drone has to fly. For this purpose, several cleaning phases have to be performed in the VEM system (Fig. 2).

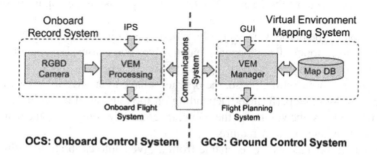

Fig. 2.   VEM system and relation with the AiRT system.

The phases that VEM processing does are:

1. Filter the cloud of points to avoid outliers.
2. Clean and register the points.
3. Simplify the points obtained. For example, points very closed to each other.
4. Update the final reliable set of points.

After each of these steps, the VEM processing sends data to the VEM manager, to update the Map DB and correct the Flight Planning System at the same time that the On-board Flight System is updated. The first step after having captured a depth image by the camera is to filter the data. The current technology has some limitations that produces artefacts in the captured data. For example, most cameras have a working range, with minimum and maximum distances: any part of the scene closer than the minimum distance or farther than the maximum distance will produce an anomalous value in the corresponding pixel (outliers). It is common to have a depth value meaning "infinity", in those pixels outside of the working range. Depending also on the technology, it is also common having sudden "spikes" in the depth image around sudden changes in the depth of the captured scene. It is necessary to discard such anomalous pixels before integrating the captured depth image into the map. After removing the outliers in the captured depth image, there are still a number of error sources, such as noise in the data (due to quantization errors, or by the type of material captured, etc.), missing data (due to occlusions and non-uniform sampling), or misaligned scans (due to errors in the positioning system). Thus, it is necessary to perform this cleaning and registration before accepting the data into the map. The RGBD Camera used is a ZR300 camera from Intel. This camera has an integrated controller that run SLAM algorithms that let it supply cloud of points just filtered. Therefore, the OCS only has to receive the clean cloud of points and perform little more post-processing. Due to the map is created by a Drone it is necessary to calibrate the Drone and the IPS.

3.2   Auto Calibration Flight

Before starting the environment scanning, the drone has to know perfectly where the anchors are set to know accurately where it is. It is mandatory for a good point localization. The more accurate the position is set, the more precision the points are scanned. If no calibration has been done before, the first step in the VEM is to calibrate the position and orientation of the drone. Consequently, when system have no map, it is necessary a Drone flight to calibrate all components that involves two phases: IPS anchors settings and Drone auto calibration.

In the IPS Anchors Setting phase, the operators have to analyse the area where the recording is going to be performed. Depending on the number of obstacles, the radio-electric interferences, the volume of the scene, its geometry complexity the team has to decide how many anchors they require.

Since not all the anchors are reachable from a given auto calibration-testing point, this phase could be done in different steps. The only requirement is that all anchors have to have been within range of the drone in at least one-step during Drone auto calibration phase.

3.3   VEM Flight

Once Drone and IPS have been calibrated, the system is ready to scan the environment. This phase is called VEM Flight. The aim to the VEM Flight is to generate the map using the method depicted in Fig. 2. The VEM Manager has to be waiting for the order to start capturing the map. When the order is received from the GCS, the first step is to load the configuration of the hardware sources, for example, the resolution of the ZR300 Camera, the position rate of the IPS Tag, and so on. When all components are ready to work, the VEM creation starts in different phases.

Input coordination. After loading the configurations, the drone starts for capturing the environment. The OCS requires two inputs to perform this duty at same time: the images from the ZR300 sensors and the corresponding position from the IPS Tag.

Cloud Filtering. The point cloud is made from the depth image and the colours of the points are added from the colour image sensor. Some filters have to be applied on the input depth image to discard wrong depth values in a pipeline filtering schema where some filtering stages are chained one after another: a filtering stage to remove unnecessary or wrong points. For example, applying a filter to reduce the amount of points without losing the main captured geometry depending on the filter configuration values used. Use the previous filtered point cloud to remove the outlier points based on the distance to the neighbours.

Cloud Registering [7]. The next stage is registering consecutive point clouds. This allows to correctly set the new cloud of points together to the past scanned environment. In this step, the VEM Manager uses the pose (orientation of the drone, typically yaw, pitch and roll angles) of the drone captured from the IPS Tag. Notice that the ZCam is firmly set on the chassis of the drone. So, the pose of the drone is the pose of the ZCam. Then a transformation using that pose has to be applied over the corresponding point cloud to translate and rotate its points to the correct position.

Cloud addition. This lets to build a global map incrementally using consecutive clouds of points supplied constantly by the ZCam. This stage cleans the global map. Several techniques can be applied at this step. For example, a detector that determines which points are in new zones in the map and which are in already captured zones. This lets to add only the new points to the global map.

Cloud transmission. Once the new points are added to the global cloud of points, the OCS has to send them back to all the clients connected to it. Depending on the amount of power, memory or quality of the Wi-Fi link, the amount of data that can be sent back to the clients may vary. So, a LoD algorithm [8] has to be used to incrementally provide the mesh to every client.

Cloud reception. On the other side, clients are receiving the cloud of points, so they add the points received to the internal data structure. Notice that these points are clean ones. So, the client only has to increment the data structure size. No postproduction is required at the client level. Notice that the GCS may be running on any hardware the user has and there is no guarantee about the minimum requirements the user can provide. So, all the computer power has to be provided by the OCS.

Cloud visualization [9]. As the scene graph is upgraded incrementally by the continuous flow of new points from the environment, this cloud is rendered on the screen by the GCS. client. The user can interact to the cloud of points, changing the point of view angle, position or any other parameter. The cloud increments the amount of environment viewed over the time.

4   Experiments and Results

In this section, up-to-date results are shown using preliminary simulations. First, we simulate a drone VEM using Gazebo [10] and develop a preliminary program with a user interface that connects to the Gazebo port and allows to represent the point cloud provided by the simulator into the user screen. After these preliminary tests, we abandoned the simulator and moved the point clouds to the O.C.S. in order to simulate a real connection to the Zcam. This software sends up to 100 clouds of points to the clients that are connected to it. Every cloud has between 4 K to 7 K points. Every point has a 3D information and a colour information. This means three float numbers for X, Y and Z dimensions (4 bytes for every number) and a RGBA colour (one byte per colour and another one for the alpha channel). So, there is a need of 128 bits (16 bytes) per point. This means around 80 KB to 115 KB of information per frame. At 60 Hz scanning frequency, the system requires to send 5 MB of data per second. No error was considered at this point since all data was collected from a simulation without any kind of position and orientation I.P.S. error and no scanning error.

The IPS update rate describes the number of positioning that IPS can provide every second, whereas the latency describes the time delay between measuring the position and obtaining an estimate. The anchors distance, can provide positions that can vary between 100 ms to 7 ms. Additional delays can be introduced by the communication protocol between the positioning sensor and the RPAS. The i2c protocol, used to communicate components in the RPAS, may introduce delays in the order of milliseconds due to its maximum transmission speed of 1 MHz. SPI can run at 42 MHz and introduces much smaller delays. Figure 3a shows the preliminary setup of the OCS components: the final hardware configuration will be slightly different: Intel Joule 570x Developer Kit, IPS Tag, and Intel ZR300 3D Camera. Figure 3b shows the result of the OCS map generation, the GCS (biggest screen), and two clients showing the VEM.

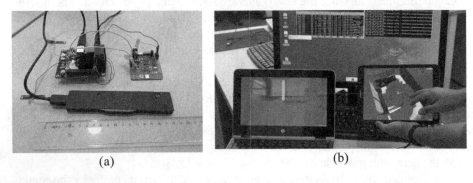

(a)   (b)

Fig. 3. (a) From top left, in clock-wise order: Intel Joule 570x Developer Kit, IPS tag and Intel ZR300. (b) Examples of the map generated by the VEM.

5   Conclusions and Future Work

This article has presented a virtual environment-mapping module assembled in an indoor drone. Its main components are a single board computer installed on-board of the drone, a 3D camera, and a single module of the positioning system. It has been implemented a bare-bones client that is able to ask the server to start scanning the environment and is able to receive portions of the map. The client then combines all the individual point clouds from the server and allows the user to explore the virtual map. The communications infrastructure between server and clients has been implemented, too. It is able to reliable connect them and recover from short losses of connectivity. Finally, it has been created a test scene in order to check that the components are behaving correctly.

Acknowledgements. This work has received funding from the European Union's Horizon 2020 research and innovation programme under grant agreement no. 732433 (reference: H2020-ICT-2016-2017, www.airt.eu).

References

1. Castillo, P., García, P., Lozano, R., Albertos, P.: Modelado y estabilización de un helicóptero con cuatro rotores. Revista Iberoamericana de Automática e Informática Industrial RIAI **4**(1), 41–57 (2007)

2. Hussein, A., Al-Kaff, A., de la Escalera, A., Armingol, J.M.: Autonomous indoor navigation of low-cost quadcopters. In: 2015 IEEE International Conference on Service Operations and Logistics, and Informatics (SOLI), pp. 133–138. IEEE, November 2015

3. Santana, L.V., Brandao, A.S., Sarcinelli-Filho, M., Carelli, R.: A trajectory tracking and 3D positioning controller for the ar. drone quadrotor. In: 2014 International Conference on Unmanned Aircraft Systems (ICUAS), pp. 756–767. IEEE, May 2014

4. Martínez, S.E., Tomas-Rodriguez, M.: Three-dimensional trajectory tracking of a quadrotor through PVA control. Revista Iberoamericana de Automática e Informática Industrial RIAI **11**(1), 54–67 (2014)

5. Heng, L., Honegger, D., Lee, G.H., Meier, L., Tanskanen, P., Fraundorfer, F., Pollefeys, M.: Autonomous visual mapping and exploration with a micro aerial vehicle. J. Field Robot. **31**(4), 654–675 (2014)

6. Munera, E., Poza-Lujan, J.L., Posadas-Yagüe, J.L., Simó-Ten, J.E., Noguera, J.F.B.: Dynamic reconfiguration of a RGBD sensor based on QoS and QoC requirements in distributed systems. Sensors **15**(8), 18080–18101 (2015)

7. Pfister, H., Zwicker, M., van Baar, J., Gross, M.: Surfels: surface elements as rendering primitives. In: SIGGRAPH (2000)

8. Lindstrom, P., Koller, D., Ribarsky, W., Hodges, L.F., Faust, N., Turner, G.A.: Real-time, continuous level of detail rendering of height fields. In: Proceedings of the 23rd Annual Conference on Computer Graphics and Interactive Techniques, pp. 109–118. ACM, August 1996

9. Preiner, R., Jeschke, S., Wimmer, M.: Auto splats: dynamic point cloud visualization on the GPU. In: Proceedings of Eurographics Symposium on Parallel Graphics and Visualization (2012)

10. Koenig, N., Howard, A.: Design and use paradigms for gazebo, an open-source multi-robot simulator. In: Proceedings of 2004 IEEE/RSJ International Conference on Intelligent Robots and Systems (IROS 2004), vol. 3, pp. 2149–2154. IEEE, September 2004

PAAMS Workshop ABAM

Network Topology and the Behaviour of Socially-Embedded Financial Markets

Olivier Brandouy[1,2] and Philippe Mathieu[1,2(✉)]

[1] GREThA UMRS 5113 – U. Bordeaux, Bordeaux, France
[2] CRISTAL UMR 9189 – U. Lille, Lille, France
philippe.mathieu@lifl.fr

Abstract. We study the impact of the network topology on various market parameters (volatility, liquidity and efficiency) when three populations or artificial trades interact (Noise, Informed and Social Traders). We show, using an agent-based set of simulations that choosing a Regular, a Erdös-Rényi or a scale free network and locating on each vertex one Noise, Informed or Social Trader, substantially modifies the dynamics of the market. The overall level of volatility, the liquidity and the resulting efficiency are impacted by this initial choice in various ways which also depends upon the proportion of Informed *vs.* Noise Traders.

1 Introduction

Financial markets have a central role in modern economies and receive from both the academic and the politic world an important amount of interest. Among others, some technical aspects in their behaviour are still discussed and scrutinized: for example, volatility is presented as a normal outcome of their behaviour, mainly (but not uniquely) driven by the "real world" stochastic they reflect. Another important aspect is their liquidity, which, at coarse grain, determines the ability of an investor to resell (to short) immediately or at very short notice one of his positions. Other technical parameters are observed, while they more or less all pertain to the same central hypothesis, the efficient market hypothesis (see [1,7,8]). If market are efficient, they reflect a certain degree of the available information regarding the economy. As such, they allow money to be allocated where it is needed and appropriately rewarded.

However, the social nature of Financial Markets, the fact they are made of human beings connected by networks (even if they seem to fade behind more-and-more automated processes) has been taken into account relatively recently for adding an extra layer of complexity in the analysis was not recognized as necessary.

In this paper we tackle this complexity (following in that other researchers like, for example, [11] or [4]) and propose a set of analysis geared at understanding their role, if any, in relation to a set of market parameters. As such, our research question is the one of a possible effect of the underlying network topology of financial markets in the emergence of price motions and beyond, market regimes. We thus follow a line that recognizes the centrality of information contagion (and reputation) in the behaviour of stock markets.

The strength of our approach derives from the agent-based philosophy we adopt, which is more and more common in computational economics (see for example [10,12,13], or [2]). Studying such a complicated set of questions can be done efficiently using an agent-based artificial market (see, in an other context [5]), for this latter is designed so to mimic some essential features of the real world (experiments over several days but with access to an intra-day information, populations of agents but heterogeneity within this population, social spacialization etc...).

The paper is organized as follows: in a first section, we describe the overall architecture of our financial market. The second section is dedicated to the agent behaviour description. The third section presents our empirical strategy and our initial results.

2   The Model

We study a simplified Economy populated with a large number of atomistic traders where only two assets can be traded: a risk-free one and a risky one A, respectively yielding a rate of return r_f and paying a random dividend. Instead of interacting uniquely through the price system, as usually proposed in the literature, these are placed within a social network and as such are embedded in a social neighbourhood. The topology of the social network can either be a regular network (RN), such a ring for example (Fig. 1a, a Barabasi-Albert [3] (BA) scale-free network (Fig. 1b) or a Erdös-Rényi random network (ER, see 1c, see [6]), with a given level of connectedness. The characteristics of these networks blatantly differ: the RN is constructed such as all agents have exactly the same number of neighbours. In the BA case, some agents can be seen as "hubs" (with lots of neighbours), while others have a very limited social neighbourhood. Finally, for the ER case, agents do have different amounts of neighbours, but by opposition with the BA case, we cannot guaranty the connectedness of the network. Through these topologies, they can share some information regarding the dividend linked to the risky asset. During the trading process, each trader receives a piece of information allowing to estimate the level of the dividend with a certain level of accuracy. Part of the simulation will consist in observing how this information can be refined through social exchanges and how communication can affect the efficiency of the market. In addition, each trader is granted a level of trust by her/his direct neighbours which may evolve regarding the accuracy of their predictions regarding the value of this asset. These aspect are described further in Subsects. 2.1 and 2.2.

2.1   Assets, Portfolio of Assets

In our artificial world, time is discretized into "periods" and "ticks". Periods can be analysed as "days", and within each of these periods, ticks can be seen as a measure of intra-day time.

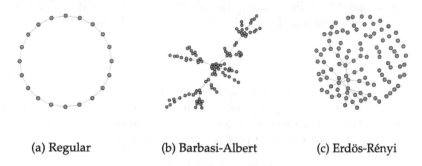

| (a) Regular | (b) Barbasi-Albert | (c) Erdös-Rényi |

Fig. 1. Three social networks structuring our OTC market

The random dividend paid to the traders allows to compute a fundamental value for the asset. For doing so, we refer to a modified version of the Gordon-Shapiro model [9]: let p_t be the price of the risky asset A; p_t can be modelled as the sum of further dividends that will be paid over time till infinity: $p_{t=0} = \sum_{t=1}^{+\infty} \frac{d_t}{(1+ke)^t}$, with ke the required rate of return for the risky asset at time t (see for example [1]).

We introduce some volatility in the dividend process: $\tilde{d}_t = d_{t-1} \times (1 + G_t)$, with $G_t \sim N(\mu, \gamma)$. In addition, we impose that $ke > G_t \forall t$.

In doing so we preserve the intuition behind the GS model: on average, dividends grow at a fixed rate, this rate being above the required rate of return ke. G_t is not observable by the agents and is never common knowledge to anyone in the economy. However these can access to an approximation of G_t, denominated $g_t \in [\underline{g_t}, \overline{g_t}]$ allowing them to perform the computation of an estimate of p_t. The framing imposed by g_t around G_t creates some level of uncertainty around G_t, the latter being ruled by a parameter in further simulations.

$$p_t \in \left[\frac{d_0\left(1 + \underline{g_t}\right)}{ke - \underline{g_t}} ; \frac{d_0\left(1 + \overline{g_t}\right)}{ke - \overline{g_t}} \right] = \left[\underline{p_t} ; \overline{p_t} \right] \tag{1}$$

So far, each investor has his own representation of the current price of the risky asset p_t and the possible next dividend through a set of information Ω_t. As we will see later, this representation may be more or less accurate, depending upon the category of agents and the information search made by each of these. In the population of artificial traders, each agent i is initially endowed with arbitrary quantities of both assets, $Q_{A,i} \geq 0$ and $Q_{r_f,i} \geq 0$.

Portfolio Construction: At the beginning of each period, agents want to maximize their expected utility in choosing θ, the proportion of risky asset A in their portfolio, so to have the highest possible value for their expected utility

$$E(U(w(1 + r_f) + \theta\tilde{\varepsilon})) \text{ with } w \text{ the financial wealth} \tag{2}$$

Let λ_i be the Arrow-Pratt absolute risk aversion coefficient, we fall in the classical case where the solution to the optimisation problem is

$$\theta^* = \frac{\mu}{\lambda_i \sigma_i^2} \tag{3}$$

In Eq. 3, μ and σ respectively denote the expected returns and the volatility of the risky asset. Knowing p_t and using g_t, investors can compute the possible boundaries for their return in one period of time conditional to the information they get. The return for the risky part of their investment:

$$r_{A,t} \in \left[log\left(\frac{\underline{p_t}}{p_{t-1}}\right); log\left(\frac{\overline{p_t}}{p_{t-1}}\right) \right] = \left[\underline{r_t}; \overline{r_t} \right] \tag{4}$$

As such, they can equally compute the expected return and, henceforth, the volatility σ of the risky asset conditional to their estimate of G_t (see Eq. 5); if we replace the population of possible returns for the asset A in t $r_{A,t}$ by X:

$$\mu(X) = \int x f(x) \, dx \qquad Var(X) = \sigma^2(X) = \int x^2 f(x) \, dx - \mu^2 \tag{5}$$

with $f(x)$ the probability density function for x. For the sake of simplicity, we use in this research a uniform PDF.[1] As such we have:

$$\mu(r_t) = \frac{1}{2}(\overline{r_t} + \underline{r_t}) \qquad Var(r_t) = \frac{1}{12}(\overline{r_t} - \underline{r_t})^2 \tag{6}$$

2.2   Agents Behaviour, Reputation and Trust

Three categories of traders co-evolve within this framework:

- *"Noise Traders"* (henceforth NT). NT only rely on a public signal ps characterized by the widest framing around G_t.
- *"Informed Traders"* (similarly "IT") who differ from the preceding NT in receiving a narrower estimate of G_t. So to speak, they receive a signal $is_i = N(\mu, \rho_i)$ allowing them to observe the true value of the risky asset with a reduced level of variance. By definition $\rho_i < \sigma^{PS}$, with σ^{PS} the standard deviation of the public signal.

---

[1] Notice that if g_t, which stands for the approximation of G_t follows a Normal distribution, it only allows agents to determine a framing for the possible price. As such, these latter must choose a "target" between the upper and the lower boundaries. This is the reason why they rely on a Uniform PDF for doing so.

– *"Social Traders"* (similarly "ST") who receive exactly the same signal as NT but can screen within their network environment, at a social distance equal to 1, if another trader, whatever his type, has a reputation large enough to be trusted in his own estimate of G_t. Said differently, ST can receive a (possibly) noisy information from their neighbours in addition to the public signal $ss_i = N(\mu, (\sigma^{PS} + \phi_t)$ with $\phi_t \in] - \sigma^{PS}, +\infty[$. The information they receive can either reduce the variance of the price estimate because it contains at least a piece truth $\phi_t \in] - \sigma^{PS}, 0]$, or it does not include anything instead of noise $\phi_t \in]0, +\infty[$. Of crucial importance here is the way ST select these information in their neighbourhood. For doing so, ST synthesize the latter following these steps:

1. Collect and archive the estimate of each neighbour in terms of possible deviation $cs_{i,t} = \left\{ \sigma^{PS}, \rho_{j,j\neq i}, \phi_{j,j\neq i} \right\}_t$; note that using the reverse relations coming from Eq. 6, ST can reconstruct te boundaries within which their neighbours believed the next dividend will be. In addition, each ST is endowed with a limited memory of k item: $cs_{i,t=1,..,k}$.

2. Make a choice in terms of information structure to use; in every case, the information chosen in the set derives from the strategy of the ST; we focus here on a single strategy where the decision is made with respect to the confidence or trust the agent has established with his/her N neighbours in time: $T_{i,j\neq i} = \left\{ T_{i,1}, T_{i,2}, \ldots, T_{i,N} \right\}_t$. One could imagine that the information in the neighbourhood is averaged, or any other aggregation technique.

3. Once the choice of information is made, the agent computes the optimal quantity of risky asset to hold θ^* and the upper and lower bounds for the price of the risky asset using the reverse relations coming from Eq. 6. The agent will then send a limit order to buy or to sell r_A in choosing respectively the upper and the lower bound as reservation prices.

4. Trust is updated at each tick, according to the appropriateness of the information transmitted by the neighbour. For doing so, the agent compares the actual dividend d_t perceived at date t and the expectations of is neighbours concerning this dividend at time $t - 1$. Let $[a, b]_{i,t}$ be the interval proposed by neighbour i at date $t - 1$. $m_{t,i} = \frac{a+b}{2}$ is the midpoint in this interval. The variation of trust linked to this information is equal to:

$$\Delta T_i = \frac{1}{(d_t - m_{t,i})^2} \times \begin{cases} -1 & \text{if } d_t - a < 0 \vee b - dt < 0, \\ 1 & \text{if } d_t - a > 0 \wedge b - dt > 0. \end{cases} \tag{7}$$

3   Empirical Settings and Results

In this section we present the way experiments have been designed, the nature of the collected data and we present our results.

3.1   Experiments

Since we are interested in understanding the role of the topology of the social network structuring the relationships among traders, we explore several network settings. The other elements of the simulations are described below:

- The total population of agents is set at $N = 500$.
- Each experiment is developed over 30 artificial days, which means that 30 dividend signals are generated and used by the agents so to decide the optimal composition of their portfolio.
- Within each day, agents are allowed to express their orders 20 times, but once by round-table cycle. Said differently, the scheduling system is such that agents are allowed to speak one time per round, 20 rounds in a day being organized. This generates pseudo intra-day prices and quotes.
- The Preferential-Attachment algorithm generates scale-free networks; the number of edges in the network is equal to $2 \times N$, N being the number of vertices.
- Our Erdos-Renyi and Regular Networks are generated so to have the same average number of edges per vertex (*i.e.*): as such, the connectedness rate c_r of a ER network for a given population of N agents is equal to $r_c = \frac{2}{N}$. The RN is, in this particular case, a circle.
- Concerning the way information is disclosed and processed:
  - NT receive a signal around the next (unknown) dividend with boundaries set at ±50%.
  - IT have a better accuracy with regard to the dividend: their boundaries are set to ±10%
  - ST receive the same information as NT but they select an information in their social neighbourhood with respect to the highest level of the trader's reputation at a social distance of 1. For each network setting, we run 12 experiments and we collect prices, quotes, and the trading volumes. All these information are linked to a time stamp.

For each network setting, we run 12 experiments and we collect prices, quotes, an the trading volumes. All these information are linked to a time stamp.

A "typical" experiment produces market motions that are *qualitatively* realistic (see Fig. 2).

3.2   Results

We are not interested in the mean return observed in our various experimental settings: this parameter should not be affected by the set of initial parameters but by the random process driving the dividend. However, the first step in our data analysis process consists in transforming observed prices p_t to returns $r_t = ln(p_t) - ln(p_{t-1})$ at a tick-by-tick level (each time a new price is observed in the market). We do not consider the return produced by a new signal emission (end-of-the day effect) so to neutralize the volatility it may trigger: we are not interested in the volatility provoked by the dividend process but rather by

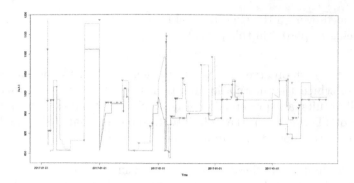

Fig. 2. Prices and quotes observed over a couple of seconds within the same day (i) Green line: best bid, (ii) Blue line: best ask, (iii) Purple triangles: prices (Color figure online)

the knowledge of each artificial agent and the one that is spread in its direct neighbourhood.

More interesting are the parameters that are used to gauge the efficiency of the market at the intra-day level:

Volatility − σ: we compute the average volatility of the market within each day using the standard deviation of the returns. We expect a higher volatility when the proportion of NT is important and when the impact of ST might be limited by the nature of the Network over which they behave (for example, in the RN setting where full connectedness is not granted).

Liquidity − λ: is simply in this case the average of stocks that are traded within a day. If a new estimate of the next dividend has little impact on the agents, whatever the reason, the exchanged volume should be relatively low compared to one observed if this information deeply modifies the composition of their optimal portfolio.

Efficiency − Ω: is the average of the absolute value of the deviation of prices with regards to the fundamental value. The lower this metric, the more efficient the market.

We first propose some graphical illustrations of our results.

In Figs. 3, 5 and 7, three matrix are nested, one for each network setting (the order is systematically the same (i): ER, (ii): PA and (iii): RN) these matrix represent using a colour (associated to a given level reported on the gauge at the right side of the matrix) one of the parameters we study (σ, λ, Ω).

For these matrix, rows are organized by mix of NT *vs.* IT. The total proportion of these sub-populations is always equal to 80% of the total population, but their proportions vary from 80% to 0%. ST always account for 20% of the population. All these figures have been chosen arbitrarily and may be discussed and challenged in an other study.

Columns simply report the values obtained during each run of the same experiment (*e.g.* 12 columns). We also provide an aggregate appreciation of the results obtained over all the experimental rounds (in Figs. 3, 6 and 8, statistical tests not being displayed in this paper).

Volatility. We first observe how volatility seems linked to the nature of the network over which the information diffusion occurs and to the proportion of NT/IT. All results are presented in Fig. 3. Not surprisingly, the higher the proportion of IT the lower the volatility (remember that Ask and Bids are constrained by the boundaries around the estimate of the dividend: since IT have a narrower estimate, prices should vary less when they populate the market). Figure 4 summarized these values in calculating the average value observed within each network setting row by row (over 12 runs). Overall, the ER setting generates the highest average level of volatility 8.926% (all population mix and runs considered). By decreasing order of volatility come respectively the RN (8.463%) and the Preferential Attachment Network (8.328%). This may be linked to a better information diffusion in the PA network, provided at least some ST are located on vertice with a high degree of connectivity. However, as we can see in Fig. 4, this appears to be particularly true when the proportion of NT becomes relatively important (30% and more). One can imagine that in this case, IT become less determinant in the price emergence and that the nature of the Network tends to play a more important role in the diffusion of the best price estimate.

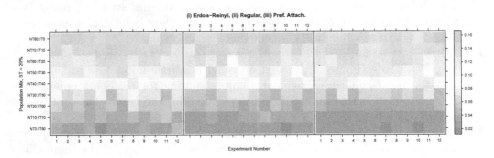

Fig. 3. Level of volatility over 20 days per experiment and mix of NT vs. IT (20% IT in any case) (i) By ranking orders, the overall highest level of volatility: (1) Erdös-Rényi, (2) Regular and (3) Preferential attachment networks (ii) Volatility is a monotonic function of the proportion of NT (iii) A similar threshold of 30% NT emerges whatever the network structure

Liquidity. The liquidity of the market is, on average, higher for the RN and the PA (resp. 471 and 464) than for the ER (446). Here again we observe a quasi linear effect: when the number of NT decreases, the liquidity of the market increases (see Fig. 5). The increase in the market liquidity is nonetheless different for each network setting: it requires 60% of IT for establishing a monotonic relationship for the ER, 50% for the RN, and 40% for the PA (see Fig. 6). Here again, if the proportion of IT *vs.* NT appears to have an impact of this parameter, the Network structure also seems to play a role in establishing different levels of liquidity.

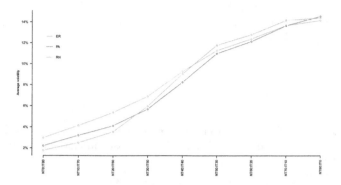

Fig. 4. Average level of volatility over all 12 experiments per mix of NT vs. IT (20% IT in any case) – The rate at which volatility increases the most can be observed for the RN case when the proportion of $NT > 20\%$

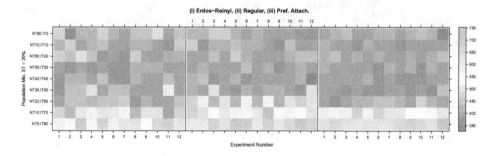

Fig. 5. Level of liquidity over 20 days per experiment and mix of NT vs. IT (20% IT in any case) (i) By ranking orders, the overall highest level of liquidity: (1) Regular and (2) Preferential Attachment and (3) Erdös-Rényi networks (ii) Liquidity decreases with higher proportions of NT (iii) The higher the availability of information, the higher the liquidity of the market

Efficiency. When it comes to efficiency, the best network structure is clearly the RN ($\Omega = 143$) while PA and RN obtain respectively values for Ω equal to 150 and 157. The overall impression in analysing Fig. 7 is that if some aggregate difference can be noticed, this seems not to be linked monotonically to the agent population mix as it was clearly the case for λ and σ. This result, although it must be confirmed and observed on larger experiments involving hundred of runs, would indicate that the single factor at play in the efficiency level (as we compute it her), would be the nature of the Network over which our artificial traders behave. This impression is also confirmed in Fig. 8.

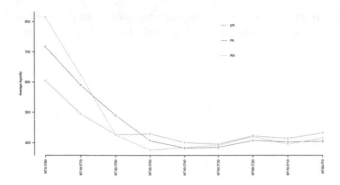

Fig. 6. Average level of liquidity over all 12 experiments per mix of NT vs. IT (20% IT in any case) – The rate at which liquidity increases monotonically varies among network settings

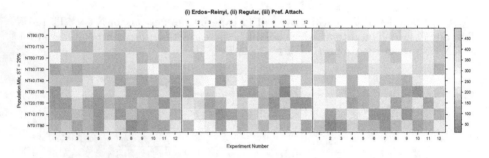

Fig. 7. Level of efficiency over 20 days per experiment and mix of NT vs. IT (20% IT in any case) (i) By ranking orders, the overall highest level of efficiency: (1) Erdös-Rényi, (2) Preferential attachment and (3) Regular networks (ii) Efficiency does not exhibit an evident relationship with the proportion of NT

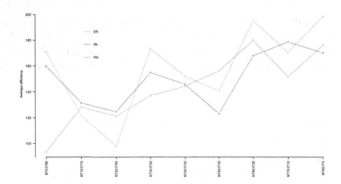

Fig. 8. Average level of efficiency over all 12 experiments per mix of NT vs. IT (20% IT in any case) – The behavior of Efficiency appears to be linked to the proportion of IT more strongly in the case of the RN setting (quasi monotonic relationship) w.r.t. the other settings where monotonicity cannot be identified

4   Conclusion

Considering that a huge proportion of financial transactions occur in OTC markets, we propose an investigation of the topology of the underlying social network over which they operate. Actually, we do not mimic a real OTC market but only focus on what we believe to be an essential feature of their nature: the underlying network. We thus address the question of the impact of this network over three essential parameters that are considered as essential for gauging market dynamics: liquidity, volatility and efficiency.

For doing so, we study how information is spread over market participants using a social-influence mechanism between three categories of agents (Noise, Informed and Social Traders). In this simplified world, traders reputation is a public signal allowing agents to estimate the reliability of the information located in their social neighbourhood, and eventually to prefer this latter to the one they own themselves. As such, the market network topology, in relation with the mix of traders populations and the signals they receive create an artificial framework geared at analysing information propagation and its subsequent, possible effects on prices, returns, and exchanged volumes.

Although simplified, this framework cannot be studied without a powerful multi-agent system. We do adopt this approach and show that, at least at some level, choosing a Regular, a Erdös-Rényi or a scale free network and locating on each node one Noise, Informed or Social Trader, substantially modifies the dynamics of the market. The overall level of volatility, the liquidity and the resulting efficiency are impacted by this initial choice in various ways which also depends upon the proportion of Informed vs. Noise Traders.

We believe these preliminary results could be explored and extended further, notably in addressing the way reputation, which is one main characteristics of the information propagation, actually evolves at fine grain and precisely modifies the dynamics within the network.

References

1. Agosto, A., Moretto, E.: Variance matters (in stochastic dividend discount models). Ann. Financ. **11**(2), 283–295 (2015)
2. Bajo, J., Mathieu, P., Escalona, M.J.: Multi-agent technologies in economics. Intell. Syst. Acc. Financ. Manag. **24**(2–3), 59–61 (2017)
3. Barabasi, A.-L., Albert, R.: Emergence of scaling in random networks. Science **286**(5439), 509–512 (1999)
4. Benhammada, S., Amblard, F., Chikhi, S.: An artificial stock market with interaction network and mimetic agents (short paper). In: International Conference on Agents and Artificial Intelligence (ICAART), Porto, Portugal, 24–26 February 2017, vol. 2, pp. 190–197. SciTePress (2017). http://www.scitepress.org/
5. Brandouy, O., Mathieu, P., Veryzhenko, I.: On the design of agent-based artificial stock markets. In: Filipe, J., Fred, A. (eds.) ICAART 2011. CCIS, vol. 271, pp. 350–364. Springer, Heidelberg (2013). https://doi.org/10.1007/978-3-642-29966-7_23

6. Erdős, P., Rényi, A.: On random graphs I. Publ. Math. (Debr.) **6**, 290–297 (1959)
7. Fama, E.F.: The behaviour of stock market prices. J. Bus. **38**, 34–105 (1965)
8. Fama, E.F., Fisher, L., Jensen, M.C., Roll, R.: The adjustment of stock prices to new information. Int. Econ. Rev. **10**(1), 1–21 (1969)
9. Gordon, M.J.: Dividends, earnings, and stock prices. Rev. Econ. Stat. **41**(2), 99–105 (1959)
10. Mathieu, P., Secq, Y.: Using LCS to exploit order book data in artificial markets. In: Nguyen, N.T., Kowalczyk, R., Corchado, J.M., Bajo, J. (eds.) Transactions on Computational Collective Intelligence XV. LNCS, vol. 8670, pp. 69–88. Springer, Heidelberg (2014). https://doi.org/10.1007/978-3-662-44750-5_4
11. Nongaillard, A., Mathieu, P.: Agent-based reallocation problem on social networks. Group Decis. Negot. **23**(5), 1067–1083 (2014)
12. Phelps, S., Parsons, S., McBurney, P.: Automated trading agents versus virtual humans: an evolutionary game-theoretic comparison of two double-auction market designs. In: Proceedings of the 6th Workshop on Agent-Mediated Electronic Commerce, New York, NY (2004)
13. Veryzhenko, I., Arena, L., Harb, E., Oriol, N.: A reexamination of high frequency trading regulation effectiveness in an artificial market framework. Trends in Practical Applications of Scalable Multi-Agent Systems, the PAAMS Collection. AISC, vol. 473, pp. 15–25. Springer, Cham (2016). https://doi.org/10.1007/978-3-319-40159-1_2

An Agent-Based Model for Detection in Economic Networks

João Brito[1(✉)], Pedro Campos[1,2(✉)], and Rui Leite[1,2]

[1] Faculty of Economics, University of Porto, Porto, Portugal
{joaogppbrito@gmail.com, pcampos@fep.up.pt}
[2] LIAAD (Laboratory of Artificial Intelligence and Decision Support), INESC TEC,
R. Dr. Roberto Frias, 4200 Porto, Portugal

Abstract. The economic impact of fraud is wide and fraud can be a critical problem when the prevention procedures are not robust. In this paper we create a model to detect fraudulent transactions, and then use a classification algorithm to assess if the agent is fraud prone or not. The model (BOND) is based on the analytics of an economic network of agents of three types: individuals, businesses and financial intermediaries. From the dataset of transactions, a sliding window of rows previously aggregated per agent has been used and machine learning (classification) algorithms have been applied. Results show that it is possible to predict the behavior of agents, based on previous transactions.

Keywords: Agent-based models · Fraud · Networks
Machine learning algorithms

1 Introduction

In a competitive environment, fraud can be a critical problem when the prevention procedures are not robust [16]. In recent years, the development of new technologies, that enhanced our way of living, have also brought new fraud methods. Traditional practices of tax evasion through illegal transactions have been improved with the use of computers and mobile communications [2]. All companies are subject to fraud risk, and this has been one of the causes of various corporate downturns, massive investment losses, significant legal costs, and erosion of confidence in respectable entities and in the capital markets to which they belong. The economic impact of fraud is wide. Estimates of the cost of crime type for North American companies vary between $ 200 and $ 600 billion [18]. Fraud can have a significant impact on a company's performance, as it can cost a company between 1 and 6 percent of its annual sales [10]. In response to these kinds of events, today it is expected that organizations assume a zero tolerance attitude towards the risk of fraud. Vigilant controls and management of organizational fraud cases send a clear signal to the public, stakeholders, and regulators about the attitude of supervisory and management bodies to the risks of fraud and tolerance that an organization presents to them [3, 13].

The purpose of this work is to create a model that is able to detect fraud transactions based on the analytics of an economic network. As it is difficult to gain access to real

© Springer International Publishing AG, part of Springer Nature 2018
J. Bajo et al. (Eds.): PAAMS 2018 Workshops, CCIS 887, pp. 105–115, 2018.
https://doi.org/10.1007/978-3-319-94779-2_10

financial data, a financial transactions network was created to generate synthetic data. The network of agents is modeled through an Agent-Based model, where the agents are of three types: individuals, businesses and financial intermediaries. Links can be of two types: between financial intermediaries (transaction lines) and between individuals and/ or businesses (connections). These two can be fixed or temporary, depending on the transaction needs of the agents. From the dataset of transactions, a sliding window of rows previously aggregated per agent has been used and machine learning (classification) algorithms have been applied: Random Forests, Neural Networks and Bayesian Networks. The goal is to detect fraudulent transactions of a given agent, and then use a classification algorithm to assess if the agent is fraud prone or not. Bayesian Networks and Random Forests algorithms performed very similarly, but Random Forests had slightly higher results. The paper is structured as follows: in Sect. 2 we introduce the problem of fraud, and the techniques we propose for this approach: agent-based modelling and networks. Section 3 contains the model. In Sect. 4 we present the main results. Conclusion is in Sect. 5.

2 Fraud, Agents, and Networks

Fraud and Detection
According to [1], economic fraud can be defined as "The use of someone's occupation for personal enrichment through the deliberate use or misapplication of the resources or assets of the employing organization". Taking into account the ability to prevent fraud, or quantify its risk and losses, it has become a potential source of competitive advantage and improvements in financial performance for companies [3, 18]. While information technologies (IT) provide new opportunities for states and businesses to create and expand their operations, they also present opportunities for individuals with criminal intent. In recent years, malicious cyber activity has become increasingly sophisticated, focused, and serious [4, 22]. Preventing and detecting fraud are related issues, but they are not similar concepts. Prevention encompasses policies, procedures, training and communication aimed at preventing fraud from occurring. Detection focuses on activities and techniques that recognize timely and promptly action whether fraud has occurred or is ongoing. While prevention techniques do not guarantee that fraud will not happen, they are the first line of defense to minimize the risk of fraud [13]. Even so, nowadays there are already several methods of detection of fraud implemented that resort to the extraction of data knowledge, statistical analysis and machine learning and artificial intelligence. They attempt to discover fraudulent acts based on anomalies and patterns in databases [2]. Several authors have used machine learning algorithms for fraud detection, as they allow for classification purposes and prediction, such as Random Forests, Bayesian Networks and Neural Networks, [6–9, 14, 20, 21], among other algorithms.

Agent Network Models as Basis for Fraud Detection
From an economic point of view, neoclassical theories see individuals as independent decision makers. Agents trade in markets, prices reflect the behavior of others, and people tune their decisions based on the information conveyed by those prices.

Typically, game theory is used in fraud detection research because it allows to study how one individual's actions influence the behavior of another. And this is where networks come in, which have been the subject of theoretical and empirical studies to investigate how these structures can influence the behavior of their constituents [23]. Networks have become particularly useful when agents interact primarily with a small part of the population, that is, with their neighbors in the network. Agent-based computational modeling is suitable for the study of networks. It is possible to program complex networks with relative ease and observe thousands of interactions between agents in these networks [12, 23, 25].

Other Related Work Using Agent Networks for Fraud Detection
Bayesian learning allied to the Dempster-Shafer theory were used to propose a credit card fraud detection model, combining current behavior data with historical data [15]. In another study, [17] used agent-based learning for detecting fraud and intruders in information network systems, namely in applications for the prevention of credit card fraud. [5] explored the application of the study of social networks in the prevention of money laundering. This phenomenon is a common illicit practice, and goes on to try to turn profits obtained illegally into legitimate assets. Money obtained illegally is generally "laundered" through transactions involving banks or other types of financial institutions. It can have a strong impact on an economy, increasing the operational risk of financial transactions and threatening the stability of financial institutions. Shamshirband et al. [19], analyzed several intrusion detection systems in mobile networks based on multi-agent systems. The authors note that the implementation of wireless sensor networks for applications such as emergency, surveillance or monitoring services always includes the permanent threat of multiple risks, intrusions and cyber-attacks. Other authors [11, 24] developed an example of such systems. The implemented network incorporates three types of peripheral agents and one central agent. The data collection agents filter and rearrange the obtained data, and then transmit the filtered information to the data analyzing agents. These are the key to the intrusion detection process as they are responsible for comprehensively analyzing the data in order to identify patterns that are out of the ordinary. There are also agents responsible for communication, who do not treat or analyze information, but only take responsibility for the dissemination of information. The central agent monitors the entire system, ensuring that the process is conducted as intended.

Network Structure
Graph theory is used to define the network structure. A population of n agents are placed in a network, G, constituting an unoriented list of pairs of agents $\{i, j\}$. In this way $i \sim j \in G$ means that the agents i and j are connected in the network G (in this case, as the network in unoriented, if $i \sim j \in G$ then $j \sim i \in G$). Networks are connected, which means that any node can reach another from another node following a path consisting of a finite number of links. The edges considered will have neither weights nor any intrinsic values that distinguishes them from other edges. Thus the importance of any edge results only from its location relative to the others.

3   BOND – An Agent-Based Model for Fraud Detection

Model Overview

BOND represents a network of financial transactions. Agents are created with a set of characteristics that represent their profile, such as location, nationality and predisposition for fraud. Using these characteristics, agents create their own financial transaction networks, which will be used to carry out transactions during the execution of the model. The design of the financial network turns out to be biased by the individual characteristics of each agent. During model execution, if an agent decides to make a transaction (send money to anybody), the agent may choose to do so legally or illegally. If the transaction is legal the agent will only move the desired amount from your account (origin) to the target account (destination). If the transaction has a fraud intention, the agent chooses to use a tiered schema, dividing the desired amount into multiple transactions from smaller amounts into different accounts, thus avoiding some reports requested by the banks. The template will produce a summary list of all transactions between agents (date, source, destination, amount, etc.). Agents can represent three types of entities individuals, businesses and financial intermediaries. Businesses are subdivided into for-profit, non-profit, trust fund or shell-type businesses. Shell corporations are companies that do not have any relevant assets and business operations, and are usually associated with illegitimate actions such as money laundering. Trust funds can also be known for suspicious financial activities. Intermediaries can be divided into formal (banks, funds) or informal (transfers that do not go through the banking system, from hand to hand). Individuals are not divided into any other subcategory. The model has been programmed using NetLogo [26].

Agent's Attributes and Initial Parameters

In the initialization process of BOND, all agents define their location and nationality (two important agent's attributes). These characteristics can only be "Native" or "Foreign". Both are defined by a user-defined percentage, which can determine which percentage of agents is of foreign nationality and is located abroad (the possibility of sending money abroad maybe seen as illegal, due to tax evasion). The parameter related to the propensity of each agent to participate in fraudulent transactions (fraud predisposition) can range from 0 to 100, and the higher the value, the higher the propensity. This value is randomly assigned, and the user can also define the percentage of agents with a high propensity to fraud. There is another variable related to the inclusion of the agent in a watch list of potential suspects. Some agents with high predispositions to be included in the list are randomly selected. The agents on this list should be monitored closely, and their inclusion here should be an important tip for fraudulent behavior.

Network Creation

Two types of links are used to create the networks in BOND. One is related to links between financial intermediaries and other agents (transaction lines); the other is related to links between individuals and/or businesses (connections). It was first assumed that each financial intermediary was linked to 40% of the remaining intermediaries. Then each individual and business creates a link with a certain number of intermediaries, this number being random between 1 and 4 (maximum of 4 accounts for example). Individuals and businesses create connections between them. Each agent in this group first determines its number of neighbors by taking a random number from an exponential distribution of mean 2 (it is shown that in several typologies the number of neighbors is well represented by this distribution). Individuals and businesses then create links to that number of agents (except financial intermediaries) without duplication. Some additional connections are also created. An individual or business that has a predisposition greater than 60% creates a connection with a trust or shell business (they are usually associated with attempted fraud and tax evasion). If they have a predisposition above 90%, they create another connection to trust or Shell-type businesses and another agent that has a predisposition above 60%. This is intended to simulate the tendency that individuals with a high propensity to seek fraudulent transactions are usually highly connected to agents with similar propensities. The connections made here are kept during the model run, but others can be created during the simulation to fit the purposes of some transactions.

The model takes into account the following attributes of each transaction: X01 – Origin agent; X02 – type of origin agent (Individual, Profit Business, Nonprofit business, Trust or Shell); X03 – Nationality of the origin; X04 – Location of origin; X05 – Situation of origin in watch list; X06 – Destination agent; X07 – type of destination agent (Individual, Profit Business, Nonprofit business, Trust or Shell); X08 – Nationality of the destination; X09 – Location of destination; X10 – Situation of destination in the watch list; X11 – amount of the transaction; X12 – Date of transaction (day); X13 Predisposition of the origin agent for the fraud.

Transactions
When BOND is executed, 5% of the total of individual agents and businesses start a transaction plan at each time period. There has to be an origin and destination agent. Origin agent proceed as follows:

1. The origin agent deletes all values from previous transactions.
2. The origin agent defines the amount to transfer (maximum 100 000).
3. The origin agent defines the destination agent (within its closest neighborhood). Two neighbors are "closest neighbors" when they are directly connected to each other. In some occasions (with a probability of 10%), one agent is chosen from out of its closest neighborhood, in order to introduce some noise.
4. The origin agent verifies if it has connections with any financial intermediary that allow for the money to get to its destination. If there is none, one new connection is created with a financial intermediary.
5. The origin agent decides how to structure the transaction. If the origin and destination agents have low predisposition for fraud (less than 60%), then all money is sent in one only transaction (called simple transaction). If both predispositions of origin and destination agent are high, but the amount is lower than 10 000, a transaction is made (a simple one). If the amount is greater than 10 000, then the origin agent decides to re-structure the transaction and divide the amount in several transactions of smaller values (called complex transaction). The origin agent chooses one or more agents of its closest network and start a sequence of transactions in such a way that the

money can reach the destination without being easily detected. Here the whole value is divided in transactions smaller than 10 000, and the source agent tries to make transactions through its network in a way that the money gets to the destination indirectly. It also avoids transferring money several times to the same intermediary agent. For example, if it has 8 transactions to make to neighbors to reach a certain node in the grid, but only has 2 neighbors that would suite that purpose, it will search for a new connection in order to dilute the transactions through more neighbors.

6. The origin agent creates a schedule for all its transactions. If the transaction is simple, then the amount is transferred directly from origin to destination. Otherwise, a scheduling of the several transaction has to be made, with heterogeneous amounts (always smaller than 10 000), to be distributed for more than one agent of its closest network.

A flowchart of the model, presenting the essential features of BOND is included in Fig. 1.

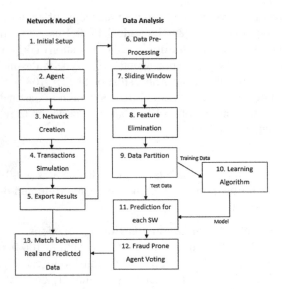

Fig. 1. Flowchart of BOND model, and the data analysis process.

4   Results

The user interface of NetLogo was used to setup the number of businesses, the number of individual people, the percentage of users that are in the watch list and the percentage of fraud prone agents. After defining these values, the remaining setup of the agents and their grid were completed by the model itself, according to the assumptions previously mentioned. Figure 2 shows an example of one simulation setup and the resulting network of transactions in NetLogo.

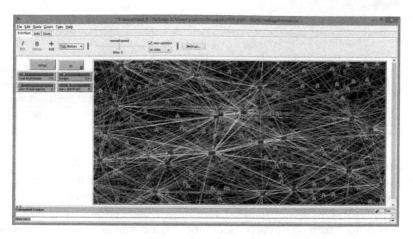

Fig. 2. Example of one simulation setup and output network in NetLogo. *Note: white lines represent the links between nodes (transaction lines and connections); nodes are the individuals (in blue); businesses (green houses) and financial intermediaries (black boxes)*: (Color figure online)

To analyze the general behavior of the model, 25 different setups were run according to the values contained in the following intervals: number of individuals [400 to 1200]; number of businesses [150 to 900], percentage of users in the watch list [2% to 11%] and percentage of fraud prone agents [4% to 21%]. The goal is to detect fraudulent transactions of a given agent, and then use that classification to assess if the agent is fraud prone or not. We consider a certain time period of transactions because of the assumption that the fraudulent agent will try to split a big amount through several transactions to several neighbors. Thus it would not make sense to analyze the transactions one by one. Taking this into account, the first step of the data processing is to sort the transactions by agent, and then by chronological order. This way it will be possible to divide the data in blocks, where each block aggregates the transactions initiated by a given agent. Once the transactions are ordered by timeline, this gives the possibility to apply a sliding window to each block of transactions. This process will look for the aggregation of the information concerning several transactions in just one line. Then, the classification algorithm will be applied in these blocks. The sliding window aggregates the information of 30 days, and the steps between each window will be of 15 days. This means that windows overlap by 15 days, allowing for a more in-depth analysis. For each window, the process should determine the following attributes: W1 – Source Agent; W2 –Source Type; W3 – Source Nationality; W4 – Source Location; W5 – Source Watch List Status; W6 – Total Transactions in the Window; W7 – Total Transactions in the Window with Trust/Shell; W8 - Total Transactions with Foreign Agents; W9 - Total Transactions with Agents in the Watch List; W10 – Average Transaction Amount; W11 – Variance Coefficient; W12 – Centrality; W13 – Fraud Suspect.

Table 1. Summary of transaction data by sliding window (SW)

	Number of SW with fraud	Average number of transactions per SW	Average number of transactions per SW with fraud	Average centrality of initiators (by sliding window)	Average centrality of initiators in fraudulent windows
Mean	1597.1	3.2	6.0	0.01	0.09
St. Dev.	1081.7	0.8	1.0	0.01	0.04

With the data resulting from the sliding windows (SW) (see Table 1 for summary) used as input, three classification algorithms were used to detect/predict the presence of fraud in every transaction window: Bayesian Networks, Neural Networks and Random Forests. The algorithms were evaluated according to the corresponding AUC (Area Under Curve) from their ROC curve (see Table 2), a common measure to assess the quality of data mining algorithms. Then, the results of each classification were used to "vote" on the likelihood of each agent being a fraud prone, and votes were then compared with the data produced by the BOND network model (the "real" data). Taking the results of Table 2 into account, it is possible to conclude that the three algorithms had successful performances. Nevertheless, the Neural Networks algorithm had slightly lower results, whether for the ROC analysis or for the voting accuracy. In addition, it had a higher standard deviation in its results and it was fairly slower in terms of running time when compared with the other two. As for the results from Bayesian Networks and Random Forests, algorithms performed very similarly for both criteria, but it is worth mentioning that Random Forests had slightly higher results with a lower corresponding standard deviation. Another important insight is the feature selection step in the classification process. As previously mentioned, before including the sliding window (SW) function, a Backward Feature Elimination is conducted, using the same algorithm used in the learning stage. According to this step it is possible to conduct the remaining of the data analysis taking into account just five variables of the SW, at a cost of an error with value 0,076 for Bayesian Networks. Those variables are: Number of Transactions; Number of Transactions with Trust/Shell; Average Transaction Amount; Variance Coefficient; Centrality. Doing the same with Random Forests, with an error of 0,035, the five variables would be: Source Type; Number of Transactions; Average Transaction Amount; Variance Coefficient; Centrality.

Table 2. Aggregated classification results based on sliding windows for the 25 scenarios

	ROC AUC for the fraudulent window prediction			Accuracy for fraudulent agent voting		
	Bayesian network	Neural networks	Random forests	Bayesian network	Neural networks	Random forests
Mean	0,9619	0,8988	0,9712	0,8972	0,8818	0,8988
Std. Dev.	0,0115	0,0232	0,0101	0,0349	0,0343	0,0311

5   Conclusions

In this paper we create a model to detect fraudulent transactions of a given agent, and then use a classification algorithm to assess if the agent is fraud prone or not. The model (BOND) is based on the analytics of an economic network of agents (modeled through an Agent-Based model). The agents are of three types: individuals, businesses and financial intermediaries. Links can be of two types: between financial intermediaries (transaction lines) and between individuals and/or businesses (connections). From the dataset of transactions, a sliding window of rows previously aggregated per agent has been used and machine learning (classification) algorithms have been applied.

Similar methodologies have already been proposed, but here the model not only identifies sets of suspicious transactions but it also draws conclusions on the agent's behavior. It achieves this by taking into account the transactions done by each agent, but more importantly by analyzing their role in their social network. The agent based model allows to insert this aspect into each set of transaction information, and the machine learning algorithms were able to incorporate them in the resulting conclusions.

Results show that it is possible to efficiently predict the behavior of agent, based on previous transactions. Five variables of the sliding window (SW) dataset have been used. The intent was to get the simulation of the agent network to replicate the behavior of regular and fraudulent agents when they do financial transactions. For the fraudulent ones, the aim was to associate a money laundering situation to actions like spreading a big amount through several small transactions, using Trust/Shell agents, or doing several transactions in a short time frame. This ended up being successfully reflected by the model and it was identified by the classification algorithms. This is showed not only by the good prediction results, but also by the feature selection step, where the selected variables are in line with fraudulent behavior assumptions that constitute the basis of BOND. Although both Random Forests and Bayesian Networks had a similar performance, both algorithms show a high value of False Negatives. Therefore, as clues for future work, we suggest that it might be interesting to explore the cost the classification function.

Also, for future work, it would be interesting to create simulations that resemble more what happens in real financial entities that handle this type of data. This would mean executing the network model more continuously (instead of standalone runs) and use the classification in parallel. For example, as the transactions are being made by agents, the classification results could be used to update information about the agents, namely their watch list status, in real time

Finally, the best fit for practical use of the model would be to serve financial companies or regulators, as a tool that helps them to analyze their financial transactions data, in order to identify suspicious money transfers and fraud prone agents. Bearing this in mind, it would be of great value if the BOND model could be applied on real financial data, so its potential impact could be better evaluated.

References

1. University of Houston system, Administrative Memorandum, 07.A.04 (2000). http://www.uh.edu/af/universityservices/policies/sam/7InfoServices/7A4.pdf
2. Bolton, R.J., Hand, D.J., Provost, F., Breiman, L.: Statistical fraud detection: a review. Stat. Sci. **17**(3), 235–249 (2002)
3. Button, M., Gee, J., Brooks, G.: Measuring the cost of fraud: an opportunity for the new competitive advantage. J. Financ. Crime **19**(1), 65–75 (2012)
4. Choo, K.K.R.: The cyber threat landscape: challenges and future research directions. Comput. Secur. **30**(8), 719–731 (2011)
5. Colladon, A.F., Remondi, E.: Using social network analysis to prevent money laundering. Expert Syst. Appl. **67**, 49–58 (2017)
6. Dheepa, V., Dhanapal, R.: Analysis of credit card fraud detection methods. Int. J. Recent Trends Eng. **2**(3), 126–128 (2009)
7. Enke, D., Thawornwong, S.: The use of data mining and neural networks for forecasting stock market returns. Expert Syst. Appl. **29**(4), 927–940 (2005)
8. Ezawa, K., Singh, M., Norton, S.: Learning goal-oriented Bayesian networks for telecommunications risk management. In: 13th International Conference on Machine Learning, pp. 139–147 (1996)
9. Friedman, N., Geiger, D., Goldszmidt, M., Provan, G., Langley, P., Smyth, P.: Bayesian network classifiers. Mach. Learn. **29**, 131–163 (1997)
10. Hogsett III, R.M., Radig, W.J.: Employee rime: the cost and some control measures. Rev. Bus. **16**(2), 9 (1994)
11. Huang, W., An, Y., Du, W.: A multi-agent-based distributed intrusion detection system. In: Advanced Computer Theory and Engineering (ICACTE), vol. 3, pp. 141–143 (2010)
12. Macal, C.M., North, M.J.: Tutorial on agent-based modeling and simulation. In: Proceedings of the 37th Conference on Winter Simulation, pp. 2–15 (2005)
13. Institute of Internal Auditors: Managing the business risk of fraud: a practical guide (2008)
14. Neil, M., Fenton, N., Tailor, M.: Using Bayesian networks to model expected and unexpected operational losses. Risk Anal. **25**(4), 963–972 (2005)
15. Panigrahi, S., Kundu, A., Sural, S., Majumdar, A.K.: Credit card fraud detection: a fusion approach using Dempster-Shafer theory and Bayesian learning. Inf. Fusion **10**(4), 354–363 (2009)
16. Phua, C., Lee, V., Smith, K., Gayler, R.: A comprehensive survey of data mining-based fraud detection research. Monash University (2010)
17. Prodromidis, A.L., Stolfo, S.J.: Agent-based distributed learning applied to fraud detection. In: Sixteenth National Conference on Artificial Intelligence (1999)
18. Schnatterly, K.: Increasing firm value through detection and prevention of white-collar crime. Strateg. Manag. J. **24**(7), 587–614 (2003)
19. Shamshirband, S., Anuar, N.B., Kiah, M.L.M., Patel, A.: An appraisal and design of a multi-agent system based cooperative wireless intrusion detection computational intelligence technique. Eng. Appl. Artif. Intell. **26**(9), 2105–2127 (2013)
20. Sun, L., Shenoy, P.P.: Using Bayesian networks for bankruptcy prediction: some methodological issues. Eur. J. Oper. Res. **180**(2), 738–753 (2007)
21. Tuyls, K., Maes, S., Vanschoenwinkel, B.: Credit card fraud detection using Bayesian and neural networks. In: Proceedings of the 1st International NAISO Congress on Neuro Fuzzy Technologies, pp. 261–270 (2002)
22. Vatis, M.: The next battlefield. Harv. Int. Rev. **28**(3), 56 (2006)

23. Wilhite, A.: Economic activity on fixed networks. In: Tesfatsion, L., Judd, K.L. (eds.) Handbook of Computational Economics, vol. 2, pp. 1013–1045. Elsevier, Amsterdam (2006)
24. Zhu, X.D., Huang, Z.Q., Zhou, H.: Design of a multi-agent based intelligent intrusion detection system. In: 2006 Proceedings of the 1st International Symposium on Pervasive Computing and Applications, pp. 290–295 (2006)
25. Namatame, A., Chen, S.H.: Agent-Based Modelling and Network Dynamics. Oxford University Press, Oxford (2016)
26. Wilensky, U.: NetLogo. http://ccl.northwestern.edu/netlogo/. Center for Connected Learning and Computer-Based Modeling, Northwestern University, Evanston, IL (1999)

Optimizing Opponents Selection in Bilateral Contracts Negotiation with Particle Swarm

Francisco Silva[1], Ricardo Faia[1], Tiago Pinto[1,2(✉)], Isabel Praça[1], and Zita Vale[1]

[1] GECAD - Knowledge Engineering and Decision Support Research Center, Institute of Engineering – Politechnic of Porto (ISEP/IPP), Porto, Portugal
{fspsa,rfmfa,tmcfp,icp,zav}@isep.ipp.pt

[2] BISITE – Research Centre, University of Salamanca, Salamanca, Spain
tpinto@usal.es

Abstract. This paper proposes a model based on particle swarm optimization to aid electricity markets players in the selection of the best player(s) to trade with, to maximize their bilateral contracts outcome. This approach is integrated in a Decision Support System (DSS) for the pre-negotiation of bilateral contracts, which provides a missing feature in the state-of-art, the possible opponents analysis. The DSS determines the best action of all the actions that the supported player can take, by applying a game theory approach. However, the analysis of all actions can easily become very time-consuming in large negotiation scenarios. The proposed approach aims to provide the DSS with an alternative method with the capability of reducing the execution time while keeping the results quality as much as possible. Both approaches are tested in a realistic case study where the supported player could take almost half a million different actions. The results show that the proposed methodology is able to provide optimal and near-optimal solutions with an huge execution time reduction.

Keywords: Automated negotiation · Bilateral contracts
Decision Support System · Electricity Markets · Game theory
Particle Swarm Optimization

1   Introduction

Over the last decades, the Electricity Markets (EMs) suffered profound changes to adapt themselves to the society's needs and the arising challenges.

This work has received funding from the European Union's Horizon 2020 research and innovation programme under the Marie Sklodowska-Curie grant agreement No 641794 (project DREAM-GO) and grant agreement No 703689 (project ADAPT); from the CONTEST project - SAICT-POL/23575/2016; and from FEDER Funds through COMPETE program and from National Funds through FCT under the project UID/EEA/00760/2013.

J. Bajo et al. (Eds.): PAAMS 2018 Workshops, CCIS 887, pp. 116–124, 2018.
https://doi.org/10.1007/978-3-319-94779-2_11

The current EMs models are a result of the previous privatization, liberalization and the international integration of national systems [1]. These changes have been motivated by the increased use of energy from renewable sources. An example of the current trend is the long-term plan of the European Union (EU) to reduce greenhouse gas emissions by 80% in 2050 [2]. The EU targeted the increase of the renewable sources share in the EU total consumption to at least 20% in 2020 and 27% in 2030. The latest results show that EU is on course to meet its objective as the share was doubled from 8.5% in 2004 to 17% in 2016.

While the evolution of the sector enriched its models, it also made them more complex, unpredictable and difficult to follow by the involved entities. Therefore, these entities need proper tools that allow them to have a better insight of the EMs operation. The EMs simulation has been proving to be a good solution as the entities are able to study the markets mechanisms and the players' relations, exploring their strategies. However, the current simulators are mostly focused in the auction-based market models, not exploring the bilateral contracts model. A relevant review [3] identifies the main phases of automated negotiation: pre-negotiation, actual negotiation and renegotiation. As result of their study, the authors identified the actual negotiation as the most explored phase while the pre-negotiation lacks further exploration, specially regarding opponents analysis.

In the literature, is possible to find some tools that support bilateral contracts negotiation such as EMCAS [4], GENIUS [5] and MAN-REM [6]. EMCAS is a multi-agent simulator that is able to simulate EMs bilateral contracts, established between a demand agent and a generation company agent. The generation agents decide the price of the demand agents' proposals that may or may not be accepted by the proposers. GENIUS is a multi-agent simulator that facilitates and evaluates the strategies of automated negotiators. The tool supports domain-independent bilateral negotiations and considers three negotiation phases: Preparation (negotiation protocol and domain), Negotiation, and Post-negotiation (negotiation analysis). MAN-REM simulates the bilateral contracts negotiation through the combination of small multi-agent simulators. The tool models the buyer, seller, distributor, and market operator (validation) agents. Three negotiation phases are considered: Pre-Negotiation (contract's preferences and response to counter-offers definition), Actual Negotiation, and Post-Negotiation (final agreement). The analysed tools present a lack of exploration of the pre-negotiation, focusing the actual negotiation. The GENIUS simulator has the most explored pre-negotiation but also lacks an opponents analysis.

The identified lack of proper opponent analysis, in the pre-negotiation phase, motivated the development of a new Decision Support System (DSS) [7]. The tool is capable to analyse the possible opponents that the supported player may face and identify the one(s) that may guarantee the best negotiation outcome. For this purpose, the DSS uses a game theory based approach, which selects the best of all the possible actions that the supported player can take, under several different scenarios. Although this approach always finds the optimal solution, its execution time greatly increases as the amount of energy to trade and the number of possible opponents increases. Thus, this paper proposes an alternative approach by using Particle Swarm Optimization (PSO) [8], a meta-heuristic algorithm, to reduce the time required to obtain a good solution.

2   Decision Support System for the Pre-negotiation of Bilateral Contracts

The developed DSS for the pre-negotiation of bilateral contracts [7] aims to aid the supported player through the process of identifying the best opponents to trade with, and how much to trade with each one, to maximize the negotiation outcome, considering its objectives. The supported player may want to maximize its profit or cost, depending if it is selling or buying, but also consider other aspects such the opponents reputation, worst scenario, most probable scenario and optimal scenario.

To reach this objective, the DSS has three phases: (i) scenarios definition, (ii) possible actions, and (iii) decision process. Firstly, the scenarios definition is fed with data by a database with historical bilateral contracts established by other players. By accessing this information, the DSS generates a set of possible scenarios that the supported player may face. Each scenario is a set of the expected prices that each possible opponent may offer for all the energy amounts between 1 and the total amount to trade.

On the second phase, following a game theory approach, the DSS generates all the possible actions (total energy's distributions among the possible opponents) that the supported player can take under each scenario [9].

After the possible actions generation, on the third and last phase, there is the need to assess the utility of each action to be able to identify the best one, regarding the objectives of the supported player. For this purpose, the utility of each action results from the weighted sum of two components: economic and reputational. The economic component quantifies how economically advantageous is an action while the reputational component measures the average reputation of the involved opponents. The weight of each component depends on the percentage of risk that the supported player is willing to face. The higher the risk the higher the weight of the economical component. The minimum risk (0%) means that only the reputational component is considered, ignoring the economic component, while maximum risk has the opposite meaning. The utility assessment is performed for every action of every scenario.

The decision process ends with the selection of the best action, which depends on the selected decision method by the supported player. For this purpose, the DSS offers three methods: Optimistic, Most Probable and Pessimistic. The Optimistic method selects the action with the highest utility value among all the scenarios. The Most Probable method selects the action with the highest utility value of the most probable scenario, the scenario that is the most likely to occur in reality. The most probable scenario is determined by using a q-learning approach which keeps evaluating the realism of the generated scenarios every time the tool's database is feeded with the real negotiation scenarios. At last, the Pessimistic decision method, is based on the mini-max game theoretic approach, by selecting the action with the highest utility of the scenario with the lowest global utility. The global utility of a scenario is the sum of the actions' utility when taken in that scenario [9].

3 Proposed Methodology

This paper proposes the use of PSO, a meta-heuristic algorithm, to determine the best action the supported player can take, without the heavy task of analysing all the possible actions.

Introduced by Kennedy and Eberhart in 1995 [8], the PSO algorithm was inspired by the movement of organisms in large swarms such as bird flocks or fish schools. The algorithm optimizes a problem by starting with an initial swarm of particles, randomly positioned in the search-space, and then moving them towards the best solution by improving their best positions over time. As result, the method is able to present good solutions but does not guarantee the optimal solution. The algorithm applies the Eqs. 1 and 2 at each iteration.

$$v_{id}^{k+1} = w \cdot v_{id}^k + c_1 \cdot r_1^k \cdot (Pbest_{id}^k - x_{id}^k) + c_2 \cdot r_2^k \cdot (Gbest_{id}^k - x_{id}^k) \qquad (1)$$

$$x_{id}^{k+1} = x_{id}^k + v_{id}^{k+1} \qquad (2)$$

Where,

- $Pbest$ - best position found by each particle,
- $Gbest$ - best position of all particles,
- v - velocity of the particle,
- x - position of the particle,
- k - iteration,
- d - parameter,
- i - particle,
- w - inertia term,
- c_1 - local attraction term,
- c_2 - global attraction term,
- $r1, r2$ - random number between $[0, 1]$.

The Algorithm 1 presents the main process of the PSO.

Algorithm 1. PSO Process

---
initialize particles with random positions and velocities
repeat
    for all particles **do**
        calculate new position   ▷ (Eqs. 1 and 2)
        calculate new position's fitness   ▷ (Eq. 3)
        if current position > *Pbest* **then**
            Pbest = current position
        end if
        if *Pbest* > *Gbest* **then**
            Gbest = *Pbest*
        end if
    end for
until stopping criteria   ▷ Gbest is the final solution

As specified in the Algorithm 1, the PSO's process begins with the assignment of a random position and velocity to each particle. At each iteration, their position is updated, by applying Eqs. 1 and 2, and evaluated by the objective function (Eq. 3). Then, if a better position is found, it becomes the local best and also global best if it is higher than the current value. When reached the stopping criteria, the process ends with the global best position as the final solution.

The process of the PSO method depends on the following parameters:

- **Swarm size** - the number of particles of the swarm. The bigger the swarm size, the bigger the covered area of the search space, in each iteration; The large swarms reduce the number of iterations but increase their complexity and, consequently, the execution time to obtain a good solution.
- **Maximum number of iterations**. This parameter must be adapted to each problem as the best value is the minimum one which guarantees a good solution. The value can be too low if it ends the search without finding a good solution and too high if only increases the execution time without improving the final solution.
- **Local and global attraction terms** - the confidence that a particle has on the previous searches of itself and its neighbours, respectively.
- **Inertia weight** - a limit to the particles movement which controls how much they can move in a single iteration.

The Eq. 3 presents the formulation of the optimization problem.

$$
f = \begin{cases} \min \left(\sum_{i=1}^{Ni} (A_i \times EP_{i,A}) \right), & \text{if negotiation type} = 1 \\ \max \left(\sum_{i=1}^{Ni} (A_i \times EP_{i,A}) \right), & \text{if negotiation type} = 2 \end{cases}
\tag{3}
$$

Where,

- i - player,
- Ni - number of players,
- A_i - amount of energy to trade with player i,
- $EP_{i,A}$ - expected price of player P for the energy amount A,
- Negotiation Type - 1 when the supported player is buying and 2 when selling.

The expected prices result from the forecasts performed by the DSS and, for the energy amounts that were not possible to forecast, an estimation process is performed. The estimation process combines a clustering mechanism with a fuzzy approach [10].

The main constraint applied to this problem is represented by Eq. 4. It guarantees that the sum of the amount to trade with each player is exactly the total amount TA that the supported player wants to trade.

$$\sum_{i=1}^{Ni} (A_i) = TA \qquad (4)$$

4   Experimental Findings

This section presents a case study to validate the proposed methodology and compare it with the game theory approach presented in Sect. 2. For this purpose, both approaches are used to solve the same scenario and their results are compared.

In this case study scenario, the supported player wants to sell 55 MWh, in a weekday context, and indicates five possible opponents that it may trade with. The supported player does not want to consider the negotiation risk, ignoring the opponents' reputation, and chooses the Most Probable decision method. In this scenario, the supported player can take 455 126 different actions. The game theory approach will evaluate each of these actions to select the most profitable one while the PSO approach will attempt the same without testing all actions.

This case study is based on real data by using real executed physical bilateral contracts declared in the Iberian Market Operator [11]. However, the dataset does not contain the contracts' established price as it is a key information and therefore it is rarely shared. The missing prices were generated by considering five different price profiles based on the real Iberian Day-ahead market price [11]. The profile 1 ranges from 70% to 130% of the market price, profile 2 is an increased version of profile 1 by 5%, profile 3 follows the market price, and profiles 4 and 5 have the opposite trend of profiles 2 and 1, respectively. The possible opponents are Player 1 (Profile 1), Player 2 (Profile 2), Player 3 (Profile 3), Player 4 (Profile 4) and Player 5 (Profile 5), which represent real players of the Iberian Market. The selected players are the most active ones in the dataset, whom frequently establishes contracts with a lower or equal energy amount than the considered for this scenario.

The PSO algorithm is executed 100 times with the following parameters: 10 particles, 150 iterations, [0.4, 0.9] inertia interval, and 1 local and global attraction terms. The DSS's price forecasts combined with the estimation methodology produced the expected prices presented in Fig. 1.

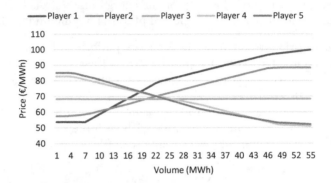

Fig. 1. Expected prices for each possible opponent

As it can be observed in Fig. 1, the expected prices for each opponent, over the different energy amounts, follow the trend of their price profile. In this scenario, it is clear that the best deal for the supported player is to sell all the energy to Player 1, which presents the highest price for 55 MWh. This was proven by the game theory approach which identified this trade as the most profitable, after an execution of 58.68 min. On the other hand, the PSO approach was able to obtain the same result, finding the optimal solution without a significant cost of time (14.07 s, 4% of the game theory approach's execution time). The Figs. 2 and 3 show the difference of the execution time of both approaches for the same scenario but different energy amounts.

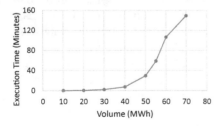

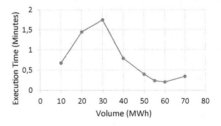

Fig. 2. Execution time of the Game Theory approach

Fig. 3. Execution time of the PSO approach

The Figs. 2 and 3 evidence the great execution time difference of both approaches. While the first approach can take up to 150 min to present a solution, for the biggest scenario observed, the PSO approach takes less than 2 min in its longest execution observed. The execution time of the game theory approach depends on the energy amount to negotiate. Even a small increase of the amount of energy to negotiate can greatly increase its execution time as the number of possible actions greatly increases. In this scenario, the supported player can take 455 126 different actions but, if the energy to negotiate is increased by 5, the number of different actions is increased by 39.6% (635 376). Regarding the PSO approach, the trend is completely different. The highest impact to the execution time is not the amount of energy but the expected prices for that amount. As it can be seen in Fig. 3, the method has longer execution times for scenarios with an higher number of good solutions, which is the case of the scenarios with an energy amount between 10 MWh and 40 MWh. On the remaining cases, the optimal solution is easier to be found, and thus quicker.

The recommended trade by both approaches results in a profit of 5489.55 €/MWh, given that the expected price of Player 1 for 55 MWh is 99.81 €/MWh. Over its 100 executions, on average, the PSO method was able to obtain a profit of 5359.61 €/MWh, with a standard deviation of 314.31 €/MWh. This way, it is possible to confirm the high efficiency of the PSO approach to solve the problem of this case study scenario, being close to the optimal solution over its 100 executions.

5   Conclusions

The development of a new DSS was motivated by the lack of opponent analysis in the pre-negotiation phase of bilateral contracts. By applying a game theory approach, the tool identifies the best action of all the possible actions that the supported player could take. However, the execution time of this approach greatly increases as the energy to trade and the number of opponents increases.

This paper proposed the use of PSO, a meta-heuristic algorithm, as an alternative approach to reduce execution time while keeping the results quality. The new approach was validated by the conducted case study as it provided optimal and near-optimal solutions in 4% of the time required by the first approach.

As future work, the proposed approach will consider the opponent's reputation. A multi-objective optimization approach will also be considered, including as additional optimization objective, the negotiation risk, based on the players' reputation.

References

1. Meeus, L., Purchala, K., Belmans, R.: Development of the internal electricity market in europe. Electr. J. **18**(6), 25–35 (2005)
2. European Commission: "Renewable energy statistics" (2018). http://ec.europa.eu/eurostat/statistics-explained/index.php/Renewable_energy_statistics. Accessed 5 Feb 2018
3. Lopes, F., Wooldridge, M., Novais, A.Q.: Negotiation among autonomous computational agents: principles, analysis and challenges. Artif. Intell. Rev. **29**(1), 1–44 (2008)

4. Veselka, T., et al.: Simulating the behavior of electricity markets with an agent-based methodology: the electric market complex adaptive systems (EMCAS) model (2002)
5. Lin, R., et al.: GENIUS: an integrated environment for supporting the design of generic automated negotiators. Comput. Intell. **30**(1), 48–70 (2014)
6. Lopes, F., Rodrigues, T., Sousa, J.: Negotiating bilateral contracts in a multi-agent electricity market: a case study. In: 2012 23rd International Workshop on Database and Expert Systems Applications, pp. 326–330 (2012)
7. Silva, F., Teixeira, B., Pinto, T., Praça, I., Marreiros, G., Vale, Z.: Decision support system for the negotiation of bilateral contracts in electricity markets. In: De Paz, J.F., Julián, V., Villarrubia, G., Marreiros, G., Novais, P. (eds.) ISAmI 2017. AISC, vol. 615, pp. 159–166. Springer, Cham (2017). https://doi.org/10.1007/978-3-319-61118-1_20
8. Eberhart, R., Kennedy, J.: A new optimizer using particle swarm theory. In: Proceedings of the Sixth International Symposium on Micro Machine and Human Science, MHS 1995, pp. 39–43, October 1995
9. Pinto, T., Vale, Z., Praça, I., Pires, E.J.S., Lopes, F.: Decision support for energy contracts negotiation with game theory and adaptive learning. Energies **8**(9), 9817–9842 (2015)
10. Faia, R., Pinto, T., Vale, Z.: Dynamic fuzzy clustering method for decision support in electricity markets negotiation. ADCAIJ Adv. Distrib. Comput. Artif. Intel. J. **5**(1), 23 (2016)
11. OMIE: "Market Results" (2018). http://www.omie.es/aplicaciones/datosftp/datosftp.jsp. Accessed 5 Feb 2018

Reputation Computational Model to Support Electricity Market Players Energy Contracts Negotiation

Jaime Rodriguez-Fernandez[1], Tiago Pinto[1,2(✉)], Francisco Silva[1],
Isabel Praça[1], Zita Vale[1], and Juan Manuel Corchado[2]

[1] GECAD – Research Group, Institute of Engineering,
Polytechnic of Porto (ISEP/IPP), Porto, Portugal
{rfmfa,tmcfp,fspsa,icp,zav}@isep.ipp.pt
[2] BISITE, University of Salamanca (US),
Calle Espejo, 12, 37007 Salamanca, Spain
{tpinto,corchado}@usal.es

Abstract. The negotiation is one of the most important phase of the process of buying and selling energy in electricity markets. Buyers and sellers know about their own trading behavior or the quality of their products. However, they can also gather data directly or indirectly from them through the exchange information before or during negotiation, even negotiators should also gather information about past behavior of the other parties, such as their trustworthiness and reputation. Hence, in this scope, reputation models play a more important role in decision-making process in the undertaken bilateral negotiation. Since the decision takes into account, not only the potential economic gain for supported player, but also the reliability of the contracts. Therefore, the reputation component represents the level of confidence that the supported player can have on the opponent's service, i.e. in this case, the level of assurance that the opponent will fulfil the conditions established in the contract. This paper proposes a reputation computational model, included in DECON, a decision support system for bilateral contract negotiation, in order to enhance the decision-making process regarding the choice of the most suitable negotiation parties.

Keywords: Bilateral contracts · Decision support system · Electricity Market
Reputation models · Negotiation process

This work has received funding from the European Union's Horizon 2020 research and innovation programme under the Marie Sklodowska-Curie grant agreement No 641794 (project DREAM-GO) and grant agreement No 703689 (project ADAPT); and from FEDER Funds through COMPETE program and from National Funds through FCT under the project UID/EEA/00760/2013.

© Springer International Publishing AG, part of Springer Nature 2018
J. Bajo et al. (Eds.): PAAMS 2018 Workshops, CCIS 887, pp. 125–133, 2018.
https://doi.org/10.1007/978-3-319-94779-2_12

1 Introduction

Trust and reputation underlies almost every face-to-face trade. The possibility for dealing with strangers significantly increases the risk for such interactions. Hence, relationships based on trust and reputation have been extensively researched the past decade as a result of the huge rise of the virtual communities such as electronic commerce, e.g. [1–3]. Several research works have concluded that seller reputation has significant influences on on-line auction prices [4, 5]. Trust and reputation have become important theme of researcher in many fields. Rather, they group together similar works that have often been of interest to audiences of the various disciplines. In this paper, we focus on how trust and reputation are acquired and used to enhance decision-making process in bilateral negotiation of energy contracts.

The last few decades, energy trade has changed significantly due to the electricity markets (EM) restructuring. Nowadays, several market models exist where each EM has its own characteristics and clearing price mechanisms. This restructuring was promoted by the liberalization and international integration of these markets [6]. Nevertheless, energy trade is essentially supported in all energy markets worldwide by means of bilateral contracts negotiation [7]. The EM liberalization process brings new challenges for the involved entities in the sector, since there are very different types of entities, both at consumers level, which may be smaller or larger; residential, commercial or industrial; urban or rural location, etc.; and at producers level, which may be based on various generation technologies such as thermal energy, co-generation, or renewable energies (e.g., solar, wind or hydro energy), among others. For this reason, it is essential for the EM participants to have an adequate analysis about the other involved players' behavior with whom they will establish a possible contract.

In is in this scope that trust and reputation play an important role. We focus our attention in computational models that use reputation to model and analyze the agents' trustworthiness throughout information exchange their own interactions. The majority of authors classify reputation from information origin standpoint, both as individual dimension when information is resulting from a direct interaction among agents, and as social dimension when information comes from a community agent that is not participating in current interaction but that has already taken part in past actions with the target agent (witness information) [8]. These systems are usually embedded in intelligent software agents as a mechanism for enabling the agent to make trust-based decisions [9]. Several research analyses of existing online reputation systems such as [10] have analyzed the feedback rating system used in eBay as a reputation system. "Reputation" is taken to be a function of the cumulative positive and non-positive ratings for a seller or buyer [11, 12]. The REGRET model developed by Sabater and Sierra [12] takes the posture that reputation is composite concept, the overall opinion on an entity is obtained as a result of the combination of different pieces of information.

Using the concept of reputation matured in the literature, and considering the need from energy negotiating players to assess the risk and quality of possible negotiations, this paper proposes a computational reputation model for enhancing support decision during the negotiation of bilateral contracts [13, 14]. The reputation model endows the proposed decision support methodology with the capability of considering, not only the potential economic gain of the supported player, but also the benefit from a point of view of the contract reliability. The implemented model is based on one of the most recognized reputation models, namely the REGRET model by Sabater and Sierra [15].

2 Proposed Reputation Computational Model

Decision making under uncertainty in EM negotiations should take into account, not only the potential economic gain for supported player, but also the reliability of the potential contracts. This way the supported player may choose to undertake negotiations with players that present a slightly lower potential profit, but compensate the loss by ensuring safer deals with players that present better reputations, which provide a different level of security, especially regarding the prospect of complying with the terms of the established contract.

The proposed computational reputation model is based on the REGRET model [12] to assess the reputation of bilateral contract negotiating players. The proposed model considers groups according to agents' type. The groups of electric power generators represent the seller players (nuclear, coal, wind, solar, among others) and energy consumer groups represent buyer players (large industries, medium-sized trade, small residential buyers). The supported player can deal both as seller and as buyer, so that players' typology will not be defined in the formulated notation for the model. As follow is presented the reputation computation model:

The reputation of competitor player p is assessed from the perspective of supported player sp. It is considered two different components of reputation in order to calculate the reputation of subject competitor player R_p:

- The individual component $R_{sp,p}$, which represents the direct observations and experience of the supported player in regard to the subject competitor player;
- The social component R_s, which considers the perspective of the group in which each player is inserted, and also the society prejudice regarding the player type (e.g., the players who represent the wind farms will trend to own a similar reputation, since they have the same problem to supply a certain amount of energy because they are equally wind speed dependent; on the other hand, regarding the consumers group it is normal the players who belong to large industries have higher reputation than the medium commerce or small players).

R_p is, therefore, defined as in (1).

$$R_p = w_i \cdot R_{sp,p} + w_s \cdot R_s \tag{1}$$

where w_i and w_s are weights that are attributed to the individual and social component, respectively. The sum of both weights should be equal to 1, and these should reflect the trust that the supported player has on its own experience and on the experience of others. $R_{sp,p}$ represents a positive or negative experience of the supported player regarding the subject competitor player. This value is updated whenever a new observation is available, and is defined in Eq. (2).

$$R_{sp,p} = \frac{NPE}{TNE} \tag{2}$$

where *NPE* represents the number of positive experiences and *TNE* the total number of experiences that the supported player has had with the subject competitor player.

The social component R_s allows using information on similar players (e.g. it is unusual that two players of the same group trend to establish different contracts), and also the use of personal experience of the group players belonging the supporter player with the subject player. R_s is defined in (3).

$$R_s = w_{gp}R_{sp,Gp} + w_{gsp}R_{Gsp,p} + w_g R_{Gsp,gp} + w_p P_s \tag{3}$$

Equation 3 shows four different social reputation with their own weights. As follow it will describe each component:

- $R_{sp,Gp}$ represents the reputation of the subject competitor player' group from the perspective of the supported player, as defined in Eq. (4).

$$R_{sp,Gp} = \sum_{pi \in Gp} w_{sp,pi} \cdot R_{sp,pi} \tag{4}$$

where $\sum_{pi \in Gp} w_{sp,pi} = 1 \cdot R_{sp,pi}$ represents the reputation of each member i of the subject competitor player' group (subject competitor player included) from the point of view of the supported player; and $w_{sp,pi}$ represents the weights that are attributed to each these individuals reputations. These weights can be defined according to the credibility of each competitor group from the supported player standpoint.

- $R_{Gsp,p}$ represents the reputation of subject competitor player from the perspective the supported player' group, as described in Eq. (5).

$$R_{Gsp,p} = \sum_{gspi \in Gsp} w_{gspi,p} \cdot R_{gspi,p} \tag{5}$$

where $\sum_{gspi \in Gsp} w_{gspi,p} = 1 \cdot R_{gspi,p}$ is the reputation of subject competitor player from the point of view of each member i of the supported player' group; and $w_{gspi,p}$ is the weights that are attributed to each these individuals reputations. These weights can be defined according to the credibility of each competitor group from the supported player standpoint.

- $R_{Gsp,gp}$ is the reputation of the subject competitor player' group from the perspective of the supported player' group, as defined in (6).

$$R_{Gsp,gp} = \sum_{gspi \in Gsp} w_{gspi,Gp} \cdot R_{gspi,Gp} \tag{6}$$

where $\sum_{gspi \in Gsp} w_{gspi,Gp} = 1 \cdot R_{gspi,Gp}$ represents the reputation of each group member where the subject competitor player is inserted (subject competitor player included) from the point of view of each member i of the supported player' group (supported player included); and $w_{gspi,Gp}$ represents the weights that are attributed to each these individuals reputations. These weights can be defined according to the credibility of each competitor group from the supported player standpoint.

- P_s represents the preconception of subject competitor player' group. This prejudice value can be attributed by default by an entity recognized as reliable, or as is described in Eq. (7).

$$P_s = \sum_{gpi \in Gp} w_{pi,Gp} \cdot R_{pi,Gp} \tag{7}$$

where $\sum_{gpi \in Gp} w_{pi,Gp} = 1 \cdot R_{pi,Gp}$ represents the reputation of each members of competitor group from the point of view of each member of opposite group, i.e., whether the supported player is a seller type, it would be the opinion of all generators groups (not only those that the supported player is belonged).

As many notions of reputation have been studied, an intuitive typology of reputation was addressed which was based on the reviewed literature. Figure 1 shows the typology tree of reputation proposed and discussed above.

In order to analyze the responses' trust that are given by each player are defined the different weights that will be attributed to their responses. These weights consider the credibility of the opinions of players. The supported player should be compared the obtained reputation responses to actual experience with the subject player in order to update the related weights and to verify the players' credibility; e.g. if a certain player attributes a large reputation value to the subject competitor player, and when the supported player establishes a contract with this opponent verifies that this player is not able to fulfill the contracted conditions, the supported player will not only update the reputation of the competitor player taking into account the bad experience, but will also update the credibility on the responses of the player that provided the misleading evaluation of the competitor player's reputation.

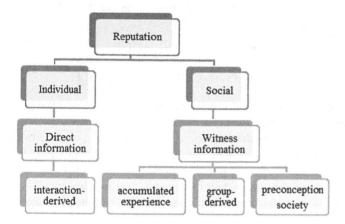

Fig. 1. Proposed reputation typology.

3   Case Study

3.1   Specifications

This section presents an experimental case with the aim of demonstrating the performance of the proposed reputation model to calculate and assess the reputation values of each subject competitor in order to be used to support the bilateral negotiation decisions in electricity market.

The study contemplates a single scenario with both player types. Energy generator or sellers, and consumers or buyers, where in turn each player is related in a group. Hence, this simulation case involves 5 consumers and 4 generators, where the supported player is a seller player. As follow it is defined the related group to each player:

- Consumers (3 groups):
    Small player → Buyer1
    Medium commerce → Buyer2, Buyer5
    Large industry → Buyer3, Buyer4
- Generators (2 groups)
    Wind farm → Seller3 (the supported player), Seller4
    Solar power plant → Seller1, Seller2

As detailed below the Table 1 presents the individual reputation values of the all buyers from the personal experience of each seller. It should be noted that no realistic reputation values referent of each competitor player, since it would require a sociologic study, which is out of the scope of this work. Hence, all reputation values were normalized ranging from 0 to 1, and it has been assumed reasonable default reputation values which were attributed to each player according to the group type belonging; e.g., if a buyer is inserted in the large industry group will have a high reputation value from the point of view of the sellers between 0.7 and 1, a medium commerce buyer will own a reputation value between 0.4 and 0.6, and a small buyer normally has a low reputation value from the perspective of sellers between 0 and 0.3.

Table 1. Buyers reputation network from the sellers' standpoint

	Buyer1	Buyer2	Buyer3	Buyer4	Buyer5
Seller1	0.3	0.4	0.8	0.9	0.5
Seller2	0.2	0.4	1.0	0.7	0.5
Seller3	**0.8**	**0.3**	**0.1**	**0.1**	**0.3**
Seller4	0.0	0.6	0.7	1.0	0.4

Table 1 shows blue light shaded cells that difference the supported player' group of other seller groups. In order to validate the influence of the personal experience of the supported player (seller3) for the reputation calculation, it can observe in Table 1 that it has supposed an opposite scenario in relation to other sellers, i.e. it has not considered reasonable reputation values, it is just that it has assumed high values of reputation in regard to small buyers and low values to large and medium buyers. This will allow an easier verification of the influence of the individual component on the proposed reputation model.

On the other hand, it will be analyzed the influence of the weights for each component. For that purpose, it has defined three simulation cases considering different weight values for the components, as both the individual component w_i as the social component w_s. For the Case 1, it is defined $w_i = 0.5$ and $w_s = 0.5$; in the Case 2, $w_i = 0.8$ and $w_s = 0.2$; and finally the Case 3, it is considered $w_i = 0.2$ and $w_s = 0.8$.

Hence, the overall goal is to allow a great analysis of the results provided by the reputation model to assess the reputation of subject competitor players, and how these results can change according to the credibility that is given to each player by means of the weights.

3.2   Results

Executing the implemented reputation model according to the previous specifications, it has been obtained the work results which will allow to assess the reputation of subject competitor players for enhancing the decision-making process of bilateral contract negotiations in electricity markets.

The following table shows the reputation result of each subject competitor player for the different cases of weights allocation that was previously mentioned, as well as the related reputation with each component. As previously was explained with detail in the Sect. 3, the individual component will represent the personal experience of the supported player between the various subject competitors; and the social component will represent the perspective of the supported player' group regarding their opinion about subject competitor players.

Table 2. Reputation of the subject competitor players considering different cases of weights allocation.

Buyer ID	1	2	3	4	5
Individual component	0.80	0.30	0.10	0.10	0.30
Social component	0.36	0.48	0.57	0.64	0.43
Reputation case 1	0.58	0.39	0.33	0.37	0.37
Reputation case 2	0.71	0.34	0.19	0.21	0.33
Reputation case 3	0.45	0.45	0.47	0.53	0.40

Observing the Table 2 it can affirm that the weights distribution has influence on the total reputation, since the social opinion about the negotiators targets does not coincide with the individual opinion of supported player.

Looking detailed to the different simulation cases, in Case 1 all reputation values are similar among the various buyers, since as the weights of social and individual components are considered equals, the contradictory opinions between the supported player and the other sellers enabling that reputations are balanced; and in this way, none of the opinions are favored. In Case 2, it is a clear example of the influence of the supported player opinion which has a greater weight for the reputation calculation, and thus, the small buyer (Buyer1) has a rather large value, and the large and medium buyers present strange reputation, much lower in comparison with the values considered as usual. The latter simulation, the Case 3 considers the smallest influence of the supported player, and reputations assume more similar values to the usual ones, i.e. large buyers (Buyer3 and Buyer4) have the highest reputation values, although the small buyer reputation is still favored by the hard influence of the supported player opinion.

In summary, this proposed scenario where the opinion of the supported player in relation to the others sellers is contrary, is an easy scenario for showing the influence of the different weights for the total reputation calculation. In this way, the reputation of the small competitors is favored, however the group of large and medium buyers present a worst reputation in comparison with reputations consider as usual (low values for small consumers, middle values for consumers of size medium and high values for large consumers). Hence, it can conclude that the obtained results provided by the proposed reputation model are according to the expected.

4   Conclusions

Pre-negotiation is a process that assumes great relevance in bilateral negotiations, as it is the phase when all the preparation and planning of the effective negotiation in energy contract negotiation is carried out. In this process, the purpose is to identify the ideal negotiators to approach the negotiations, in order to obtain the maximum possible benefit for the supported player. Therefore, an important factor in the choice of the opponents to negotiate is to take into account the ability and reputation of the latter to be able to comply with the contract. For this reason, it is crucial to develop ways for analyzing and modeling the reputation and credibility of the different potential negotiators, so that the decision-making process can be improved.

A reputation model has been proposed in this paper, showing the influence of the different weights of the social and individual components through the various simulation cases. The influence of different opinions that the supported player can present about the target negotiators has also been assessed. It can then be concluded that the results obtained by the proposed model correspond entirely to what would be expected, being therefore the model validated as fulfilling its purpose to enhance the decision support process for EM players by means of bilateral contract negotiation.

As future work, a model for the credibility of the involved players is proposed. Since the reputation model needs reputational values that are suggested by other players, these opinions may not be entirely reliable because opinions are being asked from negotiating agents, which can create a conflict of interest. A model capable of evaluating the credibility of the different players' responses would allow the automatic adaptation of the weights assigned to the responses of each player according to their credibility.

References

1. Rheingold, H.: The Virtual Community: Homesteading on the Electronic Frontier, Revised edn. MIT Press, Cambridge (2001)
2. Wellman, B.: Computer networks as social networks. Science **293**(14), 2031–2034 (2001)
3. Smith, M., Kollock, P. (eds.): Communities in Cyberspace. Routledge Press, London (1999)

4. Houser, D.E., Wooders, J.: Reputation in Internet Auctions: Theory and Evidence from eBay. working paper (2001). http://w3.arizona.edu/~econ/working_papers/Internet_Auctions.pdf
5. Dewan, S., Hsu, V.: Trust in Electronic Markets: Price Discovery in Generalist Versus Specialty Online Auctions (2001). http://databases.si.umich.edu/reputations/bib/papers/Dewan&Hsu.doc
6. Sioshansi, F.P.: Evolution of Global Electricity Markets – New Paradigms, New Challenges, New Approaches. Academic Press, London (2013)
7. Algarvio, H., Lopes, F., Santana, J.: Bilateral contracting in multi-agent energy markets: forward contracts and risk management. In: Bajo, J., et al. (eds.) PAAMS 2015. CCIS, vol. 524, pp. 260–269. Springer, Cham (2015). https://doi.org/10.1007/978-3-319-19033-4_22
8. Gutowska, A., Buckley, K.: Computing reputation metric in multi-agent e-commerce reputation system. In: International Conference on Distributed Computing Systems, Beijing (2008)
9. Sabater, J., Sierra, C.: Review on computational trust and reputation models. Artif. Intel. Rev. **24**, 33–60 (2005)
10. Resnick, P., Zeckhauser, R.: Trust among strangers in internet transactions: empirical analysis of eBay's reputation system. In: NBER Workshop on Empirical Studies of Electronic Commerce Paper (2000)
11. Resnick, P., Kuwabara, K., Zeckhauser, R., Friedman, E.: Reputation systems. Commun. ACM **43**(12), 45–48 (2000)
12. Sabater, J., Sierra, C.: REGREAT: a reputation model for gregarious societies (2001)
13. Pinto, T.: Decision Support for the Strategic Behaviour of Electricity Market Players. Doctorate Degree. University of Trás-os-Montes e Alto Douro (2016)
14. Pinto, T., Vale, Z., Praça, I., Solteiro, E.J., Lopes, F.: Decision support for energy contracts negotiation with game theory and adaptive learning. Energies **8**, 9817–9842 (2015)
15. Sabater, J., Sierra, C.: Review on computational trust and reputation models. Artif. Intel. Rev. **24**(1), 33–60 (2005)

PAAMS Workshop AMSC

Script Language to Describe Agent's Behaviors

Pawel Pawlewski[✉]

Poznan University of Technology, ul.Strzelecka 11, 60-965 Poznań, Poland
pawel.pawlewski@put.poznan.pl

Abstract. The paper presents the results of research carried out in recent years in the area of modeling and simulation of production and assembly systems. The main goal of the article is to show the practical application of ABS in the simulation modeling of production and assembly systems as well as the benefits resulting from it. The most important points of the article are the presentation of the originality of this approach in the context of traditional methodologies for building simulation models of manufacturing systems, the discussion of solutions proposed in commercial simulation programs, suggesting a language describing the behavior of agents carrying out the flow of materials in the production process and showing the model built in the described way.

Keywords: Agents · Intralogistics systems · Simulation · Modeling

1 Introduction

The article presents the results of research carried out in recent years in the area of modeling and simulation of production and assembly systems. In these studies, simulation software based on discrete event simulation (DES) was used. The collected experience and observations allowed to identify the research gap in simulation modeling. This gap has already been noticed by the author [1], which on the one hand resulted in the concept of description of the processes implemented in the production system using a multimodal approach. On the other hand, the concept of modeling production systems based on the DES/ABS approach was created.

The author's earlier work [2] presents the concept of using the DES approach to model the main processes and ABS to model the simulation of supporting processes. This was used in modeling the assembly process of city buses.

The research work has been continuing in another car industry enterprise. The process is performed on several welding stations, where welding operations are carried out successively and then the assembly and packaging operation of the product is carried out. It is a pipeline production. The researchers attempt to model the flow of parts and assemblies. The article presents the effects of the instigations that have been carried out so far.

The main goal of the article is to show the practical application of ABS in the simulation modeling of production and assembly systems and the benefits resulting from it.

The most important points of the article are the presentation of the originality of this approach in the context of traditional methodologies for building simulation models of

© Springer International Publishing AG, part of Springer Nature 2018
J. Bajo et al. (Eds.): PAAMS 2018 Workshops, CCIS 887, pp. 137–148, 2018.
https://doi.org/10.1007/978-3-319-94779-2_13

manufacturing systems, the discussion of solutions proposed in commercial simulation programs, suggesting a language describing the behavior of agents carrying out the flow of materials in the production process and showing the model built in the described way.

The main contribution of the author is to define a scripting language that allows modeling the behavior of agents carrying out the flow of materials. This language is understandable and accepted by production and logistics engineers. This script language was implemented in a commercial simulation program.

This paper is organized as follows. Section 2 describes mixed Discrete Events and Agents Based approach to model manufacturing processes. Section 3 defines the problem – how to organize and maintain a management system for parts, components, subassemblies and other materials that are delivered to the enterprise from suppliers. The solution based on script language is presented in Sect. 4. Section 5 contains the set of instructions forming the script language which is sufficient to describe behaviors of agents and which is sufficient to model the flow of parts in production and assembling system. The case study is presented in Sect. 6. Section 7 provides conclusions and plans for further research.

2 Simulation Methods – Agent Based Approach

On the one hand, simulation is modeling, i.e. mapping of the real system, under-standing the system behavior, virtual (and visual) assessment of possible consequences of actions, and on the other hand it is experimenting and testing ideas and alternatives before making decisions on actions and resource involvement [3–5]. Simulation is a collection of methods and techniques, such as discrete simulation, continuous simu-lations (including systems dynamics), Monte Carlo method (including static simula-tions in a spreadsheet), managerial games, qualitative simulation, agent simulation and others. It is assumed [6] that at the macro-strategic level, where the application areas are market and competition, social systems, ecosystems, product or project manage-ment, human resources and health systems, The simulation modeling methods based on system dynamics and, in part, on agent modeling are primarily applied. The medium level (tactical), consisting of applications related to power grids, financial management, supply chains, health care, business processes, is primarily the domain of agent modeling. However, at the micro-operational level, where we take into account indi-vidual objects, exact dimensions, speeds, distances and times, discrete event modeling methods (process approach) and agent modeling are used. This refers to applications in the area of production, services, battlefields, pedestrian traffic, warehouse logistics, computer hardware or physical systems.

From the point of view of the research area described in this article, methods based on discrete events and agent modeling are of interest because they are used at the tactical level and, above all, at the operational level. Generally, it can be concluded that the discrete-based approach is a process-based approach and agent-based modeling can be compared to a task-driven approach [6].

The author's earlier work [2] proposes a mixed DES and ABS approach for modeling the operation of work teams across multiple production lines. Typically, simulation tools use a process-driven approach, where the flow of parts between processes create demands on resources; i.e., a part moves to a work-station and demands resources to complete an operation. While this methodology is fine for many applications, it does not allow resources to complete tasks which are not flow related. In this case, a task-driven approach is needed; e.g., an operator (mobile resource) performs a set of inspections on idle equipment when not engaged in process work. The task-based approach enables an operator (task executor) to create tasks or activities that are independent of processing activities. Such tasks may require travel and acquisition of other tools or resources. As such, the task-driven approach incorporates "intelligence" into resources by enabling them to decide what jobs to do and when. Many situations in industry can be modeled using DES process approach, but for many support processes, such as logistics processes with teams of operators performing the work, the ABS approach is more effective, as illustrated in Fig. 1.

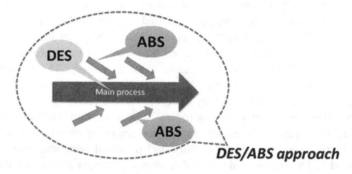

Fig. 1. Example material flows and spatial relationships in an in-plant logistics system.

Agent based modeling is a relatively new method compared to system dynamics and discrete event modeling. Agent based modeling offers a modeler another way to look at the system. You may not know how the system behaves or be able to identify its key variables and dependencies, or recognize the process flow, but you can have an insight into how the system objects behave. It is possible to start building the model by identifying the objects (agents) and defining their behaviors. Next, it is possible to connect the created agents and allow them to interact or put them in an environment which has its own dynamics. The system's global behavior emerges from many concurrent individual behaviors [7].

There is no standard language for agent based modeling, and the structure of an agent based model comes from graphical editors or scripts. There are many ways to specify an agent's behavior. Frequently, an agent has a notion of state and its actions and reactions depend on the state; then the behavior is best defined with statecharts. Sometimes the behavior is defined in rules executed by means of special events [7].

Academics still debate which properties an object should have to be an "agent": proactive and reactive qualities, spatial awareness, an ability to learn, social ability, "intellect", etc. In applied agent based modeling, however, you will find all kinds of agents: some communicate while others live in total isolation, some live in a space while others live without a space, and some learn and adapt while others never change their behavior patterns. According to [8], agent characteristic can be defined as:

1. identifiable, a discrete individual with set of characteristics and rules governing its behaviors and decision-making capabilities,
2. autonomous and self-directed,
3. situated, living in an environment where it interacts with other agents – has protocols for interaction with other agents,
4. goal directed – having goals to achieve,
5. flexible – having the ability to learn and adapt its behaviors based on experiences.

3   Problem Definition

The goal of the research is to organize and maintain a management system for parts, components, subassemblies and other materials that are delivered to the enterprise from suppliers. The challenge is to find the answer to the question of how to design (re-design) such a logistic system which, slimmed down with as much waste as possible, will ensure the most effective flow of materials inside the factory. The word flow has a special meaning here – it can be compared to the bloodstream of a living organism. The internal logistics system, with its delivery routes, is like the cardiovascular system of an organism. We have here arteries (supply routes) supplying nutrients (purchased parts) and veins – taking away contaminants (empty containers for parts), so as to keep the cells of the body (production nests) healthy and provided with what they need and when they need it. The arteries and veins of this system (supply routes) are also used to transfer signals from cells (production sockets) to the nervous system (production control department) with the level of nutrient demand (materials and purchased parts).

The researchers have analyzed and modeled the manufacturing system in the automotive industry. The process is performed on several welding stations, where welding operations are carried out successively and then the assembly and packaging operation of the product are carried out. It is a pipeline production. The researchers attempted to model the flow of parts which flow in containers. Therefore, the conclusion that appeared was that it is best to focus on the flow of containers. In the analyzed system, the flow area was defined from the so-called supermarket where there are already prepared containers with parts for the buffer with containers of finished products, which is located in front of the finished goods warehouse. The warehouse flows were not analyzed and modeled before the supermarket and after the container buffer with ready products.

The containers "flowed" from the supermarket to the fields of workstations, where the welding operation was carried out, then the assembly (in containers or on the logistic trolley) "floated" to the next workstation, up to the buffer in front of the finished product warehouse. The assembly operations were modeled taking into account the operation time (described with the appropriate statistical distribution), disruptions (failures) and planned breaks. The focus was on the flow. The containers themselves do not flow through the system – there is always a mechanism that causes this flow. Containers, as found in the supermarket, are static – they have no initiative to flow (this is not in line with the process approach). As a result, the focus was on how the flow is implemented and provoked. The mechanism that realizes the flow is well known to all: in case of a non-automatic flow, it is operators who use various means of transport such as pallets, logistic trucks, forklifts, logistic trains who constitute the flow and in case of an automatic flow it is robots, conveyors, agv trucks. Generally, in the subject literature this is considered separately as internal transport. Production flow management is the management of mechanisms that realize this flow.

Therefore, an approach to simulation modeling based on three levels of the analysis of the production system was developed:

1. Level 1 - the level of intralogistics of the workstation,
2. Level 2 - the level of intralogistics of the line/cell,
3. Level 3 - the level of intralogistics of the production system (factory).

It is assumed that under the concept of intralogistics we understand processes related to the flow of materials requiring coordination in time and space. At level 1, inside the workstation, it is the flow of parts - from the container in the storage location to the machine or work table, and further the flow of the assembly from the machine, the table to the container (transport truck). At level 2, it is the flow of containers (including logistic trolleys) between the stations forming the production line/cell. However, at level 3, this is the flow between the supermarket and the production lines/cells and further to the buffers in front of the finished product warehouse. At this level, containers with parts/products can flow in groups, for example as part of a logistic train (tugger with a few trolleys with containers).

Each workstation includes an area on which a container with parts is deposited. This area is identified and addressed by given coordinates in space X, Y, Z and rotations relative to individual axes: RotX, RotY, RotZ. This area is called storage location. Both the supermarket and the buffer in front of the finished product warehouse also contain such locations.

4   Solution Based on Script Language

It should be noted here that in any simulation program it is possible to build such a mounting system – using a process and task approach. However, each time it is done from the beginning. The level of detail offered by simulation programs, e.g. FlexSim, Anylogic, etc. is too deep. The language function available at this level includes several hundred functions [9]. To implement a model based on a multimodal approach [1], a language consisting of 57 instructions, which proved to be sufficient, was defined.

One instruction - for example "Load a Part from a Container" that performs the removal of a part from a container located in a specific storage field has the form of:

$$P\_08 \text{ LoadFromTote 1} \tag{1}$$

P_08 is the identifier of the reloading place where the container with the parts is located, LoadFromTote is the name of the instruction and 1 is the number defining how many parts should be taken (in this case one part). This simple instruction in the FlexSim simulation program is broken down into several instructions shown in Fig. 2.

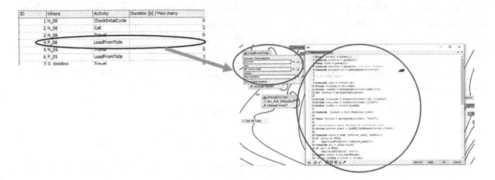

Fig. 2. Implementation of instructions for the developed description language of cyclic processes in the FlexSim program – own study.

As mentioned above, the level of detail offered by simulation programs is too deep. There was a concept to use the simulation program as SOS – a simulation operating system. As a result, a four-level behavioral model has been developed as shown in Fig. 3.

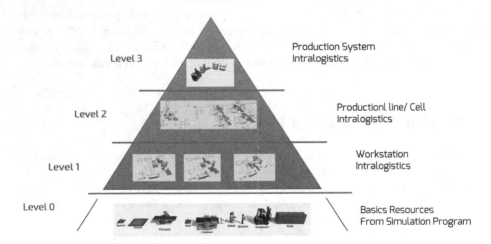

Fig. 3. Four levels of manufacturing system analysis & modeling – own study.

Many simulation programs are available in the market [10]. We chose FlexSim due to the following features [3]:

1. ease of use in a real size with drag and drop technology,
2. built-in 3D modeling,

3. loading CAD files (e.g. .dwg) directly into a model,
4. sophisticated pre-built objects, such as ASRS vehicle, Crane, Robot, Elevator,
5. enhanced modeling of conveyors,
6. fitting the shape of trucks and their parameters – in actual values,
7. built-in experimentation tool and link to optimizer (OptQuest),
8. task-executer and task-sequence technologies.

Flexsim Simulation Software is a powerful, yet easy to use, tool for building three-dimensional computer models of operational systems and analyzing their performance. Simulation can be performed at significantly lower cost than experimenting with a real system. It also helps users to understand, visualize, and validate the operation of a proposed system before it is implemented. Since 2015 FlexSim has had the ability to create custom objects that has been able to easily incorporate logic needed to model complex business processes [11].

5 Agent Script Language

During our research works, based on experiences and relations with engineers from industry we developed a set of instructions which form the script language to describe the agent behaviors. As an agent we consider, as mentioned in previous section, a mechanism that realizes the flow and is well known to all – in case of non-automatic flow, it is operators who use various means of transport such as pallets, logistic trucks, forklifts, logistic trains who make up the flow, and in case of an automatic flow it is robots, conveyors, agv trucks. We analyze the level 1 of a manufacturing system (Fig. 4) and at this level we analyze the workstation where we can distinguish 6 basic objects (Table 1):

1. Operator – employee, he performs the tasks in a working cell,
2. Parts – components needful to produce subassemblies and ready products,
3. Container – object designed for storage of parts. It can have a specified type, dimensions, color, etc.,
4. Storage Location – objects dedicated to storage the containers with components or products,

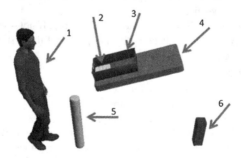

Fig. 4. Basic objects form the work environment of an operator (agent) – own study.

Table 1. Script language for agent's behavior describing – set of commands.

1	*Travel*
	(a) *Travel* - Operator is moving to a specific location in the model space
2	*Loading/unloading*
	(a) *Load* - Loading a certain number of parts from a shelf
	(b) *LoadFromTote* - Picking a certain number of parts from a container located at a storage location
	(c) *Unload* - Unloading a certain number of parts onto a shelf
	(d) *UnloadToTote* - Unloading a certain number of parts to a container located at a shelf
	(e) *GrabTote* - Picking up a tote
	(f) *ReleaseTote* - Unloading a tote to a location
	(g) *GrabEmptyTote* - Loading an empty tote from the storage location
3	*Operations*
	(a) *Rework* - Repair operation performed with use of a rework table for a specified time
	(b) *Welding* - Welding operation performed at a welding table for a specified time
	(c) *QualityCheck* - Quality control performed at a Control Table by an operator for a specified time
	(d) *SetAssembly* - Setting the number of parts needed for the assembling process realization. It should be used before assembly operation
	(e) *Assembly* - Assembly operation performed with use of AssemblyTable
	(f) *SetDisassembly* - Setting the number of parts that will be obtained by disassembling process realization. It should be used before disassembly operation
	(g) *Disassembly* - Disassembly operation performed with use of a DisassemblyTable
	(h) *Wait* - Waiting for a certain time
4	*Controlling 1 (for Containers)*
	(i) *CheckToteWait* - Checking by an operator if the container is on the shelf – if not the operator will wait for the container
	(j) *CheckPartInToteWait* - Checking by an operator if the part (in a container) is on the shelf – if not the operator will wait for the part
	(k) *CheckPartOnTableWait* - Checking by an operator if the part is on the table – if not the operator will wait
	(l) *CheckOneEmptyToteWait* - Checking by an operator if the empty container is on the shelf – if not the operator will wait for the empty container
	(m) *CheckPartInToteCall* - Checking by an operator if the part is in the container on the shelf – if not the operator will call the specified table
	(n) *CheckToteCall* - Checking by an operator if the container is on the shelf – if not operator will call the specified table
	(o) *CheckEmptyAreaWait* - Checking if the shelf is empty. If not – wait for an empty area
	(p) *CheckFirstEmptyToteWait* - Checking by an operator if the first container on the shelf is empty– if not the operator will wait
5	*Controling 2 (for Cycles)*
	(a) *Call* - Run the task list number N for a current operator
	(b) *StartOperator* - Activate another operator
	(c) *SetCycles* - Set the number of cycles to perform
	(d) *CheckCycles* - Check if the designated number of cycles is performed. Two options: Not – the operator will perform the next operation from a table (if the next operation is "Call" the operator will start the execution of a task list in designated table again). Yes – operator will skip the next operation from a table

5. Node – a virtual object, which defines the point in the model space. Each container/table/trailer has one node assigned, which informs the operator where he should go to find a specific object (e.g. welding table). It is important to include the ergonomics in a simulation model. Usually the model contractor sets manually the locations of nodes,

6. InNode – a node dedicated to intralogistics workers.

6 Case Study

To show the possibilities and utility of the designed script language, a simple assembling cell was designed. This cell is composed of (Fig. 5):

Fig. 5. The view of the assembling cell simulation model in FlexSim – own study.

1. One assembling station Ass_01,
2. Three locations of containers with parts P_01, P_02, P_03,
3. One location for the container with assembled product - P_04.

Figure 5 shows the assembling cell with names of basic objects – according to Fig. 5 – left side, and the view of the model during simulation where the operator works (assembles) – right side.

The operator performs the following procedure: he travels to node N_01 and checks that container with parts is in location P_01, if no, he waits, if yes, he picks the part from the tote from P_01 and travels to P_02 for the next part. When he has two parts, he travels to the location G_Ass_01 and puts parts on the table Ass_01 to assemble. This work continues for 30 s. Afterwards, he travels to location N_03 to pick the third part and to take it to the Ass_01 table for the second assembling operation which continues for 45 s. It means that the third part is assembled in combination with the two previous parts. When the final product is ready, the operator takes it to the location N_04 to put it into the container at the location P_04. The whole procedure of this work is described in the script language – Table 2.

Table 2. Example of using script language to model the work of operator in an assembling cell.

ID	Where	Activity		ID	Where	Activity	
1	N_01	Travel	0	16	P_03	CheckToteWait	0
2	P_01	CheckToteWait	0	17	P_03	CheckPartInToteWait	0
3	P_01	CheckPartInToteWait	0	18	P_03	LoadFromTote	1
4	P_01	LoadFromTote	1	19	G_Ass_01	Travel	0
5	N_02	Travel	0	20	WKS_01/Ass_01	Unload	1
6	P_02	CheckToteWait	0	21	WKS_01/Ass_01	Assembly	45
7	P_02	CheckPartInToteWait	0	22	WKS_01/Ass_01	CheckPartOnTableWait	1
8	P_02	LoadFromTote	1	23	WKS_01/Ass_01/	Load	1
9	G_Ass_01	Travel	0	24	N_04	Travel	0
10	WKS_01/Ass_01	Unload	2	25	P_04	CheckToteWait	0
11	WKS_01/Ass_01	Assembly	30	26	P_04	UnloadToTote	1
12	WKS_01/Ass_01	CheckPartOnTableWait	1	27	0	CheckCycles	0
13	WKS_01/Ass_01	Load	1	28	0	Call	2
14	WKS_01/Ass_01	Unload	1	29	P_04	BlockTrolley	0
15	N_03	Travel	0	30	LT_01/Ou_01	StartOperator	2

As mentioned in Sect. 4, we incorporated the designed script language into Flex-Sim. It means that we prepared a translator in FlexSim. Based on data from the company (automotive) we prepared a simulation model of a part of the plant. A lot of production lines work there in the same production hall. The car components are assembled like seats for cars, SUV's etc. Figure 6 shows the view of this model: it contains some welding cells, assembling and packing lines. The deliveries from Supermarket to the lines are performed using logistics trains based on MilkRun idea. The logistics trains (with 4 trolleys) can be seen in the middle of Fig. 6.

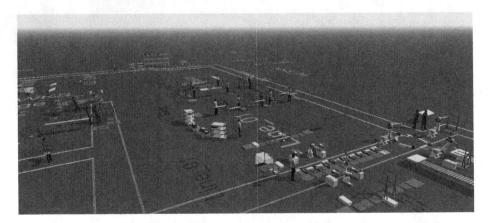

Fig. 6. The view of the part of plant built using script language – own study.

7 Conclusions and Future Research

The paper defines a scripting language that allows to model the behavior of agents carrying out the flow of materials. Researchers have built a few models based on this approach and presented this kind of modeling to industry representatives, whose reaction has been promising.

The directions for further work are as follows:

1. completing the work on the language describing the activities carried out by the operators (flow mechanisms), especially since the previously developed instructions of this language are understandable and accepted by production and logistics engineers,
2. preparing the environment for simulation modeling (using available simulation software as the equivalent of the operating system),
3. developing the model components at the workstation level,
4. formally describing the whole – using the formal apparatus offered by the authors of works from the area of multimodal cyclic processes models,
5. preparing technologies for collecting and preparing data in the enterprise for simulation modeling.

The main purpose of this work is to prepare a technology that answers the question of how to prepare data in an enterprise to build a simulation model quickly, and without having deep knowledge about simulation modeling, with use of the given tool offered on the market. The purpose of using this technology is to solve problems in the area of production and assembly regarding: design and modification of the layout of the production plant/production space, design and redesign (improvement) of intralogistics (Milk Run), work balancing and Yamazumi analyzes.

Acknowledgements. The work was carried out as part of the POIR.01.01.01-00-0485/17 project, "Development of a new type of logistic trolley and methods of collision-free and deadlock-free implementation of intralogistics processes", financed by NCBiR.

References

1. Pawlewski, P.: Multimodal approach to modeling of manufacturing processes. Procedia CIRP **17**, 716–720 (2014). Variety Management in Manufacturing—Proceedings of the 47th CIRP Conference on Manufacturing Systems
2. Pawlewski, P., Kluska, K.: Modeling and simulation of bus assembling process using DES/ABS approach. ADCAIJ: Adv. Distrib. Comput. Artif. Intell. J. **6**(1), 59–72 (2017). ISSN 2255-2863
3. Beaverstock, M., Greenwood, A., Nordgren, W.: Applied Simulation. Modeling and Analysis using Flexsim. Flexsim Software Products Inc., Canyon Park Technology Center, Orem (2017)
4. Gregor, M., Medvecky, S.: Application of digital engineering and simulation in the design of products and production systems. Manag. Prod. Eng. Rev. **1**(1), 71–84 (2010)

5. Ingalls, R.G.: Introduction to simulation. In: Mason, S.J., Hill, R.R., Monch, L., Rose, O., Jefferson, T., Fowler, J.W. (eds.) Proceedings of the 2008 Winter Simulation Conference. Institute of Electrical and Electronics Engineers, Inc., Piscataway (2008)
6. Borshchev, A.: The Big Book of Simulation Modeling. Anylogic North America, Chicago (2013)
7. Weimer, Ch.W., Miller, J.O., Hill, R.R.: Introduction to agent based modeling. In: Roeder, T.M.K., Frazier, P.I., Szechtman, R., Zhou, E., Huschka, T., Chick, S.E. (eds.) Proceedings of the 2016 Winter Simulation Conference (2016)
8. Macal, Ch.M., North, M.J.: Agent-based modeling and simulation: desktop ABMS. In: Henderson, S.G., Biller, B., Hsieh, M.H., Shortle, J., Tew, D.J., Barton, R.R. (eds.) Proceedings of the 2007 Winter Simulation Conference (WSC) (2007)
9. Cassandras, C.G., Lafortune, S.: Introduction to Discrete Event Systems. Kluwer, Dordrecht (1999)
10. Dias, L., Pereiro, G., Vilk, P., Oliveira, J.: Discrete simulation tools ranking - a commercial software packages comparison based on popularity. http://repositorium.sdum.uminho.pt/bitstream/1822/15634/1/ISC_2011_Veneza_5_10.pdf. Accessed Feb 2018
11. FlexSim. http://www.flexsim.com/. Accessed Feb 2018

Multi-agent Systems Approach to Industry 4.0: Enabling Collaboration Considering a Blockchain for Knowledge Representation

Pedro Pinheiro[1,2], Mário Macedo[1,2], Ricardo Barbosa[2,3](✉),
Ricardo Santos[1,2](✉), and Paulo Novais[3]

[1] ESTG.IPP School of Management and Technology,
Institute Polytechnic of Porto, Porto, Portugal
{8140403,8140183,rmb,rjs}@estg.ipp.pt
[2] CIICESI, Center for Research and Innovation in Business Sciences
and Information Systems, Felgueiras, Porto, Portugal
[3] ISLab/ALGORITMI Center, University of Minho, Braga, Portugal
pjon@di.uminho.pt

Abstract. Industrial processes are facing major changes with the arrival of a new revolution: Industry 4.0. By introducing blockchain technology on this environment, conditions are met to accelerate and improve the concepts associated with this new revolution. By looking at industries as an intelligent ambient, where there is a big amount of data being exchanged and created, is possible to gather data and create knowledge about the interactions, and other entities. In this work we propose a model that uses blockchain and multi-agent systems to help represent an entity in a network of entities and help the decision-making process by providing additional knowledge.

Keywords: Industry 4.0 · Blockchain · Multi-agent systems
Decision-making

1 Introduction

The industry is facing one of the biggest changes to date, with the introduction of technologies that aims to start a new revolution that will impact the overall performance, quality, and controllability of the manufacturing process [1], often called industry 4.0 (I4.0) [2]. At the same time, Ambient Intelligence is starting to become more present in the current society, where people are surrounded by intelligent interfaces, that can be applied to an industrial intelligent environment [3], where the creation of data happens at an exponential rate and can be used in decision-making. This way, industries will be able to make strategical and tactical decisions in real time, allowing for a bigger involvement from the customers in

© Springer International Publishing AG, part of Springer Nature 2018
J. Bajo et al. (Eds.): PAAMS 2018 Workshops, CCIS 887, pp. 149–160, 2018.
https://doi.org/10.1007/978-3-319-94779-2_14

the manufacturing of tailor made and personalized products [4]. The problems become how to represent an industry, enabling it to answer these challenges.

Our proposal consists of using blockchain and a multi-agent system (MAS) to represent an industry in an environment where there is a necessity to collaborate and compete one with each other's. The objective is to create a model that can aid the decision-making processes, regarding which entity should one rely on to solve the existing dependencies. The model will have two components that will allow a representation of the interactions, reasoning, and knowledge of an entity.

This paper is structured as follow. In Sect. 2 is described a state of the art of industry 4.0 and how blockchain can help accelerate this revolution. In Sect. 3 is described a state of the art of decision making in ambient intelligence and in industry. The fourth section contains an explanation of MAS, as well as some of the applications of this type of systems in the industry. In Sect. 5 we present our proposal and describe our model in detail. Finally, in the sixth section we conclude this work with a small conclusion and an overview of the future work.

2   Industry 4.0

The 21st century is marked by a digital transformation, with a constant innovation in the various fields of technology that affects the way products are manufactured and how services are provided [5]. The world has seen three industrial revolutions [5] and since the mechanisation that marked the first revolution, subsequent revolutions have resulted in radical changes in manufacturing processes [6]. The increasing automation, the use of electronics and the use of technology to gain better control of industrial manufacturing processes were the basis of the third industrial revolution [7].

With the recently emerging technologies, like Internet of Things (IoT), wireless sensor networks, big data, cloud computing, embedded systems, and mobile Internet [2], starting to be adopted and brought into the manufacturing environment, it is easy to realize that such technologies will lead the industry into a fourth stage of industrialisation [7]. The advances in this fields, created a new concept, the concept of Industry 4.0 (I4.0), first introduced by the German industry in 2011 [6]. The key idea of I4.0 is the creation of new values for the industry, trough the creation of new business models, and the resolution of various social problems [1]. Under the I4.0 concept, the increasing usage of social networks, and adoption of new technologies, has influenced consumers opinions on product manufacturing, personalisation and delivery, requiring factories to become self-aware, self-maintenance and capable of making market predictions [8].

Smart factories are formed by the advanced manufacturing capabilities associated with a digital infrastructure that must be able to capture, generate and spread intelligence [9]. In I4.0, the future of all manufacturing process is based on the concept of a smart factory [10]. Smart factory demands a shift from independent to interactive, from close to open and from stable to dynamic, to take advantage of the value chain of manufacturing and decentralised manufacturing resources [10].

One basis of I4.0 are the Cyber-Physical Systems (CPS), which are defined as the technology for managing interconnected systems between its physical assets and its computational capabilities [11]. Combining the CPS with another factor, the consumer, results in a Social Cyber Physical System [10]. This system combines the characteristics of service production and productive service and introduces a new factor: the consumer. The introduction of the consumer element in this system enables enterprises to address consumer demands more easily and offer personalised products and services [10].

2.1   Blockchain as the Engine for Industry 4.0

The Blockchain technology was introduced as a solution to the problem of making a database both secure and widely distributed [12], resulting in a technology that combines peer-to-peer networks, cryptographic algorithms and a decentralisation mechanism [13], enabling fully trusting interactions between individuals without the need for a trusted intermediary [14]. In a blockchain anyone can add data, review this data, but no one can change it, making this a complete and immutable network of activities [15]. Blockchain operates on a decentralised network, where does not exist consensus regarding the state of data, creating an environment where is easy for two or more entities, that may not know each other, to exchange value safely [15].

Another concept that exists in blockchain are the smart contracts, which are digital contracts that make sure that contractual conditions are meet before any value is exchanged, reducing the amount of human involvement required to create, execute, and enforce a contract [15]. This type of contracts allows rules to be created in a simpler, faster way [13].

Blockchain technology can bring many advantages to the industry, such as transparency, since every transaction is public to its participants, increasing trust [12]. With Industry 4.0 (I4.0) there is an increase importance in products that are tailor made to meet consumers expectations. This creates new demands in the supply chain, making it smarter, more transparent and efficient, and requesting industries to have a clearer vision of the suppliers [4]. With the application of blockchain to this solution is possible to keep transparent and immutable records from the supply chain and sharing data between the vendors and the corporations becomes simpler, as well enabling a faster assessment from the corporation regarding which vendor to use and set a registry of products, tracking their progression through different points of the supply process [14].

Another key component belonging to I4.0 is the concern for security risks, since a lot of information regarding new products and intellectual property, for instance, will have to be protected against abuse [4]. Storing data on blockchain, takes advantage of all its properties and guaranties a level of security necessary for integration of I4.0, since data stored on the blockchain is immutable. Furthermore, the decentralised and distributed structure of blockchain creates a peer-to-peer network where the risk of failure is mitigated, since there is no central point where a failure might happen [15]. It's clear then, that the concepts associated with blockchain, generates value to the integration of I4.0, through key concepts such as trust, transparency, security and data persistence, that can be easily obtained if the utilisation of the blockchain technology is adopted by the industry.

3   The Decision-Making Process

The decision-making process is a constant presence in everyday life and its shown in all kinds of situations, from choosing what clothes to wear, what medicine to prescribe to a patient, to what is going to be next product that is going to boost sales, demonstrating the importance of this process [16]. Decisions are based on the will to fulfil previous settled goals, that are mainly displayed because of their attachment to an individual or group self-interests, and it's a process that can be divided in sub-decisions and tasks [17,18]. When a decision is made, a certain result is going to be produced, becoming necessary to evaluate it to understand if the goal was reached.

The evaluation process is a hard task to carry out, since it uses the results until a decision was made in the decision-making process [16], to assign a positive or a negative connotation to the decision made [16]. The effectiveness of a decision is an uncertainty, since the process of deciding can be influenced by the variables used in the process itself. The outcome of the process and the expected output depending on the activity or situation where the process in being made [16], but there are some factors that increase the effectiveness like having access to the complete and accurate information [18]. The decision-making process is a very difficult and complex task because of the need to consider every factor, each one with a different importance to the final decision [18]. Such importance can be established by assuming a set of variables, like category of decision, previous acquainted knowledge, expectations of specific situations and personal preferences [16,18].

3.1   Decision-Making in Ambient Intelligence

The concept of Ambient Intelligence (AmI) was introduced by the European Commission's Information Society Technologies Advisory Group in 2001 and was based on the principle that at some point, humans will be surrounded by intelligent interfaces supported by computing and networking technology [3,17,19]. The vision is focused on people necessities [20], with emphasis on more user-friendly and efficient services to enable a better support for user-empowerment and human interactions [3], assigning a special perspective to technical fields like ubiquitous computing [21], pervasive and proactive computing, ambient computing, embedded computing and smart objects [20].

AmI refers to a digital environment that supports daily activities of people and will be presented on everyday objects like clothes, materials and vehicles [17], and its implementation came due to the evolution of the technology in the recent years, creating the possibility of making this vision a reality [22]. Components likes smart materials, micro-electromechanical systems, sensor technologies, embedded systems, ubiquitous communication, input/output technology and adaptive software are part of the components of Ambient Intelligence and their aggregation will enable a move from the concept to reality [20].

AmI can produce a great amount of data about some environment, becoming a unique tool to take in consideration during the demanding decision-making process [17]. This process has in its characteristics the necessity of using great amounts of information to produce a good decision, but most of the times this task is hard. With the aggregation of decision-making and AmI, becomes possible to make decisions, adapted to the variables of a specific environment. This capacity to adapt and to have the versatility to make the correct decision in every situation and context can be obtained based on the data, that has its origin in multiple sources inside the AmI like a network of computers or IoT devices, that is then analysed producing concrete information and knowledge about the environment, enabling an improved decision-making process.

3.2   Decision-Making in Industry

I4.0 allows an approximation between the digital and the physical environments presents on an industry context, creating a synchronisation between them, and defining the conditions that can enable an increase in the quality of the processes, and the products [23]. Technologies like sensors, machines, IT systems [24] allow the organisation to be more aware of what is going on inside the business systems, creating an increase in overall production, not only in physical boundaries but also beyond them too, and creating the opportunities for making better decisions [23]. Such changes in the organisations are not only reflected in the technologies, changing other fragments like, making the transition from centralised processes to the decentralisation of data-generation and decision making [25].

In industry, the process of decision-making and their consequences will be different, because of the inclusion of the data from multiple sources, like the production equipment and customer-management systems and will allow to make better decisions with access to more quantity and quality of information [20]. The decisions could be make in very contexts like strategic, tactical, operational and real-time, that will be related to multiple phases of the process of production and even business decisions [23], improving the quality of such decisions. The processes of the organisations will be better, their flexibility and efficacy will increase, the products made will be customised, a reduction of costs in the products will happen, and the processes will be optimised [26,27].

The process of decision making will be a crucial part in the future, but also the present of the organisations, with the number of people involved in this process increasing [26], changing the way people see the multiple industries and interact with them.

4   Multi-agent Systems

Multi-agent systems (MAS) are intelligent systems, where autonomous agents dwell in a world with no control, or persistent knowledge [28]. This infrastructure has been studied as a solution to manage widely distributed systems [29], especially when it comes to industrial applications, given the wide spectrum of problems these systems can tackle [30].

An agent is any entity that senses its environment and acts over it, performing a task continuously [31], with a strong autonomy [32], in a shifting environment, coexisting with other entities and processes [33]. A MAS is a network of agents, that work together to solve problems that a single agent wouldn't be able to solve [31] and can be applied to a variety of operating environments and development platforms [32].

MAS are a set of agents, that interact by exchanging knowledge and by negotiating with each other to achieve a certain goal, which is done in a dynamic, unpredictable and open environment, where these systems are usually embedded [28]. These systems are formed by a set of main characteristics: autonomy (giving agents the possibility to be responsible by their own activities), complexity, adaptability (that adjusts the agents to the environment), concurrency, communication, distribution, mobility, security, and openness [28].

The core of a MAS are its interactions, since is where all its main characteristics are shown and it's also what gives support to the communication and coordination of activities. The management of this activities is crucial to guarantee that MAS are an alternative to design decision-making systems, based on a decentralisation of functions using a set of distributed entities (agents) [34]. For this reason, MAS biggest advantages are flexibility, scalability, autonomy and reduction of problem complexity [29]. The characteristics of this systems put then in a position where they can be particularly helpful in problems with dynamic, uncertain, and distributed nature.

4.1   Multi-agent Systems in Industry

Industrial applications can benefit from MAS, especially those covering the modelling of objects, methodologies and organisations [30]. The application of MAS in industry, in areas such as manufacturing enterprise integration, supply chain management, manufacturing planning, scheduling and holonic manufacturing systems [28], aims to solve a range of complex industrial problems: bringing robustness, scalability, reconfigurability and productivity, all of which can give a greater competitive advantage [34].

MAS have found its useful application in the most various sectors such as manufacturing, healthcare and business, making this a tool widely used in fields such as production, simulation, maintenance, information and communication [33]. The first industrial MAS projects were undertaken as early as the mid-90s, and they usually focused on areas such as automotive, logistics, production planning and manufacturing [34]. One example is MetaMorphII, a multi-agent architecture to support enterprise integration [28], as well Production 2000+, a multi-agent based system working non-stop for five years, installed at the factory plant of Daimler Chrysler, that aimed at an increase of production of cylinder heads [34]. Another example is an agent-based system created to schedule in real-time, cargo assignments to vessels in a very large crude carrier fleet used to carry out transcontinental transportations of oil [35].

Now with the recent changes in technology MAS are aiming at other areas of industry such as production planning, supply chain, logistics, energy and smart grids, buildings and home automations [34]. In supply chain some work has already been done with the development of a prototype to be applied to an automotive supply chain, where was tested the potential of establishing a MAS-based system to support decision-making processes in a multi-level supply chain environment [36]. The fields where this technology has been applied, and where its likely to be applied, yield agent technology as a suitable factor to consider in real world implementations in I4.0, which is driven by internet-based services, smart manufacturing and service innovations, developing needs to be addressed, such as competitiveness in the manufacturing enterprise, increase difficulty in decision-making, communication and collaboration, that can be seen across the whole industry [33].

5   Proposal Description

Organisations, belonging to different kind of industries, have established between them a business process collaboration, that typically operates in a supply chain, to introduce major benefits into their business activities, as well to be able to respond to an ever more demanding consumer. With the introduction of I4.0, industries need to be able to provide a faster response to tailor made, and highly personalised consumer needs. This necessity will create a bigger demand in the supply chain and will constitute the need for better communications to integrate suppliers and consumers [4].

In a set of entities, where all have services and/or products to offer and necessities that rely on other entity's available services, becomes harder to make a quick and easy decision regarding which other entity to depend. There are always going to exist a set of dependencies established between two, or more, entities sharing value in a supply chain, since the processes that compose this type of activities are prone to establish a link and in a large supply chain is hard to have an overall idea of all transactions made [15]. The main problem is the fact that in an environment where industries need to make fast and reliable decisions, there is no prominent way of knowing which other corporation to depend on, creating a situation that can bring many deficits to the manufacturing processes.

Despite the existing work on supply chains analysis, our approach aims to solve a more specific problem: the problem of dependencies and how to improve the decision-making process in an environment formed by a set of multiple entities, with different purposes and objectives. The objective of our proposal is to project a model, that uses the above referenced technologies, to represent an entity so that an improvement in decision-making can be made, enabling any entity to make a better choice when it comes to who rely on to complement its manufacturing needs.

5.1   Model Presentation

The model presented on this work, represented in Fig. 1, aims to be an entry point to solve inter-entities dependencies representation, in the industry environment, to improve decision-making when it comes to choose what other entity to establish communications with.

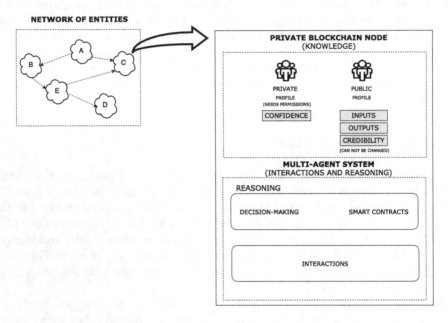

Fig. 1. Model proposal, that represents a multi-agent system and blockchain, integrated on a network of entities

This model begins to encapsulate a set of industries as a network of entities with inherent relations established between them, that represent the multiple industry processes created, to meet their business goals. For each entity on this network, there is a recurrent process happening where first an interaction is established with other entity then, using the data gathered from the interaction, a reasoning process happens from were something is learnt so that it can be used for future processes. The model tries to represent this logic using two different components to handle knowledge representation, reasoning, and interactions: blockchain, and a MAS.

In this model, the use of a private blockchain is adopted to create the possibility of setting permissions to access the data, regardless of whether it's a reading or writing operation. The use of a blockchain helps maintaining the authenticity, transparency and immutability of the data, giving it more security. The blockchain will be formed by a public and private profile of the entity to guarantee that an entity has information about the network, about the other entities, and about its own profile [37]. This information will get more precise along the time and through interactions done by the entity [37].

The private profile, contains data about the confidence of the entity in the network and its remaining entities and its represented by a value from a set of confidence levels. This private profile needs permissions to be accessed, ensuring that only the entity to which it relates can access its information. Regarding the public profile, it contains mostly accessible information about the entity and what it represents to the network and stores the following variables:

1. Inputs - represent the needs of the entity, namely what it needs from the other entities in the network in order to fulfil its business processes, for instance raw materials;
2. Outputs - what it has to offer to the network and to its entities. This will ultimately represent the input of some other entity, and it can range from something like a product to a service;
3. Credibility - corresponds to how credible we are to the network and to each entity. Despite being stored in the public part of the profile, so the other entities can see our level of credibility, this value can not be changed even by the entity to whom it refers, setting permissions to only allow the value to be read.

The way these profiles are settled allow for a scenario where, for instance, an entity B has a low level of credibility in the network, but because previous interactions with entity A were successful, entity A has a high level of confidence in B which enables it to rely on this entity to establish future interactions.

The other component of this model uses a MAS, since these systems are suited for modelling distributed problems [38], where multiple agents interact with each other to achieve local and global objectives [29], making this the adequate component to yield the core processes that an entity establishes within the network. This MAS component is formed by two layers, the interaction layer and the reasoning layer.

The interaction layer is responsible for the communications between entities [37], gathering any type of interaction established between two entities in the network, creating a history of interactions that can be used as a point of reference in the future.

The reasoning layer is formed by the decision-making module and the smart contract module. The decision-making module will provide the intended support to the entity in the choice of the preferable entity to get its inputs. The smart contract module is where a set of rules will be established to create a reliable way of exchanging value with the preferable entity, guaranteeing the compliance of the terms.

The main components that form the proposed model are in constant relation, since the interaction layer from the MAS generates the data that creates or updates the knowledge in the blockchain, and this knowledge is used in the reasoning layer of the MAS component to produce smart contracts and mainly improve decision-making. We believe that this model can deal with the complex dependencies established between entities and to provide with a solution to help industries make a better decision regarding which entity choose to answer its business needs.

6   Conclusion and Future Work

With the introduction of industry 4.0 the advances in the industrial environment are creating a new standard for industries, with a focus on a consumer that is more aware of its needs, and that is demanding more personalised solutions. This demand creates a more dependent industry, where entities need to cooperate to stay competitive, with an associated need of storing and processing all available data in order to generate knowledge about the multiple interactions, that can contribute to the decision-making process by including consumers needs and preferences.

In this work, we described an initial introduction of a model that aims to solve the problem previously described. With this model, we believe it becomes possible for an entity, that operates in a network of entities, to have a faster assessment of the others elements in the network, like the needs of other entities and, therefore, become capable of making a faster and improved choice when it comes to interact with other entity.

In the future, our plans are to dwell into the decision-making process, assigning classes to the choices available, as well setting categories to the confidence and credibility variables, to create a more solid and complete knowledge base. Other characteristic of this model that needs to be address is how the knowledge base is going to be updated and in what circumstances, for instance when a entity changes its outputs, enabling other entities to have access to the updated information. This knowledge update is directly correlated and dependable on another crucial need, knowledge representation. During the development of this model, some problems, that will be addressed in the future, were identified such as how to handle the limited computing and energy resources of some industrial devices, that becomes a critical problem when blockchain is applied to industrial systems, as result of the mining process [39].

References

1. Kang, H.S., Lee, J.Y., Choi, S., Kim, H., Park, J.H., Son, J.Y., Kim, B.H., Noh, S.D.: Smart manufacturing: past research, present findings, and future directions. Int. J. Precis. Eng. Manuf. - Green Technol. **3**(1), 111–128 (2016)
2. Wang, S., Wan, J., Li, D., Zhang, C.: Implementing smart factory of industrie 4.0: an outlook. Int. J. Distrib. Sens. Netw. **12**(1), 3159805 (2016)
3. Ducatel, K., Bogdanowicz, M., Scapolo, F., Leijten, J., Burgelman, J.C.: ISTAG scenarios for ambient intelligence in 2010. Society, p. 58 (2001)
4. Deloitte: Industry 4.0. Challenges and solutions for the digital transformation and use of exponential technologies. Deloitte, pp. 1–30 (2015)
5. Roland Berger Strategy Consultants, Blanchet, M., Rinn, T., de Thieulloy, G., von Thaden, G.: Industry 4.0. The new industrial revolution. How Europe will succeed (2014)

6. Qin, J., Liu, Y., Grosvenor, R.: A categorical framework of manufacturing for Industry 4.0 and beyond. Procedia CIRP **52**, 173–178 (2016)
7. Shrouf, F., Ordieres, J., Miragliotta, G.: Smart factories in Industry 4.0: A review of the concept and of energy management approached in production based on the Internet of Things paradigm. In: IEEE International Conference on Industrial Engineering and Engineering Management, January 2015, pp. 697–701 (2014)
8. Lee, J., Kao, H.A., Yang, S.: Service innovation and smart analytics for Industry 4.0 and big data environment. Procedia CIRP **16**, 3–8 (2014)
9. Longo, F., Nicoletti, L., Padovano, A.: Smart operators in Industry 4.0: a human-centered approach to enhance operators' capabilities and competencies within the new smart factory context. Comput. Ind. Eng. **113**, 144–159 (2017)
10. Zhang, F., Liu, M., Shen, W.: Operation modes of smart factory for high-end equipment manufacturing in the internet and big data era. Smc 2017.Org (2017)
11. Lee, J., Bagheri, B., Kao, H.A.: A cyber-physical systems architecture for Industry 4.0-based manufacturing systems. Manuf. Lett. **3**, 18–23 (2015)
12. Rabah, K.: Overview of blockchain as the engine of the 4th industrial revolution. Mara Res. J. Bus. Manag. **1**(1), 125–135 (2016). The Africa Premier Research Publishing Hub www.mrjournals.org
13. Wright, A., De Filippi, P.: Decentralized blockchain technology and the rise of Lex Cryptographia. SSRN Electron. J. 1–58 (2015)
14. Bahga, A., Madisetti, V.K.: Blockchain platform for industrial internet of things. J. Softw. Eng. Appl. **9**, 533–546 (2016)
15. Abeyratne, S.A., Monfared, R.P.: Blockchain ready manufacturing supply chain using distributed ledger. Int. J. Res. Eng. Technol. **05**(09), 1–10 (2016)
16. Hamilton, J.G., Lillie, S.E., Alden, D.L., Scherer, L., Oser, M., Rini, C., Tanaka, M., Baleix, J., Brewster, M., Craddock Lee, S., Goldstein, M.K., Jacobson, R.M., Myers, R.E., Zikmund-Fisher, B.J., Waters, E.A.: What is a good medical decision? A research agenda guided by perspectives from multiple stakeholders. J. Behav. Med. **40**(1), 52–68 (2017)
17. Santos, R., Marreiros, G., Ramos, C., Bulas-Cruz, J.: Argumentative agents for ambient intelligence ubiquitous environments. In: Proceedings of Artificial Intelligence Techniques for Ambient Intelligence. 18th European Conference on Artificial Intelligence, ECAI 2008 (2008)
18. Dean, J.W., Sharfman, M.P.: Does decision process matter? A study of strategic decision-making effectiveness. Acad. Manag. J. **39**(2), 368–396 (1996)
19. Marreiros, G., Santos, R., Freitas, C., Ramos, C., Neves, J., Bulas-Cruz, J.: LAID - a smart decision room with ambient intelligence for group decision making and argumentation support considering emotional aspects. Int. J. Smart Home **2**(2), 77–93 (2008)
20. Veronica, I.C., Mirela, G., Maria, B.D.: Modern approaces in the context of ambient intelligence. Ann. Univ. Oradea Econ. Sci. Ser. **18**(4), 963–968 (2009)
21. Marreiros, G., Santos, R., Ramos, C., Neves, J., Novais, P., Machado, J., Bulas-Cruz, J.: Ambient intelligence in emotion based ubiquitous decision making. In: Proceeedings of the International Joint Conference on Artificial Intelligence (IJCAI 2007) - 2nd Workshop on Artificial Intelligence Techniques for Ambient Intelligence (AITAm I 2007), pp. 86–91 (2007)
22. Cook, D.J., Augusto, J.C., Jakkula, V.R.: Ambient intelligence: technologies, applications, and opportunities. Pervasive Mob. Comput. **5**(4), 277–298 (2009)
23. Marques, M., Agostinho, C., Zacharewicz, G., Jardim-Goncalves, R.: Decentralized decision support for intelligent manufacturing in Industry 4.0. J. Ambient Intell. Smart Environ. **9**(3), 299–313 (2017)

24. Rüßmann, M., Lorenz, M., Gerbert, P., Waldner, M., Justus, J., Engel, P., Harnisch, M.: Industry 4.0. The future of productivity and growth in manufacturing. Boston Consulting, pp. 1–5, April 2015
25. Upasani, K., Bakshi, M., Pandhare, V., Lad, B.K.: Distributed maintenance planning in manufacturing industries. Comput. Ind. Eng. **108**, 1–14 (2017)
26. Dory, T., Waldbuesser, P.: Connected cognitive entity management: new challenges for executive decision-making. In: Proceedings of 6th IEEE Conference on Cognitive Infocommunications, CogInfoCom 2015, pp. 235–240 (2016)
27. Rai, A., Kannan, R.J.: Membrane computing based scalable distributed learning and collaborative decision making for cyber physical systems. In: 2017 IEEE 26th International Conference on Enabling Technologies: Infrastructure for Collaborative Enterprises (WETICE), pp. 24–27 (2017)
28. Oprea, M.: Applications of multi-agent systems, pp. 239–270 (2004)
29. Eddy, Y.S., Xun, S., Eddy, Y.S.F., Member, S., Gooi, H.B., Member, S.: Multi agent system for distributed management of microgrids. IEEE Trans. Power Syst. **30**(1), 24–34 (2014)
30. Aldea, A., Bañares-Alcántara, R., Jiménez, L., Moreno, A., Martínez, J., Riaño, D.: The scope of application of multi-agent systems in the process industry: three case studies. Expert Syst. Appl. **26**(1 SPEC.ISS.), 39–47 (2004)
31. Glavic, M.: Agents and multi-agent systems: a short introduction for power engineers, pp. 1–21 (2006)
32. Zhao, J.Y., Wang, Y.J., Xi, X.: Simulation of steel production logistics system based on multi-agents. Int. J. Simul. Model. **16**(1), 167–175 (2017)
33. Adeyeri, M.K., Mpofu, K., Adenuga Olukorede, T.: Integration of agent technology into manufacturing enterprise: a review and platform for Industry 4.0. In: Proceedings of 5th International Conference on Industrial Engineering and Operations Management, IEOM 2015 (2015)
34. Leitão, P., Maík, V., Vrba, P.: Past, present, and future of industrial agent applications. IEEE Trans. Ind. Inform. **9**(4), 2360–2372 (2013)
35. Himoff, J., Skobelev, P., Wooldridge, M.: MAGENTA technology: multi-agent systems for industrial logistics. In: Proceedings of the Fourth International Joint Conference on Autonomous Agents and Multiagent Systems, AAMAS 2005, February 2016, pp. 60–66 (2005)
36. Hernández, J.E., Mula, J., Poler, R., Lyons, A.C.: Collaborative planning in multi-tier supply chains supported by a negotiation-based mechanism and multi-agent system. Group Decis. Negot. **23**(2), 235–269 (2014)
37. Marreiros, G., Santos, R., Ramos, C., Neves, J., Bulas-Cruz, J.: ABS4GD: a multi-agent system that simulates group decision processes considering emotional and argumentative aspects. In: AAAI Spring Symposium Series, pp. 88–95 (2008)
38. Marreiros, G., Santos, R., Ramos, C., Neves, J.: Context-aware emotion-based model for group decision making. IEEE Intell. Syst. Mag. **25**(2), 31–39 (2010)
39. Xiong, Z., Zhang, Y., Niyato, D., Wang, P., Han, Z.: When mobile blockchain meets edge computing: challenges and applications, pp. 1–17 (2017)

Agents in Logistics and Supply Chain

Patrycja Hoffa-Dabrowska$^{(\boxtimes)}$ and Kamila Kluska

Faculty of Engineering Management, Chair of Production Engineering
and Logistics, Poznan University of Technology,
Strzelecka 11, 60-965 Poznan, Poland
patrycja.hoffa-dabrowska@put.poznan.pl,
kamila.kluska@put.poznan.pl

Abstract. Agents technology is popular in many different scientific area. One of them is logistics and supply chain. Agent is characterized by many features, as: mobility and intelligence, autonomy, the ability to monitor the environment at all times. Authors in this article focus on aspect of agents in logistics and supply chain. In this area 3 types of agents can be distinguished: searching agents, monitoring agents and managing agents. Describing the agents topic author decided to present basic information about Discrete-Event Simulation (DES) and Agent Based Simulation (ABS), which are used in logistics also. In this article are presented examples of using each mentioned method of simulation in logistics area.

Keywords: Logistics · Intralogistics · Supply chain · Agents

1 Introduction

Agent-based systems are complex systems, which synthesize contributions from many different research area, as: artificial intelligence, software engineering, robotics and distributed computing [1]. Agent systems are used to solve problems in the situation of dispersion of decision-making entities. They are used also in situation when variety of decision-making methods are used [2]. Systems based on this technology are an effective tool for solving complexity problems [3].

In this article authors described basic information about agent systems (Sect. 2). In the next section authors analyzed this topic in literature – they present the popularity of agents system in different area, detailing the logistic and supply chain. In Sect. 4 the different types of agents in logistics and supply chain are presented. In next section the differences between the Discrete-Event Simulation (DES) and Agent Based Simulation (ABS) are described. Authors show basic information and give examples of using each method in logistic area. At the end are conclusion about roles of agents system.

2 Agents System – Basic Information

The agent colloquially means "someone delegated to work in a specific place and there performing specific tasks in accordance with the previously adopted assumptions" [4]. In relation to IT aspects, it should be mentioned (said) about programming agent - it is a

J. Bajo et al. (Eds.): PAAMS 2018 Workshops, CCIS 887, pp. 161–171, 2018.
https://doi.org/10.1007/978-3-319-94779-2_15

program that performs tasks remotely (on a different computer or computer network) in accordance with the user's assumptions [4, 5].

Features of the agent [5, 6]:

- operates in a defined environment, which it influences through its behavior, decisions made;
- works autonomously to achieve the goal, which is imposed on him by the user,
- has the ability to monitor the observed area for 24 h; in the case of reviewing the available offers without reaching the goal, it goes into a sleep state; when the new offer will appear it will resume to work,
- it is intelligent, what means that it learns from the information gathered, its further activities are better and better in relation to the assumed goal, in addition in this way it adapts to the changing conditions of the environment in which it is located;
- it is characterized by mobility, what means that it can change the environment in which it works in order to achieve its goal.

In the case of agents the features: mobility and intelligence are contradictory - the more mobile is the agent, the less intelligent it is, and vice versa. This situation is caused because for more intelligence agent it is necessary to create a complex code, which is difficult to send to other places for which the agent "travels". This problem is solved by creating a group of mobile agents (gathering information) and intelligent (managing) agents, which work together for a specific purpose.

3　Agents in the Literature

Agent systems are a popular topic in various scientific fields. In order to show the popularity of this method, it was decided to make a literature background, based on chosen open bases at Poznan University of technology. It is worth mentioning that agent technology is not a new solution, although it has been very popular for over a dozen years, which is confirmed by numerous scientific publications and periodically organized conferences and workshops, such as [7, 8]:

- International Conference on Practical Applications of Agents and Multi-Agent Systems (PAAMS),
- International Conference on Autonomous Agents and Multiagent Systems (AAMAS),
- International Conference on Agents and Artificial Intelligence (ICAART),
- International Workshop on Multi-Agent Systems and Simulation (MAS&S),
- Workshop on Service Orientation in Holonic and Multi-Agent Manufacturing (SOHOMA),
- Conference on Multiagent System Technologies (MATES),
- International Conference on Intelligent Virtual Agents (IVA).

In order to show the popularity of the agent technology issue, authors decided to analyze the number of articles about agents in selected journal databases. The databases available at the Poznan University of Technology were analyzed.

The following databases were selected:

- ScienceDirect/Elsevier,
- Taylor and Francis Group - Online Journals,
- Springer/ScienceDirect.

Selected databases have been searched for the following issues:

- agent,
- agent system,
- agent + logistic,
- agent + supply chain.

The authors chose these four issues to show the popularity of agents and agent systems, especially with take into account the use of agents in logistics and the supply chain. Depending on the database, it was possible to search for articles according to various criteria. Authors decide to show how many articles were published in last year, and in 5 year period – from 2013 to 2017 (not to 2018 because of beginning of this year) and also how many articles are in the analyzed database.

The first analyzed database is ScienceDirect/Elsevier, in which authors searched mentioned issue in title, abstract or keywords. Results of this research are presented at Fig. 1.

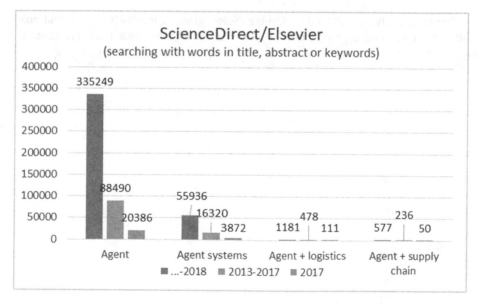

Fig. 1. Number of articles of analyzed issue in ScienceDirect/Elsevier database. Source: own study based on PUT access at 19.02.2018.

The second analyzed database is Taylor and Francis Group - Online Journals, in which authors searched defined topics in title or keywords. Results of this research are presented at Fig. 2.

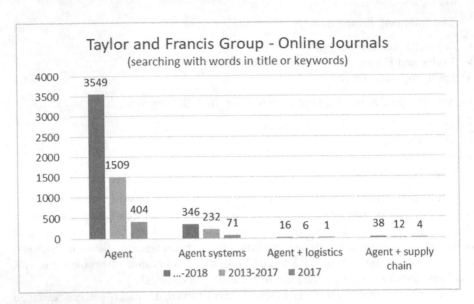

Fig. 2. Number of articles of analyzed issue in Taylor and Francis Group - Online Journals database. Source: own study based on PUT access at 19.02.2018.

The third analyzed database is Springer/ScienceDirect, in which authors had possibility to search defined topics only in title. Results of this research are presented at Fig. 3.

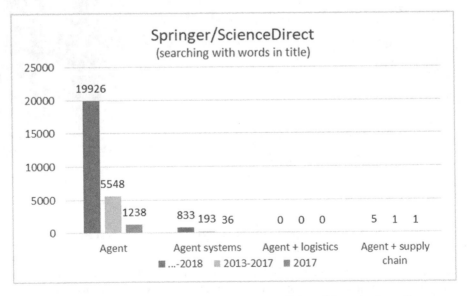

Fig. 3. Number of articles of analyzed issue in Springer/ScienceDirect database. Source: own study based on PUT access at 19.02.2018.

Analyzed results presented in Figs. 1, 2 and 3 we can see that the issue of an agent is still popular, what shows the number of articles in 2017. For first and third databases articles from 2017 are about 6% of all articles in this topic. At second databases is around 11%. For issue of agent systems the share of articles from 2017 in relation to all articles is about (in order of mentioning the databases): 6%, 20%, 4%. The share of articles about using agents in logistics and supply chain is small according to all articles. It can means that it is a research gap, which should be filled.

Describing the agent technology it is important to mention about one of the basic advantages of this technology - the possibility of using it also on mobile devices (laptops, palmtops), which increases its range of use. High software mobility and autonomous sourcing of information in a distributed environment promote the using of the discussed technology in logistics. Due to the overload of information exchanged within a given supply chain, consisting of many entities located in different places, the technology facilitating the filtration of information and supporting management seem to be useful [4].

4   Types of Agents in Logistics and Supply Chain

In logistics different classification of agents can be found. One of them, referring to the supply chain, is presented in [6]. In logistics context three types of agents can be distinguished [4, 5]:

- Searching agents – their purpose is to search the information according to specific criteria. These agents are characterized by mobility - what means that, if the defined goal has not been fully achieved, agents can independently change the location of their activity, and they remembered the previously obtained information. An example of using: searching for information about the cheapest raw materials, products, services in offers of potential suppliers on electronic products-services exchanges, or searching the transport means closest to the place of the transport order. The agent, after searching the advertising database, sends the most attractive offer to the person who delegated it. In addition, the agent may also be able to decide on the purchase of a product or service (this option depends on the autonomy level which was granted to it).
- Monitoring agents – it means intelligent agents, but not very mobile. Their tasks include reacting to received information about events. The reaction can be different, depends on defined rules of conduct. An example of using this type of agents is to use them to inform about the technical condition of the car (tire pressure, radiator temperature, engine revolutions, etc.) deviating from the accepted standard. In this situation, the agent contacts the user (application) informing about the occurrence of the state of emergency. Another example of using agent technology in logistics is use the agent for reporting stock shortages and automatically make an order in the proper supplier. Next application of monitoring agents is to connect them with mobile agents and use them in shipment tracking systems, so-called Track & Trace.
- Managing agents – these agents have both characteristics of an intelligent agent and a mobile agent. Their task is searching offers in different locations and comparing

only these offers, which meet the criteria set by the user. Their task is also determine the terms and form of transactions with agents representing business partners. Example of using this type of agents: the transport offers exchanges.

5 DES and ABS in Logistics

In context of logistics and supply chain, the two trends can be distinguished in events simulation: Discrete-Event Simulation (DES) and Agent Based Simulation (ABS).

DES is used to present the continuous processes from reality in a non-continuous way, i.e. defining the moment of events affecting the process, defining them. An event should be understood as the occurrence of a change in the state of the system at a certain point in time that can trigger the change of object attributes or start or stop operations in the process. Examples of such events in logistic context:

- truck's driveway under the loading ramp,
- the moment of ending of unloading process of a lorry,
- reaching a certain level of stock by a given product.

ABS helps better understand the real world systems in which individual entities with autonomous behaviors are presented or modeled. Modeling using ABS should pay attention to the behavior and characteristics of individual agents, and also to the relationship between the agent and the agent, and also between the agent and the environment in which it is located [9].

Referring ABS to the modeling of logistic processes, it can be defined that individual participants in the supply chain (supplier, producer, distributor, wholesaler) will be represented by an agent with specific characteristics. Also, forklift operators on the company will be represented by an agent. Each of these objects will have a different individual goal, but the common will have the same: production and delivery of a given product to a specific point/customer.

In order to more detailed application of agent technologies in logistics, it was decided to present it on an example. Figure 4 shows the part of the enterprise - production hall and warehouse. Three lathes have been distinguished on the production hall - each of them is operated by an individual operator. In addition, there are two employees in the analyzed environment - forklift operators.

Each employee is treated as an individual agent who has specific characteristics and his goal to achieve. The main goal is common - to realized the order. There may be (or not) interactions between operators of the lathes - it depends on the work organization: if every operator constantly works only on his machine and does not take into account the work of others, the direct relations with other lathe operators do not take place; if the operators exchange at work, or the products are machined on different lathe, these relationships definitely occur. In presented case at Fig. 4, between forklift operators the relationships definitely occur because work of lathe operators is dependent on forklift operators (if they bring the goods at right time or not) and in the second way – the work of forklift operators is dependent on lathe operators (how and when they get information about demand of goods). So this agents have to cooperate with each other and inform each other.

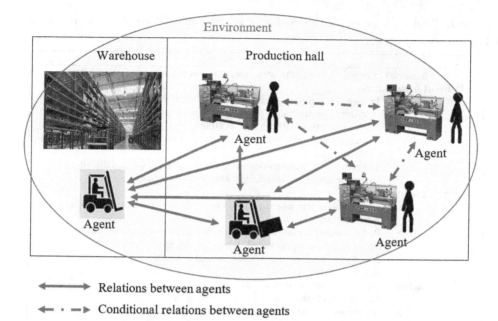

Fig. 4. The enterprise model in agent approach. Source: own study using Google graphics.

This case is also applicable to the supply chain issues, because the specified objects with various functions do not have to be limited by the area of a single building. What's more, the use of agents in simulation is arbitrary. It results from the approach to the problem, knowledge and skills of the modeler - regardless of the subject of project or area of the company. An example of using agents in processes realized in supply chain is presented in [12]. The use of agents for logistics is very wide, therefore in the next section describes an example of simulation modeling of intralogistics processes based on the milk-run concept.

6   Agents in Intralogistics

Greenwood et al. [10] proposed a framework for simulation modeling of intralogistics systems based on milk-run concept. It is a support for agent-based modeling, because it provides all physical elements, activities and decision variables necessary to model the work of individual objects in the system. Table 1 shows the framework.

The third level of the framework concerns the decision-making processes carried out by the objects, built on the basis of traditionally available task-executers in FlexSim [11]. A certain intelligence, the ability to make decisions based on specific criteria, as well as the advanced communication between these objects means that they can be treated as an agents. The agents' intelligence results from extensive algorithms that contain the logic of their behavior, analytical and computational mechanisms, which allows them to work autonomously.

Table 1. Framework for simulation modeling of in-plant, milk-run logistics systems. Source: [10]

	Physical elements

1	a. **Material** to be transported; attributes: size, location of source and use points
	b. **Logistics train**
	    a. **Trailer** containing material to be transported; different types
	        i. trailer type attributes: shape, size, configuration (storage arragement), capacity; numer of each type available
	        ii. train composition: numer of each type of trailer and arragement of trailers on a train
	    b. **Tugger**, lead vehicle, guides train; attributes: size, speed, reliability
	    c. **Operator** attributes: speed, shift and break schedules
	c. **Logistics network**
	    a. Source/use points where material is available or used; a nodes in a network; attribute: location
	    b. Paths, routes between nodes on which logistics train move; attributes: distance, shape (straight, curved, combination), speed limit
	    c. Source/use storage- area where material is actually stored; attributes: location, capacity
	d. **Relationships** among physical elements
	    a. Material has both a source point and use point
	    b. Source and use points are connected through paths
	    c. Source and use points each have an associated storage area
	    d. Each storage area has a means to provide material to be moved (at source) or material that has been delivered to be consumed (at use)
	    e. Material is transported on a trailer
	    f. Operator drives the train by means of the tugger; trailers follow the tugger

	Operational activities

2	Operational activities – interactions among physical elements creating system dynamics
	a. **Path Travel**
	        i. horizontal movement between points considering speed, shape, distance
	        ii. trailers and tugger independently conform to path shape
	        iii. handling of disturbances – intersections, other trains, etc.
	b. **Train Positioning** – placing the trailer associated with a material at a source/use point
	c. **Load/Unload** material between trailers and storage areas by an operator
	d. **Source/use mechanism** – means to either produce materials to be moved or consume material once moved (create demand for material)
	e. **Reliability/Availability** – breakdowns and recharging on tuggers; lunch and personal breaks for operators

	Decision variables
3	Decision variables – drive the bahavior and performance of the system; defines the work plan for a specified period of time through the 4Ws (what, where, when, who) and 2Hs (How much and How) a. **What** – set of tasks in m[a, b, q] b. **Where** – location of activities, a(x, y). A travel path is formed between locations c. **How much** – quantity of material handled d. **When** – time a material is handled in an use area; expressed as an absolute time or position in a sequence of route activities e. **How** material is moved – specific transport and possibly location on trailer f. **Who** – which train (tugger and operator) material and trailer are connected

Agent-based simulation is necessary to model the behavior of the milk-run objects, which is characterized by complex and coordinated cooperation over time. This cooperation allows, inter alia, for a coordinated movement along a transport route, and positioning of parts of logistics train at bus-stops with maintaining appropriate spatial relations. In addition, the agent simulation modeling allows to take into account the interdependencies of logistic trains. It means avoiding collisions, obeying traffic rules at intersections, stopping the train in designated area when the bus-stop is blocked by another logistic train.

The milk-run objects are: the train operator, tugger and trailers. Figure 5 shows the logistics train and the implementation of the loading process in simulation model.

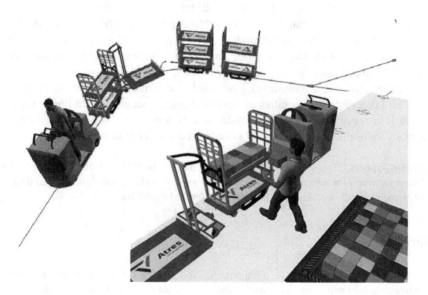

Fig. 5. The logistics train and implementation of loading activity in simulation model. Source: own study using FlexSim.

The operator's intelligence allows to receive and process orders, select and launch a tugger, inform that the train is ready to run, move it, make a decision to stop the train at a given stop, perform loading and unloading operations, etc.

The tugger's intelligence allows to select specific trailers, provide them with the information needed to form the logistics train, and also train traffic management.

Trolleys are independent objects whose tasks are synchronized with the tugger movement. Trolleys travels along transport routes and enables the positioning of a logistics train.

7 Conclusions

Agents technology is the important issue in many science disciplines, also in logistics and supply chain. Authors showed in this article the popularity of this issue. Analyzed the number of articles in three chosen bases they showed the role of agents in science. Agents technology is used in logistics area. Three types of agents can be distinguished in logistics: searching, monitoring, and managing agents. Each of them is characterized by other features and has other roles, what have been described in this article.

It is worth to pay attention for the growing role of agent modeling in logistics and the supply chain. Agents based simulation (ABS) is perfect for simulation the processes, in which the individual entities with autonomous behaviors are modeled. In ABS the goal of individual agents and relationships between them are very important. The agents communicate with each other and cooperate. This main features makes ABS the perfect method for modelling the logistics and supply chain processes, in which autonomous of single entities, cooperation between them and information flow are very important.

The paper provides a multi-level framework for simulation modeling of milk-run systems and describes the specifics of agents in such systems. Agent-based modeling approach is necessary for modeling the decision processes and movement of elements of logistics train, due to complex and coordinated cooperation over time.

Acknowledgements. The work was carried out as part of the POIR.01.01.01-00-0485/17 project, "Development of a new type of logistic trolley and methods of collision-free and deadlock-free implementation of intralogistics processes", financed by NCBiR.

References

1. Zambonelli, F., Jennings, N.R., Omicini, A., Wooldridge, M.J.: Agent-oriented software engineering for internet applications. In: Omicini, A., Zambonelli, F., Klusch, M., Tolksdorf, R. (eds.) Coordination of Internet Agents, pp. 326–346. Springer, Heidelberg (2001). https://doi.org/10.1007/978-3-662-04401-8_13
2. Stanek, S., Pańkowska, M.B., Żytniewski, M.K.: Realizacja agentów oprogramowania z wykorzystaniem środowiska JAVA. In: Porębska-Miąc, T., Sroka, H. (eds.) Systemy Wspomagania Organizacji SWO 2005. Akademia Ekonomiczna, Katowice (2005)
3. Li, J., Sheng, Z.: A multi-agent model for the reasoning of uncertainty information of supply chains. Int. J. Prod. Res. **49**, 5737–5753 (2011)
4. Wieczerzycki, W.,Wieliński, J.: Zastosowanie technologii agentowej w logistyce. Logistyka **4**, 42–45 (2003)
5. Kawa, A.: Konfigurowanie łańcucha dostaw. Teoria, instrumenty i technologie. Uniwersytetu Ekonomicznego w Poznaniu, Wyd (2011). https://doi.org/10.13140/rg.2.1.1448.4006
6. Kawa, A.: Organizowanie łańcuchów dostaw z wykorzystaniem technologii agentowej na przykładzie branży komputerowej, Prace Naukowe Politechniki Warszawskiej. Transport 01/2008; Systemy Logistyczne, Teoria i Praktyka, pp. 1–10 (2008)
7. http://wikicfp.com/cfp. Accessed 17 Feb 2018
8. https://easychair.org/cfp. Accessed 17 Feb 2018

9. Macal, C.M., North, M.J.: Introductory tutorial: agent-based modeling and simulation. In: Winter Simulation Conference, pp. 362–376 (2013)

10. Greenwood, A.G., Kluska, K., Pawlewski, P.: A multi-level framework for simulating milk-run, in-plant logistics operations. In: Bajo, J., et al. (eds.) PAAMS 2017. CCIS, vol. 722, pp. 209–220. Springer, Cham (2017). https://doi.org/10.1007/978-3-319-60285-1_18

11. Greenwood, A.G., Kluska, K., Pawlewski, P.: A hybrid modeling approach for simulating milk-run in-plant logistics operations. In: Bajo, J., et al. (eds.) PAAMS 2017. CCIS, vol. 722, pp. 221–231. Springer, Cham (2017). https://doi.org/10.1007/978-3-319-60285-1_19

12. Grzybowska, K., Hoffa-Dabrowska, P.: Analysis of the survival of complex systems with an actions coordination mechanism. In: Bajo, J., et al. (eds.) PAAMS 2017. CCIS, vol. 722, pp. 197–208. Springer, Cham (2017). https://doi.org/10.1007/978-3-319-60285-1_17

Automatic Verification of Design Rules in PCB Manufacturing

João Ramos[1(⊠)], Patrícia Rocha[2], Flávio Vilarinho[2], António Silva[2],
Marcos Andrade[2], João Varajão[2], Luis Magalhães[2], Pedro Ribeiro[3],
and Luis César Freitas[3]

[1] Centro Algoritmi, Department of Informatics, University of Minho,
Campus de Gualtar, 4710-057 Braga, Portugal
jramos@di.uminho.pt
[2] Centro Algoritmi, Department of Information Systems, University of Minho,
Campus de Azurem, 4804-533 Guimarães, Portugal
{b7673,b7232,b7216,b7963}@algoritmi.uminho.pt,
{varajao,lmagalhaes}@dsi.uminho.pt
[3] Bosch Car Multimedia Portugal, SA, Braga, Portugal
{pedro.ribeiro2,luis.freitas}@pt.bosch.com

Abstract. Nowadays, electronics can be found in almost every available
device. At the core of electronic devices there are Printed Circuit Boards
(PCB). To create a suitable PCB there is the need of complying with
several constraints, both concerning electrical and layout design. Thus,
the design rules related to the PCB manufacturing and assembly are
very important since these restrictions are fundamental to ensure the
creation of a viable physical PCB. Electrical Computer Aided Design
(ECAD) tools are able to automatically verify such rules, but they only
consider a subset of the total required rules. The remaining rules are
currently manually checked, which may increase the occurrence of errors
and, consequently, increase the overall costs in designing and in the manufacturing process of a PCB. Being the design a crucial phase in the
manufacturing procedure, a software system that automatically verifies
all design rules and produce the corresponding assessment report is fundamental. Such software system is addressed in this paper.

Keywords: Printed Circuit Board · Design collaboration
Rule-based design · Data exchange

This work was funded by the project "iFACTORY: Novas Capacidades de Indus-
trialização", with reference 002814 supported by FEDER trough "Portugal 2020
Programa Operacional Competitividade e Internacionalização" (COMPETE 2020).
This work has been supported by COMPETE: POCI-01-0145-FEDER-007043
and FCT - Fundação para a Ciência e a Tecnologia within the Project Scope:
UID/CEC/00319/2013.

© Springer International Publishing AG, part of Springer Nature 2018
J. Bajo et al. (Eds.): PAAMS 2018 Workshops, CCIS 887, pp. 172–180, 2018.
https://doi.org/10.1007/978-3-319-94779-2_16

1   Introduction

In today's industry, considering the electronics area, one may consider the PCB the most common way of assembling electronic circuits [4]. These are made by one or more insulated layers in which several elements, like capacitors, resistances, and coils, are inserted. There are also copper patterns that connect these elements. The position of the elements is fundamental for the correct functioning of the PCB since these may cause various forms of errors into a circuit due, for example, to the electromagnetic interference or the heat that a component may induce in other. Thus, despite placing the elements in a PCB, designers must pay special attention to the electrical characteristics since these may interfere in the performance of the PCB, specially when considering high precision or high speed PCBs.

A successful development of a PCB may usually be seen as a PCB with a long living period. However, to achieve such goal there is the need of maintenance, repair and overhaul (MRO) services that must be provided by the manufacturer [13]. In the maintenance domain there are three identified applications, namely functional testing, obsolescence management and redesign processes. The former is related with the identification of errors and malfunctions, which is achieved through inspection processes. The obsolescence management defines the period, based for example on mathematical formulas, in which the manufacturer will keep a stock of spare parts of will give repair solutions for existing PCBs. The later addresses overhauling processes where the initial PCB layout may be adapted, modified or completely redesigned. In this step, outdated components must be replaced by renewed developments. This is used whenever a potentially appropriate spare part is obsolete [13]. The MRO processes of electronic devices are specially challenging in companies that have long-term products like aviation industry, rail transport or plant manufacturing [7]. The functionality of a PCB must be tested and possible faults must be detected and repaired. When facing an obsolete PCB and there are not any spare parts available, redesign is the only alternative, which may be time consuming and have high costs.

To avoid the completely redesign processes after the manufacturing process and to reduce MRO services that may be needed, a good PCB layout design must be assured.

The manufacturing process of a PCB includes different stakeholders, which includes multidisciplinar teams that may be internal teams of the company, but also external teams that may manufacture the PCB and assemble its components. There is also the possibility of having internal teams over different countries according to the affiliates of the company. Each stakeholder has his own interest in particular parts of the PCB design and use different data to validate the design. The correct exchange of information is extremely important [12] in order to maintain a good involvement of all parts.

Despite the features of ECAD tools, the number of rules and constraints that need to be manually verified is high. Indeed, these tools are not able to completely check the conformity of the PCB design and layout. Some of these rules have to be manually verified by a company collaborator, which may lead to deviations in the design. The design rules are usually structured in extensive documents and may be difficult to assess. The non-verification of all design rules does not prevent the physical manufacture of the PCB. However, when not considering the machinery constraints in the design rules, the large scale production may be compromised, since the robotic arm that, for example, assembly a component may not have sufficient room to operate. The existence of standards or ontologies to define the design rules may be considered an important step for the layout design since it may structure every required rule.

In this paper it is described a tool that is able to automatically verify the rules for producing the PCB. The non-conformity of the PCB with the rules does not mean that the PCB may not be physically produced. The conformity with the existing rules assure that the PCB may be mass produced by the company using the existing machinery.

This paper is organized as follows: Sect. 2 presents a short review on PCB design, specifically in the data exchange between different teams. Section 3 briefly describes current practices for modeling rules. In Sect. 4 is presented the system that automatically verifies the layout of the PCB according to the defined guidelines. Finally, in Sect. 5 the main conclusions are drawn.

2   PCB Design

Considered as the basic component in the electronic products, the design of a PCB is extremely important since it also allows for a modular architecture of the products. The large scale production of a PCB is preceded by a design and evaluation phases where the layout of the PCB is defined and tested in order to assess if it complies with the company guidelines. This process involves several stakeholders and each one evaluates different aspects of the PCB. Figure 1 is

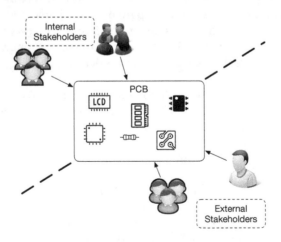

Fig. 1. Schematic of teams (internal and external to the company) involved in the PCB design process

a schematic of all partners involved in the layout design. Indeed, the exchange of information between team is crucial, but, due to the assessed features, the type of format used by each may significantly vary. Indeed, as Abrantes et al. describe in [3], there is a large set of formats which, if not correctly transmitted and treated, may led to the loss of information when sending the results from one team to another.

Abrantes et al. [3] studied and compared different ECAD file formats considering the PCB objects and their properties. Despite the development of neutral ECAD files formats, there is still a low adoption of such standards by ECAD tool vendors [6]. Thus, there are, for example proprietary ECAD file formats, IDF (Intermediate Data Format) [9], IDX (Incremental Data eXchange), STEP AP210 [10], ODB++ [1], and IPC - 2581 [8]. Abrantes et al. [3] concluded that there is a lack of standardization and the attempts to create one have failed since they were not adopted by ECAD tool developers.

3   Rule Modeling

Design rules for manufacturing process define the set of constraints that need to be checked and met in order to produce a PCB. These rules, primarily defined under the form of check lists have been progressively converted and included in automated processes through CAD/CAM systems. According to the specificity of the analysis of the PCB, the development of such rules is usually limited to software tools that included them in a hard coded manner. There are also other proprietary approaches like the one developed by Boeing [10] or Samsung [11]. Here, the rules are coded and the applications/systems developed in accordance with the necessities and specificities of each PCB.

As described by Abrantes et al. [2] there are different rule-based practices according to the application domain. Indeed, the lack of a standardization due to,

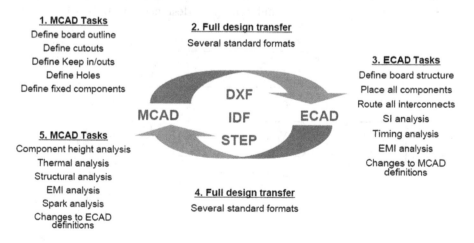

Fig. 2. Concurrent engineering between ECAD and MCAD, retrieved from [5]

for example, companies competitiveness, turns the development of ECAD tools to be domain specific (Fig. 2). In [2], the authors developed an ontology through which they were able to convert the process rule documents into rules written in natural language form. Though the definition of this ontology the rules have to be written with the same structure, removing possible deviations when one tries to read and understand long and exhaustive documents. This ontology was previously created by the research team and through it an ECAD tool (described in Sect. 4) that automatically verifies the PCB layout design is being developed. This system improves the verification coverage that is currently supported by the adopted ECAD tools and reduces the need of human inspection.

4   Rule Assessment Tool

The manufacture of a PCB is preceded by a complex and long process involving multiple stakeholders, which may be part of the same company or from an external one. This process, the design of the PCB, needs a collaborative activity over these different teams since each deals and assess different parts of the PCB. For this process there are multiple tools that, with the information stored in a database or inserted by the operator, assist in the decision process by providing an analysis of the PCB design. The exchange of information between Mechanical Computer-Aided Design (MCAD) and ECAD is essential to ensure the correct design of the PCB [5,10], but the lack of a standardization turn this a hard process.

The integration of ECAD/MCAD may be seen as being complementary to each other, since electrical design may be dependent on the mechanical one and vice-versa. Indeed, the physical layout is a balance between the space available between components and the mechanical constraints, considering the size of the components of the PCB [5].

Considering the physical layout of the PCB it is important to ensure that the available machinery is able to manufacture the designed PCB. To this process

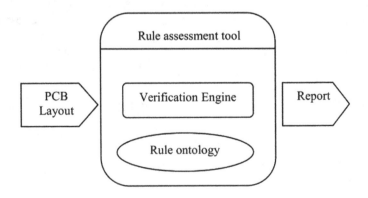

Fig. 3. Overview of the rule assessment tool, extracted from [2]

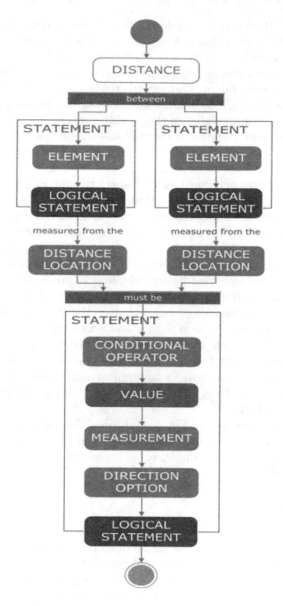

Fig. 4. Distance rule category model, retrieved from [2]

there is a large set of constraints that have to be met. The developed assessment tool may be fundamental to support the decision of the engineer since it may evaluate a large set of constraints in the PCB layout, i.e., before creating the physical PCB.

Adopted ECAD/MCAD tools by the company, in which the rule assessment tool is under development, allow the parametrization of some parameters in the pre-existent rules. However, these rules are mainly focused in the PCB concept, i.e., in assessing if the PCB that is being developed will operate correctly. Available tools may not consider the design constraints and the mass production of such PCBs may be compromised since the user cannot manually add such particular manufacturing constraints. Through the rule assessment tool one, according to the authorization levels, may add design rules considering not only the clients' requisites, but constraints related to the available machinery.

Figure 3 presents an overview of the rule assessment tool. During the design phase of the PCB the engineer inputs the current PCB layout into the system that, considering the rules defined through the ontology and the verification engine, verifies if every component, with respect to that PCB, is in accordance with the defined guidelines. After the verification process, the tool generates a report identifying the guidelines that are violated. Using the rule assessment tool the iterative process of designing a PCB may be reduced since a higher number of violated guidelines is identified in earlier stages of the development process. The overall costs may also be reduced since the human error is mitigated and possible deviations are identified before the physical production of the PCB.

To increase the functionality of the tool and also to better understand and create guidelines, there is a rule ontology that establishes the parameters of the guidelines. This may also be seen as a standardization of existing guidelines, removing possible mistakes in existing documents due to, for example, a missing necessary parameter that had to be defined. The rule ontology as been defined in [2]. The rule assessment tool provides a graphical user interface to generate rules considering the defined ontology. It is assumed that all rules may be represented using the same ontology.

The example depicted in the Fig. 4 establishes the ontology for the distance rule category. In this case the user has to define the distance between elements, stating that it must be, for example, equal (conditional operator) to 5 (value) mm (measurement).

5   Conclusion

The PCB design is essential for a successful manufacturing process. Indeed, being this one of the basic component of electronic devices, it is of the most importance that when produced in a large scale, the PCB respects all constraints and all rules regarding its manufacturing process. When one or both situations occur, then the producing costs will increase due to scrap or to rework to rectify the already produced PCBs.

ECAD tools assist in the electronic design and automatically check a set of design rules with respect to the available guidelines. MCAD tools are also an important set of tools since through them is possible to establish the physical layout of the PCB. However, the exchange of information between these different tools, even when considering several ECAD tools, may not be an easier process due to a lack of data standardization and proprietary software. Indeed, not all rules are automatically verified by such tools and there is the need of a human visual inspection. This manual process is prone to human error, which may increase the manufacture process due to the late detection of a deviation.

With the development of the assessment tool there is a double goal: develop an ontology and automatically verify the PCB guidelines. With the former is possible to ensure that all guidelines are identically structured, leading to a standardization inside the organization. This may also reduce deviations when reading and interpreting existing documentation. Through the later is possible to assist in the PCB design since a broader set of rules is automatically verified in the design process, i.e., before the PCB manufacturing process. Thus, using the assessment tool the stakeholder may take better decisions since the system indicates which guidelines are not met or which component locations should be checked. The human error is reduced since the number of checked rules is greater and, consequently, the overall costs are reduced.

References

1. ODB++ Specification v7.0. Mentor Graphics Corporation (2010). https://www.odb-sa.com/wp-content/uploads/ODB_Format_Description_v7.pdf
2. Abrantes, R., Basto, M., Varajao, J., Magalhaes, L., Ribeiro, P., Freitas, L.C.: Rule ontology for automatic design verification application to PCB manufacturing and assembly. In: IECON 2017 - 43rd Annual Conference of the IEEE Industrial Electronics Society, pp. 3403–3409. IEEE, October 2017. https://doi.org/10.1109/IECON.2017.8216576, http://ieeexplore.ieee.org/document/8216576/
3. Abrantes, R., Silva, A.M., Varajao, J., Magalhaes, L., Ribeiro, P., Freitas, L.C.: Data exchange format requirements and analysis collaboration in PCB design. In: IECON 2017 - 43rd Annual Conference of the IEEE Industrial Electronics Society, pp. 3413–3418. IEEE, October 2017. https://doi.org/10.1109/IECON.2017.8216578, http://ieeexplore.ieee.org/document/8216578/
4. Bryant, J.: PCB design issues. In: Op Amp Applications Handbook, pp. 629–652. Elsevier (2005). https://doi.org/10.1016/B978-075067844-5/50150-8. http://linkinghub.elsevier.com/retrieve/pii/B9780750678445501508
5. Chen, K., Schaefer, D.: MCAD-ECAD integration: overview and future research perspectives. In: Design and Manufacturing, vol. 3, pp. 123–132. ASME (2007). https://doi.org/10.1115/IMECE2007-41705, http://proceedings.asmedigitalcollection.asme.org/proceeding.aspx?articleid=1598857
6. Gielingh, W.: An assessment of the current state of product data technologies. Comput.-Aided Des. **40**(7), 750–759 (2008). https://doi.org/10.1016/j.cad.2008.06.003. http://linkinghub.elsevier.com/retrieve/pii/S0010448508001139
7. Grosser, H., Beckmann-Dobrev, B., Politz, F., Stark, R.: Computer vision analysis of 3D scanned circuit boards for functional testing and redesign. In: Procedia CIRP - 2nd International Through-life Engineering Services Conference, vol. 11, pp. 229–233 (2013). https://doi.org/10.1016/j.procir.2013.07.040
8. IPC: IPC-2581B Generic Requirements for Printed Board Assembly Products Manufacturing Description Data and Transfer Methodology (2013). http://www.ipc.org/TOC/IPC-2581B.pdf
9. Kehmeier, D., Makoski, T.: Intermediate Data Format (IDF) Version 4.0. Intermedius Design Integration, LLC (1998). https://www.simplifiedsolutionsinc.com/images/idf_v40_spec.pdf

10. Smith, G.L.: Utilization of STEP AP 210 at The Boeing Company (2002). https://doi.org/10.1016/S0010-4485(01)00190-7
11. Son, S., Na, S., Kim, K., Lee, S.: Collaborative design environment between ECAD and MCAD engineers in high-tech products development. Int. J. Prod. Res. (2014). https://doi.org/10.1080/00207543.2014.918289
12. Song, I.H., Chung, S.C.: Web-based CAD viewer with dimensional verification capability through the STEP translation server. J. Mech. Sci. Technol. (2007). https://doi.org/10.1007/BF03179040
13. Stark, R., Grosser, H., Beckmann-Dobrev, B., Kind, S.: Advanced technologies in life cycle engineering. In: Procedia CIRP - 3rd International Conference on Through-life Engineering Services, pp. 3–14 (2014). https://doi.org/10.1016/j.procir.2014.07.118

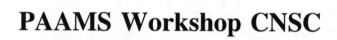

PAAMS Workshop CNSC

ABIBA: An Agent-Based Computing System for Behaviour Analysis Used in Human-Agent Interaction

Can Cui[1]($\boxtimes$), Dave Murray-Rust[2], David Robertson[1], and Kristin Nicodemus[3]

[1] School of Informatics, The University of Edinburgh, Edinburgh, UK
c.cui@ed.ac.uk, dr@inf.ed.ac.uk
[2] School of Design, The University of Edinburgh, Edinburgh, UK
[3] Institute of Genetics and Molecular Medicine, The University of Edinburgh, Edinburgh, UK

Abstract. We build an agent-based system for supporting correlation analysis between human behavioural and non-behavioural patterns. A novel social norm specification language is leveraged to create an interaction model based communication engine for choreographing distributed systems, offering a communication environment for multiple interacting players. Categorising sets of players based on their interaction behaviours allows labelling the other patterns, which the system uses to further its understanding relationship between the two traits. While existing analysis methods are manually applied, non-user-editable and typically opaque, the system offers an end-to-end computing framework and protocols which are modifiable for specific users. Evaluation for this system relies on tests for categories of people who are mentally depressed, where traditional questionnaire-based methods are superseded by methods that use more objective behavioural tests. This approach to evaluation through behavioural experimentation is intended not only to classify sub-types of depression cases which would facilitate elucidation of aetiology but evaluates system performance in a real-world scenario.

Keywords: Multiagent system · Social norm · Interaction simulation
Behaviour analysis · Human-agent interaction
Computational psychiatry

1 Introduction

In this work, we leverage social norms to propose a novel agent-based framework for human-agent interaction analysis. Social norms are the customary rules that govern individuals' social behaviours. The concept of social norms is suitable for building agent-based system because the agents have to follow basic rules of interactions to complete certain cooperate tasks. We use the Lightweight Coordination Calculus (LCC) introduced in [7] to specify the social norms. The multiagent systems traditionally use electronic institutions (and other forms of the

© Springer International Publishing AG, part of Springer Nature 2018
J. Bajo et al. (Eds.): PAAMS 2018 Workshops, CCIS 887, pp. 183–195, 2018.
https://doi.org/10.1007/978-3-319-94779-2_17

executable social norm) to ensure that the behaviours of each agent stay within the confines of the appropriate social norm. In this work, by contrast, we have the principal (additional) purpose that we use electronic institutions to elicit behaviours from agents that can then be used to cluster and classify them into different sets. For this purpose, we build the Agent-based Interaction Behaviour Analysis System (ABIBA) which can manage multi-agent interactions analysis. The system is an end-to-end solution for the system users who plan analyse agents behavioural patterns through multi-agent interactions. The users can obtain the analysis results without mastering many topic unrelated engineering skills for building the interaction and collection platform. Their only job is to make experimental protocols which the system will follow to create agents and hold the interactions. Regarding agents' patterns analysis, the users can choose the system to do specific predesigned tasks or build the ones themselves from results from the previous interactions.

To show how reasoning for the behavioural analysis can be automated and, as proof of concept, we have started a case study in which our system is used to support the study about understanding the aetiology of Major Depressive Disorder (MDD). MDD is a clinically significant degree of depression that is highly prevalent in the population [12]. It's vital for the society to understand MDD further. Even though many works have made valuable contributions to the task, the traditional research methods are time-consuming for researchers to ascertain participants in the task experiment and analyse the data from various domains. The ABIBA system will help researchers more efficiently manage behavioural research and develop data analysis.

The remainder of the paper is structured as follow: After reviewing the related work in Sect. 2, we present details about ABIBA system in Sect. 3. In Sect. 4 we explain the behaviour experiments focused on MDD including experimental instruments, experimental protocols and behavioural analysis.

2   Related Work

Most existing works on normative multi-agent system area focus on building framework demonstrating agents to behave under social norms while the purpose of our work is to analyse the emergent behaviours of agents when they interact with each other. [3] uses model checking approaches to verify agents' behaviours against predefined models, [1] concentrates on evaluating BDI agent design against the requirements. These approaches typically concentrated on testing, debugging and verification of multi-agent system [9] which only verify the multi-agent system is working properly while we need to abstract behavioural features from agents interaction for further analysis. Although work like [10] is closer to part of our work that they obtain agents' behavioural features by building a context model from agent interaction protocols, its purpose is still different from us. [10] is presenting a novel mechanism based on agent communication languages and interaction protocols for describing agents' behavioural features, but we focus on proposing an agent-based computing framework which aims to explore the relationship between their behavioural and non-behavioural patterns.

Regarding the analysis of the relationship between human behavioural features and MDD conditions, [11] exploits users' actions on social media to build an MDD prediction model, [2] explores the connection between depression and non-behavioural information. These contributions reveal several insights regarding characteristics of people with MDD, which can give inspiration to the analysis part of our work. But they do not take advantage of social norms appeared in interactions to analyse participants' behaviours. Differently, our system takes advantages of the norm specifications to analyse people's behavioural patterns. Some works try to analyse people's behavioural traits in ultimatum game which is carried out in our case study: [5] evaluates MDD's impact on decision-making in the ultimatum game, [6] explore people's genomic features variants on decision making in the ultimatum game. These studies have a weakness that once the researchers need to analyse new behavioural traits, they have to rebuild whole experiment system. Our method will give a practical, efficient, end-to-end solution for researchers to design behaviour experiment and analysis between samples' behavioural and non-behavioural patterns. The following sections present more details about ABIBA system and behaviour experiment.

3 ABIBA (Agent-Based Interaction Behaviour Analysis) System

3.1 System Computing Framework

ABIBA system is an automated, end-to-end, agent-based behaviour analysis system. It provides tools for the designers to make experiment protocols which describe agents' behaviour rules. The system will create several agents following the designers' protocol. Then the human players will control some of the agents to interact with other agents which are controlled by the system. The system leverages statistical analysis techniques like principal component analysis, correlation analysis and co-training methods to extract valuable information from collected interaction behaviours and classify agents into different clusters. Besides, the system can use data mining techniques to describe relationships between agents' behavioural patterns and non-behavioural traits like genomic information. Although in the case study, the system applies the analysis on the agents controlled by human players, the targeted agents can also be other entities like machines in industrial systems.

Figure 1 shows the system's working framework. There are two tasks the system will complete: sample analysis (shown in the bottom left light blue square) and population application. Sample analysis includes three steps: interaction data analysis, non-behavioural data analysis and relationship analysis. Interaction data analysis consists of interaction data collection and interaction data analysis. The two parts are carried out automatically by the interaction analysis subsystem. The system users will design interaction protocols which the system follows to maintain multi-agent interactions. The protocols define agents' behavioural rules like the agents' actions, actions' triggering constraints and

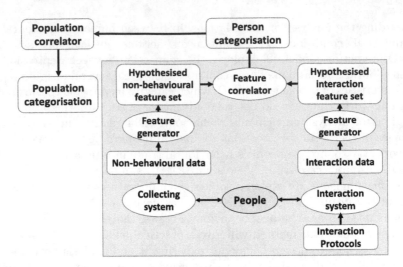

Fig. 1. ABIBA system working framework (Color figure online)

agents' state transformation condition. Sections 3.2 and 4.3 gives more details about the two concepts. Then the system follows the protocols to create multiple agents who follow the protocols to interact with each other. Finally, the interaction analysis subsystem will store agents' actions, extract their behaviour features for categorising them into subsets. Regarding non-behavioural patterns analysis, the system reads interaction players' non-behavioural patterns and extract typical features from these patterns. The system will explore the relationship between the two kinds of patterns like building a statistical classifier. The next section will explain the essential concepts in LCC.

3.2   Lightweight Coordination Calculus

Lightweight Coordination Calculus (LCC) [4,8] is a comparatively simple but flexible, practical, executable specification language. We use it to design interaction protocols specifying multi-agent interaction. LCC is the first process calculi defining social norm used directly in the computation of multi-agent system [7].

To let readers better some critical concepts of LCC calculus used in ABIBA, we need to firstly sketch a framework for describing the multi-agent interaction in our system. The multi-agent interactions are presented as dialogic activities, called "scenes", involving different groups of agents playing various roles. The roles' descriptions are made in electronic institutions which define the roles' identities, their behavioural rules in the form of interaction protocols. In each activity, each agent follows its role's protocol to interact with others. Before agent makes any action, it will check if the action is allowed by their behavioural rules. We use LCC as specification description tool to design the protocols. If the readers want to explore more details about LCC [7,8] will be helpful by giving comprehensive explanations about LCC syntax, computing framework and application examples. An example of LCC implementation is shown in Fig. 2. It's a part of the protocol used in our case study experiment which defines a role "proposer":

```
a(proposer(Total),P)::=
    offer(X)=>a(responder(Total),R)<--e(offernum(X, R))
    then
    decide(D,X)<=a(responder(Total),R)
    then
    k(fair(D,X,Total,R)).
```

Fig. 2. LCC implementation of the proposer in ultimatum game protocol

The protocol presents two sorts of information:

1. Role's information: LCC protocol uses "a(N(V), I)" to define role's information, "N" is the role's name, "V" is the role's trait and "I" is the role's identity. Figure 2 uses "a(proposer(Total),P)" to define a role with name("proposer"), trait("Total") and an identity("P").
2. Role's interaction actions: LCC protocol defines the role's actions in a form of exchanging messages: "M(X)=>a(N(V), I)<-e(Y)". "M(X)" is the message, "M" is its name, "X" is its content. "=>" means sending a message and "<=" stands for receiving a message. Sometimes the role has to satisfy a constraint to make an action. The constraint is "e(Y)" following "<-". In Fig. 2, the role will firstly send a message when the constraint "e(offernum(X, R))" is satisfied. "then" is a state connector which defines the relationship between the actions. In Fig. 2, the proposer will get the message, "decide(D, X)" from the responder after sending the offer message. Sometimes a role obtains new knowledge, "k(L(X))", from the interaction. In Fig. 2, the role gets knowledge "k(fair(D, X, Total, R))" after it receives the reply message.

3.3   Interaction Analysis

Interaction Environment. Once the system user complete the interaction protocol, the system follows them to build an environment for multiple agents to interact. Figure 3 shows the structure of the interaction environment. The human players can join the interactions through their PC or mobile phones. We call data generated from the human-system interaction as "interaction data". The system transforms this kind of data into the "experimental data" for the system's interaction engine. The interaction engine is responsible for maintaining multi-agents interactions.

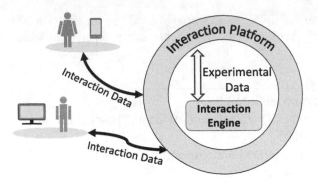

Fig. 3. Interaction environment

Interaction Engine. We have constructed an interaction engine based on LSCitter [4] inside the ABIBA system to manage multi-agent interactions. The engine follows the interaction protocol to create multiple virtual agents in a digital environment. Some of these agents, called "representative agents", are controlled by the entities from outside like human players in the case study. Whenever a virtual agent sends a message, the interaction engine will check the behavioural rule defined in the interaction protocols. In the case, the interaction engine will contact the human players about their choices. Once the engine receives the player's reply, the representative agents send the selected message. This is shown in Fig. 4.

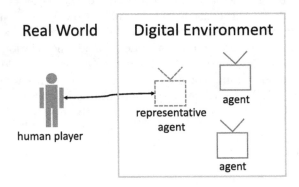

Fig. 4. The digital environment and the outside environment

The interaction engine has four parts: an agent engine, a protocol processor, a group communication unit and a server. Figure 5 shows the structure.

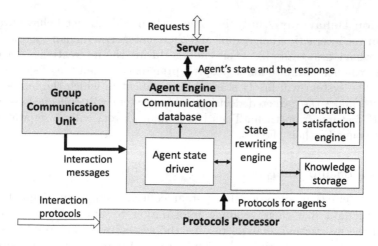

Fig. 5. Interaction engine structure

The agent engine is responsible for creating agents. There are following elements inside the engine:

1. A state rewriting engine which changes agent state as the interaction progresses.
2. An agent state driver which keeps track of where the agents are in any given interaction.
3. A constraint satisfaction engine which brings facts and knowledge into the interactions, base on which the rewriting engine can rewrite the agent's state.
4. A knowledge storage engine which allows the agent to store knowledge. It is mostly the same as the satisfaction engine but may be different particularly if different kinds of satisfaction and storage are used, and the precedence is different.
5. A communication database which stores the agent's sent and received messages in an interaction.

The protocol processor reads the interaction protocol files, then parses the files into the protocols which describe all roles' information and their actions. The agents will follow the protocol to communicate with each other. The group communication unit offers communication service which agent relies on to send and receive messages with each other.

The server in the interaction engine supports the communication between the engine and the outside environment. Take the case study as an example, each time a representative has to send a message, the agent engine will follow the protocols to send a request to the server about the human player's choice. Then the server contacts a web browser used by the player. When the player makes a response like submitting a number, the browser replies interaction engine and waits for the new request from the engine. Then the server reads the reply and sends a response to the agent engine. Finally, the representative agent sends the message with the input information.

Interaction Behaviour Analysis. The system will extract behavioural features from the interaction behaviour, and then, categorise human samples based on their behavioural traits like their choices during the interactions. For example, the researcher wants to know people's preferences when they face a specific problem. The system will firstly start an experiment in which the human players have to make the targeted decisions. The system will collect these inputs and create features from them. Then the human players will be separated into different groups by their choices.

3.4 Relationship Analysis

After the interaction analysis, the system collects human participants' non-behavioural data like their genomic information to build new feature sets. Based on the interaction analysis results, the system will explore the relationship between human participants' behavioural and non-behavioural traits. The aim of the relationship analysis is to build a behaviour prediction model with non-behavioural data as input and behavioural patterns as output. In the case study, the system clusters samples into different groups by extracting their typical behavioural patterns from their actions in the experiments; then it uses the behavioural patterns as labels to build a classifier with samples' non-behavioural information (genomic data in this case) as features. The classifier reads people's non-behavioural data and predicts their potential behaviour patterns without additional interaction experiments. In the next section, we will show more details about the case study including experimental participants, experimental process and experimental instruments.

4 Case Study

4.1 Experimental Participants

In collaboration with the MRC Institution of Genetics and Molecular Medicine (IGMM) in the College of Medicine Veterinary and Medicine who aims to break new ground in understanding the aetiology of MDD, the ABIBA system will support a behaviour experiment for the Generation Scotland cohort study (N = 21000).

4.2 Experimental Process

The ABIBA system will follow the protocols designed by the researchers and interact with the human participants. Then the system will analyse the relationship between participants' behavioural and non-behavioural patterns, consequently, provides the results to the researchers.

In the experiment, the researcher will firstly inform the human players about the game rules. Then the players choose their roles and exchange messages with other agents through the interfaces. There are two games for the players to play: the ultimatum game and the trust game.

The Ultimatum Game Rule. There are two roles in the ultimatum game: a proposer and a responder. At the beginning of the game, the proposer is given an amount of money. Then the proposer offers a part from the given money to the responder and waits for the reply. Finally, the responder accepts or rejects the offer. If the responder accepts the offer, it gets the amount of money, and the proposer gets the rest; if not, they will get nothing. For example, the proposer was given £10 and offers £5 to the responder. If the responder chooses to accept it, the responder gets £5, and the proposer gets the left £5; if the responder rejects the offer, they get nothing.

The Trust Game Rule. There are also two players in the trust game: an investor and a trustee. Firstly, the investor receives some money like £10. Then, the investor gives some amount to the trustee, say £4. Then the offer will be multiplied by a factor, like 3. The trustee will get the tripled offer, £12 in this case. Finally, the trustee repays a part of £12 to the investor, such as £3. Consequently, the investor gets £9 $(9 = 10-4+3)$ and the trustee gets £9 $(9 = 4*3-3)$.

4.3 Experimental Instrument

Game Interface. Human participants will use the Generation Scotland website to as interface to play the game. Figure 6 shows how the interaction works: At first, the agent engine sends a state request to the server inside the interaction engine. The request is about the amount the "proposer's offer". Then the server sends a request to the web browser. The web page presents "How much do you want to offer?" and waits for the human player to enter their answer. The player enters the number into the text box and submits it. The web browser sends a request to the interaction engine. Then the server translates the request into

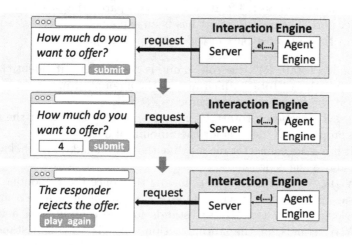

Fig. 6. Interactions in the ultimatum game

an understandable message for the agent engine. After reading the message, the agent engine drives the proposer agent to send a message to the responder agent. When the interaction engine gets the reply from the responder agent, it shows the reply on the web page, in Fig. 6 the reply is "The responder rejects the offer".

Game Protocols. The ABIBA system will follow the game protocol to organise the experiment. Section 3.2 has given an example of the protocol written by LCC. In the following part of this section, we will introduce the protocols used in the case study. Figures 7 and 8 are the two protocols:

```
a(proposer(Total),P)::=
offer(X)=>a(responder(Total),R)<--e(offernum(X, R))
then
decide(D,X)<=a(responder(Total),R)
then
k(fair(D,X,Total,R)).

a(responder(Total),R)::=
offer(X)<=a(proposer(Total),P)
then
decide(D,X)=>a(proposer(Total),P)<--e(acceptornot(D, X)).
```

Fig. 7. The ultimatum game protocol

The ultimatum game protocol. The protocol is designed on the basis of the game rule mentioned in Sect. 4.2. It contains two parts: the proposer part and the responder part. The proposer part has been explained in Sect. 3.2, so we will only interpret the responder part in the below paragraph:

1. "a (responder(Total), R)": the role' name is "responder", its identity is "R", its characteristic is "Total" which means the amount of money given to the proposer at the beginning of the game.
2. "offer(X) <= a(proposer(Total), P)": the responder will wait for the message from the proposer. "X" stands for the amount of offer.
3. "then": it is a state connector means that the role should do the below action once the above one is done.
4. "k(get(Wi))< −−i(Wi is X*Rate)" means that once the responder receives the message about offer, it will compute the amount it will own and store the knowledge. "i(Wi is X*Rate)" stands for the computation action and "k(get(Wi))" stands for the storing action. "i()" is a symbol standing for computing action and "is" means assignment values from the right side to the left.

5. "decide(D, X) => a(proposer(Total), P) < −− e(acceptornot (D, X))": after the responder finishes the above actions, it reply to the proposer. When the responder satisfies the constraint "e(acceptornot (D, X))" by find true value for decision variable "D", it will send its decision message, "decide(D, X)", to the proposer.

The trust game protocol is shown in Fig. 8. In this protocol, there are also two roles, five actions and two constraints: the investor part: "a(investor(Total, Rate), I)" and "a(trustee(Rate), T)" define two the roles: an "investor" and a "trustee". "I" and "T" stand for identities of two roles. "Total" is the amount the investor gets at the beginning of the game. "Rate" is the times the investor's offer will be multiplied.

1. the investor part:
   (a) "offer(X) => a(trustee(Rate), T) < −− e(invest(X, T))": the investor will offer some money to the trustee when the constraint, "e(invest(X, T))", is satisfied. "X" stands for the number.
   (b) "repay(Y)<=a(trustee(Rate), T)": the investor waits for the reply form the trustee after sending the offer.
   (c) "k(own(Pi)) <− i(Pi is Total+(Y − X))": when the investor agent receives the repay message from the "trustee" agent, it will calculate the amount it finally has and store the amount.
2. the trustee part:
   (a) "offer(X) <= a(investor(_, Rate), I)": the trustee waits for the message from the investor.

```
a(investor(Total,Rate), I)::=
offer(X)=>a(trustee(Rate), T)<--e(invest(X, T))
then
repay(Y)<=a(trustee(Rate),T)
then
k(own(Pi))<--i(Pi is Total+(Y-X)).

a(trustee(Rate),T)::=
offer(X)<=a(investor(_,Rate),I)
then
k(get(Wi))<--i(Wi is X*Rate)
then
repay(Y)=>a(investor(_,Rate),I)<--e(repay(Y, I))
then
k(own(Pt))<--i(Pt is Wi-Y).
```

Fig. 8. The trust game protocol

(b) "k(get(Wi))<–i(Wi is X*Rate)": when it gets the message, it will calculate the total amount it gets, "i(Wi is X*Rate)".

(c) "repay(Y) => a(investor(_, Rate), I) < −− e(repay(Y, I))": once constraint, "e(repay(Y, I))", is satisfied, the trustee will repay to the investor by sending "repay(Y)". "Y" stands for the repay amount.

(d) "k(own(Pt)) <– i(Pt is Wi-Y)": after repaying the offer, the trustee will calculate the remaining amount and store the amount.

5   Following Work

In summary, he ABIBA system takes advantage of specification language LCC to offer an end-to-end solution for agent interaction behaviour analysis. It exploits social norm theory to build an agent interaction model for organising multiple player experiments. To test the system function and performance, we apply ABIBA to a case study about behaviour and biologic patterns analysis among people with MDD in cooperation with the IGMM and Generation Scotland. We will collect data starting with 200 people for a pilot study to be sure things run smoothly. We anticipate publishing the specific results of the behavioural experiments in a future paper since these will require detailed analysis concerning genotypic information.

References

1. Abushark, Y., Thangarajah, J., Miller, T., Harland, J., Winikoff, M.: Early detection of design faults relative to requirement specifications in agent-based models. In: Proceedings of the 2015 International Conference on Autonomous Agents and Multiagent Systems, AAMAS 2015, pp. 1071–1079. International Foundation for Autonomous Agents and Multiagent Systems, Richland (2015)
2. Kessler, R.C., van Loo, H.M., Wardenaar, K.J., Bossarte, R.M., Brenner, L.A., Cai, T., Ebert, D.D., Hwang, I., Li, J., de Jonge, P., Nierenberg, A.A., Petukhova, M.V., Rosellini, A.J., Sampson, N.A., Schoevers, R.A., Wilcox, M.A., Zaslavsky, A.M.: Testing a machine-learning algorithm to predict the persistence and severity of major depressive disorder from baseline self-reports. Mol. Psychiatry 21(10), 1366–1371 (2016)
3. Lomuscio, A., Qu, H., Raimondi, F.: MCMAS: an open-source model checker for the verification of multi-agent systems. Int. J. Softw. Tools Technol. Transf. 19(1), 9–30 (2017)
4. Murray-Rust, D., Robertson, D.: LSCitter: building social machines by augmenting existing social networks with interaction models (2014)
5. Radke, S., Schäfer, I.C., Müller, B.W., de Bruijn, E.R.: Do different fairness contexts and facial emotions motivate 'irrational' social decision-making in major depression? An exploratory patient study. Psychiatry Res. 210(2), 438–443 (2013)
6. Reuter, M., Felten, A., Penz, S., Mainzer, A., Markett, S., Montag, C.: The influence of dopaminergic gene variants on decision making in the ultimatum game. Front. Hum. Neurosci. 7(June), 242 (2013)

7. Robertson, D.: A lightweight coordination calculus for agent systems. In: Leite, J., Omicini, A., Torroni, P., Yolum, I. (eds.) DALT 2004. LNCS (LNAI), vol. 3476, pp. 183–197. Springer, Heidelberg (2005). https://doi.org/10.1007/11493402_11
8. Robertson, D.: Lightweight coordination calculus for agent systems: retrospective and prospective. In: Sakama, C., Sardina, S., Vasconcelos, W., Winikoff, M. (eds.) DALT 2011. LNCS (LNAI), vol. 7169, pp. 84–89. Springer, Heidelberg (2012). https://doi.org/10.1007/978-3-642-29113-5_7
9. Serrano, E., Muñoz, A., Botia, J.: An approach to debug interactions in multi-agent system software tests. Inf. Sci. **205**, 38–57 (2012)
10. Serrano, E., Rovatsos, M., Botía, J.A.: Data mining agent conversations: a qualitative approach to multiagent systems analysis. Inf. Sci. **230**, 132–146 (2013)
11. Shickel, B., Heesacker, M., Benton, S., Rashidi, P.: Hashtag healthcare: from tweets to mental health journals using deep transfer learning, pp. 1–10 (2017)
12. The National Institute for Health and Care Excellence: Depression: The NICE Guideline on the Management of Depression in Adults (2009)

Using Crowdsourcing
for the Development of Online Emotional
Support Agents

Lenin Medeiros[(✉)] and Tibor Bosse

Behavioural Informatics Group, Vrije Universiteit Amsterdam,
De Boelelaan 1081, 1081 HV Amsterdam, Netherlands
{l.medeiros,t.bosse}@vu.nl

Abstract. This paper describes several steps towards the development
of an online agent (or socialbot) that provides emotional support to
stressed users. In particular, we present an empirical study that was
conducted with the aim to investigate how people help each other to
cope with stressful situations via online social networks. To this end,
around 10.000 tweets about stressful situations were collected. Then,
using crowdsourcing, these tweets were classified into stress categories,
and supportive replies to them were collected, which were also classified into categories. Contingency tables were constructed in order to
explore which types of support were most frequently used in which circumstances. The resulting values can be used as parameters for a previously developed algorithm that automatically constructs support messages. This allows our agent to generate supportive messages that are
more similar to the support messages that human beings send via social
media.

1 Introduction

From time to time, every human being is confronted with negative events such
as broken relationships, work problems, loss of family members or health issues.
These so-called 'everyday problems' are known to be important sources of stress
[1]. To help people to cope with everyday stress, emotional support from peers
seems to be a promising means [2]. A specific type of emotional support is
Computer-Mediated Emotional Support (CMES). Through CMES, large numbers of people use the Internet to seek and provide emotional support for their
everyday problems [3–5]. Nearly 40% of all American Internet users seek support
from online peers [6].

One of the most frequent forms of CMES is the use of online social networks
[7], since this type of support only requires sending a short text message at
appropriate moments. Indeed, sharing problems and showing affection are some
of the most common reasons why people use social media [8].

Nevertheless, when using social media, helpful emotional support is not
always available. Some people simply have fewer friends than others and, besides

© Springer International Publishing AG, part of Springer Nature 2018
J. Bajo et al. (Eds.): PAAMS 2018 Workshops, CCIS 887, pp. 196–209, 2018.
https://doi.org/10.1007/978-3-319-94779-2_18

that, users do not always want to share their problems online, in particular when these problems are very personal. Finally, peers are sometimes reluctant to provide support, as people who provide emotional support are more vulnerable to developing stress-related complaints themselves, as suggested in [9].

To deal with these issues, the use of *Computer-Generated Emotional Support* (CGES) in online social networks is an interesting possibility. This paper is part of a project that explores the pros and cons of this solution. To this end, the concept of 'artificial friends' is introduced: social agents that help people deal with their 'everyday problems' via social media. The idea is that these agents analyze text messages that people share online, and generate appropriate responses to these messages with the purpose of comforting them and alleviating their stress. This vision was inspired by a number of promising recent initiatives regarding support agents in other domains, such as bullying [10].

As a first step in that direction, we developed a prototype of such an artificial friend in the form of a chatbot for the Telegram Messenger App [11]. This prototype consists of three main modules which are intended to: (1) process text messages based on keyword search and classifies them into categories of problems, (2) select appropriate support strategies based on psychological theories of emotion regulation, and (3) generate appropriate responses based on the output of the first two modules. The acceptability of the agent has been evaluated in a pilot study, with promising results. Nevertheless, the pilot study also led to the conclusion that there was room for improvement of the agent's algorithms to classify incoming messages and generate appropriate response messages, probably due to the ad hoc implementation of these modules [12].

Therefore, the purpose of the current paper is to gain more precise insight in (1) the types of problems that people share via online social networks, and (2) the types of strategies people use to help each other cope with these problems. To achieve this, a series of crowdsourcing experiments is conducted, and the data obtained through the experiments are systematically analyzed (cf. [13]). In the future, we will use these results to improve the agent's algorithms in such a way that it generates support that better resembles the peer support provided by real social media users. Assuming that this type of support is appreciated more than the ad hoc support messages used so far, this endeavor is expected to improve the acceptability of our artificial friend.

The remainder of this paper is structured as follows. Section 2 reviews the existing literature in the area of (both Computer-Mediated and Computer-Generated) Emotional Support. Section 3 presents the design of the crowdsourcing experiment conducted to acquire the relevant data to improve our agent. The results of the experiment are presented in Sect. 4. Finally, Sect. 5 concludes the paper with a discussion.

2   Related Work

2.1   Emotional Regulation

The main theory underlying our research is proposed by Gross [14], who defines *emotional regulation* as the process people undertake to regulate their own emotional responses to a given (mostly negative) stimulus. In his work, five different emotional regulation strategies are identified, of which four are used in this work [15]: (1) *situation selection* (SS) – to select situations based on how likely they will lead to undesired emotional states, (2) *situation modification* (SM) – to modify situations to make them less likely to lead to undesired emotional states, (3) *attentional deployment* (AD) – to avoid thinking about potential stressful situations and (4) *cognitive change* (CC) – to think about a given situation from a different perspective (i.e. re-interpret the situation) in order to modify its emotional significance. The current paper addresses a study to check to what extent people use such techniques, in an interpersonal way, in order to provide emotional support to their peers. Inspired by Heaney et al. [2], we add a fifth strategy in our research [16], namely *general emotional support* (GES) – "to provide support by only providing empathy, love, trust and/or caring". This strategy is assumed to be always applicable.

2.2   Computer-Mediated Emotional Support

Peer support or peer-to-peer support, as defined by Kim et al. [17], is the process in which people with strong social ties seek for and send supportive information to each other. Often, this happens within social networks (e.g., groups of friends). It has been shown in previous works that this approach might lead to health promotion [2]. Some evidence of this was provided by Cohen and Wills [18] and Cobb [19], among others, who found a positive relation between social support and how people deal with stressful situations and their health-related consequences.

In some circumstances, for instance when support seekers have limited mobility, as suggested by Caplan and Turner [20], such a process might be mediated by software. For these cases, researchers often use the term *Computer-Mediated Emotional Support*, as mentioned in the previous section. Among many researchers, Braithwaite et al. [3] presented a model to explicate emotional distress reduction via CMES in people with disabilities; White and Dorman [21] performed a study on health-related on-line support groups; and Wright and Bell [5] and Walther and Boyd [4] performed literature reviews of research about on-line mutual support groups on the Internet, social support and computer-mediated communication. In sum, all of these studies conclude that CMES is a promising approach for providing emotional and empathic support to users that are seeking for this.

2.3   Computer-Generated Emotional Support

In addition to using computers as mediators, in certain occasions it may be useful to create software that provides emotional support to humans directly. Gockley et al. [22], in their study on avatars that are able to socially interact with humans, address challenges regarding design decisions for systems that simulate real and functional characters building human-robot relationships. Indeed, empathic robots can make users more likely to see them as friends or colleagues, as demonstrated by Leite et al. [23].

For various target user groups, such as victims of cyberbullying [10], emotionally supporting agents have been developed before. The research conducted by Kindness et al. [13] deserves special mention since it shares some interesting similarities with our work. Like the current paper, the study by Kindness and colleagues also aims to find out which support strategies are most appropriate in which stressful situations, with the long-term aim to develop CGES. However, while we analyze so-called everyday problems (or daily-life stressful situations) and respective support messages via Twitter, in their work the context is Community First Responders (CFRs) dealing with medical emergencies. Therefore, their stressors are directly related to the ones experienced by CFRs while performing their tasks (e.g., time pressure or physical demand). In both works the main goal is to computationally generate emotional support messages tailored to stressors. While their support strategies are not directly based on the strategies by Gross [14], their set of support strategies can roughly be mapped to ours in the following way: (1) *emotional reflection* – GES, (2) *directed action* – SM, and (3) *praise, emotional advice* and *reassurance* – CC. Note that in their work there is no occurrence of AD and SM, since the stressed actors cannot stop facing the potential stressful situations because dealing with them is part of their tasks.

To summarize, our goal is to explore the possibilities of a socially interactive agent that is able to provide emotional support to stressed users that are experiencing daily-life stressful situations. Such support messages should be tailored to these situations. In the respective human-robot interaction, the user has to feel comfortable enough to share problems with a virtual agent. To do that, the approach taken in this paper is to create the supportive messages in such a way that they resemble the strategies used by human users. This does not mean that we claim that this is necessarily the optimal approach for dealing with stress. We are just investigating how to develop an intelligent piece of software, a chatbot (or *socialbot*), that would be able to provide the same kind of support messages to a stressed user as if it were one of his or her human peers. In the next section we describe the method to investigate how people seek for and provide online emotional support tailored to certain types of stressful situations.

3   Method

In order to better understand how people help each other to cope with stressful situations via social networks, an empirical study was conducted. All the data we collected during this research is available in a MongoDB hosting service (mLab)[1]. All the scripts we used to collect and analyze the data are also available[2].

3.1   First Experiment

In this experiment we were guided by the following question: What are the most common types of stressful situations shared by users via Twitter? We executed a Python script to collect data from Twitter via a query using some of the keywords presented in the bags of words used by our chatbot prototype. We used exactly 6 keywords for each stressful situation. We searched for tweets containing these keywords in combination with some negative sentiment represented by the string `":("` (i.e., a sad emoticon). For example, the string `"disease :("` was used as one of the query criteria to crawl potential tweets about health problems. We also searched for tweets containing keywords together with the string `"#stressed"`, indicating that the user is feeling stressed (e.g., `"girlfriend #stressed"`, returns potential tweets about relationship problems). The complete list of keywords we used to perform the queries is presented in Table 1. Hence, we executed 12 queries per stressful situation category. We also executed two final queries to search for tweets that do not contain any of the terms we used to collect the rest of the data (these tweets were supposed to be classified as 'other'). We put a threshold of 300 tweets per query. For each query the API returned tweets from a 7 days time window.

Table 1. Types of stressful situations and respective keywords.

Type of Situation	Keywords
Death	"died :(", "passed away :(", "rip :(", "rest in peace :(", "funeral :(", "death :(", "died #stressed", "passed away #stressed", "rip #stressed", "rest in peace #stressed", "funeral #stressed", "death #stressed"
Finances	"money :(", "debts :(", "salary :(", "expenses :(", "dollars :(", "euros :(", "money #stressed", "debts #stressed", "salary #stressed", "expenses #stressed", "dollars #stressed", "euros #stressed"
Health	"disease :(", "ill :(", "hospital :(", "sick :(", "diagnosed :(", "health :(", "disease #stressed", "ill #stressed", "hospital #stressed", "sick #stressed", "diagnosed #stressed", "health #stressed"
Relationships	"relationship :(", "girlfriend :(", "boyfriend :(", "wife :(", "husband :(", "crush :(", "relationship #stressed", "girlfriend #stressed", "boyfriend #stressed", "wife #stressed", "husband #stressed", "crush #stressed"
School	"exams :(", "test :(", "grade :(", "teacher :(", "studies :(", "school :(", "exams #stressed", "test #stressed", "grade #stressed", "teacher #stressed", "studies #stressed", "school #stressed"
Work	"work :(", "job :(", "project :(", "workload :(", "office :(", "boss :(", "work #stressed", "job #stressed", "project #stressed", "workload #stressed", "office #stressed", "boss #stressed"

---

[1] https://mlab.com/databases/collected_data_from_twitter.

[2] https://goo.gl/w49Zv3.

For each tweet, four questions were asked to the participants (see Fig. 1). First, we checked whether they could read and understand the tweet (question 1). After that, we requested participants to decide whether a given tweet was about a stressful situation (question 2) or not, and asked them to classify the stressful situation into one of the predefined categories (question 3). Each tweet was analyzed by three different participants. Only when all of them provided the same answers for both questions we considered a given tweet as useful. Question 3 was a multiple-choice question whose options were the stressful situation categories used to collect the tweets. When the answer was 'Other', the participant would have to inform us what was the classification, in his or her opinion, via an open text input. We ended up with around one thousand of tweets classified as useful. More details about the results are described in Sect. 4. We then took a subset of useful tweets as input for the experiment described in the next section.

1. Can you read and understand this tweet? I.e., is it available and written in English?
○ Yes
○ No

2. Would you classify this tweet as a description of a personal daily-life problem?
○ Yes
○ No

3. To which category does the problem shared in the tweet belong? Select one option from the list below.

- select one -	⬍

4. If you answered "Other" above, what would be the name of the new category?

Fig. 1. Questions asked in the first crowdsourcing experiment.

3.2   Second Experiment

The main research question of this second experiment was the following: How do people support their stressed friends via Twitter? We believe that, by answering this question, we could have insight into the types of support people use when helping their peers cope with stress on-line, as well as what are the most used support strategies for each type of stress. To achieve that, we performed another experiment using the resulting data from the first experiment. This second experiment was divided into two parts. For both parts we used 70 useful tweets per category according to what was stated in the previous section. We did not change the set of tweets among both parts, so all of the tweets passed trough the same procedure.

In the first part (see Fig. 2), participants were asked to read the tweets and think about how they would reply to them, as if they were posted by one of their peers, and select the option that was most suitable according to them. There were 5 options: one for each type of support strategy, as defined in Sect. 2.1. These options were based on the message templates used by our chatbot prototype, and were carefully created in such a way that they fit the five support strategies.

Each tweet was analyzed by two participants. We verified how many times a given support strategy was used for each one of the stressors, resulting in a contingency table. Then, based on this table, we performed chi-squared tests to check whether the distributions of these two variables (stressful situation and support strategy) were independent or not. Finally, an additional simulation-based analysis was conducted to find out whether the most frequently used strategy was used significantly more often than the other.

1. Can you read and understand this tweet? I.e., is it available and written in English?
○ Yes
○ No

2. If a friend of yours has shared this tweet with you, which of the following answers would be most appropriate in your opinion? Please, use 140 Characters at maximum.

> ✓ - select one -
> I'm so sorry to hear this from you. Take care!
> Think positively! I'm sure this situation will eventually make you stronger.
> Don't think too much about it. Let your mind be focused on other things!
> I'm sure you have other things to deal with, just put your energy there and avoid facing this situation!
> Try to think on how you could change this situation. I bet you'll manage to deal with it!

Fig. 2. Questions asked in the first part of the second crowdsourcing experiment (multiple choice questions).

In the second part (see Fig. 3) we only included participants that were not involved in the first trial described above. They were asked to read the tweets and to come up with replies via an open text input field. We did not provide any information to them, other than the tweets. Again, we took two different participants to process each tweet. Then, all the answers provided by them were classified via a final crowdsourcing process, in which (new) participants had to tag the replies using up to 5 labels (each label representing one of the support categories). They did this by relating the replies to the options from the first part of the experiment (see Fig. 4). In this case, again two different users processed the same message. As in the first part of the experiment, we also performed chi-squared tests and simulations. Then, we compared the results obtained from both parts of this second experiment. The results are reported in Sect. 4.

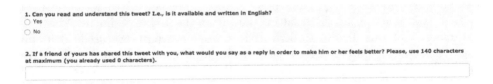

1. Can you read and understand this tweet? I.e., is it available and written in English?
○ Yes
○ No

2. If a friend of yours has shared this tweet with you, what would you say as a reply in order to make him or her feels better? Please, use 140 characters at maximum (you already used 0 characters).

Fig. 3. Questions asked in the second part of the second crowdsourcing experiment (open ended questions).

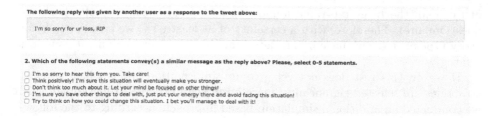

The following reply was given by another user as a response to the tweet above:

I'm so sorry for ur loss, RIP

2. Which of the following statements convey(s) a similar message as the reply above? Please, select 0-5 statements.

☐ I'm so sorry to hear this from you. Take care!
☐ Think positively! I'm sure this situation will eventually make you stronger.
☐ Don't think too much about it. Let your mind be focused on other things!
☐ I'm sure you have other things to deal with, just put your energy there and avoid facing this situation!
☐ Try to think on how you could change this situation. I bet you'll manage to deal with it!

Fig. 4. Questions asked to categorize the results of the open ended questions.

4   Results

After executing the first experiment, as stated in Sect. 3.1, we ended up with the following results (see Fig. 5): problems about school appeared as the most common type, followed by relationships and health. Then, we have death, work, and finances, respectively, as least common. We can relate the frequency of messages about school to the work performed by Smith and Brenner [24], among others, since they report that the majority of people that use Twitter is young (hence they are more likely to be part of educational environments). This might explain the difference with the results from the pilot study [16], which were not based on Twitter data: there, problems about relationships seemed to be the most common ones.

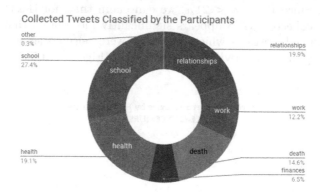

Fig. 5. Useful tweets classified by our participants in the first experiment.

We collected supportive replies to the tweets via crowdsourcing. We obtained the distribution of support categories over stressors presented in Figs. 6 and 7 for the first and the second experiments, respectively.

In order to check statistically if the support strategies, selected via both multiple-choice and open questionnaires, are correlated with the stressful situations, we performed chi-squared tests for each of the stressors. With 4 degrees of freedom, the biggest p-value found was 0.03 (relationships; multiple-choice questionnaire). Therefore, with a certainty of at least 95%, we can conclude for every type of stress we have in our data that there is a correlation with support strategy.

However, this test does not yet give any information about which support strategies are selected significantly more often than others. To investigate this, we conducted an additional simulation-based approach, according to the following logic. If both variables (type of stress and support strategy) were unrelated, then for each stressor, a given support strategy would be selected by the participants with a probability equal to 20% and 16.67%, for both questionnaires, respectively. We used this fact to analyze whether certain strategies were used significantly more than average by simulating this selection process 2 million times. Then, we counted, for each support category, how many times we obtained a value at least equal to the one we observed in our empirical data. If the mean was less than 5% (i.e., the significance level α of 0.05), we could say we found a statistically relevant number. As an example, for death, we randomly selected 134 support strategies (which is the total number of answers we collected for 'death' via crowdsourcing) 2 million times. In our experiment, GES was chosen as a support strategy for death 62 out of the 134 times (depicted by the green bar in the Death category in Fig. 6. However, in our simulation-based approach, the percentage of the 2 million simulations in which GES was selected at least 62 times was less than 1%. Similarly, the second most common support strategy in our observed data for death was AD, which was selected 31 times in the real experiment. In our simulations, this strategy was chosen more than 31 times in about 21%. Since $1\% < \alpha < 21\%$, we can claim that, for the tweets about death that we collected, GES appears significantly more often than any other type of support. All cases in which strategies were selected significantly more than average are highlighted via the red arrows in Figs. 6 and 7.

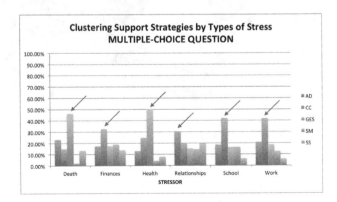

Fig. 6. Useful tweets classified by our participants in the first experiment. (Color figure online)

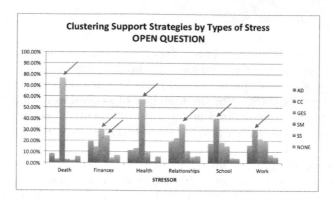

Fig. 7. Useful tweets classified by our participants in the second experiment. (Color figure online)

For the resultant data from the second part of the second experiment, after having the supportive replies analyzed by human users, we performed exactly the same tests and simulations as described above. Figure 7 presents the respective distributions of support strategies over stressful situations for this part of the experiment. Note that, since in this case the participants were allowed to select up to 5 tags for each supportive reply they had to analyze, in some cases they just did not select any tag, which is why the additional category NONE is included.

The most popular type of support for the majority of the types of stress is GES, which is clearly the most generic one. This was expected because people can always select this strategy if they are in doubt about the more specific strategies. However, for school and work we obtained a different result: CC. This may be explained by the fact that stressful situations in these domains are more open for different interpretations (e.g., 'you may lose this job, but there are probably much better jobs out there'). In addition, we also performed the simulation-based approach discussed before, to find out what are the the most frequent support strategies.

As we were also expecting, the number of times GES was selected was significant in all stressful situations, except for problems about school and work, which most significant support strategy was CC.

When we compare Figs. 6 and 7, via checking the red arrows, we clearly see that we can find at least one 'best' strategy for all the stressful situations, except for finances and relationships. This comparison is interesting because we can reduce any bias related to both selection processes of the support strategies, since they were performed by different sets of participants in different approaches (multiple-choice versus text input). Therefore we can claim that tweets about health and death, in our dataset, are more likely to receive replies using GES as supportive strategy. Tweets reporting problems about school or work are more likely to lead to CC. Finally, we could not draw any significant conclusions regarding the tweets about financial or relationships problems.

5   Discussion

The research discussed in this paper departed from the idea that intelligent agents can, under the right circumstances, play the role of a social companion that 'listens to' a person's problems and provides emotional support. Although this idea has been explored before in a number of studies, as in [13], research on how such support can be realized in the form of a chatbot on social media (or socialbot) is still in its infancy. One of the advantages of this approach is that such a system is relatively simple to develop (e.g., no sophisticated multi-modal interaction is required), while having access to large numbers of users and data. The main purpose of such a bot would be to identify users with mild signs of everyday stress, and help them in an initial phase of their problem, by providing them a platform where they can share their situation. Another use could be to bring them into contact with other social media users with similar problems.

The main achievement of the current paper is that we now have a clear overview of both stressful situations and respective support strategies that people typically share via social media and use to help their peers cope with these undesired life events. The most common stressful situation turned out to be typical 'everyday' topics like school, relationships, health and work, which confirms existing social science research about everyday stress [1]. To categorize the strategies, the choice was made to use the well-known emotion regulation strategies introduced by Gross [14] as categories. Although these strategies were originally introduced in the context of self-regulation, recently they have also been used in the context of inter-personal emotion management [25].

Based on empirical data about people's online behavior obtained via crowd-sourcing experiments, the relation between stressful situations and corresponding support strategies was studied. This has resulted in a better understanding of which types of emotional support people typically provide for which type of problem. For instance, general emotional support was found to be (by far) the most frequently used support strategy in case of problems related to death and health, whereas cognitive change was the most often used strategy in situations related to school and work. Finally, for finances and relationships, the results turned out to be more ambiguous, which suggests that these categories could be explored in more detail in the future (e.g., splitting them into sub-categories).

These results are useful from a Social Science as well as an Artificial Intelligence perspective. From a Social Science perspective, they provide more insight into the online (peer-support) behavior of social media users. From an AI perspective, the results provide useful information for further improvement of our support agent, and of CGES systems in general. In particular, the statistics found through the experiment could serve as starting point to fine-tune the support algorithm that is used in the current version of our chatbot. For example, in case the agent is faced with a user that shares a problem related to school, it could show preference to provide support via cognitive change. One of the challenges for future research is to test if such an algorithm increases acceptance of the agent, compared to the more ad hoc algorithm that is currently used [12].

Having said that, it is important to note that the aim so far is to create an agent that provides online support that is similar to the support that human beings provide. However, this does not necessarily mean that this type of support is most effective in alleviating people's stress. Indeed, human beings are not always perfect in providing emotional support [26], and the extent to which their support is effective depends on many factors. In fact, people's preference for certain messages may depend on individual characteristics (such as gender) as well as specific circumstances [27]. Therefore, it seems promising to enable the agent to personalize its strategies (e.g., to dynamically switch between them).

Also the method used to classify the messages could be improved in the future: for instance, unsupervised learning could be used to automatically cluster tweets about similar stressful situations. Additionally, we could check how people actually provide support, instead of asking them about what they would do. This analysis could be performed by looking at tweets people sent as replies to the messages we collected.

Other directions for follow-up research involve the use of more sophisticated algorithms to classify messages into stress categories. For instance, a Vector Space Model could be used to create a representation of the text in the messages. In addition, more sophisticated algorithms could be used to manage the conversation. As an example, instead of addressing only one-shot ('question-answer') interactions, more complex types of interaction could be explored, in order to make longer human-agent conversations possible. To this end, the notion of dialog trees and multiple choice interaction could be used, to keep the interaction manageable without restricting the user's freedom. Also, the conversation could be split into separate phases, as in done in [10]. In that work, the interaction between a user (a child who is victim of cyberbullying) and an 'artificial buddy' is split into five phases such as 'welcome' and 'gather information'.

Once the final version of the agent is available, a systematic evaluation will be conducted. This will be done both through usability studies (to investigate to what extent users accept emotional support from such a system) and by actually measuring its effectiveness in helping people cope with everyday stress.

Acknowledgements. The authors would like to thank the Brazilian government and to state that Lenin Medeiros' stay at VU Amsterdam was funded by Science without Borders/CNPq (reference number: 235134/2014-7).

References

1. Burks, N., Martin, B.: Everyday problems and life change events: ongoing versus acute sources of stress. J. Hum. Stress **11**(1), 27–35 (1985)
2. Heaney, C.A., Israel, B.A.: Social networks and social support. In: Health Behavior and Health Education: Theory, Research, and Practice, vol. 4, pp. 189–210 (2008)
3. Braithwaite, D.O., Waldron, V.R., Finn, J.: Communication of social support in computer-mediated groups for people with disabilities. Health Commun. **11**(2), 123–151 (1999)

4. Walther, J.B., Boyd, S.: Attraction to computer-mediated social support. In: Communication Technology and Society: Audience Adoption and Uses, pp. 153–188 (2002)
5. Wright, K.B., Bell, S.B.: Health-related support groups on the internet: linking empirical findings to social support and computer-mediated communication theory. J. Health Psychol. **8**(1), 39–54 (2003)
6. Fox, S.: Peer-to-peer Healthcare. Pew Internet & American Life Project (2011)
7. van Breda, W., Treur, J., van Wissen, A.: Analysis and support of lifestyle via emotions using social media. In: Aberer, K., Flache, A., Jager, W., Liu, L., Tang, J., Guéret, C. (eds.) SocInfo 2012. LNCS, vol. 7710, pp. 275–291. Springer, Heidelberg (2012). https://doi.org/10.1007/978-3-642-35386-4_21
8. Quan-Haase, A., Young, A.L.: Uses and gratifications of social media: a comparison of facebook and instant messaging. Bull. Sci. Technol. Soc. **30**(5), 350–361 (2010)
9. Medeiros, L., Sikkes, R., Treur, J.: Modelling a mutual support network for coping with stress. In: Nguyen, N.-T., Manolopoulos, Y., Iliadis, L., Trawiński, B. (eds.) ICCCI 2016. LNCS (LNAI), vol. 9875, pp. 64–77. Springer, Cham (2016). https://doi.org/10.1007/978-3-319-45243-2_6
10. van der Zwaan, J.M., Dignum, V., Jonker, C.M.: A conversation model enabling intelligent agents to give emotional support. In: Ding, W., Jiang, H., Ali, M., Li, M. (eds.) Modern Advances in Intelligent Systems and Tools, pp. 47–52. Springer, Heidelberg (2012). https://doi.org/10.1007/978-3-642-30732-4_6
11. Medeiros, L., Bosse, T.: An empathic agent that alleviates stress by providing support via social media. In: Proceedings of the 16th Conference on Autonomous Agents and MultiAgent Systems, pp. 1634–1636. International Foundation for Autonomous Agents and Multiagent Systems (2017)
12. Medeiros, L., Bosse, T.: Testing the acceptability of social support agents in online communities. In: Nguyen, N.T., Papadopoulos, G.A., Jędrzejowicz, P., Trawiński, B., Vossen, G. (eds.) ICCCI 2017. LNCS (LNAI), vol. 10448, pp. 125–136. Springer, Cham (2017). https://doi.org/10.1007/978-3-319-67074-4_13
13. Kindness, P., Masthoff, J., Mellish, C.: Designing emotional support messages tailored to stressors. Int. J. Hum Comput Stud. **97**, 1–22 (2017)
14. Gross, J.J.: Emotion regulation: affective, cognitive, and social consequences. Psychophysiology **39**(3), 281–291 (2002)
15. Gross, J.J.: Emotion Regulation: Conceptual and Empirical Foundations (2014)
16. Medeiros, L., Bosse, T.: Empirical analysis of social support provided via social media. In: Spiro, E., Ahn, Y.-Y. (eds.) SocInfo 2016. LNCS, vol. 10047, pp. 439–453. Springer, Cham (2016). https://doi.org/10.1007/978-3-319-47874-6_30
17. Kim, H.S., Sherman, D.K., Taylor, S.E.: Culture and social support. Am. Psychol. **63**(6), 518 (2008)
18. Cohen, S., Wills, T.A.: Stress, social support, and the buffering hypothesis. Psychol. Bull. **98**(2), 310 (1985)
19. Cobb, S.: Social support as a moderator of life stress. Psychosom. Med. **38**(5), 300–314 (1976)
20. Caplan, S.E., Turner, J.S.: Bringing theory to research on computer-mediated comforting communication. Comput. Hum. Behav. **23**(2), 985–998 (2007)
21. White, M., Dorman, S.M.: Receiving social support online: implications for health education. Health Educ. Res. **16**(6), 693–707 (2001)
22. Gockley, R., Bruce, A., Forlizzi, J., Michalowski, M., Mundell, A., Rosenthal, S., Sellner, B., Simmons, R., Snipes, K., Schultz, A.C., et al.: Designing robots for long-term social interaction. In: 2005 IEEE/RSJ International Conference on Intelligent Robots and Systems, (IROS 2005), pp. 1338–1343. IEEE (2005)

23. Leite, I., Pereira, A., Mascarenhas, S., Martinho, C., Prada, R., Paiva, A.: The influence of empathy in human-robot relations. Int. J. Hum Comput Stud. **71**(3), 250–260 (2013)

24. Smith, A., Brenner, J.: Twitter use 2012. Pew Internet & American Life Project, vol. 4 (2012)

25. Williams, M.: Building genuine trust through interpersonal emotion management: a threat regulation model of trust and collaboration across boundaries. Acad. Manag. Rev. **32**(2), 595–621 (2007)

26. Burleson, B.R.: Emotional support skills. In: Handbook of Communication and Social Interaction Skills, pp. 551–594 (2003)

27. Spottswood, E.L., Walther, J.B., Holmstrom, A.J., Ellison, N.B.: Person-centered emotional support and gender attributions in computer-mediated communication. Hum. Commun. Res. **39**(3), 295–316 (2013)

On "Influencers" and Their Impact on the Diffusion of Digital Platforms

Juan Manuel Sanchez-Cartas[(✉)] and Gonzalo Leon

Universidad Politecnica de Madrid, Campus de Montegancedo, Madrid, Spain
{juanmanuel.sanchez,gonzalo.leon}@upm.es

Abstract. We simulate the impact of influencers in the adoption of digital multi-sided platforms. We consider four metrics to identify influencers: degree, betweenness, closeness and page rank, and we test how they shape the adoption, prices, and profits of digital multi-sided platforms using an agent-based model. We simulate the market adoption with and without those influencers. We find that adoption is lower and grows slower without influencers. This result is also valid even when one side has influencers, but the other one has not. Depending on the network we assume, the role of influencers is different. In some cases, the launching fails, in others, it is slower only. We also find that prices are sensitive to influencers. However, the effect on prices depends on which centrality measure we consider. Companies use prices as a tool to counterbalance the influence of influencers in profits. Lastly, we show that profits are very sensitive to influencers, without them, profits are lower.

Keywords: Two-sided markets · Digital platforms · Influencers
Node removal · Small-world networks

1 Introduction

Influencers, people who influence other people, are the marketing tool of the social media era. Many of those influencers are well-known because their role in shaping opinions in Twitter, Instagram or Youtube. They are capable of reaching a lot of people, and as Google points out, they are trendsetters more important than other celebrities[1]. Although influencers play a relevant role in transmitting information in the social media, it is not evident which features make them relevant[2]. Is it their followers? Is it their position in the networks? There are many open questions about the role of influencers. Although influencers and their role in the Internet is a trendy topic, there is a lack of works in which the role of influencers is addressed. Companies assume that influencers are essential

---

[1] https://www.thinkwithgoogle.com/consumer-insights/youtube-stars-influence/.
[2] Influencers can be passive or active. Active ones are those who are targeted by companies to promote their products. Passive ones are those who are not directly targeted by companies. In this work, we focus in passive influencers.

© Springer International Publishing AG, part of Springer Nature 2018
J. Bajo et al. (Eds.): PAAMS 2018 Workshops, CCIS 887, pp. 210–222, 2018.
https://doi.org/10.1007/978-3-319-94779-2_19

in their marketing campaigns, but it is not clear to what extent they modify the behavior of these companies. We simulate a theoretical market in which two price-competing multi-sided platforms compete for users and developers during the take-off phase of those platforms. We use four metrics of network centrality to identify influencers. We show the adoption is overestimated when we do not consider the price competition. Platforms do not want to maximize adoption, they want to earn profits, and they face a trade-off between boosting adoption and earning profits. We also show that adoption is higher and faster when there are influencers. Without influencers, the profits, the adoption, and the speed of adoption are much lower than the case with them. We also show that the speed of adoption may be overestimated if we only assume a word-of-mouth process. We find that prices are sensitive to influencers, but that influence depends on which centrality measure we consider. Lastly, an interesting result is that, in all the cases, independently of what centrality measure we consider, profits are higher with influencers. They help in accelerating adoption and profits.

2   Node Removal, Network Robustness and the Role of Influencers in Infection/Adoption Processes

Intuitively, we can consider an "influencer" as a node that plays a relevant role in the diffusion of information in a network. The role of those influencers in the network performance has been studied in a lot of disciplines[3].

But not all nodes are equal. In some networks, there are nodes that are more important than others, and we need to identify them. For example, [8, Chap. 7] points out that a network with a scale-free distribution is vulnerable to the removal of the most connected nodes. If we remove those nodes, the network can fail to have a giant component. The relevance of some nodes has led to the study of node removal or node isolation in different fields. For example, [10] studies the relevance of critical nodes in the air transport network. They consider four different measures to identify those nodes, and they find that some nodes play a key role in the connectivity of the network. Other works prefer to use synthetic indexes to identify the "influential" nodes, one example is [11]. They consider three metrics to measure the vulnerability of a network, and they create a synthetic index with those metrics. These works have not only pointed out the relevance of some nodes but also, that we require several metrics to identify influencers.

We are interested in the impact of node removal in the launching of digital platforms. However, to the best of our knowledge, there is no work which addresses this case. Nonetheless, we can find works that address the role of those influential nodes in the diffusion of information, such as [12]. They study the role of "super mediators", a type of influential nodes recognized by the difference between their degree and the average degree of the network when one

---

[3] See for a global perspective [8, Chap. 7]. But there are examples in epidemiology, [15], network robustness, [11] or diffusion of information, [12].

node is removed. Other authors also address the impact of node removal in different network topologies, such as [1] or [7]. The former shows that, in the case of homogeneous networks or random networks, there is no significant difference when some nodes are isolated, but when considering scale-free or small-world networks, the removal of critical nodes may have a relevant impact on the performance of the network. This evidence is also corroborated by [7]. However, these works do not consider the impact on the diffusion when the process is also influenced by changes in other variables, such as prices.

On the other hand, there is no work which addresses how the adoption of products is influenced by the removal of relevant nodes. Nonetheless, there are many works that study the diffusion of products. Examples of those works are [2,9] or [16]. They consider the impact of stand-alone values, prices, network topologies, etc. Lastly, some works have emphasized the relevant role of influencers in the adoption of platforms, such as [3] or [4]. However, they only point out that role, but they do not analyze this topic in depth.

3   Market Framework, Diffusion of Information and Node Removal

Let's consider that two platforms launch a digital service. For example, an application market, such as the App Store or the Play store, in which users and developers get in touch. As the market framework, we consider the framework proposed by [6], but with some modifications. In this framework, there are two platforms that compete in prices for users and developers.

Both, users and developers, only adopt the platform that maximizes his/her utility, and if the utility is non-negative. We define the utility of the i-user who adopts the platform j as follows[4]

$$U_{ij} = \theta_{i,j}^u - t_u * |l_j - x_i| - p_{u,j} + \delta_u n_d \tag{1}$$

All users (and developers) pay a price for using the platform. That price is the same for all users (developers) and depends on each platform ($p_{u,j}$). Each user/developer has a constant stand-alone value when consuming platform j ($\theta_{i,j}^u$), and a specific set of tastes that we represent with their position (x_i) in the Hotelling segment, $[0, 1]$. Each platform offers a service that coincides with a specific set of tastes (l_j). We assume that platforms are totally differentiated between them. So, they will be at the extremes of the Hotelling segment. The difference between the service offered by platforms and the users' tastes is considered a cost that is weighted by a parameter (t_u) commonly called "transportation cost or nuisance cost". In this way, the expression $t_u * |l_j - x_i|$ represents the disutility of having a product that does not fit users' tastes perfectly. All users (and developers) value the presence of developers (users) in the other part of

---

[4] The developers' utility function is symmetric. Despite this symmetry, users value the number of developers on the platform, and developers the number of users. The platform has to be able to fix prices that attract both groups at the same time.

the market. In this way, the larger the number of developers in the platforms, the larger the utility that users obtain from using the platform (n_d)[5]. Up to this point, we have described the market framework proposed by [6]. Nonetheless, we need to relax some of their assumptions to address the role of influencers. We assume that users (and developers) are linked with other users (developers) in a network. This network has no impact on utilities, but it is through the network that users (and developers) are informed about the platforms following an infection process. This framework is similar to the one proposed by [6]. However, there are relevant differences:

- When a user or developer considers the possibility of adopting a platform, he/she assesses the stand-alone value of the platform $(\theta^u_{i,j})$. We assume it is normally distributed with a positive mean. In this way, we can simulate the presence of early-adopters, laggards, etc.
- Agents are not fully informed. In our framework, some users and developers do not know the platforms at the beginning.
- In the original framework, all users and developers have non-negative utilities. In our framework, some users and developers would have a negative utility if they use the platform. So, adoption may not be total.
- In the original framework, there is no adoption process. All users consume one of the platforms from the very beginning. In our framework, there is an adoption process.
- In the original framework, no network is considered. In our framework, we assume a network among users and another one among developers.

The two platforms compete in prices during one hundred periods[6]. At each moment, there will be three types of users and developers: Those who do not know any platform, those who know one platform only, and those who know both platforms. Although we consider the framework proposed by Hagiu and Halaburda, we do not assume their equilibrium equations. If we assume that, it will make no sense to simulate adoption because one of their main assumptions is that there is no adoption process. Instead, we consider their utility and profit functions, and we fix the platforms' prices by using an algorithm proposed in a previous work, [13]. It allows us to simulate the price competition without using the equilibrium equations. Users and developers choose the platform which provides them the largest non-negative utility. Platforms evaluate the impact on their profits of a small change (0.1) in prices. If that change is profitable, they will increase or decrease the price by that quantity. If not, they will maintain the current price[7].

---

[5] The parameter δ_u controls how users value the presence of an additional developer. For simplicity's sake and without loss of generality, we assume that this value is constant and equal for all users and developers, $\delta_u = \delta_d = \delta$.

[6] We define a period as an iteration in the simulation model. We choose one hundred iterations arbitrarily. Other number of iterations can be considered as well.

[7] Profitability is measured in terms of net profits. In this framework, it is the sum of the revenues on users' and developers' sides. Formally: $n_d * p_{d,j} + n_u * p_{u,j}$.

3.1 Infection Process and Node Removal

We assume that 5% of users and developers know the platforms at the beginning of the simulations[8]. These users and developers represent the "innovators". They can "infect" others users or developers with their information. We consider that the process of adoption follows an infection process as in [9] or [5]. Once users (or developers) know one platform, there is a probability of infecting other users in his/her network with that information. The infection process depends on consuming the platform: users and developers have to consume to infect other agents with their information about platforms. However, if a user (or developer) knows one platform only, he/she will spread the information about that platform only. If that user (or developer) knows the two platforms, he/she will only spread information about the platform he/she consume. Lastly, if they know one or two platforms but they do not consume any platform, they will not spread the information[9]. On the other hand, there is no a standard definition of "influencer". We only know that influencers play an important role because they influence other people, so we have to consider different influence measures. Influencers can be relevant because of their degree (how connected a node is), closeness (how easily can a node reach other nodes), betweenness (how important is a node in terms of connectivity), or because of other neighbors' characteristics. To identify those influential nodes, we consider four centrality measures: degree, closeness, betweenness and page rank[10]. Then, we order the agents by their relevance in each metric. For each metric, we remove the 10% with the largest values[11]. We analyze three cases: When no node is removed, when only the 10% is removed in one of the sides (users or developers), and when the 10% is removed in both sides (users and developers).

4   Simulations

We simulate the market in NetLogo, [14], which has been extensively used in the literature of diffusion of innovations, [2,9,16], etc. We create a world with 314 users and 314 developers, and two platforms[12]. We consider three types of networks: small-world, preferential attachment, and random. The first two are

---

[8] We choose 5% of innovators because it is a common assumption throughout the diffusion of innovation literature.

[9] The probability depends on the normalized degree of each node. The higher the degree, the higher the chance of being infected. We divided the degree of each user/developer by 4. In this way, the most connected node will only be infected in 1 out of 4 cases.

[10] The page rank of a node is the proportion of time that an agent walking forever at random on the network would spend at one node. Nodes that are connected to a lot of other nodes that are themselves well-connected get a higher page rank.

[11] The experiment has been carried out by removing the 5% and 15% also. The conclusions are the same.

[12] The number of users and developers is arbitrarily selected. We can consider other numbers, and conclusions will not change.

created following the algorithm of the "network" extension of Netlogo. The small-world network is created by considering the proximity between agents in the simulated world and adding some random links (1% chance)[13]. The "innovators" are selected by clustering. Therefore, all innovators are less than one node away from one another. To study the role of "influencers" in the diffusion process, we need to know the relationship among the different centrality measures that we consider. As we observe in Table 1, most of the cases are partly correlated. Therefore, each centrality measure addresses different types of "influence". These correlations are robust to different network topologies, so the interpretation of influence does not seem to depend on the network topology we assume.

Table 1. Correlations

Measures	Betweeness & degree	Betweeness & closeness	Betweeness & page rank	Degree & closeness	Degree & page rank	Closeness & page rank
Small-world correlations						
Average	.5585	.7298	.6480	.7420	.9453	.6861
Std. dev.	.0464	.0463	.0367	.0427	.0134	.0390
Preferential-attachment correlations						
Average	.7678	.3079	.7574	.2911	.7754	−.0120
Std. dev.	.0226	.0474	.0228	.0477	.0267	.0414
Random network correlations						
Average	.9323	.8124	.9243	.8064	.9616	.7357
Std. dev.	.0075	.0375	.0120	.0373	.0086	.0246

4.1   The Infection with Price Competing Platforms

Traditionally, adoption processes have been analyzed as stochastic processes of infection in which some nodes infect other nodes following a probability or a threshold distribution. However, the process of adoption may be influenced by prices or users' perception of products. Let's consider first that prices are exogenously fixed at zero. In this way, we can focus on the "infection" process. This case may represent the diffusion of open source platforms, such as Python or Android, in which no one pays for using them. But also, this case allows us to establish a framework in which we can compare the impact of prices in the adoption process. In Table 2, we observe the average infection in each network after 100 periods. The results are in accordance to those of literature: The scale-free networks are very sensitive to the removal of the higher degree nodes, [8, Chap. 7], and the small-world networks are the most robust ones, [11]. Nonetheless, the overall adoption cannot be directly compared with other works because it depends not only on the network topology but also, on the utility functions that we assume for users and developers, and on the word-of-mouth process.

---

[13] These networks are generated following the G(n, p) variant of the ErdõsRènyi model, the BarabàsiAlbert algorithm for preferential attachment networks, and the Watts-Strogatz small-world network. For each network topology, we simulate 150 runs.

Table 2. Average adoption in the different networks

Networks & removal	Small-world network	Preferential-attachment network	Random network
No removal	83.05%	33.88%	74.11%
Betweeness (one-side)	73.52%	2.62%	49.22%
Betweeness (both)	71.91%	2.52%	44.26%
Closeness (one-side)	74.30%	1.15%	54.42%
Closeness (both)	73.53%	0.75%	51.47%
Degree (one-side)	74.88%	2.59%	47.98%
Degree (both)	74.31%	2.59%	42.62%
Page rank (one-side)	74.32%	2.81%	48.80%
Page rank (both)	72.92%	2.75%	45.79%

Both, the overall adoption and the speed of adoption, are affected by the node removal. Obviously, this removal reduces the adoption. Let's introduce the idea of price competition between two platforms. We start all the simulations fixing a zero price and then, we let the platforms choose the prices that increase their profits at each step. At the same time, the spread of information among users and developers keeps going on. This situation can be considered as the simulation of the launching of a private platform such as Wolfram Mathematica. Let's begin analyzing the degree centrality. The degree is the most common and simple centrality measure in the literature. So, it makes sense to adopt it as a common framework to compare the three network topologies. In Table 3, we compare the three networks in three different cases: No removal, removal of 10% of users, and removal of 10% of users and developers. The first interesting result is that the preferential attachment network is critically damaged if we remove the 10% of agents with the larger degrees. This is not new. What is new is that, even when platforms can use the prices to try to boost adoption, the network is so critically damaged that nothing can be done. The launching will fail. If we adopt the other three centrality measures, we have the same conclusion.

On the other hand, a striking result in both, small-world network and random network, is that the adoption is lower in all the cases than in the previous case. This result is what we observe in reality, the number of users of Wolfram Mathematica is much smaller than the number of Python users[14]. This result seems to be counter-intuitive because platforms are limiting the adoption of their products. However, the intuition is straightforward. A private platform has to face a trade-off between adoption and profits. If the platforms want to earn profits, they have to fix positive prices on one side at least. A positive level of prices may change some users' decisions, given that the number of users is lower, fewer developers will enter the platform. Because the number of developers is lower, fewer users will enter the platform, and so on. As we observe in Table 3, when

---

[14] We only consider the adoption, not the profitability. We will analyze it later.

Table 3. Average adoption and profits at the end of the simulations

Networks & sides without influencers	Small-world		Preferential attachment		Random	
	Average adoption	Average profits	Average adoption	Average profits	Average adoption	Average profits
No influencers removal	45.98%	0.2340	8.55%	0.0456	19%	0.0901
Betweeness (one side)	30.43%	0.1847	1.17%	0.0196	8%	0.0518
Betweeness (both)	29.77%	0.1467	1.12%	0.0022	4.63%	0.0207
Closeness (one side)	35.46%	0.1956	0.96%	0.0192	10.79%	0.0482
Closeness (both)	28.32%	0.1393	0.43%	0.0012	6.90%	−0.0632
Degree (one side)	35.69%	0.1958	1.23%	0.0220	6.3%	0.0056
Degree (both)	35.68%	0.1645	1.35%	0.0025	4.5%	0.0178
Page rank (one side)	35.17%	0.1977	1.16%	0.0177	6.41%	0.0565
Page rank (both)	31.53%	0.16	1.15%	0.0038	4.25%	0.0192

we remove 10% of higher-degree agents, the percentage of users who adopt the platform in the random network case falls more than 50%. In contrast, in the small-world network, it "only" falls 23%. Also, it does not matter if we remove the 10% of users or the 10% of users and developers, the overall adoption will be similar. Except in the small-world network, we can consider that platforms fail in launching their platforms, so there is no point in analyzing those cases. This result also emphasizes two issues: (a) the well-known fact in the literature that small-world networks are more resilient than the random or preferential attachment networks to the removal of some relevant nodes, and (b) the topology of the network is important. Let's consider now the other three centrality measures in the small-world network case.[15]

4.2   Adoption

In Table 3, we have observed the first interesting difference between the cases with and without influencers. In the latter, platform adoption is lower. However, the level of adoption depends on the centrality measure we assume. But the adoption is clearly lower. In this sense, there are no big differences between the cases in which we remove the influencers on one side or both. However, it is interesting that the effect in the final adoption depends on the metric we consider. For example, if we consider the betweenness, although we have removed the 10% more influential, the drop in demands is more than 10%. In fact, the demand is around fifteen percentage points lower than in the case with those influencers. However, with the rest of metrics, the drop is around ten percentage points if we only consider one side, but when we consider both sides, that drop is slightly lower. On the other hand, we observe that the speed of adoption is slower when we remove the influencers. They are the catalyst that guarantees a quick

---

[15] Networks are critically damaged when we remove the influencers in the random and preferential attachment networks.

launch. In Table 4, we observe that, in all the cases, the speed of adoption is two times faster with influencers than without them. However, in comparison with a case with only an infection process, the speed is significantly slower.[16] Lastly, in the cases in which we consider the closeness and the page rank measures, the adoption of platforms is slightly different when we only remove 10% of users than when we remove the 10% of users and developers. This is the first evidence we find that different centrality measures influence the adoption process of platforms differently. In Table 2, we depict the final adoption of platforms when prices were zero. In that case, there was no such difference in the adoption process, so this difference seems to be the consequence of how platforms fix prices.

Table 4. Derivates of adoption. First 25 iterations

Speed of adoption	Betweeness	Closeness	Degree	Page rank
Original case	.0132	.0134	.0127	.0126
One side	.0061	.0072	.0077	.0075
Both	.0058	.0051	.007	.0063

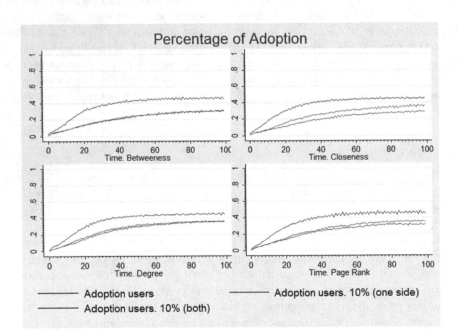

Fig. 1. Adoption of products with and without the 10% influentials

---

[16] In the same simulations but without platforms fixing prices, the speed of infection is around 3–4% per iteration.

4.3   Prices

In Fig. 2, we compare the prices of the four previous cases. Our results show that there are differences in how platforms fix prices when we remove users with large closeness or page rank metrics than when we remove users with large betweenness or degree metrics. This result suggests that the most connected users play a different role than those who are "close" to everyone in the network. Nonetheless, there is always a case in which prices are similar with and without influencers. The intuition of this result is the following. When we consider the betweenness and the degree metrics, we remove those nodes that are either very connected or those who play a relevant role in connecting other nodes. So, when we remove those nodes, the information spreads more asymmetrically. In this situation, platforms have market power over some users because they do not know about the existence of competitors. Therefore, platforms have an incentive to fix higher prices. Nonetheless, when we remove 10% of influencers in both sides (users and developers), we are again in a symmetric framework. Therefore, prices behave symmetrically (in both sides). On the other hand, when we consider the closeness and the page-rank metrics, we pay attention to nodes that are "close" to the rest of nodes in the network (closeness), or to nodes that attract a lot of "traffic" from other nodes. This case is interesting because prices behave differently. The intuition is the following. The closeness measures the distance to all other nodes. The page-rank pays attention to how important neighbors are. So, when we remove the nodes that seem to be the most important ones under these metrics, we may not disrupt the flow of information enough. Only when we remove the 10% of users and developers, we remove enough agents to affect how the information flows. If we pay attention to Fig. 1, only in these cases the overall level of adoption is different when we remove users only or users and developers. This change happens after ten iterations, the exact same moment in which prices start to rise in Fig. 2.

4.4   Profits

In Fig. 3, we compare the profits that platforms earn when we remove the influencers in the four cases analyzed in the previous section. In all cases, profits grow faster and are larger when there are influencers. In contrast with prices, which behavior depends on the centrality metric we assume, profits behave in a similar way. This result points out that the different price behavior of the previous section may be the way in which platforms mitigates the removal of some nodes. On the other hand, independently of what centrality metric we use, influencers have an impact on profits. In Table 3 and in Fig. 3, we observe that the cases without influencers have lower profits. We can summarize the role of influencers in two points: Profits are more sensitive than demands to influencers, and the way platforms react to the absence of those influencers vary among the different centrality measures.

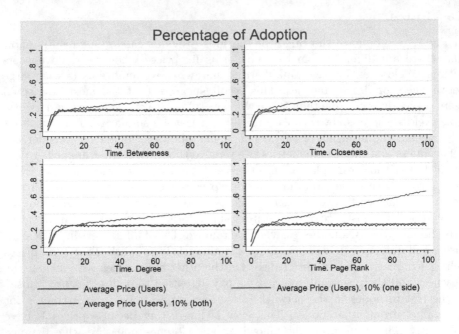

Fig. 2. Average prices on users' side with and without the 10% influentials

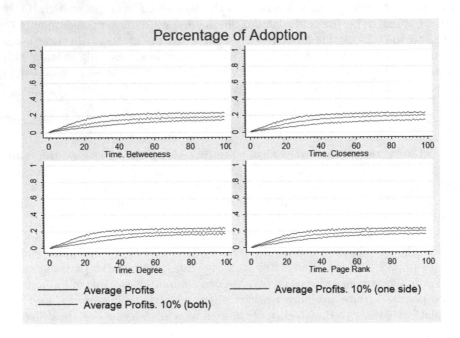

Fig. 3. Average profits with and without the 10% influentials

5 Conclusions

We simulate a multi-sided market with two price-competing platforms that are launching a digital service that requires users and developers. We focus on the role played by influencers in the adoption process. We identify influencers by four metrics of centrality, and we simulate the adoption, prices, and profits of those platforms when we remove those influencers. We find that a simple word-of-mouth process overestimates both, the adoption and the speed of adoption. We also find that adoption is lower and grows slower without influencers. When we consider the role of prices, adoption is lower because platforms want to earn profits, so they have to fix positive prices. We find that prices are sensitive to influencers but, that influence depends on which centrality metric we consider. The closeness and the page-rank metrics lead to large prices if we remove influencers on both sides of the market. The degree and the betweenness metric lead to large prices if we only remove influencers on one side of the market. Lastly, we show that, independently of what centrality measure we consider, profits are higher when there are influencers.

References

1. Crucitti, P., Latora, V., Rapisarda, A., Marchiori, M.: Efficiency of scale-free networks. Phys. A **320**, 642 (2002)
2. Diao, J., Zhu, K., Gao, Y.: Agent-based simulation of durables dynamic pricing. Syst. Eng. Procedia **2**, 205–212 (2011)
3. Evans, D.S.: Platform Economics: Essays on Multi-sided Businesses. Competition Policy International (2011)
4. Evans, D.S., Schmalensee, R.: Failure to launch: critical mass in platform businesses. Rev. Netw. Econ. **9**(4) (2010)
5. Günther, M., Stummer, C., Wakolbinger, L.M., Wildpaner, M.: An agent-based simulation approach for the new product diffusion of a novel biomass fuel. J. Oper. Res. Soc. **62**(1), 12–20 (2011)
6. Hagiu, A., Hałaburda, H.: Information and two-sided platform profits. Int. J. Ind. Organ. **34**, 25–35 (2014)
7. Huang, J., Jin, X.: Preventing rumor spreading on small-world networks. J. Syst. Sci. Complex. **24**(3), 449–456 (2011)
8. Jackson, M.: Social and Economic Networks. Princeton University Press, Princeton (2010)
9. Kim, S., Lee, K., Cho, J.K., Kim, C.O.: Agent-based diffusion model for an automobile market with fuzzy topsis-based product adoption process. Expert Syst. Appl. **38**(6), 7270–7276 (2011)
10. Lordan, O., Sallan, J.M., Simo, P., Gonzalez-Prieto, D.: Robustness of the air transport network. Transp. Res. Part E: Logist. Transp. Rev. **68**, 155–163 (2014)
11. Mishkovski, I., Biey, M., Kocarev, L.: Vulnerability of complex networks. Commun. Nonlinear Sci. Numer. Simul. **16**(1), 341–349 (2011)
12. Saito, K., Kimura, M., Ohara, K., Motoda, H.: Super mediator-a new centrality measure of node importance for information diffusion over social network. Inf. Sci. **329**, 985–1000 (2016)

13. Sanchez-Cartas, J.M.: Agent-based models and industrial organization theory. A price-competition algorithm for agent-based models based on game theory. Complex Adapt. Syst. Model. **6**(2), 2 (2017)
14. Wilensky, U.: Netlogo (1999). https://ccl.northwestern.edu/netlogo/
15. Zanette, D.H., Kuperman, M.: Effects of immunization in small-world epidemics. Physica A: Stat. Mech. Appl. **309**(3), 445–452 (2002)
16. Zhang, T., Zhang, D.: Agent-based simulation of consumer purchase decision-making and the decoy effect. J. Bus. Res. **60**(8), 912–922 (2007)

Household Occupancy Detection
Based on Electric Energy Consumption

Alberto L. Barriuso$^{(\boxtimes)}$, Álvaro Lozano, Daniel H. de la Iglesia,
Gabriel Villarrubia, and Juan F. de Paz

Department of Computer Science and Automation, University of Salamanca,
Plaza de la Merced, s/n, 37008 Salamanca, Spain
{albarriuso,loza,danihiglesias,gvg,fcofds}@usal.es

Abstract. It is possible to detect the presence of residents in a home by monitoring its energy consumption. Currently, the state of the art provides us with a number of approaches. Some studies leverage intrusive systems which require user interaction. Others employ sensors to detect the presence of people in a non-intrusive way. In this article, we propose the use of a sensor network for measuring electric energy consumption in a home. A multi-agent system is used to manage the data generated by the deployed sensor network in an intelligent way. A non-intrusive occupation monitoring algorithm was designed to determine when a house is occupied and when it is empty.

Keywords: Multi-agent system · NIOM · PANGEA

1 Introduction

Occupancy detection techniques have been widely studied in recent years. The scientific community's great interest in obtaining knowledge on human presence in buildings owes to its large number of applications.

Up until now, presence detection has frequently been applied to the field of energy consumption optimization [1]. Heating, ventilation and cooling (HVAC) and lighting systems can make use of the building's presence information, inasmuch as they could automatically operate in real-time. Thus, energy consumption can be reduced, enhancing the building energetic efficiency [2]. By applying these techniques not only energy can be saved, but the residents level of comfort could be improved, by maintaining a warm temperature when the residents are at home [3]. Likewise, occupancy patterns can be useful for incentivized-based forms of Demand Response (DR) [1]. DR systems aim to modify the consumption patterns in response to (i) the change in the price of electricity over time or (ii) to incentive payments designed to induce lower electricity use at times of high wholesale market prices [4]. Another field where occupancy detection is widely applied is health monitoring, we can find several examples where elders or hospital patients behavior is studied in order to improve the different health-care services offered to them [5, 6].

© Springer International Publishing AG, part of Springer Nature 2018
J. Bajo et al. (Eds.): PAAMS 2018 Workshops, CCIS 887, pp. 223–231, 2018.
https://doi.org/10.1007/978-3-319-94779-2_20

The Smart Grid concept is also making considerable progress. It can be defined as "the use of sensors, communications, computational ability and control in some form to enhance the overall functionality of the electric power delivery system" [7]. The European Union and the United States are taking many initiatives to ensure the implementation of this kind of technologies, one such initiative is the European Electricity Grid Initiative -within the framework of the Strategic Energy Technology Plan- [8] or the Energy Independence and Security Act [9]. Consequently, in the near future all the households will be equipped with new intelligent meters. For this reason, the load curve data will be accessible to smart metering operators.

As demonstrated in [10], load curve analysis can be an illuminating praxis that should be considered in day-to-day operations, system reliability and energy planning. The analysis of these data is becoming of great importance in a particular area: the demand side management (DSM) of smart grids. However, this kind of data can reveal additional information; non-intrusive appliance load monitoring (NILM) techniques are able to disaggregate a household's electrical consumption into particular data [11]. Following the lines of research in the load curve analysis, household occupancy can also be studied according to its electrical consumption. The state of the art contains previous works in this area [12], however there is still a lot of room for improvement.. For this reason, we purpose a multi-agent system for the detection of presence in the home based on electric energy consumption. Concretely, our proposal focuses on the deployment of a sensor network based on the Cloogy project [13], for consumption monitoring. By executing the occupancy algorithm presented in this work on the data collected by the sensor network, it was possible to detect the presence of people in a home.

The paper is organized as follows: Sect. 2 reviews the current state of the art in occupancy detection techniques. Our review includes sensor-based systems and proposals which analyze the household's load curve. Section 3 presents the proposed system, describing both the theoretical and the practical details. Section 4 describes the conducted case study in which the system was implemented in order to validate its operability. Section 5 outlines the obtained results. The closing Sect. 6 draws conclusions on the conducted work- Moreover, and future lines of research are defined.

2 Background

Occupancy monitoring has been the focus of many studies. The majority of works employed sensors for this purpose, however their approaches vary greatly. Some studies only used a single sensor while others used multiple sensors. It is common to opt for the second choice, since the fusion of several sources of information improves the performance of occupancy detection methods. Another varying feature is the kind of sensor or sensors used. [14] makes a survey of the current approaches that use sensor networks for real-time building occupancy estimation. This survey is summarized in Table 1, where the systems have been classified into: (i) method: terminal or non-terminal based, whether the system required users to carry a terminal or no, (ii) function: defines the ability of the system to detect, identify and track individuals in the environment, (iii) infrastructure: where a distinction is established between explicit and implicit infrastructures, depending if the purpose of the infrastructure is just the detection of occupancy, or if the occupancy detection is inferred from certain data sources.

Table 1. Classification of occupancy detection systems [14]

Sensors	Method		Infrastructure		Infrastructure	
	Terminal	Non-terminal	Individualized	Non-individualized	Implicit	Explicit
C02 sensors	X	✓	X	✓	X	✓
PIR sensor	X	✓	X	✓	X	✓
Ultrasonic sensors	X	✓	X	✓	X	✓
Image sensors	X	✓	X	✓	✓	✓
Sound sensors	X	✓	X	✓	X	✓
EM signals	✓	X	X	✓	✓	✓
Power meters	X	✓	X	✓	X	✓
Computer app	X	✓	X	✓	✓	✓
Sensor fusion	✓	✓	✓	✓	✓	✓

Notwithstanding, adapting this kind of approach implies the intrusion of these sensors in the household environment; the installation of these devices may be bothersome for the residents, or in some cases, the house itself may not be able to put up with the installation of a sensor architecture. This is why a non-sensor dependent and therefore non-intrusive alternative is sought.

As mentioned in Sect. 1, governments are taking many initiatives and are investing in smarter grids, in order to increase exponentially the number of houses with installed smart meters. Smart meters offer a non-intrusive way of detecting occupation. To this end, the data they register need to be analyzed and the consumptions that imply human activity must be identified.

In Fig. 1 we can see a common architecture of a smart metering system. The main components that conform a smart metering system are [15]: (i) **smart metering devices** -*smart meter (SM)* -: responsible for calculating in detail the electrical consumption, they are able to communicate this information through a network; (ii) a **data gathering device** -*data concentrator (DC)* -: it is in charge of gathering the data provided by SMs. Frequently, these devices act as master nodes of a communication subnetwork

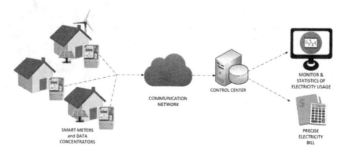

Fig. 1. Smart metering system architecture.

conformed by themselves and a group of SMs; (iii) a **communication system**, where quality, time and security of the data flow must be guaranteed, and (iv) a **centralized management and control system**, -*control center (CC)* - which will store and process all the received data.

3 Proposed System

The architecture proposed in this work is detailed below. Each of the elements that make up the system will be explained in detail. The diagram in Fig. 2 shows the main elements that make up the proposed system. The PANGEA platform [16] was chosen for the design of the architecture, which facilitates the creation of virtual agent organizations and their integration with different light hardware devices. Different virtual organizations are in charge of carrying out specific tasks, such as data collection and management or coordination and security.

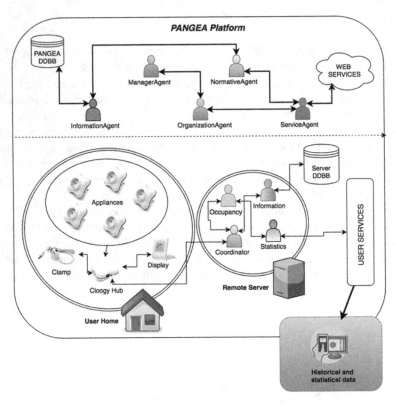

Fig. 2. General diagram of the proposed architecture for the detection of occupancy based on electric energy consumption.

The first element of the architecture is the organization of the user's home. Within the house, all the sensors involved in the non-intrusive occupancy detection system are displayed. These commercial sensors from the VPS company (Virtual Power Solutions) [17] are available on the website of the Cloogy project [13] and are simple to install in a domestic electrical network.

The first and the central element of the system deployed in the user's home is the *Cloogy hub*, this device is responsible for receiving data from each of the nodes of the system. The *clamp* is the device responsible for recording from the electrical panel, the entire household's electricity consumption data. The *display* is responsible for displaying the house's consumption information in real time. Finally, the smart plugs are responsible for monitoring the electrical consumption of any individual household appliance, reading its consumption independently of the rest of the equipment. All the data processed by the deployed sensor network are sent in real time to the system's central server.

The remote server organization has the following roles: Coordinator, statistics, information and occupancy. The coordinating agent is in charge of managing the information that comes from the sensor devices. The information agent is responsible for storing all recorded data, while the statistics agent is responsible for collecting and displaying the data and statistics obtained in the system to the platform users. Lastly, the occupancy agent is in charge of analysing the data generated by all load reading devices and then determines whether the house is occupied or not.

3.1 Occupancy Agent

The main task of the occupancy agent is to determine whether people are present or absent in a household from the readings of the available reading devices (clamp and smart plugs). For the occupancy agent to accomplish this objective, the collected information must go through several preprocessing tasks.

The algorithm executed by this agent requires a minimal setup, at least a clamp for the whole load consumption reading and 0 to N smart plugs installed in the household appliances. Depending on the setup of smart plugs in the household, occupancy detection will become more accurate, this will be explained in more detail later on.

At the time of installing the smart plug, the web page will ask the user to select the kind of appliances connected to the smart plug from a list of possible appliances. However, since this task can be tedious for users it, can be automated with appliance classification [18, 19]. We classified these devices into two types of appliances: Human Interaction Appliances and Non-Human Interaction Appliances (HIA and NHIA). On one hand, HIA require, as their name points out, human interaction in order to change from one of their possible power states to another, for instance a television needs a Human Interaction Event (HIE) to be switched on. On the other hand, NHIA do not require human interaction to change their power state. This method assumes that HIA appliances are activated by people. Therefore we exclude the cases where the user sets a timer to change the power state of their HIA.

Therefore, as illustrated in Fig. 3, a distinction has been made between HIA and NHIA. The data collected by HIA will be processed in order to search HIE which directly implies human presence, these events will later be used to increase the accuracy of the occupancy algorithm applied to the consumption of the entire household. In addition, the load coming from monitored NHIA will also be discarded by the occupancy algorithm since this load is not indicative of human presence.

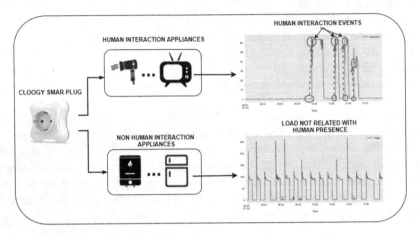

Fig. 3. Human interaction appliances and non-human interaction appliances

Figure 4 shows how the occupancy agent executes the occupancy algorithm. This algorithm is based on the algorithm of Dong Chen et al. NIOM [12] however in this case we intend to increase its performance and solve its drawbacks using additional information from smart plugs.

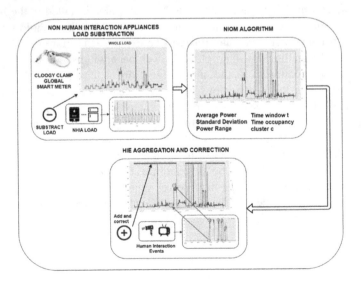

Fig. 4. Algorithm flowchart process

The occupancy algorithm carries out the following steps: (i) collection and exclusion of the NHIA load from the whole load. (ii) execution of the NIOM algorithm on the already processed load (iii) aggregation of HIE to the results of the NIOM algorithm and occupancy values correction. After this process the inferred occupancy state is stored.

One of the greatest drawbacks of the NIOM algorithm is its sensibility to NHIA loads, this generates false positive in the occupancy results. Thanks to the exclusion of NHIA load in the algorithm the accuracy of the algorithm is improved. Another drawback of the NIOM algorithm is its lack of sensibility to human presence in a household,, it doesn't detect slight changes in load consumption and only changes the state from non-occupancy to occupancy when the consumption increases significantly. This trait of the NIOM would get worse if NHIA loads were included. The inclusion of HIE and the exclusion of NHIA load improves the presence detection accuracy.

4 Results

The DRED dataset [20] was used to test and evaluate the performance of the proposed platform. Dredd is an open-access dataset from the Netherlands, it provides data from several sensors which measured electricity, resident occupancy and ambient parameters in a household over a 6 month period. The presence data provided by this dataset were used to measure the performance of the proposed system. First, the household was evaluated considering the total household consumption, while different HIA and NHIA data were progressively included in the subsequent evaluations of the algorithm. In this process, it was demonstrated that both the exclusion of the NHIA, and the use of the HIA as an occupancy indicator, have improved the results rendered by the NIOM algorithm. Figure 5 shows a snapshot of the visualization tool used to visualize both the household's electric energy consumption and the algorithm's output.

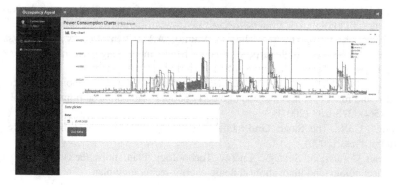

Fig. 5. Algorithm flowchart process

5 Conclusions

The detection of human presence in buildings is of growing interest to the scientific community, this is because such knowledge has numerous applications. Most probably, in the near future all the households will be equipped with new intelligent meters. For this reason, load curve data will be useful when deducing human presence in a household. Several state-of-the-art algorithms have been developed in this line of research. Thus, the following article proposes an improved version of the NIOM algorithm by including the consumption data of individual appliances.

Acknowledgements. The present work was done and funded in the scope of H2020 DREAM-GO Project (Marie Sklodowska-Curie grant agreement No. 641794). The research of Daniel Hernández de la Iglesia has been co-financed by the European Social Fund and Junta de Castilla y León (Operational Programme 2014–2020 for Castilla y León, EDU/529/2017 BOCYL). Álvaro Lozano is supported by the pre-doctoral fellowship from the University of Salamanca and Banco Santander. This work was supported by the Spanish Ministry, Ministerio de Economía y Competitividad and FEDER funds. The research of Alberto López Barriuso has been co-financed by the European Social Fund and Junta de Castilla y León (Operational Programme 2014–2020 for Castilla y León, EDU/128/2015 BOCYL).

References

1. Chaney, J., Hugh Owens, E., Peacock, A.D.: An evidence based approach to determining residential occupancy and its role in demand response management. Energy Build. **125**, 254–266 (2016)
2. Tang, G., Wu, K., Lei, J., Xiao, W.: SHARK: sparse human action recovery with knowledge of appliances and load curve data. Cyber-Phys. Syst. **1**(2–4), 113–131 (2015)
3. Kleiminger, W., Beckel, C., Santini, S.: Household occupancy monitoring using electricity meters. In: Proceedings of the 2015 ACM International Joint Conference on Pervasive and Ubiquitous Computing - UbiComp 2015, pp. 975–986 (2015)
4. Federal Energy Regulatory Commission: Assessment of Demand Response & Advanced Metering (2015)
5. Junnila, S., Kailanto, H., Merilahti, J., Vainio, A.M., Vehkaoja, A., Zakrzewski, M., Hyttinen, J.: Wireless, multipurpose in-home health monitoring platform: two case trials. IEEE Trans. Inf. Technol. Biomed. **14**(2), 447–455 (2010)
6. Kaushik, A.R., Celler, B.G.: Characterization of PIR detector for monitoring occupancy patterns and functional health status of elderly people living alone at home. Technol. Health Care **15**(4), 273–288 (2007)
7. Gellings, C.W.: The Smart Grid : Enabling Energy Efficiency and Demand Response. Fairmont Press (2009)
8. European Comission: Strategic Energy Technology Plan. https://ec.europa.eu/energy/en/topics/technology-and-innovation/strategic-energy-technology-plan
9. U.S. Government: Energy Independence and Security Act
10. Tang, G., Wu, K., Lei, J., Bi, Z., Tang, J.: From landscape to portrait: a new approach for outlier detection in load curve data. IEEE Trans. Smart Grid **5**(4), 1764–1773 (2014)
11. Stankovic, L., Stankovic, V., Liao, J., Wilson, C.: Measuring the energy intensity of domestic activities from smart meter data. Appl. Energy **183**, 1565–1580 (2016)

12. Chen, D., Barker, S., Subbaswamy, A., Irwin, D., Shenoy, P.: Non-intrusive occupancy monitoring using smart meters. In: 5th ACM Workshop on Embedded Systems For Energy-Efficient Buildings – BuildSys 2013, pp. 1–8 (2013)
13. Cloogy—Eficiência Energética—Residências e Empresas. https://www.cloogy.pt/. Accessed 20 Jan 2018
14. Labeodan, T., Zeiler, W., Boxem, G., Zhao, Y.: Occupancy measurement in commercial office buildings for demand-driven control applications—A survey and detection system evaluation. Energy Build. **93**, 303–314 (2015)
15. Uribe-Pérez, N., Hernández, L., de la Vega, D., Angulo, I.: State of the art and trends review of smart metering in electricity grids. Appl. Sci. **6**(3), 1–24 (2016)
16. Zato, C., Villarrubia, G., Sánchez, A., Barri, I., et al.: PANGEA – platform for automatic construction of organizations of intelligent agents. In: Omatu, S., De Paz Santana, J.F., González, S.R., Molina, J.M., Bernardos, A.M., Rodríguez, J.M.C. (eds.) Distributed Computing and Artificial Intelligence. AISC, vol. 151, pp. 229–239. Springer, Heidelberg (2012). https://doi.org/10.1007/978-3-642-28765-7_27
17. VPS - Energy Efficiency and Automated Demand Response. https://www.vps.energy/. Accessed 20 Jan 2018
18. Aftab, M., Chau, C.-K.: Smart power plugs for efficient online classification and tracking of appliance behavior (2017)
19. de la Iglesia, D.H., Barriuso, A.L., Murciego, Á.L., Herrero, J.R., Landeck, J., de Paz, J.F., Corchado, J.M.: Single appliance automatic recognition: comparison of classifiers. In: De la Prieta, F., Vale, Z., Antunes, L., Pinto, T., Campbell, A.T., Julián, V., Neves, A.J.R., Moreno, M.N. (eds.) PAAMS 2017. AISC, vol. 619, pp. 115–124. Springer, Cham (2018). https://doi.org/10.1007/978-3-319-61578-3_11
20. Uttama Nambi, A.S.N., Reyes Lua, A., Prasad, V.R.: LocED. In: Proceedings of the 2nd ACM International Conference on Embedded Systems for Energy-Efficient Built Environments - BuildSys 2015, pp. 45–54 (2015)

PAAMS Workshop ISCIF

Information Fusion and Machine Learning in Spatial Prediction for Local Agricultural Markets

Washington R. Padilla[1], Jesús García[2(✉)], and José M. Molina[2]

[1] Research Group Ideia Geoca,
Salesian Polytechnic University of Quito-Ecuador Engineer Systems,
Quito, Ecuador
wpadillaa@ups.edu.ec
[2] Applied Artificial Intelligence Group, Carlos III University, Madrid, Spain
jgherrer@inf.uc3m.es, molina@ia.uc3m.es

Abstract. This research explores information fusion and data mining techniques and proposes a methodology to improve predictions based on strong associations among agricultural products, which allows prediction for future consumption in local markets in the Andean region of Ecuador using spatial prediction techniques. This commercial activity is performed using Alternative Marketing Circuits (CIALCO), seeking to establish a direct relationship between producer and consumer prices, and promote buying and selling among family groups.

Keywords: Data fusion · Alternative circuits of commercialization
Associations mining · Predictive analysis

1 Introduction

The goal of this research is to increase the incomes of small farmers in the Andean region of Ecuador, preventing their migration to large population centers. The CIALCO acronym comes from using the first two letters of the words Alternative Circuit marketing (in Spanish 'Circuito Alternativo de Comercialización'). There are several types of circuits, this study is limited to information of groups involved in circuits of fair type, defined as specific places where agricultural producers meet periodically to conduct its business [1].

The analysis is based on information from 2014, provided by the General Coordination Network Marketing Ministry of Agriculture, and Livestock of Ecuador. It contains the weekly performance of sales of agricultural products made by small farmers located in Ecuador's central highlands specifically the provinces of Tungurahua and Chimborazo. The country Ecuador is crossed by the Equatorial line, i.e., its territory is located both north and south from latitude zero. The provinces of Tungurahua and Chimborazo are in the south and central region, and the information has been collected on the sale of agricultural products in these alternative marketing circuits, which seek to establish a direct relationship between producers and consumers.

© Springer International Publishing AG, part of Springer Nature 2018
J. Bajo et al. (Eds.): PAAMS 2018 Workshops, CCIS 887, pp. 235–246, 2018.
https://doi.org/10.1007/978-3-319-94779-2_21

The available data contains information about the number and volume of sales of products such as vegetables, legumes, meat, dairy, fruits, tubers and processed products, finding an average of 1,200 items per month divided on a weekly basis.

This research is aimed at finding patterns in the behavior of consumption of agricultural products, using Information Fusion of spatially distributed information of several products and learned knowledge about relationships among these products to predict future situations. In this work, we apply Artificial Intelligence techniques over the market fused data, to extract association rules for improving the prediction on the behavior of consumption of agricultural products to establish better policies to potentiate local operations.

2 Machine Learning for Prediction

In data mining it is very important to look for causal relations between variables to predict changes in some variables based on knowledge of other ones. An association rule of the form $\{A\} \Rightarrow \{B\}$ can be interpreted as: "if A appears then B also will appear", and aims to identify relationships not explicit between categorical attributes. The set A is called antecedent of the rule and B is called consequent. In order to assess the quality of association rules, the most common metrics are support, confidence and lift [2]:

- The **support** of a rule is defined as the number of instances that the rule covers with respect to the total set.

  $\sup_a(x) = |x|$, $\sup_r(x) = \frac{|x|}{|D|}$, being D the total set of transactions.

  If antecedent A and consequent B are considered, the support is the intersection set:
  $\sup_a(A \Rightarrow B) = \sup_a(A \cap B)$

- The **confidence** of a rule indicates the accuracy of its predictions; it is defined as the percentage of times that the consequent B is met among the instances selected by the antecedent A.

  $\mathrm{conf}(A \Rightarrow B) = \frac{\sup_a(A \Rightarrow B)}{\sup_a(A)} = \frac{A \cap B}{|A|}$.

- The **lift** of a rule (Dr, Experfy On line courses, 2016) is the ratio of the observed support with respect to that expected if X and Y were independent

  $\mathrm{lift} = \frac{\sup(X \Rightarrow Y)}{\sup(X) \times \sup(Y)}$,

Among the existing algorithms for association rule discovery, *Apriori* algorithm [3] is the most representative technique for this task. As can be seen in [4], it searches for trends based on the performance parameters mentioned above, based on prior knowledge or "a priori" frequent sets. It is summarized below:

Step 1: Generate all item sets L with a single element; this set is used to form
a new set with two, three or more elements
all possible pairs which are taken Sup equals minsup
Step 2: For every frequent item set L' found:
      For each subset J, of L'
           Determine all association rules of the form:
           If L'-J→J
           Select those rules whose confidence is greater or equal than
     minconf
Repeat Step 1, including next element into L

However, in many applications the patterns are time varying, the entities may follow periodic patterns such as trajectories, transportation, etc., that are not considered by this basic algorithm. The problem in this case is discovering the patterns from data considering temporal attributes and describe how they vary in time. There is abundant bibliography for discovering temporal patterns in sequence databases, usually dealt as sequence mining (or frequent patterns search) and temporal data association.

For the first case, there are extensions of Apriori algorithm considering lists of objects ordered in time as items, being the searched result the associations in form of sequences of items. Some cases derived from Apriori are GSP for spatio-time associations [5, 6] algorithms.

As a different alternative, the paradigm of temporal association rules are discussed by different authors, considering rules within temporal frames, also based on Apriori mining schema extended to consider temporal support [Che00], or even meta-rules describing how relationships vary in time [7].

A series of studies conducted in various fields of science try to use the rules of association as a criterion to establish future estimates, so we can see some jobs such as [8] analyze the stock of a supermarket, or in [9] predict admission decisions by students. Finally, works like [10] have explored relationships between association rules and a fuzzy classification.

As complementary to temporal data association, time series analysis builds hypotheses about cause-effect relationships that can be expressed in terms of forecasting. In simple statistical methods, the hypothesis that X causes Y implies a correlation between X and Y, which in turn implies that Y can be predicted from X. More generally, the hypothesis on the effect of X on Y is tested to see if the scores on Y can be predicted more accurately from a model that includes X that of a model that excludes X. There is abundant bibliography in time-series regresion, both with classical models [11] and application of advanced machine learning techniques (neural networks, support vector regression, etc.) [12].

The use of spatial data analysis and regression is very usual with geo-located data in multiple domains. In [13] an explanation of the mathematical development of kriging and cokriging based on substitution models within the framework of optimization is made [14], they basically propose to improve the construction of the variogram using information of magnitude and direction applied to data of the National Network of the Geomagnetic Observatories of China. As mentioned in [15], "in the geographical space everything is related to everything, but the closest spaces are more related to each other".

This work establishes a group of products that have the highest ratio of marketing associativity (Apriori algorithm association rules), determined the one with the highest consumption, prediction to future with time series and sales estimation in a specific area, in the Two cases are investigated on the improvement in estimation processes of future commercial behavior using the association set.

3   Knowledge Extraction Process

Figure 1 sketches the methodology of five steps used to obtain the predictions of product sales, detailed in the pseudocode below. It starts defining the products to be studied, generates the files to be processed, searches for the best association rules in the data sets, makes predictions and finally evaluates the improvements.

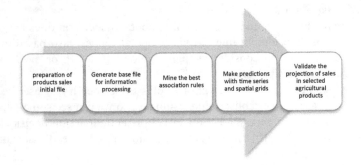

Fig. 1. Methodological description

1. Prepare the information
    1.1. Delete records without information
    1.2. Standardize value of similar records
    1.3. Establish units of measurement valid
    1.4. Generate the set of products for the study

2. Generate the database ready for pattern search
3. Obtain the best rules of Association

    3.1. Discredit the archive of products sold
    3.2. Apply *Apriori* algorithm to obtain the best rules of Association
    3.3. Establish the set of associated products

4. Make predictions (using spatial estimation)
5. Compare error metrics of single-product prediction vs. the predictions using associated products

3.1 Data Preparation of Initial File with Transactions (Vegetables and Legumes)

This process begins by validating the data originally provided, deletes non-significant information, and standardizes product names and units of measure.

The information provided includes data collected weekly in fairs of CIALCO type, in the provinces of Napo, Chimborazo and Tungurahua belonging to the central area of the Andes in Ecuador. A subset of products included in the analysis are presented in Table 1, with the names in Spanish (in the original dataset), and their corresponding names in English and scientific names.

The record contains the products that are part of the marketing, the value of sales,

Table 1. Set of products

Spanish name	scientific name	English name
Acelga	Beta vulgaris var. cicla	Chard
Ajo	Allium sativum	Garlic
Arveja	Pisum sativum	Vetch
Babaco	Carica pentagona	Babaco
Brócoli	Brassica oleracea italica	Broccoli
....	....	....
Vainita	Phaseolus Vulgaris L	Green beans
Zanahoria	Daucus carota	Carrot
Zapallo	Cucurbita máxima	Pumpkin

date and fair to which the transaction belongs. The data sheet contains all the recorded transactions, organized in packages named "canastas" (baskets), each one representing a sale of certain products, containing the products present in each purchase, and implicitly also contains the spatial geo-localization of the operation (the location of fair) and the time stamp (date) of operation. If part of the transaction is the label with the character 's', otherwise 'no' for all months of 2014 as can be seen in Fig. 2.

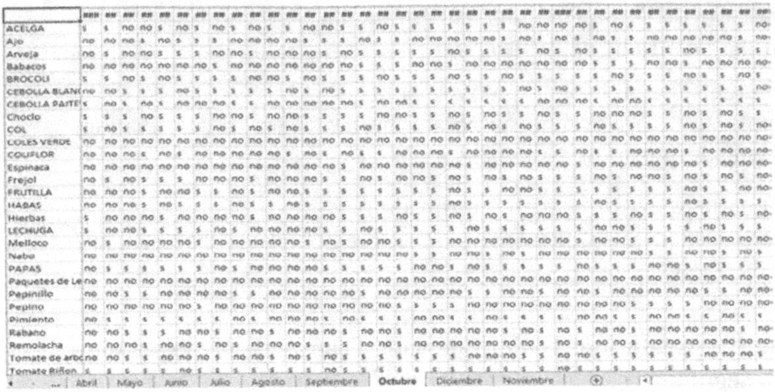

Fig. 2. Transactions with products contained in each sale ("canasta")

The initial information has been subject to a data cleansing process in which homogenization is done, mainly in the names of products, values for unit sales and elimination of products that do not have relevant information for this study. In order to find association rules information must be quantized, so we can identify whether an agricultural product is part of the procurement process. To optimize the process of searching for the best association rules, the 'no' symbol has been replaced by '?' symbol in the first place. The reason for this operation was to focus the search only in "positive" rules, those relating the presence of products and avoid the search of those rules relating absence of products. The main reason for this decision was that transactions in the dataset select sparse products in the table, so most of values would be negative.

3.2   Search for Best Association Rules

The data file contained 549 pre-processed transactions containing subsets of the 31 elements acquired. In the search for association rules, the first condition was that the value of **support** is higher or equal to 0.4, implying the number of times that appears in the database must be greater than 220 to ensures this constraint. The subsets of data with a single element (14 items) and with 2 elements (15 items) are shown in Fig. 3.

Among the elements that make up the subset of data L1 and L2, we obtain the subset of data that satisfy the minimum confidence value equal to 0.8, as can be verified in Fig. 4. For example, the white onion appears 338 times in L1, while the intersection between white onion and kidney tomato appears in L2 293 times, whose confidence for this example is 293/338 = 0.86. As a result, it is obtained that the kidney tomato is found in the five resulting association rules on the consequent side.

```
Attributes:   31                              Large Itemsets L(1):
              Acelga                          Arveja=t 222
              Ajo                             Brocoli=t 327
              Arveja                          CebollaBlanca=t 338
              Babacos                         Cebolla Paiteña=t 280
              Brocoli                         Choclo=t 257
              CebollaBlanca                   Col=t 282
              Cebolla Paiteña                 Frutilla=t 228
              Choclo                          Habas=t 308
              Col                             Lechuga=t 294
              Col Verde                       Papas=t 329
              Coliflor                        Pimiento=t 256
              Espinaca                        Tomate de arbol=t 312
              Frejol                          Tomate Riñon=t 431
              Frutilla                        Zanahoria=t 374
              Habas
              Hierbas                         Size of set of large itemsets L(2): 15
              Lechuga
              Melloco                         Large Itemsets L(2):
              Nabo                            Brocoli=t Tomate Riñon=t 269
              Papas                           Brocoli=t Zanahoria=t 225
              Paquetes de Legumbres           CebollaBlanca=t Habas=t 224
              Pepinillo                       CebollaBlanca=t Papas=t 225
              Pepino                          CebollaBlanca=t Tomate Riñon=t 293
              Pimiento                        CebollaBlanca=t Zanahoria=t 227
              Rabano                          Col=t Tomate Riñon=t 230
              Remolacha                       Habas=t Tomate Riñon=t 245
              Tomate de arbol                 Habas=t Zanahoria=t 221
              Tomate Riñon                    Lechuga=t Papas=t 225
              Vainita                         Lechuga=t Tomate Riñon=t 222
              Zanahoria                       Papas=t Tomate Riñon=t 254
              Zapallo                         Papas=t Zanahoria=t 246
=== Associator model (full training set) ===   Tomate de arbol=t Tomate Riñon=t 268
                                              Tomate Riñon=t Zanahoria=t 311
```

b.- Total Items   c.- Subset Item sets

Fig. 3. Item sets for search of association rules

```
Apriori
=======

Minimum support: 0.4 (220 instances)
Minimum metric <confidence>: 0.8
Number of cycles performed: 12

Generated sets of large itemsets:

Size of set of large itemsets L(1): 14

Size of set of large itemsets L(2): 15

Best rules found:

1. CebollaBlanca=t 338 ==> Tomate Riñon=t 293    <conf:(0.87)> lift:(1.1) lev:(0.05) [27] conv:(1.55)
2. Tomate de arbol=t 312 ==> Tomate Riñon=t 268    <conf:(0.86)> lift:(1.09) lev:(0.04) [23] conv:(1.49)
3. Zanahoria=t 374 ==> Tomate Riñon=t 311    <conf:(0.83)> lift:(1.06) lev:(0.03) [17] conv:(1.26)
4. Brocoli=t 327 ==> Tomate Riñon=t 269    <conf:(0.82)> lift:(1.05) lev:(0.02) [12] conv:(1.19)
5. Col=t 282 ==> Tomate Riñon=t 230    <conf:(0.82)> lift:(1.04) lev:(0.02) [8] conv:(1.14)
```

Fig. 4. Best association rules

4 Spatial Estimation

4.1 Data Preparation for Spatial Analysis

To implement the proposed methodology we use the mathematical algorithms found in the R Studio language, version 1.0.143 [17] and in Weka 3.7 [16]. The first activity is centered in the creation of the grid or mesh to determine the prediction area, a dimension structure is defined cellcentre.offset $x = -79.1085$, $y = -2.531218$, cellsize $x = 0.05$, $y = 0.05$, cells.dim $x = 21$; $y = 32$. In the sector of the equatorial line one degree of length equals 111.32 km, the distance occupied in length by the two provinces xmin $= -79.133499$,

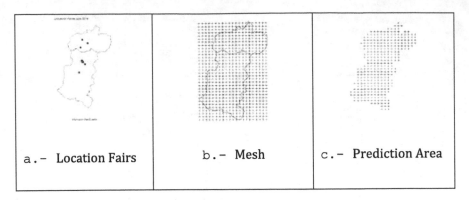

Fig. 5. Location of fairs and prediction mesh

xmax = −78.0834991 is 1.049 degrees, the equivalent to 116 km, for the conformation of the grid, the distance between cells is 5.84 km (Fig. 5).

The data used correspond to the commercialization of the input variable (kidney tomato) in the month of July 2014, corresponding to the provinces of Tungurahua and Chimborazo. Figure 6a displays the geolocation (coordinates that represent the latitude and longitude) for each of the fairs of CIALCO type considered in the study, being the last column the values of the commercialization for kidney tomato. In Fig. 6b, we can see the behavior of the variable, we can identify that 50% of the data is between the values of 20 and 60 that the median is 31.50 and the average is 39.65.

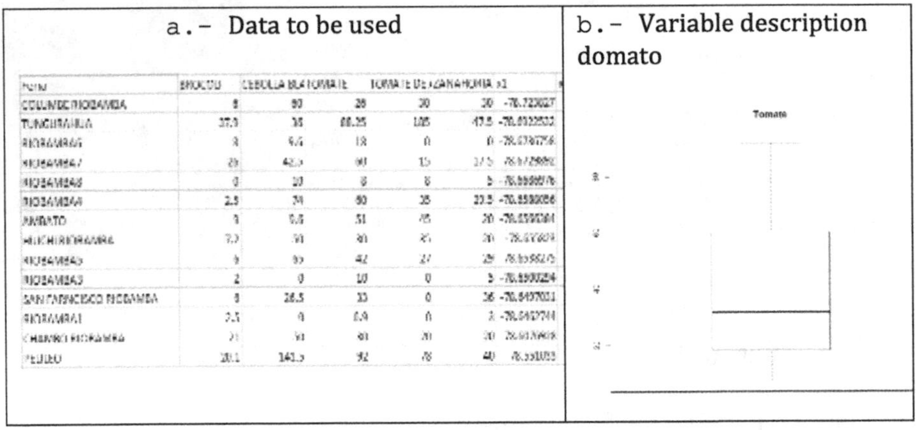

Fig. 6. Analysis of tomato variable

For the selected tomato variable, the methodology described above has been applied and the results of each task are presented in the following subsections

4.2   Kriging Based on Experimental and Adjusted Spatial Variograms

Figure 7, at the left side, shows the distribution of points when calculating the experimental variogram with the data used. The distance between the points that identify the fairs is expressed in tenths of a degree, and between each jump there is a distribution of two fairs. At the right side, the adjusted variogram can be observed using the experimental variogram and a model variogram of spherical type.

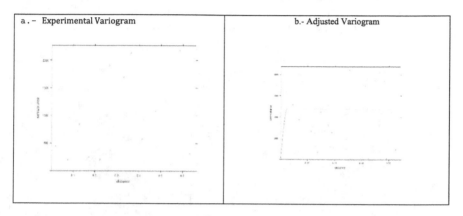

Fig. 7. Tomato sales variogram

Using the continuous function of the adjusted variogram, the tomato consumption prediction values are obtained based on distance and spatial correlation in the following way:

Krige (TOMATE ∼ 1, FJespacial, spgrid, model = m), ∼ 1 defines a single constant predictor.

Based on the ordinary kriging method, considered the best unbiased linear estimator type, the results shown in Fig. 8 can be appreciated. The values found in the interpolation vary especially in two foci on which the predictions were generated. The values closest to the points of information are more influenced than those located further.

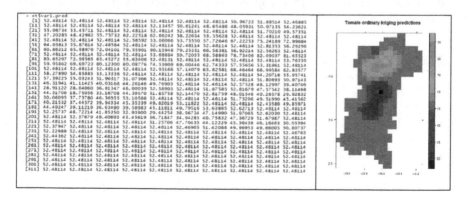

Fig. 8. Spatial estimation using (single) tomato variable kriging

4.3 Extended Model for Multivariable Prediction Based on Associated Products

To carry out a prediction with multiple variables, we extend the spatial prediction as result of interrelation with the products found from the association rules. The set of associated products in the commercialization with the highest incidence in the process were identified, in particular the five products resulting from A priori algorithm are {tomato, brocoli, white onion, tree tomato, carrot}. In the same way as for the future estimate made for the tomato variable, we proceed to estimate the spatial distribution of this variable considering the associated products, as shown in Fig. 9.

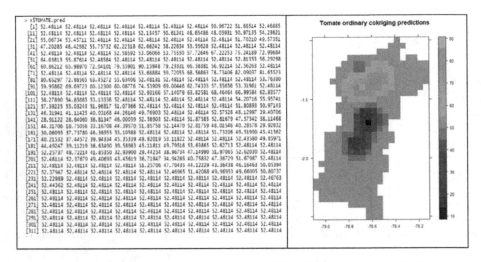

Fig. 9. Multivariable prediction

4.4 Comparison of Cross Validation Results Obtained in the Two Cases (CVu-CVmv)

To perform the validation of the prediction data, the procedure known as "leave-one-out" cross-validation (LOOCV) was applied. As can be seen in Fig. 10, the average of the residuals has a value of 0.7.

```
> summary(cvtom)
Object of class SpatialPointsDataFrame
Coordinates:
          min        max
x -78.723827 -78.551033
y  -1.888003  -1.257143
Is projected: NA
proj4string : [NA]
Number of points: 14
Data attributes:
    var1.pred         var1.var         observed          residual          zscore             fold
Min.   :16.05    Min.   :  23.76   Min.   : 6.90    Min.   :-51.0621   Min.   :-7.9858    Min.   : 1.00
1st Qu.:23.75    1st Qu.:  69.43   1st Qu.:20.00    1st Qu.:-19.6668   1st Qu.:-0.7889    1st Qu.: 4.25
Median :36.58    Median : 142.48   Median :31.50    Median :  4.4379   Median : 0.2507    Median : 7.50
Mean   :38.93    Mean   : 823.78   Mean   :39.65    Mean   :  0.7189   Mean   :-0.1132    Mean   : 7.50
3rd Qu.:56.27    3rd Qu.:1993.55   3rd Qu.:57.75    3rd Qu.: 21.3920   3rd Qu.: 0.9124    3rd Qu.:10.75
Max.   :62.74    Max.   :2496.56   Max.   :92.00    Max.   : 44.1241   Max.   : 9.0169    Max.   :14.00
```

Fig. 10. Cross validation for tomato sales prediction

5   Conclusions

In summary, the method has two stages. The first one established a consumption prediction using geostatistical techniques such as the variogram to find a continuous function to interpolate the estimated values of product sales in points with no available observations. Based on the functions of kriging, the sales values of products are established according to their spatial location and the influence of their close neighbours. To finalize this phase, a cross validation is carried out using the Leave-one-out cross-validation evaluation, which allows verifying the error of estimated future values. In the second stage, the Apriori algorithm was used to search the products that have the greatest associativity with the selected variable: tomato, broccoli, tree tomato, white onion and carrot. Based on this multivariable set, the prediction values are calculated using the same procedure described in the first stage.

Acknowledgements. This work was supported in part by Project MINECO TEC2017-88048-C2-2-R and by Commercial Coordination Network, Ministry of Agriculture, Livestock, Aquaculture and Fisheries Ecuador.

References

1. Padilla, W.R., García, H.J.: CIALCO: Alternative marketing channels. Commun. Comput. Inf. Sci. **616**, 313–321 (2016)
2. Zulfikar, W.B., Wahana, A., Uriawan, W., Lukman, N.: Implementation of association rules with apriori algorithm for increasing the quality of promotion. In: 2016 4th International Conference on Cyber and IT Service Management, pp. 1–5 (2016)
3. Association Rules. http://www.saedsayad.com/association_rules.htm. Accedido 12 dic 2017
4. Patil, S.D., Deshmukh, R.R., Kirange, D.K.: Adaptive apriori algorithm for frequent itemset mining. In: 2016 International Conference System Modeling Advancement in Research Trends (SMART), pp. 7–13 (2016)
5. Chang, C.-C., Li, Y.-C., Lee, J.-S.: An efficient algorithm for incremental mining of association rules. In: 15th International Workshop on Research Issues in Data Engineering: Stream Data Mining and Applications (RIDE-SDMA 2005), pp. 3–10 (2005)
6. Zaki, M.J.: SPADE: an efficient algorithm for mining frequent sequences. Mach. Learn. **42**, 31–60 (2001)
7. https://www.hhl.de/fileadmin/LS/micro/Download/Spiliopoulou_2000_HigherOrderMining.pdf
8. Asadifar, S., Kahani, M.: Semantic association rule mining: a new approach for stock market prediction. In: 2017 2nd Conference on Swarm Intelligence and Evolutionary Computation (CSIEC), pp. 106–111 (2017)
9. Mane, R.V., Ghorpade, V.R.: Predicting student admission decisions by association rule mining with pattern growth approach. In: 2016 International Conference on Electrical, Electronics, Communication, Computer and Optimization Techniques (ICEECCOT), pp. 202–207 (2016)
10. Kumar, P.S.V.V.S.R., Maddireddi, L.R.D.P., Anantha Lakshmi, V., Dirisala, J.N.K.: Novel fuzzy classification approaches based on optimisation of association rules. In: 2016 2nd International Conference on Applied and Theoretical Computing and Communication Technology (iCATccT), pp. 1–5 (2016)

11. http://www.ARMA15.pdf
12. Mitsa, T.: Temporal Data Mining. CRC Press (2010). https://www.crcpress.com/Temporal-Data-Mining/Mitsa/p/book/9781420089769. Accedido 12 dic 2017
13. Won, K.S., Ray, T.: Performance of kriging and cokriging based surrogate models within the unified framework for surrogate assisted optimization. In: Proceedings of the 2004 Congress on Evolutionary Computation (IEEE Cat. No. 04TH8753), vol. 2, pp. 1577–1585 (2004)
14. Chen, D., Liu, D., Li, Y., Meng, L., Yang, X.: Improve spatiotemporal kriging with magnitude and direction information in variogram construction. Chin. J. Electron. 25(3), 527–532 (2016)
15. Celemín, J.P.: Autocorrelación espacial e indicadores locales de asociación espacial: Importancia, estructura y aplicación. Rev. Univ. Geogr. 18(1), 11–31 (20090
16. Weka 3 - Data Mining with Open Source Machine Learning Software in Java. [En línea]. Disponible en: http://www.cs.waikato.ac.nz/ml/weka/. Accedido 28 sep 2017
17. RStudio – Open source and enterprise-ready professional software for R. [En línea]. Disponible en: https://www.rstudio.com/. Accedido 08 dic 2017

SMEC-3D: A Multi-agent 3D Game to Cognitive Stimulation

Priscilla Braz[1], Vera Maria B. Werneck[2], Herbet de Souza Cunha[3],
and Rosa Maria E. Moreira da Costa[2(✉)]

[1] Centro Universitário CARIOCA, Rio de Janeiro, Brazil
priscillaf.abreu@gmail.com
[2] Universidade do Estado do Rio de Janeiro, Rio de Janeiro, Brazil
{vera,rosa}@ime.uerj.br
[3] Petrobrás, Rio de Janeiro, Brazil

Abstract. Multi-agents are being increasingly used in many areas, especially in Health Systems. In a game the agents' paradigm provides more autonomy, intelligence and pro-activity. In this context, Multi-agents systems can be used to control the user performance, by adapting the interface to the difficulty tasks level. This paper aims at describing the development process of SMEC-3D, a cognitive stimulation game that integrates Virtual Reality and Multi-agent technologies. The SMEC-3D modeling process used i* (i-star) framework to model the goals, agents, domain, plans and tasks. The game objective is to improve attention and memory of patients with neuropsychiatric disorders. The paper describes the development process specially the agents' methodology. The resulted SMEC-3D game showed that the combination of tools and programming languages applied to this experiment worked efficiently.

Keywords: Multi-agents system · Serious games · Cognitive stimulation

1 Introduction

Multi-agent Systems (MAS) have been integrated into systems in different knowledge domains and have provided automated control strategies, decreasing the control of human intervention for the performance of processes and software tests.

In parallel, Virtual Reality (VR) technology has been used, with positive results, in different cognitive rehabilitation processes [1–3]. Three-dimensional (3-D) virtual environments offer opportunities to develop motivational activities, facilitating repetitive tasks in playful scenarios with no risk to users. In general, during activities using commercial games, therapists control the activities difficulty level according to the user's performance. Cognitive rehabilitation (CR) systems usually do not perform this control automatically. In the CR domain games can be added as an additional treatment strategy in the rehabilitation of various dysfunctions, increasing the motivation of patients. In fact, games can provide a fun activity that motivates patients to continue therapy [4]. The term "Serious games" is used for computer games designed to educate and train people, simulating situations of the real world that are impossible to perform in a

J. Bajo et al. (Eds.): PAAMS 2018 Workshops, CCIS 887, pp. 247–258, 2018.
https://doi.org/10.1007/978-3-319-94779-2_22

controlled environment for different reasons such as time, safety or cost, among others [5]. Serious games are used for purposes other than mere entertainment. The MAS strategies can be integrated in 3-D serious game to increase the possibilities of offering a personal control based on the performance of the users. In this situation, the users would feel more independent and the therapist would have new possibilities to monitor their performance through reports and messages sent by the system.

This paper aims at describing the modeling and developing strategies to integrate into a serious game, intelligent agents for stimulation the cognitive activities of patients that have different types of neuropsychiatric disorders. The SMEC-3D integrates a group of agents that are engaged to manage and monitor the performance of the users while navigating in the environment. The game offers activities to stimulate memory, attention and concentration functions.

This paper is organized in sections: Sect. 2 presents the general concepts related to this project. Section 3 describes the development methodology and the game. This section also presents the results of case study done by an expert. Section 4 discusses the results and presents future perspectives.

2   General Concepts

In recent years, cognitive rehabilitation processes have explored the potential of Virtual Reality and Serious Games technologies. 3-D virtual environments have been used to train motor skills and stimulate cognitive processes, such as visual perception, attention and memory [5, 6].

In general, Serious Games explore strategies that support users in learning new concepts and in recovering cognitive or motor skills [5]. These games provide possibilities for education and at the same time provide entertainment [5, 7].

Virtual Reality has potential to support rehabilitation processes, in that it allows individuals to interact and train within realistic and interesting virtual environments. The control of movement and interaction with scene objects is accomplished by sensors that capture body movements. In the cognitive rehabilitation area, virtual environments are designed to be more enjoyable than traditional therapy procedures [8]. In this sense, several 3-D environments have been developed for different disabilities [2–4, 6].

Often, many interventions are required during patient navigation in these environments, provoking distractions and consequently reducing the user immersion level. The application of intelligent agents can help to decrease this problem, by reducing the therapists' actions.

Multi-agent techniques have been applied in different areas, exploring various methodologies and programming languages [9]. Every agent must have autonomy to manage its internal state and to achieve its goals automatically [10, 11]. Some examples of integrating MAS with Health VR environments have been developed especially with education and training focus [12–14]. These works explored different technologies and methodologies for modeling and construct the systems. Our research group has conducted some experiments with RV languages and agent frameworks, developing and comparing some combinations of these technologies [15]. However, these experiments used few agents with limited functionalities. In order to explore new combinations of modeling methodologies, VR languages and frameworks for MAS development, the SMEC-3D was proposed and will be described next.

There are several proposals for modeling multi-agent systems in the literature. In this context, we highlight the work of Werneck et al. [9], which reviewed and com-pared methodologies for modeling multi-agent systems. Considering this fact and the discussions, we decided to adopt the i* framework [16], that supports requirement analysis and high-level design in an agent-oriented system development paradigm.

The i* framework [16] proposes two main models: SD model (Strategic Dependency) and SR Model (Strategic Rationale). The SD Diagram identifies actors (users and/ or agents), the tasks and the resources needed to process the tasks. The SD is used to present the dependencies among the actors. The SR model promotes a clear mapping of the logic process for the goals to be achieved, the tasks performed, the resources made available, and the soft goals reached. This model provides the internal strategy of each actor (agents) by representation of intentionality, allowing a greater visibility of the way to reach the solution.

3 SMEC-3D

SMEC-3D integrates MAS technologies with VR and the game objective is to stimulate the patients' cognitive abilities as attention, concentration and memory. The agents control the activities difficulty levels.

According to Hight [17], game users are motivated to play, with the possibility of obtaining new knowledge. Pan et al. [18] reinforce this idea from observing some experiments and conclude that users can learn while playing games. In this sense, the SMEC-3D stimulates users to increase or recover impaired cognitive functions due to illness or accidents. Another aspect that can contribute to increase users playing these games is that they can carry out the activities alone, without feeling embarrassed or uneasy on account of making mistakes.

The game has two rooms (living room and kitchen). The living room has book-shelves, with balls or cubes of different colors that are randomly shown on a table and the patient must choose which is similar on the shelves. The agents will monitor the time and the user interactions with the environment. They will control the right and wrong answers and combine these data with the information on the patients' impairments. The therapist is responsible to register the patient's personal data in the system.

This game has eight levels of difficulty. At each level, the patient will have 10 rounds and should have at least seven correct answers to proceed to the next level. If the minimum items are not reached, the patient will remain in the current level. It can occur up to four times. Otherwise, the session will end.

The second game takes place in a kitchen, contains objects that are used in the individual's daily life. In this phase, the degree of difficulty is greater than the first exercises, because the objects are different and are distributed in various places: on the table, on the stove, on the floor, etc. The game's difficulty level will rise by increasing the number of objects to be selected and by introducing distracters such as noises.

In general, the activities offered by the environment do not have a winning condition for the user. According to his performance, the level of activity becomes more difficult or easier. Thus, Hight [17] points out that this happens in many games, and exemplifies citing the game "Tetris" [19], which becomes more complex until the user decides to stop, or the game ends when the player misses too many pieces. In this case, the idea of victory comes from comparing his current performance with previous ones or comparing his results with those from other players. The SMEC-3D gives points to users according to wrong and corrects answers. Thus, the SMEC-3D challenge is to exceed a previous result or to be placed ahead of others players.

A systematic process to guide the creation of this environment led us to follow a model and we applied the pipeline presented in Fig. 1.

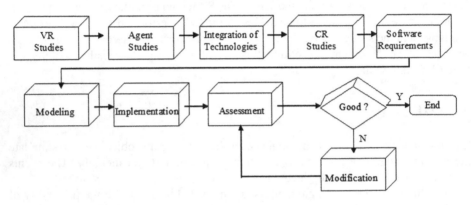

Fig. 1. The pipeline used to develop the SMEC-3D project

The studies made at the two first pipeline stages stressed that there were few experiments integrating MAS in VR systems, and the implementation details were never clear.

The third stage required a long research work, which sought to find the structure to support VR and MAS integration. We created two environments with serious games features [15] that were built with JAVA3D [20] and X3D (eXtensible 3D) [21] languages. To implement the agents we first studied different authoring tools such as NetLogo tool [22] and JADE (Java Agent Development Framework) framework [23]. However, they did not produce acceptable results, since they were not easily integrated with the JAVA3D and X3D. Then, we decided to use the structure provided by the JAVA [24] and JAVAScript [25] languages. Comparing the results from these two experiments, we realized that the JAVA3D has a smaller learning curve than the X3D, because it uses the same structure as JAVA, such as library calls, which are widespread and well known.

3.1 Software Requirements

After these studies, we began the elicitation of software requirements with a physician. We discussed the levels of difficulties, each task's control time and the cognitive functions associated with the tasks. We concluded that the tasks would be simple and should work with the attention and memory processes. Therefore, the first game stimulates the attention focus, the divided attention and the work memory. The second one also stimulates these functions, but shows a scene that can be associated with a known space where patients perform day-to-day activities.

A lexical catalog (Table 1) described the requirements specification to support the agents' identification. Four agents were defined for planning patient care, controlling the interactions in the games, analyzing the patient performance and setting up the environment.

Table 1. Part of the SMEC-3D lexicon catalog

Name:	Treatment Planner Agent
Concept:	Software Agent responsible to construct and suggest a **treatment plan** for the **patient** according to their specificities.
Classification:	Object
Impact (s):	The **Planner Agent** create a **treatment plan** using the data of the **patient**. The **Planner Agent** changes the **treatment plan** of the **patient** from the request of the **analyzer agent**.
Synonymou(s):	Planner Agent.
Name:	Patient
Concept:	Person who is in rehabilitation treatment using rehabilitation software.
Classification:	Subject
Impact (s):	The patient who plays the game.
Synonymou(s):	user.
Name:	Game history
Concept:	Set of data of **patient** performance in **games** since registering in the system.
Classification:	Object
Impact (s):	The history of the **game** is stored in **Smec-3D** by the **controler agent.**
Synonymou(s):	history, patient game history.

The Planner Agent is responsible for planning a treatment protocol considering the patient data that is registered by the therapist. For this, it combines the user data with a list of relevant protocols. On this basis, a new protocol can be defined or an existing protocol can be customized.

The primary goal of the Controller Agent is to monitor the game. To reach it, this agent monitors every user interaction in the game by capturing the user's answers, evaluating it, storing information on the history and suggesting the next task. It has some options: "Continue in the same level", "Change the difficulty level", "Change the game" or "Finish the game". In some of these cases, the game scene needs to be modified. Thus, this agent communicates via messages with the Environment Customizer Agent, which is responsible for those changes.

The Environment Customizer Agent is responsible for making changes in the scenes. These changes can be: "Change the level of difficulty", "Change the game" or "Change activities". All changes are performed from a request "send to the Controller Agent" via message exchange.

The Analyzer Agent is responsible for evaluating patient performance throughout the treatment considering the need for changes in the planned treatment. Before that, he gets information about the treatment protocol, the user's performance in past activities, makes a comparison between the expected and obtained results from this, and decides to stay with the same protocol or suggest changes to it.

3.2   I* Modeling

The SMEC-3D SD Diagram (Strategic Dependency) is presented in Fig. 2 by defining the relations dependencies among the actors. For example, the physician depends on the planner to define the protocol game based on the analyzer that changes the protocol depending on the patient game interaction history provided by the controller.

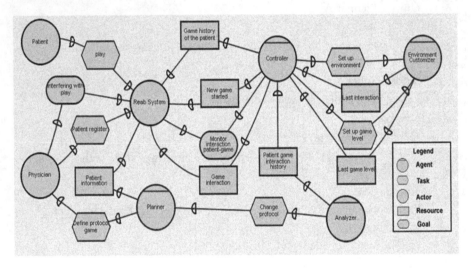

Fig. 2. Strategic dependency model

The Planner Agent SR Model (Fig. 3) presents the strategies of the planner agent whose main goal is to define the treatment protocol. For this, this agent needs to capture the specificities of the patient as well as the existing protocols considered relevant to the case. Based on the patient information the agent will analyze the compatibility of the protocols and decide whether to customize an existing protocol or whether to define a new protocol.

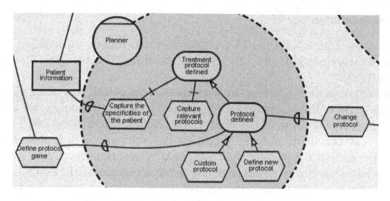

Fig. 3. Strategic rationale model of planner agent

Figure 4 presents the goals and tasks of the Controller Agent. The goals of this agent are: "Wait for a new game", "Monitor the game" and "Propose the next iteration". Upon detecting the start of a new game, the agent monitors each patient interaction in the proposed activities. For this reason, these interactions are captured, evaluated and the assessment data are stored in the history. After all activities were evaluated, a new iteration will be proposed. This iteration may continue in the same game, change the game level, end or change the game. In the case of changing the difficulty level or the game, the agent communicates with the Environment Customizer Agent to make these modifications.

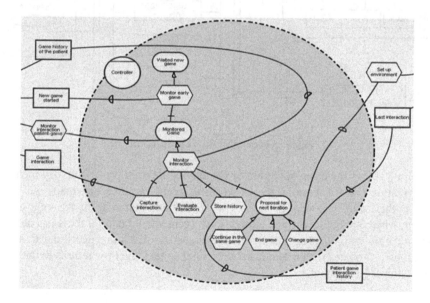

Fig. 4. Strategic rationale model of controller agent

3.3 Implementation

SMEC-3D adopted the X3D and JAVA languages, the framework JADE [23] and a relational database MySQL [26]. To integrate these four technologies, we used the NetBeans IDE [27].

From the agents modeling step, we implemented the central part of the model: the 'Controller' and the 'Environment Customizer' agents that are responsible for capturing and assessing the user's actions in the game, then making the changes. Thus, the environment will offer activities for registered users and will monitor their performance as they play the games. The integration of these two agents, classify the SMEC-3D as a hybrid application, which combines cognitive and reactive agents. The Controller Agent can be considered as a cognitive agent, because it is proactive, since it is able to take the initiative to achieve their goals, makes decisions based on past actions and interacts with other agents by exchanging messages.

The Environment Customizer agent can be considered reactive, because it is based on a stimulus-response model. It waits for requests to perform the actions.

Figure 5 shows an architectural representation of the global environment, adapted from Gomes [28].

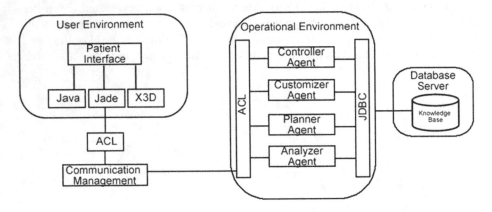

Fig. 5. Global SMEC-3D architecture

Figure 6 shows the basic operation of the agents' internal processing. By means of an information control module, the Controlling agent captures and maps the user's actions in the scene. The mapped actions are submitted to an analysis through rules of behavior, where are defined which attitudes the agent should take. If there is a need for communication with other agents, a message is sent, so that some decisions are made. In case there is no need to communicate with other agents, the flow returns to the information control component.

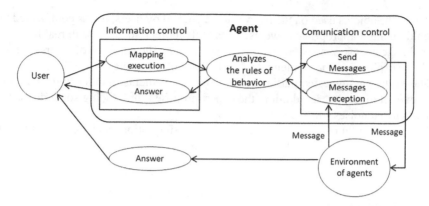

Fig. 6. Basic agents internal processing

The agents need a relational database and an operating environment where they will be hosted. The MySQL database has drivers that are compatible with the JAVA (JDBC).

The cooperation process among agents uses the recognition mechanism of the actions taken by other agents through the receipt of messages. These messages send process information and share the data stored in the database.

Figure 7 presents two games scenes.

Fig. 7. Two scenes from the SMEC-3D game: (a) showing the bookshelves and the table where the object is presented (b) the kitchen and the table where the object to be searched is presented

A case study was conducted with a psychiatrist to evaluate the prototype based on a script following quality concepts. First the psychiatrist simulates the patient interaction. Initial explanations about the game objective and the tasks were given and after he used the game. After that, he answered some questions about the software usability. The psychiatrist also used the software in the role of an expert. They discussed some details of the motivations for software development and how the agents interfere in the users' navigation. Thus, in the "Discussion phase", some changes were proposed.

After that process the psychiatrist considered that it was easy to learn how to perform the activities in the game. Also, he classified it as easy to navigate through. The response time of the application as well as the attractiveness and realism of the scenes were appropriate.

About the objects used on the shelves to be clicked by users, it was commented that it would be more appropriate if we used elements more associated with real life rather than using geometric shapes. He also proposed that only the variation of colors or shapes should be explored in the challenges of each phase of the game.

The evaluator suggested putting some distracter elements in order to include some extra level of difficulty. In addition, the expert proposed introducing some distracters, such as sudden noises.

The new version of the game considered these suggestions and we used only balls as objects for the first game. In the second game we included some noises such as a barking dog.

4   Conclusions

This paper introduced the work associated with the development of the Smec-3D serious game. It discussed particular challengers involved in building multi-agent VR system as therapeutic technology for cognitive stimulation.

Advances in computer technology need to spread through all society. It includes people with different disabilities who need access to more motivating treatment strategies, minimizing their motor and cognitive impairments. At the other side, therapists must have new possibilities to monitor the patients' evolution at distance, reducing the need for constant face-to-face contacts. In this case, some exercises could be done at home, increasing the rehabilitation possibilities.

Virtual Reality technology has been greatly explored in this area and the integration of multi-agents in the navigation control of users of virtual 3-D environment will open new perspectives for automation treatment protocols. Additional research should consider new intelligent approaches, the use of motion trackers, and the adoption of RV development tools that increase users' interaction with scenes and their level of presence.

Multi-agent systems need to be backed up by a specific methodology, with efficient requirements-gathering strategies and well-defined process support. In this case, we consider that the methodology i* provided formal technical elements that were able to support the understanding and development of the system. Also, we consider that this study has emphasized the need to integrate a multidisciplinary team to overcome some challenges of modeling, implementing and using complex systems.

Acknowledgments. This work is part of the "Instituto Nacional de Ciencia e Tecnologia - Medicina Assistida por Computação Cientifica" (Medicine assisted by Scientific Computation), Brazil. Grant E-26/170.030/2008.

References

1. Anderson, K.R., Woodbury, M.L., Phillips, K., Gauthier, L.V.: Virtual reality video games to promote movement recovery in stroke rehabilitation: a guide for clinicians. Arch. Phys. Med. Rehabil. **96**(5), 973–976 (2015)
2. Gamito, P., Oliveira, J., Coelho, C., et al.: Cognitive training on stroke patients via virtual reality-based serious games. Disabil. Rehabil. **39**(4), 385–388 (2017)
3. Burdea, G.C., Polistico, K., House, G.P., Liu, R.R., Muñiz, R., Macaro, N.A., Slater, L.M.: Novel integrative virtual rehabilitation reduces symptomatology of primary progressive aphasia-a case report. Int. J. Neurosci. **125**(12), 949–958 (2015)
4. Berger-Vachon, C.: Virtual reality and disability. Technol. Disabil. **18**, 163–165 (2006)
5. Connolly, T.M., Boyle, E.A., MacArthur, E., Hainey, T., Boyle, J.M.: A systematic literature review of empirical evidence on computer games and serious games. Comput. Educ. **59**(2), 661–686 (2012)
6. Lange, B.S., Requejo, P., Flynn, S.M., Rizzo, A.A., Valero-Cuevas, F.J., Baker, L., Winstein, C.: The potential of virtual reality and gaming to assist successful aging with disability. Phys. Med. Rehabil. Clin, North Am. **21**(2), 339–356 (2010)
7. Howes, S.C., Charles, D.K., Marley, J., Pedlow, K., McDonough, S.M.: Gaming for health: systematic review and meta-analysis of the physical and cognitive effects of active computer gaming in older adults. Phys. Ther. **97**(12), 1122–1137 (2017)
8. Laver, K., George, S., Thomas, S., Deutsch, J.E., Crotty, M.: Virtual reality for stroke rehabilitation. Stroke **43**(2), e20–e21 (2012)
9. Werneck, V.M.B., Costa, R.M.E.M., Cysneiros, L.M.: Modelling multi-agents systems using different methodologies. In: Alkhateeb, F., Maghayreh, E., Doush, I.A. (eds.) Multi-Agent System: Modelling, Interactions, Simulations and Case Studies, pp. 77–96. Intech, Rijeka (2011)
10. Wooldridge, M.J.: An Introduction to Multi-Agent Systems. Wiley, Chichester (2009)
11. Russell, S., Norvig, P.: Artificial Intelligence: A Modern Approach, 3rd edn. Prentice Hall, Englewood Cliffs (2009)
12. Riedmann, P., et al.: RIVALE: a prototype realistic immersive virtual agent-based learning environment case study for learning requirements elicitation skills. In: Proceedings of the AIS SIG-ED IAIM 2013 Conference (2013)
13. Ferreira, V.M.F., Carvalho, J.C.C., Werneck, V.M.B., da Costa, R.M.E.M.: Developing an educational medical game using AgilePASSI multi-agent methodology. In: IEEE 28th International Symposium on Computer-Based Medical Systems, pp. 298–303 (2015)
14. Vaughan, N., Gabrys, B., Dubey, V.N.: An overview of self-adaptive technologies within virtual reality training. Comput. Sci. Rev. **22**, 65–87 (2016)
15. da Costa, R.M.E.M., Mendonca, I., Souza, D.S.: Exploring the intelligent agents for controlling user navigation in 3D games for cognitive stimulation. In: 8th International Conference on Disability, Virtual Reality and Associated Technologies, vol. 1, pp. 1–6 (2010)
16. Yu, E.: Modeling strategic relationships for process reengineering. In: Yu, E., Giorgini, P., Maiden, N., Mylopoulos, J. (eds.) Social Modeling Engineering (2011)
17. Hight, J., Novak, J.: Game Development Essentials: Game Project Management. Thomson, Clifton Park (2007)
18. Pan, Z., Cheok, A.D., Yang, H., Zhu, J., Shi, J.: Virtual reality and mixed reality for virtual learning environments. Comput. Graph. **30**, 20–28 (2006)
19. Tetris. http://www.tetris.com. Accessed Feb 2018
20. JAVA3D. http://java.sun.com/javase/technologies/desktop/java3d/. Accessed Feb 2018

21. Brutzman, D., Daly, L.: X3D: 3D Graphics for Web Authors. Morgan Kaufmann Publishers, Los Altos (2007)
22. NETLogo. http://ccl.northwestern.edu/netlogo. Accessed Feb 2018
23. JADE. http://jade.tilab.com/. Accessed Feb 2018
24. JAVA. http://www.java.com/pt_BR/. Accessed Feb 2018
25. JAVAScript. http://www.javascript.com/. Accessed Feb 2018
26. MySQL. http://www.mysql.com. Accessed Feb 2018
27. Netbeans. http://netbeans.org/. Accessed Feb 2018
28. Gomes, E.R.: A model based on intelligent agents FIPA platform for distance learning environments. Final Work, Federal University of Pelotas, RS, Brasil (2005). (in Portuguese)

How Machine Learning Could Detect Anomalies on Thinger.io Platform?

Nayat Sanchez-Pi[1]([✉]), Luis Martí[2], Álvaro Luis Bustamante[3], and José M. Molina[3]

[1] Institute of Mathematics and Statistics, Rio de Janeiro State University, Rio de Janeiro, Brazil
nayat@ime.uerj.br
[2] Institute of Computing, Fluminense Federal Univertity, Niterói, Brazil
lmarti@ic.uff.br
[3] Computer Science Department, Carlos III University of Madrid, Madrid, Spain
{alvaro,molina}@ia.uc3m.es

Abstract. This research explores the capacity of Machine Learning techniques to detect anomalies and how incorporate this capacity to thinger.io platform. Thinger.io is a IoT opensource platform that allows to create an IoT environment using any hardware available on market. In this paper, several ML techniques are proposed to detect anomalies in the platform.

Keywords: Predictive analysis · Machine Learning · Time series · IoT

1 Introduction

Ambient Intelligence (AmI) envisions a future information society where users are "proactively, but sensibly" provided with services that support their activities in everyday life [4]. AmI scenarios depict intelligent environments capable of unobtrusively recognize the presence of individuals and seamlessly react to them [11]. To achieve this goal, AmI systems embed a multitude of sensors in the environment that acquire and exploit data in order to generate an adequate response through actuators, using communication systems and computational processes. Sensor and Actuator deployment and communications should be developed using the Internet of Thing paradigm.

The Internet of Things (IoT) is generally conceptualized as connecting "things" to the Internet to provide some kind of utility, such as remote sensing or remote actuation [31]. It relies on the same basic concepts than M2M (Machine to Machine) [18], or even can be seen as an evolution of wireless sensor and actuator networks (WSAN) [2]. However, aside from the new underlying technologies that appears in this domain, i.e., new communication protocols, cheaper network interfaces, battery friendly devices, etc., the underlying idea is to be able to deploy an intelligent, invisible network, which can be monitored,

© Springer International Publishing AG, part of Springer Nature 2018
J. Bajo et al. (Eds.): PAAMS 2018 Workshops, CCIS 887, pp. 259–269, 2018.
https://doi.org/10.1007/978-3-319-94779-2_23

controlled and programmed. Therefore, IoT technologies and products, generally requires a connection to the Internet to allow multiple devices and services to interact each other [1].

In the 1990s, the Internet began to proliferate in professional and consumer environments, but was still very limited by poor data networks (unstable connections, low bandwidth, etc.). In 2000, the Internet connection became the norm for several applications, and today is indispensable for numerous companies, industries, and consumer products, which requires remote information access. However, many of these connected applications still require human interaction and monitoring through applications and interfaces. The real idea behind the IoT is to build an invisible technology that works in the background to behave dynamically in the way our "things" act as we want. The possibilities offered by IoT systems are numerous, and can be applied to several fields, from Smart Homes, Smart Cities, Connected Car, Industry 4.0, Smart Farming, etc.

In general, the IoT can be applied to any process or environment which requires a monitoring or remote actuation, generally over the Internet. It can be used for monitoring fuel consumption, control cultivation processes, supervise storage conditions, control pollution, irrigation systems, etc. There are also many recent developments related to monitoring chronic patients or older people (associated to the HealtCare term), agriculture (Smart Farming), power generation systems, etc.

Till the date, in the world it is possible to find about 5 billion connected devices, while the predictions in the IoT talk about 50 billion connected by 2020. These large-scale numbers introduce numerous technological challenges at the infrastructure and computing level that need to be developed [3]. In this paper, we explain the open problems in IoT and present a free platform named thinger.io. A specific development is explained: software and hardware, and form this development we explain how ML techniques could be useful to be incorporated in thinger.io to detect anomalies in sensor values.

2   Open Problems in IoT

Inside IoT platform, some problems appears at different levels [24]:

1. Monitoring a complex environment: Monitoring the real-world environment is a big challenge given the number of variables that can be sensed nowadays. There are multiple sensors that can be used to monitor temperature, humidity, presence, people location, ultraviolet radiation, air quality, hazard gases, pressure, proximity, acceleration, etc. [1,30]. So, it is important to research and select the available sensors that can be used to achieve the desired tasks, taking into account the integration in the environment in a transparent way (ubiquitous computing). In some cases, such as in wearable devices [26], the sensors must be small enough, so they can be integrated in devices with constrained dimensions.

2. Connectivity: Today it is possible to find several ways to connect devices to the Internet, such as the well-known wireless networks (WiFi, Bluetooth 4.0, 6LoWPAN), mobile networks (4G LTE), wired networks (Ethernet, Fiber Optics), etc. [14]. Such variety of interfaces allows a broad way to connect intelligent sensors to the Internet, but at the same time it opens technological challenges in the infrastructures that support them, such cloud computing systems [15]. This involves working with optimized network protocols to work with sensors with limited resources, dealing with the scalability of computing architectures to support the concurrent connection of millions of devices, and the availability of permanent access that requires such devices. In addition, it is necessary to think in standard ways of communication between devices, self-discovery, etc. This way, devices from different manufacturers can interact between them to generate the expected intelligent behavior.

3. Autonomy: Although there are several types of sensors and actuators that can be integrated in intelligent IoT environments, there are still many challenges regarding the autonomy of its deployment. Many devices must be powered by batteries, which provides limited time of use, like in wereables, or devices deployed in remote areas. So, it could be necessary to perform multiple optimizations at different levels of the IoT architecture to extend the life time of a deployment [25]. It is possible to optimize in different areas like protocols to save bandwidth, sensing periods, power saving mode of devices and sensors, etc. [28]

4. Security: Devices deployed in our environment can be monitoring personal information, or even interact with our resources and nearby elements, like those present in homes or the industry. This way, the security in the IoT ecosystem is a real concern, to avoid leaking sensitive data, or granting access to non-authorized actors to actuate over our environment, like our home, or car. This way it is required to have secure clouds, secure connections, anonymity in the information stored in the cloud, etc. [29]

3   IoT Platform

The IoT platform used for the experiment is an open source alternative, called thinger.io. Thinger.io is relatively new to the IoT ecosystem but is being used extensively in different research projects [13,20,21], or even for education [17]. It provides a ready to use cloud service for connecting devices to the Internet to perform any remote sensing or actuation over the Internet. It offers a free tier for connecting a limited number of devices, but It is also possible to install the software outside the cloud for a private management of the data and devices connected to the platform, without any limitation [29].

This platform is hardware agnostic, so it is possible to connect any device with Internet connectivity, from Arduino devices, Raspberry Pi, Sigfox devices, Lora solutions over gateways, or ARM devices, to mention a few. The platform provides some out of the box features like device registry; bi-directional communication in real-time, both for sensing or actuation; data and configuration

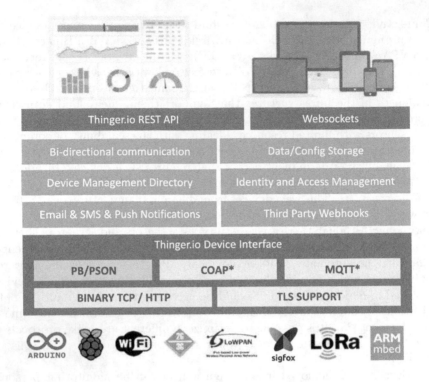

Fig. 1. The architecture of thinger.io.

storage, so it is possible to store time series data; identity and access management (IAM), to allow third party entities to access the platform and device resources over REST/Websocket APIs; third party webhooks, so the devices can easily call other web services, send emails, SMS, push data to other clouds, etc. It also provides a web interface to manage all the resources and generate dashboards for remote monitoring. The general overview of this platform is available at Fig. 1.

The main feature used in this platform, for the purpose of this paper, is related with the "Data Buckets", where a bucket is a resource for storing time series data. This way, a data bucket is a time series storage where devices can push information when required. Each data point is automatically timestamped in the cloud at reception time, as IoT devices do not use to handle a RTC by themselves (Real-time Clock). This information is stored in the cloud in secure, efficient, and scalable solutions (Dynamo DB from Amazon Web Services). The information stored in a bucket can be both displayed in a dashboard inside the console interface or exported in ARFF, JSON, or CSV for its offline analysis.

The information analyzed in this paper is the result of almost 1 year of recording from different sensors (all integrated in the same device) with a 5 min sampling interval. The second feature required to be configured in his platform is associated to the device registry in the "Devices" section. Each device in Thinger.io must be registered, so they can present their own credentials to interact with the platform resources, like storying information from sensors. In our setup it is required to provide access to a single device, which is described in the hardware section.

4 Hardware

The hardware used for the experiment relies on a board that is a complete Internet of Things development kit, called Climastick, that integrates WiFi connectivity along with a set of powerful sensors to provide environmental and motion sensing. This way, it is possible to create several connected projects easily. It is fully compatible with the Thinger.io cloud infrastructure, as it provides easy to use libraries that can be used in the Arduino IDE. This device is shown in Figs. 2a and b.

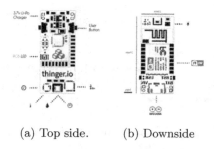

(a) Top side.   (b) Downside

Fig. 2. Hardware

It includes environmental sensing for temperature, relative humidity, barometric pressure, and lux intensity. It also includes an Inertial Measurements Unit (IMU), integrating an accelerometer, a gyroscope, and a digital compass. It can be used in remote areas, as it incorporates a Li-Po Charger, which is able to charge (and be powered by) batteries from a solar panel or the built-in USB. Finally, it also provides some features like an RGB Led, or a user button. The complete set of specifications are available at Figs. 3 and 4. This device is fully compatible with the Arduino Environment, as it can be programmed directly from the Arduino IDE. There are libraries for reading the sensors and connecting the board to the Thinger.io Cloud or other Internet services. With this device, using the Thinger.io platform in the cloud, the device will be sensing the environment for temperature (from two different sensors BME280 and SI7021), humidity (BME280), barometric pressure (BME280), altitude (based on the barometric pressure), and light intensity (TSL2561). The sensors specifications are available at Fig. 4. The device will be sampling this information every 5 min. The device will enter in a deep sleep mode (power saving mode, without Internet connection) after sampling the information to avoid self-heating the board and affect temperature readings. All the sensor readings are taken at the same time, immediately after the board initialization.

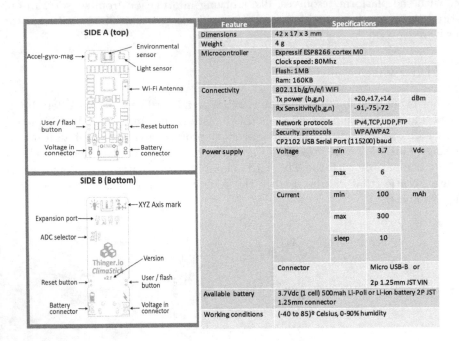

Fig. 3. Climastick board information

Feature	Specifications					
	Sensor	Variable	Range	Resolution	Accuracy	Condition
Embedded Sensors **(I2C)**	BME280	Temperature	(-40 , 85) ºC	0.01 ºC	(+0.5 , +1) ºC	
		Relative humidity	(0 , 100) %Rh	0.01 %Rh	(+1 , +3) %Rh	(0 , 60) ºC
		Barometric pressure	(300 , 1100) hPa	0.18 hPa	(+0.1 , +1)hPa	TCOP 25-65 ºC, 900 hPa
	SI7021	Temperature	(−10,85) ºC	0.01 ºC	+0.3 ºC	(-10,85) ºC
	TSL2561	Light	(0 , 65535) Lux	0.01 Lux	+3.5 lux	(-30,70)ºC (0,95)%Rh
	MPU-9250	Magnetometer	+4800µT	0.6 µT/LSB	+500µT	(-40 , 85) ºC
		Accelerometer	+16 g	2048 LSB/g	(2-16)LSB/g	92Hz total RMS noise
		Gyroscope	+2000º/sec	16.4º/sec	0.01º/s /√Hz	
						LPF range (5-250KHz)
Voltage sensor	ADC	VIN / BAT voltage	(0 , 5) Vdc	1. Vdc (10 bit ADC)	0.1 Vdc	(-10 , 60) ºC
Buttons	1 Reset button		Pulled-up to 3.3Vdc, ground when is push			
	1 Flash / User button (GPIO-0)		Pulled-up to 3.3Vdc, ground when is push			
Other	User LED (GPIO-13)		Up to 1024 analog stepping			
	Serial Port Tx LED (GPIO-2)		PWM frequency range is between 100Hz and 1Khz, 14 bit resolution			
	P1 Digital aux port (GPIO12)					
	ADC external port (if selected)		Completely float circuit, no build-in pulls or filter.			

Fig. 4. Board specifications

5   Machine Learning to Detect Anomalies

Methods for detection of intrusion attacks [7,27] can be grouped in two main classes: (1) signature-based IDSs, that look for a *priori* known patterns of attacks in system activities, (2) anomaly-based IDSs, which model the normal behavior of the system/network under supervision and flag deviations from normal as anomalous, and hence, possible attacks. Signature-based IDSs can detect known attacks for which patterns have been discerned. However, it is impossible for them to detect new or unknown attacks, as, by their very nature, they do not possess a known pattern for such attacks. This fact limits the applicability of this class of IDS in IoT scenarios, where low or little maintenance can be expected and the multiplicity of devices implies that many more patterns should be elaborated than are practically discovered and maintained. Anomalies themselves can have a positive or negative nature, depending on their context and interpretation. The importance of anomaly detection is a consequence of the fact that anomalies in data translate to significant actionable information in a wide variety of application domains. The correct detection of such types of unusual information empowers the decision maker with the capacity to act on the system in order to adequately react, avoid, or correct the situations associated with them.

Anomaly detection has seen extensive study and use in a wide variety of applications such as fraud and intrusion detection [12], fault detection in safety critical systems [19], finance [6] or industrial systems [32], among many others.

Anomaly-based IDSs learn to model normal system behaviour and detect deviations from it, they are capable of detecting known and unknown attacks. This is a special case of semi-supervised learning [8].

Anomaly detection can be posed as a particular case of the classification problem in which data items must be tagged as either 'normal' or 'anomalous'. A classifier correctly detects instances that correspond to each of the two categories. Because of this fact, the existing metrics devised to assess the quality of a classification algorithm are also applicable in this context. When dealing with anomaly detection, the dataset is generally highly unbalanced, as, by their very nature, there are fewer 'anomalous' instances available than 'normal' ones. If only the classification accuracy is used, the error contribution of the anomalies will be reduced and hence the model will be biased to not recognize them. Furthermore, as already mentioned, the anomaly detection problem requires that the classifier not only be able to correctly classify the 'normal' and 'anomalous' instances present in the training dataset, but also be capable of detecting when a given input falls in an area that was not covered by data of the training set and, therefore, also can be interpreted as an anomaly.

The clonal selection algorithm (CLONALG) [10] is one of the computational implementations of this principle and an illustrative way of presenting the underlying concepts of clonal selection.

The CLONALG model involves the selection of antibodies (candidate solutions) based on affinity either by matching against an antigen pattern or via evaluation of a pattern by a cost function.

Selected antibodies are subjected to cloning proportional to affinity, and to hypermutation of clones inversely proportional to clone affinity. After repeating this process for all the elements of the set of elements to be recognized (of for a sufficient amount of times in case of function optimization), the algorithm returns the set of antibodies as solution to the problem. The resultant clonal-set competes with the existent antibody population for membership in the next generation. In addition, low-affinity population members are replaced by randomly generated antibodies. The pattern recognition variation of the algorithm includes the maintenance of a memory solution setwhich in its entirety represents a solution to the problem.

Negative selection [9] another paradigm is widespread in the field of immune systems. It aims at deleting self-reactive lymphocytes during their maturation (auto-immunity). Such lymphocytes can occur because the building blocks of antibodies (produced by B-cells) are different gene segments that are randomly composed and undergo a further somatic hypermutation process.

The negative selection of T-cells occurs within the thymus which provides a protected environment rich in antigen presenting cells that present self-antigens. Immature T-cells that strongly bind these self-antigens are eliminated. Thus, the remaining T-cells, which can recognize foreign antigens, are not self-reactive. The negative selection mechanism has mainly inspired the negative selection algorithm (NSA) [16] from a computational perspective. Given a set of 'normal' data instances – the self – as input, the NSA performs a loop where, at each iteration, it randomly generates immature immune cells (detectors) and tries to match each cell with all the instances in the self via an affinity function. If that immune cell matches at least one instance in the self it is discarded, otherwise, it is promoted to a mature cell and output by the algorithm. This iterative process is repeated until almost all the non-self-space has been covered by the generated immune cells, or a maximum number of detectors is reached.

In the literature, hyper-spheres [16] and/or hyper-rectangles [5] have been used as the geometrical structures of the detectors.

The Voronoi diagram-based Evolutionary Algorithm (VorEAl) [22,23],was proposed as an anomaly detection algorithm with success. VorEAl evolves Voronoi diagrams that are used to classify data in an anomaly detection context [7]. VorEAl applies a multi-objective optimization principle that allows it to build models of operation that are a compact representation of normal operation while still taking into account known anomalies. VorEAl is particularly suitable for the IoT domain because of low computational footprint at exploitation time. This is because it represents the areas of the input space as Voronoi cells. These cells can be represented as a k-d tree. Therefore, the computational complexity of computing a VorEAl prediction for a Voronoi diagram of m cells is, on the average case, of $O(log m)$ and, in the worst case, $O(m)$.

6   Conclusions

Sensor data is fundamental for AmI developments. Usually, AmI projects are developed using IoT platforms (public or private) based on Cloud services.

IoT platforms captures information from deployed sensors which collects huge amounts of data. This massive number of online devices raises new security and privacy challenges that, combined with the current state of world affairs, call for special attention to these issues. In particular, anomalies in deployed sensors is a crucial point for AmI developments, if system does not acquire real data, reasoning system could not understand the environment to take the appropriate decision. In this paper, we introduce the use of ML techniques in the context of IoT intrusion detection.

Acknowledgements. This work was supported in part by Project MINECO TEC2017-88048-C2-2-R, FAPERJ APQ1 Project 211.500/2015, FAPERJ APQ1 Project 211.451/2015, CNPq Universal 430082/2016-9, FAPERJ JCNE E-26/203.287/2017, Project Prociência 2017-038625-0, CNPq PQ 312792/2017-4.

References

1. Abbasi, A.Z., Islam, N., Shaikh, Z.A., et al.: A review of wireless sensors and networks' applications in agriculture. Comput. Stand. Interfaces **36**(2), 263–270 (2014)
2. Alemdar, H., Ersoy, C.: Wireless sensor networks for healthcare: a survey. Comput. Netw. **54**(15), 2688–2710 (2010)
3. Atzori, L., Iera, A., Morabito, G.: The internet of things: a survey. Comput. Netw. **54**(15), 2787–2805 (2010)
4. Augusto, J., Shapiro, D.: Advances in Ambient Intelligence, vol. 164. IOS Press Inc., Amsterdam (2007)
5. Aziz, A., Salama, M., ella Hassanien, A., El-Ola Hanafi, S.: Detectors generation using genetic algorithm for a negative selection inspired anomaly network intrusion detection system. In: Proceedings of the Federated Conference on Computer Science and Information Systems, pp. 597–602, September 2012
6. Borrajo, M.L., Baruque, B., Corchado, E., Bajo, J., Corchado, J.M.: Hybrid neural intelligent system to predict business failure in small-to-medium-size enterprises. Int. J. Neural Syst. **21**(04), 277–296 (2011)
7. Chandola, V., Banerjee, A., Kumar, V.: Anomaly detection: a survey. ACM Comput. Surv. (CSUR) **41**(3), 15 (2009)
8. Chapelle, O., Schlkopf, B., Zien, A.: Semi-Supervised Learning, 1st edn. MIT Press, Cambridge (2010)
9. Dasgupta, D., Niño, L.F.: Immunological Computation: Theory and Applications. CRC Press, Boca Raton (2009)
10. De Castro, L.N., Von Zuben, F.J.: Learning and optimization using the clonal selection principle. IEEE Trans. Evol. Comput. **6**(3), 239–251 (2002)
11. Ducatel, K., Bogdanowicz, M., Scapolo, F., Leijten, J., Burgelman, J.: Scenarios for ambient intelligence 2010, ISTAG Report, European Commission. Institute for Prospective Technological Studies, Seville (2001). ftp://ftp.cordis.lu/pub/ist/docs/istagscenarios2010.pdf
12. Eskin, E., Arnold, A., Prerau, M., Portnoy, L., Stolfo, S.: A geometric framework for unsupervised anomaly detection. In: Barbará, D., Jajodia, S. (eds.) Applications of data mining in computer security. ADIS, vol. 6, pp. 77–101. Springer, Boston (2002). https://doi.org/10.1007/978-1-4615-0953-0_4

13. Fisher, D.K., Fletcher, R.S., Anapalli, S.S., Pringle III, H.: Development of an open-source cloud-connected sensor-monitoring platform. Adv. Internet Things **8**(01), 1 (2017)

14. Florez, J., Rojas, J., López, D.: Evaluación de tecnologías de comunicación para redes vehiculares de última generación. Redes de Ingeniería **1**(1), 12–23 (2012)

15. Gubbi, J., Buyya, R., Marusic, S., Palaniswami, M.: Internet of things (IoT): a vision, architectural elements, and future directions. Future Gener. Comput. Syst. **29**(7), 1645–1660 (2013)

16. Ji, Z., Dasgupta, D.: Real-valued negative selection algorithm with variable-sized detectors. In: Deb, K. (ed.) GECCO 2004. LNCS, vol. 3102, pp. 287–298. Springer, Heidelberg (2004). https://doi.org/10.1007/978-3-540-24854-5_30

17. Kamar, I., Chatterjee, P., Hamie, A.: Internet of things in learning systems-a perspective of platforms. Int. J. Adv. Res. Comput. Sci. **7**(2), 52–56 (2016)

18. Kim, J., Lee, J., Kim, J., Yun, J.: M2M service platforms: survey, issues, and enabling technologies. IEEE Commun. Surv. Tutor. **16**(1), 61–76 (2014)

19. King, S., King, D., Astley, K., Tarassenko, L., Hayton, P., Utete, S.: The use of novelty detection techniques for monitoring high-integrity plant. In: Proceedings of the 2002 International Conference on Control Applications, vol. 1, pp. 221–226. IEEE (2002)

20. La Ode Hasnuddin, S.S., Abidin, M.S.: Internet of things for early detection of lanslides. In: Prosiding Seminar Nasional Riset Kuantitatif Terapan 2017, vol. 1 (2018)

21. Likotiko, E., Petrov, D., Mwangoka, J., Hilleringmann, U.: Real time solid waste monitoring using cloud and sensors technologies. Online J. Sci. Technol. **8**(1), 106–116 (2018)

22. Martí, L., Fansi-Tchango, A., Navarro, L., Schoenauer, M.: Anomaly detection with the voronoi diagram evolutionary algorithm. In: Handl, J., Hart, E., Lewis, P.R., López-Ibáñez, M., Ochoa, G., Paechter, B. (eds.) PPSN 2016. LNCS, vol. 9921, pp. 697–706. Springer, Cham (2016). https://doi.org/10.1007/978-3-319-45823-6_65

23. Martí, L., Fansi Tchango, A., Navarro, L., Schoenauer, M.: VorAIS: a multi-objective voronoi diagram-based artificial immune system. In: Proceedings of the 2016 on Genetic and Evolutionary Computation Conference Companion, pp. 11–12. ACM (2016)

24. Miorandi, D., Sicari, S., De Pellegrini, F., Chlamtac, I.: Internet of things: vision, applications and research challenges. Ad Hoc Netw. **10**(7), 1497–1516 (2012)

25. Pantazis, N.A., Nikolidakis, S.A., Vergados, D.D.: Energy-efficient routing protocols in wireless sensor networks: a survey. IEEE Commun. Surv. Tutor. **15**(2), 551–591 (2013)

26. Patel, S., Park, H., Bonato, P., Chan, L., Rodgers, M.: A review of wearable sensors and systems with application in rehabilitation. J. Neuroeng. Rehabil. **9**(1), 21 (2012)

27. Shafi, K., Abbass, H.A.: Biologically-inspired complex adaptive systems approaches to network intrusion detection. Inf. Secur. Tech. Rep. **12**(4), 209–217 (2007)

28. Sudevalayam, S., Kulkarni, P.: Energy harvesting sensor nodes: survey and implications. IEEE Commun. Surv. Tutor. **13**(3), 443–461 (2011)

29. Suo, H., Wan, J., Zou, C., Liu, J.: Security in the internet of things: a review. In: 2012 International Conference on Computer Science and Electronics Engineering (ICCSEE), vol. 3, pp. 648–651. IEEE (2012)

30. Suryadevara, N., Gaddam, A., Rayudu, R., Mukhopadhyay, S.: Wireless sensors network based safe home to care elderly people: behaviour detection. Sens. Actuators A Phys. **186**, 277–283 (2012)

31. Weber, R.H.: Internet of things-new security and privacy challenges. Comput. Law Secur. Rev. **26**(1), 23–30 (2010)
32. Woźniak, M., Graña, M., Corchado, E.: A survey of multiple classifier systems as hybrid systems. Inf. Fusion **16**, 3–17 (2014). Special Issue on Information Fusion in Hybrid Intelligent Fusion Systems, http://www.sciencedirect.com/science/article/pii/S156625351300047X

AIDE-VR: Extending a Virtual Living Lab Framework Using Virtual Reality

Thiago Vieira de Aguiar[✉], Nayat Sánchez-Pi[✉],
and Vera Maria Benjamim Werneck[✉]

Rio de Janeiro State University, Rio de Janeiro, Brazil
thiago.vieiradeaguiar@gmail.com, {nayat,vera}@ime.uerj.br
http://www.uerj.br/

Abstract. The Ambient Intelligence Development Environment (AIDE) tool allows developers of Ambient Assisted Living (AAL) solutions to test their projects in a virtual environment. The simulation reduces the onus on systems development in AAL, proving to be an adequate tool for the adoption of agile methodologies in AAL projects. This work presents the implementation of an extension of AIDE that enables designers to test their solutions with the end user through the virtual reality environment. AIDE-VR extends the simulations of the first tool to be used with the end users of the product in an immersive experience through the use of virtual reality.

Keywords: Virtual Living Lab · Human-Centered Design
Virtual reality

1 Introduction

A solution in Ambient Assisted Living (AAL) aims to accompany and support people with special needs like whether elderly and people with physical and mental limitations, within their coexistence places [1,2].

How it's a relatively sensitive scenario and it involves users with limitations, it's possible to affirm that the acceptance of these users to the solution is an important metric in the validation of these systems, since these have as main objective, to increase the autonomy of the individuals in their environments.

As a way of seeking to gain the relative acceptance of the user to the developed solutions, the approach called Human-centered Design (HCD) proposes the involvement of the same in the entire process of product construction.

Agile methodologies, such as the Scrum framework, encompass this approach and propose an iterative process of development where, at each iteration, the user performs an evaluation on the product in developement.

However, solutions in AAL require an expressive set of hardware and the industry has not yet defined protocols and standards that allow the development of systems independent of the platforms on which they will be deployed.

© Springer International Publishing AG, part of Springer Nature 2018
J. Bajo et al. (Eds.): PAAMS 2018 Workshops, CCIS 887, pp. 270–281, 2018.
https://doi.org/10.1007/978-3-319-94779-2_24

Therefore, the adoption of agile methodologies can considerably increase the cost of an AAL project, since it would require the acquisition of hardware for user evaluations. In this evaluation, several factors could further increase the project's cost such as the non-adequacy of the user to the acquired hardware. Moreover, the evolution of technology may render obsolete, at advanced stages of the project, some or the set of hardware, acquiring previously, at the beginning of the project.

Using HCD methodologies for user involvement, applying physical prototypes in AAL domain, is costly and time consuming, because that combines software artifacts, devices and physical environments [2].

To solve this problem and to promote relative decrease in the possible onus on such projects, the concept of Virtual Living Lab (VLL) was defined, which suggests the creation of virtual environments for the validation of AAL solutions.

These virtual environments are equipped with devices, also virtual, that simulate the behavior of the set of hardware required by the project, allowing to perform tests in a very inexpensive way and also allows several data collects to be performed in simulated executions.

Ambient Intelligence Developmnet Environment (AIDE) emerge as a tool for easy development and rapid prototyping of AmI systems, adopting the idea of VLL and offering a virtual environment for simulations aimed at creating AAL solutions [3].

However, the presented tool is limited cause it creates a non-participative simulations, that is, there is no interaction on the part of the end users of the product, because it has the interaction engineer with focus, having as main objective, to offer for the engineer, a virtual environment for product evaluation.

It is important to note that this tool does not aim at developing solutions in AAL, but in creating a virtual environments for AAL developers to evaluate their solutions.

This work presents a proposal to extend the AIDE tool, which allows the developer to make available to the end user of the product in development to evaluate this through an environment in virtual reality.

2 Theoretical Foundation

This section presents the theoretical foundations involved in this work. These concepts are Ambient Intelligence, Ambient Assisted Living, Virtual Living Lab and Virtual Reality.

2.1 Ambient Intelligence

Ambient Intelligence (AmI) is a discipline built on the concepts of ubiquitous computing, customizable systems, and user-centered human-machine interaction design [4]. This information technology paradigm is intended to increase people's ability through digital environments that are responsive, adaptive, and responsive to human needs, skills, gestures and emotions [5].

The key technologies required by an AmI are [18]: unobtrusive hardware; communication infrastructure; dynamic and massively distributed device networks; relatively natural and human interfaces; reliability and safety.

2.2 Ambient Assisted Living

As a consequence of AmI's development, Ambient Assisted Living (AAL) emerges as an important tool in the strategies needed to address social challenges related to population aging.

The AAL theme arises from the application of the concepts of domotics and intelligent houses in the resolution of problems related to the inhabitants with limitations, helped by networks of sensors and actuators and systems of autonomous action through the concept of AmI [6].

It aims to providing assistance to people people with special needs (whether elderly, people with physical and mental limitations, etc.) in their environments of coexistence to promoting the increase of the people's autonomy [1].

As specific objectives of an AAL has, to prolong the permanence of individuals in their family environments, increasing their autonomy, self-confidence and mobility; to support the maintenance of health status and its functional capabilities; to promote a healthier lifestyle for individuals at risk; increase security, prevent social isolation and; to support caregivers [7].

Regarding quality issues in an AAL, [8] points out the following aspects, like: cost, ease of use and usability, adequacy, confidence and security and adaptability.

It is important to note that user interaction in AAL services is one of the most complex interaction projects when it comes to usability engineering. In an AAL environment, the modalities of interaction that can be used are speech recognition systems, gestural systems, context sensitive systems, visual, auditory or tactile interaction [9].

The philosophy of Virtual Living Lab, below, proposes to reduce costs in the development of this type of solution.

2.3 Virtual Living Lab

In an AAL project, it's need a set of hardware devices to make it capable of perceiving their environment and exchanging information with it.

Moreover, it is possible to affirm that such solutions need to reach a high level of acceptability of users in view of its objective That is, the user experience of AAL solutions needs to be considered as one of the key validation metrics for this type of solution.

However, in order to reach such a level of acceptability, the constant participation of the end user is required in all its development, allowing its rapid return in relation to the solution, this feedback, perceived through tests of the solution [10].

Thus the use of agile methodologies, such as Scrum and the use of HCD, are presented as a way to meet this need, thus ensuring that the user is part of all stages of the solution development process.

As a result of the quest to increase the success of AAL projects, the philosophy of Virtual Living Lab (VLL) has emerged. It is a low-cost computer simulation, allowing to reduce costs, reproducing AAL environments, which includes not only the inhabitants of the environment, but also the systems involved, as well as the sensors and actuators [12].

The implementation of these virtual laboratories, allows to evaluate the solution developed using few financial resources, simulating physical equipment, such as sensors, through virtual representations, located in virtual environments. In addition, it allows users to evaluate the solution without being subject to the inherent risks of project failures [13], making it easier to adopt agile methodologies.

The application of the HCD methodology, allowing the user to be involved in the development process and the creation of physical prototypes are both costly and time consuming. The adoption of virtual reality techniques for the construction of virtual prototypes offers users the possibility of experimenting and interacting with the proposed solution before its implementation or implantation [2].

However, it is important to note that when using agile methodologies and HCD, the user's contact with a viable prototype or a viable minimum product is proposed, while in the use of a virtual environment, it is important to search for an experience that involves as much of the user's perceptions as possible, since he will not be in contact with a real product, for this, the use of virtual reality is shown as an adequate option.

2.4 Virtual Reality

The science that studies the concept of virtual reality works to define and create interactive interfaces that are closer to the human senses, developing and applying complex techniques with the intention of replacing real-world sensory information with synthetic stimuli. The goal of immersive virtual environments is to allow the user to experience a computer-generated world as if it were real, producing a sense of presence in the user's mind [14].

Virtual reality offers the possibility of three-dimensional environments and intuitive "transparent" interfaces in the sense that the computer interface is not visible to the user. Further, their three-dimensional display and interaction capabilities allows for significantly enhanced three-dimensional perception and interaction over conventional three-dimensional computer graphics.

VR techniques are very suited to create Virtual Prototypes that offer the beneficiaries the possibility to visualize and interact with proposed solutions before they exist [2].

Therefore, virtual reality presents itself as a appropriate human-machine interaction to be applied in the adoption of VLL environments for use in testing activities with the end-user of the solution under development.

3   Related Works

[9] describes a modeling framework for validate the usability and accessibility of AAL using the HCD methodology. This framework, VAALID is a advanced computer aid engineering tools that will allow developers of AAL products and services to optimize and make more efficient the whole process of User Interaction design, and to validate usability and accessibility at all development stages, following a user centred design process.

The VAALID uses Virtual Reality technologies to provide an immersive environment with 3D virtual ambients where AAL users can experience a new product, interactively [10]. Each user can navigate and interact with the simulated scene to test the developed services. Such an environment can be developed through the language VRML[1].

How a evolution of the search [2] presents the VAALID IDE that is an integrated development and simulation environment which pretends speed up the iterations through the HCD cycle, offers an advanced, integrated, computer aided design environment to development VR representation and simulation of AAL Solutions, to integrate the planning phase of aal solutions and their testing and evaluation.

Another tool, Ambient Intelligence Development Environment[2] (AIDE) [3] is a framework to produces a 3D simulation that represents the results of the interactions between an AAL system and some virtual character [3], thus allowing the incorporation of AAL services in this virtual environment [11].

The simulation deals with physical models supported by the open source engine JMonkeyEngine[3] [3] which is a Java based game engine.

Therefore, AIDE allows developers to observe the interaction between avatars, which have behaviors defined by them, through their own diagrams and the AAL environment, equipped with a multi-agent system.

This tool, however, is limited to simulating the behaviors defined by the developer, following strictly their diagrams. Such simulations do not allow user interaction with the environment. It presents itself as a suitable alternative for the development team to run tests on the proposed solution, evaluating, for example, if the algorithms developed are responding properly, but can not evaluate the user experience in the interaction with the environment [15].

All this tools has limitations, the first, the project is centered in VR using InstantReality where the definition of the scenarios is closed and deterministic due to, in part, lack of a physics engine. Besides, theirs models are concerned with AAL applications and user interaction with the applications but no with the

---

[1] http://www.web3d.org/x3d-vrml-most-widely-used-3d-formats.

[2] http://grasia.fdi.ucm.es/aide/.

[3] http://jmonkeyengine.org/.

daily activities and her behaviour in the physical space. Therefore, this approach does not allow automatic tests because a user is always necessary [11].

The limitations of the AIDE tool; not allowing the end user to dive with the simulation and aware that this tool has as its main focus the interaction engineer or the developer.

So, it has been proposed an extension of this second to make possible its usefulness to the user, offering an immersive experience when the interaction with the virtual environment, in order to allow a more satisfactory evaluation of the product under development. Such an extension was titled AIDE-VR.

AIDE was selected because it's builded from a game engine, that has a serveral resources to implemented virtual environment.

4   PROSPOSAL: AIDE-VR

As a proposal to extend the tool presented, AIDE, a version was implemented that allows the developer to provide to the end user with an immersive experience where the user are to also has the option of interacting with the environment in an active way, surpassing the role of mere spectator of the simulation and assuming the role of protagonist in the presented scene.

As seen previously, virtual reality techniques provide an immersive user experience that gives the user the perception that he is present in the environment that is being presented to him. With this, the adoption of this interaction method presents itself promising to increase the reliability when applying AAL product tests by end users.

Moreover, just as the solution itself, which is intended for a real environment, an AAL, is presented in "virtual mode", so the evaluation of the solution by the user may not involve a level of perception of the solution that is appropriate to a correct assessment of the product by him. Thus, just as the solution itself was "immersed" in the simulation, in the VLL, immersing itself is presented as the best interaction alternative.

As the base tool, AIDE, is built through the game engine JMonkeyEngine (JME), it brings together a collection of features that facilitate not only the implementation of virtual environments, like physics simulation algorithms or assets to enrich the scene, but also the possibility of adopting specific libraries, such as those that allow the implementation of an interface in virtual reality.

Having already available, add-ons to work with virtual reality, simply adapt the tool AIDE to work with such interaction mechanism. The version 3 (JME3) of JMonkeyEngine has a wide range of support for Virtual Reality (VR).

The library required to implement virtual reality in JME is JMonkeyVR. The package that implements this library for the hardware available for the experiments, the Oculus Rift, is the Legacy: Oculus Rift 0.5. In this, the main class, OVRApplication, must be used to extend the PHATApplication class of the AIDE tool.

This second class is responsible for starting the simulation hardware configurations and executing the simulated scene update loop.

With the implementation of the OVRApplication class, PHAT
Application takes on the responsibility of to start the virtual reality hardware,
a graphical user interface and an icon for the user to interact with the environment.

4.1   Features of the Extension

The developed extension has, how the main purpose, to allow the end user of the
product in development to have a more immersible experience possible, through
the simulation of a virtual environment explored through virtual reality.

This objective is based on the premise that, in order for a user to actually
experiment with the product to be developed, in accordance with HCD approach
and agile methodology, he must experience, in the test, something as close as
possible to what he will experience when using the final product.

With this, what is offered to the developer, with the extension in question,
AIDE-VR, is a simulation for the evaluation of its solutions that allows to the
same, to present to the end user an experience of its product in development in
a virtual reality environment.

The Fig. 1 presents the same environment available in the AIDE tool, but
running with the implemented extension, AIDE-VR.

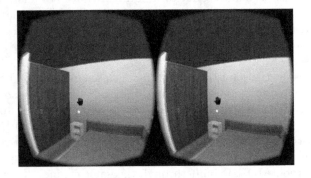

Fig. 1. AIDE-VR - 3D virtual environment.

In addition, along with the inherent immersion of the virtual reality experience, the user acquires the ability to engage in the scene as an active actor of the
same, assuming a first-person perspective, acquiring an active role in the simulation, interacting with the elements of the simulation, colliding up with obstacles,
and even interfering with the activities of the other simulation avatars.

How the result of this ability, the user has the possibility change the plot
predefined by the developer and, with this, to observe the results of his own
action on the environment and, therefore, its action on the solution, on the
product that is being presented to it.

With this, the user can be able, with more accurately, evaluate how the
solution presented satisfies him as a potential user of the product.

4.2 Tool Evaluation

As a way of evaluating the extension, was proposed use cases similar to those presented in the AIDE tool.

The basic scenario presented in AIDE, simulates the conviviality of two characters, an elderly person with Parkinson's syndrome and another character without limitations, who plays a caregiver role.

The technologies already implemented in the tool are presence sensors, fall sensors (accelerometer), camera, sensors of opened door and microphone.

In the first scenario, the caregiver is alerted to the fall of the elder. He also receives information from the room in which the elderly person has suffered the fall, allowing him to readily assist him.

In a second simulation, with a scenario similar to the first one, the caregiver is alerted to the need for the elderly to ingest a particular remedy because their blood pressure is inadequate. The elderly is sitting on the sofa in the living room watching TV. In this scenario, the caregiver is alerted to the need for the medication, in addition to being informed of the location where the medicine box and the elderly meet.

The Fig. 2 displays the user's vision when viewing another avatar of the scene.

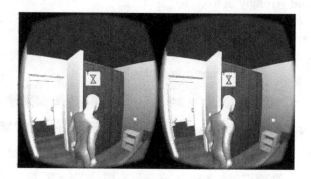

Fig. 2. AIDE-VR - Avatars.

As a third scenario, also with a similar plot to the previous ones, however, this time the caregiver is alerted that the elderly person presents abnormal conditions and that he should immediately contact the emergency service and inform the abnormal conditions identified.

These three scenarios were performed through a usability test with a group of participants who, after the experiment, they answered a satisfaction questionnaire based on the SUS method [16].

The usability test, in relation to the scenarios presented, resulted in an approximate result, in the first scenario, 90% of the participants concluded the activity, among them, 10% needed help. In the second scenario, 81% concluded, with 44% of them, with the help of the mediator. In the third scenario, all concluded, with 27% being helped. Figure 3 shows the results.

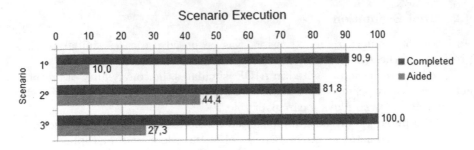

Fig. 3. Result of the usability test.

The result obtained with the experiment, in the application of the satisfaction questionnaire, and using the definitions of the subject of [17], that is presented in Fig. 4, indicates good results in the usability dimension, suggesting to pay more attention to the question of user satisfaction. These topics relate the questions presented in the satisfaction questionnaire to the usability categories: satisfaction, minimizing errors, easy of memorize, efficiency and learning facility; using a five-level scale: strongly disagree, disagree slightly, not disagree or agree, slightly agree and strongly agree.

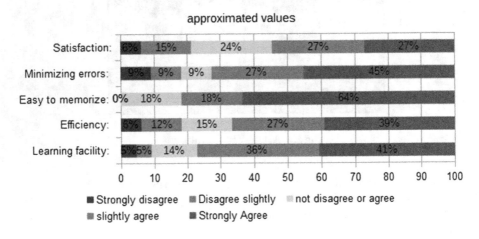

Fig. 4. Summary of the SUS questionnaire.

The execution of the presented scenarios allowed the identification of the particularities between the two tools.

In the first tool, AIDE, all simulations are summarized in the user observing the actions performed by the avatars, of both characters. In this, the user had the possibility to navigate the scene, as an observer, but in a passive way, his actions do not interfere in the simulation. In this case, the user assumes a third-person view.

In this tool, it is possible to perform repeated executions of the simulation, allowing the collection of data in a systematic way. But, since artificial intelligence has not been implemented in the characters, one can "prevent" the execution of the other's task without generating a reaction.

In the second tool, AIDE-VR, the user starts to have active role in the simulation, assuming a first-person view. Therefore, in the first scenario, when the elderly person fell, if the user, in the role of the caregiver, did not act on the environment, the elderly person would remain fallen.

When the user's view assumes the third-person perspective, it is assumed that he interprets his avatar as "I interacting in the environment through him (the avatar)", but when he assumes the perspective in the first-person, the user interprets the scene as "I interacting in the environment".

In the second scenario, the recovery of the elderly, the restoration of their normal health condition, depended exclusively on the user who, in the role of caregiver, had the responsibility of administering the necessary medicine for the elderly.

As well as in the third scenario that, without the action of the user, still in the role of the caregiver, the elderly would not receive the necessary care for the maintenance of their health.

The Table 1 presents a comparative summary of the features offered by the two tools.

Table 1. Features of tools.

Features	AIDE	AIDE-VR
User view	3-person	1-person
Navigating on the virtual environment	yes	yes
User is a character in the scene	no	yes
User interacts with simulation elements	no	yes
User changes the default storyline	no	yes
Systematic repetition of the simulation	yes	yes

5   Conclusions

The VLL's philosophy, proposed as a promising approach for the reduction of the costs involved in the AAL solution development process, can go further by offering tools that make it possible to adopt methodologies and practices aimed at user involvement in the production process of a solution.

When speaking of solutions tested in virtual environments, this involvement should bring to the referred user an experience that goes beyond their basic senses such as vision and hearing, also assuming their more subjective perceptions as the sensation of immersion in these environments, because once they are evaluating a product, it should have the maximum impression it would have if in a real environment, testing a real product.

Currently, the most immersive way to be applied in virtual environments are the virtual reality techniques.

The extension of the AIDE tool, presented in this work and entitled AIDE-VR, offers the developer or the interaction engineer the possibility of adopting such a tool for use in the evaluation process by the end users of their product in development.

Therefore, it offers the developer a better adaptation to agile methods such as Scrum and the HCD approach, thereby enabling the construction of solutions with a relative increase in user satisfaction with the product.

The adoption of these methods aims to facilitate the identification of problems of adequacy of the product to the needs of the end user, since, assuming the commitment proposed by the HCD, the user will be in constant contact with the solution in development, giving a return of what is really necessary develop, making the final product as suitable as possible to its needs.

In addition, with the adoption of agile methodologies, from the initial iterations, the user will be evaluating the system and constantly demonstrating if the solution is easy to use, if it has a relatively adequate usability for its limitations.

However, while such practices are possible without the use of the tool presented, the cost of deploying a test environment, with all the necessary resources and being relatively safe for the user, often leads to the adoption of such practices, infeasible. With this, the use of tools that implement the concept of VLL, are presented as an alternative to allow the use of agile methods and of the HCD relatively cheaply.

Therefore, the AIDE-VR tool can be an alternative to help with the quality of AAL products when it comes to cost, usability and suitability.

References

1. Cunha, M., Fuks, H.: AmbLEDs para ambientes de moradia assistidos em cidades inteligentes. In: Proceedings of the 13th Brazilian Symposium on Human Factors in Computing Systems, Sociedade Brasileira de Computação, pp. 409–412 (2014)
2. Sala, P., Kamieth, F., Mocholí, J.B., Naranjo, J.C.: Virtual reality for AAL services interaction design and evaluation. In: Stephanidis, C. (ed.) UAHCI 2011. LNCS, vol. 6767, pp. 220–229. Springer, Heidelberg (2011). https://doi.org/10.1007/978-3-642-21666-4_25
3. Gómez-Sanz, J.J., Sánchez, P.C.: A multiple data stream management framework for ambient assisted living emulation. In: De Pietro, G., Gallo, L., Howlett, R.J., Jain, L.C. (eds.) Intelligent Interactive Multimedia Systems and Services 2016. SIST, vol. 55, pp. 695–703. Springer, Cham (2016). https://doi.org/10.1007/978-3-319-39345-2_62
4. Sánchez Pi, N.: Intelligent techniques for context-aware systems (2011)

5. Acampora, G., Cook, D.J., Rashidi, P., Vasilakos, A.V.: A survey on ambient intelligence in healthcare. In: Proceedings of the IEEE, vol. 101, no. 12, pp. 2470–2494. IEEE (2013)
6. Ferreira, J.M.R.: Middleware para ambient assisted living: casos de estudo (2013)
7. Leitão, A.C.C.: Modelos de negócio para ambient assisted living (2012)
8. Ribeiro, D.A.G.: Modelação em contextos de ambient-assisted living (2013)
9. Naranjo, J.-C., Fernandez, C., Sala, P., Hellenschmidt, M., Mercalli, F.: A modelling framework for ambient assisted living validation. In: Stephanidis, C. (ed.) UAHCI 2009. LNCS, vol. 5615, pp. 228–237. Springer, Heidelberg (2009). https://doi.org/10.1007/978-3-642-02710-9_26
10. Fernández-Llatas, C., Mocholí, J.B., Sala, P., Naranjo, J.C., Pileggi, S.F., Guillén, S., Traver, V.: Ambient assisted living spaces validation by services and devices simulation. In: 2011 Annual International Conference of the IEEE Engineering in Medicine and Biology Society, pp. 1785–1788. IEEE (2011)
11. Campillo-Sanchez, P., Gómez-Sanz, J.J., Botía, J.A.: PHAT: physical human activity tester. In: Pan, J.-S., Polycarpou, M.M., Woźniak, M., de Carvalho, A.C.P.L.F., Quintián, H., Corchado, E. (eds.) HAIS 2013. LNCS (LNAI), vol. 8073, pp. 41–50. Springer, Heidelberg (2013). https://doi.org/10.1007/978-3-642-40846-5_5
12. Gómez-Sanz, J.J., Cardenas, M., Pax, R., Campillo, P.: Building prototypes through 3D simulations. In: Demazeau, Y., Ito, T., Bajo, J., Escalona, M.J. (eds.) PAAMS 2016. LNCS (LNAI), vol. 9662, pp. 299–301. Springer, Cham (2016). https://doi.org/10.1007/978-3-319-39324-7
13. Prendinger, H., Gajananan, K., Zaki, A.B., Fares, A., Molenaar, R., Urbano, D., van Lint, H., Gomaa, W.: Tokyo virtual living lab: Designing smart cities based on the 3D internet. IEEE Internet Comput. 17(6), 30–38 (2013)
14. Bowman, D.A., McMahan, R.P.: Virtual reality: how much immersion is enough? Computer 40(7), 36–43 (2007)
15. de Aguiar, T.V., Sánchez-Pi, N., Werneck, V.M.B.: Virtual Living Lab com AIDE Utilizando Metodologias Ágeis (2016)
16. Brooke, J.: SUS-A quick and dirty usability scale. Usability Eval. Ind. 189(194), 4–7 (1996)
17. Tenório, J.M., Cohrs, F.M., Sdepanian, V.L., Pisa, I.T., de Fátima, M.H.: Desenvolvimento e avaliação de um protocolo eletrônico para atendimento e monitoramento do paciente com doença celíaca. Revista de Informática Teórica e Aplicada 17(2), 210–220 (2010)
18. Friedewald, M., Da Costa, O., et al.: Science and technology roadmapping: ambient intelligence in everyday life (Am I@ Life Karlsruhe: Fraunhofer-Institut für System- und Innovationsforschung (FhG-ISI) (2003)

PAAMS Workshop MASGES

Multi Agent System Application for Electrical Load Shedding Management: Experiment in Senegal Power Grid

M. Al Mansour Kebe[✉], Mamadou L. Ndiaye, and Claude Lishou

Ecole Superieure Polytechnique, Universite Cheikh Anta Diop,
BP 5085, Dakar Fann, Senegal
manskebe@gmail.com

Abstract. This paper proposes a multi-agent approach for power grid load shedding programming. Known as the most complex machine ever made by man, power grid is an essential pillar of all national economies. Its complexity and size make it vulnerable. Load shedding is usually an emergency control process against electrical networks with low production capacity. In this study, a system named MASLA, a Multi Agent System based Load Shedding Algorithm, which explores the load shedding planning is proposed. In electrical distribution system, power is delivered to customers through feeders which are a combination of electrical lines and medium voltage transformer substations. Depending on its power, a feeder may serve very large number of customers of different types (industrial, residential, ...). Hence, Feeder Agent and Load Agent are defined in a power grid and a negotiation takes place between them, considering customer's level of priority to select which one will be significantly impacted in a possible emergency outage. The model is implemented using a multi agent platform and a case study using the Senegalese power grid revealed that the proposed approach is useful and feasible for companies facing frequent disruption of electricity supply.

Keywords: Multi agent system · Complex system · Power grid
Power cut · Load shedding · Knapsack problem

1 Introduction

Electrical energy is essential in the life of modern societies. Indeed, nobody imagines going about their daily activities without their mobile phones, computers, televisions or radios and yet all these amenities require electricity to function. In developing countries, power companies face disruption of electricity supply and customers undergo several hours of power outage throughout the year, a situation that can severely impact the economy and the social stability depending on when and where these outages occur. It is therefore important to implement an optimization system of these power cuts that reduces the impact for the customer in a fair model. Even though power outages are similar from the customers' point of view, and may just differentiated by their duration and impact, the reasons for their occurrences are numerous. Given the distribution network we can mention: the lack of sufficient production, sudden disconnection of one or more power

© Springer International Publishing AG, part of Springer Nature 2018
J. Bajo et al. (Eds.): PAAMS 2018 Workshops, CCIS 887, pp. 285–298, 2018.
https://doi.org/10.1007/978-3-319-94779-2_25

generating units from the power grid, precautionary measures to avoid losing power grid equipments due to overload, preventive maintenance.

A very important factor to consider is the level of customer supply priority. Indeed, when the amount of energy generated is not sufficient, it is important to consider the priority level based on customer criticality (such as hospitals, public services, special events), to ensure the safety and stability of the country.

Information on the level of priority will be used to build an energy resource allocation plan. A model defining a realistic mechanism of what can be called a smart shedding which, unlike conventional shedding, allows negotiation among the agents of the system to select those who will be shed. The proposed model will optimize customer's power outage duration from a multi-agent system taking into consideration various constraints.

The main contribution of this paper is the development of a multi-agent system for generating a well-controlled electrical load shedding planning which consider correct amount of load to meet the power deficit while keeping load priority based on some factors to reduce the impact of load shedding for both utilities and consumers.

The rest of the paper is structured as follows: Sect. 2 presents the background of the study, including complexity of the power grid, frequency control and literature review. The third section elaborates on the model of the proposed system. Section 4 describes the proposed multi-agent system along with the relevant implementation modalities. Section 5 presents the findings of a case study on Senegal's power grid followed by discussions on the proposed approach.

2   Background

2.1   Complexity of the Power Grid and Frequency Control

Power grid, commonly referred as the greatest and most complex machine ever made by man, is one of the most complex systems within a country [1, 2]. This complexity is due to the huge number of its components and their multiple interactions. From multiple production power plants, through transmission and distribution grids, power needs to be delivered in a very reliable way to each customer in every place of a country. As Schewe [1] expressed with such accurate humor, the power grid snakes its way to the bedroom, and climbs right up into the lamp next to your pillow, being there while you sleep and waiting for you in the morning.

Maintaining the equilibrium of this complex system goes through a real time true-distributed control of all system parameters. In these parameters, electrical frequency or 'frequency' is the main criterion of power grid system quality and security because it is [3]:

- a global variable of interconnected networks that have the same value in all parts of the network,
- an indicator of the balance between supply and demand,
- critically important for the smooth operation of all users and particularly the manufacturing and industrial sectors.

Controlling power frequency, which needs to be at 50 Hz (or 60 Hz) and stay in range between ±1% of this value, is highly problematic and requires the involvement of great power generation units that must have a reserve of power allowing to meet quickly increasing customer demand. In a case of a sudden generating unit failure or when there is insufficient reserve or Automatic Generation Control (AGC) mechanism, load shedding remains the easiest and most reliable way to restore electric power grid stability [4] and avoid general power system collapse known as blackout.

Load Shedding Scheme: Frequency based load shedding is an emergency protection strategy, implemented through electrical protection relay on each power grid feeder. Whenever frequency of the system falls below predetermined thresholds, parts of the system load are shed in some predetermined steps. Sometimes for more security, it is necessary to consider the frequency's rate of change (known also as frequency gradient). For instance, the European Network of Transmission System Operators for Electricity (ENTSOE) has recommended the following steps for under-frequency load shedding [5]:

- The first stage of automatic load shedding should be initiated at 49 Hz.
- At 49 Hz, at least 5% of total consumption should be shed.
- A stepwise 50% of the nominal load should be disconnected by using under-frequency relays in the frequency range of 49.0-48.0 Hz.
- In each step of load shedding, a disconnection of no more than 10% of the load is advised.
- The maximum disconnection delay should be 350 ms including breakers' operating time.

In the Senegalese power grid, the load shedding scheme is a combination of four (04) under-frequency value called frequency stage (or block) and three (03) threshold of frequency gradient (Tables 1 and 2).

Table 1. Senegal under frequency load shedding stage scheme

Under frequency stage	Stage 1	Stage 2	Stage 3	Stage 4
Threshold	49 Hz	48,5 Hz	48 Hz	47,5 Hz
Quantity of power to cut	20%	25%	25%	(x)
Temporisation	200 ms	200 ms	200 ms	0 ms

The percentage of load in Stage 4 (x) is not determined. To that stage belong the feeders which are not part of previous stages, except the feeders with disabled from load shedding program.

Table 2. Senegal under frequency load shedding gradient frequency

Gradient frequency stage	Stage 1	Stage 2	Stage 3
Threshold	1.2 Hz/s	2.5 Hz/s	3.2 Hz/s
Associated under frequency stage	Stage 1 and 2	Stage 1, 2 and 3	All stages
Temporisation	0 ms	0 ms	0 ms

This power grid issue known as Under-Frequency Load Shedding (UFLS) is classic and very largely addressed in literature [6, 7].

Power Companies Facing High Disruption of Electricity Supply: While power cuts are rare in developed countries (because demand is accurately forecasted, adequate infrastructure investment is scheduled and networks are well managed), they are common or even a normal daily event in many developing countries where electricity generation capacity is underfunded and/or infrastructure is poorly managed [8].

As a vivid illustration, the Senegalese power utility (Senelec) had to proceed in 2014 to 238 load shedding operations due to lack of power reserve and many successive tripping's of the generation units and network faults. In 2014 Senelec recorded 985 generations unit tripping's and 28,219 disruptions to the high-voltage and medium-voltage electricity networks [9].

It is known that when a power grid utility has neither sufficient power reserve nor automatic generation control mechanism, it is a day to day struggle to avoid black-out and load shedding are very frequent. Designing a well-controlled load shedding planning is of a great significance in this regard.

3 Literature Review and Use of Multi Agent System Within Power Grid

As previously noted, ensuring reliability and maintaining equilibrium of a power grid goes through a real time and true– distributed control of all system parameters. A Modern solution to this need for control is provided with the use of products and services from the Information Technologies.

To address the load shedding issue, reliable techniques are required to provide fast and accurate load shedding to prevent collapse in the power system. Computational intelligence techniques, due to their robustness and flexibility in dealing with complex non-linear systems, could be an option in addressing this problem. In [10] a comprehensive review of application of computational intelligence techniques for load shedding in power systems is addressed including techniques like artificial neural networks, genetic algorithms, fuzzy logic control, adaptive neuro-fuzzy inference system, and particle swarm optimization. The review paper discusses the limitation of these computational intelligence techniques, which restricts their usage in load shedding in real time.

Moreover, Multi Agents System (MAS) which builds on theories and concepts from many areas such as computer science, artificial intelligence, distributed systems, social sciences, economics, organization and so on [11], is a good candidate for power grid system. While other technologies provide good modelling approach to arrive at an optimal solution, MAS offers a way of viewing the world so it can intuitively represent a real world situation of interacting entities. For that reason, MAS are suitable applicant for smartgrid system that can be considered as a distributed information system, because it is intrinsically distributed with the sensors, actuators, and decision system spread in the grid. As a conclusion, the multiagent systems is a natural approach for studies, modeling and simulation of smart grids.

Researches are very active in this field and many applications are being designed using this paradigm. In 2007, McArthur et al. [12, 13] conducted a comprehensive study on the use of multi agents systems within power systems. The most active domains in this study are system modelization, simulation and control of distributed system. In 2015, Moradi et al. [14] confirmed the growing interest and importance of the use of multi agent system in power grid, thanks to the trending topic of 'smart grid'. For instance, the work of Pipattanasomporn et al. [15] presents a method for design and implementation of a multi-agent system aimed at intelligent management of power grid. The work of Logenthiran et al. [16] showcases a MAS for the real-time operation of a micro grid. A MAS application to perform a diagnostic of the network disruption is described in the works of Wang [17] and Rehtanz [18] published a book on "autonomous systems and intelligent agents in power system control operation" which summarizes several case studies.

While load shedding questions are poorly discussed in regard to conventional power grids as far as using multi agent system, the question has recently been well addressed through microgrid point of view with many studies about load Shedding management in an islanded microgrid [19–21]:

Two algorithms have been proposed through exploration of recent related work

- In a **distributed algorithm**: Auctions are a great way to represent and solve distributed resource allocation problems. They require all components to send their bids to a centralized auctioneer who then determines the winners. The allocation will attempt the optimization of a target function, usually the auctioneer's revenue or the bidders' revenue. However, in most cases, this optimization is computationally intensive (NP-complete) and heuristics should be used.
- In a **centralized algorithm**, feeder-level groups are formed among the loads. In a group, the demand for the highest consumption is shed to the specific level of power consumption. Other demands in the group are then shed alternatively. After the cycling, if a supply demand gap remains, the next group is selected and the process continues until the gap is resolved. All components in a microgrid cooperate for a common goal, e.g., the maximization of system performance.

The main idea of the study is to benchmark from algorithm developed in the area of microgrid regarding load shedding and to apply them for improving operation in main power grid that are still very stressed especially in developing countries.

4 Modelization of the Load Shedding Application

4.1 The Design of Load Shedding Scheme

With the deregulation of the electricity market, elaboration of the load shedding program requires cooperation between Transmission System Operators (TSOs) and Distribution System Operators (DSOs). While the policy is set out by the TSOs, which are responsible for the balance of the system, the design and operational implementation of the power grid defense plan, including the selection of which customer's power to cut, are the sole responsibility of the DSOs.

Currently, the design of the load shedding plan is conducted considering the sensitivity of feeder and priority level. Consequently, feeders for Hospitals, official buildings, water pumping stations, telecommunication stations and other targeted users are systematically excluded from load shedding schedule. The load shedding program update is motivated by:

- An exceptional application for exclusion from load shedding: They come from Government Authorities responsible for giving information about events requiring stable supply of electricity, such as cultural or sport exhibitions, the President internal travels and meetings etc. In this case, the feeder in question is excluded from load shedding plan and is replaced by an equivalent one (similar load size) to maintain the equilibrium of the overall system.
- The Commissioning of a new feeder by choosing the stage which will be assigned to the feeder and rearranging the whole system is to ensure global equilibria.
- A large variation of feeder loads due to climatic change or distribution feeder reconfiguration.

4.2   Definition of Customer's Level of Priority

Even if power needs to be delivered in a very reliable way to each customer in every part of a country, customers don't have the same sensitivity as far as emergency power cut is concerned. In fact, the impact of power cuts is not the same for every user. With use of enterprise Customer Information System (CIS) or with the help of Standardized Industrial Classification (SIC) [22], we can adopt the Classification of all customers with a level of priority assigned to them as described on Table 3. In most cases, a feeder supplies a very large number of customers of different types: a mix of residential, commercial, government and institutions with different levels of priority. A Level of Priority must be assigned to each feeder with consideration of combinations of all customer types within this feeder to obtain a representative Level of Priority. In this study, we adopt the following rules:

Rule 1: When a feeder supplies an Emergency Customer, it will be classified as Emergency Feeder with 0 assigned as level of priority;
Rule 2: When a feeder contains a Strategic Customer, the feeder will be classified as Strategic Feeder with 1 assigned as level of priority;
Rule 3: When a feeder supplies an Event, the feeder will be classified as Temporary Critical Feeder with 1 assigned as level of priority;
Rule 4: Depending on the level of representativeness of Important or Standard customers on a feeder, it will be classified as an Important Feeder with 2 assigned as level of priority or Standard Feeder with 3 assigned as level of priority. For such endeavour, a dynamic weight coefficient is defined (see Table 4). Taking into

consideration of all individual customers (from 0 to n), the feeder's priority level (PL) is calculated as follows:

$$PL = 1 + \sum_{i=0}^{n} W_i \frac{P_i}{P_f} T_{peak_i} \tag{1}$$

with:

- P_f: total load of the feeder
- P_i: load of individual customer
- W_i: Weight factor (see Table 4)
- $Tpeak_i$: coefficient which takes into account time dependency of the PL and is set to 0 between 19 h and 23 h and to 1 otherwise. $Tpeak_i$ enables to takes into account the rise in insecurity (burglar udand other types of crime for example) in many residential areas, plunged in total darkness when power cut occurs at night.

Table 3. Definition of customers' level of priority

Level of priority	Customer classes	Concerned sector
0	Emergency	Customers with power interruption will face safety hazards e.g.: hospitals and health services, police stations, fire stations, important telecommunication services, and state institutions (palaces, ministry, army etc.)
1	Strategic	Customers with power interruption will suffer serious financial damage or public hazard problems e.g., major banks, oil refinery plants, high technology plants, electronic media, central and antennas for communications emergency, airports, railway stations and bus stations, water pumping stations, ...
1	Momentary critical	important events such as a football match, a concert, visits of the President, ... (are time dependent)
2	Important	Customers with power interruption will be detrimental to public interest or cause breakdown of logistic chains or idle labour e.g., schools, universities, companies, industry, markets, supermarkets, shopping center, sports, entertainment facilities
3	Standard	Customers with power interruption will experience minor outage cost such as food spoilage or heat in the absence of air conditioning: residential area, apartment, buildings, houses, traffic lights

Table 4. Customer's level of priority weight coefficient

Customer class	Weight coefficient (W)
Important	0.25
Standard	1

Based on the following, we can make a mathematical formulation of the optimization problem.

4.3   Mathematical Formulation of the Problem

The problem may be stated as an optimization problem as follows:

Given a feeder f_i comprised of Medium Voltage Substations MVs_i which is also a set of Low Voltage customers LVc_i; all the feeders f_i of the power grid need to be allocated to the 4 stages of load shedding scheme considering:

An objective: get the power of each stage PS_j which is a percentage of the total power of the grid as defined in Table 1

A constraint: Feeder level of priority LP_i and PS limitation as expressed in Eq. (2.1) below

Cost function: - see Eq. (2.2) below

- minimization of Economic or Social impact of the load shedding (by reducing Non-Supplied Energy NSE_i) in case of power cut
- minimization of Power Cut duration Cd_i for all customers:

$$
\begin{cases}
\sum_{i=0}^{n}(f_i \cdot Pf_i) \leq PS_j \ with \ f_i \in [0;1] & (2.1) \\[2mm]
\min z = \sum_{i=0}^{n} Cd_i \cdot f_i \ \ or \min z' = \sum_{i=0}^{n} ENS_i \cdot f_i & (2.2) \\[2mm]
\max v = \sum PL_i & (2.3) \\[2mm]
if \ j \in [0;1] => \begin{cases} w = \prod PL_i \neq 0 \\ w = \prod PL_i \neq 1 \end{cases} & (2.4)
\end{cases}
$$

where:

- f_i: feeder variable; If feeder f_i is selected, $f_i = 1$ else $f_i = 0$,
- Pf_i, Power rate of feeder f_i composed of Medium Voltage Substations PS_j: the power rate of each stage of the load shedding planning,
- PL_i: Priority Level of feeder f_i
- $Cd_{i:\ last}$ Power Cut duration for feeder
- ENS_i represent the Energy Non-Supplied (ENS) due to power cut for each feeder
- i varies from 0 to n which is the number of all feeders
- j varies from 0 to m which is the number of all load shedding stages.

Through this formulation, it can be noted there is an NP-complete problem which can be approached as a knapsack problem [23, 24] or more precisely a multidimensional knapsack problem if the number of stages (j) is considered.

5 MASLA - Multi Agent System Based Load Shedding Algorithm

This section presents the MASLA system architecture which comprises Supervisor Agent, Feeder Agent and Load Agent. Negotiation process is one of the key processes for the MASLA system to successfully attain its goal.

5.1 Composition of the Multi Agent System

Supervisor Agent (SA). The SA's role is to ensure the stability of the power grid and represent the world agent with a global vision of the system. The SA knows the peak demand of power grid, the frequency, the different stages of the load shedding planning. The SA is also in charge of initialisation of the system by creating Feeder Agent and Load Agent.

Feeder Agent (FA). The Feeder Agent represents a feeder which is a combination of electrical lines and medium voltage transformer substation that supplies very large amounts of customers of different types. The FA is characterized by its Power Rates, level of priority, Energy Non-Supplied (ENS) in case of power cut, date-time of last power cut.

Load Agent (LA). The Load Agent is a group of customers such as a small district represented by a medium voltage substation. The LA has the same characteristics as the Feeder Agent: Power Rate, level of criticality, Non-Supplied Energy (ENS), date-time of last power cut.

5.2 Negotiation Process Between Agents

The negotiation process takes place via the FIPA Contract-Net. The call for proposals from Supervisor agent allows the agents to proceed to biddings and find a solution to our NP Complete problem (Fig. 1).

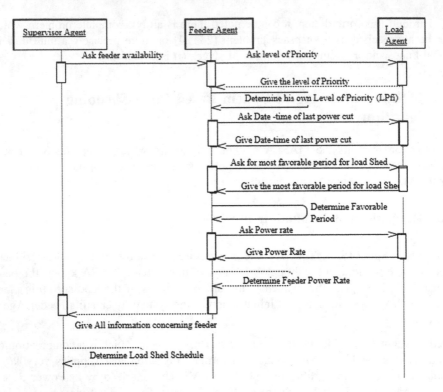

Fig. 1. Sequence diagram showing the negotiation process between agents

5.3   Multi-agent System Design and Implementation

To implement a multi-agent system, there are a number of open-source agent platforms available in the literature which helps developers to build a complex agent system in a simplified manner [25]. The GAMA platform [26] was chosen to implement our system. This platform is a new trend which enables multi agent development through an intuitive interface and programming language GAML. GAMA has the advantage of implementing many features like FIPA compliance, Geographical Information System (SIG) and the ability to build spatially explicit multi-agent simulation which is one feature of power grid system.

Figure 2 shows the architecture of the platform including interaction with database and importation of daily power system disturbance report that allows update of feeder data.

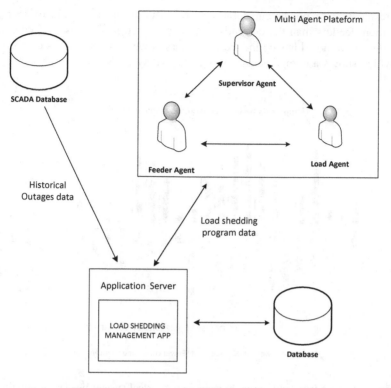

Fig. 2. Architecture of MASLA platform system

6   Test Case in the Senegalese Power Grid

In order to demonstrate the feasibility of the proposed approach, it has been applied to the Senegalese Power grid which is composed of 9 High Voltage Substations and 35 feeders, and has a peak load of 507 MW.

Only the cost function of minimization of Power Cut duration is considered in this case study.

In highly disturbed utilities, the load shedding protection mechanism operates every day. As a result, customers face many power cuts in a week in addition to other causes of power supply interruption due to equipment failure (underground power cable damage, aging of the equipment, ...) which are very common in developing countries [27, 28].

Dataset used for the case study are provided by Senegal Power Company (Senelec) dispatching control room. Regarding multi agent implementation, 01 supervisor agent, 35 feeders agents and 2000 loads agents were implemented corresponding to provided data for the test case. In July 2016, the UnderFrequency Load Shedding (UFLS) worked 16 times. Using these disturbances data, simulation is done to compare the real system with the multi agent approach.

As result, system power cut durations are reduced (from 42 min to 18 min)and involve more feeders than the currently used system (16 feeders vs 27 feeders).

The proposed model has optimized customers power cut duration as can be seen in Fig. 3 which shows a comparison between the two systems.

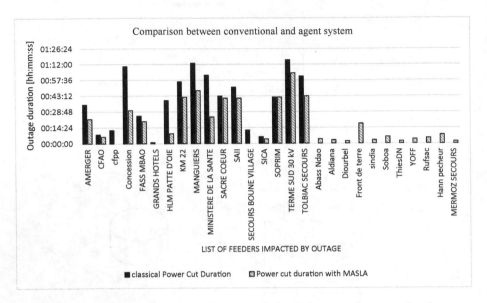

Fig. 3. Comparison between multi agent and classical system power cut duration

We not that MASLA system power cut durations per feeder are reduced and involve more feeders compared with the current conventional used system. As expected impact for customers are reduce and we have a more faithful model since more customers are impacted.

7   Conclusion and Future Work

In this paper, a multi agent system application for electrical load shedding management is presented. Following a literature review, the question is formulated as an optimization problem that is shown to be an NP Hard Problem. The paper proposes a method for planning load shedding in which a negotiation is done between customers, considering their level of priority to select which one will be impacted in a possible emergency power cut using Multi-Agent System. To demonstrate the effectiveness of the proposed multi agent methodology to achieve the MASLA function, the distribution system of Senegal has been taken as a case study. Known methods from microgrid have been applied to improve stressed conventional power grid with traditional load shedding scheme showing its effectiveness. In future work, the application will be considered with more accurate data combined with economic cost function in the Senegalese Power grid and real-time implementation with SCADA system.

References

1. Schewe, P.: The Grid: A Journey Through the Heart of Our Electrified World. J. Henry Press, Washington, D.C (2007)
2. Mei, S., Zhang, X., Cao, M.: Power Grid Complexity. Springer, Heidelberg (2011). https://doi.org/10.1007/978-3-642-16211-4
3. Ameli, M.T., Moslehpour, S., Khoshmakani, H.: Presentation and comparison of the various methods of load-shedding for frequency control in Iran power networks. In: IJME-INTERTECH Conference (2006), pp. 315–320 (2006). http://citeseerx.ist.psu.edu/viewdoc/download?doi=10.1.1.607.7554&rep=rep1&type=pdf
4. Diouf, E.: Frequency control ancillary services in large interconnected systems. Ph.D. dissertation. The University of Manchester (2013)
5. ENTSOE: Entsoe network code on emergency and restoration, 25 March 2015. https://www.entsoe.eu/major-projects/network-code-development/emergency-and-restoration/Pages/default.aspx. Accessed 12 Dec 2016
6. Zhang, Z., Wang, Z., Fang, P.: Study on emergency load shedding based on frequency and voltage stability. Int. J. Control Autom. **7**(2), 119–130 (2014). https://doi.org/10.14257/ijca.2014.7.2.12
7. Lu, M., ZainalAbidin, W., Masri, T., Lee, D., Chen, S.: Underfrequency load shedding (UFLS) schemes–a survey. Int. J. Appl. Eng. Res. **11**(1), 456–472 (2016). https://www.ripublication.com/ijaer16/ijaerv11n1_70.pdf
8. Wikipedia: Rolling blackout—Wikipedia, the free encyclopaedia (2016). https://en.wikipedia.org/w/index.php?title=RollingBlackout&oldid=750326314
9. Senelec: Rapport annuel mouvements d'energie (2014)
10. Laghari, J.A., Mokhlis, H., Bakar, A.H.A., et al.: Application of computational intelligence techniques for load shedding in power systems: a review. Energ. Convers. Manag. 75, 130–140 (2013). http://dx.doi.org/10.1016/j.enconman.2013.06.010
11. de Oliveira Saraiva, F., Asada, E.N.: Multi-agent systems applied to topological reconfiguration of smart power distribution systems. In: 2014 International Joint Conference on Neural Networks (IJCNN), pp. 2812–2819. IEEE (2014). https://doi.org/10.1109/ijcnn.2014.6889791
12. McArthur, S.D., Davidson, E.M., Catterson, V.M., Dimeas, A.L., Hatziargyriou, N.D., Ponci, F., Funabashi, T.: Multi-agent systems for power engineering applications part i: Concepts, approaches, and technical challenges. IEEE Trans. Power Syst. **22**(4), 1743–1752 (2007). https://doi.org/10.1109/TPWRS.2007.908471
13. McArthur, S.D., Davidson, E.M., Catterson, V.M., Dimeas, A.L., Hatziargyriou, N.D., Ponci, F., Funabashi, T.: Multi-agent systems for power engineering applications part ii: technologies, standards, and tools for building multi-agent systems. IEEE Trans. Power Syst. **22**(4), 1753–1759 (2007). https://doi.org/10.1109/TPWRS.2007.908472
14. Moradi, M.H., Razini, S., Hosseinian, S.M.: State of art of multiagent systems in power engineering: a review. Renew. Sustain. Energy Rev. **58**, 814–824 (2016). https://doi.org/10.1016/j.rser.2015.12.339
15. Pipattanasomporn, M., Feroze, H., Rahman, S.: Multi-agent systems in a distributed smart grid: design and implementation. In: Power Systems Conference and Exposition, 2009 PSCE 2009 IEEE/PES, pp. 1–8. IEEE (2009). https://doi.org/10.1109/psce.2009.4840087
16. Logenthiran, T., Srinivasan, D., Khambadkone, A.M., Aung, H.N.: Multiagent system for real-time operation of a microgrid in real-time digital simulator. IEEE Trans. Smart Grid **3**(2), 925–933 (2012). https://doi.org/10.1109/TSG.2012.2189028

17. Wang, H.: Multi-agent co-ordination for the secondary voltage control in power-system contingencies. IEE Proc.-Gener. Transm. Distrib. **148**(1), 61–66 (2001). https://doi.org/10. 1049/ip-gtd:20010025
18. Rehtanz, C.: Autonomous Systems and Intelligent Agents in Power System Control and Operation. Springer, Berlin (2003). https://doi.org/10.1007/978-3-662-05955-5
19. Choi, Y., Lim, Y., Kim, H.M.: Optimal load shedding for maximizing satisfaction in an Islanded microgrid. Energies **10**(1), 45 (2017). https://doi.org/10.3390/en10010045
20. Lim, Y., Park, J., Kim, H.-M., Kinoshita, T.: A bargaining approach to optimizing load shedding in islanded microgrid operation. IETE Tech. Rev. **30**, 483–489 (2013). https://doi. org/10.4103/0256-4602.125669
21. Lim, Y., Kim, H.M., Kinoshita, T.: Distributed load-shedding system for agent-based autonomous microgrid operations. Energies **7**(1), 385–401 (2014). https://doi.org/10.3390/ en7010385
22. Wang, P., Billinton, R.: Optimum load-shedding technique to reduce the total customer interruption cost in a distribution system. IEE Proc.-Gener. Transm. Distrib. **147**(1), 51–56 (2000). https://doi.org/10.1049/ip-gtd:20000002
23. Wikipedia: Knapsack problem—Wikipedia, the free encyclopaedia (2016). https://en. wikipedia.org/w/index.php?title=Knapsackproblem&oldid=753008280. Accessed 4 Dec 2016
24. Bernhard, K., Vygen, J.: Combinatorial Optimization: Theory and Algorithms. Springer, Heidelberg (2008). ISBN 978-3-540-71844-4
25. Kravari, K., Bassiliades, N.: A survey of agent platforms. J. Artif. Soc. Soc. Simul. **18**(1), 11 (2015). https://doi.org/10.18564/jasss.2661
26. GAMA Platform: Documentation sur la plateforme gama (2016). https://github.com/gama-platform/gama/wiki. Accessed 4 Dec 2016
27. Musa, B.: Outage analysis on distribution feeder in North East Nigeria. J. Multi. Eng. Sci. Technol. (JMEST) **2**(1), 149–152 (2015). ISSN: 3159-0040
28. Onishi, N.: Weak power grids in Africa's stunt economies and fire up tempers depending on their system size, system inertia and generation mix (2015). http://www.nytimes.com/2015/ 07/03/world/africa/weak-power-grids-in-africa-stunteconomies-and-fire-up-tempers.html. Accessed 01 Dec 2016

A Fuzzy-Based Multi-agent Model to Control the Micro-grid Operation Based on Energy Market Dynamics

Santiago Gil[✉], Oscar M. Salazar, and Demetrio A. Ovalle

Departamento de Ciencias de la Computación y de la Decisión, Facultad de Minas, Universidad Nacional de Colombia, Carrera 80 No. 65-223, Medellín, Colombia
{sagilar,omsalazaro,dovalle}@unal.edu.co

Abstract. The concept of distributed generation and renewable energy has increased the need for using Smartgrids which are electric micro-grids having intelligent characteristics that provide autonomy to the system not only to improve their operation but also to make it easier for users their management. The aim of this paper is to propose a fuzzy-based Multi-Agent Model to control a micro-grid by determining optimal operation states based on real-time process conditions and energy market dynamics. The Prometheus methodology is used for the MAS architecture design and development. The implementation of the system is carried out using Java, the JADE framework and the JFuzzyLogic library. Based on the proposed fuzzy MAS model, a prototype was implemented and validated through a case study. Results obtained demonstrate the effectiveness of this approach to automatically manage the states of a micro-grid when connected to external grid in a dynamic energy market environment. It is also possible to extend this application for different micro-grid applications involving other power generation, storage, and consumption capabilities.

Keywords: Micro-grid operation control · Real time systems · Smartgrids
Energy market dynamics · Fuzzy logic · Prometheus methodology

1 Introduction

The concept of distributed generation and renewable energies has increased the need for using the electric micro-grids, which supply a necessity in the electric energy sector which is in progress [1, 2]. The micro-grids can work in a manual way, but it is suitable to operate automatically and autonomously to ease the users its handle. In that situation where it is adopted the term of Smartgrid, micro-grids that exhibit intelligent characteristics and provide autonomy to improve its operation.

In the field of micro-grids or more commonly named Smartgrids, it has become usual the development of projects to propose different solutions or improvements on their operations; one of these approaches is the control of micro-grids, in which it is usually used methods and techniques from automation and artificial intelligent disciplines to give the "Smart" attribute to such a power system. Using some of these techniques, or

© Springer International Publishing AG, part of Springer Nature 2018
J. Bajo et al. (Eds.): PAAMS 2018 Workshops, CCIS 887, pp. 299–311, 2018.
https://doi.org/10.1007/978-3-319-94779-2_26

the combination of both, it is possible to characterize the micro-grid in an autonomous way, and every time in a more efficient and intelligent way.

A technique that could be used for the smart micro-grid control modeling is multi-agent system (MAS) approach. In fact, intelligent agents have some characteristics that allow micro-grids to effectively work on control tasks, as follow [3–5]: reactivity: respond immediately to changes perceived in their environment; task distribution: each agent has well-defined functionalities and identifies such problems to solve; proactivity: agents take initiative to solve problems; cooperation and coordination: perform tasks through the exchange of messages with other agents through a common language; autonomy: agents do not require the direct intervention of human beings to operate; deliberation: each agent has the ability to perform internal reasoning processes which allow it to make suitable decisions; mobility: can move from one node to another through the network; adaptation: from the changes in the environment switch its behavior and thus improve its performance, and parallelism: the system can improve its performance through the execution of tasks performed in parallel by agents.

This research work proposes a multi-agent system approach to control a micro-grid operation, by determining the next operation state using a fuzzy logic system [6] that uses –in real time execution– the energy market dynamics and micro-grid operation conditions. In fact, fuzzy logic approach allows systems to handle the uncertainty given by non-deterministic conditions present in real time energy systems.

In addition, it is offered to the user a consumption recommendation mechanism based on energy prices by displaying most expensive and cheapest hours to consume electric power. The design of the MAS architecture is based on Prometheus [7] methodology which covers the following three phases: System Specification, Architecture Design and Detailed Design. The implementation of system is carried out in an application using JAVA, JADE framework and JFuzzyLogic library. The application is integrated with MATLAB platform by means of MATLAB Engine API, where it is simulated the micro-grid operation. The energy price information is obtained from a web REST service.

2   Related Works

This section presents some related works within the research field and compares them in order to identify their strengths and weaknesses.

Wang et al. [8] propose the development of a multi-agent system for a micro-grid in a building, where there is a central agent which interacts with the process and data, and executes an optimization function to maximize the users' comfort by means of Particle Swarm Optimization (PSO) technique. The other local agents interact directly with the lowest level devices to perform the control logic by means of a fuzzy-based PID control loop which determines the power requirements that needs the device to keep high comfort.

Cheah et al. [9] develop an operation platform for a university campus micro-grid, which has some functionalities for the micro-grid operation and services for the system users. The main functionality the system deploys is that the user can schedule an energy consumption plan, and moreover, the system gives recommendations to the user based on the energy price, power consumption, peak hours, and user habits information gathered from the process, thus enabling the user to subscribe to the most economical consumption plan.

Li et al. [10] design a system to control the AGC (Automatic Generation Control) and AVC (Automatic Voltage Control) through a multi-agent system with the purpose of regulation and drops avoidance of the grid, implemented in an electric micro-grid named Cyber Physical Microgrid System (CPMS). The agents represent the distributed processing required in distributed generation, where each one acts directly over a generator set within the generation system, obtaining a physical connection (among devices and machines) and a logical connection that means the communication among agents.

Kouluri and Pandey [11] implement a multi-agent system for the control and regulation of a distributed micro-grid in critical conditions, where the system determines the micro-grid Connected/Disconnected states when detecting events that affect the micro-grid. The MAS implementation is performed by means of JADE framework, which is integrated with MATLAB/SIMULINK, where the power system model runs. The bridge between JAVA and MATLAB is done by means of MACSimJX Toolbox. This work considers 2 operation states: connected to and disconnected from external grid, and 3 agent types: control agent, DER agent, and load agent.

Feron and Monti [12] propose a Virtual Power Plant (VPP) with the goal of optimizing consumption price based on energy price interacting with the energy market. The optimization is carried out using Linear Programming (LP) and a multi-agent system, which consists in 4 agents, 3 of them are located in the physical process and the last is located in the high-level layer responsible of the system planning. The devices can generate or consume power, and they enter into an offer market, where the optimization is responsible of reducing the overall energy cost in the VPP system.

From previous reviewed research works it is possible to highlight a lack of autonomy within the system to automatically manage the micro-grid operation control by considering several states. Our approach involves the switch among 6 different states autonomously as well as a feedback mechanism offered by a recommendation system to the user. The switch among states is determined by means of the micro-grid operation conditions and also using the energy price values supplied by a real-time environment. The above is achieved through the integration of fuzzy logic techniques within a multi-agent system.

3   Model Proposed

The proposed model was developed following the Prometheus methodology alignments for Multi-Agent systems design. The Prometheus methodology proposes, as mentioned above, the following three phases: System Specification, Architecture Design and Detailed Design. The System Specification involves the definition of the following elements: goals, scenarios, roles, actions and perceptions. The main goal of the proposed system is to control the micro-grid operation to become it a Smartgrid. This approach includes some of the main parts of a micro-grid system to be functional considering the energy market dynamics. They are proposed the following sub-goals to achieve the main goal: interact with the user, manage micro-grid operation, supervise micro-grid operation, process energy price information, show recommendations to the user. In order to satisfy the proposed sub-goals, the following scenarios are defined: (1) User interface scenario, which points all the graphical information given and received to/by the user. (2) Operation scenario, which points the functionality of the cyber-physical process, (3) Energy market dynamics processing scenario, which points the acquisition, storing and processing related to energy price in the system. According to the Prometheus methodology, the following roles can be defined: (1) Energy market dynamics processor, (2) Price information getter, (3) Interface, (4) Micro-grid operation manager. The defined roles are grouped into agents, obtaining the next 3 agents: (1) Interface Agent, (2) Energy market Agent and, (3) Micro-grid control Agent, in which only the Energy market energy covers two roles (1 & 2). The system has a very reactive part, which belongs to the physical process, where the Micro-grid control Agent takes place, received perceptions (System conditions) from and making actions (Results from the operation changes) to the different actors of the process (Loads, batteries, micro-grid and external grid).

3.1 Energy-Market Agent Based on Fuzzy Logic

The Energy-Market Agent receives the perception about the energy price and performs the inferential mechanism applied on the control operation of the system, and finally, the Interface Agent interacts with the user and generate recommendations based on the most expensive and cheapest times of power consumption. At this time, it is only used one database, where it is stored the energy price information to make the operation inference and the user recommendation.

The design phase of the Prometheus methodology defines the system overview (see Fig. 1) where agents interact not only with the databases —that store information of the

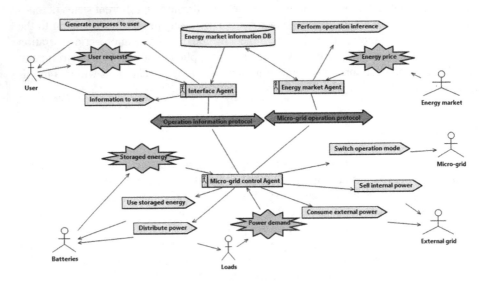

Fig. 1. Multi-agent system overview.

system entities— but also with other agents through communication protocols, and this allows to perform the functionalities of the proposed system efficiently.

The main capacity of the Energy-Market Agent is founded on the fuzzy inference of the micro-grid operation based on process conditions and energy price, always finding such a result in which it is possible to obtain a high economy throughput. In order to achieve this capacity, it is used a fuzzy logic mechanism, to obtain a result depending on the concerning variables.

The Fuzzy Inference System is divided into 2 fuzzy modules each one with 2 inputs, 1 output, and 9 fuzzy rules; when the power relation is satisfied (i.e. *power relation = generation − demand ≥ 0*), in this way, it works with the first inference, otherwise it works with the second one. The basis on which the designed fuzzy rules work can be described as follows:

RULE_1: IF higher energy price AND higher power availability THEN work in island mode AND sell the free power to external grid.

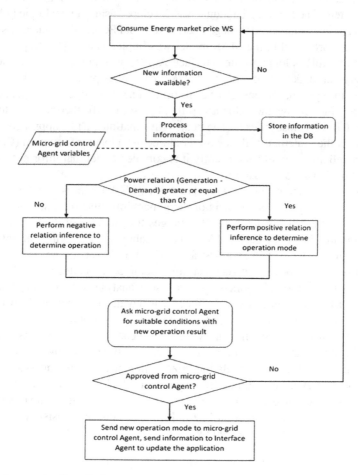

Fig. 2. Main capacity flow diagram concerning the inference of the micro-grid operation mode.

RULE_2: IF higher energy price AND lower power availability THEN work in connected mode using all the available power.

RULE_3: IF lower energy price AND higher power availability THEN work in island mode AND store the free power into batteries.

RULE_4: IF lower energy price AND lower power availability THEN work in connected mode AND consume external power AND store the available power into batteries.

Figure 2 presents the flow diagram concerning the main capacity of the Energy-Market Agent.

4   Model Implementation and Validation

The implementation of the fuzzy-based multi-agent system was carried out under Java platform with the JADE [13] framework in a Java application. The Java application was integrated with Matlab and Simulink via Matlab Engine API, where it ran the variables of the micro-grid system. The fuzzy logic module was developed using JFuzzyLogic [14] library. The used database was managed through PostgreSQL and PGAdmin4 manager system.

Every agent proposed in the MAS model was implemented. The graphical part of the application –that belongs to the Interface Agent– was implemented through Java Swing library and makes it possible to watch the changes produced in the conditions and results of the system. The energy price information is consumed from an open REST Web Service which brings the value and time [15], so, it is further possible to store in the Postgres DB with those indexes. The treated information is a first approach to process information on the system, the ideal case would be get a local information (Colombia), from a more reliable source, but currently it is complex to get that information in real-time offered by private organizations.

The micro-grid system can be adapted to work with different power characteristics, it only needs to change the parameters of the generation capability, storage capability and power demand analysis, to change the ranges for the rules of the Fuzzy Inference System. Currently the Fuzzy-based MAS concerns about the following variables for the operation of the power system as a first approach: Power generation, Power demand, Stored energy, Energy price. But such variables could be expanded as needed.

It is not on the scope of this work the power system analysis, we used the power system variables to verify the functionality when integrating it with the price variable in a real-time environment. The proposed micro-grid can generate up to 660 kW and store up to 440 kWh; based on those values the Fuzzy Logic Inference Systems were designed, but as mentioned before, it can be applied for whatever capabilities of the power system.

On the one hand, the positive relation Fuzzy Inference System consists of 2 inputs: price and stored energy, and 1 output: free-operation, which always activates the internal consumption state and also activates one of the two following states, sale or storage. On the other hand, the negative relation Fuzzy Inference System consists of two inputs: price and available power represented by:

$$\text{Generated power} + \text{stored energy}/1h \tag{1}$$

As well, the system has only one output: external-operation, which always activates the external consumption state (i.e. the micro-grid requires power supply from external grid), and also activates one of the two following states, complete consumption (full supply from external grid) or partial consumption (partial supply from external grid). Finally, the standby state appears when there are not enough suitable conditions to make decisions in order to switch among operation states. Such conditions concern communication problems, lack of energy prices due to web services unavailability, switch to manual operation, among others.

Figure 3 shows the prototype user interface displaying the information of the process. Below at left in the figure, it is shown the kWh average price graph obtained from one day long, the current average price in USD cents, and the time it was released. Below at right, it is deployed the Interface Agent recommendation being offered to the user and, current variables values of the power system. The current variables values are linked from MATLAB using MATLAB Engine API via the matlab.engine.shareEngine('matlab_microgrid') command in MATLAB Command Window.

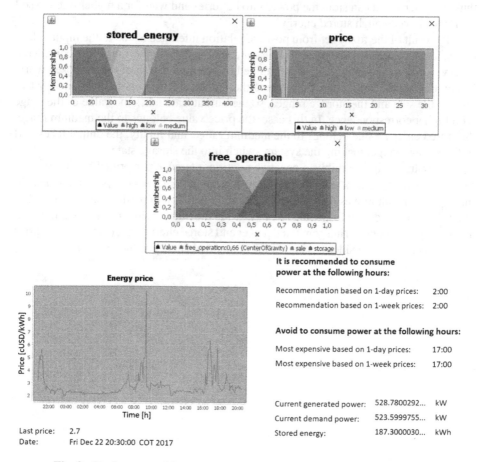

Fig. 3. Deployment of the system interface for a positive relation inference.

We can conclude that the Interface Agent recommendations offered to the user suggest a better way to save money when consuming power; in the posted recommendations the Interface Agent shows that the cheapest hour to consume power is at 2:00 am and the most expensive time is at 5:00 pm (17:00) – It covers all hour long (2:00 am–2:59 am, 5:00 pm–5:59 pm). The recommendations have 2 ways to calculate, the first one is by means of 1-day energy prices, considering as reference yesterday values, and the second one, by means of 1-week energy prices, considering as reference current week values. Normally, yesterday and week recommendations are identical, but it changes when they are non-working days, like Sundays or holydays, where yesterday recommendations vary in comparison to week recommendations, and it would help to identify some patterns, if it were the case.

Results obtained from the Energy-Market Agent –deployed in Fig. 3– shows a positive relation inference (because *generated power* > *power demand*), where the result moves to the storage state. The result of switching to the storage state is due to the following reasoning: (1) the current stored energy compared to the batteries capability is not enough and, (2) the price of the kWh is not too high to obtain a high profitability; thus, the micro-grid can store the power into batteries and wait for a higher price to sell energy or have enough stored energy.

The result of the fuzzy set from positive relation inference is due to the input values the system is concerned, the price and the stored energy; the inputs ranges are considered as low, medium and high values, determined by the application of the proposed work. Depending on the weighing of the inputs the output, the free operation, consider two ranges, the sale and the storage ranges, so the output state takes the value of the range with higher correspondence. In this case, the price value belongs to the medium range, the stored energy value belongs to the medium range, and finally, the output takes part of the storage range, making the system switch into the storage state.

By contrast, Fig. 4 exhibits a negative relation inference performed by the Energy-Market Agent since it is possible to affirm that *generated power* < *power demand*. In this case the result moves the state from external operation to partial consumption. The obtained result is due to following reasoning: (1) the micro-grid has enough amount of available power considering generated power and stored energy and, (2) the energy price is not too cheap to consider buying all the demanded energy to the external grid.

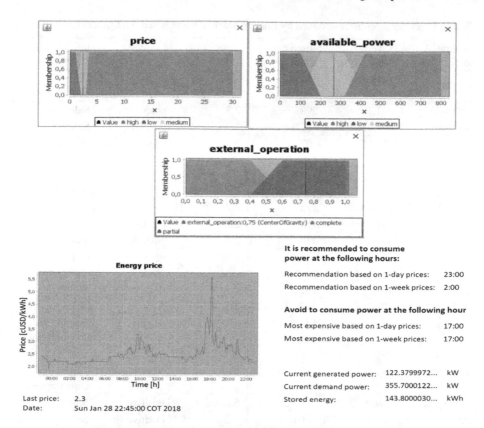

Fig. 4. Deployment of the system interface for a negative relation inference.

The result of the fuzzy set from negative relation inference is similar to the positive one, but with the price and the available power inputs and the same ranges. The output, the external operation, consider two ranges, the complete consumption and partial consumption ranges, so the output state takes the value of the range with higher correspondence. In this case, the price value belongs to the medium range, the available power value belongs to the medium range, and finally, the output takes part of the partial consumption range, making the system switch into the partial consumption state. Table 1 shows some results of both fuzzy systems with different conditions in the power system and the energy price, where it is possible to appreciate the responses of the fuzzy inferences for those conditions; they meet the behavior of the rules described in Sect. 3: for higher prices the system tends to be in sale or partial consumption states, but for lower prices the system tends to be in storage or complete consumption states, always depending on enough power conditions.

Table 1. Fuzzy inferences obtained by Energy-Market Agent based on different conditions.

Generated power [kW]	Power demand [kW]	Stored energy [kWh]	Energy price [cUSD/kWh]	Power relation	Inference result
43.4	284.3	15.9	2.3	negative	Complete consumption
520.4	423.3	298.78	2.3	positive	Sale
480.75	456.93	87.3	2.3	positive	Storage
125.5	415.85	63.4	2.3	negative	Partial consumption
87.5	415.85	32.4	2.2	negative	Complete consumption
457.57	432.13	275.2	2.2	positive	Sale
457.57	432.13	160.9	2.2	positive	Storage
655.9	315.67	438.2	2.2	positive	Sale
2.2	587.03	1.5	2.0	negative	Complete consumption
244.65	187.3	192.4	2.5	positive	Storage
244.65	187.3	205.2	2.5	positive	Sale
122.38	355.7	143.8	2.7	negative	Partial consumption
336.55	289.42	256.7	2.7	positive	Sale
112.15	487.3	56.5	5.8	Negative	Partial consumption
95.1	69.0	6.72	5.6	Positive	Sale
57.8	45.9	0.0	5.2	Positive	Sale
192.55	452.12	19.68	4.6	Negative	Partial consumption
351.88	307.25	48.5	3.9	Positive	Sale
277.32	389.1	35.6	3.4	Negative	Partial consumption
28.1	293.67	9.3	3.4	Negative	Complete consumption

It is important to highlight that the changes among states, when conditions vary in the system, can easily be seen because the designed Fuzzy Inference System enables the micro-grid to operate autonomously in a smart way. The results satisfy the expected behavior the multi-agent micro-grid control system was design for.

Figure 5 shows the communication sequence diagram among agents –obtained from JADE Sniffer Agent–, where it is shown the proposal given by the Energy-Market Agent with the new operation state as a result of the fuzzy inference sent to the Micro-Grid Control Agent as well as the accepted proposal message from Micro-Grid Control Agent, due to such a proposal complies with the process requirements. Other messages from Micro-Grid Control Agent are sent to the Interface Agent and Energy-Market Agent to update the process conditions to the entire MAS.

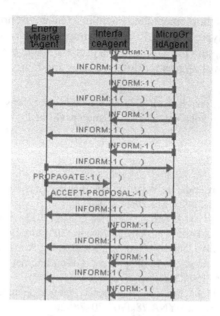

Fig. 5. Communication sequence diagram among agents.

In our approach we verified the useful of using Fuzzy Logic Inference Systems to manage the transition among states within the energy system because the conditions to trip the transitions are not fully deterministic, and it could be difficult to determine what exact values to define in multiple comparison transitions (e.g. $price \geq p_0$ AND stored energy $\geq se_0$ makes change to **sale** state) and so on for every case or rule that could appear to manage transitions. The use of Fuzzy Logic techniques avoids these complex and non-deterministic operations and ensures a high throughput of the system.

5 Conclusions and Future Work

The proposed fuzzy-based MAS achieves a good approach to control the micro-grid operation considering energy market dynamics, as well as, it gives useful information to the user. The Energy-Market Agent inference algorithm overcomes a difficult constraint in automation to manage non-deterministic conditions to switch among states, and in fact, it enables the micro-grid to operate in a smarter way, even a human would have a difficult task if s/he would have to decide when to change among states. An important thing to highlight is that the system is scalable to work with any micro-grid power system, and more variables and agents could be added to enhance the performance of the system, and additionally, that works in a real-time environment. Obtained results prove the effectiveness of the proposed model to work with the base rules described above in literal 3 and comply them. As future work, we intend to increase the number of agents and context variables of the system to enhance the performance of the MAS.

In addition, we pretend to implement the system in a real environment over a real micro-grid or a physical prototype. Finally, in order to improve the recommendation system, we will develop consumption profiles based on process management and user operation information, and relations/patterns for different days and hours.

Acknowledgments. The research work presented in this paper was partially funded by the master's studies Sapiencia scholarship offered to Santiago Gil in 2017.

References

1. Hatziargyriou, N.: Microgrids: the key to unlock distributed energy resources? IEEE Power & Energy Magazine, pp. 26–28, May/June 2008
2. Deloitte, El futuro del sector de energía eléctrica global (2015). https://www2.deloitte.com/content/dam/Deloitte/mx/Documents/energy-resources/Futuro_Energia_Electrica.pdf
3. Carrera, Á., Iglesias, C.A., García-Algarra, J., Kolařík, D.: A real-life application of multi-agent systems for fault diagnosis in the provision of an Internet business service. J. Netw. Comput. Appl. **37**, 146–154 (2014)
4. Duque, N.D., Ovalle, D.A.: Artificial Intelligence planning techniques for adaptive virtual course construction. Revista DYNA **78**(170), 70–78 (2011)
5. Salazar, O.M., Ovalle, D.A., Duque, N.D.: Adaptive and personalized educational ubiquitous multi-agent system using context-awareness services and mobile devices. In: Zaphiris, P., Ioannou, A. (eds.) LCT 2015. LNCS, vol. 9192, pp. 301–312. Springer, Cham (2015). https://doi.org/10.1007/978-3-319-20609-7_29
6. Cingolani, P., Alcalá-Fdez, J., JFuzzyLogic: a robust and flexible Fuzzy-Logic inference system language implementation. In: WCCI 2012 IEEE World Congress on Computational Intelligence, 10–15 June 2012, Brisbane, Australia (2012)
7. Padgham, L., Thangarajah, J., Winikoff, M.: Tool support for agent development using the Prometheus methodology. In: IEEE Fifth International Conference on Quality Software - QSIC (2005)
8. Wang, Z., Yang R., Wang, L.: Intelligent multi-agent control for integrated building and micro-grid systems. In: ISGT 2011, Hilton Anaheim, CA, pp. 1–7 (2011). https://doi.org/10.1109/isgt.2011.5759134
9. Cheah, P.H., Zhang, R., Gooi, H.B., Yu, H., Foo, M.K.: Consumer energy portal and home energy management system for smart grid applications. In: 10th International Power and Energy Conference 2012 (IPEC), Ho Chi Minh City, pp. 407–411 (2012). https://doi.org/10.1109/asscc.2012.6523302
10. Li, Z., Zang, C., Zeng, P., Yu, H., Li, H.: MAS based distributed automatic generation control for cyber-physical microgrid system. IEEE/CAA J. Automatica Sinica **3**(1), 78–89 (2016). https://doi.org/10.1109/jas.2016.7373765
11. Kouluri, M.K, Pandey, R.K.: Intelligent agent based micro grid control. In: 2nd International Conference on Intelligent Agent & Multi-Agent Systems 2011, Chennai, pp. 62–66 (2011). https://doi.org/10.1109/iama.2011.6049007
12. Feron, B., Monti, A.: An agent based approach for Virtual Power Plant valuing thermal flexibility in energy markets. In: 2017 IEEE Manchester PowerTech, Manchester, pp. 1–6 (2017). https://doi.org/10.1109/ptc.2017.7981126

13. Bellifemine, F., Bergenti, F., Caire, G., Poggi, A.: Jade—a java agent development framework. In: Bordini, R.H., Dastani, M., Dix, J., El Fallah, Seghrouchni.A. (eds.) Multi-Agent Programming: Languages, Platforms and Applications, vol. 15, pp. 125–147. Springer, Boston (2005). https://doi.org/10.1007/0-387-26350-0_5
14. Cingolani, P., Alcalá-Fdez, J.: jFuzzyLogic: a java library to design fuzzy logic controllers according to the standard for fuzzy control programming. Int. J. Comput. Intell. Syst. **6**, 61–75 (2013)
15. ComEd: Comed hourly pricing program (2018). https://hourlypricing.comed.com/, WS: https://hourlypricing.comed.com/api?type=currenthouraverage&format=json. Accessed 26 Jan 2018

Coalitions of End-Use Customers in Retail Electricity Markets: A Real-World Case Study Involving Five Schools for Children

Hugo Algarvio[1,2(✉)], Fernando Lopes[2], and João Santana[1]

[1] Instituto Superior Técnico, Universidade de Lisboa, INESC-ID, Lisbon, Portugal
{hugo.algarvio,jsantana}@tecnico.ulisboa.pt
[2] LNEG-National Research Institute, Est. Paço do Lumiar 22, Lisbon, Portugal
fernando.lopes@lneg.pt

Abstract. The key mechanisms for purchasing and selling electrical energy include electricity pools and bilateral contracts. This article is devoted to bilateral contracting, which is modeled as a negotiation process involving an iterative exchange of offers and counter-offers. It focuses on coalitions of end-use consumers and describes a case study involving five schools for children located in England. The schools decide to ally into a coalition to strengthen their bargaining positions and, hopefully, to obtain better tariffs. To this end, they rely on a coordinator agent, who is defined from the group of five schools, by selecting either the "most powerful" school or the "best negotiator" school. The coordinator takes decisions according to either a "majority" rule, a "consensus" rule, or an "unanimity" rule. The simulations are performed with an agent-based system, called MATREM (for Multi-agent TRading in Electricity Markets). Although preliminary, the results suggest that coalition formation and management is beneficial to end-use customers, since the price agreed in the new forward contracts is more favorable to these agents, particularly when the coordinator is the "best negotiator" agent and considers the "unanimity" decision rule.

Keywords: Electricity markets · Bilateral contracts
Customer coalitions · Trading strategies · Decision rules
MATREM system

1 Introduction

The liberalization of electricity markets (EMs) has led to the establishment of a wholesale market, where competing generators offer their energy to retailers, and a retail market, in which retailers ensure delivery to end-use customers [1, 2].

H. Algarvio and F. Lopes—This work was supported by "Fundação para a Ciência e Tecnologia" with references UID/CEC/50021/2013 and PD/BD/105863/2014.

© Springer International Publishing AG, part of Springer Nature 2018
J. Bajo et al. (Eds.): PAAMS 2018 Workshops, CCIS 887, pp. 312–320, 2018.
https://doi.org/10.1007/978-3-319-94779-2_27

Because of transaction costs, only largest consumers choose to purchase energy directly on the wholesale market. Most small and medium consumers purchase energy from retailers, who in turn buy it in the wholesale market [3].

This paper focuses on retail markets, which differ from their more traditional counterparts because energy cannot be efficiently held in stock or stored (as tangible goods can). The following two types of agents are of particular importance to the paper: retailer or supplier agents (representing business units that sell electricity to end-use customers) and consumer or customer agents (including commercial, industrial and other electricity consumers). The agents are able to negotiate and sign forward bilateral contracts—that is, agreements between two parties to exchange a specific amount of electric power at a certain future time for a specific price. To this end, they are equipped with a negotiation model that handles two-party and multi-issue negotiation (see, e.g., [4]). The negotiation process involves an iterative exchange of offers and counter-offers. An offer is, essentially, a set of issue-value pairs—such as "energy price = 50 £/MWh", "contract duration = 12 months", and so on—and a counter-offer is an offer made in response to a previous offer.

Now, a particular end-use customer can either negotiate directly with a single retailer agent a mutually acceptable agreement or negotiate concurrently with several different retailers to obtain a better agreement. Alternatively, two or more customers can ally into a coalition to strengthen their bargaining positions and pursue a superior negotiation outcome (see, e.g., [5,6]). Alliances of two or more customers can potentially increase their bargaining power during bilateral contracting of electricity. Furthermore, a coalition of end-use customers can negotiate concurrently with several retailers to pursue a more superior outcome.

This paper centers on contract negotiation between a single retailer and a coalition of end-use customers. It is an extension of the work presented in [7,8]. Specifically, it presents a case study involving five schools for children located in England. The schools decide to sign up for a new time-of-use tariff characterized by two different energy prices for two different blocks of time (peak and off-peak) of a 24-h day. To this end, they decide to ally into a coalition in order to negotiate a better energy tariff. Also, they rely on a coordinator agent, defined by selecting either the "most powerful" school (i.e., the school with the higher consumption levels) or the "best negotiator" school (i.e., the school with the lower electricity prices). The coordinator takes decisions about the submission of new offers and acceptance of incoming offers according to either a "majority" decision rule (three of the customers must are in agreement), a "consensus" rule (four of the customers must are in agreement), or an "unanimity" rule (all customers must are in agreement). The simulations are performed with the agent-based system MATREM (for Multi-agent TRading in Electricity). The system supports a power exchange, a derivatives exchange, and a bilateral marketplace for negotiating tailored (or customized) bilateral contracts. Furthermore, MATREM supports coalitions of end-user customers.

The remainder of this paper is structured as follows. Section 2 presents an overview of the MATREM simulator, focusing on the bilateral marketplace and the various types of market entities supported by the tool. Section 3 presents the case study and discusses the simulation results. Finally, Sect. 4 states the conclusions and outlines some avenues for future work.

2   The MATREM System: An Overview

MATREM allows the user to conduct a wide range of simulations regarding the behavior of energy markets under a variety of conditions.[1] The tool supports a power exchange and a derivatives exchange. The power exchange comprises a day-ahead market and a shorter-term market known as intra-day market. The day-ahead market (DAM) buys energy from sellers and sells energy to buyers in advance of time when the energy is produced and consumed (see, e.g., [9]). The intra-day market sets prices and schedules a few hours ahead to facilitate balancing on advance of real time. The derivatives exchange comprises a futures market for trading standardized bilateral contracts. This exchange uses an electronic trading system that automatically matches the bids and offers from various market participants.

The tool also supports a bilateral marketplace for negotiating the details of tailored (or customized) long-term bilateral contracts (see, e.g., [10]). Buyers and sellers are equipped with a negotiation model that handles two-party and multi-issue negotiation. The negotiation process involves three main phases or stages: (i) pre-negotiation (focuses on preparation and planning for negotiation), (ii) actual negotiation (seeks a solution for a dispute and is characterized by movement toward a mutually acceptable agreement), and (iii) post-negotiation (centers on details and implementation of a final agreement).

Currently, the tool supports four key types of entities participating in the aforementioned markets, namely generating companies (GenCos), retailers (RetailCos), aggregators and consumers, and also two key types of entities responsible for all markets, specifically market operators (MOs) and system operators (SOs). Worthy to mention is the possibility of two or more customers to ally into a coalition to strengthen their bargaining positions and pursue a superior negotiation outcome. The customers can come together to pool their efforts in search for a solution that meets common or overlapping goals. In other words, various customers can intentionally form a coalition who interacts and negotiates with a seller agent (e.g., a RetailCo agent) to achieve a desired outcome that meets shared objectives (but see, e.g., [7,8]).

The tool considers two main types of software agents: market agents and assistant agents. Market agents represent the entities that take part in the different simulated markets. Assistant agents are categorized into interface managers (responsible for managing the interfaces of the simulated markets) and intelligent assistants (provide support to the user in making strategic decisions). Both market and assistant agents are computer systems capable of flexible action and

---

[1] See [12] for a detailed description of the MATREM system and [13] for its classification according to a number of specific dimensions related to both liberalized electricity markets and intelligent agents.

able to interact, when appropriate, with other agents to meet their design objectives. They are currently being developed using the JAVA Agent Development Framework (JADE), which is an open source platform for peer-to-peer agent based applications [11].

The target platform for MATREM is a 32/64-bit microcomputer running Microsoft Windows. A graphical interface allows the user to specify, monitor and steer all simulations. The interface is fully integrated into the Windows environment and employs the familiar look of other desktop Windows applications. Agent communication is done by sending and receiving messages.

3   Case Study

This case study extends the case study presented in [8], which analyzes the impact of customer coalitions on energy tariffs during bilateral contracting of electricity. The main agents are now five end-use customers (a_1, a_2, a_3, a_4, and a_5) and a retailer (a_s). More specifically, the customers represent five schools for children located in England:

- a_1: St George's College, Weybridge Road, Addlestone, Surrey[2]
- a_2: St George's Junior School, Thames Street, Weybridge, Surrey[3]
- a_3: Ludgrove School, Ludgrove, Wokingham, Berkshire[4]
- a_4: Thames Ditton Infant School, Speer Road, Thames Ditton, Surrey[5]
- a_5: Ashley CofE Primary School, Ashley Road, Walton-on-Thames, Surrey[6]

Table 1 presents the daily average energy quantities, the electricity tariffs and the annual average costs for all customers. The data is based on real consumption patterns and tariffs.[7]

The end-use customers decide to sign up for a new time-of-use tariff (characterized by two different energy prices for two different blocks of time, namely peak and off-peak). To this end, they decide to ally into a coalition to strengthen their bargaining positions. Also, they decide to rely on a trusted coordinator agent (a_c), who can interact and negotiate directly with the retailer agent a mutually acceptable agreement and, hopefully, a better tariff for all customers. The contract duration is set to 365 days.

The negotiating agenda includes the energy prices for the two periods of a 24 hour day. Negotiation proceeds by an iterative exchange of offers and counter-offers. At a specific period of the negotiation process, each agent prepares a new offer by considering the previous offer and also a specific negotiation strategy. The coordinator agent pursues either a "low-priority concession making" strategy [4] or an "energy dependent concession making" strategy [14]. The retailer

---

[2] http://www.stgeorgesweybridge.com/college/why-st-georges-college.
[3] http://www.stgeorgesweybridge.com/junior-school.
[4] http://www.ludgrove.net/.
[5] http://www.thames-ditton-infant.surrey.sch.uk/.
[6] http://www.ashleyschool.org.uk/.
[7] http://www.ecodriver.co.uk (accessed on April 2017).

agent makes concession throughout negotiation according to the total amount of energy that the customers are expecting to consume in a given daily pricing period (see [7] for details about the strategy).

The coordinator sends team decisions to the retailer and broadcasts decisions from the retailer to the team members. These two agents—the coordinator and the retailer—interact according to the rules of an alternating offers protocol [15]. Also, the coordinator interacts with all customers, helping them in two key decisions: which offer should be sent to the retailer and whether a counter-offer received from the retailer should be accepted. Typically, whenever the mediator receives an offer from the retailer, it communicates the offer to all customers and opens a voting process, where each customer states whether or not the offer is acceptable. The votes can be either positive (1), if the offer is acceptable, or negative (0), if the offer is not acceptable. The votes are submitted to the coordinator, who counts the number of acceptances (positive votes) and makes a decision based on a specific decision rule (see, e.g., [6]). In this work, we consider the following three decision rules: a "majority" rule (three of the customers must are in agreement), a "consensus" rule (four of the customers must are in agreement), and an "unanimity" rule (all customers must are in agreement).

Table 1. Daily average quantities, tariffs and annual costs of customers

	Period	End-use Customer				
		a_1	a_2	a_3	a_4	a_5
Daily average energy (MWh)	Peak	0.980	0.365	0.138	0.121	0.075
	Off-peak	0.629	0.220	0.072	0.017	0.024
Energy tariff (£/MWh)	Peak	96.00	96.00	94.00	80.00	163.50
	Off-peak	60.00	60.00	69.00	80.00	163.50
Annual cost (thousand £)		48.11	17.60	6.54	4.02	5.90

Part I: the coordinator agent is the "most powerful" school. The first part of the case study considers that the coordinator agent is the St George's College (agent a_1)—that is, the agent with the consumption pattern corresponding to 0.980 MW/h during the peak period and 0.629 MW/h during the off-peak period. This choice assumes that bargaining power is a function of a single criterion, namely the amount of energy that a customer is willing to purchase.[8] The coordinator pursues a "low-priority concession making" strategy during the course of the negotiation with the retailer agent. This means that this agent (and naturally all customers) places greater emphasis on the key negotiation issue—that is, the peak price—and often yields on the less important or low-priority issue (i.e., the off-peak price).

---

[8] Certainly, bargaining power should be modeled by a more complex function. Broadly speaking, bargaining power is the potential to alter the attitudes and behaviors of others that an individual brings to a given negotiation situation (but see, e.g.,. [16]).

Table 2. Simulation results (Part I of the case study)

Decision rule		Period	End-use customer				
			a_1	a_2	a_3	a_4	a_5
Majority	Energy tariff (£/MWh)	Peak	92.7	92.7	92.7	92.7	92.7
		Off-peak	66.9	66.9	66.9	66.9	66.9
	Annual cost (k£)		48.5	17.7	6.4	4.5	3.1
	Annual benefit (£)		−432	−124	117	−481	2782
Consensus	Energy tariff (£/MWh)	Peak	93.9	93.9	93.9	93.9	93.9
		Off-peak	64.7	64.7	64.7	64.7	64.7
	Annual cost (k£)		48.4	17.7	6.4	4.5	3.1
	Annual benefit (£)		−356	−108	114	−520	2769
Unanimity	Energy tariff (£/MWh)	Peak	92.1	92.1	92.1	92.1	92.1
		Off-peak	66.4	66.4	66.4	66.4	66.4
	Annual cost (k£)		48.2	17.6	6.3	4.4	3.1
	Annual benefit (£)		−115	−9	158	−454	2802

The simulation results are presented in Table 2, namely the new energy tariffs, the corresponding average annual costs, and the annual financial benefits. Notice that three different simulations were performed: a simulation where the coordinator adopts the majority rule, another one where the coordinator adopts the consensus rule, and a final one where the coordinator adopts the unanimity rule. Clearly, each of the new tariffs is better for customers a_3 and a_5, since the new peak and off-peak prices are lower than the current peak and off-peak prices, respectively. For agent a_3 (Ludgrove School), the annual gains are considerable: £117.06 (majority rule), £114.43 (consensus rule), and £158.45 (unanimity rule). And for agent a_5 (Ashley CofE Primary School), the annual gains are quite significant: £2782.84 (majority rule), £2769.27 (consensus rule) and £2802.36 (unanimity rule).

Apparently, the new tariffs are also better for customers a_1 and a_2—in all simulations, the new peak prices are lower than the current peak price (although the new off-peak prices are higher than the current off-peak price). However, these tariffs result in annual losses for both customers. For customer a_1 (St George's College), the losses are considerable: −£432.82 (majority rule), −£356.98 (consensus rule), and −£115.69 (unanimity rule). And although less considerable for customer a_2 (St George's Junior School), the losses are important: −£124.85 (majority rule), −£108.06 (consensus rule) and −£9.54 (unanimity rule).

The new tariffs are, however, worse for agent a_4 (Thames Ditton Infant School)—the new peak prices are considerably higher than the current peak price. The annual losses are quite significant: −£481.43 (majority rule), −£520.78 (consensus rule), and −£454.23 (unanimity rule). This result is not a surprise, at least in part, since the current tariff of this school is considerably better than the current tariffs of all the other schools.

Table 3. Simulation results (Part II of the case study)

Decision rule		Period	End-use customer				
			a_1	a_2	a_3	a_4	a_5
Majority	Energy tariff (£/MWh)	Peak	91.6	91.6	91.6	91.6	91.6
		Off-peak	65.9	65.9	65.9	65.9	65.9
	Annual cost (k£)		47.9	17.5	6.3	4.4	3.0
	Annual benefit (£)		181	98	197	−428	2820
Consensus	Energy tariff (£/MWh)	Peak	91.2	91.2	91.2	91.2	91.2
		Off-peak	65.4	65.4	65.4	65.4	65.4
	Annual cost (k£)		47.6	17.4	6.3	4.4	3.0
	Annual benefit (£)		455	198	233	−404	2837
Unanimity	Energy tariff (£/MWh)	Peak	83.1	83.1	83.1	83.1	83.1
		Off-peak	74.9	74.9	74.9	74.9	74.9
	Annual cost (k£)		46.9	17.0	6.1	4.1	2.9
	Annual benefit (£)		1163	511	390	−107	2975

Part II: the coordinator agent is the "best negotiator" school. The second and last part of the case study considers that the coordinator agent is the Thames Ditton Infant School (agent a_4)—that is, the agent with the tariff corresponding to 80 £/MWh (peak and off-peak periods). This choice assumes that this agent is a skilled negotiator, namely a negotiator with the ability to: (i) explore a wide range of options for action, (ii) work hard to find a common ground with the opponent, (iii) spent more time considering the long-term implications of the issues at stake, and (iv) set a "range" of acceptable settlements. Put simply, the other agents are assumed to be "average" negotiators (when compared with a_4).

The coordinator pursues an "energy dependent concession making" strategy throughout negotiation. The simulation results are presented in Table 3. Again, three different simulations were performed (each involving a different decision rule).

Clearly, the new tariff resulting from the third simulation (unanimity rule) is significantly better for customers a_1, a_2, a_3 and a_5—the new peak and off-peak prices are considerably lower than the current peak and off-peak prices, respectively. Also, each of the new three tariffs is better for customers a_3 and a_5. Again, for customer a_3 (Ludgrove School), the annual gains are considerable: £197.28 (majority rule), £233.04 (consensus rule), and £390.13 (unanimity rule). And for customer a_5 (Ashley CofE Primary School), the annual gains are quite significant: £2820.70 (majority rule), £2837.59 (consensus rule), and £2975.38 (unanimity rule).

The new tariffs resulting from both the first simulation (majority rule) and the second simulation (consensus rule) are significantly better for customers a_1 and a_2—in both simulations, the new peak prices are considerably lower than the current peak price (although the new off-peak prices are higher than the current off-peak price). These tariffs lead now to considerable annual gains for the two customers. For customer a_1 (St George's College), the gains are £181.53 (majority rule) and £455.26 (consensus rule). And for customer a_2 (St George's Junior School), the annual gains are as follows: £98.55 (majority rule) and £198.10 (consensus rule).

Finally, the new tariffs resulting from all simulations seem to be worse for agent a_4. In fact, they lead to significant annual losses, namely $-£428.60$ (majority rule), $-£404.99$ (consensus rule), and $-£107.47$ (unanimity rule). Again, at least in part, this results was expected.

4   Conclusion

This article investigated how coalitions of end-use customers could strengthen their bargaining positions and lead to superior negotiation outcomes. To this end, it presented a case study involving five schools for children located in England. The schools decided to negotiate a new contract and to ally into a coalition. They relied on a trusted coordinator agent who has negotiated directly with a retailer agent a mutually acceptable agreement. Although preliminary, the simulation results do suggest the following:

1. The technical decision of the end-use customers to ally into a coalition may be considered a high-quality group decision, since the new tariffs are more favorable to the majority of customers.
2. The decision to select the agent with the lower electricity prices to act as coordinator seems to be a wise decision—the resulting tariffs are considerably better (when compared with the tariffs obtained by considering as coordinator the agent with the higher consumption levels).
3. The decision to adopt an "unanimity" decision rule seems to be another wise decision—the new tariffs are more favorable than the tariffs obtained by considering the "majority" and "consensus" rules.

In the future, we intend to study other types of coalitions, especially coalitions involving entities from the primary and domestic sectors, and also to analyze the impact of new decision rules on contract negotiation outcomes. We also intend to study the impact of competition, by considering a coalition of end-use customers negotiating concurrently with several retailers to pursue a more superior outcome.

References

1. Shahidehpour, M., Yamin, H., Li, Z.: Market Operations in Electric Power Systems. Wiley, Chichester (2002)
2. Lopes, F., Coelho, H. (eds.): Electricity Markets with Increasing Levels of Renewable Generation: Structure, Operation, Agent-based Simulation and Emerging Designs. Springer, Cham (2018). https://doi.org/10.1007/978-3-319-74263-2

3. Kirschen, D., Strbac, G.: Fundamentals of Power System Economics. Wiley, Chichester (2004)
4. Lopes, F., Coelho, H.: Strategic and Tactical behaviour in automated negotiation. Int. J. Artif. Intell. 4(S10), 35–63 (2010)
5. Klusch, M., Gerber, A.: Dynamic coalition formation among rational agents. IEEE Intell. Syst. 17(3), 42–47 (2002)
6. Sánchez-Anguix, V., Julián, V., Botti, V., García-Fornes, A.: Studying the impact of negotiation environments on negotiation teams performance. Inf. Sci. 219, 17–40 (2013)
7. Algarvio, H., Lopes, F., Santana, J.: Multi-agent retail energy markets: bilateral contracting and coalitions of end-use customers. In: 12th International Conference on the European Energy Market (EEM 2015), pp. 1–5. IEEE (2015)
8. Algarvio, H., Lopes, F., Santana, J.: Multi-agent retail energy markets: contract negotiation, customer coalitions and a real-world case study. In: Demazeau, Y., Ito, T., Bajo, J., Escalona, M.J. (eds.) PAAMS 2016. LNCS (LNAI), vol. 9662, pp. 13–23. Springer, Cham (2016). https://doi.org/10.1007/978-3-319-39324-7_2
9. Lopes, F., Sá, J., Santana, J.: Renewable generation, support policies and the merit order effect: a comprehensive overview and the case of wind power in Portugal. In: Lopes, F., Coelho, H. (eds.) Electricity Markets with Increasing Levels of Renewable Generation: Structure, Operation, Agent-based Simulation, and Emerging Designs. SSDC, vol. 144, pp. 227–263. Springer, Cham (2018). https://doi.org/10.1007/978-3-319-74263-2_9
10. Sousa, F., Lopes, F., Santana, J.: Contracts for difference and risk management in multi-agent energy markets. In: Demazeau, Y., Decker, K.S., Bajo Pérez, J., de la Prieta, F. (eds.) PAAMS 2015. LNCS (LNAI), vol. 9086, pp. 155–164. Springer, Cham (2015). https://doi.org/10.1007/978-3-319-18944-4_13
11. Bellifemine, F., Caire, G., Greenwood, D.: Developing Multi-Agent Systems with JADE. Wiley, Chichester (2007)
12. Lopes, F.: MATREM: an agent-based simulation tool for electricity markets. In: Lopes, F., Coelho, H. (eds.) Electricity Markets with Increasing Levels of Renewable Generation: Structure, Operation, Agent-based Simulation, and Emerging Designs. SSDC, vol. 144, pp. 189–225. Springer, Cham (2018). https://doi.org/10.1007/978-3-319-74263-2_8
13. Lopes, F., Coelho, H.: Electricity markets and intelligent agents part ii: agent architectures and capabilities. In: Lopes, F., Coelho, H. (eds.) Electricity Markets with Increasing Levels of Renewable Generation: Structure, Operation, Agent-based Simulation, and Emerging Designs. SSDC, vol. 144, pp. 49–77. Springer, Cham (2018). https://doi.org/10.1007/978-3-319-74263-2_3
14. Lopes, F., Algarvio, H., Coelho, H.: Bilateral contracting in multi-agent electricity markets: negotiation strategies and a case study. In: International Conference on the European Energy Market (EEM 2013), pp. 1–8. IEEE (2013)
15. Osborne, M., Rubinstein, A.: Bargaining and Markets. Academic Press, London (1990)
16. Lewicki, R., Barry, B., Saunders, D.: Negotiation. McGraw Hill, New York (2010)

Distributed Multi-agent Based Energy Management of Smart Micro-grids: Autonomous Participation of Agents in Power Imbalance Handling

Sajad Ghorbani[1]([⊠]), Roozbeh Morsali[2], Rainer Unland[1,3],
and Ryszard Kowalczyk[2,4]

[1] Institute of Computer Science and Business Information Systems,
University of Duisburg-Essen, Essen, Germany
{sajad.ghorbani,rainer.unland}@icb.uni-due.de
[2] Swinburne University of Technology, Melbourne, Australia
{rmorsali,rkowalczyk}@swin.edu.au
[3] Department of Information Systems,
Poznan University of Economics, Poznan, Poland
[4] Systems Research Institute, Polish Academy of Sciences, Warsaw, Poland

Abstract. Micro-grids are known as a means of localization of renewable energy production and consumption. However, due to the intermittent nature of renewable energy sources, one of the main challenges in Micro-grid energy control and management is to handle any deviation from the prior forecasted power generation/consumption. Our proposed distributed multi-agent algorithm tries to handle power imbalance situations in a PV-based grid connected Micro-grid through optimizing a combination of storage usage, load curtailment, and main grid power purchase. In this model, the users' consumption preferences are considered as an important factor in the decision making. We first devise a community of consumers with various energy usage preferences and then investigate the performance of our proposed algorithm over multiple scenarios having different users' reactions to the energy conservation requests. The results obtained show the convergence and feasibility of the proposed algorithm. Moreover, the cost of imbalance handling is considerably reduced, preserving the level of satisfaction in the community, as the inconvenience effect of load curtailment is compensated by paying back to the consumers.

Keywords: Smart grid · Micro-grid · Multi-agent systems
Energy management · Distributed control

1 Introduction

As the share of green electricity production in the market grows, the electricity grid is getting bigger and more complex. Localization of electricity production and consumption in Micro-grids will help to overcome this complexity. However, power production in majority of Micro-grids is highly dependent on renewable energy resources [1–4] which are intermittent in nature. Therefore, *Power Imbalance* situations happens when there is a

© Springer International Publishing AG, part of Springer Nature 2018
J. Bajo et al. (Eds.): PAAMS 2018 Workshops, CCIS 887, pp. 321–332, 2018.
https://doi.org/10.1007/978-3-319-94779-2_28

deviation from the forecasted power generation/consumption. The main optimization problem here is to find a combination of energy storage, back-up generation, and importing power from the grid to handle the power imbalance issue. There has been lots of research in the field of Microgrid Control and Management addressing the mentioned issue by means of various demand-side management schemes [2, 5]. Majority of the proposed approaches use the blind curtailment to decrease the cost of handling the power imbalance. However, in order to maximize the users' participation in any demand-side management program, taking into account the socio-economic factors seems to be inevitable.

One way to consider factors like consumers' level of satisfaction is to define utility values for their appliances. In some studies, the utility function of different appliances are either defined by their power consumption level [6–8] or based on their type [9, 10]. The problem of the approaches that consider power rating as a measurement for utility function can be seen by comparing, for instance, the consumption of lighting and TV. The TV consumption is about 100 times the amount of energy that lighting uses, which shows the lack of these approaches to determine the users' consumption preferences. For the second approaches, even if all the utility functions of different appliances can be defined, the satisfaction level that different users get from using the same appliances are not the same. In fact, this is the individual users' preferences which determine the priority of consumption. In this paper, we proposed a Distributed Autonomous Multi-agent model for handling unforeseen events in Micro-grid energy management, that considers individual users' convenience as an important factor in the decision making. In our model, autonomous user agents are responsible for reflecting the users' convenience level and performing local optimization based on users' consumption priorities. Utilizing the flexibility that Multi-agent Systems [11] provide, make them a suitable platform to model the Micro-grid energy management systems [12, 13]. Authors in [14, 15], introduced the concept of unified *Energy Agent* in which any component of the energy grid can be represented by an agent and all the energy conversion happening in the grid environment can be modelled through the proposed Multi-agent based platform. The storage management of Micro-grids [16], Distributed Energy Resource (DER) management [17], and holonic control of a network of Micro-grids [18] are among the other applications of Multi-agent systems in electricity grid management. The model of agent-based imbalance handling considering user inconvenience in load curtailment is introduced by authors in [19]. This work is an extension to our previous proposed distributed algorithm. We improved the model and investigate the practicality of it for a large community of Micro-grid users with different behaviors in negotiation. In the next section, the system model along with the mathematical models of *Power Imbalance* and *User Inconvenience* in load curtailment are briefly described. Then, the overall system and the proposed distributed Multi-agent based algorithm to handle power imbalance are defined. In Sect. 3, the performance of the proposed distributed algorithm is evaluated over multiple scenarios modeling various community behaviors in a PV-based Microgrid.

2 System Model

As mentioned before, the main goal of the proposed algorithm is to solve the power imbalance problem in Micro-grids by choosing an optimized combination of storage, load curtailment, and purchasing power from the grid (Fig. 1), taking the inconvenience caused by each combination to the consumers into account. A possible solution to this problem is the combination of importing power from the main grid and the curtailment from the load side. This combination should be able to meet two main objectives; the overall cost of imbalance handling must be minimized, and in case of any curtailment, the effect of that on the users' level of satisfaction should be mitigated. The Multi-agent system that we devised for this purpose consists of four types of agents. The *Micro-grid Control Agent, User Agent, Storage Agent*, and *Grid Agent*. Table 1 shows the agents and their roles in the proposed Multi-agent set-up.

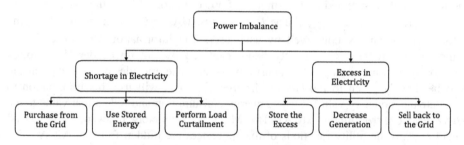

Fig. 1. Possible solutions for the power imbalance situations [19]

Table 1. Agent in the proposed Multi-agent imbalance handling system

Agent	Role
Micro-grid Control Agent	• monitor the actual PV generation and actual load, and calculate the amount of power imbalance at each time-slot (t) • perform the optimization and calculates the cost of imbalance and the user share
User agent	• capture the user's consumption priorities • participate in load curtailment by sending proposals to Micro-grid Control agent
Storage agent	• charge and discharge the storage unit upon the request from Micro-grid Control agent
Grid agent	• purchase the needed energy or sell back the excess energy from/to the main grid based on the requests from Micro-grid Control agent

The *Micro-grid Control Agent* (MCA) is constantly monitor the forecasted and actual generation to detect the amount of deviated energy form the forecast PV generation in each time-slot t. The *User Agent* (UA) captures the respective user's consumption priorities and translating them to monetary values. In the imbalance situation UAs reflect those values as proposals to the MCA. It is assumed that UAs are physically connected to the appliances and can switch them on and off upon request from the MCA. *Storage agent* (SA) is responsible of managing storage units and receives the charging or discharging commands from the MCA. Finally, *Grid agent* (GA) which is connected to the main grid will import or export (in case of over production) the amount of energy demanded by the MCA.

To explain how the proposed distributed algorithm works, we first need to briefly introduce the model of *Power Imbalance* and the model of *Inconvenience*.

2.1 Models of Power Imbalance and Inconvenience

In each time-slot t the amount of deviated power from the prior forecast is $\Delta E_g = E_{g,f} - E_{g,a}$, where E_g is the power generated (kWh) and subscripts f and a indicate the forecast and actual generation, respectively. In case of any deviation, the amount of energy shortage (E_{shrt}) should be first supplied by the energy stored (E_{strg}) in the batteries and the energy conserved (E_{cnsr}) from the load curtailment. If not enough, the rest should be supplied by the amount of power imported from the main grid with the cost $f_g \left(E_{shrt} - E_{strg} - E_{cnsr} \right)$. The *User Agents* (UAs) are responsible to determine the amount of energy conserved by each user. The information about users' consumption preferences is constantly being captured by the respective UA through monitoring the time of use, power consumption, etc. The priorities of consumption can also be directly given to the UA by the user. The UA will use this information to calculate the monetary value of user's energy consumption and reflect that value to the *Micro-grid Control Agent* (MCA). The MCA is completely unaware of the UAs' calculation, as the utility functions of the appliances are hidden from the MCA.

If the process of Imbalance handling leads to any load curtailment, there will be a satisfaction drop (I_u) to the affected users. As the consumption priorities may vary between individual users, each user may experience different amount of inconvenience which can be shown as $I_u = \sum_{i=1}^{M} I_{u,i}$ for user u^{th}, where M is the number of affected appliances. The overall variation in the community's satisfaction level is $I = \sum_{u=1}^{N} \sum_{i=1}^{M} I_{u,i}$, where N is the number of users participated in the load curtailment. Therefore, the total cost of imbalance based on above calculation is $C_{Imb} = f_{Imb}(E_{shrt}, E_{cnsr}, I) = f_g \left(E_{shrt} - E_{strg} - E_{cnsr} \right) + I$, where the function f_g returns the cost of energy that should be imported from the main grid.

2.2 Distributed Multi-agent Imbalance Handling Algorithm

The main objective of the proposed Multi-Agent algorithm is to minimize the imbalance cost (C_{Imb}) in each time slot in a distributed manner. Algorithm starts with checking the amount of energy shortage (E_{shrt}). In case of any shortage ($E_{shrt} > 0$), the priority is to use the accumulated stored energy in the battery until the time slot t, $E_{strg}(t)$. Then, only when the battery is run out of energy, the cost of importing needed power from the grid and share of every user in the cost are calculated. In the next step, the User Agents (UAs) which want to participate in the load curtailment will return the energy conservation ($E_{cnsr,u}$) amount and inconvenience cost (I_u) of their respective users to the micro-grid control agent (MCA) as proposals (Fig. 2).

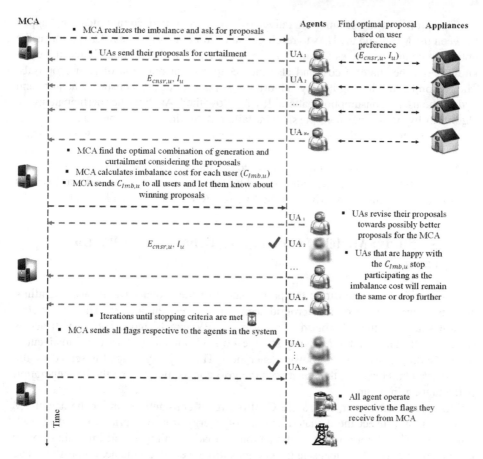

Fig. 2. Schematic representation of the data communications between the MCA and agents in the proposed distributed imbalance handling algorithm

These proposals represent the utility values of appliances which will be turned off or their usage will be postponed by user. Utility functions of the appliances are either unknown or hidden from the MCA. This will hide the detailed information about individual users' consumption from the central entity. The MCA will calculate the minimum imbalance cost as optimal solution based on all combination of the proposals received from the user agents, hence, if any UA tries to misrepresent the inconvenience cost, the chance of it being accepted will be very low. This makes the proposed algorithm strategy proof. The proposals are simple numbers representing monetary values of consumption for the specific users on a certain time-slot. The calculation of the user priorities is out of scope of this research and it is assumed different costs representing the priorities of different users in the simulations.

The proposed algorithm is iterative and on each round communication happen between the MCA and the UAs to reach global minimum costs. The MCA performs the optimization and computes C_{Imb} and user costs $(C_{Imb,u})$, and consequently lets the users know about the share of cost and also the acceptance or rejection of their proposals. The reason behind having iterative algorithm is that user agents constantly acquire and update the users' consumption pattern. It will allow the UAs to further participate in the algorithm by proposing more possible curtailments in the future time sluts.

As the iterations advance the C_{Imb} is being reduced until it is not greater than a given tolerance value (ε). The same local optimizations are done at users' level. The stopping criteria here is a tolerance value determined by each user (ε_u).

After performing the algorithm and finding the optimal solution, the control signals are going to be sent by the MCA to the Storage Agent and the Grid Agent.

3 Case Study: Model of Community Behavior in a PV Based Microgrid

In this section, to demonstrate the performance of the proposed imbalance handling algorithm, we apply it on a Microgrid scenario in a residential area. The power generation source in this Microgrid is an array of PV panels and a battery will act as storage unit. The need for having storage come from the fact that the load curve normally differs from the PV power generation. The majority of load is served by the PV generation. However, there is a possible grid connectivity, since the PV generation is fluctuating in nature.

As mentioned earlier, Microgrid Control Agent constantly monitor the actual PV generation and detect the deviated amount of energy from the prior forecast in each time-slot t. There is a possible combination of load curtailment and importing power from the main grid to compensate the energy shortage effect on the next time-slots. The curtailment than happen to the load is determined by the proposals received from User Agents. In the following, we first model a community of users with various types of consumption and a simple User Agent which capture the user's consumption preferences.

3.1 Model of Community Behavior in the Negotiations

In [20] authors characterized the energy consumption pattern by segmentation of the household in residential sector. They investigated the influence of different factors, namely, social class, family dimension, contracted power, number of rooms in the household, and different tariffs on the consumption. We consider three levels of social class for the costumers in our Microgrid. Users in different social classes have different consumption priorities. This will affect their decisions in case of any participation in load curtailment plan. Social class A refers to the consumers for whom the less inconvenience is more important than cost. For the users in social class C the cost incurred is rather more important that the inconvenience. Finally, consumption importance and preferences for the users in social class B is close to retail electricity price of the grid. Table 2 shows the hourly and daily inconvenience cost for the users in different social classes. We consider two scenarios for our Microgrid community. In scenario 1, 30% of the population are from class A, 30% are from class B, and 40% are from class C. In scenario 2, 20% of the population are from social class A, 60% are from class B, and 20% are from class C.

Table 2. Different user classes with their preferences in negotiations

Social class	A	B	C
Hourly cost (C_h)	0.4 [€/kWh]	0.25 [€/kWh]	0.1 [€/kWh]
Daily cost (C_d)	4 [€]	2.5 [€]	1 [€]
Inconvenience cost (I_c)	0.36 [€/kWh]	0.33 [€/kWh]	0.3 [€/kWh]
Scenario 1	30%	30%	40%
Scenario 2	20%	60%	20%

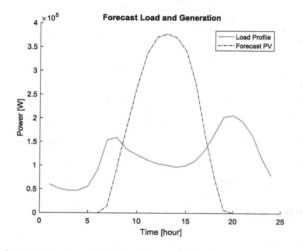

Fig. 3. Total load profile for 100 households; forecast PV generation

To generate the population in every scenario we randomized the amount of daily and hourly cost around ±30%. Figure 3 shows the total load and the PV generation forecast which are used in our simulations.

3.2 PV-Based Microgrid Model

We consider a Micro-grid situated in a residential area, consisting of 100 households. The needed electricity to serve the loads is provided by an array of Photovoltaic (PV) panels with the overall size of 400 kW. As the power produced by the PVs is not constant 24 h a day, the given Micro-grids is equipped with a battery. The size of the battery is about 30% of the PV production capacity which can store excess solar generation and discharge it later in the evening. The battery degradation effect due to charge/discharge cycles is ignored in the calculation. There is also a possibility of grid connectivity which is useful to handle the peak in morning and sell back the excess of PV generation that cannot be stored. The price of purchasing power from the grid is around retail electricity price, fixed at 30 cents per kWh, and the price for selling the excess electricity is also flat at 20 cents per kWh. Considering the Micro-grid in a balanced mode, the net share of main grid in 24 h is about 4% of the total load. The rest is provided by PV if it produces 100% of the forecasted generation capacity. All the simulations are run on a PC with Intel (Core i7) processor with 24 GB RAM, using MATLAB R2016b release.

Imbalance Scenario. In case of any deviation from the forecast, the algorithm is initiated to compensate the effect of power shortage. The realistic PV-generation shortage may happen due to the cloud coverage [21]. Since the proposed algorithm is working based on hourly intervals, for the sake of simplicity we assume 10% shortfalls in PV-generation and increase it stepwise. Figure 4 illustrates the performance of the proposed algorithm in different scenarios.

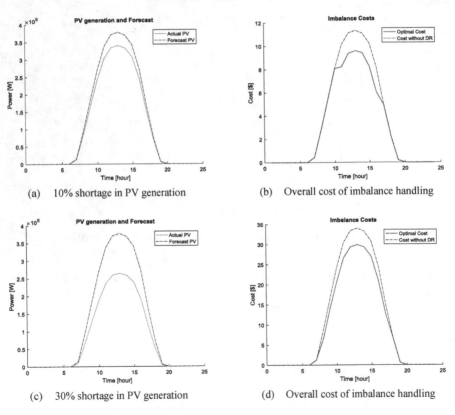

(a)   10% shortage in PV generation   (b)   Overall cost of imbalance handling

(c)   30% shortage in PV generation   (d)   Overall cost of imbalance handling

Fig. 4. Shortage scenarios in PV generation and; cost reduction by proposed algorithm

Algorithm is run for various shortage scenarios and on different community behaviors. As the population is produced by randomizing Scenario 1 and 2 of three social classes mentioned in Sect. 3.1, the obtained result in each run might be slightly different. Hence, the average value of multiple run for the same scenario is considered as final cost for the imbalance handling. Table 2 shows the results.

Table 3. Simulation result. Imbalance handling with/without using proposed algorithm

Shortage in PV generation	Grid purchase ($) (no curtailment)	Optimal cost scenario 1	Optimal cost scenario 2
10%	86.32	73.18	76.22
20%	172.64	146.46	147.88
30%	258.97	223.55	226.92
40%	345.28	301.41	300.76
50%	431.61	379.15	379.89
60%	517.93	456.41	457.90
70%	604.25	530.33	536.14

As can be seen in Table 3, in all the assumed shortage scenarios, the cost of handling the imbalance is considerably less than the cost of importing power from the grid. Comparison between the result of scenario 1 and scenario 2, in which the shares of social classes are not the same, does not show a significant difference in the final cost of imbalance handling and proposed algorithm will converge to an optimum cost with various user distributions. In the simulation setup, we removed the effect of users' hourly consumption rates on their share of cost. However, there still more user sensitivity analysis needs to be performed to model possible user reactions to, for instance, different pricing schemes.

Figure 5 shows that the amount of energy which can be conserved by the proposed distributed algorithm are close to the amount of imbalance in each run of the algorithm.

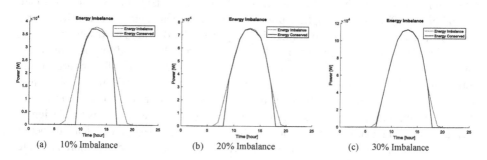

(a) 10% Imbalance	(b) 20% Imbalance	(c) 30% Imbalance

Fig. 5. The amount of energy imbalance vs. the energy conserved by running the proposed algorithm

4 Discussion

In the proposed imbalance handing strategy, the major part of the decision making is being done by the user agents. As the information about the users' consumption are hidden from the central entity (MCA), it is not practical that the MCA accepts only a portion of received proposal by each user. This may seem to reduce the flexibility of the model. However, due to high number of consumers in the residential Micro-grid and the amount of power proposed by each user agent, the effect of having not breakable proposals is negligible. It is worth mentioning that the Multi-agent imbalance handling model is working on the planning layer of Micro-grid. Therefore, the storage facilities act as a buffer and provide the required time to perform the algorithm for the next hours. At the moment, the storage agent and grid agent have simple functionalities. The charge and discharge functions of the storage agent could be done based on the smart storage strategies first introduced in [16]. Moreover, the capability of market analysis can be embedded into the grid agent. The current grid agent trades the electricity based on the feed-in tariff and fixed retail electricity price.

5 Conclusion and Future Work

In this paper, we addressed the problem of handling unforeseen events in Micro-grid energy management, considering individual users' convenience as an important factor in the decision making. In our distributed Multi-agent based model, autonomous agents are responsible for reflecting the users' convenience level and performing local optimization based on users' consumption priorities. By so doing, the utility functions for modelling the appliances are hidden from the Micro-grid central agent. The inconvenience caused by load curtailment is taken into account as a monetary cost along with the power purchase cost from the main grid. This guarantee that if load curtailment is applied there will be no satisfaction drop in the community due to it, as the inconvenience is calculated in the costs and can be paid to the respective users as incentives.

We demonstrated the performance of the proposed imbalance handling algorithm, by applying it on a PV-based Micro-grid scenario in a residential area. To investigate the effect of different consumption priorities in curtailment plans, we consider three levels of social class for the costumers in the given Micro-grid. The results show the feasibility of the proposed algorithm in different scenarios developed for the evaluation. The simulation results also indicate that the proposed algorithm will converge to an optimum cost having various user distributions. However, there still more user sensitivity analysis needs to be performed to model possible user reactions in the power imbalance situation. One of the area in which this work can be extended is the design of user agent. Using learning techniques in the user agent's design will lead to better capturing the respective user's consumption priorities, and consequently, more accurate proposals in the time of power imbalance.

References

1. Barnes, M., Kondoh, J., Asano, H., Oyarzabal, J., Ventakaramanan, G., Lasseter, R., Hatziargyriou, N., Green, T.: Real-world microgrids-an overview. In: 2007 IEEE International Conference on System of Systems Engineering, pp. 1–8 (2007)
2. Bayindir, R., Hossain, E., Kabalci, E., Perez, R.: A comprehensive study on microgrid technology. Int. J. Renew. Energy Res. (IJRER) **4**, 1094–1107 (2014)
3. Hatziargyriou, N., Asano, H., Iravani, R., Marnay, C.: Microgrids. IEEE Power Energy Mag. **5**, 78–94 (2007)
4. Planas, E., Andreu, J., Gárate, J.I., de Alegra, I.M., Ibarra, E.: AC and DC technology in microgrids: a review. Renew. Sustain. Energy Rev. **43**, 726–749 (2015)
5. Olivares, D.E., Mehrizi-Sani, A., Etemadi, A.H., Cañizares, C.A., Iravani, R., Kazerani, M., Hajimiragha, A.H., Gomis-Bellmunt, O., Saeedifard, M., Palma-Behnke, R., Jiménez-Estévez, G.A., Hatziargyriou, N.D.: Trends in microgrid control. IEEE Trans. Smart Grid **5**, 1905–1919 (2014)
6. Samadi, P., Mohsenian-Rad, A.H., Schober, R., Wong, V.W.S., Jatskevich, J.: Optimal real-time pricing algorithm based on utility maximization for smart grid. In: 2010 First IEEE International Conference on Smart Grid Communications, pp. 415–420 (2010)
7. Remani, T., Jasmin, E.A., TP, I.A.: Load scheduling with maximum demand using binary particle swarm optimization. In: 2015 International Conference on Technological Advancements in Power and Energy (TAP Energy), pp. 294–298 (2015)
8. Yang, P., Tang, G., Nehorai, A.: A game-theoretic approach for optimal time-of-use electricity pricing. IEEE Trans. Power Syst. **28**, 884–892 (2013)
9. Li, N., Chen, L., Low, S.H.: Optimal demand response based on utility maximization in power networks. In: 2011 IEEE Power and Energy Society General Meeting, pp. 1–8 (2011)
10. Mohajeryami, S., Schwarz, P., Baboli, P.T.: Including the behavioral aspects of customers in demand response model: real time pricing versus peak time rebate. In: 2015 North American Power Symposium (NAPS), pp. 1–6 (2015)
11. Wooldridge, M.: An Introduction to Multiagent Systems. Wiley, Hoboken (2009)
12. Kantamneni, A., Brown, L.E., Parker, G., Weaver, W.W.: Survey of multi-agent systems for microgrid control. Eng. Appl. Artif. Intell. **45**, 192–203 (2015)
13. Rohbogner, G., Hahnel, U.J., Benoit, P., Fey, S.: Multi-agent systems' asset for smart grid applications. Comput. Sci. Inf. Syst. **10**, 1799–1822 (2013)
14. Derksen, C., Unland, R.: The EOM: an adaptive energy option, state and assessment model for open hybrid energy systems. In: Proceedings of the 2016 Federated Conference on Computer Science and Information Systems, FedCSIS 2016, Gdansk, Poland, 11–14 September 2016, pp. 1507–1515 (2016)
15. Loose, N., Nurdin, Y., Ghorbani, S., Derksen, C., Unland, R.: Evaluation of aggregated systems in smart grids: an example use-case for the energy option model. In: Bajo, J., Escalona, M.J., Giroux, S., Hoffa-Dąbrowska, P., Julián, V., Novais, P., Sánchez-Pi, N., Unland, R., Azambuja-Silveira, R. (eds.) PAAMS 2016. CCIS, vol. 616, pp. 369–380. Springer, Cham (2016). https://doi.org/10.1007/978-3-319-39387-2_31
16. Morsali, R., Ghorbani, S., Kowalczyk, R., Unland, R.: On battery management strategies in multi-agent microgrid management. In: Abramowicz, W. (ed.) BIS 2017. LNBIP, vol. 303, pp. 191–202. Springer, Cham (2017). https://doi.org/10.1007/978-3-319-69023-0_17
17. Nunna, H.K., Doolla, S.: Multiagent-based distributed-energy-resource management for intelligent microgrids. IEEE Trans. Ind. Electron. **60**, 1678–1687 (2013)

18. Ghorbani, S., Unland, R.: A holonic multi-agent control system for networks of micro-grids. In: Klusch, M., Unland, R., Shehory, O., Pokahr, A., Ahrndt, S. (eds.) MATES 2016. LNCS (LNAI), vol. 9872, pp. 231–238. Springer, Cham (2016). https://doi.org/10.1007/978-3-319-45889-2_17
19. Ghorbani, S., Rahmani, R., Unland, R.: Multi-agent autonomous decision making in smart micro-grids' energy management: a decentralized approach. In: Berndt, J.O., Petta, P., Unland, R. (eds.) MATES 2017. LNCS (LNAI), vol. 10413, pp. 223–237. Springer, Cham (2017). https://doi.org/10.1007/978-3-319-64798-2_14
20. Pombeiro, H., Pina, A., Silva, C.: Analyzing residential electricity consumption patterns based on consumer's segmentation. In: International Workshop on Information Technology for Energy Applications, pp. 29–38, Lisbon, Portugal (2012)
21. Seyedmahmoudian, M., Mekhilef, S., Rahmani, R., Yusof, R., Renani, E.T.: Analytical modeling of partially shaded photovoltaic systems. Energies 6, 128–144 (2013)

PAAMS Workshop MASLE

Design of an Agent-Based Learning Environment for High-Risk Doorstep Scam Victims

Laura M. van der Lubbe[1](✉), Tibor Bosse[1], and Charlotte Gerritsen[2]

[1] VU Amsterdam, De Boelelaan 1081, 1081 HV Amsterdam, The Netherlands
{l.m.vander.lubbe,t.bosse}@vu.nl
[2] Netherlands Institute for Study of Crime and Law Enforcement,
De Boelelaan 1077, 1081 HV Amsterdam, The Netherlands
cgerritsen@nscr.nl

Abstract. Doorstep scams are scams, often happening at the front door, in which a con artist has a convincing, but fraudulent, story with the purpose of coming into your house and/or stealing money. Various campaigns to educate people exist, but they do not focus on the verbal skills people can use to prevent themselves from becoming a victim. This paper describes the conceptual design of a proposed training application. This application will provide an agent-based learning environment for high-risk doorstep scam victims. In order to create a training application, field research has been done to the content and progress of doorstep scams, which is used to create interactive scenarios.

Keywords: Virtual agent-based learning · Resilience training
Interactive scenarios

1 Introduction

Doorstep scams are scams in which a con artist has a convincing, but fraudulent, story with the purpose of coming into your house and/or stealing money. Elderly people are at a high risk of becoming victims of such scams, often with a high emotional impact. Various campaigns and information websites (e.g. 'Scam awareness month'[1]) exist to warn and educate people on this phenomenon. In such campaigns, people are often educated on how to prevent doorstep scams from happening, or how to prevent intruders from coming in their houses, with behavioral tips such as opening the door with the chain on. However, besides behavioral actions in order to prevent a doorstep scam from happening, verbal skills (such as refusal assertiveness) are also important to be more resilient against doorstep scams. There is no large scale prevention campaign known that

---

[1] www.citizensadvice.org.uk/about-us/campaigns/current_campaigns/scams-awareness-month/.

© Springer International Publishing AG, part of Springer Nature 2018
J. Bajo et al. (Eds.): PAAMS 2018 Workshops, CCIS 887, pp. 335–347, 2018.
https://doi.org/10.1007/978-3-319-94779-2_29

focuses on the conversation that takes place within a doorstep scam, and the verbal skills needed to prevent these scams from happening. On a smaller scale, actors are sometimes used to play a doorstep scam scenario with a group of people within larger meetings.

The Dutch ministry of Safety and Justice acknowledges doorstep scams as high impact crimes. They have funded this research in which, together with a large Dutch elderly organization called KBO-PCOB[2], a virtual training is under development. With this training, people learn how to interact (what to say and how to use their voice) with the use of virtual agents in a simulated world, in order to improve their resilience against doorstep scams. Within this research the main target group is elderly users, however the training could also be useful for other users. The advantages of a virtual training are that the training is available at any time and for a larger audience, that it can be used multiple times and it offers an opportunity to adjust to the user. Within other domains there has already been research towards using virtual agents for trainings that normally were performed using actors [3,4], which is considered to be less costly and more easy to control. Furthermore, previous research has shown that virtual trainings or serious games are effective learning resources [11,12,19,30].

This paper provides a conceptual design for a virtual training for verbal skills to improve the resilience against doorstep scams. First Sect. 2 provides an overview of related literature. Within Sect. 2.1 the domain of doorstep scams is further explained, followed by an overview of related interventions, both for the target group (Sect. 2.2) as well as for the learning purpose of this training (Sect. 2.3). Section 3 describes a conceptual design of the training proposed in this project. Finally, Sect. 4 summarizes the contribution of this paper and explains the future steps in the development of the training.

2   Doorstep Scams and Related Interventions

2.1   Doorstep Scams

Doorstep scams appear often appear at the doorstep, but also on the street or on the phone. The introduction stated that educational programs around doorstep scams often provide people with behavioral actions they can use to prevent doorstep scams. In contrast, the proposed training application focuses on the verbal skills that can prevent a doorstep scam from happening.

The content and progress of the stories told during doorstep scams have not been studied earlier. Therefore a field study has been done to better understand the content and progress of doorstep scams. For this field study the following sources have been used: a focus group meeting with the partner KBO-PCOB, various conversations with domain experts, (news) articles and reports.

---

[2] www.kbo-pcob.nl.

An overview of frequently encountered doorstep scam stories, based on the field study, is provided below:

- Stories at the door:
  - The electricity, gas, or water, needs to be checked by the con artist, therefore he/she must enter your home.
  - The con artist has a delivery (package, flowers) that he/she wants to give to the victim. Either this is an excuse to enter the house or it is an excuse to seduce the victim to do a small payment (e.g. delivery costs), often with the purpose to steal more money from the victim than just the payment.
  - A con artist in the role of handyman wants to do some job for the victim, however he/she asks (a large amount of) money that needs to be payed right away. The job will not be done (correctly), but the money is taken.
- Stories on the phone
  - The con artist calls with a story about fraudulent payments made, pretending to be the bank. He/she will ask private information, such as their debit/credit card PIN.
  - The con artist tells the victim that he/she has won a price, but in order to claim the price the victim needs to give information or make a small payment.
  - The con artist calls pretending to do a survey and asks the victim to give personal information. This information is later used to do a financial scam or identity theft.
- Stories on the street
  - The con artist claims to be collecting money or selling something for charity. Either the money is not used for charity or the con artist uses this to be able to easily pickpocket the target.
  - The con artist sells a newspaper or magazine, however the victim ends up with a long and expensive subscription.
  - The con artist sells some goods at the street, either the prize is too high (or the quality too low) or the good turns out to be completely worthless.

The fact that doorstep scams are a serious problem at the moment can be derived from the number of campaigns and news articles that can be found on the subject. However, it is hard to find statistics about the scope of the problem. This is due to the fact that there are multiple criminal activities associated with doorstep scams, which makes the registration inconclusive. Furthermore, often victims do not report a doorstep scam [15], for example due to shame.

2.2 Serious Games for Elderly Users

Various types of serious games targeting elderly users are used to address different difficulties the target group faces. An often used type of game is the exergame, a game in which the player has to perform some sort of physical activity. Mostly these games are used to address problems that have to do with physical activity of the elderly users and related problems. However, research has also been done towards using exergames for seniors with subsyndromal depression [22]. Various exergames focus at balance and postural control. An often used technology for these sorts of exergames are the Nintendo Wii Fit, sometimes together with the additional Balance Board (e.g. [12,29]). Other technologies used are, for example, a step pad training [23], or Xbox Kinect games (such as [29]). Besides this, exergames are for example used to promote active aging [12].

Serious games for elderly users can be used to address problems with cognitive abilities. So called brain training games, such as Brain Age [19], improve the player's attention and memory skills. While these games are often designed especially to serve as a serious game, the research of Whitlock et al. [31] found that an existing game, World of Warcraft, improved the attention and spatial orientation of the players. Furthermore, Shang-Ti et al. [25] used an XBox 360 Kinect game to improve the selective attention of players.

Serious games for elderly do not only address physical or cognitive abilities, but it can also be used to enhance the users' social contacts, for example intergenerational interactions [5]. SilverGame [24] is a platform consisting of different activities to promote social activities. The activities also serve as entertainment and promote exercise.

2.3 Virtual Trainings for Social Skills and Resilience Against Scams

This research aims to improve verbal resilience against doorstep scams. This section gives an overview of other types of (computer-based) trainings that exist, within a broader scope of related trainings.

Phishing Training. Phishing is using social engineering techniques to obtain sensitive information[3], often performed via e-mail(s). Social engineering refers to using psychological manipulation to make people perform certain actions or disclose certain information[4]. Although this research is focused at doorstep scams, it is considered relevant to look at the domain of phishing, since social engineering techniques are also used in doorstep scams.

Educating people about phishing and online safety can be done in different ways, for example using cartoons [27]. Robila and Ragucci [21] tested user education consisting of quantitative testing and social context aware examples. The students that followed this education showed better phishing identification skills and gave a positive evaluation of the education they received.

Assertiveness Training. Being assertive means that you are behaving confident and that you dare to say what you think or believe[5]. This is a form of verbal resilience. Winship and Kelley [32] used a verbal response model to train assertiveness. Participants that were trained using this model showed an

---

[3] Definition based on: en.wikipedia.org/wiki/Phishing.

[4] Definition based on: en.wikipedia.org/wiki/Social_engineering_(security).

[5] Definition: dictionary.cambridge.org/dictionary/english/assertive.

increase in their assertive behavior. Another research showed that assertiveness training within a group can also be effective [20]. Furthermore, verbal modeling and therapist coaching can increase the refusal of unreasonable requests [14].

Saying No. Saying no, or refusal skills, are part of assertiveness trainings, applied in various domains among which are smoking behavior, drugs usage, shoplifting and rape prevention. There are various ways in which somebody can say no: you can simply say no, make aversive statements, give a reason for not accepting an offer, change the subject or walk away [18]. In order to learn students to resist direct and indirect pressures to engage in negative behaviors, an effective prevention program should both show different verbal strategies as well as the need to be assertive when refusing an offer [16]. Even though nonverbal assertive skills can be used for different types of situations, practicing verbal strategies with specific situations is also needed [18].

Verbal resilience also means that you use your voice in a assertive way. Nonverbal assertive skills that can be measured within the voice are for example: speaking firmly or authoritative [17], duration of a reply [1], medium latency of the response [1,7], the loud volume of the voice [1,7], and the medium fluency [7]. A way to measure assertiveness through behaviors is the Behavioral Assertiveness Test - Revised (BAT-R) [6], however the validation for this test is mixed [1]. One remark made is that for example the volume of voice is not unique for assertiveness.

Within this research saying no, although often implicitly, is an important aspect of the assertive behavior taught to the player. As suggested within the research of Nichols et al. [18] it is important to give verbal strategies for specific situations; this is done in the proposed virtual training.

Social Skill Training with Virtual Agents. Although some of the above-mentioned trainings are virtual, there are no examples mentioned yet of training programs for assertiveness with a virtual agent. Virtual agents are used for many different types of training programs, among which are social skills. For example the automated social skills trainer (ASST) [28], in which human-agent interaction takes place via user speech and language interaction. The proposed training focuses mostly on communication, previous research has been done in the same field, however no comparable virtual trainings are found. deLearyous [30] is a serious game used to train interpersonal communication skills. Players learn how to use Leary's Rose in their advantage. The communication with the agent is in this case performed by unconstrained written language input. Another serious game to train interpersonal communication skills is Communicate! [11]. This game is used to train communication in a consultation setting. The interaction with the agent in this game is via multiple choice.

3   Conceptual Design of the Training Application

The platform for which the virtual training will be developed is a tablet. Since this is an often used platform by elderly people, KBO-PCOB posed this requirement. The application consists of two components: the training scenarios and the game layer. The next subsections will discuss these components.

Besides choosing a suitable platform for the target group, it is also important to keep the target group in mind when designing the game. Tailoring a serious game to the elderly target group reduces the risks of factors, such as information overload, that reduce the efficiency of the game for this target group [12]. Not only the content and game play of the game must be tailored to the target group, also specific design principles [2] will be used to adjust the game design to the target group. This includes high contrasts and a larger font type.

3.1   Training Scenarios

The training scenarios consist of different components that together form an interactive training scenario with tailored feedback.

A **three-dimensional environment** will be created using the game engine Unity[6]. The environment will feature a small part of a residential area. Within this residential area there will be a decorated street, that can be used for the scenarios that take place on the street. Furthermore, one of the houses within the environment will be partly furnished to feature the scenarios taking place at the front door and phone scenarios that take place in the living room. Figure 1 shows the different view points within a prototype of the environment.

The **virtual agents** used within the scenarios, playing the role of doorstep scam artist, will be modeled using iClone[7]. With this software several agents will be created, which will be used in different scenarios. For each scenario at least two similar agents will be created, one female and one male. The outfits of the virtual agents need to suit the scenarios. In some scenarios this means that working uniforms have to be recreated using the same type of colors and adding

Fig. 1. Screenshots of the prototype environment with different virtual agents

---

[6] www.unity3d.com/.

[7] www.reallusion.com/iclone/.

a certain corporate logo. Figure 1 shows two prototype agents in the prototype environment.

In order to create credible facial expressions during talking, Facial Motion Capture[8] software, with a plug-in for iClone, will be used to map human actors' expressions to the virtual agents' faces. Furthermore, the actors' voice will be recorded, which will be used as the speech of the virtual agents.

The **interactive conversations** are interactive scripts of a doorstep scam, represented in a conversation tree. Within these conversation trees, vertices represent either atomic agent behaviours or decision nodes (which enable the user to select a response), whereas edges represent transitions between nodes. They are turn-based, always starting and ending with the virtual agent. Each round the player is offered three choices as response to the agent. In general these choices are of a good, moderate and bad level, influencing the conversation in the same way. Good in this context means assertive, bad means submissive. In general the outcomes of a conversation have the same mapping: good means no scam happened, and bad means that a scam happened.

Based on the information obtained during the field study a general outline is made for all the scenarios:

1. Background: getting to know the background of the story the con artist is telling.
2. Identity: getting to know about the identity of the con artist and his/her relation to the story that has been told.
3. Alternative: finding out alternatives to the suggested behavior by the con artist.

In each scenario these three aspects can be found in this order. It depends on the specific scenario how these aspects are addressed. Following the same outline in each scenario gives the players guidance for other (real life) doorstep scams.

For the prototype of the application six different scenarios (see Table 1) are written, based on the most heard about stories told during doorstep scams (see Sect. 2.1). To ensure that the scenarios are credible, they have been evaluated with various domain experts provided by the KBO-PCOB.

Table 1. Overview of the scenarios

	Location	Short description	Goal con artist
1	Front door	Energy meter check	Enter the house
2	Front door	Package delivery	Enter the house with package
3	Phone	Fraudulent bank activity	Gain personal bank information
4	Phone	Lottery won	Gain personal information
5	Street	Money for charity	Collect money for non-existing charity
6	Street	Sell bracelet for charity	Sell overpriced/fake bracelets

---

[8] www.facewaretech.com.

As stated in Sect. 2.1, people often do not report a doorstep scam. To motivate them to do so they are offered an opportunity to make a report in the application at the end of the scenario, they will receive feedback on this decision.

As stated in Sect. 2.3 being assertive is not only represented in the content of your message, but also in the way the message is communicated. The application addresses both: the content is represented in the different choices provided by the interactive conversation, the **speech analysis** module addresses the influence of how the message is communicated. The technique used for this module is based on the research of Formolo and Bosse [8], the technical details of the module are beyond the scope of this paper.

The speech analysis will be a separate module which is only available when the tablet is online, and it can be turned off and on by the player. When this module is turned on the player will not only be asked to make a choice within the scenario, the player is also asked to say this choice aloud and record this (within the application). The progress of the interactive scenario is then no longer only determined by the choices made, but also by the level of assertiveness measured in the voice of the player. When the speech analysis module is not used, each reaction of the player directly leads to a reaction of the virtual agent. However, when the module is turned on in some cases one choice of the player can lead to two different reactions by the agent, determined by the level of assertiveness.

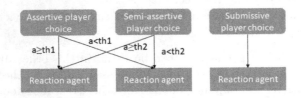

Fig. 2. Flow scenario taking speech analysis into account

Figure 2 shows the flow when speech analysis is taken into account. When no speech analysis is performed the flow chart does not have thresholds and diagonal lines. A high assertiveness score (a) means a very assertive reaction. When a player has a high assertiveness score this will lead to the reaction normally given to a assertive player choice, although this might not be the most assertive choice when looking at the content. This also works the other way around. Threshold1 (th1) is lower than threshold2 (th2), since a very assertive player choice needs a little bit less assertive voice to have an assertive impact on the virtual agent.

After each training scenario the player will receive feedback. This feedback consists of a general reaction on the outcome achieved (whether or not you became a victim of a doorstep scam) and some general tips for the specific scenario. Besides this there is also **tailored feedback**. As mentioned in the section about the Interactive Conversations, each scenario follows a general outline. For each scenario variables are defined within the three steps in the scenario, for example asking the identification of the virtual agent. These variables are linked to a specific moment in the conversation. The feedback is tailored to the variables that are not reached within the conversation that has been held. So for example when the player did not ask the identification of the virtual agent, the player will receive feedback afterwards on asking identification during conversations.

The tone of the feedback is positive. The goal of the feedback is to inform and educate players, not to punish them for wrong behavior. This positive tone can be found in the general formulation of the sentences as well as in the fact that the feedback suggests other types of behavior instead of telling the player what not to do. Since the general outline of the different scenarios is comparable, players can use the feedback for different scenarios. Furthermore, since the scenarios are comparable to real world doorstep scams, the feedback is also reusable in different possible real world doorstep scams.

3.2   Game Layer

Goh et al. [9] give an overview of several strengths of serious games. One of these strengths is the fact that serious games offer covert learning, in combination with an already existing positive attitude towards games this makes serious games an easier accepted platform for learning. Furthermore, serious games are seen as fun and motivational since players want to achieve goals within the game. Another important strength of serious games is the feeling of control players have; they can practice a scenario as many times as they want to master a skill and they always have the option to shut down the tablet, giving them a feeling of safety.

Greitzer [10] defines four levels of engagement for computer-based trainings (see Fig. 3). The proposed training aims at level three engagement, in which a limited amount of branching within the interactive scenario follows the choices of the player.

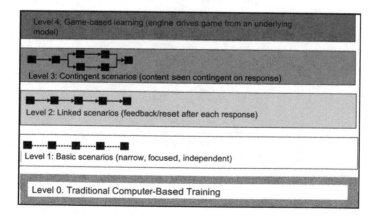

Fig. 3. Levels of engagement for computer-based trainings [10]

Siang and Radha Krishna [26] created, based on the hierarchy of needs from Maslow [13], a hierarchy of players' needs (see Fig. 4). This hierarchy can help game designers to guide the motivation of players. The game layer of the application will be built around the actual training scenarios with the purpose of motivating players to (repeatedly) do the training. The players' needs of Siang and Radha Krishna [26] are addressed in the following way:

- Rules need: The players will receive an explanation about the rules of the game at the beginning, as well as instructions while they are playing.
- Safety need: The player will receive feedback at the end of each training scenario. The positive tone of the feedback will give them the feeling that they can handle the scenarios. Furthermore, when the player falls for a doorstep scam within the training this will not affect the player in real life.
- Belongingness need: The feedback that the players receive after each scenario helps them to improve their resilience against doorstep scams as they can use the feedback for other scenarios as well.
- Esteem need: The players have control over the scenarios since they can make choices influencing the progress of the scenario, as well as the option to quit a scenario. Furthermore, by the feedback received from the game, the players will be encouraged, boosting their esteem.
- Need to know and understand: By repeatedly training different scenarios players will improve their resilience skills, which gives them the ability to train with even more advanced scenarios that can be unlocked at a certain skill level.
- Aesthetic need: Several state of the art game development techniques have been used to build a 3D-environment with credible virtual agents.
- Self actualisation need: (Advanced) players can play scenarios multiple times to test the reaction the virtual agent gives on different reactions, allowing them to test different reaction strategies.

Fig. 4. Hierarchy of players' needs [26]

4   Conclusion and Future Work

Within this paper the content of doorstep scams was investigated in order to create a virtual agent-based learning environment for high-risk potential victims of doorstep scams. With a field study the general structure and content of doorstep scams was explored, which was used to create various interactive scenarios. These interactive scenarios will be used within a virtual training application. The aim of this virtual training application is to improve the verbal skills of the users, in order to empower their verbal resilience against doorstep scams. No other large scale interventions are known that serve the same purpose. The application that is currently being developed can be used in an individual setting, but it can also be used as a tool for group interventions.

The conceptual design and the scenarios are used to create a prototype of the application. Besides developing the application the speech analysis must also be trained specifically for identifying assertive and submissive voices. Furthermore various evaluation meetings will be arranged to improve the prototype. Once a prototype of the application is working, it will be evaluated with a small focus group of possible users (elderly people).

References

1. Bellack, A.S., Hersen, M., Turner, S.M.: Role-play tests for assessing social skills: are they valid? Behav. Ther. **9**(3), 448–461 (1978)
2. Blendinger, K.: Tablet-applications for the elderly: specific usability guidelines, p. 117 (2015)
3. Bosse, T., Gerritsen, C.: Towards serious gaming for communication training - a pilot study with police academy students. In: Poppe, R., Meyer, J.-J., Veltkamp, R., Dastani, M. (eds.) INTETAIN 2016 2016. LNICST, vol. 178, pp. 13–22. Springer, Cham (2017). https://doi.org/10.1007/978-3-319-49616-0_2
4. Bosse, T., Gerritsen, C., De Man, J.: An intelligent system for aggression de-escalation training. In: ECAI, pp. 1805–1811 (2016)
5. Chua, P.H., Jung, Y., Lwin, M.O., Theng, Y.L.: Let's play together: effects of video-game play on intergenerational perceptions among youth and elderly participants. Comput. Hum. Behav. **29**(6), 2303–2311 (2013)
6. Eisler, R.M., Hersen, M., Miller, P.M., Blanchard, E.B.: Situational determinants of assertive behaviors. J. Consult. Clin. Psychol. **43**(3), 330–340 (1975)
7. Eisler, R.M., Miller, P.M., Hersen, M.: Components of assertive behavior. J. Clin. Psychol. **29**(3), 295–299 (1973)
8. Formolo, D., Bosse, T.: Human vs. computer performance in voice-based recognition of interpersonal stance. In: Kurosu, M. (ed.) HCI 2017. LNCS, vol. 10271, pp. 672–686. Springer, Cham (2017). https://doi.org/10.1007/978-3-319-58071-5_51
9. Goh, D.H., Ang, R.P., Tan, H.C.: Strategies for designing effective psychotherapeutic gaming interventions for children and adolescents. Comput. Hum. Behav. **24**(5), 2217–2235 (2008)
10. Greitzer, F.L.: Ingredients of effective and engaging online learning (2005)
11. Jeuring, J., et al.: Communicate! — a serious game for communication skills —. In: Conole, G., Klobučar, T., Rensing, C., Konert, J., Lavoué, É. (eds.) EC-TEL 2015. LNCS, vol. 9307, pp. 513–517. Springer, Cham (2015). https://doi.org/10.1007/978-3-319-24258-3_49

12. Konstantinidis, E.I., Billis, A.S., Mouzakidis, C.A., Zilidou, V.I., Antoniou, P.E., Bamidis, P.D.: Design, implementation, and wide pilot deployment of FitForAll: an easy to use exergaming platform improving physical fitness and life quality of senior citizens. IEEE J. Biomed. Health Inform. **20**(1), 189–200 (2016)
13. Maslow, A.H.: Motivation and Personality, 3rd edn. Revised by: Frager, R., Fadiman, J., McReynolds, C., Cox, R. Harper and Row Publishers Inc., New York (1987)
14. McFall, R.M., Lillesand, D.B.: Behavior rehearsal with modeling and coaching in assertion training. J. Abnorm. Psychol. **77**(3), 313–23 (1971)
15. van der Meer, P.A.M.: Onderzoeksrapport Veiligheid 2017 (version 1.0). Technical report Commissioned by KBO-PCOB (2017)
16. Miller-Day, M.A., Alberts, J., Hecht, M.L., Trost, M.R., Krizek, R.L.: Adolescent Relationships and Drug Use. Lawrence Erlbaum Associates, London (2014)
17. Nichols, T.R., Birnel, S., Graber, J.A., Brooks-Gunn, J., Botvin, G.J.: Refusal skill ability: an examination of adolescent perceptions of effectiveness. J. Primary Prevent. **31**(3), 127–37 (2010)
18. Nichols, T.R., Graber, J.A., Brooks-Gunn, J., Botvin, G.J.: Ways to say no: refusal skill strategies among urban adolescents. Am. J. Health Behav. **30**(3), 227–236 (2006)
19. Nouchi, R., Taki, Y., Takeuchi, H., Hashizume, H., Akitsuki, Y., Shigemune, Y., Sekiguchi, A., Kotozaki, Y., Tsukiura, T., Yomogida, Y., Kawashima, R.: Brain training game improves executive functions and processing speed in the elderly: a randomized controlled trial. PLoS ONE **7**(1), e29676 (2012)
20. Rathus, S.A.: An experimental investigation of assertive training in a group setting. J. Behav. Ther. Exp. Psychiatry **3**(2), 81–86 (1972)
21. Robila, S.A., Ragucci, J.W.: Don't be a phish: steps in user education. ACM SIGCSE Bull. **38**, 237–241 (2006)
22. Rosenberg, D., Depp, C.A., Vahia, I.V., Reichstadt, J., Palmer, B.W., Kerr, J., Norman, G., Jeste, D.V.: Exergames for subsyndromal depression in older adults: a pilot study of a novel intervention. Am. J. Geriatr. Psychiatry **18**(3), 221–226 (2010)
23. Schoene, D., Lord, S.R., Delbaere, K., Severino, C., Davies, T.A., Smith, S.T.: A randomized controlled pilot study of home-based step training in older people using videogame technology. PLoS ONE **8**(3), e57734 (2013)
24. Senger, J., et al.: Serious gaming: enhancing the quality of life among the elderly through play with the multimedia platform SilverGame. In: Wichert, R., Eberhardt, B. (eds.) Ambient Assisted Living. ATSC, pp. 317–331. Springer, Heidelberg (2012). https://doi.org/10.1007/978-3-642-27491-6_23
25. Shang-Ti, C., Chiang, I.T., Liu, E.Z.F., Chang, M.: Effects of improvement on selective attention: developing appropriate somatosensory video game interventions for institutional-dwelling elderly with disabilities. Turk. Online J. Educ. Technol. **11**(4), 409–417 (2012)
26. Siang, A.C., Radha Krishna, R.: Theories of learning: a computer game perspective. In: 2003 Proceedings Fifth International Symposium on Multimedia Software Engineering, pp. 239–245 (2003)
27. Srikwan, S., Jakobsson, M.: Using cartoons to teach internet security. Cryptologia **32**(2), 137–154 (2008)
28. Tanaka, H., Sakti, S., Neubig, G., Toda, T., Negoro, H., Iwasaka, H., Nakamura, S.: Teaching social communication skills through human-agent interaction. ACM Trans. Interact. Intell. Syst. **6**(2), 1–26 (2016)

29. Taylor, L.M., Maddison, R., Pfaeffli, L.A., Rawstorn, J.C., Gant, N., Kerse, N.M.: Activity and energy expenditure in older people playing active video games. Arch. Phys. Med. Rehabil. **93**(12), 2281–2286 (2012)
30. Vaassen, F., Wauters, J., Van Broeckhoven, F., Van Overveldt, M., Daelemans, W., Eneman, K.: deLearyous: training interpersonal communication skills using unconstrained text input. In: Proceedings of the European Conference on Games Based Learning, pp. 505–513 (2012)
31. Whitlock, L.A., McLaughlin, A.C., Allaire, J.C.: Individual differences in response to cognitive training: using a multi-modal, attentionally demanding game-based intervention for older adults. Comput. Hum. Behav. **28**(4), 1091–1096 (2012)
32. Winship, B.J., Kelley, J.D.: A verbal response model of assertiveness. J. Couns. Psychol. **23**(3), 215–220 (1976)

Significant Educational Content Based Learning Model Using Public Ontologies and Multiagent Systems

Felipe Demarchi$^{(\boxtimes)}$, Elder Rizzon Santos$^{(\boxtimes)}$,
and Ricardo Azambuja Silveira$^{(\boxtimes)}$

Federal University of Santa Catarina, Florianópolis, Brazil
felipedemarchi26@gmail.com,
{elder.santos, ricardo.silveira}@ufsc.br

Abstract. The Semantic Web offers a structure to support generation of significant learning contents for Web based intelligent learning environments by using public knowledge bases known as public ontologies, available on the Web. Prior research has therefore been undertaken into allowing agents societies to navigate through these knowledge bases, in search of answers to queries. In addition, research is emerging into using this knowledge to contribute to the area of education, in terms of creating virtual learning environments. This work proposes a model for agents that allows access to ontologies related to a given domain of knowledge available on the Web, allowing these agents to use this knowledge in the construction and formulation of questions for the production of relevant and updated content for the student. Several efforts have been made to integrate agents with ontologies, which allow a greater knowledge for the agent based on a local ontology. However, no proposal has yet combined the ability to use the semantic data available on the Web in conjunction with a consolidated BDI agent framework for the production of meaningful content for virtual learning environments. Therefore, this work proposes a model for a virtual learning environment that uses agents developed using the Jason interpreter, with its ability to access ontologies available on the Web to update its belief base and generate significant content for the student. To validate this approach, a case study of an educational quiz is presented that uses this information to identify questions and check the answers obtained.

Keywords: Semantic Web · BDI agents · Virtual learning environments

1 Introduction

The emergence of the Semantic Web has brought several challenges in terms of making the application of this concept possible. In order to solve these, research has emerged regarding the integration between intelligent agents and ontologies, thus allowing use of the knowledge available from the Semantic Web to contribute to the area of education, in the creation of virtual learning environments.

© Springer International Publishing AG, part of Springer Nature 2018
J. Bajo et al. (Eds.): PAAMS 2018 Workshops, CCIS 887, pp. 348–359, 2018.
https://doi.org/10.1007/978-3-319-94779-2_30

According to Berners-Lee, Hendler and Lassila [2], the Semantic Web aims to bring a meaningful content structure to Web pages, allowing virtual agents to move between these pages performing specific tasks for users. In order to do this, it is necessary to use knowledge representation from the various ontologies that are available on the Web; the great power offered by the Semantic Web will be accessible when agents can collect the information available in the various bases of knowledge representation, process this information and share the results with other agents.

For our definition of agents, we consider the notation presented by Wooldridge and Jennings [12] according to which an agent consists of a system that is situated within some environment and can perform autonomous actions in this environment to reach its objectives. It has the properties of autonomy, social ability, reactivity and proactivity.

Another concept necessary for the context of the Semantic Web refers to ontologies; Gruber [8] defines an ontology as an explicit specification of a conceptualization, understood as a simplified and abstract vision of the world that it is meant to represent for some purpose. Antoniou and Van Harmelen [1] point out that an ontology consists of a finite list of terms, and that the relationship between these terms, which define important concepts, is formed by the classes and objects of the domain.

Based on this, it is possible to identify the possibilities of using these concepts of the Semantic Web in virtual learning environments, in order to take advantage of the information available in knowledge representation bases to produce content relevant to a particular virtual learning environment.

Many works have been developed in order to allow agents to use ontologies as a knowledge base. Dikenelli et al. [6], Moreira et al. [11] Klapiscak and Bordini [9], Mascardi et al. [10], Campos [4] and Freitas et al. [7] are all proposals that allow the integration between agents and ontologies as a knowledge base. However, these proposals do not consider the context of virtual learning environments in defining agents' access to ontologies.

This paper briefly presents the proposed model integration of a Jason-BDI agent structure with public ontologies such as DBPedia, in order to produce a virtual learning environment for the development of an educational quiz about geography. The quiz can create questions and answers defined through searches of these knowledge bases available on the Semantic Web to the students. We presented a detailed description of the model in previous work [5] and, in this paper, the formulation of the learning content generation is described.

This paper is organized as follows. Related works are described in Sect. 2. Section 3 presents a structure based on remote ontologies for the formulation of questions and answers. In Sect. 4, the proposed agent model is presented. In Sect. 5, a case study is described that validates the proposed model. Finally, Sect. 6 presents the conclusions and future work.

2 Related Works

In this section, we review the main works presented in [5] that perform an integration between agents and ontologies, and that use ontologies as the agents' knowledge base.

SEAGENT [6] allows agents to have as their internal knowledge a local ontology allowing communication between agents. In order to perform this communication, it uses ontology matching between the ontologies of the two agents, allowing agents with heterogeneous ontologies to communicate with each other.

AgentSpeak-DL [11] is a BDI agent-oriented programming language using descriptive logic and ontologies of the AgentSpeak language, which uses predicate logic. To do this, it incorporates ontological knowledge with the agent, developing the necessary changes in language semantics to allow execution based on these ontologies.

JASDL [9] (Jason AgentSpeak-DescriptionLogic) uses the Jason interpreter to implement the theoretical proposal presented by AgentSpeak-DL.

CooL-AgentSpeak [10] is an extension of the AgentSpeak-DL language that allows alignment between the local heterogeneous ontologies present in different agents. It makes use of an agent with this alignment capability called Ontology Agent, which is consulted whenever it is necessary to perform an alignment between the ontologies of two agents.

PySA [4] proposes a Python BDI agent implementation that defines URIs (Uniform Resource Identifiers) as agent beliefs that point to online data available on the Semantic Web, and more specifically in DBPedia.

Freitas et al. [7] propose an approach that allows the interaction of agents and ontologies using a coded layer based on CArtAgO. In this approach, any agent-oriented language with support for this artifact can use this implementation to perform the integration between agents and local ontologies. One of the main contributions of this work is to allow an agent to have access to more than one ontology as a knowledge base.

In analyzing the above-mentioned works, it is possible to identify that many efforts are being applied to research concerning the integration between agents and ontologies, with the aim of contributing to research related to the Semantic Web. However, although many works allow the use of ontologies as the agents' knowledge base, and in some cases allow communication between the agents present in multi-agent systems, only the work of Campos [4] integrates the agent with an ontology available remotely, from a proper implementation of the agent, without applying a consolidated agent structure.

Another point that can be observed is that none of these papers deal with the use of knowledge bases for the production of updated content for virtual learning environments. When searching for knowledge in databases such as DBPedia and Wikidata, up-to-date information is guaranteed for the production of content.

3   Development of Questions and Answers

Currently, there are several widely available remote knowledge bases, with the main ones including DBPedia, Wikidata and GeoNames. In order to access these ontologies, services are available that allow querying with the SPARQL language (SPARQL Protocol and RDF Query Language), which allows access to triples composed of Subject-Predicate-Object and stored in RDF format.

In order to work with a virtual learning environment that uses data available from remote ontologies for the production of its content, and having as its theme the production of an educational geography quiz, it was decided to establish a table that will serve as a basis for identifying the predicates that can be used to produce certain types of questions, as well as the words that should be used in the formation of this question.

For this, it was necessary to establish a pattern for the question format that the virtual learning environment will be able to answer, defining questions that start with the words "how many", "who", "where", "when" and "what". It was possible to identify patterns of predicates, some of which are indicated in Table 1.

Table 1. Relationships between question types and predicates.

Question tipe	DBPedia predicates	Word
Where	dbo:country	Located
	dbo:isPartOf	Located
	geo:lat	On the map
	geo:long	On the map
When	dbo:foundingDate	Founded
Who	dbo:leaderName	Leader
What	foaf:nick	Nick
	dbo:capital	Capital of
	dbo:currency	Currency
	dbo:officialLanguage	Language
	dbo:largestCity	Largest city
How Many	dbo:populationTotal	People has

In addition, an important relationship that can be observed is owl:sameAs, which identifies the relationship between the entity in DBPedia and entities in other knowledge bases such as GeoNames and Wikidata; this increases the amount of knowledge it is possible to obtain from these ontologies.

With a predetermined object for formalizing the questions, and based on table of relationships between the question type and the predicates, it is possible to allow an agent to examine this information and produce meaningful questions for the context, comparing the answer given by the student with the objects obtained from the established predicates.

To exemplify the DBPedia knowledge base queries, we will assume that we want to ask questions about the "Florianópolis" object. In this case, the bases of the queries in SPARQL for the preparation of questions will have a URI obtained from the following query:

```
SELECT ?p WHERE {
        ?p rdfs:label 'Florianópolis'@EN . (1)
}
```

By this means, it is possible to link question types to predicates for question generation. When we get the WHERE question type, you can see a link to the dbo:-country predicate, which has "located" as the base word for the question. In this case, this would be: "Where is Florianópolis located?" and the answer would be obtained from the following SPARQL query:

```
SELECT ?country WHERE {
        ?p rdfs:label 'Florianópolis'@EN .
        ?p dbo:country ?country . (2)
}
```

This query will return the "Brazil" object, indicating that Florianópolis is located in Brazil. It is also important to note that this object, which was obtained by the query, serves as the basis for further queries regarding this matter.

By obtaining this mapping of the predicates that answer each type of question, it is possible to develop an agent model for application to a virtual learning environment, so that the agent can formulate questions for the student based on the table of relationships between the types of questions and their predicates; an agent can also use the insight gained from the responses to populate their belief base and produce new questions from it. See [5] for details.

4 Proposed Agent Model

In order to apply the concepts of the Semantic Web to a consolidated agent model, we chose to use the architecture and the reasoning cycle of the Jason interpreter.

This interpreter uses 10 steps for the execution of an agent's reasoning cycle. The first four steps relate to obtaining information for the belief base, and the remaining steps are related to the selection of events and plans that make it possible to reach the objectives of the agent [3].

The main point to be modified is the use of URIs that point to available knowledge bases on the Semantic Web as agent beliefs; in the context of this proposal, these are URIs that point to existing entities in DBPedia. Figure 1 shows the details of the execution cycle of the agent responsible for formulating the questions.

We must assume that our scenario will have at least two agents in communication: one responsible for the preparation of the questions and another for presenting and obtaining the student's answers. These will be called Question Agent (QA) and Answer Agent (AA), respectively.

The QA agent should start with a belief that points to an existing URI in the DBPedia knowledge base, and from there begins the process of obtaining terms and formulating questions based on the table of relationships between question types and predicates.

This agent will update the belief base in two situations: (1) upon receiving a response from agent AA, and (2) by adding a new URI to its belief base.

The agent events for the formulation of the questions are based on the predicates in the table of relationships with the question types; thus, an event will be generated to deal with each of the predicates, allowing each reasoning cycle of an agent to deal with one event, that is, with one type of question. In addition, it will also contain an event which checks the response received from the AA agent.

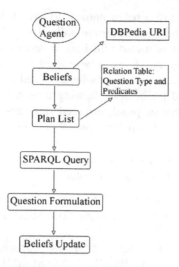

Fig. 1. Agent execution cycle.

In order to formulate the questions, each of the question types indicated in the relationship table has a plan for execution based on the type of question, the predicate and the base word(s), using the URI that the agent has as belief, for the formulation of the question. To be considered an applicable plan, its context should be based on a SPARQL query that will be performed using the URI and the predicate obtained in the previous steps. If the search result is empty, it means that the URI being used has no relation to the predicate in question; it will therefore not be considered an applicable plan. In order to obtain a validation of the response sent by agent AA, a plan is considered applicable with the annotation [source(AA)].

Finally, after selecting an applicable plan for formulating a question, it is executed by sending it to the agent AA, who will be responsible for presenting the questions and obtaining the answers. To validate the response sent by the AA agent, a SPARQL search is performed and the search result compared with the response sent by the agent. In this case, if the result points to an object that represents a URI, it will be added to the agent's belief base for future formulation of questions.

In this way, we have a BDI agent that has beliefs that point to URIs available on the Semantic Web, formulates questions based on these pre-established URIs and predicates, and updates its belief base with new URIs found from the answers obtained for the questions. This allows the agent to expand the number of questions that can be formulated for the student, always maintaining their relevance to the contents.

5   Case Study

To exemplify the execution of the agent cycle for the formulation of the questions, a case study was chosen with reference to a geography quiz, which demonstrates the steps performed by the agent and the updates.

The agent named QA have a belief named uri, which is a list that will begin its process with a URI about the city of Florianópolis as a belief, which will point to the DBPedia resource. In addition, it also will have a belief called number of questions, responsible for managing the questions to be made based on the URI.

The events will be generated from this belief based on the table of relationships between question types and predicates, allowing a search of plans for each type of question. For this, a number of pre-determined questions were used based on the quantity of predicates that point to information about the geography theme, defining a belief called num_of_questions, responsible for managing the questions and defining based on which URI the questions will be generated. In the case of the URI used as an example, the following events will be generated:

```
+!generateQuestions : num_of_questions(X) & X = 0 < - !ques-
tion("where", "dbo:country", "located");  - + num_of_ques-
tions(X + 1).
+!generateQuestions : num_of_questions(X) & X = 1 < - !ques-
tion("when", "dbo:founding", "located");  - + num_of_ques-
tions(X + 1).
+!generateQuestions : num_of_questions(X) & X = 2 < - !re-
moveUri; - + num_of_questions(0); !generateQuestions.
```

The next step to be performed by QA is the selection of one of these events to define the relevant plans; following the execution of the reasoning cycle of the Jason interpreter, these consist of the unification of the event triggering the plan with the selected event. The selection of events follows the pattern of the interpreter, which selects the first event from the list. Thus, the relevant plan consists of:

```
+!question(Type, Predicate, Word) : ... < - ... .
```

In order to select the relevant plans, only the triggering event is required, as shown above, since the unification of the selected event takes place at this stage of the definition of the plan. After listing the relevant plan, the applicability or otherwise of this plan is defined. In the context of the educational quiz, plans that return some information from the SPARQL query will be considered applicable based on the information obtained; this query is performed by an internal event named searchdb-pedia added to the Jason interpreter, which performs the SPARQL search and returns a true value if the search finds some information, or false if it returns empty.

This internal event added to the implementation of the interpreter is primarily responsible for the communication between the agent and the knowledge base. In addition, this is the event that will determine whether or not a plan is applicable.

Not all relevant plans are applicable to the URI referring to the city of Florianópolis. Figure 2 illustrates the properties related to this URI, demonstrating that some predicates such as dbo:capital and dbo:largestCity do not apply because they are not present in the URI in question.

Of the predicates that apply to the URI and which can generate questions about the subject, there are two types of possible returns: the literal values, such as the result obtained from dbo:foundingDate, dbo:populationTotal and foaf:nick predicates, and the objects that point to other URIs, such as dbo:isPartOf, dbo:leaderName and dbo:country. This last case, upon receipt of the student's response, generates new beliefs for agents based on these URIs.

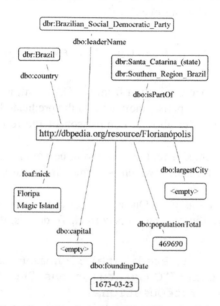

Fig. 2. Properties related to the URI referencing Florianópolis.

The definitions of the plans, in the context of the return of the internal searchdb-pedia event, then have the following format:

```
+!question (Uri, Type, Predicate, Word) : uri(L) & L = [H|T] &
.searchdbpedia(H, Predicate) < - .send(AA, achieve, q(H,
Type, Predicate, Word)).
```

Returning to the case study of the quiz, and following the standard implementation of the interpreter which selects the first applicable plan that matches, the plan that will be selected is that of the predicate dbo:country, which is present in the Florianópolis entity of DBPedia.

After selecting this applicable plan, the intentions will be executed; in this case, the information will be sent to the Answer Agent (AA), leaving the Question Agent (QA) awaiting the response to carry out the validation of this. It is important to point out that information is sent to the agent AA that allows the return of the response to the QA, in order to be able to compare the response sent from a new SPARQL query; that is, the URI and the predicate will be necessary in the returned results.

In this case, QA will send a message containing the following elements: the URI referring to the Florianópolis entity, the type corresponding to the plan in the relationship table, in this case the "where" type; the dbo:country predicate, which was used to perform the SPARQL query for this plan; and the reference word for the formulation of the question, which in this case is "located".

The execution of the Answer Agent is simpler. It awaits the message sent from QA to pose the question to the student and sends the response back to the agent. Therefore, this agent will have the following event:

```
+q(Uri, Type, Predicate, Word) [source(qa)] < - .print(Type,
"is ", Uri, "", Word);.send(qa, achieve, answer(Answer, Uri,
Predicate)).
```

On receiving the message originating from the QA agent, it will print the question to the student and send the response, the URI and the predicate back to the QA agent; the latter two are necessary to allow a comparison of the response with the search result.

In the case study presented here, the question to be presented to the student will be "Where is Florianópolis located?", which is formed from the information sent to the AA agent.

Returning to the execution of the Question Agent, this receives the message sent by the Answer Agent and verifies whether it is correct. To do this, the QA agent will have the following events:

```
+answer(Answer, Uri, Predicate) :.checkanswer(Answer, Uri,
Predicate) < -.print("Congratulations!"); !verifyUri(Uri,
Predicate); !generateQuestions.
+answer(Answer, Uri, Predicate) : not.checkanswer(Answer,
Uri, Predicate) < -.print("Wrong answer!"); !
generateQuestions.
```

In this case, we have two events that can deal with the AA's response; both will check the response sent based on the SPARQL query performed from the URI and the predicate in question. This is done by an internal event added to the architecture of the Jason interpreter, returning true or false according to the result of the verification. If the response is correct, the agent displays a congratulatory message and executes the verifyUri goal to verify whether this response is a URI or a literal value. If the answer is wrong, only a message is displayed indicating the error.

Assuming that the student responded correctly, stating that the city of Florianópolis is located in Brazil, the corresponding objective will be executed, with the checkanswer internal event returning true, presenting the congratulatory message and calling the verifyUri goal.

This goal will check whether the response corresponds to a URI that points to another DBPedia entity or whether it is a literal value. This also happens from an internal event added to the interpreter, which will return true or false. If true, it will add this URI on the list of URIs of the agent's belief base, as shown below:

```
+!verifyUri(URI, Predicate) :.checkuri(Uri, Predicate,
X) < - !addUri(X).
```

In the case of the question concerning the location of the city of Florianópolis, the search result corresponds to a DBPedia URI named dbr:Brazil. In this case, this URI is added on the list of URIs of the agent's belief base.

Regardless of a right or wrong response, or whether or not a new belief is added to the agent, the agent cycle is restarted and a new question is formulated.

If, as in our example, a new belief has been added to the QA agent, it will expand its number of questions by running the corresponding events. From Fig. 3 it is possible to observe the new intentions that will be obtained from the URI corresponding to Brazil.

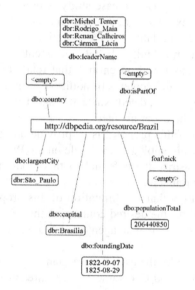

Fig. 3. Properties related to the URI referencing Brazil.

Following this, agent QA will also list as applicable plans the questions regarding the entity Brazil. As can be seen from Fig. 3, questions can be formulated regarding the name of the leader, the largest city, its date of foundation, capital and total population, not considering as applicable those queries that return empty (nick, isPartOf and country).

Using the URIs as agent beliefs allows the use of a BDI agent structure applied to a virtual learning environment. There are several advantages to the use of Semantic Web data for the formulation of an educational quiz; for example, when using data available remotely, the agents will always be accessing updated data for the formulation of the questions. For example, when new elections take place and the presidency of a country changes, the predicate dbo:leaderName will change to the name of the new leader of the government. Another benefit is that the agent can use this semantic data and the links between the entities to expand the content while maintaining the relevance of the subject. As presented in this case study, the city of Florianópolis is the starting point for expanding the knowledge of the agent to the state and country where this city is located.

6 Conclusion

This research relates to the use of the concept of the Semantic Web to produce relevant and updated content for a virtual learning environment, integrating intelligent agents with remote ontologies available on the Web. In order to follow the principles of a BDI agent model, the use of the Jason interpreter is proposed; this is a consolidated agent model based on the AgentSpeak language.

In order to do this, creation and modification of the internal events of the Jason interpreter are proposed, in order to allow an agent to perform SPARQL queries on remote ontologies (specifically DBPedia), and to return the necessary information for the production of the contents of the virtual learning environment.

In order to validate this approach, a case study is presented for the creation of an educational quiz in the context of geography, which uses only information available in remote ontologies for the formulation of the questions related to the context. It is possible to observe that from an initial belief, the agent can produce questions and expand the bank of questions based on entities that relate to the initial belief, while maintaining the coherence of the content. In addition, it is important to mention that this information will always be updated; since the agent uses remote ontologies, the knowledge base will keep the agent updated.

The main contribution of this proposal is to provide an operational model for the integration of BDI agents with ontologies available on the Web to implement a learning environment, and to demonstrate the potential of this model in the creation of active and dynamic learning environments.

It is important to point out that one limitation of this proposal is the fact that pre-defined predicates are used for the desired context, in this case, a geography quiz. It is not part of the scope of this work that an agent can obtain new predicates from the URI that it has as a belief.

Finally, future work includes the use of more than one remote ontology for content generation, such as Wikidata and GeoNames; it has already been observed that these can be obtained from the predicate owl:sameAs. Another option is the dynamic generation of the table of relationships between the question types and the predicates, expanding the possibility of creating an educational quiz to other contexts.

References

1. Antoniou, G., Van Harmelen, F.: A Semantic Web Primer, 2nd edn. The MIT Press, London (2008)
2. Berners-Lee, T., Hendler, J., Lassila, O.: The Semantic Web. Scientific American, May 2001 (2001). https://pdfs.semanticscholar.org/566c/1c6bd366b4c9e07fc37eb372771690d5ba31. pdf. Accessed 15 Oct 2017
3. Bordini, R.H., Hübner, J.F., Wooldrige, M.: Programming Multi-Agent Systems in AgentSpeak Using Jason. Wiley, England (2007)
4. Campos, D.: Representação de Dados Semânticos em Agentes BDI. Dissertation (MSc.), Federal University of Santa Catarina (2014)

5. Demarchi, F., Santos, E.R., Silveira, R.A.: Integration between agents and remote ontologies for the use of content on the semantic web. In: Proceedings of ICAART 2018 – 10° International Conference on Agents and Artificial Intelligence. Funchal, Maddira, Portugal (2018)
6. Dikenelli, O., Erdur, R.C., Gumus O.: SEAGENT: a platform for developing semantic web based multi agent systems. In: Proceedings of the Fourth International Joint Conference on Antonomous Agent and Multiagent Systems, pp. 1271–1272. ACM, Utrecht (2005)
7. Freitas, A., Panisson, A.R., Hilgert, L., Meneguzzi, F., Vieira, R., Bordini, R.H.: Integrating ontologies with multi-agent systems through CArtAgO artifacts. In: IEEE/WIC/ACM International Conference on Web Intelligence and Intelligent Agent Technology, pp. 143–150. IEEE, Singapore (2015)
8. Gruber, T.R.: Toward principles for the design of ontologies used for knowledge sharing? Int. J. Hum Comput Stud. **43**(5–6), 907–928 (1995)
9. Klapiscak, T., Bordini, R.H.: JASDL: a practical programming approach combining agent and semantic web technologies. In: Baldoni, M., Son, T.C., van Riemsdijk, M.B., Winikoff, M. (eds.) DALT 2008. LNCS (LNAI), vol. 5397, pp. 91–110. Springer, Heidelberg (2009). https://doi.org/10.1007/978-3-540-93920-7_7
10. Mascardi, V., Ancona, D., Bordini, R.H., Ricci, A.: CooL-AgentSpeak: enhancing AgentSpeak-DL agents with plan exchange, ontology services. In: IEEE/WIC/ACM International Conference on Web Intelligence and Intelligent Agent Technology, pp. 109–116. IEEE, Lyon (2011)
11. Moreira, Á.F., Vieira, R., Bordini, R.H., Hübner, J.F.: Agent-oriented programming with underlying ontological reasoning. In: Baldoni, M., Endriss, U., Omicini, A., Torroni, P. (eds.) DALT 2005. LNCS (LNAI), vol. 3904, pp. 155–170. Springer, Heidelberg (2006). https://doi.org/10.1007/11691792_10
12. Wooldrige, M., Jennings, N.R.: Intelligent agents: theory and practice. Knowl. Eng. Rev. **10** (2), 115–152 (1995)

Multi-agents for Simulate Preferences of Students in LO Selection

Luis Felipe Londoño, Néstor Darío Duque-Méndez[✉]
and Valentina Tabares-Morales

Universidad Nacional de Colombia, Sede Manizales, Manizales, Colombia
{lflondonor, ndduqueme, vtabaresm}@unal.edu.co

Abstract. The selection of educational material that allows to address the diversity of students in the class-room is a problem faced by teachers in their daily work. The difficulty increases as you wish to attend to a greater number of traits in the trainees, for example, their predominant learning styles and their conditions of disability, to cite some cases. A valid alternative to include different profiles of students and to evaluate the type of materials available is to simulate students with different characteristics and evaluate the relevance of available educational resources. This article presents an interactive tool that supports the teacher in this task, simulating the behavior of students through agents, providing each one with different learning styles and special education needs related to any disability condition. The multi-agent system recommends learning objects (LO) stored in a repository, according to the preferences of agents, which were guide by rules defined according to their characteristics and associated with the metadata of the resources. The appropriate materials are chosen for all students selected by the teacher.

Keywords: Simulation multi-agent · Selection of learning objects
Multi-agents system

1 Introduction

The teacher is often faced with the problem of what teaching materials to select for their teaching work. The selection is not easy, as it has to consider several aspects such as, among others, the teaching objectives, the educational context, the needs of the students their abilities, cognitive styles, experience and skills [1]. It is fundamental to choose the resources and didactic materials properly because they are fundamental tools for the development and enrichment of the teaching-learning process of the students [2, 3].

The selection of educational material that allows to address the diversity of students in the classroom is a problem faced by teachers in their daily work. The difficulty increases as you wish to attend to a greater number of traits in the trainees, for example, their predominant learning styles and their conditions of disability, to cite some cases.

The simulations have been presented as a valid alternative to include different profiles of users and from there to evaluate the behavior in different situations [4–7].

Simulations based on agents have reported important results and good number of papers have been published showing the application of this approach [8, 9]. The basic unit of a multi-agent simulation is the agent. An agent is any actor in a system, any entity that can generate events that affect itself and other agents. Simulations consist of groups of many interacting agents [8].

This article presents an interactive tool that supports the teacher in this task, simulating the behavior of students through the agents, providing each one with different learning styles and special education needs related to any disability condition.

The multi-agent system recommends the learning objects (LO) that are stored in a repository, according to the preferences of the agents, which are guide by rules defined according to their characteristics and associated with the metadata of the resources. The appropriate materials are chosen for all students selected by the teacher. The proposal was validating in real environment.

This article is organized as follows: Sect. 2 is a revision the main related concepts and related work in this area; Sect. 3 describes the proposed model. Section 4 shows the experimental work. Finally, the main conclusions and future research directions, it shows in Sect. 5.

2 Concepts and Related Works

Below are briefly some concepts related to the proposal:

Learning Objects (LO) is a resource or digital content that facilitates the appropriation of knowledge to the users due to the characteristics and structure of the learning object [10].

Learning Objects Repositories are platforms where the learning objects are stored so that the people can access more easily to the them [11, 12].

Learning Styles (LS) are recognized as relevant in the learning process. According to Felder (1996) we should be aware of the differences that students have to process information in order to offer them dynamic educational materials adjusted to individual learning preferences [8].

Multi-Agent Systems (MAS) is composed of multiple interacting agents within an environment. MAS being emergent computing approaches widely spread in several e-learning areas providing solutions for complex and restrictive systems. In contrast with conventional computing approaches, MAS has special features such as customization, intelligence, accessibility, safety, task distribution, decision making, among others [13].

Educational Recommender Systems aim to provide students with search relevant results adapted to their needs or preferences and delivering those educational contents such as LO that could be closer than expected [14].

Simulation can been use in any situation involving random entities or variables. Simulation models are typically made up of separate but interacting networks, which often have looping and feedback characteristics. This can be made clearer by constructing a model for the specific example [15].

The following part lists some works related to the proposal:

In [15] a simulation based on the knowledge of the phones users is describe. The goals of the simulation are to facilitate communication between product engineers and testers and make predictions of some aspects of usability.

Works like [4, 5] show that recently exist a lot of where works simulators are used or created for different goals. This is because in areas like health, made virtual simulations is the bests tool to the medical training, because how it shows in the work [6] where a systematic review is performed of one hundred articles about simulators and it concludes that the 75% of the articles shows the positive effects that had the simulators in the appropriation of knowledge.

The spectrum of simulation programs in health ranges from simple, informal experiences to complex multidisciplinary training sessions [16], your paper presents simulation programs as a teaching method for perioperative nurses.

In [7] shows the SIMBA simulator (SIMulator for Business Administration), this is a powerful tool to support the decision-making process of business managers and business education. In this work also it is proposed a reinforcement learning (RL), for the creation of smart agents that can handle virtual companies in SIMBA.

The multi-agent systems are a new technology that right now is having more and more force, for this reason in works like [9] a multi-agents system are used to do the simulation of the behavior of the people in an evacuation after a disaster. This with the objective of capture information to create contingency plans and recommendations for the optimization of the evacuation process.

Another way in which agents can being use is in a recommendation system and in [17, 18] shows the use of agents and multi-agents systems for recommendations of learning objects, learning resources and media content is a good strategy.

However, in none of the works founded multi-agent system are used to do a simulation for validating a system recommendation, which is the purpose in this work.

3   Proposal

The main purpose of this work is to simulate the behavior of students through agents, providing each one with different learning styles and special education needs related to any disability condition. A multi-agent system (MAS) is proposed, this makes recommendations of LO stored in a repository, according to the preferences of the agents, which are guided by rules defined according to their characteristics and associated with the metadata of the resources. The appropriate materials are chosen for all students selected by the teacher.

The model presented in Fig. 1 is proposed from the analysis and design made of MAS. This model explains the architecture of the multi-agent system and the interactions between agents.

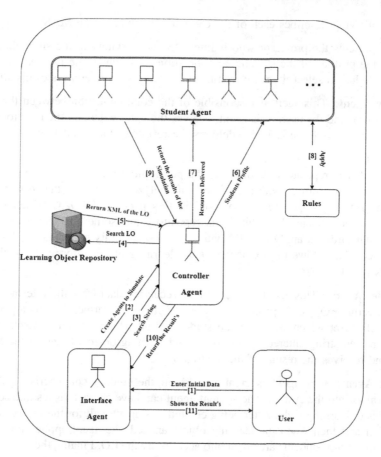

Fig. 1. Multiagent system model for simulation

Figure 1 shows the model that was purpose for this multi-agent that performs the simulation of student preferences in the LO selection. This model shows that the simulation has four modules; the first module goes from step one to step two and denote the user interaction with the interface and upload the file with the agents that it going to be create. The second module is the communication between the interface and de controller agent and goes from step two to step three and also include the step ten, the third module goes from step four to step eight and is where the controller agent sends the characteristics of the agents that the simulation going to create. The fourth module is when the agents created receive the resources and change their preferences according to the resources goes from step nine to step eleven.

The following describes each of the elements involved in the MAS:

User: Represents the professor who is interested in carrying out the simulation, also indicates the profiles of the students and the subject on which the LO search will be perform. He has to select the recovered LO to identify the preferences of his students.

Interface Agent: This agent is responsible of the communication between the multi-agent platform and the user. This agent receives the dates enters by the user for do the simulation and search the LO, also delivers the results of the simulation.

Learning Object Repository: This is the repository from where the learning objects are retrieved. The repository should offer the possibility of delivering the metadata set of each LO in xml format, with the purpose of analyze and execute the corresponding rules. The learning object repository used in this paper is FROAC (Federación de Objetos de Aprendizaje Colombia); this repository has some characteristics, as the metadata standard that apply is LOM with others accessibility metadata and had some web services that allows the exchange of the learning object information with other platforms [10, 19].

Controller Agent: This agent is in charge of receiving data from the Interface Agent and the Learning Object Repository. The main activity performed by this agent is the creation of those, which will simulate students, find which learning objects comply with the search string entered by the user, send learning objects found to the Student Agent and receives the results of the simulation.

Student Agent: This agent is create based on the student characteristics that the teacher enters into the system. The student agent can have characteristics like sensorial disabilities or learning style. After being created this agent wait for the LO selected by the teacher and then when the learning object arrived, the agent applies the rules to identify how many students are taken into account by the LO. Finally, the agent returns the results to the controller agent that highlight the students, who could have a better acceptance of that content.

Each student agent executes a system of production rules in order to determine if the chosen LO would meet their preferences. Two sets of rules are used; the first set applies rules related to the student's learning style, where a hybrid model that combines the Felder and Silverman model and the VARK model is used [20]. For the second set, rules related to special education needs associated with sensory disabilities are execute. Below in Table 1 are some of the rules implemented.

Table 1. Production rules

Learning Style Rules	• LearningStyle (Auditory-Global) ∧ [LearningResourceType (narrativeText ∨ lecture ∨ audio ∨ video)] ∧ [InteractivityLevel (medium ∨ high)] ∧ [InteractivityType (Expositive ∨ Mixed)] • LearningStyle (Auditory-Sequential) ∧ [LearningResourceType (narrativeText ∨ lecture ∨ audio ∨ video)] ∧ [InteractivityLevel (low ∨ very low)] ∧ [InteractivityType (Expositive ∨ Mixed)] • LearningStyle (Kinesthetic-Global) ∧ [LearningResourceType (selfAssesment ∨ exercise ∨ problemStament ∨ simulation)] ∧ [InteractivityLevel (medium ∨ high ∨ very high)] ∨ [InteractivityType (Active ∨ Mixed)] • LearningStyle (Kinesthetic-Sequential) ∧ [LearningResourceType (selfAssesment ∨ exercise ∨ problemStament ∨ experiment ∨ simulation)] ∧ [InteractivityLevel (medium ∨ high)] ∨ [InteractivityType (Active ∨ Mixed)] • LearningStyle (Reader-Global) ∧ [LearningResourceType (narrativeText ∨ presentation)] ∧ [InteractivityLevel (medium ∨ high)] ∧ [InteractivityType (Expositive ∨ Mixed)] • LearningStyle (Reader-Sequential) ∧ [LearningResourceType (narrativeText ∨ presentation ∨ questionnaire)] ∧ [InteractivityLevel (medium ∨ low ∨ very low)] ∧ [InteractivityType (Expositive ∨ Mixed)] • LearningStyle (Visual-Global) ∧ [LearningResourceType (selfAssesment ∨ table ∨ diagram ∨ figure ∨ graph)] ∧ [InteractivityLevel (low ∨ very low ∨ medium ∨ high ∨ very high)] ∨ [InteractivityType (Active ∨ Mixed)] • LearningStyle (Visual-Sequential) ∧ [LearningResourceType (selfAssesment ∨ slide ∨ diagram ∨ questionnaire ∨ simulation)] ∧ [InteractivityLevel (low ∨ very low ∨ medium)] ∨ [InteractivityType (Active ∨ Mixed)]
Special Education Needs Rules	• Disability (Null visual) ∧ [audiodescription (yes)] ∧ [Interactivity Level (medium) ∨ Interactivity Level (low) ∨ Interactivity Level (very low)] ∨ [format (audio) ∨ format (video)] • Disability (Low visual) ∧ [audiodescription (yes)] ∧ [Interactivity Level (high) ∨ Interactivity Level (medium) ∨ Interactivity Level (low)] ∨ [format (audio) ∨ format (video)] • Disability (Null hearing) ∧ [HasTextAlternative (yes)] ∧ [Interactivity Level (medium) ∨ Interactivity Level (low) ∨ Interactivity Level (very low)] • Disability (Low hearing) ∧ [HasTextAlternative (yes)] ∧ [Interactivity Level (medium) ∨ Interactivity Level (low) ∨ Interactivity Level (very low)] ∨ [format (text) ∨ format (image) ∨ format (application)]

4   Experimental Work

The multi-agent system developed to the validation of this work was create in JAVA, using the framework JADE (Java Agent Development Kit), also was used the library Swing to build the graphic interface that is used by the agent for the interchange of dates with the user.

In this platform, the information of the learning objects is retrieved from FROAC, which has a service that returns the xml with the metadata of each resource.

Figure 2 shows the main interface of the simulator. The teacher must upload a file to the system with the data of the students of the simulation, and then he has to enter a search string on the subject of the class. The system performs the search of the learning objects in FROAC and lists the results, where the teacher has the possibility of selecting LO to identify what would be the students' preference in front of this resource. The results of the simulation are present in the lower part, highlighting those students who could have a better acceptance of that content, according to the rules established for it.

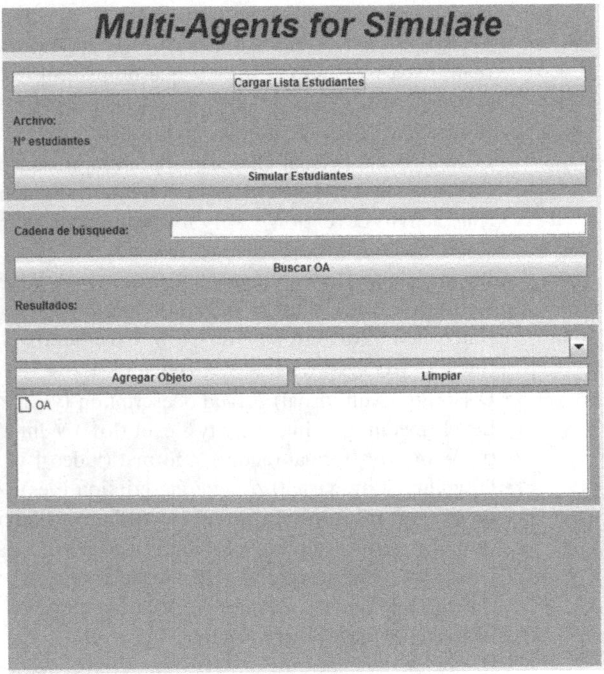

Fig. 2. Multiagent system model for simulation

Three cases were defining for the experimentation of the multi-agent system. In the first case, 20 students with different learning styles were simulate. In the second case, 20 students with different special educational needs associated specifically with sensory disabilities were simulate. Finally, for the third case, 20 students were simulating, of which 10 had defined a learning style and the rest had a special need. In Table 2 the profiles of the students simulated in each case are shown.

Table 2. Characteristics to simulate

Characteristics	Case 1	Case 2	Case 3
Visual-Global	5		2
Visual-Sequential	4		2
Auditory-Global	1		1
Auditory-Sequential	1		1
Reader-Global	1		1
Reader-Sequential	1		1
Kinesthetic-Global	3		1
Kinesthetic-Sequential	4		1
Hearing Disability - Null		5	2
Hearing Disability - Low		6	3
Visual Disability - Null		5	2
Visual Disability - Low		4	3

For the execution of the three cases, the search strings "water" and "environment" are applied, the teacher selected the same educational resources; with the purpose to identify the behavior of students with different profiles according to the type of material that was deliver.

Figure 3 shows the result that the teacher would obtain by selecting the 3 LO defined, for case 1 of the simulation. As can be seen, 12 of the 20 simulated students are highlighted in the interface for the first search string and 18 of the 20 simulated students are highlighted in the interface for the second search string. Which indicates that, with the characteristics of material selected, these students could be benefit according to the preferences they would have according to their profile.

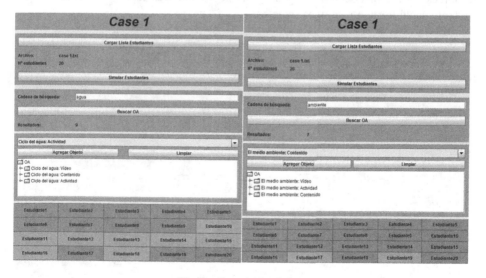

Fig. 3. Case 1 simulation

Results for case 2 are presented in Fig. 4 It is emphasized that in this case with the three selected resources it would be possible to cover the preferences of all students, since their metadata indicate that they have the necessary requirements to meet the diversity presented there.

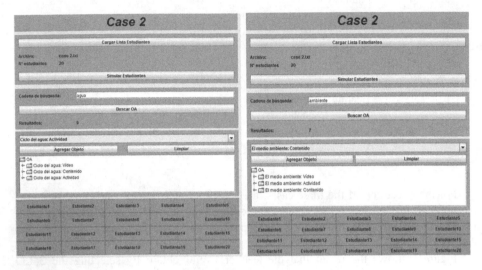

Fig. 4. Case 2 simulation

Finally, in Fig. 5, the simulation of case 3 is observe, where learning styles and special needs are contemplating. For this scenario, when selecting the 3 test LOs, the system reports that 17 out of 20 students would have a greater preference for these resources for the first search string and for the second was report that 18 of the 20 students could use the resources selected.

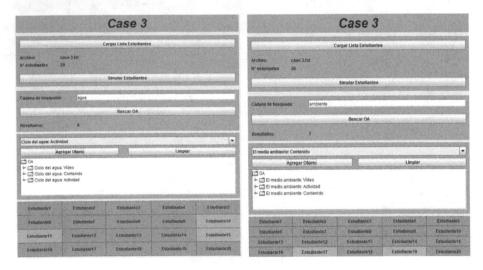

Fig. 5. Case 3 simulation

The developed of the simulation shows potential for the multi-agent system in issues of educational informatics and especially in problems of allocation of educational resources. Because the teacher could know how many of his students accept or not the LO that him considered to applied in his class. This allows that the teacher can design his class using a minimum amount of LO to explain or support a subject and attending to all its students.

5 Conclusions and Future Work

The developed of the simulation shows potential for the multi-agent system in issues of educational informatics and especially in problems of allocation of educational resources for a group of students with diverse styles of learning and special education needs.

The simulation allows us to identify that the diversity of students requires different types of educational materials that can meet the expectations of a heterogeneous group.

The system can been use for the teacher to manage the allocation of educational resources to a group of students, to verify how many students properly receive the assigned educational resource, determine whether an educational resource designed for a particular learning style or education need really fits for the students.

The simulation allows reducing times that the teacher would take in verifying if the educational resources are adapted according to the learning styles of its students.

As future work, it is expecting to make a comparison between the results of the simulations carried out and those obtained after providing resources to real students and establishing their level of LO acceptance. As well, it is working in the possibility of determining the type of material that remains pending to be designed or built to cover the students that according to the simulation would not accept the available resources.

References

1. Macías, R.D.: ¿Qué materiales didácticos seleccionar y cuándo? TINKUY **11**, 107–119 (2009)
2. Klašnja-Milićević, A., Ivanović, M., Nanopoulos, A.: Recommender systems in e-learning environments: a survey of the state-of-the-art and possible extensions. Artif. Intell. Rev. **44** (4), 571–604 (2015)
3. Salehi, M., Kamalabadi, I.N.: Hybrid recommendation approach for learning material based on sequential pattern of the accessed material and the learner's preference tree. Knowl.-Based Syst. **48**, 57–69 (2013)
4. Holzinger, A., Kickmeier-Rust, M.D., Wassertheurer, S., Hessinger, M.: Learning performance with interactive simulations in medical education: lessons learned from results of learning complex physiological models with the HAEMOdynamics SIMulator. Comput. Educ. **52**(2), 292–301 (2009)
5. Abboudi, H., Khan, M.S., Aboumarzouk, O., Guru, K.A., Challacombe, B., Dasgupta, P., Ahmed, K.: Current status of validation for robotic surgery simulators a systematic review. BJU Int. **111**(2), 194–205 (2013)
6. Ravert, P.: An integrative review of computer-based simulation in the education process. Comput. Inform. Nurs. **20**(5), 203–208 (2002)

7. Garcia, J., Borrajo, F., Fernandez, F.: Reinforcement learning for decision-making in a business simulator. Int. J. Inf. Technol. Decis. Mak. **11**(5), 935–960 (2012)
8. Minar, N., Burkhart, R., Langton, C., Askenazi, M.: The Swarm Simulation System : A Toolkit for Building Multi-agent Simulations. Mexico (1996)
9. Bunea, G., Leon, F., Atanasiu, G.M.: Postdisaster evacuation scenarios using multiagent system. J. Comput. Civ. Eng. **30**(6), 5016002 (2016)
10. Duque, N., Ovalle, D., Moreno, J.: Objetos de Aprendizaje, Repositorios y Federaciones. Conocimento para todos (2014)
11. López Guzmán, C., García Peñalvo, F.J.: Los Repositorios de Objetos de Aprendizaje como soporte a un entorno e-learning. Universidad de Salamanca (2005)
12. Solano, I.M.: Repositorios de objetos de aprendizaje para la enseñanza superior: Dspace. Herram. telemáticas para la enseñanza Univ. en el Espac. Eur. Educ. Super, p. 18 (2007)
13. Ahmad, S., Bokhari, M.: A new approach to multi agent based architecture for secure and effective e-learning. Int. J. Comput. Appl. **46**(22), 26–29 (2012)
14. Rodríguez, P.A., Ovalle, Demetrio A., Duque, N.D.: A student-centered hybrid recommender system to provide relevant learning objects from repositories. In: Zaphiris, P., Ioannou, A. (eds.) LCT 2015. LNCS, vol. 9192, pp. 291–300. Springer, Cham (2015). https://doi.org/10.1007/978-3-319-20609-7_28
15. Reynolds, R.A.: Simulation technique. In: Reynolds, R.A. (ed.) Computer Methods for Architects. Elsevier Ltd. (1980)
16. Hemingway, M., Fitzgerald, B.: Designing effective simulation programs. AORN J. **104**(6), P13–P14 (2016)
17. Tabares, V., Duque, N., Rodríguez, P., Giraldo, M., Ovalle, D.: Plataforma Adaptativa para la Búsqueda y Recuperación de Recursos Educativos Digitales. XI Conferencia Latinoamericana de Objetos y Tecnologías de Aprendizaje (2016)
18. Tabares, V., Duque, N., Rodríguez, P., Giraldo, M., Ovalle, D.: Análisis de Características del Perfil de Usuario para un Sistema de Recomendación de Objetos de Aprendizaje. IX Conferencia Latinoamericana de Objetos y Tecnologías de Aprendizaje, pp. 487–493R (2014)
19. Londoño, L.F., Tabares, V., Duque, N.: Evolución en la Accesibilidad de la Federación de Repositorios de Objetos de Aprendizaje Colombia – FROAC. Rev. Ing. e Innovación, **3**(1) (2015)
20. Felder, R., Silverman, L.: Learning and teaching styles in engineering education. Eng. Educ. **78**(June), 674–681 (1988)

Monitoring Students' Attention in a Classroom Through Computer Vision

Daniel Canedo[✉], Alina Trifan, and António J. R. Neves

IEETA/DETI, University of Aveiro, 3810-193 Aveiro, Portugal
{danielduartecanedo,alina.trifan,an}@ua.pt

Abstract. Monitoring classrooms using cameras is a non-invasive approach of digitizing students' behaviour. Understanding students' attention span and what type of behaviours may indicate a lack of attention is fundamental for understanding and consequently improving the dynamics of a lecture. Recent studies show useful information regarding classrooms and their students' behaviour throughout the lecture. In this paper we start by presenting an overview about the state of the art on this topic, presenting what we consider to be the most robust and efficient Computer Vision techniques for monitoring classrooms. After the analysis of relevant state of the art, we propose an agent that is theoretically capable of tracking the students' attention and output that data. The main goal of this paper is to contribute to the development of an autonomous agent able to provide information to both teachers and students and we present preliminary results on this topic. We believe this autonomous agent features the best solution for monitoring classrooms since it uses the most suited state of the art approaches for each individual role.

Keywords: Class monitoring · Learning environment
Face Detection · Face Recognition · Face Tracking · Pose estimation

1 Introduction

The studies presented on [1] show that the student engagement is linked positively to desirable learning outcomes, such as critical thinking and grades obtained in a subject. The student engagement and attention depend on several factors. One important factor that influences the preservation of the student engagement is the teacher [2]. Teachers' positive emotions are likely to induce students' positive emotions, referred to as "emotional contagion". Therefore, positive teacher emotions may not only be essential for the wellbeing of teachers but they may also affect students' wellbeing and, in turn, learning in class. This suggests that teachers' ability to connect well with students can be beneficial regarding students' attention.

Additionally, [3] complements that the size of a classroom influences the students' attention. In large classes, the teacher will have to use up more time to

© Springer International Publishing AG, part of Springer Nature 2018
J. Bajo et al. (Eds.): PAAMS 2018 Workshops, CCIS 887, pp. 371–378, 2018.
https://doi.org/10.1007/978-3-319-94779-2_32

draw students' attention, which is emotionally exhausting. In contrast, smaller classes seem to allow an environment in which students are less likely to receive corrective talk from their teachers, since they are naturally more engaged to the class. This appears to be a more productive educational environment.

However, [4] showed that only 46% to 67% of the students pay attention during a class. This means that up to half of the students could not be productive in their learning. It is important to recognize the potential factors that may lead to this scenario and in which situations of the class the students tend to lose their focus more than others. With this information in hands, the teachers can search for possible problems during their classes and try to correct them, which may benefit the learning efficiency of their students.

The first contribution of this paper is a thorough revision of the state of the art on monitoring classrooms. There is already some work done in this area, such as apps and social networks for monitoring the students activities as mentioned in [5] or Teacher Assistance apps as shown in [6]. However, as the title suggests, our main focus is a non-invasive approach using cameras placed in convenient spots of the classroom.

We first review state of the art techniques on Computer Vision that are useful in a classroom environment. This review is focused on Face Detection, Face Recognition, Facial Features and Pose Estimation. Firstly we need to acquire the regions of interest in the classroom. Those regions of interest are the students' faces, which can be obtained through Face Detection. After obtaining them, we can extract their Facial Features. This component is not only important for measuring the students' attention, but also for Face Recognition. We need to make sure that the identification process is as accurate as possible, since we obviously don't want to assign information to the wrong students. As for the Pose Estimation, we can use it to measure certain behaviours and relate them to the attention level of the students.

After studying the state of the art, we propose an autonomous agent concatenating the most suited techniques for monitoring a classroom, showing some preliminary results. We must considerate the working distance in our scenario. Since the cameras need to capture the whole classroom, they need to be placed far away from the students, which inputs low resolutions faces for our proposed agent.

Lastly, we make a brief conclusion of what was presented in this paper.

2   Understanding Attention in Large Classrooms

In this section we present the state of the art techniques on Computer Vision that are useful in a classroom, divided into several subsections, corresponding to useful approaches we have identified for monitoring students' attention.

2.1   Camera Self-calibration

The classroom environment is not uniform, its luminosity changes as the day goes by. Opening or closing the windows, turning on or turning off the lights are also causes for an irregular luminosity during a day of classes. All of these situations induce different image intensities, therefore the camera needs to be calibrated to capture analyzable and uniform images. Maintaining the uniformity of the input images increases the Face Recognition accuracy. Comparing faces that are within the same conditions is obviously more accurate than comparing faces that are within different conditions. A study of [7] proves this point: an image that is not calibrated would potentially deteriorate the accuracy of Face Detection and Face Recognition.

A work presented in [8] showed a calibration of the most important parameters of the vision system which makes algorithms for object detection efficient. They propose a self-calibration method based on the image luminance histogram. The histogram of the luminance shows how many times each intensity value appears in an image. This can easily indicate if the image is underexposed or overexposed to light. Thus, they propose the application of a Proportional-Integral controller (PI) to handle this underexposure or overexposure to light. With this method they managed to preserve the intensity uniformity of the captured images.

2.2   Face Detection and Recognition

Face Detection and Face Recognition are the most important techniques of monitoring a classroom. Assigning attention levels to the wrong student is something undesirable, so the priority is to make a proper recognition before assigning data. Despite the inevitable low resolution of the input faces because of the distance between the camera and the students, we must assure a good identification accuracy.

A work made by [9] proposed a system that uses a multi-task cascade convolution neural network (MTCNN [10]) for Face Detection and uses the ResNet-101 layers convolution neural network for Face Recognition. The MTCNN has 3 stages to output a proper Face Detection, in each stage the face that is being analyzed goes through a convolutional neural network (CNN). The first stage obtains the candidate windows and their bounding box regression vectors, merging highly overlapped candidates [11]. The second stage feeds those candidates to another CNN, which rejects a large number of false candidates. The third stage is similar to the second one, but it also outputs five facial landmarks' positions. Paired with the proposed ResNet-101 layers CNN trained with 65 million samples, they claim to achieve 98.87% accuracy rate for the Face Recognition based on the Labeled Faces in the Wild (LFW [12]) Face Recognition benchmark.

Their proposed method was developed for classrooms, so they also faced the same problems we mentioned above. They showed that their system can detect low resolution faces while preserving the Face Recognition accuracy rate and real time performance. This is the ideal state of the art solution for detecting and recognizing students in a classroom environment, therefore we will consider it in the following section of this paper.

2.3 Features and Pose Extraction

One way of measuring the students' attention that immediately comes to mind is by analyzing their eyes. However, as [13] mentioned, the accuracy of techniques like Eye Tracking tend to suffer from low resolution images. Knowing this, we can't rely on that technique for extracting data from the students. Nevertheless, there are other methods to measure the students' attention which work around the distance problem.

As a study of [14] showed, head orientation contributes 68.9% in the overall gaze direction and achieved 88.7% accuracy at determining the focus of attention. This conclusion implies that head orientation is a powerful method of measuring the students' attention.

A work presented in [15] proposed a head pose estimation algorithm by associating a few facial landmarks with 3D world coordinates. Calculating the rotation and translation of those landmarks, it's possible to transform the 3D points in world coordinates to 3D points in camera coordinates and project them onto the image plane. Consequently, a resulting line starts in the nose landmark and it is drawn to the direction in which the head is oriented to.

Although the head pose alone already has a high accuracy determining the focus of attention, paired with another technique could additionally improve the results. Students that are paying attention normally react to a stimulus in the same way. In other words, students that have their motion synchronized with the majority are assumed to be paying attention. An example of this synchronization is when the class has to write down something important if the teacher tells them to [16].

The work described in [17] proposes a real time multi-person 2D pose estimation (OpenPose). The image to be analyzed is fed to a CNN, predicting a set of 2D confidence maps of body part locations and a set of 2D vector fields of part affinities, encoding the degree of association between parts. Using non-maximum suppression they are able to obtain the body part candidates. The set of 2D vector fields of part affinities has the role of eliminating wrong associations in a multi-person scenario (where the classroom is included).

The OpenPose average precision on detecting the body parts (head, shoulders, elbows, wrists, hip, knees and ankles) is claimed to be between 75% and 80% based on the MPII Multi-Person Dataset test, beating the precision of the other state of the art solutions.

With this body pose estimation, students' motion can be tracked. Concatenating this output with the head pose estimation's output, we might have an approach of calculating the attention of a classroom that presents a satisfactorily high accuracy.

3 Proposed Agent and Preliminary Results

The overview presented in the previous section led to the proposal of the following autonomous agent for monitoring classrooms. In Fig. 1 we present its workflow diagram.

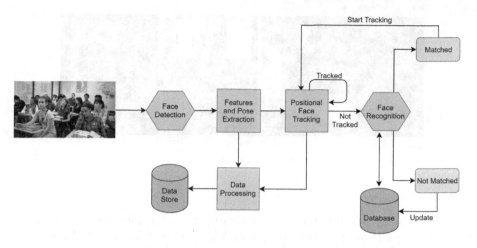

Fig. 1. Workflow diagram of the proposed autonomous agent.

The proposed agent receives an image from an acquisition module that captures the images of the classroom. This module analyzes the image and calibrates the camera parameters (Fig. 2) using the camera self-calibration approach mentioned in the previous section.

Fig. 2. From left to right, an image captured with some of the parameters of the camera set to higher values and the corresponding image obtained after the calibration.

In Fig. 2 the importance of camera calibration is explained. In the left image, it would be difficult to detect the face since the image has high intensity values. The right image is the resulting image obtained after the calibration, which homogenized the intensity values of the face, making it simpler to be detected.

Afterwards we propose the use of the MTCNN mentioned above for the Face Detection block. This block is responsible to feed the Features and Pose Extraction block with images of the students' faces, which has the role of retrieving their facial features and body pose. We propose the adjustment of the head pose estimation approach mentioned previously for estimating the head orientation and the use of OpenPose for the body pose estimation (Fig. 3).

Fig. 3. From left to right, preliminary results of the head pose estimation and the body pose estimation.

At this point, there is the need of identifying the students before assigning them the data regarding their attention. We propose a block called Positional Face Tracking to assist the Face Recognition block, which is responsible for tracking the students' faces by comparing their actual position with their previous position. Since the students usually are sat down on their chairs, we can avoid that the proposed agent would keep on trying to recognize them (which has a significant computational cost and reduces the frames per second) by adding this type of tracking. However, if certain student moves out of place, the tracking may fail. If this is the case, the proposed agent would advance to the Face Recognition block and try to recognize the respective student. We propose the ResNet-101 layers CNN mentioned in the previous section for the Face Recognition block.

In Fig. 4 we show a preliminary result of our proposed autonomous agent prototype, obtained from a real environment. The students were participating in a workshop about Computer Vision organized at our University.

Fig. 4. Preliminary result of Positional Face Tracking, Face Recognition and Attention Levels in a real scenario during a workshop at our University.

In the beginning of the referred workshop, we registered the students that agreed to participate in the experiment through a NFC Reader, which automatically turned on the camera, storing images of their faces. We trained their aligned faces using the ResNet-101 layers CNN and turned on the proposed agent prototype. When the students were identified through the Face Recognition block, the agent started tracking their faces and their attention. Since the prototype assumes that the students looking towards the camera are paying attention, the students in Fig. 4 have low attention levels despite their obvious focus on the lecture. However, the target position can be configured beforehand and will be considered in future experiments. Although we used a static Database in this experiment, we propose a dynamic Database that would assign a unique ID to each student and store their faces automatically, providing more autonomy to the agent.

The data regarding the students' attention was saved into vectors during the lecture. When the agent was turned off, the Data Processing block calculated the averages of the attention levels for each student and stored them into the Data Store block. For this block, we propose an online database that is updated at the end of the class, being accessible to both teachers and students.

4   Conclusion

In this paper we proposed an agent for monitoring classrooms. We made a research about the potentially best state of the art on Computer Vision techniques that may be applied in a classroom environment. By putting them together in a workflow that theoretically handles problems like false positives or losing track of a student, we proposed an autonomous agent showing some of the preliminary results of its prototype. We believe that this agent has the potential of transforming the classroom in a sensing environment, by providing guidance and feedback not only to the teachers on how to improve their teaching role during a class, as well as to the students on how to improve their behaviour in the classroom and consequently increase their academic performance. The long term goal of our research is to provide visual feedback to the teachers regarding the average level of students' attention, and provide counseling to the students regarding their behaviour during the class. Such counseling can be, for example, the identification of lecture periods in which students were less watchful and the corresponding topics that potentially need extra attention.

Acknowledgments. This work was supported by the Integrated Programme of SR&TD SOCA (Ref. CENTRO-01-0145-FEDER-000010), co-funded by Centro 2020 program, Portugal 2020, European Union, through the European Regional Development Fund.

References

1. Carini, R.M., Kuh, G.D., Klein, S.P.: Student engagement and student learning: testing the linkages. Res. High. Educ. **47**(1), 1–32 (2006)
2. Hagenauer, G., Tina, H., Volet, S.E.: Teacher emotions in the classroom: associations with students' engagement, classroom discipline and the interpersonal teacher-student relationship. Eur. J. Psychol. Educ. **30**(4), 385–403 (2015)
3. Blatchford, P., Bassett, P., Brown, P.: Examining the effect of class size on classroom engagement and teacher-pupil interaction: differences in relation to pupil prior attainment and primary vs. secondary schools. Learn. Instr. **21**(6), 715–730 (2011)
4. Raca, M., Kidzinski, L., Dillenbourg, P.: Translating head motion into attention-towards processing of student's body-language. In: Proceedings of the 8th International Conference on Educational Data Mining. No. EPFL-CONF-207803 (2015). APA
5. Carchiolo, V., et al.: Monitoring students activities in CS courses. In: 2016 15th RoEduNet Conference: Networking in Education and Research. IEEE (2016)
6. Gutierrez-Santos, S., et al.: Scalable monitoring of student interaction indicators in exploratory learning environments. In: Proceedings of the 25th International Conference Companion on World Wide Web. International World Wide Web Conferences Steering Committee (2016)
7. Zhao, W., et al.: Face recognition: a literature survey. ACM Comput. Surv. (CSUR) **35**(4), 399–458 (2003)
8. Neves, A.J.R., Trifan, A., Cunha, B.: Self-calibration of colormetric parameters in vision systems for autonomous soccer robots. In: Behnke, S., Veloso, M., Visser, A., Xiong, R. (eds.) RoboCup 2013. LNCS (LNAI), vol. 8371, pp. 183–194. Springer, Heidelberg (2014). https://doi.org/10.1007/978-3-662-44468-9_17
9. Fu, R., et al.: University classroom attendance based on deep learning. In: 2017 10th International Conference on Intelligent Computation Technology and Automation (ICICTA). IEEE (2017)
10. Zhang, K., et al.: Joint face detection and alignment using multitask cascaded convolutional networks. IEEE Sig. Process. Lett. **23**(10), 1499–1503 (2016)
11. Farfade, S.S., Saberian, M.J., Li, L.-J.: Multi-view face detection using deep convolutional neural networks. In: Proceedings of the 5th ACM on International Conference on Multimedia Retrieval. ACM (2015)
12. Huang, G.B., et al.: Labeled faces in the wild: a database for studying face recognition in unconstrained environments. Technical report, vol. 1, no. 2, pp. 07–49, University of Massachusetts, Amherst (2007)
13. Krafka, K., et al.: Eye tracking for everyone. arXiv preprint arXiv:1606.05814 (2016)
14. Stiefelhagen, R., Zhu, J.: Head orientation and gaze direction in meetings. In: CHI 2002 Extended Abstracts on Human Factors in Computing Systems. ACM (2002)
15. Head Pose Estimation using OpenCV and Dlib. https://www.learnopencv.com/head-pose-estimation-using-opencv-and-dlib/
16. Raca, M., Dillenbourg, P.: System for assessing classroom attention. In: Proceedings of the Third International Conference on Learning Analytics and Knowledge. ACM (2013)
17. Cao, Z., et al.: Realtime multi-person 2d pose estimation using part affinity fields. In: CVPR, vol. 1, no. 2 (2017)

PAAMS Workshop SCIA

An Ontology for Sustainable Intelligent Transportation Systems

Adriana Giret[✉], Vicente Julian, Carlos Carrascosa, and Miguel Rebollo

Dpto. Sistemas Informáticos y Computación,
Universitat Politècnica de València, Valencia, Spain
{agiret,vinglada,carrasco,mrebollo}@dsic.upv.es
http://www.gti-ia.dsic.upv.es/

Abstract. Nowadays, the need of Intelligent Transportation Systems software tools and services for Sustainable Transportation is urgent. This paper proposes an ontology specially tailored for Intelligent Transportation System characterization. The main features of the proposed ontology is the ability to incorporate sustainable variables when characterizing a transportation system, and the coverage of open fleet concepts together with its dynamic features. Moreover, it is enhanced to facilitate its integration with other intelligent components that in a wider and complete application tool can provide intelligent computation over the data specified with the proposed ontology.

Keywords: Ontology · Intelligent Transportation Systems
Sustainability

1 Introduction

An issue that has triggered concerns over the recent decades relates to the capacity of the global economy to accommodate an enduring demographic, economic and resource consumption growth. Since a growing share of the global population is urbanized, sustainability has increasingly become focused on urban areas. Major cities are requiring a vast array of supporting infrastructures including energy, water, sewers and transport. A key to urban sustainability issues is linked with the provision and maintenance of a wide range of urban infrastructure. Every city has specific infrastructure and environmental problems. Transportation, as a core component supporting the interactions and the development of socioeconomic systems, has also been the object of much consideration about to what extent it is sustainable. Sustainable transportation can be defined as the capacity to support the mobility needs of people, freight and information in a manner that is the least damageable to the environment [12]. Components for evaluating sustainability include the particular vehicles used for road, water or air transport; the source of energy; and the infrastructure used to accommodate the transport (roads, railways, airways, waterways, canals and terminals).

© Springer International Publishing AG, part of Springer Nature 2018
J. Bajo et al. (Eds.): PAAMS 2018 Workshops, CCIS 887, pp. 381–391, 2018.
https://doi.org/10.1007/978-3-319-94779-2_33

Transportation sustainability is largely being measured by transportation system effectiveness and efficiency as well as the environmental and climate impacts of the system [6].

In addition to Sustainable Transportation another concept that lately is more and more demanding solutions is "Intelligent Transport Systems" (ITS). ITS is a generic term for the integrated application of communications, control and information processing technologies to the transport system. The resulting benefits save lives, time, money, energy and the environment and stimulate economic performance. In this sense the two concepts are closely related, being the second a supporter for achieving the goals of the first.

ITS covers all modes of transport and considers all elements: the vehicles, the infrastructure, the drivers and users all interacting together dynamically. The main function of ITS is to provide services and information for the full spectrum of users in particular drivers, passengers, vehicle owners and operators, but also vulnerable road users like pedestrians and cyclists and support safe and efficient traffic management by the transport network operators. The intention is to improve the operation of the entire transport system. With ITS, road users such as motorists, freight and commercial fleet operators and public transport customers can make better judgements on their travel decisions. Factors such as traffic conditions, road maintenance or construction work may potentially impact on travel times; weather conditions will affect the road network and safety.

This work is motivated and inspired by the need of ITS software tools/services for Sustainable Transportation. Sustainable transportation is now often used to indicate a shift in the mentality of the community of transportation analysts to represent a vision of a transportation system that attempts to provide services that minimize harm to the environment. In order to facilitate the development of such tools there is an urgent need to provide ontologies that can express all the features of a transportation system together with the sustainable concepts and data that must be also included as first class goals in any optimization systems for improving mobility in urban areas. Moreover, the proposed approach follows an open transportation fleet paradigm[1].

Section 2 summarizes the most relevant state-of-the-art works on ITS ontology and reveals the lack of a proper treatment of sustainability issues by those works. Section 3 describes the proposed ontology. Section 4 provides an overview description of a framework in which the proposed ontology is integrated. Section 5 cites a few sample applications that were implemented using the ontology. Finally, Sect. 6 summarizes the conclusions and future works.

2   Related Work

In [5] an ontology-driven architecture to improve the driving environment through a traffic sensor network is proposed.

---

[1] Open fleets extend the traditional fleet concept towards a new dimension of openness: vehicles may interact with their environment in a Smart city [9], or join and leave the fleet at any time.

The work described in [7] presents the state of research in Intelligent Transportation System ontologies relying on results from the EU-funded research project T-TRANS. In particular, it first compares approaches of structuring Intelligent Transportation Systems. In a second step, the shortcomings of these approaches are discussed and the relationships of Intelligent Transportation System concepts are demonstrated by linking Intelligent Transportation System applications with technologies.

On the other hand the authors of [14] study a unified representation of urban transport information using urban transport ontology in order to solve the problems of ontology mergence and equivalence verification in semantic fusion of traffic information integration.

One of the most used ontology for Intelligent Transportation Systems is the one proposed in [3]. The authors propose an ontology that is enhanced for the personalization of user interfaces for developing transportation interactive systems by model-driven engineering.

In [13] the authors propose two ontologies for way-finding with multiple transportation modes. Whereas the work described in [8] proposes a system that is based on public transportation ontology.

From this literature review we can conclude that sustainability variables and features are not taken into account by any work and the new concept of open fleets is still no included in any ontology from the specialized state-of-the-art.

3   The Ontology for Sustainable Intelligent Transportation Systems

The public transport system plays an integral role in any Sustainable Intelligent Transportation System since urban areas rely on public transport services. Public transport infrastructure systems such as bus, tram, metro and rail are the key designs for mobility. As discussed in [1] an urban public transport network is a complex system which is a result of interaction between a set of distributed and evolving entities such as the means of public transport, people and the network infrastructure. The complexity of the public transport system is further amplified by other dynamic parameters such as traffic jams, unexpected events such as accidents and changes in routes, weather, sustainable features such as air quality, CO_2 emissions from transportation means, etc. To this end we propose an Intelligent Transportation System Ontology as a way to coupe with the specification of the different elements in a transportation model.

The Intelligent Transportation System Ontology is based on the work of [3]. Nevertheless, other works such as [13] that proposes two ontologies for way-finding with multiple transportation modes, and [8] in which a system is proposed based on public transportation ontology, were also taken into account for the ontology definition.

The ontology proposed is complete in terms of the six dimensions defined in [3] and extended with the open fleets concept and the sustainable specific attributes and/or relationships that are key in order to realize the optimized movement of passengers, objects (products, parcels, etc.) in the city. Following the ontology is described with special focus on its original elements.

Figure 1 shows the different ontology concepts that built up the model and deal specifically with the transportation multi-modality or transportation mode. In the proposed ontology there are three modes. (i) Public to which pertain the modes that are provided by transportation operators, with transportation lines running in a transportation network following a schedule (see Fig. 2 for a detailed view). (ii) Private to which pertain Cars, Bicycles, Trucks, and Motorcycle that can again be Owned or Rented by citizens/users. For the case of rented Private Transports there are two possibilities: with driver or without driver. The former case applies to Taxis and or Uber like systems, in which the user pays for the itinerary to the owner of the transport. (iii) Priority to which pertain special type of transports such as: Ambulance, Police Car and Fire Truck. Vehicle Type is used to describe the features of the different modes, and are key for reasoning purposes in any application tool for intelligent transportation systems, i.e. when a given transport must be considered for recommendations issues to the users that are willing to move in an optimized way. The optimized recommendation might consider two main goals: maximize the economic compensation of the users (for example, choosing the cheaper routes and/or transportation means, the fastest or shortest route), and; to minimize the harm to the environment (in terms of CO_2 emissions). The arguments and/or variables that are taken into account for these two goals in the Vehicle Type description are: the price features and the sustainable features related to CO_2 emissions per passenger and per product/parcel volume. In addition these arguments are combined with the GPS Location, Number of Seats and Parcels Capacity in order to infer an

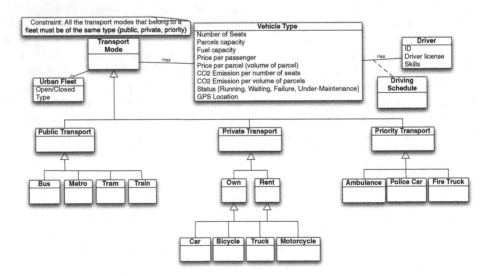

Fig. 1. Main ontology concepts of the Intelligent Transportation System Ontology

optimized recommendation to the user that at all time tries to achieve the two mentioned goals.

An Urban Fleet (see Fig. 1) is defined as a group of transports in which all the transports belong to the same Transportation Mode. It can be Open or Close. An Open Urban Fleet is one that can change dynamically, i.e. a transport owner can decide to enter or exit the fleet at any time. A Close Urban Fleet is one in which no new transport owners can decide to enter the fleet in a dynamic fashion.

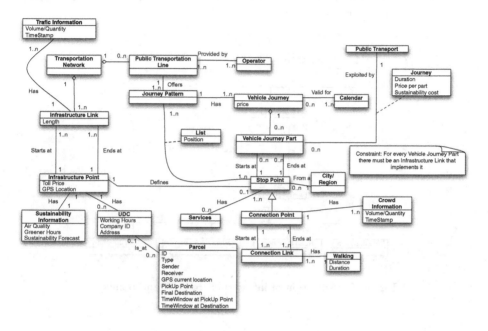

Fig. 2. Ontology definition of the transportation network

Figure 2 presents the Transportation Network ontology. It is defined by the set of Infrastructure Links that defines the transportation infrastructure itself and the set of Public Transportation Lines that runs in the network. An Infrastructure Links connects Infrastructure Points (see Fig. 3): railway junctions, wire junctions, road junctions (a road junction is valid for cars, trucks, and maybe bikes), and bike-lane junctions (an special type of road junction only valid for bikes). An Infrastructure Link can be a: road element, wire element, railway element, bike-lane element. Moreover a road element must be categorized as bike or no-bike allowed. Every Infrastructure Link has a Traffic Information associated that is used in order to infer recommendations to the users about timing issues when intending to move trough the given Infrastructure Link. Moreover, every Infrastructure Point is associated with Sustainability Information about Air Quality, "Greener" Hours to navigate the point, and Sustainability Forecast

386   A. Giret et al.

(mainly about CO2 data). The Sustainability Information is intended to be taken into account by for example a recommender model when analyzing the sustainability cost for the overall system for the given itinerary (a route made up of connected Infrastructure Links).

A Public Transportation Line (Fig. 2) is provided by an Operator and offers a set of Journey Patterns. The description of the Public Transportation Line is based on the work of [3] augmented with sustainability features and the Crowd Information associated with the Connection Points in a line.

Finally Fig. 4 shows the specification for User in the system and products/parcels that can be transported in an urban area.

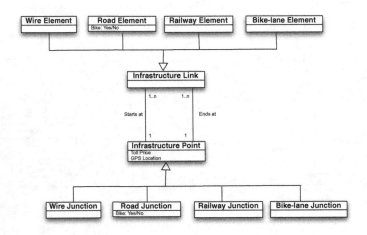

Fig. 3. Classification of infrastructure links and points

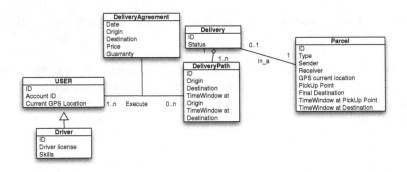

Fig. 4. Users, deliveries and parcels

4   A Framework that Incorporates the Ontology

The ontology presented in this paper can be used as it, in an isolated way, by any application. Nevertheless, it is important to direct the reader attention towards an intelligent framework specially tailored to the development and execution of intelligent applications for transportation systems. The Framework is called SURF and was originally presented in [2]. This framework is made up by a series of services and utilities that can support open fleet managements. Figure 5 shows the architecture devised for open fleet management divided into four layers, which are the following:

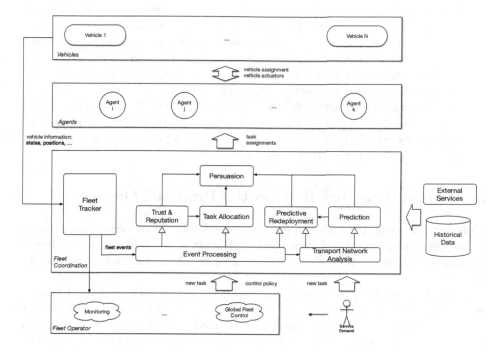

Fig. 5. General view of the SURF framework

- "Fleet Operator", which includes the basic components used for global fleet control and monitoring. This layer represents the control operator of the system which is in charge of supervising the global operation of the system.
- "Fleet Coordination", this is the heart of the framework, with all the different perception inputs, provide information about vehicle status, position, ... and they also receive information to be displayed to the vehicle driver. As its main goals, this layer follows the operational states and positions of the vehicles determining whether or not a re-calculation of task assignments and/or deployment of idle vehicles should be done. This layer is divided into

different modules, the most important ones are the following: a Fleet Tracker, which receives information about the operational states and positions of the available vehicles; the Event Processing, which analyses the incoming events and determines which are the modules that must receive these events; the Task Allocation module calculates the global assignment of all pending tasks to agents/vehicles; the Predictive Redeployment module, obtains adequate positions for all idle agents/vehicles at a specific moment; the Persuasion module provides actions to agents that tend to improve the overall performance of the system; and, the Trust and Reputation module is in charge of modeling the expected behavior of agents/vehicles in the system using previous situations.

- Agent Organization, it is formed by the agents which manage the different urban transport entities. In this case, one agent can be in charge of a vehicle or a fleet. Their main goals are task assignments and vehicle deployments allowing the coordination. Agent receives possible tasks to do from the Fleet Coordination layer, but they may not follow a certain global strategy rejecting task assignments and also leaving the fleet.

- Vehicle layer, it is formed by the vehicles and public transport stations forming the fleet including the drivers (this could be optional in case of autonomous vehicles). This layer can be seen as a set of sensors and actuators which are included in each vehicle.

5   Applications that Rely on the Proposed Ontology

This section briefly presents three sample applications that were implemented using the ontology proposed. Nevertheless, the list of possible new and different applications is large and can get longer as new ideas and user requirements appear.

One of the issues to be addressed in Smart Cities concerns the **smart transport of parcels inside a city** [9], commonly known as last mile delivery. Our approach for parcels' last mile delivery is named *CALMeD SURF* [11] and is based on crowdsourcing, taking advantage of the movements of the citizens in the urban area, that move for their own needs. This application is addressed as a mobile phone app for: customers that want to deliver a parcel, and users that want to serve as occasional deliverers in an urban area. The main idea is that the users register in the application (as customer or deliverer), and *CALMeD SURF* will locate them in the city on real-time. In this way, when there is a parcel delivery request, the system uses a graph, that is dynamically generated from the active users and the instantiated transportation ontology, where each node is either a user (a potential deliverer, and/or customer) or a delivery center/office. The system proposes optimized parcels delivery paths to the crowd of potential deliverers (those who are closest to the calculated delivery path) to participate. If some of the potential deliverers rejects the proposal, it calculates an alternative path (i.e. a new path and a new set of potential deliverers) in order to achieve the parcel delivery goal. The calculated path may include several deliverers that may pass the parcel from one to another (connecting sub-paths). One of the optimization criteria used by the system, closely related with the goal of minimizing the harm to the environment, is to minimize the deviation of the deliverers from the path to their own destinations. Trying in this way to minimize new emissions originated by movements that are solely used for parcel deliveries.

Nowadays, one of the most popular urban transport systems in order to aid in reducing emissions is the **shared vehicles system**. One such system is the shared bicycle system which have an special interest due to its characteristics. The distribution/balancing of bicycles over time and space through the different pick up/drop off stations in the city network is one of the key problems to solve in order to maintain an efficient bike sharing system. Traditional approaches rely on the service provider for balancing the system, but this approach, in general, adds extra costs. Our proposal [4] consists on an multi-agent system that includes user actions as a balancing mechanism, taking advantage of their trips to optimize the overall balance of the system. The proposed approach, when necessary, tries to persuade the user to deviate slightly from its origin/destination by providing appropriate arguments and incentives. With this information the multi-agent system analyses the transportation network (specified using the ontology presented in this paper), scoring alternative stations and routes and making offers to balance the bikes across the stations.

One of the most used online web-services and/or mobile apps every day are applications for **route planning**, getting not only the route according to the means of transport that the user selects, but also recommendations of places of interest that can be found along the way. Unfortunately, these applications do not consider the profile of the end users, and generate the same routes for a person who has a disability as for those who do not. In [10] we propose a model for a recommendation system based on the user profile to generate automatic and personalized routes on foot or on public transportation for people with disabilities. The proposed solution extends the ontology described in previous section in order to add and extend the user profile definition for disabilities characterization and the network structure elements description.

6   Conclusions

This paper has proposed an ontology for Sustainable Intelligent Transportation Systems. Bearing in mind that sustainable transportation can be defined as the capacity to support the mobility needs of people, freight and information in a manner that is the least damageable to the environment, and the urgent need to have a way by which sustainability features are specified and taken into account by the tools that support this system, the proposed ontology can be considered an important contribution to the research and development field. The ontology is complete in terms of the six dimensions defined in [3] and extended with the open fleets concept and the sustainable specific attributes and/or relationships that are key in order to realize the optimized movement of passengers, objects (products, parcels, etc.) in the city.

Three sample applications that uses the ontology were also summarized, illustrating in this way the advantage that any application tool can get from using a more complete ontology that integrates open fleets and sustainability concepts.

As future work, we are working on more applications that uses the ontology and the SURF framework in order to provide different type of intelligent services for optimizing the movement of people and products in urban areas.

Acknowledgement. This research was carried out as a part of the SURF project under the grant TIN2015-65515-C4-1-R by the Spanish government.

References

1. Beamon, B.M.: Supply chain design and analysis: models and methods. Int. J. Prod. Econ. **55**(3), 281–294 (1998)
2. Billhardt, H., Fernández, A., Lujak, M., Ossowski, S., Julián, V., De Paz, J.F., Hernández, J.Z.: Towards smart open dynamic fleets. In: Rovatsos, M., Vouros, G., Julian, V. (eds.) EUMAS/AT -2015. LNCS (LNAI), vol. 9571, pp. 410–424. Springer, Cham (2016). https://doi.org/10.1007/978-3-319-33509-4_32
3. de Oliveira, K.M., Bacha, F., Mnasser, H., Abed, M.: Transportation ontology definition and application for the content personalization of user interfaces. Expert Syst. Appl. **40**(8), 3145–3159 (2013)
4. Diez, C., Sanchez-Anguix V., Palanca, J., Julian, V., Giret, A.: Station status forecasting module for a multi-agent proposal to improve efficiency on bike-sharing usage. In: Proceedings of the 5th International Conference on Agreement Technologies 2017 (2017)
5. Fernandez, S., Hadfi, R., Marsa-Maestre, I., Velasco, J.R.: Ontology-based architecture for intelligent transportation systems using a traffic sensor network. Sensors (Basel) **16**, 1287 (2016)
6. Mihyeon Jeon, C., Amekudzi, A.: Addressing sustainability in transportation systems: definitions, indicators, and metrics. J. Infrastruct. Syst. **11**, 31–50 (2015)
7. Kellberger, S., Castelli, L., Piera, M.A.: Development of an intelligent transport system ontology - linking applications and technologies across different transport modes. In: European Transport Conference 2013 (2013)
8. Mnasser, H., Oliveira, K., Khemaja, M., Abed, M.: Towards an ontology-based transportation system for user travel planning. IFAC Proc. Volumes **43**(8), 604–611 (2010). 12th IFAC Symposium on Large Scale Systems: Theory and Applications
9. Neirotti, P., De Marco, A., Cagliano, A.C., Mangano, G., Scorrano, F.: Current trends in smart city initiatives: some stylised facts. Cities **38**, 25–36 (2014)
10. Peralta, A., Giret, A.: Recommender system of walking or public transportation routes for disabled users. In: Submitted to The Workshop on Smart Cities and Intelligent Agents 2018 (2018)
11. Rebollo, M., Giret, A., Carrascosa, C., Julian, V.: The multi-agent layer of calmed surf. In: Proceedings of the 5th International Conference on Agreement Technologies 2017 (2017)
12. Rodrigue, J.-P.: The Geography of Transport Systems. Routledge, Abingdon (2017)

13. Timpf, S.: Ontologies of wayfinding: a traveler's perspective. Netw. Spat. Econ. **2**(1), 9–33 (2002)
14. Yang, W.-D., Wang, T.: The fusion model of intelligent transportation systems based on the urban traffic ontology. Phys. Procedia **25**, 917–923 (2012). International Conference on Solid State Devices and Materials Science, 1–2 April 2012, Macao

Recommender System of Walking or Public Transportation Routes for Disabled Users

Andrea Peralta Bravo[1] and Adriana Giret[2(✉)]

[1] Departamento de Tecnología en Análisis de Sistemas,
Instituto Tecnológico del Azuay,
Octavio Chacón Moscoso 1-98 y Primera Transversal, 010108 Cuenca, Ecuador
andrea.peralta@tecazuay.edu.ec
[2] Departamento de Sistemas Informáticos y Computación,
Universitat Politècnica de València, Camino de Vera s/n, 46022 Valencia, Spain
agiret@dsic.upv.es

Abstract. Nowadays, the advance of the technology has allowed to develop applications and systems to facilitate the daily life of the people. One of the most used field by thousands of people every day is to generate routes to go from one place to another, obtaining not only the route according to the means of transport that the user selects, but also can get recommendations of places of interest that can be found along the way. Unfortunately, these applications do not consider the profile of the end users, and generate the same routes for a person who has a disability as for those who do not. In this article, we propose a model to create a recommendation system based on the user profile to generate automatic and personalized routes on foot or on public transportation for people with disabilities.

Keywords: Recommender systems · Planning routes

1 Introduction

According to World Health Organization (WHO), by the year 2016, one million people had some type of disability; it corresponds to 15% of world's population. For this reason, WHO has sought to raise awareness among the rest of the population to reflect on the rights of people with disabilities. Many countries worldwide have worked hard to ensure that people with disabilities are included in all areas of everyday life.

The year 2003 was established by European Union (EU) as "The European year of people with disabilities", in which each of the EU member states decided to complement and carry out national measures in order to generate the necessary conditions to achieve effective inclusion and full participation of persons with disabilities in accordance with EU human rights provisions on disability; in addition, it was agreed that by 2010, progress has been achieved in various areas such as the possibility of employment, access to goods and services, among others [1].

Good results have been achieved and people with disabilities have been included in many social and workplaces in the most countries, where they have created coupled environments so that all people have access without any restrictions; however, there are still many fields in which it is necessary to continue working and one of them is the technological field.

© Springer International Publishing AG, part of Springer Nature 2018
J. Bajo et al. (Eds.): PAAMS 2018 Workshops, CCIS 887, pp. 392–403, 2018.
https://doi.org/10.1007/978-3-319-94779-2_34

Everyone knows that technology is an important part of our life; computers, cellphones and tablets are devices that we use all the time. So, we can find thousands applications that helps us to do many tasks, but most of them don't consider the profile of end users. An example are the applications oriented to mobility, that although they facilitate us the shortest route to go from one site to another, this is not always the most adequate for all.

As a solution, this paper presents a model to create a recommender system based on the user profile to generate routes on foot or on public transportation for people with disabilities. The rest of this paper is organized as follows: In Sect. 2 we talk about related works, while Sect. 3 presents the architecture of the model that we propose and its evaluation is described in Sect. 4. Finally, conclusions and future works are addressed in Sect. 5.

2 Related Works

Many works have been carried out in order to obtain recommender systems that allow people with disabilities to mobilize using public transport or walking, with greater ease. For example, Mancini [2] proposes a framework to help users with mobility impairments, to transport them from one point to another. This is based on the creation of a road map with different levels of detail, it can be modified at runtime in case there is an obstacle that makes it difficult to use the initial plan. An algorithm A* is used to find the optimal path between two points.

In other studies, Kulyukin [3] contributes to the investigation of a hypothesis, the same argues that, if a route is described verbally in detail, users with disabilities can use their skills of orientation, mobility and problem solving to follow the detailed route successfully. To do this, a standard algorithm is presented that is used to find new paths in the previously mentioned routes.

On the other hand, Hsu [4], designs and implements an intelligent recommendation system, it allows developing a support system for decision making for tourist attractions, this allows to reduce unnecessary costs in the search for information through the creation of communities in which they share interest and characteristics. By means of Nearest Neighbor Algorithm, the data entered by new users is compared and the most compatible community is selected, this will give the user the suggestions and feedback that he needs based on his community. For this purpose, Bayesian networks are also used to evaluate and compare the factors that affect consumer behavior.

Karimanzira [5], presents an investigation based on the mobility independence of people with disabilities through diffuse logic to eliminate non-viable journeys. For this, a modification of the A* or Dijkstra algorithm was used.

Idress [6] proposes a prototype based on mobility in interior spaces using QR codes. They are located in sections on the floor, a scanner returns the position of the user, as well as the question of the next point to reach and, through the algorithm A*, the shortest path between two points is searched.

Neis [7] proposes the generation of a routing network based on geodata collected by collaboration, these are provided by the OpenStreetMap Project. The algorithm was tested and evaluated in selected areas of Europe, resulting in generated extended networks, which include information about the sidewalk.

Kammoun [8] describes a routing algorithm adapted for users with visual deficiency. The objective of the study was to find the most adapted route that connects the points of origin and destination and that allows to provide people with visual problems a scarce but useful mental representation of the itinerary and the environment that surrounds them, for this the Dijkstra algorithm was used, and will be used in NAVIG (Navigation Assisted by Artificial Vision and GNSS).

Kilincarslan [9] makes a comparison between two algorithms A* that describes the route from one point to another and then the use of a standard algorithm used at the time of execution for people with visual deficiency. For the tests, a shopping center was used as a case study and both algorithms were tested in the development environment by means of simulations performed with the data collected in the environment.

On the other hand, Holone [10] has combined accessibility and routing maps planning for people with mobility problems. The authors have developed a prototype that presents a client software and a server responsible for the calculation of routes. This prototype allows users to annotations to better the route calculation.

The server uses a standard algorithm to find the shortest route between two points in a geographic network. The calculation of the shortest route is made by distance so it deals with inaccessible segments as if they were longer than they really are and thus avoids locations inaccessible to the user when there is an alternative route.

Once the route is completed, users can add feedback to the server indicating if the route was good, uncomfortable or inaccessible, thus improving the data it presents.

Karimi [11], in his work focuses on the calculation of routes and navigation for people with visual disability as for mobility problems. In this work a hybrid prototype is developed, which not only performs the calculation of the best route by using the D* algorithm, but also allows users to share routes, points and areas of interest, where the possibilities of accessibility are indicated, mobility challenges, etc. that allows other users to choose the route better. The authors believe that this work will allow finding better solutions when it comes to finding optimal routes for people with disabilities.

Neis [12], presents an algorithm for the calculation of routes for people with disabilities. This algorithm presents two stages, in the first, Data preparation, a network of routes is generated and it is evaluated if the street segments present additional parameters that may be important. In the second stage generates routes that can be used for people with disabilities based on all the relevant information that was obtained in the previous step. The authors conclude that by applying an algorithm for the calculation

Ferrari [13], presents a method that establishes a ranking on the accessibility, for people with wheelchairs, of the different routes of a city. As a case study he uses the city of London. As an optimization criterion they use the fastest route, number of maximum transshipments, maximum time walking and speed when hiking. The authors propose the use of this ranking along with the route planner of the city itself in order to improve the results.

Sobek [14], proposes a web route planner for people with mobility problems. For this he uses the Dijkstra algorithm. In addition, it allows users to visualize the route and find problems in this one that the algorithm has not taken into account. The authors indicate that this application is still not valid for people with vision problems.

By other hand, Menkens [15] presents, a web application that allows finding the optimal route for people in wheelchairs. This application allows users to view and add points of interest, to inform other users of problems or places. To ensure the best route and that obstacles will not be encountered, the authors use the Barrierefreie project Wegplanung based on the algorithm A* and also takes into account the characteristics of the street/sidewalk, obstacles or possible problems identified by other users.

After evaluating the aforementioned studies, we can conclude that the algorithms mostly used in the construction of recommender systems for people with disabilities, correspond to those that offer better results in terms of calculation of routes between two geographical points. The most used approach is the Dijkstra algorithm, because it allows obtaining optimal results. Similarly, standard algorithms based on heuristics were used because, when they are customized, good results are obtained in the features they wish to optimize.

On the other hand, it is concluded that although there have been several approaches to designs and implementations of recommender systems, there are still many aspects in which work must continue, including:

- Optimize the modeling of sidewalks and pedestrian crossings, due to the fact that most of the works reviewed are not mentioned or modeled superficially.
- Refine the detection of obstacles for those with blindness and deafness.
- Design a recommendation system that allows personalizing the search for routes according to the type of disability.
- Design multiplatform systems in order to facilitate the use of them.

3 Model Design

3.1 Base System

This recommender system is based on the work carried out by Káthia de Oliveira and other "Transportation ontology definition and application for the content personalization of user interfaces" [16], which is the model of an ontology used to generate customized user interfaces for interactive urban transport system; the transportation ontology is used to provide personalization of the content through the model-driven architecture (MDA).

This model integrates specific knowledge about transport system and information about user and the context in which the system is being used. In this way, three levels of MDA abstraction are defined:

- Computation independent model (CIM): To establish the user interaction with a high level of abstraction, represented as a model of user interface tasks.
- Platform independent model (PIM): To introduce the structure of the user interface using content customization.
- Platform specific model (PSM): To specify the user interface for a specific platform.

3.2   Proposed Recommender System's Conceptual Design and Modular Structure

Figure 1 shows the structure of the recommender system. It has a modular structure, which allows each element to perform a specific task and thus obtain the desired results.

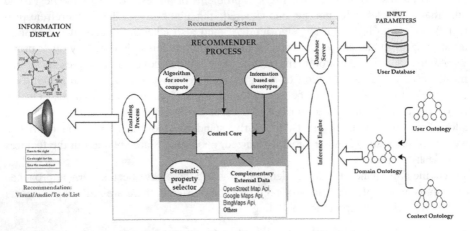

Fig. 1. Recommender system's structure

Input Parameters. The set of input parameters has two components responsible for providing the necessary information for the recommender to work correctly.

The first component is a database server. It is responsible for storing all data that will be used by the application. The second component is a domain ontology that is the base for the user ontology and context ontology.

- **User Ontology**

Its objective is to facilitate the recovery of the relevant information of the users taking into consideration the profile to which it belongs. To this end, the ontology proposed by De Oliveira [16] was modified, enhancing it with concepts and attributes to categorize and specify the user disabilities. Figure 2 shows the ontology.

- **Context Ontology**

Figure 3 shows the ontology fragment that represents the information relevant for routes planning in a city or country.

Base on this model, new attributes are considered that allow taking into account new parameters that are required to facilitate the mobility of people with disabilities. To this end, the established recommendations made by Verswyvel [17] in his study "Accessibility Regulations" were taken into consideration.

The new parameters considered in the means of transport are: Number of Seats for people with disabilities, access ramp, audio stop notice, visual stop notice, access guide dog, wheelchair space and wheelchair seat belt; also, in the road junction three attributes were added: Time traffic light, crosswalk and access ramp; on the other hand, two entities were created: Street Characteristics and Services. In the first one, the attributes are: surface, stairs, sidewalk's width, sidewalk's slope, barriers and diving islands; in the second, the attributes are: seats elevator, access ramp, electric stairs, advice information audio and advice information visual.

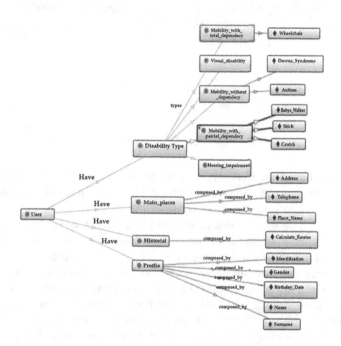

Fig. 2. User ontology

Recommender System. The recommender system is composed by three elements: recommender preprocess, recommender process and translating process.

Recommender preprocess is divided in database server and inference engine. The first one is used to process the stored information in the input database. The second one is responsible for mapping the ontologies with the corresponding contextual model. To carry out this process, the concepts established in the contextual model are considered and related to the elements of the ontology. This concept is analyzed always trying to find the elements of the ontology that can influence the concept of contextual model. Once an element is found, it is assigned an ontological concept. In this way, the information provided to the recommendation process will be personalized, depending on the context.

On the other hand, the recommender process is responsible to take data obtained in the recommender preprocess to get a result for the user. This element is composed by 5 components:

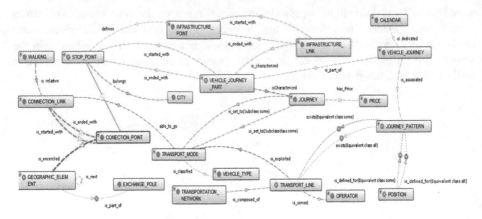

Fig. 3. Context ontology

- **Information based on stereotypes:** For the inclusion of this component, many stereotypes were considered: one group for each type of disability, and these in turn are subdivided into subgroups that consider the different means of transport. This scheme is based on the fact that people with the same type of disability will have relatively similar preferences to move from one place to other. However, this doesn't mean that these considerations are not modifiable, since the user can define the preferences that best suit their needs. For the construction of stereotypes, all parameters that must be taken into account to compute the route for a person with disabilities were considered. Table 1 has been constructed based on referential values obtained from [17, 18], in which each parameter takes a weight (low, medium, high) according to the impact it causes in the person with a specific type of disability. The defined weights allow establishing new criteria that must be considered when generating the route, that is, it will not be taken into account only that the distance is the shortest, but that it is the optimal.
- **Algorithm for route computing:** It defines the algorithm that will be used to find the optimal path between two points. There are several algorithms that facilitate this task, but the Dijkstra is the most suitable for this case since in order to generate the route it uses both the distance and the weights of the links to obtain the route that best suits the needs of the user.

The Dijkstra algorithm takes the weights established in Table 1 and assigns them a numerical value: High = 100, Medium = 50 and Low = 25; for each link, according to the user profile, each parameter is reviewed to obtain the calculation coefficients that would affect the proposed Eq. (1) are obtained:

$$link\ value = D + 100 \times NH + 50 \times NM + 25 \times NL \tag{1}$$

Where NH is the number of parameters with a value high; NM is the number of parameters with a value medium; NL is the number of parameters with a value low; and D is the distance between the points of the link.

Table 1. Construction of stereotypes for each type of disability

Means of Transport	Parameters	Values	Weights						
			Autism	Down's Syndrome	Walking Stick/Crutches	Walker	Wheelchair	Deafness	Blindness
Walking	Surface	Concrete	Low	Low	Low	Low	Low	Low	Low
		Pavement	Low	Low	Low	Low	Low	Low	Low
		Asphalt	Low	Low	Low	Medium	Medium	Low	Medium
		Rock	Low	Low	Medium	High	High	Low	High
		Cobblestones	Low	Low	Medium	High	High	Low	High
		Gravel	Low	Low	High	High	High	Low	High
		Grass	Low	Low	High	High	High	Low	Medium
	Stairs	Yes	Low	Low	High	High	High	Low	Medium
		No	Low	Low	Low	Low	Low	Low	Low
	Sidewalk width	> 2 m	Low	Low	Low	Low	Low	Low	Low
		< 2 m	Low	Low	Medium	High	High	Low	Medium
	Slopes	> 1.20 m	Low	Low	Medium	High	High	Low	Medium
		< 1.20 m	Low	Low	Low	Low	Low	Low	Low
		In the corner	Medium	Medium	High	High	High	Low	High
		On the sides	Low	Low	Medium	High	High	Low	Medium
		In the middle	Low	Low	Medium	High	High	Low	Medium
		Without Barrier	Low	Low	Low	Low	Low	Low	Low
	Pedestrian Crossing	With Elevator	Low	Low	Low	Low	Low	Low	Low
		With Normal Stairs	Low	Low	Medium	High	High	Low	High
		With electric Stairs	Low	Low	Low	Medium	High	Low	Low
	Entrance Ramp	Yes	Low	Low	Low	Low	High	Low	Low
		No	Low	Low	Medium	High	High	Low	High

In this way, when generating the route, the value of the link will be considered instead of just the distances, therefore, the user would obtain a route according to their needs.

- **Semantic property selector:** This element aims to consider the interests of the user to modify the stereotypes indicated above, that is, that the user has the ability to establish what their preferences are to compute the route. In this way, the recommender will prioritize what is established in this element instead of the information based on stereotypes. In addition, each time the user completes a route, the recommendation system, through implicit feedback, modifies user preferences, so that the next time a route is calculated, it better fits the needs of the user. On the other hand, each time the user executes a route, he/she will have the possibility of evaluating it, and the preferences of the user will be adjusted so that the recommendation system improves for the next time it is used.
- **Complementary external data:** This element is incorporated in order for the recommender system to be enriched by external information from various APIs that are available and can be used to provide more information to the user. For example, showing various points of interest such as restaurants, museums, parks, etc. that are found by the route traced and that could be of interest to the user needs and/or likes.

- **Control Core:** It becomes the most important part of the recommendation system since it constitutes its central block in which the main classes and functions are grouped to link the user profile with the generated routes to obtain the final recommendation. The control core takes all the characteristics of the submodules previously described and follows this sequence of steps:

  1. Take the preferences of the user and modifies the weights of the corresponding parameters considering the user profile and the type of disability that the user has.
  2. Take the start and end point of the route and assign reference values to all possible roads based on previously established weights.
  3. Execute the algorithm for route calculation considering only the paths that are viable for the user.
  4. Receive the route and send it to the translation process.

The last element is translating process; its objective is to take the result sent by the control nucleus and transform it into an ordered list of instructions that can be presented to the user when sent to the Information Display module. This process is dependent on the software tools used for the development of the recommender system and the format in which the control core sends the information.

Information Display. The objective of this module is to take the list of instructions that make up the path generated in the translating process and present it to the end user.

The final recommendation must be presented to the user in different multimedia formats according to the type of disability they have. In this way, the formats in which the recommendation of the system is shown should be: audio, ordered detailed list or visual map. Table 2 shows the different types of disability together with the multimedia format.

Table 2. Multimedia Format for each type of disability

Disability		Multimedia Formats
Mobility without dependency	Autism	Detailed List, Visual
	Down's Syndrome	Detailed List, Visual, Audio
Mobility with partial dependency	Walking Stick	Audio, Visual
	Crutches	Audio
	Walker	Audio
Mobility with total dependency	Wheelchair	Audio Visual
Deafness		Visual
Blindness		Audio

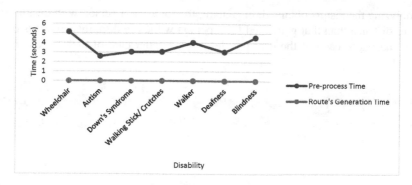

Fig. 4. Comparison of average times obtained for each user profiles

4 Evaluation

To validate the model, different experiments were carried out, in which an application was developed that allowed to establish nodes and random links where each of them had different characteristics that must be taken into account for the generation of routes for a person with disabilities.

The recommendation system was executed 10 times, in each execution the type of disability was modified and different routes were obtained for each of them taking into account that the starting node and the final node were the same for all the user profiles. According to the type of disability, in each node the time taken by the recommender to carry out the pre-process was taken into account, as well as the time it took to calculate the route once all the parameters had been met.

Analyzing the results obtained, it can be seen that the time required to establish the weights of the stereotypes is greater when the type of disability has more parameters to consider. While, in what refers to computing the route, the most relevant thing is that the time is minimal, and this is because the well-established weights make it easier to compute the route. Figure 4 shows a comparison of the average times obtained for each user profiles.

In summary, the proposed recommender system model fulfills its objective of generating routes for people with disabilities based on the user profile and preferences without considering only the distance between the two points, but it can also be seen that the more parameters have to consider for the user profile more time it takes the recommender to perform the pre-process information. On the other hand, routes were generated for users who do not have any disabilities and were compared with the routes generated for users with disabilities. An example of this can be seen in Fig. 5a, which is a route for a person with a wheelchair and Fig. 5b which is a route for a person without a disability. As you can see, the routes generated are different. This is because for people without disabilities only the distance factor will be considered, while for people with disabilities, the characteristics of the road to be traveled will be taken into consideration.

Analyzing the results obtained, in general, the route for a person with disability has a greater distance than that generated for a person without a disability, but it is the one that best adapts to each of the user profiles, taking better care of their needs.

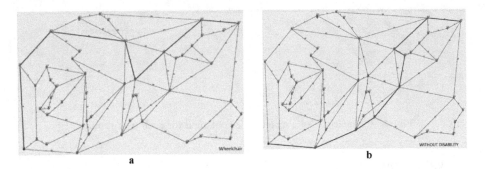

Fig. 5. a. Route generated for a person with a wheelchair. **b.** Route generated for a person without disabilities

5   Conclusions and Future Works

Currently, several approaches have been made to make recommendation system models that allow the generation of routes for people with disabilities, the majority being for those who suffer some physical or visual disability. For this reason, a modular recommender system was proposed, which takes into account the different user profiles to obtain optimal routes for people with disabilities.

The model takes as a starting point a database as well as a set of ontologies that serve as a source of information in order to facilitate the exchange of data in an agile way between different data sources, always prioritizing the information in which the user is interested. On the other hand, when considering the different parameters that must be taken into account for each of the user profiles, it is guaranteed that the route generated by the recommender will be the most optimal for a certain user profile and thanks to the visualization module of information, the user has all the facilities to follow the generated route without problems. The model works correctly, however, the biggest problem is the lack of information on the characteristics that are relevant to the recommender, such as data on sidewalks, surfaces, public transport stops, etc.

For this reason, the model could be expanded so that, by means of external tools such as Open Street Map that have the necessary structure to enter the information that is not currently available and allow obtaining the desired results with real data.

Finally, the model could be extended so that a future also allows the detection of external phenomena such as, for example, detection of traffic jams, climatic conditions, temporary barriers, etc., that allow generating better results for the user.

Acknowledgement. This research was carried out as a part of the SURF project under the grant TIN2015-65515-C4-1-R by the Spanish government.

References

1. Mabbett, D.: The development of rights-based social policy in the european union: the example of disability rights. JCMS: J. Comput. Mark. Stud. **43**(1), 97–120 (2005)
2. Mancini, A., Zingaretti, P.: Point to point navigation for people with mobility impairments. In: 2014 IEEE/ASME 10th International Conference on de Mechatronic and Embedded Systems and Applications (MESA), pp. 1–6, IEEE (2014)
3. Kulyukin, V., Nicholson, J.: Toward blind travel supports through verbal route directions: a path inference algorithm for inferring new route descriptions from existing route descriptions. Open Rehabil. J. **5**, 22–40 (2012)
4. Hsu, F.-M., Lin, Y.-T., Ho, T.-K.: Design and implementation of an intelligent recommendation system for tourist attractions: the integration of EBM model, bayesian network and Google Maps. Expert Syst. Appl. **39**(3), 3257–3264 (2012)
5. Karimanzira, D., Otto, P., Wernstedt, J.: Application of machine learning methods to route planning and navigation for disabled people. In: MIC 2006: Proceedings of the 25th IASTED International conference on Modeling, Indentification, and Control, pp. 366–371, ACTA Press (2006)
6. Idrees, A., Iqbal, Z., Ishfaq, M.: An efficient indoor navigation technique to find optimal route for blinds using QR codes. In: 2015 IEEE 10th Conference on de Industrial Electronics and Applications (ICIEA), pp. 690–695. IEEE (2015)
7. Neis, P., Zielstra, D.: Generation of a tailored routing network for disabled people based on collaboratively collected geodata. Appl. Geogr. **47**, 70–77 (2014)
8. Kammoun, S., Dramas, F., Oriolaand, B., Jouffrais, C.: Route selection algorithm for blind pedestrian. In: Control Automation and Systems (ICCAS), pp. 2223–2228. IEEE (2010)
9. Kasemsuppakorn, P., Karimi, H.: Personalised routing for wheelchair navigation. J. Location Based Serv. **3**(1), 24–54 (2009)
10. Holone, H., Gunnar, M.: People helping computers helping people: navigation for people with mobility problems by sharing accessibility annotations. In: Computers Helping People with Special Needs, pp. 1093–1100 (2008)
11. Karimi, H.A., Dias, M.B., Pearlman, J., Zimmerman, G.J.: Wayfinding and navigation for people with disabilities using social navigation networks. EAI Endorsed Trans. Collaborative Comput. **1**(2), e5 (2014)
12. Neis, P., Zielstra, D.: Generation of a tailored routing network for disabled people based on collaboratively collected geodata. Appl. Geogr. **47**, 70–77 (2014)
13. Ferrari, L., Berlingerio, M., Calabrese, F., Reades, J.: Improving the accessibility of urban transportation networks for people with disabilities. Transp. Res. Part C: Emerg. Technol. **45**, 27–40 (2014)
14. Sobek, A., Harvey, M.: U-Access: a web-based system for routing pedestrians of differing abilities. J. Geog. Syst. **8**(3), 269–287 (2006)
15. Menkens, C., Sussmann, J., Al-Ali, M., Breitsameter, E., Frtunik, J., Nendel, T., Schneiderbauer, T.: EasyWheel-a mobile social navigation and support system for wheelchair users. In: Information Technology: New Generations (ITNG), 2011, pp. 859–866. IEEE (2011)
16. De Oliveira, K.M., Bacha, F., Mnasser, H., Abed, M.: Transportation ontology definition and application for the content personalization of user interfaces. Expert Syst. Appl. **8**(40), 3145–3159 (2013)
17. Verswyvel, S.: Accessibility Regulations (2003)
18. National Roads Authority: Pedestrian Crossing Specification and Guidance (2011)

Situation Awareness Cognitive Agent
for Vehicle Geolocation in Tunnels

Felipe Fernández[1], Ángel Sánchez[2(✉)], Adrián Suárez[2],
and José F. Vélez[2]

[1] Technical University of Madrid, Campus de Montegancedo,
28660 Madrid, Spain
felipefernandez@fi.upm.es
[2] Rey Juan Carlos University, 28933 Móstoles (Madrid), Spain
{angel.sanchez,adrian.suarez,jose.velez}@urjc.es

Abstract. The integration of geolocation, big data and cognitive agents has become one of the most boosting business tools of the digital era. By definition, geolocation represents the use of different technologies in a variety of applications to help locate humans and objects. To really achieve smart services, companies also require accessing huge volumes of related information to draw meaningful conclusions. With big data, it is possible to establish connections between a wide range of associated information, and use it to improve available services or create new ones. Today, the influence of geolocation, cloud data science and involved cognitive agents impacts many application fields, which include: safety and security, marketing, beacon technology, geofencing, location-sensitive services, transportation and logistics, healthcare, urban governance, intelligent buildings and smart cities, intelligent transport systems, advanced driver assistance systems, and autonomous and semi-autonomous vehicles. To address these challenges, this paper presents a general associative-cognitive architecture framework to develop goal-oriented hybrid human-machine situation-awareness systems focused on the perception and comprehension of the elements of an environment and the estimation of their future state for decision-making activities. The architecture framework presented emphasizes the role of the associated reality as a novel cognitive agent and the involved semantic structures, to improve the capabilities of the corresponding system, processes and services. As a proof of concept, a particular situation awareness agent for geolocation of vehicles in tunnels is shown, that uses cloud data association, vision-based detection of traffic signs and landmarks, and semantic roadmaps.

Keywords: Geolocation · Vehicle location · Situation awareness
Cognitive architecture · Multi-agent systems · Smart city infrastructures
Semantic roadmaps

© Springer International Publishing AG, part of Springer Nature 2018
J. Bajo et al. (Eds.): PAAMS 2018 Workshops, CCIS 887, pp. 404–415, 2018.
https://doi.org/10.1007/978-3-319-94779-2_35

1   Introduction

Today cognitive agents, big data, analytics hubs and geolocation techniques are going to completely redefine many business models and how we react on available information – in our work, in our homes, when we travel and drive, how we enjoy sports and entertainment, etc. These elements can assist to decision-making processes and really improve the involved services and business results.

In many different processes, suitable information and knowledge, context awareness and a timely understanding and accurate assessment of a concrete situation are crucial to improve the corresponding decision-making activities.

In these fields, it is needed a cognitive perspective that fosters the ability to determine quickly the context and relevance of involved events. Specially, a common cognitive problem in critical real-time systems is the necessity of managing the corresponding environment and context information in an efficient way. The involved Situation Awareness (SA) systems, Endsley 1995 Model [1–3], focus on the challenges related to three basic cognitive agents: (1) perception (observation) of the elements of a particular environment and their state, within a time-space volume (window), (2) comprehension (understanding) of their meaning and (3) projection (prediction-estimation) of their state in the future.

However, a still open research challenge in situation awareness systems [4–6] is to develop integrated goal-oriented adaptive supervisory platforms and frameworks that support higher-level semantic cognitive activities, integrate associated context and historical knowledge, learning capabilities and robust decision support. From a cognitive perspective, the main situation awareness challenges, for real time systems, usually lay in integrating timestamped data fusion techniques, data semantic analysis, alarms and events management, and expert rules knowledge.

To also address context and content aware problems [7, 8], related data fusion [9, 10], to extract meaning and relevance, and to have a deep understanding of the systems of interest, a general cognitive architecture framework is presented in this paper, which emphasizes the role of associated reality as new cognitive agent to improve perception, understanding and prediction of the involved human-machine interactive systems.

As a proof of concept of the cognitive situation awareness architecture framework presented, a particular agent for geolocation of vehicles in tunnels is shown, where GPS services are not available (that can originate an insufficient position awareness). The application uses an onboard video camera with traffic signs recognition (and other possible landmarks), common vehicle sensors, cloud data association and semantic video databases (reference and real-time semantic roadmaps). There are not many related papers on applications which use a SA approach for becoming the driver more aware of the current traffic situations [11].

The paper is organized as follows. In Sect. 2, we discuss main cognitive architecture framework concepts applied to situation awareness systems, and introduce the associated reality cognitive agent for human-machine systems. Section 3 describes a specific cognitive architecture for improving the robustness of vehicle geolocation which uses a semantic real-time roadmap and a semantic reference roadmap, specifically designed for advanced driver assistance systems. Section 4 summarizes the use case for vehicle positioning that we have developed using the presented framework. Finally, Sect. 5 discusses the conclusions and further research.

2 Cognitive Architecture Framework for Situation Awareness

Mainly due to economic and efficiency reasons, cognitive agents require a simple mental representation of objects and situation features relevant for the involved goals, which is essential for development of the involved systems and services.

An *Associated Reality* (AsR) goal-oriented cognitive agent or *copilot agent*, for situation awareness services, in hybrid human-machine interactive systems, captures, modelizes, combines, aggregates, stores and recovers, direct or indirect related real-time information and knowledge, using multiples sources, from a particular viewpoint.

To improve the situation awareness of a system, it is very convenient to explicitly define an AsR cognitive agent, with associated data, information and knowledge about the system of interest and its environment (associative mental model), in order to have a deep understanding of the problem and for making reliable predictions. Without this associative proactive cognitive agent, it will be harder to have a sagacious situation awareness system.

An AsR cognitive agent can significantly improve the observability, controllability and situation awareness of the system of interest. It implies a hybrid human-machine ecosystem sharing the considered goals and objectives, and a continuous vigilance and alertness for extracting relevant associated information and drawing inferences and conclusions.

These cognitive agents should perceive, analyze and associate the available information about the system and its environment to improve their knowledge and make better decisions in the future.

Following Endsley's approach [6–8] and explicitly adding the association phase, a general AsR cognitive agent for situation awareness can be decomposed into the following four basic subagents, with different feedback loops in the corresponding process areas:

1. Perception of the elements and state space of a particular environment.
2. Comprehension-fusion of their meaning.
3. *Association* with the related information.
4. Prediction-estimation of their state in the future.

Figure 1 depicts the derived situation awareness cognitive architecture for situation awareness. Its main elements of are:

$$AsR = (Specification, Control, Management, AsR\ cognitive\ agent, Decisions, Actions)$$

The main innovation aspect of this architecture framework is the AsR cognitive layer, which contains an active cognitive agent for situation awareness with associative knowledge. This structure basically emulates some associative properties of human and mammals brain for situation awareness activities.

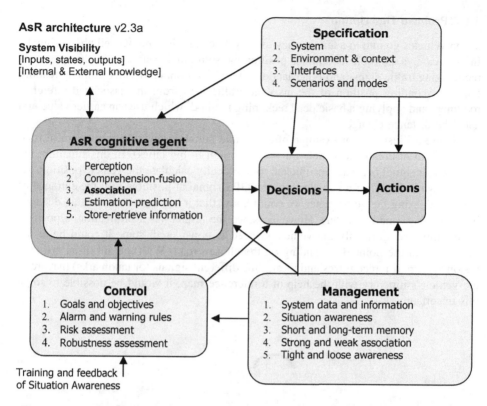

Fig. 1. AsR architecture for situation awareness with an associated reality cognitive agent.

The AsR cognitive agent provides the basis to perceive (capture), comprehend (analyze) and associate (relate) the corresponding semantic information, make estimations (predictions), and also store and retrieve the corresponding semantic databases.

3 Cognitive Architecture for Vehicle Geolocation

This section describes the proposed particular associative cognitive model for improving vehicle geolocation using an onboard video camera and common vehicle sensors. First, a short description of the problem is presented. Then the overall system architecture and geolocation rules are described. Next, the image-based landmark detection method is summarized. Finally, an example of an RDF semantic model for tunnels is shown.

3.1 Problem Description

When vehicles go into in a tunnel, they usually lose the GPS and 4G cell phone signals. In this case, a possible additional positioning solution considered in this paper, is recognizing traffic signs (and other landmarks) with an onboard video camera, reading the corresponding position of the involved traffic sign from the associated reference roadmap, and applying a basic dead reckoning method, which uses an earlier value and adds the distance change.

Figure 2 illustrates an example of a possible situation awareness problem in road tunnels with bifurcations (which are very common in big cities). In this situation, the velocimeter signal is clearly insufficient to univocally calculate the vehicle position. As it is shown in Fig. 2, if a vehicle loses the GPS signal at position T, at the entrance of the tunnel, using the velocimeter we could know that it has travelled a certain distance in a time (e.g. one kilometer). However, since the tunnel has a bifurcation, a position uncertainty occurs if only the vehicle's speed is considered, since it could be at the point A or at the point B depending on the chosen road. With the aid of an artificial vision system, if it recognizes and locates the different signals (or landmarks) that are in the vehicle's itinerary with the help of a reference map, it would be possible to solve this uncertainty.

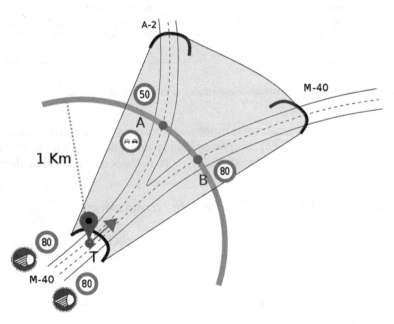

Fig. 2. A possible lack of situation awareness in tunnels with bifurcations: a reference semantic map is defined to estimate the correct vehicle position using visually-detected traffic signs with the corresponding onboard video camera.

3.2 High Level Architecture for Vehicle Positioning

We propose a solution for determining current position of a vehicle inside a tunnel, which is based on the system architecture shown by Fig. 3. We distinguish three types of components: current signals, software agents and repositories.

- Current signals provide data to the system to perform the complete vehicle geolocation task in real time. These include: GPS, 4G cell phone signals, vehicle signals (like those supplied by velocimeter and other inertial sensors), and an onboard video signal.
- Software agents provide different system components functionalities and send information other related ones. Considered software agents include: intelligent video analysis (i.e. for video-based detection of scene landmarks), estimation of current vehicle position (and optionally estimation of traffic density) in-tunnel and out-tunnel (pre-tunnel and post-tunnel), and vehicle situation awareness which properly associates information from the vehicle, the tunnel infrastructure and other system model components.
- Repositories with associated-annotated data and information provide required complementary knowledge for situation awareness in vehicle geolocation. These repositories include: the *reference semantic map* which contains previously associated-annotated information of considered reference landmarks, and the *real-time semantic map* which combines information from the reference semantic map and an intelligent video analysis agent to estimate more accurately the current vehicle position. The system models provide some required contextual information for real-time vehicle positioning (including a dead reckoning method for estimating the position and an additional method for estimating traffic density, among others). The involved system includes alarm rules databases which can be activated according to detected scenario and context.

One key component of this architecture is the reference semantic map, which provides a landmark positional scene information of a previously observed tunnel region (i.e. inside the tunnel and in surrounding adjacent road regions). Commonly, the exact position of these landmarks is provided by organizations dedicated to the design, maintenance and control of traffic infrastructures. Using these reference maps, the real-time semantic map and some vehicle signals (e.g. velocimeter information), it is possible to estimate the vehicle position according to some rules like the presented one in the next subsection.

Analyzed landmarks mainly include the present traffic signals but other elements, like traffic information panels, can also be considered. The current traffic density can additionally be estimated using the processed video signal together with some system model for such purpose. A matching between the reference semantic roadmap and the current real-time semantic map allows estimating vehicle's position by using the corresponding sequence of landmarks and involved adjacent spatial intervals.

In case of not detecting an expected landmark in the current spatial interval, we can continuously using the dead reckoning method (included in the systems model repository) from the previous spatial interval to estimate the vehicle position, but with less accuracy. A set of alarms and events could be triggered using the corresponding rule database.

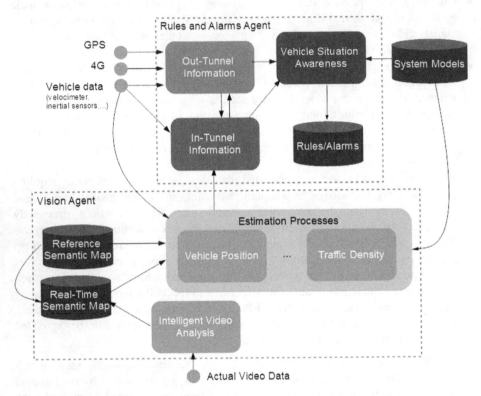

Fig. 3. Overall system architecture for vehicle geolocation in tunnels.

3.3   Estimation Rule for Vehicle Geolocation Using Landmarks

For the prototype, the following basic dead reckoning rule is considered to determine the vehicle geolocation, in the corresponding *sequence of adjacent spatial intervals*, considering the possible traffic signal occlusions or false and miss detections.

IF < landmark of the beginning of spatial interval is detected>
   THEN   < landmark is currently validated>;
              <current position is computed as current landmark position plus vehicle
                  average velocity by elapsed time from present detected landmark>
   ELSE   <activate a "non-detection" event>;
              <current position is computed as previous landmark position plus vehicle
                  average velocity by elapsed time from previous detected landmark>

3.4 Image Processing-Based Landmark Detection

Automatic real-time traffic sign detection and recognition has been a challenging research area in computer vision applications since more than twenty years [12, 13]. Along these years, many researchers have applied the top-most classification techniques to these problems for intelligent vehicles. Both problems present important difficulties when solved in non-restricted conditions due to geometric distortions of traffic signs caused by image perspective and to highly-varying illumination conditions of the scenes where signs can appear. In 2013, a paper by Mathias et al. [14] analyzed and experimented with the current traffic sign detection and recognition algorithms and determined that most effective methods used variants of HOG features for detection, and sparse representations for classification. More recently, different works adopted deep learning paradigm for considered traffic sign problems. For example, a model which uses Extreme Learning Machines (ELM) on HOG features is presented in [15]. Other example of this trend is a work by Zeng et al. [16] which integrates Convolutional Neural Networks (CNN) for feature learning with and ELM architecture for the recognition of signs.

Regarding the datasets used for the experimentation on traffic sign problems, since their emergence in 2013, the German Traffic Sign Detection (GTSDB) and Recognition (GTSRB) Benchmarks [13] are some of the most used ones.

To accurately detect traffic signs presenting large variability conditions (i.e. natural illumination outside the tunnel and artificial illumination inside the tunnel), we used the TensorFlow Object Detection API [17], which contains an Inception-type model. This general pre-trained deep-learning model is used to build a system able to accurately detect signal images in videos. This is carried out by applying transfer learning [18] on the pre-trained model for the GTSDB. This way, an accuracy of above 95% is achieved when detecting the traffic signs. Figure 4 shows some sample images of this dataset.

Fig. 4. Sample traffic signs of the GTSDB dataset.

3.5 Knowledge Representation Model for a Tunnel Infrastructure

Resource Description Framework (RDF) is a type of AI modelling for knowledge representation. Semantic models can be represented in RDF as directed graphs (semantic networks) where nodes represent concepts and arcs represent properties. Figure 5 shows a RDF graph example of some basic knowledge corresponding to the considered tunnel infrastructure.

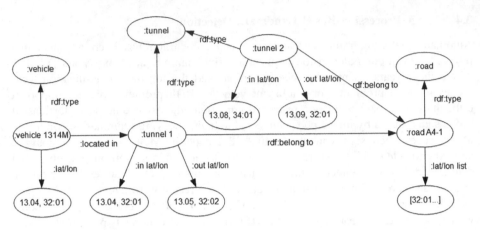

Fig. 5. Example of knowledge representation of tunnel infrastructure using RDF.

4 Use Case for Vehicle Positioning in Tunnels

Figure 6 shows a concrete application sample of the proposed framework for vehicle positioning inside a tunnel. In this figure, a sequence of sample frames corresponding to the scene view captured by a video camera placed at car dashboard is shown. Additional data regarding vehicle and landmarks positioning were acquired using a local GPS and some information provided by Spanish National Department of Traffic (DGT). Figure 6 (a) shows the view before entering inside the tunnel (i.e. pre-tunnel region), Figs. 6(b) and (c) respectively show two frames in the tunnel (i.e. in-tunnel region) and Fig. 6(d) shows the vehicle's view after exiting the tunnel and the start of a new tunnel (i.e. post-tunnel region). Tables 1 and 2 respectively illustrate and sketch of the reference semantic map (built from a previous tour of the vehicle through this tunnel) and the real-time semantic map (which is being built from the current tour). In the reference semantic map, we have completed the positional information (i.e. longitude, latitude, road and KM position) of the detected in-tunnel landmarks, while in the real time semantic map this information is missing due to lack of GPS and 4G signals inside the tunnel. This additional data can be recovered using the corresponding precise reference semantic map with specified positions and distances, and the currently detected landmarks, or using a reference semantic map with approximate positions and distances computed by a dead reckoning method, using vehicle sensors on a previous travel.

Tables 1 and 2 respectively show the reference semantic map and real-time (current) semantic map of the tunnel scene shown in Fig. 6. The reference semantic map was built in a previous tour on the same tunnel. It contains for each landmark (i.e. table row) the following information: current time, latitude and longitude (LAT/LONG), kilometric point (KM) and road, and landmark description(s) (e.g. traffic sign types). The real-time semantic map and vehicle's position estimations are built for the current tour through the tunnel. The reference semantic map, the image-based landmark detections and the specified dead reckoning method for geolocation inside the tunnel (see Subsect. 3.3) are used to determine LAT/LONG and (KM, Road) of traffic signs

Fig. 6. Sequence frames of a current vehicle tour through a tunnel: (a) out-tunnel (i.e. pre-tunnel) region, (b) and (c) in-tunnel region, and (d) out-tunnel (i.e. post-tunnel) region. Rectangles in red correspond to real-time automatically detected landmarks (e.g. traffic signals) in current frame, and green rectangles correspond to other detected landmarks (e.g. tunnel lights) which are less relevant to determine the vehicle's position. (Color figure online)

Table 1. Reference semantic map corresponding to tunnel scene of Fig. 6.

Frame	Time	LAT/LONG	(KM, Road)	Traffic sign 1	Traffic sign 2
(a)	12:13:19	40.4201/-3.8858	(72.45, M50)	Forbidden overtake trucks	Road direction right
(b)	12:13:26	40.4215/-3.8853	(72.81, M50)	Speed limit 100 km	
(c)	12:13:28	40.4225/-3.8850	(72.93, M50)	Minimal distance 70 m	
(d)	12:13:43	40.4275/-3.8826	(73.51, M50)	Speed limit 100 km	Minimal distance 70 m

Table 2. Real-time (current) semantic map corresponding to tunnel scene of Fig. 6.

Frame	Time	LAT/LONG	(KM, Road)	Traffic sign 1	Traffic sign 2
(a)	13:44:27	40.4201/-3.8858	(72.65, M50)	Forbidden overtake trucks	Road direction right
(b)				Speed limit 100 km	
(c)	13:44:37	**40.4225/-3.8850**	**(72.93, M50)**	Minimal distance 70 m	
(d)	13:44:52	40.4275/-3.8826	(73.51, M50)	Speed limit 100 km	Minimal distance 70 m

inside the tunnel. Note that the empty second row of Table 2 means that landmark in image (b) has not been detected in the current tour and an "Abnormal detection" condition (e.g. sign hiding) was applied. After that missing event, a later traffic sign in image (c) was correctly detected and its position (in bold) was determined using the reference semantic map.

5   Conclusions

This paper has presented a general cognitive architecture framework for situation awareness systems based on the explicit inclusion of the associated reality cognitive agent, to empower the development and management of these systems in different application fields. The corresponding approach emphasizes the role of this associative agent as a copilot or personal assistant for hybrid human-machine cognitive agents, which combines and models related information of the system of interest and its environment, for improving the corresponding processes and services.

A situation awareness architecture was defined, with data fusion and semantic roadmap schemas, to manage the corresponding systems. The corresponding associative situation awareness cognitive agent supports reference semantic roadmaps schemas, and a simple and flexible declarative rule style for building the corresponding processes and services.

As a proof of concept, a particular demonstration prototype for vehicle geolocation in tunnels was presented, in order to improve the robustness of advanced driver assistance systems, using an onboard video camera and common standard vehicle sensors. In the future we plan to extend the defined goal-oriented associative cognitive agent, to develop more real-time applications in different scenarios and contexts.

It is also planned a continuous development of the associative architecture defined for situation awareness agents, to expand the application fields, and to optimize its fundamental principles and the considered semantic roadmaps. Some other critical applications are also envisaged in the field of advanced driver assistance systems, semi-autonomous and fully autonomous vehicles.

Acknowledgements. This work has been supported by the Spanish Ministry of Economy y Competitiveness under project number TIN2014-57458-R.

References

1. Endsley, M.R.: Towards a theory of situation awareness in dynamic systems. Hum. Factors **37**(1), 32–64 (1995)
2. Endsley, M.R., Jones, D.G.: Designing for Situation Awareness: An Approach to Human-Centred Design. Taylor & Francis, London (2012)
3. Nowak, C., Lambert, D.: The semantic challenge for situation assessments. In: IEEE 8th International Conference on Information Fusion, July 2005, Los Alamitos (2005)
4. Baader, F., et al.: A novel architecture for situation awareness systems. In: Giese, M., Waaler, A. (eds.) TABLEAUX 2009. LNCS (LNAI), vol. 5607, pp. 77–92. Springer, Heidelberg (2009). https://doi.org/10.1007/978-3-642-02716-1_7

5. Kokar, M.M., Matheus, C.J., Baclawski, K.: Ontology-based situation awareness. Inf. Fusion **10**(1), 83–98 (2009)
6. Kokar, M.M., Endsley, M.R.: Situation awareness and cognitive modeling. In: IEEE Intelligent Systems, Cyber-Physical-Social Systems, pp. 2–7, May–June 2012
7. Ulicny, B., et al.: Augmenting the analyst via situation-dependent reasoning with trust-annotated facts. In: Proceedings of the 2011 IEEE International Multi-Disciplinary Conference Cognitive Methods in Situation Awareness and Decision Support, pp. 17–24. IEEE (2011)
8. Laing, C., Vickers, P.: Context informed intelligent information infrastructures for better situational awareness. In: International Conference on Cyber Situational Awareness, Data Analytics and Assessment (CyberSA), 8–9 June 2015
9. Steinberg, A.N., et al.: Revisions to the JDL data fusion model. In: Proceedings of the SPIE Sensor Fusion: Architectures, Algorithms and Applications, pp. 430–441 (1999)
10. Lundquist, C.: Automotive sensor fusion for situation awareness. Ph.D. thesis, Department of Electrical Engineering, Linköping University, Sweden (2009)
11. Golestan, K., Soua, R., Karray, F., Kamel, M.S.: Situation awareness within the context of connected cars. Inf. Fusion **29**, 68–83 (2016)
12. Aghdam, H.H., Heravi, E.J.: Guide to Convolutional Neural Networks. A Practical Application to Traffic-Sign Detection and Classification. Springer, Heidelberg (2017). https://doi.org/10.1007/978-3-319-57550-6
13. Houben, S., Stallkamp, J., Salmen, J., Schlipsing, M., Igel, C.: Detection of traffic signs in real-world images: the German Traffic Sign Detection Benchmark (GTSDB). In: Proceedings International Joint Conference on Neural Networks (2013)
14. Mathias, M., Timofte, R., Benenson, R., Van Gool, L.: Traffic sign recognition - how far are we from the solution? In: Proceedings of the International Joint Conference on Neural Networks (2013)
15. Sun, Z.L., Wang, H., Lau, W.S., Seet, G., Wang, D.: Application of BW-ELM model on traffic sign recognition. Neurocomputing **128**, 153–159 (2014)
16. Zeng, Y., Xu, X., Fang, Y., Zhao, K.: Traffic sign recognition using deep convolutional networks and extreme learning machine. In: He, X., Gao, X., Zhang, Y., Zhou, Z.-H., Liu, Z.-Y., Fu, B., Hu, F., Zhang, Z. (eds.) IScIDE 2015. LNCS, vol. 9242, pp. 272–280. Springer, Cham (2015). https://doi.org/10.1007/978-3-319-23989-7_28
17. TensorFlow Models Repository. https://github.com/tensorflow/models. Accessed 04 Feb 2018
18. Szegedy, C., et al.: Going deeper with convolutions. In: Proceedings of the 2015 IEEE Conference on Computer Vision and Pattern Recognition (2015)

Provider Recommendation in Heterogeneous Transportation Fleets

Miguel Ángel Rodríguez-García⬤, Alberto Fernández$^{(\boxtimes)}$⬤,
and Holger Billhardt⬤

Universidad Rey Juan Carlos, Madrid, Spain
{miguel.rodriguez,alberto.fernandez,
holger.billhardt}@urjc.es

Abstract. Nowadays, transportation is a critical sector of our lives, not only for the movement of people, but also to be capable to move goods around the world. Although providing such services can be seen as a very tiny problem in our society, behind it, there is a complex sector that requires sophisticated models and specific software to analyse a vast amount of information coming from different sources in order to provide a sustainable and efficient service. Given such a complex field, various issues have come up like the search of optimised routes, efficient assignment of vehicles, reduction of gas emissions, cost optimization problems, etc. In most cases, the provided approaches are focused on addressing the optimization problem considering fleets with identical features. In this work, we present HVSRec, a heterogeneous fleet semantic recommender system that integrates mechanisms to manage vehicles of different nature and characteristics efficiently. The platform is aimed to connect customers that request a transportation of a certain good with drivers that are offering transportation services with their own vehicle.

Keywords: Fleet management systems · Heterogeneous fleets
Semantic recommendation systems

1 Introduction

In recent years, transportation holds an essential place in daily life. It is an enormous industry that employs millions of people in order to provide efficient delivery services [1]. Its primary business is focused on managing services to move people or goods by using different types of vehicles which range from municipal buses, bicycles to large trucks.

The transportation sector has an incredible impact on the economic development of society. According to the U.S. Department of Commerce [2] the investment in this industry came to $1.48 trillion in 2015, and it represented the 8 percent of the GDP (Gross Domestic Product). In Europe, a report provided by The European Commission [3] categorises transport as a relevant sector that has a significant impact on growth and employment, reaching 10 millions of employees and 5% of GDP.

The sector is considered a complex field with several players and decision levels, and high investments during the transportation process [4]. This complicated environment exposes various challenges that have raised a great interest in the research community.

© Springer International Publishing AG, part of Springer Nature 2018
J. Bajo et al. (Eds.): PAAMS 2018 Workshops, CCIS 887, pp. 416–427, 2018.
https://doi.org/10.1007/978-3-319-94779-2_36

Route optimisation problem, fleet management, dynamic assignment problem and equipment selection problem are some of the research lines in this domain. In the literature, for the routes optimization problem classical approaches but also modern heuristics and metaheuristics have been proposed to solve such a problem [5, 6]. Regarding fleet management, the analysed issues deal mainly with the dispatching of vehicles to carry out demanded services efficiently. To address this issue, different techniques have been proposed. For instance Krisnamurthy et al. propose a column generation algorithm [7] to manage the travel time spent from the slowest automobile. On the contrary, Langevin et al. [8] propose an innovative algorithm based on dynamic programming to solve the assignment and the routing problems simultaneously. For its part, the ability to select the optimised equipment has been another relevant issue broadly investigated in fleet management. Especially, in industry sectors related to resource extraction (logistics, mining, metallurgy, etc.) [9–12]. However, with the arrival of ICT (Information Communication Technology) new transportation models have emerged facilitating the appearing of diverse companies like Uber, Lift, etc. in which the classic model based on delivery driver and customer has been softened allowing that everyone who has a vehicle can offer a transportation service. Hence, this new disruptive model provides a more complicated version of the fleet management problem where mixed fleets, vehicles with different features, can also be considered in the model.

Despite the success of the analysed solutions, in most cases they are quite technical, which means that they are very focused on developing an efficient algorithm that solves the considered problem. However, in real life, there are parameters like associated costs, different preferable features of different vehicles, driver interests, and others, that should be incorporated when creating a real-world model. Therefore, we need a standard language that integrates all these pieces of information in a management system. In this sense, Semantic Web technologies offer knowledge representation models to convert data flows coming from different formats in a standardized format, RDF. These conceptual models have been successfully employed in recommender systems of different fields [13, 14]. However, to the best of our knowledge, they have not been applied for fleet management recommendation.

In this paper, we present HVSRec (Heterogeneous Vehicle Semantic Recommendation) platform, whose goal is to coordinate the assignment of transportation delivery providers to customers. HVSRec aims to address environments with dynamic product delivery demand, autonomous transportation providers with vehicles of different types and, thus, capabilities.

The remainder of the manuscript is organised as follows: in the next section, we will introduce the overall architecture of the HVSRec system and explain its main modules. In Sect. 3, we explain in more detail how delivery requests are matched with transportation providers. Finally, in Sect. 4, we sum up our work and propose future lines of work.

2   Architecture

In this section, we describe the architecture of the HVSRec platform. It comprises three main modules: (i) the *HVSRec Population*, which aims for retrieving information about cars from online repositories and it is also responsible for semantically describing such data by using the RDF standard; (ii) the *HVSRec Recommender* module that is in charge of generating the recommendations of transportation providers on demand, and finally, (iii) the *HVSRec API* module, that represents the system's front-end, providing access to the recommender service from the outside. Figure 1 depicts the module decomposition of the platform.

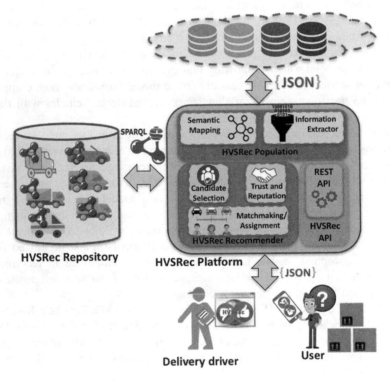

Fig. 1. Architecture of the system.

We define two different roles in the platform. First, the drivers (or providers) who offer their vehicles for a delivery service. Second, customers (or clients) who request a transportation service of some product or good from one place to another. The HVSRec platform works as follows: delivery providers utilise the front-end app to register the vehicles that they want to offer. For each vehicle, the *HVSRec Population* module retrieves technical details about it, like engine capacity, type of energy used (diesel, petrol, electric, etc.), gross vehicle weight rating, etc. To translate such information into RDF, we have taken advantage of ontologies to describe these details semantically.

With regard to the customers, they utilise the front-end app to query for delivery services. When a user asks for such a service, a complete description of the demanded service must be provided, indicating the kind of good and size, among others. After the *HVSRec API* receives such details it asks the recommender for a list of vehicles that match the given description. The recommender queries the repository for a list of vehicles and driver that satisfy the demanded requirements. Furthermore, the user and delivery driver profile will be analysed by a *trust and reputation* module to check their behaviour on the platform. Finally, the user will get a list of recommended providers he can contact.

In the following sections, we will analyse the function of each module and sub-modules in depth.

2.1 HVSRec Platform

The HVSRec Platform represents the core of the system and it carries out primary functions such as populating the semantic repository, recommendation tasks and online query services. Different modules that we will describe in the following sections perform these functions.

HVSRec Population Module. Its principal aim is to populate the repository with details about vehicles retrieved from external online databases. To extract the information, we have developed several scripts in Java that utilise RESTful web services technology to query online databases and retrieve the data in a lightweight data-interchange format. Currently, different web pages provide information about cars such as *auto-data.net*, which provides technical specification of more than 50 different brands; Car DataBase API that contributes with more than 31000 specifications of a broad number of brands; *emunds.com* that offers an API to retrieve technical details from luxury ranging vehicles to new brands; and finally the National Highway Traffic Safety Administration[1] (NHTSA) that provides different ways to gather information on vehicles and their specifications. Table 1 stands for an excerpt of information gathered from Car DataBase API.

Table 1. Information obtained from Car DataBase API about Audi A6 2008.

Technical feature	Specification
Brand	Audi
Model	A6
Name	A6 Allroad quattro (4F, C6 facelift 2008)
Engine	3.2 FSI V6 (256 Hp) quattro Tiptronic
Max Weight	2430
Fuel	Petrol (Gasoline)

---

[1] https://www.nhtsa.gov/.

The technical features collected from the API are entirely accurate. In the example described in Table 1, the Audi A6 Allroad Quattro has been described in detail. Various specific features have been retrieved such as engine, type of fuel used, and so on. Once the information extraction module gathers the data, these are converted into RDF format. To carry out this conversion, we have developed a systematically way of transforming information adequately. We have taken advantage of knowledge representation to build a conceptual model capable of describing such features semantically. The model is described in detail in Sect. 2.2.

HVSRec Recommender. It is responsible for the primary function of this platform. Given a description of a delivery request, it will try to find vehicles capable of providing the demanded service. In order to accomplish its task, the module needs to orchestrate two components: (i) the repository from which it has to build the list of recommendations, and (ii) the user queries coming from the API. In order to optimise the recommendation list, it analyses the available providers from three different points of view: viability of the transportation, the trustworthiness of the service provider, and the cost of the service. Regarding the latter, we examine the distance between the service and the pickup location, as well as the fare the driver of a vehicle wants to charge for a service. For viability, we check whether the size and weight of the packages match with the maximum capacities of vehicles, etc. On the other hand, *trust and reputation* of customers and service providers allows for establishing differences in the expected service quality. After a delivery service finishes, both customer and driver can rate each other evaluating the provided service/behaviour. This information is used to update the trust and reputation component. In general, including trust will promote seriousness among drivers and customers, e.g., drivers with higher ratings will have higher probability of being selected for a transportation service than those with low reputation. More details are given in Sect. 3.

HVSRec API. The API provides an entry point to the system for clients and drivers. It implements a set of subroutines that provides a simple way of connecting the two parts of the application: the front-end and the back-end. To develop this API, we have used RESTful Web Services, one of the most broadly-used technologies that has been converted into a de facto standard in Web applications development. By using this technology, users can directly interact with the services provided by the system. Among the different offered services, users will be able to register themselves in the system, ask for recommendations, register their vehicles, rate services or clients, etc.

The language that we picked to interact with the API is JSON, a lightweight data-interchange format easily interpretable. Thus, the API receives user queries in JSON format and these are then transformed into specific commands. The recommender module takes these commands and employs some of its components to build a response. As a result, depending on the required service, the API module will receive a list of objects which is transform into JSON format. Finally, users will receive their response in their respective apps on possibly different devices.

2.2   HVSRec Repository

The repository is the data store of the platform. It stores car details extracted from online databases. To allow easy integration of data flows of different nature, we use RDF as a standardized format to represent the information. As a triple-store, we decide to use the widely extended repository Virtuoso[2], which provides a set of very extensive libraries in the domain of semantic web applications and that offer public functions to access and work quite efficiently.

To store information in the repository, it is required to have an ontology model that provides a semantic description of information about cars. Before developing our own ontology, we have analyzed several works in which models to represent the car application domain have been developed. Among the analyzed approaches a high percentage are focused on smart cars industry. They mainly use ontologies to design a standardized way of integrating information coming from different physical devices. For instance, the Automotive Ontology Community Group which has the aim (among others) to utilize ontologies for a better interoperability in the automotive industry[3]. Although, the group seems quite active, there is still nothing materialized. The Web page specifies some of the vocabularies that are being used by renowned companies, but it seems that there is still work coming out. In the same line, Feld and Müller [15] introduces the Automotive Ontology that aims at integrating different devices in smart cars. This model represents the core of an application that provides an abstract layer capable of representing information extracted from different devices semantically. A similar approach is proposed by Sun et al. [16] where they present an infrastructure framework for modelling a general architecture for a smart car. In particular, the monitoring system relies on a hierarchical context model that utilizes three ontologies to provide a semantic representation of the read events. Another approach is Zhao et al. [17], where they introduce a Knowledge Base and an Intelligent Speed Adaptation (ISA) system capable of detecting over speed in driving environments in real time. Their knowledge base system contains three different ontologies: Map ontology, Control Ontology and Car Ontology which contains a clear taxonomy that represent different types of vehicles, their installed sensors and used engine. Finally, a very simple approach is given by Mizoguchi in [18] which provides a basic introduction about Ontological Engineering providing a further explanation of what is the difference between ontology and a knowledge base. Here, he introduces a clear taxonomy that classifies the vehicles application domain.

The different analyzed approaches give us a better understanding of the application domain to model. Finally, we came up with a mixed model in between Zhao et al. [17] and Mizoguchi [18]. Figure 2 shows the taxonomy of the implemented model and its main concepts. There are three main groups (first level concepts): (i) a *Vehicle* taxonomy including different types of vehicles, (ii) *CarParts*, with physical car elements, and (iii) type of *Fuel* used, such as fossil, hydrogen, electric or a combination of them (*Multiple_fuel*), such as hybrid cars.

---

[2] https://virtuoso.openlinksw.com/.

[3] https://www.w3.org/community/gao/.

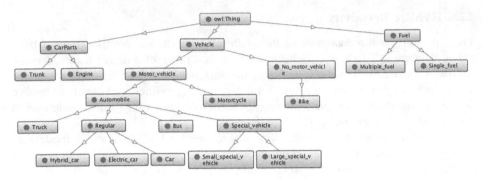

Fig. 2. Vehicle ontology.

Beyond the vehicle taxonomy, we have also defined a set of data properties which are extremely relevant for the recommender module. For instance: *max_weight* will limit the maximum weight that the vehicle can carry and it will be determined in the Trunk class, *max_lenght*, *max_width* and *max_height* stand for the dimensions of the Vehicle; *cost_per_km* will differ from the type of selected vehicle. A truck is expected to cost more than a van, for instance.

2.3 HVSRec Application

Its principal aim is to facilitate users to access services provided by the platform. To do so, it contains a set of graphic interfaces that facilitate its usage. In the application, we have set two types of profiles: customer and provider role. The customer role stands for users who wish to move packages to other location, and the provider role represents drivers who want to offer their vehicles for delivery services.

3   Recommending Vehicles for Delivery Services

In this section we describe the process of recommending delivery service providers to customers. This task consists of several phases. First, vehicles from the HVSRec repository are filtered so as to select those compatible with the product to be transported, e.g. size, weight, etc. Then, the reputation of providers is evaluated and the price for the service is determined and the most appropriate providers are selected to be returned as a possible list of candidates to the customer.

3.1   Candidate Selection

The first step for recommending delivery service providers is to filter out those whose vehicles are not able to transport the customer's packages. We generate a SPARQL query from the package description that checks the different constraints including size, weight, width and height.

For example, the SPARQL query that returns vehicles a package with the following characteristics {weight = 10 kg, length = 100 cm, width = 60 cm, height = 30 cm} is:

```
PREFIX rdf: <http://www.w3.org/1999/02/22-rdf-syntax-ns#>
PREFIX hvsr: <http://ia.urjc.es/onto/hvsr>
SELECT ?provider
WHERE {
    ?provider hvsr:has_vehicle ?veh.
    ?veh hvsr:max_weight ?weight.
    ?veh hvsr:max_lenght ?length.
    ?veh hvsr:max_width ?width.
    ?veh hvsr:max_height ?height.
    FILTER (?length >= 100 && ?width >= 60 &&
            ?height >= 30 && ?weight >= 10)
}
```

3.2 Trust and Reputation

When a provider is recommended to a customer, the customer would be interested in estimating the provider's expected behaviour, which is commonly estimated by his reputation. Although less frequent, also the provider might want to know the reputation of the customer. We use a trust and reputation mechanism to provide such information.

We apply an adaptation of the models proposed by Ramchurn et al. [19] and Hermoso et al. [20]. In the following description we focus on a customer's perspective, the same approach is followed for the provider.

The confidence a customer c has on a service provider p is calculated as a combination of his local experience with $p(e_c(p))$ and the provider's reputation $R(p)$ (the global opinion of other users with that provider). Usually, if a customer has had many previous interactions with a given provider, his confidence is mainly based on their previous experiences. This is modelled as the reliability $r_c(p)$ on their own experience with p. However, if there have been very few or no interactions at all, the confidence is mostly based on the reputation. In summary, the confidence $C_c(p)$ that a customer c has on a delivery service provider p can be estimated as:

$$C_c(p) = r_c(p) * e_c(p) + (1 - r_c(p)) * R(p) \tag{1}$$

In our system, recommendations of service providers to costumers are accompanied by values that represent the reputation of a particular provider, e.g. the aggregated evaluation of the trustworthiness of the provider as perceived by other customers. A customer can use this information in conjunction with his own experience (like in Eq. (1)) in order to evaluate his subjective trust in each proposed provider. A customer will use this information (together with other parameters, like the price of a delivery service) to take its decision on which provider to choose for a service. After a transaction has taken place, both, provider and customer, can evaluate each other and the reputation information is updated.

In many cases, a provider behaves differently for distinct types of products. For example, that a provider performs well delivering books does not mean he will also be good transporting furniture or frozen food. The used model also accounts for different types of interactions (in our case, transportation need) and roles played by the agents participating in it. Actually, Eq. (1) is a simplification, and we apply it for the same type of transportation need. If for a given type of delivery service there are not enough previous evaluations for a given provider then, we follow the approach of [20], which allows inferring the confidence under the assumption that agents behave similarly when they play similar roles, i.e. providers perform similarly when they transport similar type of goods. For example, if someone has a good reputation transporting fruit he is expected to be good transporting similar goods. We implement this by calculating the similarity between products in a taxonomy that is used to tag and classify them.

3.3   Matchmaking/Assignment

A set of transportation providers are recommended to customers by analysing several attributes including trust and reputation, vehicle appropriateness, cost of vehicle, distance from vehicle to customer, distance to destination and usage of green energy.

This process is carried out after the candidate selection phase, so all providers considered in this phase are in principle capable of transporting the customer's product. We apply an additional filter here, only those providers with a confidence (trust and reputation) above a certain threshold θ are considered. As mentioned before, the reputation is also shown to the customers at the end of the whole process such that they can use it to make the final decision.

Each vehicle has, among other characteristics, the cost per kilometre (denoted by $cost\_km(v)$) for vehicle usage. This value represents the actual cost of the usage of a vehicle for his owner and should include petrol consumption and other expenses, like maintenance cost, taxes, etc.

We are interested in reaching assignments with as low costs as possible. Costs help to find appropriate vehicles according to their size. For example, a motorcycle seems to be more appropriate to deliver a letter than a truck. It should be noted that the cost implicitly includes a reference to the type of vehicle (e.g., a truck will have a higher cost than a motorcycle). Furthermore, environmental costs (e.g., CO_2 emissions) could be included in the cost of a vehicle or green energy vehicles may become less costly due to incentives like tax reductions, free parking, etc.

We define the cost of a vehicle v for a product p with following this function:

$$Cost(v, p) = cost\_km(v) * (D_o + D_d) \tag{2}$$

Where, D_o is the distance from candidate vehicle v to origin of product p, and D_d the distance from origin to destination of p.

Furthermore, we assume, different delivery service providers may have different fares per km (*fare(v)*), that specify the net income they request for doing any delivery service. With these two parameters the price a customer has to pay for sending p with provider v is calculated by the following equation:

$$Price(v,p) = Cost(v,p) + fare(v) * (D_o + D_d) + O \qquad (3)$$

The price takes into account both, the fare and the cost of a vehicle, as well as a certain overhead for the mediation service (O).

We are interested in recommending providers with lower price (in general with lower costs) and also with higher reputation. Therefore, when a new customer requests a service, the HVSRec system combines a set of the k providers with lowest price and the m providers with the highest reputation. This set is returned to the customer together with information of all the detailed information (price, reputation, vehicle type and specifications, driver information, etc.), and the costumer can then select a provider.

4   Conclusion

In this work, we present an ontology-based recommender for transport services in heterogeneous fleets. In particular, we have introduced the architecture of the platform describing its operation. Then, we have decomposed it in its separate modules to analyse their principal objectives in detail. During this analysis, we have introduced the car ontology that we have extended from two others models to describe information about cars semantically.

As future work, we would like to enrich the ontology with more technical details about the cars, especially, data about the capacity of the trunk. By using this information, the platform will be able to manage more precisely the amount of packages that can be transported by vehicles. From this weakness, we realised that the packet dimension details like weight, height and width are vital to managing the truck's free capacity significant feature that has a high impact over delivers planning, costs of delivery services, routes planning, among others. Therefore, we think that integrating such property will help us to optimise the performance of the recommender.

User profiles have not been integrated into the semantic repository. However, we think to express their details semantically it will improve the accuracy of the trust and reputation module. Hence, we plan to use well-known ontologies for describing persons like FOAF.

With regards to the quality of the recommendations, we plan to prepare several experiments to evaluate the accuracy of the recommendation service.

We are also working on optimizing the assignments of the transportation requests to the service providers. Here, the idea is to reduce costs or to promote specific assignments (e.g., more environmental friendly vehicles), maintaining at the same time to quality of the service from the point of view of the customers. The basis for a possible optimization is the fact that the situation in the system changes dynamically and at given points in time, a better assignment solution than proposed initially may exist. We think about two different approaches to deal with this issue. The first idea consists in not assigning or recommending service providers immediately, but instead use a time interval to identify possible better recommendations e.g., due to the appearance of new providers, or to aggregate several requests in a global assignment/recommendation process (similar to the work proposed in [21]). The second idea is based on dynamic re-assignments of providers that have already been selected for a delivery service, if such a re-assignment can reduce the overall cost of the currently engaged transportation services. Here, an incentive approach may be necessary in order to persuade drivers to accept changes in their currently assigned service tasks.

Finally, we believe the description expressed by users can provide valuable information that would be significant to consider when recommendations are demanded. Therefore, we plan to implement more dynamic forms which enable users to give a detailed description of the service that they need. In this regard, we think that combining Semantic Web and Natural Language Processing techniques can help us to achieve a better understanding of the real requirements that users' demand which would directly impact in the quality of the recommendations.

Acknowledgments. Work partially supported by the Autonomous Region of Madrid (grant "MOSI-AGIL-CM" (S2013/ICE-3019) co-funded by EU Structural Funds FSE and FEDER), project "SURF" (TIN2015-65515-C4-4-R (MINECO/FEDER)) funded by the Spanish Ministry of Economy and Competitiveness, and through the Excellence Research Group GES2ME (Ref. 30VCPIGI05) co-funded by URJC and Santander Bank.

References

1. https://www.wetfeet.com/articles/industry-overview-transportation. Accessed 11 Feb 2018
2. https://www.selectusa.gov/logistics-and-transportation-industry-united-states. Accessed 11 Feb 2018
3. https://ec.europa.eu/jrc/en/research-topic/transport-sector-economic-analysis. Accessed 11 Feb 2018
4. Crainic, T.G., Laporte, G.: Fleet Management and Logistics. Springer, New York (2012). https://doi.org/10.1007/978-1-4615-5755-5
5. Laporte, G., Gendreau, M., Potvin, J.Y., Semet, F.: Classical and modern heuristics for the vehicle routing problem. Int. Trans. Oper. Res. **7**(4–5), 285–300 (2000)
6. Barthélemy, T., Rossi, A., Sevaux, M., Sörensen, K.: Metaheuristic approach for the clustered VRP. In: EU/MEeting: 10th Anniversary of the Metaheuristics Community-Université de Bretagne Sud, France (2010)
7. Krishnamurthy, N.N., Batta, R., Karwan, M.H.: Developing conflict-free routes for automated guided vehicles. Oper. Res. **41**(6), 1077–1090 (1993)
8. Langevin, A., Lauzon, D., Riopel, D.: Dispatching, routing, and scheduling of two automated guided vehicles in a flexible manufacturing system. Int. J. Flex. Manuf. Syst. **8**(3), 247–262 (1996)
9. Burt, C.N., Caccetta, L.: Equipment selection for surface mining: a review. Interfaces **44**(2), 143–162 (2014)
10. El-Moslmani, K., Alkass, S., Al-Hussein, M.: A computer module for multi-loaders-multi-trucks fleet selection for earthmoving projects. In: Proceedings of the Canadian Society for Civil Engineering Annual Conference, GE-107, Montréal (2002)

11. Burt, C., Caccetta, L., Welgama, P., Fouché, L.: Equipment selection with heterogeneous fleets for multiple-period schedules. J. Oper. Res. Soc. **62**(8), 1498–1509 (2011)
12. Aykul, H., Yalcin, E., Ediz, I.G., Dixon-Hardy, D.W., Akcakoca, H.: Equipment selection for high selective excavation surface coal mining. J. S. Afr. Inst. Min. Metall. **107**(3), 195 (2007)
13. Colombo-Mendoza, L.O., Valencia-García, R., Rodríguez-González, A., Alor-Hernández, G., Samper-Zapater, J.J.: RecomMetz: a context-aware knowledge-based mobile recommender system for movie showtimes. Expert Syst. Appl. **42**(3), 1202–1222 (2015)
14. Rodríguez-García, M.Á., Colombo-Mendoza, L.O., Valencia-García, R., Lopez-Lorca, Antonio A., Beydoun, G.: Ontology-based music recommender system. In: Omatu, S., Malluhi, Q.M., Gonzalez, S.R., Bocewicz, G., Bucciarelli, E., Giulioni, G., Iqba, F. (eds.) Distributed Computing and Artificial Intelligence, 12th International Conference. AISC, vol. 373, pp. 39–46. Springer, Cham (2015). https://doi.org/10.1007/978-3-319-19638-1_5
15. Feld, M., Müller, C.: The automotive ontology: managing knowledge inside the vehicle and sharing it between cars. In: Proceedings of the 3rd International Conference on Automotive User Interfaces and Interactive Vehicular Applications, pp. 79–86 (2011)
16. Sun, J., Wu, Z.H., Pan, G.: Context-aware smart car: from model to prototype. J. Zhejiang Univ. Sci. A **10**(7), 1049–1059 (2009)
17. Zhao, L., Ichise, R., Yoshikawa, T., Naito, T., Kakinami, T., Sasaki, Y.: Ontology-based decision making on uncontrolled intersections and narrow roads. In: IEEE IV Intelligent Vehicles Symposium, pp. 83–88 (2015)
18. Mizoguchi, R.: Part 1: introduction to ontological engineering. New Gener. Comput. **21**(4), 365–384 (2003)
19. Ramchurn, S.D., Sierra, C., Godó, L., Jennings, N.R.: A computational trust model for multi-agent interactions based on confidence and reputation. In: Proceedings of 6th International Workshop of Deception, Fraud and Trust in Agent Societies, pp. 69–75 (2003)
20. Hermoso, R., Billhardt, H., Ossowski, S.: Integrating trust in virtual organisations. In: Noriega, P., Vázquez-Salceda, J., Boella, G., Boissier, O., Dignum, V., Fornara, N., Matson, E. (eds.) COIN -2006. LNCS (LNAI), vol. 4386, pp. 19–31. Springer, Heidelberg (2007). https://doi.org/10.1007/978-3-540-74459-7_2
21. Billhardt, H., Fernández, A., Lujak, M., Ossowski, S., Julián, V., de Paz, J.F., Hernández, J.: Coordinating open fleets. A taxi assignment example. AI Commun. **30**(1), 37–52 (2017)

A Bike Sharing System Simulator

Alberto Fernández[1(✉)], Sandra Timón[1], Carlos Ruiz[1],
Tao Cumplido[2], Holger Billhardt[1], and Jürgen Dunkel[2]

[1] CETINIA, University Rey Juan Carlos, Madrid, Spain
{alberto.fernandez, sandra.timon, carlos.ruiz,
holger.billhardt}@urjc.es
[2] Computer Science Department, Hochschule Hannover, Hanover, Germany
taocumplido@gmail.com, juergen.dunkel@hs-hannover.de

Abstract. Bike-sharing systems are becoming very popular in big cities. They provide a cheap and green mean of transportation used for commuting and leisure. Being a shared limited resource, it is common to reach imbalanced situations where some stations have either no bikes or only empty slots, thus decreasing the performance of the system. To solve such situations, trucks are typically used to move bikes among stations in order to reach a more homogeneous distribution. Recently, research works are focusing on a complementary action to reduce imbalances consisting in incentivizing users to take (or return) bikes from stations with many bikes rather than those with few bikes, e.g. by fare discounts. In this paper, we present simulator for analyzing bike-sharing systems. Several user generation distributions can be configured. The simulator is specifically designed with the aim of evaluating incentive-based rebalancing strategies. The paper describes in detail the characteristics and potential of the simulator, including several experiments.

Keywords: Bike sharing · Simulator · Smart transportation

1 Introduction

Nowadays, due to the great pollution produced by motor vehicles and since not everyone can afford to acquire and maintain one, bike-sharing systems have emerged in big cities to try to palliate these problems. These systems allow citizens to move between different geographical points in a simple and economical way, as they can rent a bike at any station and return it at a different one. Also, some of these bike-sharing systems offer the possibility of making bike or slot reservations, which is even more convenient for the users. However, resources in bike-sharing systems, i.e. stations and, consequently, bikes and slots, are limited. Therefore, it is important to manage these resources as efficiently as possible so as to provide a good quality of service and user experience. To this aim, it is necessary that each station has the appropriate number of bikes and slots at each moment, so that a user who arrives at a station to rent a bike (or wants to reserve a bike) can find available bikes, or the one who arrives at a station to return a bike (or wants to reserve a slot) finds an available slot.

J. Bajo et al. (Eds.): PAAMS 2018 Workshops, CCIS 887, pp. 428–440, 2018.
https://doi.org/10.1007/978-3-319-94779-2_37

Traditionally, bike balancing has been done by trucks that transport bikes from some stations to others. Some research has focused on optimizing the static balancing problem [1–3], where the routes of trucks at night or off-peak periods are optimized. More recently, the dynamic problem has been considered, which involves predicting the demand on each station in the next period and optimizing the distribution of bikes in stations so as to maximize the number of trips (i.e. reduce the number of "no-service" situations) [4–6]. While those approaches only consider trucks as the means to rebalance the bike-sharing system, there are other works that try to incentivize bike users to collaborate in the system rebalancing [7–10], typically by dynamically modifying rental prices. Using prices as incentives is also common in static strategies, for example BiciMAD[1] introduces discounts on final rental price if the user hires a bike at a station with more available bikes or if he returns it to a station with many empty slots.

While most current systems are station-based, the development of location technologies (e.g. GPS) have provoked the appearance of several floating systems [1, 12]. In such systems, bikes can be left "floating" anywhere in the city so the problem of finding an empty slot is avoided. In those systems, the problem is to keep the different areas of the city covered with available bikes.

In this paper we present a simulator that allows analyzing the behavior of station-based bike-sharing systems. The ultimate goal of the simulator is to help to evaluate dynamic rebalancing algorithms based on user incentives in different settings. In this sense, different user types (behaviors) can be defined and different balancing strategies can be implemented. Although some simulation models exist [11], to the best of our knowledge, there are no available simulators of this kind. Chemla et al. [7] presented an open-source simulator for evaluating their proposed algorithms for dynamic balancing but, unfortunately, the simulator is no longer available.

The rest of the paper is organized as follows. In Sect. 2 we introduce the kind of systems this simulator is aimed at. Section 3 details the architecture and its components. Some experiments are presented in Sect. 4. We conclude the paper in Sect. 5.

2 Context and Problem Description

In this paper we envision a system that dynamically provides incentives to persuade users to help in the balancing of the distributions of bikes in the city. We concentrate on station-based systems, e.g., bikes can only be taken or left at fixed stations in the city and each station has a fixed number of slots to hold available bikes. Furthermore, we consider that users can make reservations on stations, either of a bike or of a slot to leave a bike. The global architecture of the envisioned system is presented in Fig. 1.

There is a *physical infrastructure* consisting on bikes and stations, which a fixed number of slots. The information about the current situation of the stations and bikes is received by the fleet operator, which can use that information to provide more or less *dynamic management* of the stations. For example, different incentives could be given to users to try and keep the system balanced. Such incentives might be fixed (e.g. in

---

[1] Public bike sharing system of Madrid (Spain): https://www.bicimad.com/.

Madrid a discount is given if a bike is taken from a station with more than 70% of occupancy) or could be modified dynamically. Through smartphones or web applications users may access recommendation services, such as station information, booking bikes/slots, routes searches between stations, etc. Those recommendation services, created by the system operator or third party providers, make use of the dynamic management of stations (e.g. state or prices), so they could recommend/incentivize booking a bike in a station with some discount.

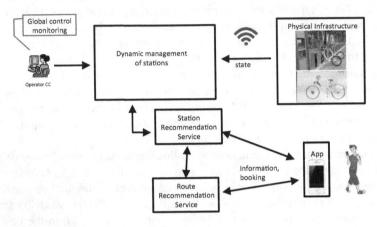

Fig. 1. Bike sharing system.

The dynamic management of stations along with recommendation services are fundamental to try and keep the system as efficient as possible, i.e. reduce or mitigate imbalances. In order to design and compare different dynamic balancing strategies, a bike sharing simulator is required.

The aim of this paper is to present a simulator we have designed as general as possible in order to evaluate different balancing strategies and also allowing the definition of different types of users with different behaviors.

In the simulator, a user can appear in the system at any point in the simulated area (we will see more details in Sect. 3.3), which includes stations. The first thing a user has to decide is which station he wants to take a bike from and whether he wants to reserve it before moving there. That decision is on the user behavior model and might be taken using support applications (information, recommendation, etc.). Once the user arrives at the chosen station, it may happen that there are no available bikes (even if there were some when the user consulted the information). In that case, the user must decide whether to choose a new station (and possible reservation) or to leave the system without rental. The same situation may also happen even for users having bookings since the expiration time could occur before arriving at the station.

In case that the user successfully hired a bike, the destination is decided, which can be a particular station, or the user just uses the bike to "go around". In the latter case the user eventually decides to return the bike at any point in the city (this allows for simulating users that rent bikes for fun without knowing the destination at rental time).

In case the user knows the target station, he must decide whether to make a reservation of a slot or not. Now, the situation is very similar to rental: there might be no empty slots when the user arrives at a station. In this case, the user does not have the option of leaving the system. Instead has to search for a new station to leave the bike.

3 Architecture

In this section we describe the architecture of our simulator, which is depicted in Fig. 2. The core of the simulator comprises (i) a bike sharing system infrastructure, (ii) user management and (iii) an event-based simulator engine.

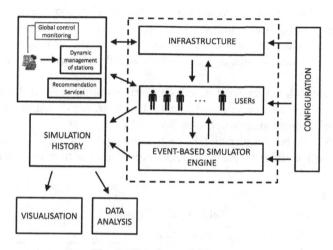

Fig. 2. Simulator architecture.

The bike sharing *infrastructure* represents the stations and bikes in the simulator. It contains information about the location of stations, number of empty bikes and slots, etc. and manages the rentals and bookings of bikes and slots. The *user management* includes different types of users and manages the interaction of them with the infrastructure as well as the information and recommendation services provided by the bike fleet operator. The *event-based simulator engine* is the main component of the core. It is in charge of processing the different events that occur in the system (new users, rentals, returns, bookings, etc.), triggering new events when necessary.

A *configuration* module is in charge of setting the parameters of a specific simulation, such as the infrastructure used, types and probability distribution of users, simulation time, geographical area to simulate, etc. During the simulation, users, depending on their behavior, can use *operator's services* to make decisions such as which station to take a bike from. In that module is where balancing algorithms can be implemented.

The simulation track is stored in a *simulation history*, which can be used later for graphical visualization and/or data analysis. This architecture allows us to decouple the simulation from its visualization and analysis. When the simulation is run the results are stored. The *Visualization* component shows the evolution of the simulation on a map. It can load a different simulation from a file, so this is a functionality that can be used without executing any simulation. The same is applied to *data analysis:* the statistics of any pre-recorded simulation can be analyzed.

In the following we describe in more detail the main building blocks of the simulator.

3.1   Simulator Engine

There are two main approaches to implement simulators. In continuous simulation, a fixed time-step is defined and the system is updated every step. In many steps there might not be any changes with respect to the previous one. On the other hand, in discrete or event-based simulation, the system is only updated when a new event occurs.

Our simulator follows an event-based approach, since the state of the system only changes when new events occur (see Table 1). However, the visualization component uses a continue simulation approach (see Sect. 3.5).

Table 1 shows a brief explanation of each event type. Although not detailed there, each event type has different parameters, among others the time in which the event takes place.

Table 1. Event types.

Event type	Description
User Appears	It represents the user appearance and, consequently, the moment when he determines the station where he wants to rent a bike from and whether he wants to make a bike reservation
User Arrives at Station to Rent Bike Without Reservation	It is not sure that the user will be able to take a bike: it depends on if the station has bikes available
User Arrives at Station to Rent Bike With Reservation	It is sure the user will be able to take a bike from the station
Bike Reservation Timeout	A bike reservation has expired before the user arrived at the destination station while the reservation was active (valid)
User Wants to Return Bike	The user has cycled somewhere in the city and now has decided he wants to go to a station to return the bike
User Arrives at Station to Return Bike Without Reservation	As the station may not have available slots, it is not sure the user will be able to return his bike there
User Arrives at Station to Return Bike With Reservation	A user is returning a bike because he had a reservation of an empty slot
Slot Reservation Timeout	It means the slot reservation has expired before the user arrived at the destination station

The simulation engine operation is based on a priority queue of events (ordered by the time instant they happen). Initially, all the *"User Appears"* events for the whole simulation are introduced (they are generated at the beginning of the simulation or loaded from a file). Then, the events are processed in order. The execution of events may require some decisions to be made by the user model associated to the event, and it usually creates and inserts new events into the queue.

For example, event *User Appears(user1,100)* states that *user1* appears at instant t = 100. When that event is processed, *user1* must decide (her user model is invoked) the station she wants to rent a bike from and whether she wants to make a reservation. Then, the route and arrival time are calculated[2], and the corresponding arrival event is inserted into the queue (*User Arrives at Station to Rent Bike With/Without Reservation*). In addition, if the user decided to book a bike, the *Bike Reservation Timeout* is also added with the established maximum reservation time (it is a system configuration parameter).

3.2   User Management

Users are responsible of making decisions on different moments of the simulation in which they are invoked by the simulator engine when processing the events. Our simulator easily allows using different types of users in the same simulation.

Each kind of user has his own implementation for the decision methods, which gives them their particular behavior, usually defined by a set of configuration parameters. There are different types of decisions to be made, for example, leaving the system (after a bike reservation timeout, after arriving at a station without available bikes…), making bike or slot reservations, deciding the destination station after renting it or to cycle somewhere in the city before deciding where to return it, etc.

An interesting issue is how users choose stations to hire or return bikes. They can use a recommendation system that provides information about fleet state as well as incentives to keep the fleet as balanced as possible. Users process that information to make decisions based on their behavior model. For example, one user might not want to go to a station located further than 500 m whatever discount he gets, while other might have a more complex decision function (e.g. combining distance and incentives).

Currently, our simulator provides the following types of users:

- *Uninformed.* This user tries to take/return bikes from the nearest station. He does not have information about availability of bikes/slots, so it may happen that there is no availability when the user arrives at the station.
- *Informed.* It is an informed user that knows the state of the fleet and only goes to stations with available bikes/slots. He chooses target stations by the shortest distance.
- *Obedient.* It contacts the recommender system and always follows its suggestions. Therefore, he is the perfect user from the dynamic balancing system's point of view.
- *Informed-R.* It is like *Informed* but making reservations before going to stations.
- *Obedient-R.* It is like *Obedient* but making reservations before going to stations.

---

[2] We use OpenStreetMap (OSM): https://www.openstreetmap.org.

- *Random.* This user randomly makes most of his decisions.
- *Commuter.* He always goes directly from the origin to the destination station to arrive as soon as possible at work, study, etc.
- *Tourist.* His main characteristic is that, after renting a bike, he always cycles somewhere in the city before deciding where to return it.
- *Distance/Resources ratio.* He chooses lowest ratio of the distance to the station and the number of available bikes or slots it has.
- *Most available resources.* This user always goes to the station with more available bikes (for rentals) or empty slots (for returns).

3.3   Experiment Configuration

Simulation experiments are configured by providing three types of configuration parameters: infrastructure, user generation and global configuration. These configuration parameters are stored in *json* files. We are currently developing a user interface to facilitate its creation.

Infrastructure. It contains information about the stations in the system, including physical location, capacity and initial number of bikes.

User Generation. It specifies where and when users appear in the system, as well as their type. User generation is defined by *entry points*. An entry point is a user generator defined by a location in the map (longitude and latitude coordinates), radius, probability distribution (e.g. Poisson ($\lambda = 5$)), type of users, number of users (0 for no limit) and starting time. Users are generated following the indicated distribution in a random position within the circle specified by the parameter *radius* around the center *location*. Each generated user is randomly assigned a walking and cycle speed in a predefined range. Entry points provide a flexible way of configuring different types of scenarios. For example, if we know demands at stations, we can simulate it by setting entry points at each station's location (and radius = 0) and demand distribution. Different types of users can be generated at the same point by defining several entry points at the same location.

Generated users (with *type*, *position* and *time*) are stored in a file that is fed into the simulator engine. This way, we can load the same users in several experiments, for example, to evaluate different station configurations, balancing strategies, etc.

Global Configuration. Global parameters of the experiments are specified in this part. They include the maximum *reservation time*, total *simulation time*, random *seed* (optional, it can be used to generate the same sequence of random values), *bounding box* of the map (top-left and bottom-right corners), *map* (we use OSM to calculate routes and times) and *output path* for the history file. We consider time units in seconds.

3.4 Simulation History

During the execution of the simulation, a history file is generated. It includes all the information about the events that occur in the simulation, such as new users, arrivals at stations, taking/returning bikes, routes taken by the users, etc. The information is represented incrementally, i.e. at each event, the change in the system is recorded.

Simulation history is used for visualization (Sect. 3.5), which allows reproducing the result of the simulation graphically as many times as desired, without needing to execute the simulation again. This is very convenient since it separates simulation and visualization, so they do not need to be synchronized. Actually, they usually run at a different pace. For example, a simulation of one day may take a few seconds, but its visualization might last for several minutes. Furthermore, the user might want to visualize different cases already stored without executing the simulation again.

History is also used for data analysis (Sect. 3.6), where different quality measures are taken to assess the efficiency of the bike sharing system. Again, the separation of simulator engine and analysis brings several advantages. It allows executing complex simulations that may take a long time, and once finished (offline), their data can be analyzed quickly. Since executions are stored in files, they can be easily processed and their results, compared.

Furthermore, simulation histories could be used for developing demand forecast methods, e.g. histories of execution could be used as training data to machine learning algorithms.

3.5 Visualization

The aim of the visualization component is to display the produced history data of the simulation in a useful and appealing way (see Fig. 3). This includes rendering geographic data on a map and making the status of the current situation visible. Additionally, the visualization is designed and implemented in an entity-agnostic way, resulting in a pluggable architecture that allows to easily add concrete entity models. This works well with the data format used in the simulation history (Sect. 3.4).

The visualization essentially acts as a reproducer of a set of recorded data where certain entities are displayed on a map with additional status information. The reproduction can occur in two ways:

1. A step-by-step reproduction of the data. This simply takes the next or previous recorded timestamp and applies the changes.
2. A playback mode simulating real-time. This mode waits in simulated real-time for the next or previous event to occur but updates the position of moving entities in between. The speed in which real-time is simulated can be controlled. A negative factor will rewind the playback.

To render the map, data from OpenStreetMap is used. The actual entities are displayed by an interactive marker, where the actual image and interactivity can be configured for each entity individually. It is also possible to not display an entity at all. In the bike-rental simulation these are currently the reservations and bikes. In the simulation a bicycle is either parked at a station or is rented by a user to cycle around.

Both cases do not require actually displaying the bike, rather the user marker should reflect whether a user is currently a pedestrian or a cyclist. The plug-in interface allows to easily adapt to new scenarios though. For example, it would be no problem to add a display strategy for bikes that are not parked at stations but at any point in the city, as long as this information is present in the history data.

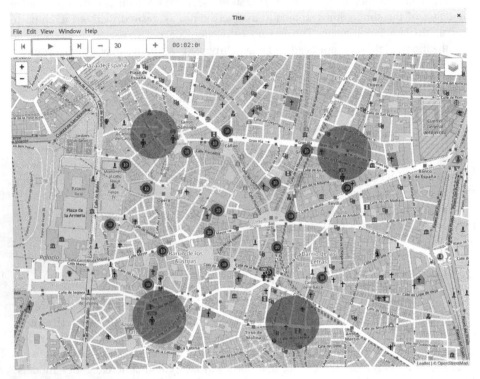

Fig. 3. Snapshot of the visualization interface. Entry points locations and radius are indicated in grey circles Small circles represent stations, with the number of available bikes shown in them. The ratio of available bikes and free slots is shown in red and green, respectively. Bike and person symbols represent users riding or walking, respectively. (Color figure online)

3.6 Data Analysis

Since the main purpose of this simulator is to assess algorithms that try to balance the number of available resources (bikes/slots) at a bike-sharing system, it provides quality measures that allow to evaluate the efficiency of those algorithms. The basic measures that provides our simulator are the following, which are stored per station and globally: *Successful hires* (*SH*, total number of bike rentals), *Failed hires* (*FH*, total number of attempts to hire a bike that failed due to unavailability), *Successful returns* (*SR*), *Failed returns* (*FR*), *Successful bike booking* (*SB*), *Failed bike bookings* (*FB*), *Successful slot booking* (*SS*), and *Failed slot bookings* (*FS*).

With the global values, we define the following quality measures (N is the total number of users, i.e. total bike demand):

- *Demand satisfaction* (*DS*): measures the ratio of users who were able to hire a bike (either at first trial or not), including those who booked a bike in advance.

$$DS = SH/N$$

- *Return satisfaction* (*RS*): measures the ratio of users who were able to return their bikes (either at first trial or not), including those who booked a dock in advance. Note that return demand is SH (those who actually hired a bike). The result should be 1, otherwise there are users who did not find an empty slot.

$$RS = SR/SH$$

- *Hire efficiency* (*HE*): it is the ratio between the number of rentals and the total rental attempts of those users who hired a bike.

$$HE = SH/(SH + FH)$$

- *Return efficiency* (*RE*): it is the ratio between the number of returns and the total return attempts:

$$RE = SR/(SH + FR)$$

All these measures are written in a *csv* format file so it can be imported into a more powerful statistical software for further analysis.

4 Evaluation

We have carried out several experiments to evaluate the simulator. We chose a 3 km square map of central Madrid and set 20 stations in real locations of the current bike-sharing system of Madrid (BiciMAD). They all have a capacity of 20 bikes. Initially, each station was set to 10 available bikes (thus, 10 empty slots too). We set four entry points. The location of those elements is shown in Fig. 3. We set a maximum of two failed attempts to rent or book a bike before leaving the system without using it.

In order to test the effect of a balancing strategy, we created a simple recommendation system that returns the stations within a range of 600 m to the user's location, sorted by the ratio of available bikes or slots, depending on whether the user wants to hire or return a bike, respectively. The goal of this paper is not proposing a good strategy, we only created one to show the potential of the simulator.

We carried out several experiments with the following types of users (presented in Sect. 3.2): *Uninformed*, *Informed*, *Obedient*, *Informed-R* and *Obedient-R*.

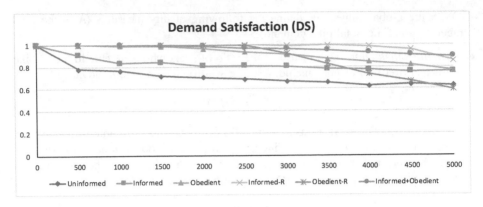

Fig. 4. Demand satisfaction execution results.

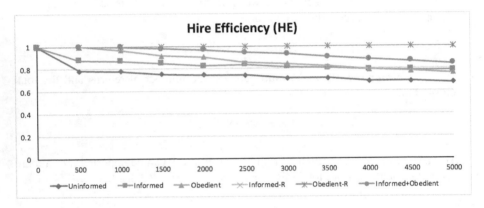

Fig. 5. Hire efficiency execution results. *Informed-R* coincides with *Obedient-R*

In order to compare the influence of the balancing strategy, we executed configurations with users of only one type in each simulation, as well as a combination of *Informed* and *Obedient* (50% of each). In order to have more precise comparison, users were generated at the same location and time for all configurations, i.e. users were generated once and stored in a file, which was loaded in every experiment.

Figure 4 shows the results of demand satisfaction (DS) for different number of users. As expected, fleet performance with *Uninformed* users is the worst of all cases. Tests with *Obedient* users outperform *Informed* since the use of a balancing strategy reduces the number of times that stations get empty. When users make reservations they get bikes at stations more frequently up to the fleet becomes highly saturated (3000 users), where *Obedient-R* starts declining. The reason is that stations assigned by the recommender are farther than usual so they keep bikes occupied (used+reserved) longer times thus other users cannot take them. However, *Informed-R* does not suffer that effect since they always go to the closer station. Hire efficiency (HE) is shown in Fig. 5. The results are in line with DS. As expected, users that make reservations always hire bikes.

5 Conclusion

In this paper we have presented a bike sharing system simulator. We described its architecture in detail and carried out some experiments so as to show the type of results that can be obtained. Stations of different size and locations can be configured, users with different behaviors can be randomly generated everywhere in a map following different probability distributions, simulation results can be stored, retrieved, graphically visualized and quality measures are taken for its analysis.

The architecture design allowed us to separate the configuration from the simulation execution, and the latter from the visualization and analysis. Thus, the simulator can generate users or load them from a file. Likewise, the visualization interface or data analysis tool can load previously stored simulation histories.

The simulator can be used with different objectives. On one hand, it can be used to assess a specific bike-sharing system infrastructure (station locations, size, etc.) before deploying it by testing how the proposed infrastructure behaves to a given expected demand. On the other hand, different incentive based strategies can be implemented and evaluated.

Currently we are working on creating graphical interfaces to assist users to create configurations. Other future lines related to the simulator include adding further quality measures (e.g. time a station is empty, extra distance walking by users, etc.). In addition, we plan to work on designing incentive based algorithms and test them with the simulator.

Acknowledgments. Work partially supported by the Autonomous Region of Madrid (grant "MOSI-AGIL-CM" (S2013/ICE-3019) co-funded by EU Structural Funds FSE and FEDER), project "SURF" (TIN2015-65515-C4-4-R (MINECO/FEDER)) funded by the Spanish Ministry of Economy and Competitiveness, and through the Excellence Research Group GES2ME (Ref. 30VCPIGI05) co-funded by URJC-Santander Bank.

References

1. Pal, A., Zhang, Y.: Free-floating bike sharing: solving real-life large-scale static rebalancing problems. Transp. Res. Part C Emerg. Technol. **80**, 92–116 (2017)
2. Erdoğan, G., Battarra, M., Calvo, R.W.: An exact algorithm for the static rebalancing problem arising in bicycle sharing systems. Eur. J. Oper. Res. **245**(3), 667–679 (2015)
3. Forma, I.A., Raviv, T., Tzur, M.: A 3-step math heuristic for the static repositioning problem in bike-sharing systems. Transp. Res. Part B Methodol. **71**, 230–247 (2015)
4. Contardo, C., Morency, C., Rousseau, L.M.: Balancing a dynamic public bike-sharing system. Technical report, vol. 4. CIRRELT (2012)
5. O'Mahony, E., Shmoys, D.B.: Data analysis and optimization for (citi) bike sharing. In: Proceedings of the Twenty-Ninth AAAI Conference on Artificial Intelligence (AAAI 2015), pp. 687–694. AAAI Press (2015)
6. Schuijbroek, J., Hampshire, R.C., Van Hoeve, W.J.: Inventory rebalancing and vehicle routing in bike sharing systems. Eur. J. Oper. Res. **257**(3), 992–1004 (2017)

7. Chemla, D., Meunier, F., Pradeau, T., Calvo, R.W., Yahiaoui, H.: Self-service bike sharing systems: simulation, repositioning, pricing (2013). https://hal.archives-ouvertes.fr/hal-00824078

8. Fricker, C., Gast, N.: Incentives and regulations in bike-sharing systems with stations of finite capacity. arXiv preprint arXiv:12011178 (2012)

9. Pfrommer, J., Warrington, J., Schildbach, G., Morari, M.: Dynamic vehicle redistribution and online price incentives in shared mobility systems. IEEE Trans. Intel. Transp. Syst. **15** (4), 1567–1578 (2014)

10. Waserhole, A., Jost, V.: Pricing in vehicle sharing systems: optimization in queuing networks with product forms OSP 2012. <hal-00751744v5> (2014)

11. Romero, J.P., Moura, J.L., Ibeas, A., Alonso, B.: A simulation tool for bicycle sharing systems in multimodal networks. Transp. Plan. Technol. **38**(6), 646–663 (2015)

12. Reiss, S., Bogenberger, K.: Optimal bike fleet management by smart relocation methods: Combining an operator-based with an user-based relocation strategy. In: IEEE 19th International Conference on Intelligent Transportation Systems (ITSC), pp. 2613–2618 (2016)

PAAMS Workshop MAS&S

Actors Based Agent Modelling and Simulation

Giulio Angiani[✉], Paolo Fornacciari, Gianfranco Lombardo,
Agostino Poggi, and Michele Tomaiuolo

Department of Engineering and Architecture,
University of Parma, Parco Area delle Scienze 181A, 43124 Parma, Italy
giulio.angiani@unipr.it
http://www.dia.unipr.it

Abstract. Agent-based modeling and simulation are some powerful techniques that are widely used with success for analyzing complex and emergent phenomena in many research and application areas. Many different reasons are behind the success of such techniques, among which an important mention goes to the availability of a great variety of software tools, that ease the development of models, as well as the execution of simulations and the analysis of results. However, the agent models provided by such tools do not offer the features of the computational agents found in multi-agent systems or distributed artificial intelligence techniques. Therefore, it is difficult to use such tools to model complex systems defined by autonomous, proactive and social entities. This paper presents an actor software library, called ActoDeS, for the development of concurrent and distributed systems, and shows how it can be a suitable mean for building flexible and scalable ABMS applications.

Keywords: Agent Based Modeling and Simulation · Actor model
Distributed simulation · Crowd simulation · Cellular automata simulation

1 Introduction

Agent-based modeling and simulation (ABMS) has been and is widely used with success for studying complex and emergent phenomena in many research and application areas, including agriculture, biomedical analysis, ecology, engineering, sociology, market analysis, artificial life, social studies, and others fields. Such studies are possible thanks to the availability of several tools and libraries that support the development of ABMS applications. Moreover, the availability of large-scale, dynamic, and heterogeneous networks of computational resources and the advent of multi-cores computers allow the development of high performance and scalable computationally intensive ABMS applications. As a matter of fact, such applications are able to manage very large and dynamic models, whose computational needs (in space and time) can be difficult to satisfy by a single machine.

The success and the diffusion of ABMS techniques is also due to the availability of software tools that ease the development of models, the execution of simulations and the analysis of results (see, for example, Mason [1], NetLogo [2], and Repast [3]). However, the limit of such tools is that their agent models show a very limited use of the features offered by the computational agents found in multi-agent systems or distributed artificial

© Springer International Publishing AG, part of Springer Nature 2018
J. Bajo et al. (Eds.): PAAMS 2018 Workshops, CCIS 887, pp. 443–455, 2018.
https://doi.org/10.1007/978-3-319-94779-2_38

intelligence techniques [4]. Therefore, modeling some kinds of problem that, for example, require complex interaction among agents, could become very difficult. Moreover, all the most known and used ABMS tools have been initially designed for the execution of simulations on a single machine and, only in a second step, they were extended for supporting distributed simulations (see, for example, D-Mason [5] and HLA_AC-TOR_REPAST [6]). It is worth noting that such extensions show a limitation in terms of reusability. In fact, the code of agents defined for a standalone execution must be modified in order to gain suitable implementations to be used in a distributed simulation.

In this paper we present an actor based software library, called ActoDeS, that provides the suitable features for simplifying the development of scalable and efficient agent based models and simulations. The next section discusses the use and the advantages of using actors in ABMS applications. Section 3 introduces the features of ActoDeS. Section 4 shows the advantages of using this software library for ABMS applications. Section 5 presents the use of ActoDeS for developing a simple ABMS application. Section 6 presents the experimentation of ActoDeS. Finally, Sect. 7 concludes the paper by discussing its main features and the directions for future work.

2   Actors for Agent Based Modelling and Simulation

Actors [7] are autonomous concurrent objects, which interact with other actors by exchanging asynchronous messages and which, in response of an incoming message, can perform some tasks, namely, sending messages to other actors, creating new actors, and designating a new behavior for processing the following messages the actor will receive.

Actors have the suitable features for defining agent models that can be used in ABMS applications and for modeling the computational agents found in MAS and DAI systems [8]. In fact, actors and computational agents share certain characteristics: (i) both react to external stimuli (i.e., they are reactive), (ii) both are self-contained, self-regulating, and self-directed, (i.e., they are autonomous), and (iii) both interact through asynchronous messages and such messages are the basis for their coordination and cooperation (i.e., they are social). Moreover, the use of messages for exchanging state information decouples the code of agents. In fact, agents do not need to access directly to the code of the other agents (i.e., their methods) to get information about them, and so the modification of the code of a type of agent should cause smaller modifications in the code of the other types of agent. Finally, the use of actors simplifies the development of real computational agents in domains where, for example, they need to coordinate themselves or cooperate through direct interactions.

Different researchers propose the use of actors for agent based simulation. For example, Jang and Agha [9] proposed an actor-based software infrastructure, called adaptive actor architecture, to support the construction of large-scale agent-based simulations, by exploiting distributed computing techniques to efficiently distribute agents across a distributed network of computers. In particular, this software infrastructure uses some optimizing techniques in order to reduce the amount of exchanged data among nodes and to support dynamic agent distribution and search. Cicirelli et al. [6] propose the use of actors for distributing Repast simulations. In particular, they defined a software infrastructure that allows: the migration of agents, a location transparent naming, and an efficient communication. This architecture allows the decomposition of a large system into sub-systems (theatres), each hosting a collection of application actors, that can be allocated on different computational nodes.

3 ActoDeS

ActoDeS (Actor Development System) is a software library for the development of concurrent and distributed systems, implemented by using the Java language. It takes advantage of concurrent objects (from here called actors), derived from the actor model [7], and of preexistent Java software libraries and solutions for supporting concurrency and distribution. The development of a standalone or distributed application consists in the definition of the behaviors assumed by its actors and its configuration. In particular, ActoDeS allows to guarantee some or others execution attributes of an application (e.g., performance, reliability, and scalability of the configuration) by using different implementations of actors and runtime components. Moreover, the deployment of an application on a distributed architecture is simplified because an actor can move to another computational node and can transparently communicate with remote actors.

In ActoDeS, an application is defined by a set of actors that interact by exchanging asynchronous messages. Actors can send messages only to known actors, i.e., actors of which they know the addresses. There are two-way for an actor to know another actor address: the second actor was created by the first one, or the address of the second actor was sent to the first one from other actors who know it. After their creation, actors can change several times their behaviors until they kill themselves.

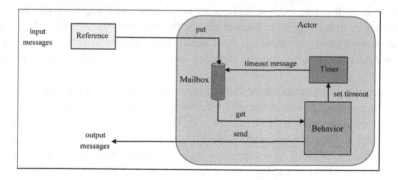

Fig. 1. Agent architecture.

Each behavior has the main duty of processing the incoming messages that match some message patterns. Therefore, if an unexpected message arrives, then the actor mailbox maintains it until a behavior will be able to process it, or a behavior kills the actor. The processing of the incoming messages is performed through some handlers, called cases. In response to a message, within such cases, an actor can send other messages, create new actors, change its local state or its behavior, set a timeout within receiving a new message and finally kill the actor. In particular, when a timeout fires, the actor sends automatically a timeout message to itself and the corresponding case is executed. Figure 1 shows a graphical representation of the architecture of an actor.

In ActoDeS, addresses, messages and message patterns are all instances of some Java classes. An actor address is represented by a reference object that acts as both system-wide unique identifier and local and remote proxy of an actor. A message is an object that contains a set of fields, maintaining the typical header information and the message content. Finally, a message pattern is an object defined as a combination of constraints on the value of some message fields.

Depending on the complexity of the application and on the availability of computing and communication resources, a system can be distributed on one or more actor spaces. Each actor space corresponds to a Java virtual machine and so a system distributed on some actor spaces can be deployed on one or more computational nodes. An actor space acts as "container" for a set of actors and provides them the necessary services for their execution. In particular, an actor space performs its tasks through three main runtime components, (i.e., controller, dispatcher and registry) and through two runtime actors (i.e., the executor and the service provider).

The controller is a runtime component that has a duty to manage the activities of an actor space. In particular, it configures and starts the runtime components and the actors of the application and manages its activities until the end of its execution.

The dispatcher is a runtime component that is meant to support the communication with the other actor spaces of the application. In particular, it creates connections to/from the other actor spaces, manages the reception of messages from the input connections, and delivers messages through the output connections. This component can be configured by using different communication technologies (the current release of the software supports ActiveMQ, ZeroMQ, MINA and RMI).

The registry is a runtime component that supports actor creation and message passing. In fact, it creates the references of new actors and supports the delivery of those messages that come from remote actors, by mapping the remote reference onto the local reference of the message final destination. Figure 2 shows an application based on two actor spaces and the delivery of messages between local and remote actors.

The executor is a runtime actor that manages the execution of the actors of an actor space and may create its initial actor(s). Of course, the duties of an executor depend on the type of implementation of its actors and, in particular, on the type of threading solutions used in their implementation. In fact, an actor can have its own thread (from here named active actors), or it can share a single thread with the other actors of the actor space (from here named passive actors). Hence, while the executors of active actors (called coordinators) delegate the large part of their work to the Java runtime environment, the executors of passive actors (called schedulers) must completely manage their execution by initializing them and by cyclically calling their method that performs a step of their execution.

The service provider is a runtime actor that offers the possibility of performing new kinds of actions (e.g., to broadcast or multicast a message and to move from an actor space to another one) to the actors of an application by providing them a set of additional services that they can employ by sending a message to the service provider.

4 ActoDeS for Agent Based Modelling and Simulation

The features of the actor model and the flexibility of its implementations make ActoDeS a suitable mean for building flexible and scalable ABMS applications. In fact, the presence of different actor implementations allows developers to choose one or another implementation depending on the features of the application domain. More-over, the availability of different executor implementations and the possibility of their specialization allow a correct and efficient scheduling of the agents in application domains that require different scheduling algorithms [10]. Finally, ABMS application developers need only to define the behaviors of the agents acting in their application.; In fact, when launching simulations with different actor and/or executor implementa-tions, or simulations which involve distributed actors among many actor spaces, the code of such behaviors does not require any modification.

ActoDeS provides an efficient implementation of broadcast and multicast; this feature is very important because agents must often diffuse information about their state to the other agents of the application. In particular, in our spatial models all the entities are actors (i.e., the environment is defined by a set of actors) and each actor diffuses its spatial information through a message at each step of the simulation. Of course, if the diffusion of such messages were implemented by a point-to-point interaction then the cost of communication would become intolerable also with a limited number of actors. However, ActoDeS provides an actor implementation, called "shared actor", that allows to avoid this kind of problem: all the actors of the application share a single mailbox that maintains all the messages sent in the previous and in the current simu-lation step. An actor can read only the messages of the previous step that are: broadcast messages, point-to-point messages of which it is the destination, and multicast mes-sages which are directed to a group of which it is a member. Moreover, this kind of solution allows to avoid the burden of maintaining a copy of the current and the next environment in order to guarantee that agents decide their actions with the same information. This is usually needed in other ABMS platforms [10]).

ActoDeS allows the management of simulations involving large number of actors. In fact, its simulation schedulers (i.e., its executors) are actors and therefore they can exchange messages. Hence, we implemented some distributed simulation algorithms by defining some executors that are able to synchronize their activities through the exchange of messages. ActoDeS also provides an executor implementation which can remove an actor from the scheduling list, store it in a persistent storage and insert it again in the scheduling list. This kind of executor is useful in the application domains that involve large number of entities and when an important part of them is active only in some parts of the simulation (e.g., the simulation of a social network). In fact, in these conditions the cost of removing, storing and adding actors can be easily balanced by the reduction of the number of actors scheduled by the executor. This reduction guarantees a smaller use of computational resources and runtime memory.

Two important features that an ABMS tool should provide are the availability of graphical tools for visualizing the evolution of simulations and tools for analyzing data obtained from simulations. ActoDes does not provide tools for the visualization of simulations and the analysis of their results, but it provides a logging service that allows the recording on files and the streaming of the Java objects describing the relevant actions of an actor (i.e., its initialization, reception, sending and processing of messages, creation of actors, change of behavior, and its shutdown). Therefore, the development of a tool for performing one of these two tasks is completely decoupled from the definition of the model and the execution of the simulation, and it requires only the processing of the logging objects generated by the simulation.

5   A Simple Modeling and Simulation Example

To show how a developer can use ActoDeS for modeling and simulating a system, we present an example that describes the "game of life" cellular automata model [11] and its simulation.

```java
public final class Alive extends Behavior {
  // Constants and instance variables definition.
  public Living(final Set<Reference> n) {
    // Variable initialization.
  }
  public void initialize(final Binder b) {
    Case c = (m) -> {
      this.alives++;
      return null;
    };
    b.bind(MessagePattern.contentPattern(new IsEqual<Object>(State.ALIVE)), c);
    c = (m) -> {
      if ((this.alives < MIN) && (this.alives > MAX)) {
        return new Dead(this.neighborhood);
      }
      else {
        this.alives = 0;
        this.neighborhood.forEach((n) -> send(n, State.ALIVE));
        return null;
      }
    };
    b.bind(CYCLEPATTERN, c);
  }
}
```

Fig. 2. The "Alive" behavior.

In the "game of life" cellular automata model, each cell interacts with its neighbor cells (usually identified by the Moore's neighborhood) and moves between an "alive" and a "dead" state on the basis of the "alive" neighbors. Therefore, each cell can be represented by an actor that moves between an "alive" and a "dead" behavior and the "alive" actors send an "alive" messages to the actors in their neighborhood at each simulation step. Figure 2 shows the code of the "alive" behavior; in particular, it defines two cases: the first processes the messages coming from the "alive" neighbors and the second processes the message notifying the end of the current simulation step coming from the executor.

To complete the model and to perform the simulation, what is still missing is the description of how the actors, representing the cellular automaton, are created and of how an actor gets the references of the actors defining its neighborhood.

```java
public final class AutomataBuilder extends Builder {
  // Constants and instance variables definition.
  public AutomataBuilder(final int w, final int h, final Map<CellFactory, Double> p) {
    // Variable initialization.
  }
  private class Data {
  // Instance variables definition.
    public Data(final Reference r, final Set<Reference> n) {
      // Variable initialization.
    }
  }
  public void build() {
    Data[][] actors = new Data[this.width][this.height];
    // Choose a cell factory on the basis of its probability.
    Chooser<CellFactory> chooser = new Chooser<>(this.pairs);
    for (int x = 0; x < this.width; x++) {
      for (int y = 0; y < this.height; y++) {
        CellFactory factory = chooser.choose();
        Set<Reference> neighbors = new HashSet<>();
        Reference r = actor(factory.create(neighbors));
        actors[x][y]= new Data(r, neighbors);
      }
    }
    for (int x = 0; x < this.width; x++) {
      for (int y = 0; y < this.height; y++) {
        setNeighbors(x, y, actors);
      }
    }
  }
  private void setNeighbors(final int x, final int y, final Data[][] d) {
    // Its code finds the neighbors for the actor with x and y coordinates.
  }
}
```

Fig. 3. The builder of the actors defining the cellular automata.

```java
public static void main(final String[] v) {
  int width  = 1000;
  int height = 1000;
  final Map<CellFactory, Double> pairs = new HashMap<>();
  pairs.put((n) -> new Alive(n), 0.3);
  pairs.put((n) -> new Dead(n), 0.7);
  final int length = 1000;
  Configuration c = Controller.INSTANCE.getConfiguration();
  c.setFilter(Logger.LOGACTIONS);
  c.addWriter(new ConsoleWriter());
  c.setExecutor(new CycleSimulator(
      new AutomataBuilder(width, height, pairs), new Length(length)));
  Controller.INSTANCE.run();
}
```

Fig. 4. The main method executing the cellular automata simulation.

As introduced above, the initial set of actors of an application is created by the executor. Of course, the types of actor to be created depend on the type of application, to do it, an executor accepts as parameter either the behavior of the initial actor or a builder object that creates the initial set of actors. ActoDeS, provides a set of builders and, in particular, a builder for creating 2D cellular automata that receives as parameters: the width and the height of the cellular automaton, the possible initial behaviors of the actors and the probability that an actor assume one of such behaviors as its initial behavior. Moreover, this builder, after the creation of the actors, assigns the set of the references of the neighbors to each initial behavior. Figure 3 provides a partial view the code of such a builder and Fig. 4 shows the code of the main method running the simulation.

6   Experimentation

We experimented and are experimenting the use of actors in different ABMS application domains. In particular, the main activities are related to the modeling and simulation of: (i) the crowd behavior in different building evacuation scenarios, (ii) the algorithms for the management of social and peer-to-peer networks [12, 13], (iii) the most known distributed and agent-based coordination algorithms (in this case, it is a mainly a teaching activity related to a "distributed systems" master course), and (iv) the most known cellular automata models (e.g., the game of life [11], the pursuit problem [14] and the traffic modelling [15]). In the following, we will discuss our work on crowd simulation and describe the algorithms we defined for performing distributed crowd and cellular automata simulations.

6.1   Crowd Simulation

The experimentation of the crowd simulation for building evacuation has be done in a 2D continuous space where pedestrians try to reach a meeting point outside the building by following either other pedestrians or a set of alternative paths towards the different meeting points. Both pedestrians and the environment are defined through actors, and, as introduced above, to reduce the message passing overhead, the simulations are performed by using the "shared actor" implementation.

The actors representing the pedestrians are defined by using the boid model [16]. A simulation is defined by a sequence of simulation steps. At each simulation step, each pedestrian receives some messages containing information about the environment and about the state (i.e., position, movement direction and speed) of other pedestrians. Then, it processes the messages, which represent entities within a certain small neighborhood around themselves, through a set of boid rules. By combining the results of the rules, it updates its state, and, finally, informs the other pedestrians about its new state by sending them a broadcast message. Moreover, when the pedestrian enter in the area of influence of a meeting point, then it moves to an "arrive" behavior that drives it to its final position. The simulation ends when all pedestrian actors run the "arrive" behavior. Also in this case, the behaviors of the pedestrian actors provide two cases: the first one processes the messages coming from other actors of the application and the second one updates the state of the actor and broadcasts it, when the actor receives a message from the executor that notifies the end of the current simulation step.

The environment is defined by actors that represent circular and polygonal obstacles, points of the paths for exiting from the building, and meeting points. In particular, circular obstacles broadcast messages containing their position and radius, polygonal obstacles broadcast messages containing a set of points that discretize their edges, path points broadcast messages containing their position and the direction towards the next point and, finally, meeting points broadcast messages containing their position. In this case, the behaviors of the environment actors provide a single case that broadcasts the actor state information, when the actor receives a message from the executor that notifies the end of the current execution step. Figure 5 shows a graphical view of a step of a crowd simulation, built from the logging data of the simulation. In particular, yellow circles represent the path points, the magenta star represents a meeting point, green and sky blue shapes represent pedestrians; sky blue pedestrians are the ones that moved to the "arrive" behavior.

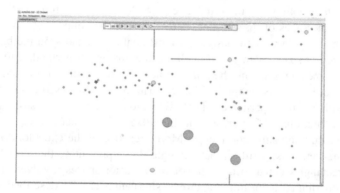

Fig. 5. A graphical view of a step of a crowd simulation. (Color figure online)

The experimentation was performed with different set of boid rules and different environments. In particular, the experimentation shows how the use of boid rules allows obtaining intelligent behaviors without using complex AI algorithms. However, the "calibration" of the model (i.e., the definition of the correct weights of the boid rules) often requires the execution of several simulations to obtain a successful evacuation where pedestrian actors both do not collide among them or with obstacles and do not lose time inside the building. Regarding the implementation of such simulation models, the definition of different kinds of pedestrian and environment actors is pretty easy; instead, the definition of their initial state is a heavy work, of course, when we want to model a complex building structure. However, ActoDeS allows to save an "image" of an application during its execution and we can use this image as initial point of another simulation.

6.2 Distributed Simulation

The modeling and simulation of complex problems can require the use of large number of actors that may determinate unacceptable simulation times, or the impossibility to run the simulation on one of the available computational nodes. In such cases, the availability of distributed algorithms and, of course, of an adequate number of computational nodes can help performing simulations. We are working on the definition and implementation of distributed simulation algorithms and, in particular, we defined two prototypes of conservative distributed algorithms for 2D crowd and cellular automata simulations. These two prototypes do not require modifications on the code of the actors used for the standalone simulations, as explained before. They require, instead, new types of executors. In fact, they must support the coordination among the executors of the actor spaces involved in a simulation, in order to correctly part the actors in the actor spaces, and to synchronize the execution of the simulation steps. The executors for crowd simulations need to move some pedestrian actors to another actor space, when they exit from their management 2D space. Moreover, they need to propagate the messages of the "border" actors near to the contiguous actor spaces.

In both the cases, actors are assigned to different actor spaces on the basis of their position in the 2D space or in the 2D cellular automaton. In particular, to reduce the propagation of messages among the different actor spaces, each actor space manages a rectangular area, which is defined by an algorithm that divides the global space in rectangles with minimal perimeters [17]. Executors manage the distribution in two phases: in the first phase they create and initialize all the other actors; in the second phase they execute the simulation steps. Moreover, one of the executors of a simulation, called master, must partition the rectangle that representing the global space in a number of rectangles equal to the number of the actor spaces involved in the simulation. The distributed algorithm for crowd simulation can be described by the following steps:

1. Master executor partitions the global rectangle and sends a rectangle to each executor (including itself).
2. Executors create all the pedestrian and environment actors positioned in its rectangle and create an additional copy of the environment actors that are managed by other actor spaces, but that can influence the behavior of the local pedestrian actors (this solution removes the need of propagating the "border" messages coming through environment actors).
3. Executors repeat until the end of the simulation:
   3.1. Perform an execution step of all its actors.
   3.2. Propagate the "border" messages to the other actor spaces.
   3.3. Move the pedestrian actors to another actor space when they exit from the local rectangle.
   3.4. Send a synchronization message to the other actor spaces and wait for the corresponding messages from the other actor spaces.

The distributed algorithms for cellular automata simulations treats 2D models where cells have a Moore neighborhood. Therefore, in a distributed simulation, the cost of the propagation of "border" messages is reduced and it is not a duty of the executors:

The executors exchange the references of the actors of the border cells for completing their neighborhood and then each actor can send messages to the neighbor actors without taking care if they are local or remote actors. In particular, the distributed algorithm for cellular automata simulation can be described by the following steps:

1. Master executor partitions the global rectangle and sends a rectangle to each executor (including itself).
2. Executors create all the actors representing the cells positioned in its rectangle.
3. Executors build the neighborhoods with the appropriate local actor references.
4. Executors ask to the other actor spaces the references for completing the neighborhoods of their actors that represent the border cells and send the references to complete the neighborhoods of the other actor spaces.
5. Executors repeat until the end of the simulation:
   5.1. Send a synchronization message to the other actor spaces and wait for the corresponding messages from the other actor spaces.
   5.2. Perform an execution step of all their actors.

7 Conclusions

This paper presented a software library, called ActoDeS, which allows the development of efficient, large, actor based applications by taking advantage of the actor model and by providing different implementations of the components supporting their execution. In particular, the library described in this paper is an evolution of a previous implementation of ActoDeS [18] which enriches the actor model with new functionalities and reduces the needed amount of the code for defining the behaviors of the actors.

ActoDeS has been extended and experimented with success in the development of ABMS applications. Of course, its current implementation does not provide all the features of the most known ABMS platforms (i.e., NetLogo, Mason and Repast); however, the use of the actor model for the definition of agents allows simplifying the development of non-trivial applications where the management of concurrent activities and the interaction among agents is of primary importance. Moreover, the implementation of some solutions that: (i) reduce the overhead of the diffusion of broadcast and multicast messages, (ii) avoid the burden of managing idle actors, and (iii) distribute actors on some actor spaces, allowing its use for simulating large and complex systems where each node can run millions of actors.

Current and future research activities are and will be dedicated to the extension of the ActoDeS library to provide new ABMS functionalities, to continue the activities in crowd, social and peer-to-peer network simulation taking in account some new relevant works, e.g., [19], to simplify the code through the use of a domain specific language [20], and to use ABMS techniques for modeling and simulating distributed systems [21], social networks [22], collaborative work [23] and security infrastructures [24].

References

1. Luke, S., Cioffi-Revilla, C., Panait, L., Sullivan, K., Balan, G.: MASON: a multi-agent simulation environment. Simulation **82**(7), 517–527 (2005)
2. Tisue, S., Wilensky, U.: Netlogo: a simple environment for modeling complexity. In: Proceedings of ICCS 2004, Boston, MA, USA, pp. 16–21 (2004)
3. North, M.J., Collier, N., Vos, J.: Experiences in creating three implementations of the repast agent modeling toolkit. ACM Trans. Model. Comput. Simul. **16**(1), 1–25 (2006)
4. Drogoul, A., Vanbergue, D., Meurisse, T.: Multi-agent based simulation: where are the agents? In: Sichman, J.S., Bousquet, F., Davidsson, P. (eds.) MABS 2002. LNCS (LNAI), vol. 2581, pp. 1–15. Springer, Heidelberg (2003). https://doi.org/10.1007/3-540-36483-8_1
5. De Chiara, R., Mancuso, A., Mazzeo, D., Scarano, V., Spagnuolo, C.: Bringing together efficiency and effectiveness in distributed simulations: the experience with D-MASON. Simulation **89**(10), 1236–1253 (2013)
6. Cicirelli, F., Furfaro, A., Giordano, A., Nigro, L.: HLA_ACTOR_REPAST: an approach to distributing repast models for high-performance simulations. Simul. Model. Pract. Theory **19**(1), 283–300 (2011)
7. Agha, G.A.: Actors: a model of concurrent computation in distributed systems (1986)
8. Kafura, D., Briot, J.P.: Actors and agents. IEEE Concurrency **6**(2), 24–29 (1998)
9. Jang, M.W., Agha, G.A.: Agent framework services to reduce agent communication overhead in large-scale agent-based simulations. Simul. Model. Pract. Theory **14**(6), 679–694 (2006)
10. Mathieu P., Yann, S.: Environment updating and agent scheduling policies in agent-based simulators. In: Proceedings of ICAART, pp. 170–175 (2012)
11. Gardner, M.: The fantastic combinations of John Conway's new solitaire game Life. Sci. Am. **223**, 120–123 (1970)
12. Bergenti, F., Franchi, E., Poggi, A.: Agent-based interpretations of classic network models. Comput. Math. Organ. Theory **19**(2), 105–127 (2013)
13. Franchi, E., Poggi, A., Tomaiuolo, M.: Blogracy: a peer-to-peer social network. Int. J. Distrib. Syst. Technol. **7**(2), 37–56 (2016)
14. Benda, M.: On optimal cooperation of knowledge sources: an empirical investigation. Technical report, Boeing Advanced Technology Center (1986)
15. Nagel, K., Wolf, D.E., Wagner, P., Simon, P.: Two-lane traffic rules for cellular automata: a systematic approach. Phys. Rev. E **58**(2), 1425–1437 (1998)
16. Reynolds, C.W.: Flocks, herds and schools: a distributed behavioral model. ACM SIGGRAPH Comput. Graph. **21**(4), 25–34 (1987)
17. Alon, N., Kleitman, D.J.: Partitioning a rectangle into small perimeter rectangles. Discrete Math. **103**(2), 111–119 (1992)
18. Bergenti, F., Poggi, A., Tomaiuolo, M.: An actor based software framework for scalable applications. In: Fortino, G., Di Fatta, G., Li, W., Ochoa, S., Cuzzocrea, A., Pathan, M. (eds.) IDCS 2014. LNCS, vol. 8729, pp. 26–35. Springer, Cham (2014). https://doi.org/10.1007/978-3-319-11692-1_3
19. Pax, R., Pavón, J.: Agent architecture for crowd simulation in indoor environments. J. Ambient Intell. Humaniz. Comput. **8**(2), 205–212 (2017)
20. Bergenti, F., Iotti, E., Monica, S., Poggi, A.: Agent-oriented model-driven development for JADE with the JADEL programming language. Comput. Lang. Syst. Struct. **50**, 142–158 (2017)

21. Negri, A., Poggi, A., Tomaiuolo, M., Turci, P.: Dynamic grid tasks composition and distribution through agents. Concurrency Comput. Pract. Exp. **18**(8), 875–885 (2005)
22. Franchi, E., Poggi, A., Tomaiuolo, M.: Social media for online collaboration in firms and organizations. Int. J. Inf. Syst. Model. Des. **7**(1), 18–31 (2016)
23. Bergenti, B., Poggi, A.: An agent-based approach to manage negotiation protocols in flexible CSCW systems: In: Proceedings of 4th International Conference on Autonomous Agents, pp. 267–268 (2000)
24. Poggi, A., Tomaiuolo, M., Vitaglione, G.: A security infrastructure for trust management in multi-agent systems. In: Falcone, R., Barber, S., Sabater-Mir, J., Singh, Munindar P. (eds.) TRUST 2003-2004. LNCS (LNAI), vol. 3577, pp. 162–179. Springer, Heidelberg (2005). https://doi.org/10.1007/11532095_10

Agent Based Modelling and Simulation of an Auction Market for Airport Slots Allocation

José Alberto Araúzo[1]($\boxtimes$), Félix Antonio Villafáñez[1],
David Poza García[1], Javier Pajares[1], and Juan Pavón[2]

[1] INSISOC Group, Universidad de Valladolid, Campus Miguel Delibes,
Paseo de Belén s/n, 47011 Valladolid, Spain
{arauzo, poza}@eii.uva.es, villafafelix@yahoo.es,
pajares@insisoc.org
[2] GRASIA, Universidad Complutense de Madrid, Ciudad Universitaria,
c/Profesor José García Santesmases 9, 28040 Madrid, Spain
jpavon@fdi.ucm.es

Abstract. Airport slot allocation is a combinatorial allocation problem involving different complex and autonomous systems. Nowadays, airport slots are allocated in a two-stage process: primary allocation is performed according to a set of administrative rules and for each airport independently, while secondary allocation is based on trading mechanisms. Several studies have raised inefficiencies in these processes. To enhance the airport slot allocation process we use an auction-based market. More specifically, we present an airport slot allocation mechanism based on a price-setting auction that has been implemented and evaluated by means of Agent-Based Modelling (ABM) and simulation techniques. The solutions obtained using our approach are compared and assessed with the ones obtained using linear programing, showing that market mechanisms can be an efficient alternative to the current administrative procedure.

Keywords: Agent-Based Modelling · Simulation · Air transport management
Airport slot allocation · Combinatorial auction

1 Introduction

Airlines that intend to fly to/from 'coordinated' airports need to obtain time slots (from now on referred to simply 'slots') for them, where a time slot is a permission given by a coordinator to use the full range of airport infrastructure necessary to operate an air service at a coordinated airport on a specific date and time for the purpose of landing or take-off. Airport coordinators allocate these slots in a two-stage process: primary and secondary slot allocation. The first one produces the main allocation; later, the second one allows the transfer of slots among airlines, subject to the coordinator's approval, so that they can try to improve what they got in the primary allocation.

The primary allocation of slots in European airports is an administrative process governed by the EU Regulation 95/93 [1], based on the global principles defined by the IATA (International Air Transport Association) Worldwide Slot Guidelines [2].

© Springer International Publishing AG, part of Springer Nature 2018
J. Bajo et al. (Eds.): PAAMS 2018 Workshops, CCIS 887, pp. 456–467, 2018.
https://doi.org/10.1007/978-3-319-94779-2_39

According to these regulations, primary allocation applies a series of criteria mainly based on historical precedence (the so called "grandfather rights").

The grandfathering system has important advantages: it reduces transaction costs and allows airlines long term planning operations. However, it prevents the competition by creating barriers to entry; regardless of the insufficient provisions for new entrants, and also, it is not an efficient system from the economic point of view [3].

In order to overcome the limitations of the grandfathering systems we propose a price-setting auction based market to solve the primary allocation in a single airport scenario, showing its application to different scenarios and comparing the results obtained with those applying linear programming optimisation techniques.

For this purpose, Sect. 2 presents several alternative approaches for primary and secondary slot allocation, Sect. 3 describes the process of modelling a combinatorial price-setting auction for the primary allocation, Sect. 4 presents simulation results, and Sect. 5 summarises the main conclusions of the study.

2 Primary Airport Slot Allocation Mechanisms

Several alternative approaches for this primary allocation have been proposed in the last years, and they can be classified in two big branches: mathematical optimisation techniques and market-based mechanisms.

Mathematical optimisation techniques use exact [4, 5] or heuristic [6] algorithms to provide the best (or close to the best) solution achievable for a pre-established problem definition, scope and constraints [7]. In [4], Zografos et al. develop an optimisation model implementing the existing rules and constraints to accommodate slot allocation to the airlines' preferences. In [5] we can see an integer linear programming model for optimisation of the airport slot allocation process on the European scale, whereas [6] provides a comparison between a local search heuristic and an algorithm based on an integer linear programming model. But in these approaches, the need for a complete specification of the problem makes them hard to apply in the real world since: (i) airlines may not be in favour of disclosing strategic information; and (ii) they might not be able to express it correctly and precisely in mathematical terms.

As an alternative, market-based mechanisms, especially those based on auctions, should provide high quality results without the need for any participant to disclose private information. Markets are based on supply and demand, which are ultimately founded on economic factors, so they can provide information about how valuable a slot is in economic terms. Besides, a market where the participants maximise their surplus is usually associated with a maximisation of the social welfare [8–10].

Among the market approaches, Rassenti et al. [11] propose a sealed-bid combinatorial auction for the allocation of airport time slots, where the airlines can submit various contingency bids for flight-compatible combinations of slots. [12, 13] propose a mechanism for slot allocation that enables airlines to pay for delay reduction or receive compensation for delay increase. Moreover, Pertuiset et al. use in [14] a Vickrey–Clarke–Groves auction to propose a primary market of slots at congested airports.

Due to the successful implementation of the price-setting auctions in other types of resource allocation problems such as multi-project scheduling [15] or job shop scheduling [16], we propose a price-setting auction based market [17, 18] to solve the primary allocation in a single airport scenario.

3   Auction Model for Airport Slot Allocation

In this paper we propose an iterative price-setting auction to solve the allocation of arrival and departure slots at a single airport, where the available number of these slots is limited according to the airport capacity constraints. Our model adds more realistic features than previous auction proposals in this field. Thus, we add rolling capacity constraints [4] to represent the real allocation conditions, and also, we consider the possibility of reject flights if theirs utilities are low and the demand exceeds the airport capacity

3.1   Formal Problem Formulation

We propose a similar problem to the one proposed by Zografos in [4], but furthermore, we include the possibility to reject flights when slots are not available to schedule all flights, or when the cost of scheduling a flight is higher than its gross utility. Gross utility is the utility that is obtained by the flight when it is scheduled in the best way as possible. This feature allows to apply the model in cases in which the demand exceeds the airport capacity and some flights must be allocated in other airports.

We assume that there are M flights that need to reserve two slots each at certain airport, one for landing (arrival) and one for taking-off (departure). For each flight m, we can define a utility function (1), which returns the value that a pair of slots (ta_m, td_m) has for that flight. This utility function is calculated as a gross utility (gu_m) minus a cost due to the deviations between the preferred slots for the flight (tra_m, trd_m) and the ones actually requested (or achieved in the allocation process) (ta_m, td_m).

$$u_m(ta_m, td_m) = gu_m - wa_m|tra_m - ta_m| - wd_m|trd_m - td_{jm}| \tag{1}$$

Where gu_m is the gross utility of flight m, tra_m the preferred slot for the arrival of the flight m, ta_m the allocated slot for the arrival of the flight m, wa_m the penalty cost of the time offset for the arrival slot of flight m, trd_m the preferred slot for the departure of the flight m, td_m the allocated slot for the departure of the flight m, and wd_m the penalty cost of the time offset for the departure slot of flight m.

The airport slot allocation problem can be formulated as a mathematical programing problem (2) in which the total utility (sum of each agent's utility) must be maximised (2.a). We also consider the possibility that the airport's slot constraints do not allow airlines to be able to schedule all their flights. The binary variable δ_m is defined to introduce this issue into the objective function: it takes the value 1 if the flight is scheduled at the airport and 0 otherwise. The formulation implicitly considers a unit of time equal to the slot duration at the airport (called 'coordination interval'). The number of total coordination intervals at the airport is T.

The solution shall satisfy two kinds of constraints: the capacity constraints (2.b–2.d); and the scheduling constraints (2.g) that force that the departure of each flight m shall happen after a minimum turnaround time (tt_m) from its arrival. We have defined three kinds of capacity constraints: the first one for arrivals (2.b), the second one for departures (2.c) and the last one for both (2.d). Furthermore, these three types of capacity constraints can be applied during one or several consecutive coordination time intervals; in the latter case they are referred to as 'rolling constraints'. The number of coordination intervals affected by a rolling constraint is denoted by T_h, where $h = \{1, 2, \ldots H\}$ is a subscript to denote and identify the rolling constraint. If $T_h = 1$ the constraint is referred only to a coordination interval, and therefore it is a standard capacity constraint.

To formulate the capacity constraints, two auxiliary set of binary variables are defined: $\delta a_{\tau m}$, which takes the value 1 when the arrival of the flight m is scheduled in τ and 0 otherwise; and $\delta d_{\tau m}$, which takes the value 1 when the departure of the flight m is scheduled in τ and 0 otherwise. These variables are defined and connected with the variables ta_m, td_m and δ_m by means of the constraints (2.e) and (2.f). The maximum number of operations allowed at each coordination interval t for each constraint h is denoted by ac_{ht} for the arrival slot constraints (2.b), dc_{ht} for the departure slot constraints (2.c) and tc_{ht} for the total slot constraints (2.d).

$$\max_{\overline{ta},\overline{td}} \; f\left(\overline{ta}, \overline{td}, \overline{\delta}\right) = \sum_{m=1}^{M} \delta_m \cdot u_m(ta_m, td_m) \tag{2.a}$$

$$\text{s.t.} \quad \sum_{j=1}^{M} \sum_{\tau=t}^{\min(T-1,t+T_h-1)} \delta a_{\tau m} \leq ac_{ht} \quad \begin{aligned} & h = 1, 2, \cdots, H \\ & t = 0, 1, 2, \ldots, T-1 \end{aligned} \tag{2.b}$$

$$\sum_{m=1}^{M} \sum_{\tau=t}^{\min(T-1,t+T_h-1)} \delta d_{\tau m} \leq dc_{ht} \quad \begin{aligned} & h = 1, 2, \cdots, H \\ & t = 0, 1, 2, \ldots, T-1 \end{aligned} \tag{2.c}$$

$$\sum_{m=1}^{M} \sum_{\tau=t}^{\min(T-1,t+T_h-1)} (\delta a_{\tau m} + \delta d_{\tau m}) \leq tc_{ht} \quad \begin{aligned} & h = 1, 2, \cdots, H \\ & t = 0, 1, 2, \ldots, T-1 \end{aligned} \tag{2.d}$$

$$\delta a_{tm} = \begin{cases} 1 & if \quad ta_m = t \quad and \quad \delta_m = 1 \quad t = 0, 1, \cdots, T-1 \\ 0 & otherwise \quad\quad\quad\quad\quad\quad\quad\quad\quad m = 1, 2, \ldots, M \end{cases} \tag{2.e}$$

$$\delta d_{tm} = \begin{cases} 1 & if \quad td_m = t \quad and \quad \delta_m = 1 \quad t = 0, 1, \cdots, T-1 \\ 0 & otherwise \quad\quad\quad\quad\quad\quad\quad\quad\quad m = 1, 2, \ldots, M \end{cases} \tag{2.f}$$

$$ta_m + tt_m \leq td_m \quad m = 1, 2, \ldots, M \tag{2.g}$$

3.2   Auction Model Design

This section presents the specification of the auction mechanism proposed, an iterative combinatorial price-setting auction, in terms of the triplet I × E × A (Institution, Environment and Agents) [19].

The Institution: Iterative Combinatorial Price-Setting Auction

The proposed iterative combinatorial price-setting auction has the following characteristics and rules [20]:

- As a price-setting auction, the auctioneer varies the prices depending on the difference between supply and demand. The supply is determined by the capacity of the airport involved in the auction, whose profile includes the definition of 'rolling constraints'.
- Several slots can be combined in one request, therefore allowing an airline to bid at the same time for all its preferred slots and preventing the risk of inefficiencies due to the inability to achieve a correspondent slot pair in another airport for a certain slot already obtained before.
- It follows the following iterative process:

  (a) Initial slot prices are communicated to the participants for individual arrival and departure slots separately. These prices can be related to certain default values, economic studies associated to operational costs, or other type of estimations.
  (b) At each iteration, the airlines make their requests for their preferred slots depending on the current prices and their internal objective functions.
  (c) The auctioneer compares the requests with the capacity constraints and modifies the prices of every slot (arrival and departure separately) according to the gradient between them. These new prices are announced and used to repeat the process in the next iteration.
  (d) The process is repeated until the stop criterion is met (maximum number of iterations, an equilibrium situation is reached, etc.).

- The auctioneer analyses the allocation produced by the auction. If there are situations where capacity constraints are still violated, the auctioneer applies a predefined tie-breaker mechanism and proposes alternative allocations that airlines are allowed to accept or reject. In any other case, airlines shall accept the slots they have requested.
- Finally, the auctioneer communicates: (i) to each airline, the slots that have been allocated at every airport; (ii) to each airport, the slots allocated to each airline.

The Environment

The environment for a particular scenario is restricted in terms of number of traders (number of airlines and airports) and number of items (slots), but the economic values and slot prices are not restricted. Generally, total supply (total amount of slots available in the airport in certain time period considered) and demand (total number of slots requested by airlines in the same time period) may not be equal, which may lead to different situations where the same auction institution may produce different outcomes.

The Agents' Behaviour

Agents' behaviour refers to the actions, communications, knowledge and routines each participant exhibit in the system. Agents will be represented and studied by means of Agent-Based Modelling techniques. In our study, we have considered three agents in the system: the airport, the coordinator and the flight agents.

The Airport Agent

It is a 'passive agent', defined only by its attributes and without any capability to initiate a communication process or make any decision. Those attributes represent the capacity constraints, which must be communicated to the coordinator when asked for them. The airport agents will receive their complete schedule with the slots allocated to airlines after the auction process.

The Coordinator Agent

So far, the coordinator's only role is to act as auctioneer and apply the auction's rules to produce a feasible allocation. The coordinator is the airport representative in the auction. He shall communicate with airports to know their capacity constraints and with airlines to inform them about the slot prices and receive their corresponding requests. The coordinator shall not require or disclose any other private information of other agents.

The coordinator shall not favor any airline nor apply any preference; for this purpose, airlines may participate anonymously in the auction. It shall establish prices for arrivals $(pa_t^{i)})$ and departures $(pd_t^{i)})$ in each coordination interval t at the auction round i.

The prices in round i are calculated by adding a set of Lagrange multipliers $(\lambda a_{ht}^{i)}, \lambda d_{ht}^{i)}, \lambda t_{ht}^{i)})$ that are the result to apply the Lagrangian Relaxation technique to every capacity constraints. They are updated every round according to the subgradient method [21]. In this case, the subgradient $(ga_{ht}^{i)}, gd_{ht}^{i)}, gt_{ht}^{i)})$ at round i is defined as the difference between capacity and demand for each capacity constraint ht of arrivals $(ga_{ht}^{i)})$ (3.a), departures $(gd_{ht}^{i)})$ (3.b) or the addition of both $(gt_{ht}^{i)})$ (3.c). In the set of formulas (3), $\delta a_{\tau m}^{i)}$ is equal to 1 if the flight m demands an arrival in the coordination interval τ at round i and 0 otherwise. $\delta a_{\tau m}^{i)}$ denotes the same concept for departures.

$$ga_{ht}^{i)} = \sum_{m=1}^{M} \sum_{\tau=t}^{\min(T-1,t+T_h-1)} \delta a_{\tau m}^{i)} - ac_{ht} \qquad \begin{matrix} h = 1,2,\cdots,H \\ t = 0,1,2,\ldots,T-1 \end{matrix} \qquad (3.a)$$

$$gd_{ht}^{i)} = \sum_{m=1}^{M} \sum_{\tau=t}^{\min(T-1,t+T_h-1)} \delta d_{\tau m}^{i)} - dc_{ht} \qquad \begin{matrix} h = 1,2,\cdots,H \\ t = 0,1,2,\ldots,T-1 \end{matrix} \qquad (3.b)$$

$$gt_{ht}^{i)} = \sum_{m=1}^{M} \sum_{\tau=t}^{\min(T-1,t+T_h-1)} \left(\delta a_{\tau m}^{i)} + \delta d_{\tau m}^{i)} \right) - tc_{ht} \qquad \begin{matrix} h = 1,2,\cdots,H \\ t = 0,1,2,\ldots,T-1 \end{matrix} \qquad (3.c)$$

The Lagrange multipliers for arrivals (λa_{ht}^{i}), departures (λd_{ht}^{i}) or both (λt_{ht}^{i}), are updated each round according to (4), where α^{i} is an update step that decreases as the auction progresses. To start the procedure the multipliers are set to zero: $\lambda a_{ht}^{0)} = \lambda d_{ht}^{0)} = \lambda t_{ht}^{0)} = 0$.

$$\lambda a_{ht}^{i)} = \max\left\{0, \lambda a_{ht}^{i-1)} + \alpha^{i)} \cdot g a_{ht}^{i)}\right\} \quad \begin{array}{l} h = 1, 2, \cdots, H \\ t = 0, 1, 2, \ldots, T-1 \end{array} \qquad (4.a)$$

$$\lambda d_{ht}^{i)} = \max\left\{0, \lambda d_{ht}^{i-1)} + \alpha^{i)} \cdot g d_{ht}^{i)}\right\} \quad \begin{array}{l} h = 1, 2, \cdots, H \\ t = 0, 1, 2, \ldots, T-1 \end{array} \qquad (4.b)$$

$$\lambda t_{ht}^{i)} = \max\left\{0, \lambda t_{ht}^{i-1)} + \alpha^{i)} \cdot g t_{ht}^{i)}\right\} \quad \begin{array}{l} h = 1, 2, \cdots, H \\ t = 0, 1, 2, \ldots, T-1 \end{array} \qquad (4.c)$$

The previous multipliers are used to calculate the prices for arrivals $(pa_{t}^{i)})$ and departures $(pd_{t}^{i)})$ for each coordination interval t at each round i, according to (5). The price for an arrival slot at a coordination interval t is calculated as the sum of all the arrival and total multipliers referred to that coordination interval; the price for departure slots is the sum of departure and total multipliers.

$$pa_{t}^{i)} = \sum_{h=1}^{H}\left(\sum_{\tau=\max(0,t-T_h+1)}^{t} \left(\lambda a_{h\tau}^{i)} + \lambda t_{h\tau}^{i)}\right)\right) \quad t = 0, 1, 2, \ldots, T-1 \qquad (5.a)$$

$$pd_{t}^{i)} = \sum_{h=1}^{H}\left(\sum_{\tau=\max(0,t-T_h+1)}^{t} \left(\lambda d_{h\tau}^{i)} + \lambda t_{h\tau}^{i)}\right)\right) \quad t = 0, 1, 2, \ldots, T-1 \qquad (5.b)$$

If the auction ends before achieving a feasible allocation which fulfils the airport's capacity constraints, the coordinator applies a feasibility and tie-breaking mechanism to the auction results in order to modify those allocations that still violate the capacity constraints, proposing alternative allocations. The feasibility procedure is based on a sorted list, in which flights are ordered according to the sum of the slot prices they have accepted to schedule their arrival and departure operations at the last round of the auction. Then, the coordinator must try to schedule the arrival and departure of each flight, following the previous list order.

The Flight Agents

In our model, the flights need to reserve slots to schedule their arrival and departure operations. There are as many flights agents as flights we consider. At each auction round, each flight m tries to maximize its surplus s_m, which is calculated as the utility $u_m(ta_m, td_m)$ that the flight gets for scheduling its arrival in ta_m and its departure in td_m, minus the price it hast to pay for the two slots, pa_{ta_m} for the arrival slot and pd_{td_m} for the departure slot.

$$s_m(\overline{pa}, \overline{pd}, ta_m, td_m) = u_m(ta_m, td_m) - pa_{ta_m} - pd_{td_m} \qquad (6)$$

where $\overline{pa} = (pa_0, pa_1, \cdots, pa_{T-1})$ and $\overline{pd} = (pd_0, pd_1, \cdots, pd_{T-1})$ are the prices calculated in the previous round.

Depending on the prices, each airline may decide to displace its requests to cheaper slots if they help to maximize their expected utility. If the price of every slot becomes so high than no positive surplus can be achieved from the flight, the airline will not bid for any of them, deciding not to operate in the airport ($\delta_m = 0$). To select the arrival and departure slots, the flight agent has to take into account the turnaround time tg_m (the scheduling constraint 7.b). Therefore, the decision problem of the flight m can be formulated as the following mathematical programing problem (7), where we have included the variable δ_m to model the allocation decision. This problem can be easily solved using an enumeration algorithm.

$$\max_{ta_m, td_m} \quad s_m^*(ta_m, td_m) = \delta_m \cdot (u_m(ta_m, td_m) - pa_{ta_m} - pd_{td_m}) \tag{7.a}$$

$$\text{s.t.} \quad ta_m + tt_m \leq td_m \tag{7.b}$$

4 Computational Experiments

To test and assess the proposed auction mechanism, we have developed an agent based simulation model. Netlogo [22, 23] has been the environment used to implement it, which is a platform that enables ABM Programming and Simulation.

In order to evaluate the auction performance, we propose six simulation scenarios with 24 coordination time intervals, but different amounts of flights to represent different 'load' scenarios which generate more complex allocation problems. They are grouped two by two, with different instances of flights' parameters for the same amount of flights: the first two scenarios have 24 flights (1a and 1b), the following two have 30 (2a and 2b), and the last two ones have 40 flights (3a and 3b).

The six scenarios have the same capacity constraints according to Table 1. It shows for h = 1, 2: the number of operations allowed (available slots) per type (arrivals, departures or total operations) along certain number ($T_1 = 1$, $T_2 = 3$) of consecutive coordination intervals [t, t + T_h].

Table 1. Airport capacity constraints for h = 1, 2. Number of available slots to schedule operations.

h	T_h	Max arrivals (ac_{ht})	Max departures (dc_{ht})	Max operations (tc_{ht})
1	1	2	2	3
2	3	5	4	8

The flight parameters have been generated randomly using a uniform distribution as follows: minimum turnaround time (tt_m) between 2 and 4, requested time for arrival (tra_m) between 0 and (23 − tt_m), requested time for departure (trd_m) in the range [tram + tt_m, tra$_m$ + 2 • tt_m], wa$_m$ between 0.1 and 3, wd$_m$ in the range [0.5 • wa$_m$, 1.5 • wa$_m$], and the gross utility (gu$_m$) between 5 and 15.

Table 2 represents the load factor of each scenario according to the number of slots demanded in the initial requests versus the different capacity constraints, which can be understood as an indicator for the level of the allocation complexity of each case. No shaded cells represent load factors below 75%, light grey shaded cells mark load factors from 75% up to 100%, and dark grey highlight load factors over 100% (there are more demanded than available slots).

Table 2. Load factor of complex scenarios according to the initially demanded slots.

			Initial request					
			Average load factor (Σ flights' requested slots / Σ airport available slots)					
		Coord. intervals	h=1, T_h=1			h=2, T_h=3		
Case	Flights		arrival	departures	total	arrival	departures	total
1a	24	24	50% (24/48)	50% (24/48)	72% (48/72)	55% (66/120)	75% (72/96)	72% (138/192)
1b	24	24	50% (24/48)	50% (24/48)	72% (48/72)	57% (68/120)	75% (72/96)	73% (140/192)
2a	30	24	63% (30/48)	63% (30/48)	83% (60/72)	73% (87/120)	87% (87/96)	92% (176/192)
2b	30	24	63% (30/48)	63% (30/48)	83% (60/72)	72% (86/120)	94% (90/96)	91% (174/192)
3a	30	24	83% (40/48)	83% (40/48)	111% (80/72)	93% (111/120)	125% (120/96)	120% (231/192)
3b	40	24	83% (40/48)	83% (40/48)	111% (80/72)	93% (112/120)	125% (120/96)	121% (232/192)

Each case has been solved both through the ABM simulation and by means of MILP (Mix Integer Linear Programing). The MILP models have been built for this purpose as proposed in Sect. 3.1, and they have been solved using OpenSolver [24].

Although the proposed problems have an explicit global objective function and can be solved by means an MILP algorithm, it has been done in this way only for comparison purposes. Our procedure never uses the global objective function, and explicit airline objective functions are used only to model the airline behaviour as a bidder. So, we can compare the efficiency of our model versus an exact mathematical optimization procedure that would be difficult to use in real environments. The MILP gives us optimal solutions whenever all the information is available, but as we argued before, airlines are reluctant to make public some of this information (strategic information, costs, revenues, etc.). Therefore, we compare MILP results with "perfect information" with auction results, where the auction coordination does not know this information and only knows data related to slot prices and slot requests.

- As we can see in the Table 3, for scenarios 1a, 1b and 2b, the auction mechanism provides schedules which are as efficient as the ones obtained with MILP. In addition, in scenarios 1a and 1b all the flights are scheduled with both methods; however in scenario 2b only 25 of the 30 flights can be scheduled.

- For scenario 2a, only 23 of 30 flights can be scheduled with the auction, while MILP optimisation schedules one flight more. Nonetheless, neither method achieves the allocation of all the existent requests despite the 'load factor' is below 100% (there are more slots than requests) because the airlines are the ones deciding not to bid attending to their utility functions.

- In scenarios 3a and 3b (the ones with load factor over 100%), neither method achieves a complete allocation for all the existent requests, but both allow to allocate the same number of flights and getting the same total utility. However, the auction still generates higher displacement cost of flights from their preferred slots, diminishing the value of the objective function versus the MILP solution. Nevertheless, a fine tune-up of the auction mechanism has not been performed yet, which is expected to improve the results; this aspect is currently under study and results will be presented in future works.

Table 3. Results for the six scenarios with different load factor (BFS: Best Feasible Scheduling, GU: Gross Utility)

Scenario	Number of requested Fligths	Number of coord. intervals	Method	Number of rounds for BFS	Number of Fligths on BFS	Total GU of Fligths	Total GU of scheduled Fligths	Total displacement costs of BFS	Objective Function for BFS
1a	24	24	Auction	54	24	224	224	17,2	206,8
	24	24	MILP		24	224	224	17.2	206.8
1b	24	24	Auction	49	24	256	256	15.6	240.4
	24	24	MILP		24	256	256	15.6	240.4
2a	30	24	Auction	162	23	307	258	41.1	216.9
	30	24	MILP		24	307	268	50.2	217.8
2b	30	24	Auction	134	25	295	267	21.4	245.6
	30	24	MILP		25	295	267	21.4	245.6
3a	40	24	Auction	354	27	400	314	20.2	293.8
	40	24	MILP		27	400	314	15.3	298.7
3b	40	24	Auction	179	28	411	320	21.5	295.5
	40	24	MILP		28	411	320	20.6	299.4

5 Conclusions

In this paper, we have studied primary auctioning of airport capacity in several demonstration scenarios, analysing the auction evolution in detail and comparing its results with MILP resolution for the same problems (perfect information).

A simulation environment based on Agent-Based Modelling has been developed from scratch to assess and validate Auction Market designs to solve slot allocation problems. This analysis is part of an ongoing study based on Experiment Design, which defines key relevant scenarios with different parameters that will be used to compare the outcome of auction markets with mathematical optimisation and administrative mechanisms.

According to the results obtained so far, iterative combinatorial auctions can be valid mechanisms for primary airport slot allocation. Depending on the scenario, auctions lead to situations where, without violating any airport capacity constraint, slots are allocated to airlines while the overall surplus is maximised. In these cases, the auction is actually leading to the optimum solution, the same one provided by the MILP optimisation. In addition, certain scenarios and agents' behaviours may also lead to situations where it is not possible to allocate all the requests, even if there is enough capacity for them, neither by means of auctions or mathematical optimisation techniques, but both may provide the best possible solution.

In this sense, auction markets can provide a way to solve the airport allocation problem in an economically optimum or sub-optimum way, where the participants do not have to disclose their private information (costs, strategies, etc.), which is a very important advantage over centralised optimisation procedures (such as linear programming) when it comes to a real life implementation. In auction markets, the only information exchanged are the slot prices and the slot requests, and when the auction process has finished, the economic value of each slot is obtained (independently for arrivals and departures), which is something unknown so far with current allocation systems.

Acknowledgements. This research has been partially financed by the project ABARNET (*Agent-Based Algorithms for Railway NETworks optimization*) financed by the Spanish Ministry of Economy, Industry and Competitiviness, with grant DPI2016-78902-P, and t*he Project Computational Models for Industrial Management (CM4IM) project*, funded by the Valladolid University General Foundation. It has also been financed by the Regional Government of Castille and Leon and the European Regional Development Fund (ERDF, FEDER), with grant VA049P17, LONJA 3D.

References

1. Council Of The European Communities, European Council Regulation (EEC) No. 95/93 of January 1993 on Common Rules for the Allocation of Slots at Community Airports, Official Journal of the European Union, L 14, 22.01.1993, p. 1, Brussels, Belgium (1993)
2. IATA: Worldwide Slot Guidelines, 8th edn. Montreal - Geneva (2017)
3. Zografos, K.G., Madas, M.A., Sched, A.K.J.: Increasing airport capacity utilisation through optimum slot scheduling: review of current developments and identification of future needs. J. Sched. **20**(1), 3–24 (2017)
4. Zografos, K., Salouras, Y., Madas, M.A.: Dealing with the efficient allocation of scarce resources at congested airports. Transp. Res. Part C Emer. Technol. **21**(1), 244–256 (2012)
5. Pellegrini, P., Bolić, T., Castelli, L., Pesenti, R.: SOSTA: an effective model for the simultaneous Optimisation of airport SloT Allocation. Transp. Res. Part E Logistics Transp. Rev. **99**, 34–53 (2017)
6. Pellegrini, P., Castelli, H., Pesenti, R.: Metaheuristic algorithms for the simultaneous slot allocation problem. IET Intel. Trans. Syst. **6**(4), 453–462 (2012)
7. Castelli, L., Pellegrini, P., Pesenti, R.: Airport slot allocation in Europe: economic efficiency and fairness. Int. J. Revenue Manag. **6**(1/2), 28–44 (2012)
8. Blumrosen, L., Nisan, N.: Combinatorial auctions. In: Algorithmic Game Theory, pp. 267–299. Cambridge University Press, Cambridge (2007)

9. Arul, S.V., Gunasekaran, A., Nachiappan, S.P., Ramasamy, B.: Development of efficient combinatorial auction mechanism for airport slot allocation. Int. J. Serv. Oper. Manag. **3**(4), 427–443 (2007)
10. Ball, M.O., Berardino, F., Hansen, M.: The use of auctions for allocating airport access rights. Transp. Res. Part A Policy Pract. (2017, in Press)
11. Rassenti, S.J., Smith, V.L., Bulfin, R.L.: A combinatorial auction mechanism for airport time slot allocation. Bell J. Econ. **13**(2), 402–417 (1982)
12. Castelli, L., Pesenti, R., Ranieri, A.: The design of a market mechanism to allocate air traffic flow management slots. Transp. Res. Part C **19**(5), 931–943 (2011)
13. Mehta, R., Vazirani, V.V.: An incentive compatible, efficient market for air traffic flow management. In: Cao, Y., Chen, J. (eds.) COCOON 2017. LNCS, vol. 10392, pp. 407–419. Springer, Cham (2017). https://doi.org/10.1007/978-3-319-62389-4_34
14. Pertuiset, T., Santos, G.: Primary auction of slots at European airports. Res. Transp. Econ. **45**, 66–71 (2014)
15. Araúzo, J.A., Pajares, J., Lopez-Paredes, A.: Simulating the dynamic scheduling of project portfolios. Simul. Model. Pract. Theory **18**(10), 1428–1441 (2010)
16. Araúzo, J.A., del-Olmo, R., Laviós, J.J., de-Benito-Martín, J.J.: Scheduling and control of flexible manufacturing systems: a holonic approach. In: RIAI-Revista Iberoamericana de Automática e Informática Industrial, vol. 12, no. 1, pp. 58–68 (2015)
17. De Vries, S., Vohra, R.V.: Combinatorial auctions: a survey. Informs J. Comput. **15**(15), 284–309 (2003)
18. Pikovsky, A.: Pricing and Bidding Strategies in Iterative Combinatorial Auctions. Doctoral dissertation, Universität München (2008)
19. Hernández, C., López-Paredes, A.: Engineering market design and computational organization. Growing the market from the bottom-up. In: Proceedings of the Workshop on Complex Behaviour in Economics, CEFI, Aix-en-Provence, France (2000)
20. Kutanoglu, E., Wu, S.D.: On combinatorial auction and Lagrangean Relaxation for distributed resource scheduling. IIE Trans. **31**(9), 813–826 (1999)
21. Fisher, M.L.: The Lagrangian relaxation method for solving integer programming problems. Manag. Sci. **50**(12 supplement), 1861–1871 (2004)
22. Allan, R.J.: Survey of agent based modelling and simulation tools, Science & Technology Facilities Council (2010)
23. Wilensky, U.: NetLogo itself. Center for Connected Learning and Computer-Based Modeling, Northwestern University, Evanston, IL (1999). http://ccl.northwestern.edu/netlogo/
24. Mason, A.J.: OpenSolver – an open source add-in to solve linear and integer progammes in excel. In: Klatte, D., Lüthi, H.J., Schmedders, K. (eds.) Operations Research Proceedings 2011, pp. 401–406. Springer, Heidelberg (2012). https://doi.org/10.1007/978-3-642-29210-1_64. http://opensolver.org

AMAK - A Framework for Developing Robust and Open Adaptive Multi-agent Systems

Alexandre Perles$^{(\boxtimes)}$, Fabrice Crasnier, and Jean-Pierre George

IRIT, University of Toulouse, Toulouse, France
{Alexandre.Perles,Fabrice.Crasnier,Jean-Pierre.George}@irit.fr

Abstract. Multi-agent systems are commonly used in various research fields such as artificial intelligence, operational research, simulation, biology, ... However, this diversity often requires that the system and agents in it are created from scratch for each new research project. In addition to the fact that this forces the developers to code similar elements anew each time, this can introduce non-negligible biases (e.g. an information accessible to every agent which shouldn't be or a scheduler executing twice due to a user interface design failure). To avoid this, we propose in this paper AMAK, a framework developed in Java™ to facilitate the design and development of a multi-agent system. First, we present the particularity of Adaptive Multi-Agent Systems. Secondly, a state of the art of the main tools and software aiming at facilitating the development of such systems is discussed. Then, we develop the architecture of the framework and the main features. The use of the framework is illustrated with an application for socio-technical ambient systems. And finally, we conclude with the perspectives of this work.

Keywords: Multi-agent system · Cooperation · Framework
Development · Java

1   Introduction

Today, companies develop ad-hoc Artificial Intelligence solutions often based on machine-learning with methods such as Gradient Boosting, Random Forest, Deep Learning and Genetic Algorithms. These methods show really great performance when the problem is well-defined and data are numerous and centralized.

But in modern society, we tend to have dynamic problems that are not completely identified/specified and involving numerous interacting entities. To solve these types of complex problems, it is necessary to reconsider the way we handle problems, notably by decentralizing the control and by adapting the solving process during time. This motivates the Multi-Agent Systems (MAS) approaches and more specifically the ones aiming for self-adaptation.

© Springer International Publishing AG, part of Springer Nature 2018
J. Bajo et al. (Eds.): PAAMS 2018 Workshops, CCIS 887, pp. 468–479, 2018.
https://doi.org/10.1007/978-3-319-94779-2_40

An Adaptive Multi-Agent System is a MAS in which agents interact with their neighborhood in a cooperative way [1] so as to adapt their behavior to disturbances they perceive. The main idea is that when agents are all cooperative at the microlevel, the global system solves the problem at the macrolevel [6].

These kinds of approaches tend to be more and more used in private and public research. The development of these systems requires to follow a bottom-up approach. It means that the focus is put on the behavior of agents [5].

To avoid common errors in the development of Adaptive Multi-Agent Systems and given the fact that the only differences between this kind of systems is in the architecture of agents and their behavior, we propose a framework integrating the common bricks useful for all adaptive multi-agent system projects.

This paper presents the framework we developed and highlights its characteristics. In the first part, more details are given on the Adaptive Multi-Agent System theory. Secondly, a state of the art of the main tools and software aiming at facilitating the development of such systems is discussed. Then, the characteristics of the framework are presented. And finally, the use of the framework is illustrated with an application for socio-technical ambient systems.

2   Adaptation in Multi-agent Systems

The need for adaptation comes from the fact that complex problems are generally not completely specified. Indeed, complex problems or systems involve numerous entities interacting dynamically and are therefore hard to solve, control or predict.

As agents are autonomous and have a limited perception (they can only perceive a small part of their environment), the adaptation in Multi-Agent Systems can come from three factors:

- The tuning of parameters: Agents can change the way they act by modifying their internal parameters based on their perception;
- The changes of interaction: An agent initially interacting with another can decide to break this link and interact with other agents;
- The addition/removal of an agent: If an agent is useless, it can decide to remove itself. Conversely, an agent can decide to create another agent if it thinks it will benefit the system.

The adequate functioning of a multi-agent system requires a cooperative behavior of agents. Cooperation is a social attitude in which agents coordinate and help each other. An agent is considered as cooperative if he tries to reduce the *criticality* in its neighborhood. The *criticality* of an agent can be defined as "the state of dissatisfaction of an agent regarding its local goal" [11]. This information can be seen as the main motivator for an agent to act, leading to a continuous self-organizing process between the agents, which is the engine for self-adaptation at the system level.

3 Existing Tools

The development of adaptive multi-agent systems can be made with almost any programming language. However, a code basis can be useful as it allows to focus on the specific features and to avoid common errors. The most used tools or frameworks are Jade (Java Agent DEvelopment Framework), GAMA (Gis & Agent-based Modelling Architecture), NetLogo, SARL and MadKit.

Jade is a Java™ framework first released in 2000. This framework allows to distribute agents in various containers. Basically, the Jade framework contains a class named Agent that must be extended by any developed agent. These agents are then controlled by two special agents with a global view of the system: The DF Agent which provides a directory with the full list of available agents and the AMS Agent which controls the platform. The main advantages of this framework are that it has been used in many projects, that it generalized the concept of behaviors and that it is compliant with the FIPA standards [2]. However, the development of systems using Jade may not be intuitive. Moreover, even if it seems adapted to the development of multi-agent systems, adaptive multi-agent systems require a more decentralized control and is notably incompatible with agents with a global view.

GAMA is a platform dedicated to agent-based modeling and simulation. The development is high-level and therefore allows to focus on the behaviors of agents. However, it requires to learn a specific programming language called GAML [15].

NetLogo is particularly useful for teaching. Packaged as a full-featured Integrated Development Environment, it provides a really simple way to experiment with multi-agent systems. It differentiates from other by its simplicity and has been used for many scientific articles. However, despite its simplicity, it also requires to learn a specific programming language [16].

SARL is a statically-typed agent-programming language. It is a specific language aiming at filling in the gaps of the Java™ language. It is based on events and has a syntax similar to a mix between Java™ and Python. However, it lacks easy rendering capacities and forces its user to learn a new language [14].

MadKit is a generic multi-agent system platform based on a organizational model. It has been developed in Java™ and has a clear structure. It is relatively easy to use however it is not really intuitive [10].

4 The AMAK Framework

The framework AMAK is an all-in-one Java™ library aiming at facilitating the development of Adaptive Multi-Agent Systems. It is presented as a jar file that must be added to Java™ projects [12]. The programming language Java™ has been chosen as it is widely used in both research and education fields. In addition to this, this language is object-oriented and programs developed with it are portable [9].

During the design and development of Adaptive Multi-Agent Systems, the focus should be made on the agents' behaviors. However, to be able to code the behavior of an agent, it is necessary to code all the related concepts which are the scheduling of agents, the plotting of data and specific algorithms (for example, determining the most critical agent). Given the bottom-up approach used in the development of such system, one small change in any part of the code can have non-negligible impact on the system overall functioning and can notably introduce biases and therefore lead to wrong results. The use of a framework allows to avoid common errors and also to save time.

By providing a set of inheritable classes and methods, the framework AMAK gives a solid basis to develop such systems. The three main abstract classes are AMAS, Agent and Environment. These concepts present in every multi-agent system have specific characteristics and comply with the Adelfe methodology designed to assist the development of adaptive multi-agent systems [4]. The Fig. 1 represents the relations between the main classes. Inheriting the AMAS class allows to develop a multi-agent system compliant with the scheduler given in AMAK. It also supports the addition and removal of agents safely at runtime. The abstract class Agent mainly contains three overridable methods: onPerceive, onDecide and onAct. These methods are common to all kind of agents as defined in [7]. Also, it can be necessary to execute specific code on each agent for example when all agents have finished their cycle. The framework contains such methods. It can be used for example to debug or to log agent states. Finally, the class Environment is abstract and must be extended by the environment of the multi-agent system. The extended class must provide direct access to any information the agents may require. Each agent belonging to the multi-agent system has a pointer to this environment and use it to perceive its part of the environment.

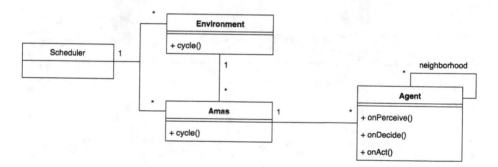

Fig. 1. Relations between the main classes

The scheduling is ensured by a specific class Scheduler which enables to execute the cycle of the AMAS and therefore the cycle of each agent synchronously (or not) with the environment. Adaptive Multi-Agent Systems have specific characteristics. Notably the fact that agents have a criticality and often use it to determine which agent should be helped. This criticality value is computed at various times directly by the framework to ensure that the value complies with the real state of the agent and that the computation is made as few often as possible. Moreover, specific algorithms are added. For example, it exists a predefined method which allows any agents to directly know which agent in its neighborhood is the most critical.

During the design and development of multi-agent systems, it is often necessary to visualize data and notably agents locations and interaction links. The module DrawableUI is an abstract class that must be extended by any rendering class you may have. This class contains a method called at each cycle (synchronized with the multi-agent system scheduler or not) that must be implemented.

The framework AMAK is also packaged with various tools generally used in such projects. The tool *AVT* (Average Value Tracker), developed by Sylvain Lemouzy [11] for the SMAC team, is a tool aiming at finding a potentially-dynamic value in a specific range given simple feedback (smaller, bigger and almost good). The problems faced by Adaptive Multi-Agent Systems are often dynamic and not completely specified. Such tool is particularly adapted.

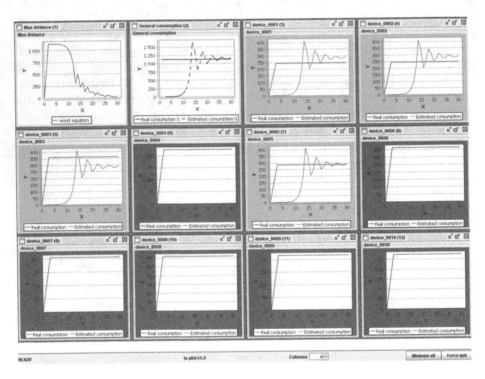

Fig. 2. Screenshot of the *LxPlot* tool used in AMAK (Color figure online)

The second integrated tool is *LxPlot* (https://bitbucket.org/perlesa/lx-plot). It exists multiple libraries for plotting data in Java™. The most used is probably JFreeChart (http://www.jfree.org/jfreechart/). However, it requires to write a lot of code to manage to display simple points. The library *LxPlot* integrates the library JFreeChart and simplifies it to allow to draw points or lines using one simple line of code. The Fig. 2 presents a screenshot of the tool *LxPlot* used in a socio-technical ambient system presented later.

Sometimes, simple piece of code can be executed a lot of times. If this code is not optimized, it can have non-negligible impact in term of computation time. To face this problem, the framework includes a simple tool called *Profiler* which allows to measure the exact time in nanoseconds taken by the execution of a piece of code.

Java^{TM} natively includes convenient classes to read or write files. However, as for the plotting library, this requires to write a lot of code to read or write a simple file. The tool *FileHandler* allows to simply read or write text, CSV and JSON files.

Finally, a multi-agent system can handle an important amount of agents (for example, the drone application is able to handle thousands of agents on a computer with a medium configuration). It, therefore, can be hard to observe what is happening during the execution. AMAK integrates convenient tools to display data and a logging system with various log levels and a tag system to filter and display only some information based on a regular expression. Moreover, by default, the logging system writes to the standard output but it can easily be rerouted to write log to a file or even send logging data through the network.

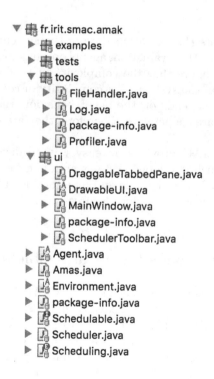

Fig. 3. Main classes of the proposed framework

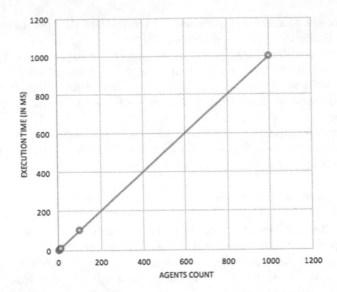

Fig. 4. Evolution of the execution time of a system developed with AMAK over the number of agents

The Fig. 4 represents the execution time of the system over the number of agents in the system. For this evaluation, agents do random actions at each cycle. It can be seen in this figure that the complexity in time evolves linearly with the number of agents in the system. The complexity of communication can't be observed as it mainly depends on the agent behavior. However, following the AMAS theory, agents are cooperative. Therefore, they are not supposed to send useless messages.

The framework AMAK provides an easy way to develop and maintain a multi-agent system. Such developed systems are open (agents can be added or removed at runtime), efficient, reliable and monitorable. The Fig. 3 presents the main classes. The framework is provided for free under the LGPL (Lesser General Public License) license [8].

5   Application to Socio-Technical Ambient Systems

Since the beginning of its development in 2017, AMAK has been used in various projects. First of all, AMAK is used in education in last year of multiple master's degrees. Given its simplicity of use and the fact that it is based on the commonly used language Java^TM, it is particularly adapted to education. It has been used in education on two examples: the solving of the philosopher's dinner problem [12] and the adaptive management of a drones fleet [13]. It allows to easily understand concepts related to the design and development of multi-agent systems. Secondly, each year, new internships and PhD students integrate the IRIT laboratory. To avoid losing too much time understanding the process of conceiving multi-agent systems, AMAK gives a robust and clear structure to start with [3].

AMAK has been used for the development of a socio-technical ambient system aiming at making emerge an ambient welfare.

An ambient environment consists of a multitude of devices, some of which measure its physical characteristics such as heat sensors, light sensors, olfactory sensors and hearing sensors while others act directly on it to modify its state such as the electric motors of the shutters to control the opening and closing of the curtains, or the switches to control the switching "on" and "off" of the ceiling or fixture. AMAK has been used for the development of the ambient socio-technical system aimed at bringing out the notion of ambient well-being of immersed humans in this environment. By simulating connected devices such as sensors and effectors, the framework allows such a system to discover the optimal combination to maximize user comfort and bring out our goal of well-being. In this research framework, learning about the environment linked to well-being is carried out using multi-agent systems related to the four characteristics of human physical comfort i.e. thermal comfort, visual comfort, olfactory comfort or the acoustic comfort we will call "MAS Comforts". The latter ones are initially responsible for learning the thermal, luminous, olfactory or auditory environments and in a second phase for providing their criticality levels to the multi-agent systems representing the ambient socio-technical system consisting of sensors and effectors scattered in the environment we call "MAS Devices". To meet the socio-economic objectives and to realize a functionality of eco-citizenship, a multi-agent system that we call "MAS Conso" must meet this objective. The Fig. 5 presents the overall architecture of the presented system.

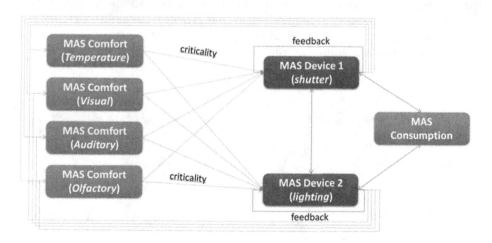

Fig. 5. Ambient system architecture

In this article, we will show the use of the AMAK framework to meet the goal of learning the power consumption of the environment using the construction of a "MAS Conso". The class "Environment" allows to build the world in which the multi-agent system will operate. Here we can set up all the elements that will interact with the system, in our case we have built a simulator to generate the necessary inputs to the system such as the power consumption of the environment as well as the states of devices present in the environment. In addition, it is easy to be able to connect graphical output interfaces to evaluate or compare the work of the "MAS Conso". The Fig. 6 presents a screenshot of a graphical output interface developed for the project.

Oracle consumption	501,00	Resolution cycle number	498
MAS consumption	479,00	Perception world	4
critical equation	501	MAS decision	INCREASE
criticality value	22.0	Treshold	2.0
Reverse matrix not possible		Linear résolution	00000

Fig. 6. Multi-agent system state

The class "AMAS" allows to define the elements of our multi-agent system and to create the agents that will intervene. Using the method "onInitialAgentsCreation()", we create our "Estimation" agent and the "Device" agents that represent the devices of the environment. The Fig. 7 presents the architecture of the "MAS Conso" and notably the links between agents. The "AMAS" class is scheduled using a "Scheduler" class that provides the ability to track the life cycles of the system, the beginning of cycles using the method "onSystemCycleBegin()" and the end using the method "onSystemCycleEnd()".

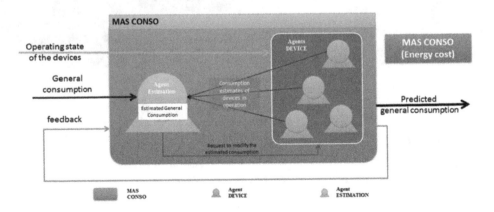

Fig. 7. MAS Conso architecture

Finally, each "Agent" is independent and respond to a schema of coopera-tive multi-agent systems, the class has an onPerceive() perception method that allows the agent to perceive a part of its environment, an onDecide() decision-making method making it possible to forge its decision on the solicitation of the neighborhood but also according to its own needs, and finally an action method onAct() allowing to act on its environment. In our "MAS CONSO", the "Esti-mation" agent aims at evaluating the power consumption of the environment. To maintain a cooperative state, he memorizes the states of the world he perceives at each change and looks for the most critical state to improve the predictions. To fulfill this objective, it perceives the total electricity consumption of the envi-ronment and solicits the device agents to obtain their prediction of consumption. It is then able to evaluate the tendency to take for Device Agents to improve their prediction. Considering these, they perceive the request of the Agent Esti-mate but, according to their own knowledge of their tendency, they will follow his recommendation or decide not to answer his request.

The flexibility of the framework makes it possible to develop these different agents while keeping them coherent. Also, this system requires to observe the evolution of different values such as the instantaneous energy consumption that is made possible thanks to the built-in tools *LxPlot*. Figure 2 is a screenshot of the data displayed using *LxPlot*. We evaluate here an environment composed of 10 devices, with each cycle of perception it is possible to observe the cooperating devices with a background of green color, those which do not follow the demand of the agent Estimation with a background of orange color and those who are not in working condition during this observation of the environment. In addition, the graphs show the consumption to be achieved for each device (red line) and the evolution of the predictions (blue line). In addition, the first graph allows the observation of the criticality defined by the distance between the actual consumption and the estimated consumption, as for the second graph, it shows the general evolution of the system on electricity consumption.

Table 1. Comparison with existing tools

	Known language	Intuitive	Flexible	Rendering capacities
Jade	+++	-	++	-
GAMA	-	++	+	++
NetLogo	-	++	-	+
SARL	-	++	++	-
MadKit	+++	+	+	+
AMAK	+++	++	+	-

6 Conclusion

The Table 1 shows the differences between the main existing tools and AMAK. As it can be seen, AMAK is less adapted to rendering data. However, it is as much (or more) intuitive as the others thanks to its simple structure, the simplicity of the method names and the use of Java™. It is also flexible and doesn't require to learn a new language.

Despite the large choices of tools and frameworks to assist the development of Adaptive Multi-Agent Systems, the proposed framework seems relevant as it provides an effective and intuitive way to develop such systems. However, it lacks the possibility to reliably execute agent simultaneously. Moreover, the rendering capacities are currently limited. Also, it has been shown that the framework respects major generic concepts of multi-agent systems development and that it maintains a linear complexity evolution over the number of agents which means that multi-agent system developed with AMAK are scalable. The perspective of this work will be to improve the rendering capacities of the framework and to use it on various projects with different natures and requirements.

References

1. Axelrod, R., Hamilton, W.: The evolution of cooperation. Science **211**(4489), 1390–1396 (1981). http://www.ncbi.nlm.nih.gov/pubmed/7466396 http://www.sciencemag.org/cgi/doi/10.1126/science.7466396
2. Bellifemine, F., Poggi, A., Rimassa, G.: JADE - A FIPA-Compliant Agent Framework (1999). https://pdfs.semanticscholar.org/19f5/4048201ce8e416b74f33 25266c34ae203f74.pdf
3. Blanc-Rouchossé, J.B.: Régulation auto-adaptative de réseau électrique intelligent. Technical report (2017)
4. Bonjean, N., Mefteh, W., Gleizes, M.P.P., Maurel, C., Migeon, F.: Adelfe 2.0, pp. 1–45 (2012)
5. Crespi, V., Galstyan, A., Lerman, K.: Top-down vs bottom-up methodologies in multi-agent system design. Auton. Robots **24**(3), 303–313 (2008). https://link.springer.com/content/pdf/10.1007%2Fs10514-007-9080-5.pdf
6. Di Marzo Serugendo, G., Gleizes, M.P., Karageorgos, A.: Self-organising Software. From Natural to Artificial Adaptation. Springer, Heidelberg (2011). https://doi.org/10.1007/978-3-642-17348-6
7. Ferber, J.: Multi-Agent Systems: An Introduction to Distributed Artificial Intelligence, vol. 222. Addison-Wesley, Reading (1999). http://jasss.soc.surrey.ac.uk/4/2/reviews/rouchier.html
8. GNU: GNU Lesser General Public License. https://www.gnu.org/licenses/lgpl-3.0.en.html
9. Gosling, J., McGilton, H.: The Java TM Programming Language Environment. No. May (1996). http://www.oracle.com/technetwork/java/intro-141325.html
10. Gutknecht, O., Ferber, J.: MadKit: a generic multi-agent platform. In: Proceedings of the Fourth International Conference on Autonomous Agents, AGENTS 2000, pp. 78–79 (2000). http://portal.acm.org/citation.cfm?id=336595.337048 %5Cnpapers2://publication/doi/10.1145/336595.337048%5Cnhttp://portal.acm.org/citation.cfm?doid=336595.337048
11. Lemouzy, S.: Systèmes interactifs auto-adaptatifs par systèmes multi-agents auto-organisateurs: application à la personnalisation de l'accès à l'information (2011). http://thesesups.ups-tlse.fr/1303/
12. Perles, A.: AMAK. https://bitbucket.org/perlesa/amak

13. Perles, A.: AMAS Exercises. https://bitbucket.org/perlesa/amas-exercises
14. Rodriguez, S., Gaud, N., Galland, S.: SARL: a general-purpose agent-oriented pro-
    gramming language. In: Proceedings of 2014 IEEE/WIC/ACM International Joint
    Conference on Web Intelligence and Intelligent Agent Technology - Workshops,
    WI-IAT 2014, vol. 3, pp. 156–165. IEEE, August 2014. http://ieeexplore.ieee.org/
    document/6928174/
15. Taillandier, P., Vo, D.-A., Amouroux, E., Drogoul, A.: GAMA: a simulation plat-
    form that integrates geographical information data, agent-based modeling and
    multi-scale control. In: Desai, N., Liu, A., Winikoff, M. (eds.) PRIMA 2010. LNCS
    (LNAI), vol. 7057, pp. 242–258. Springer, Heidelberg (2012). https://doi.org/10.
    1007/978-3-642-25920-3_17
16. Tisue, S., Wilensky, U.: NetLogo: a simple environment for modeling complexity.
    In: Conference on Complex Systems, pp. 1–10 (2004). http://ccl.sesp.northwestern.
    edu/papers/netlogo-iccs2004.pdf

Benchmarking the Agent Descriptivity of Parallel Multi-agent Simulators

Craig Shih, Caleb Yang, and Munehiro Fukuda(✉)

University of Washington, Bothell, WA 98011, USA
{cshih,yangc9,mfukuda}@uw.edu
http://depts.washington.edu/dslab/MASS/index.html

Abstract. Agent-based models (ABMs) need to populate a mega number of agents over a scalable simulation space in order to handle practical problems, (e.g., metropolitan traffic simulation and nationwide epidemic prediction). Although parallel and distributed simulation have steadily addressed their computational needs, non-computing scientists still tend to use GUI-rich, easy-to-use ABM interpretive platforms. This paper intends to identify the difficulty in using the current parallel ABM simulators and to propose their future improvements. For this purpose, we surveyed different ABM applications, modeled them as seven benchmark test cases, used them to analyze the agent descriptivity of parallel ABM simulators, and evaluated their execution performance affected by the current implementations.

Keywords: Agent-based models · Parallel simulation
Agent programmability · Benchmark tests

1 Introduction

Agent-based models (ABMs) have been highlighted as micro-simulation that models microscopic events, (e.g., transport simulation involving traffic lights, constructions, and pedestrian movements) and that observes an emergent collective group behavior of many simulation entities (which are called agents). Since not all scientists are computing specialists, GUI-rich, easy-to-use ABM interpretive platforms including NetLogo[1], Repast Symphony[2], and MASON[3] have attracted them for the last 10+ years.

Emergent worldwide tensions including globalization, urbanization, population increase, and Internet dissemination require the ABM problem size to be scaled up, which increases computation time unacceptably. For instance, FluTE, an influenza epidemic simulation model [7] takes 2 hours to simulate an unmitigated epidemic in 10 million people. Scientists have noticed that parallel computing is imperative for large-scale simulations of ABMs [8]. However ABM

---

[1] http://ccl.northwestern.edu/netlogo/.
[2] https://repast.github.io/repast_simphony.html.
[3] https://cs.gmu.edu/~eclab/projects/mason/.

J. Bajo et al. (Eds.): PAAMS 2018 Workshops, CCIS 887, pp. 480–492, 2018.
https://doi.org/10.1007/978-3-319-94779-2_41

interpretive platforms are difficult to parallelize or to speed up. In fact, NetLogo has not yet been parallelized. D-MASON[4], a distributed version of MASON has been no longer maintained for the last four years.

Contrary to these interpretive platforms, FLAME[5] and RepastHPC[6] are C/C++-based platforms that facilitate ABM parallelization over a cluster system and have successfully promoted scalable computing. EURANCE is a massively parallel agent-based simulation of European economy where FLAME populated 3,500 through to 500,000 agents [10]. RepastHPC has been tested for scalability on Blue Gene/P and achieved exascale computing on Illinois electric power transmission grid and services [26]. Despite that, as mentioned above, many scientists are still using NetLogo and Repast Symphony.

From our programming experiences with FLAME and RepastHPC [6], we observe two hurdles for non-computing specialists to clear when using these two systems: (1) tolerating limited flexibilities in programming and (2) understanding parallel-computing concepts. Based on their own design philosophy, FLAME and RepastHPC give a specific programming framework that guarantees automatic parallelization of user applications as far as they are coded in accordance with the framework. However, their learning curves are very steep. Moreover, users still need to understand underlying parallel-computing platforms such as message boards in FLAME and MPI in RepastHPC.

Given these backgrounds, we have surveyed programming styles in various ABM applications in Sect. 2; focused on two C++-based ABM parallel simulators in Sect. 3, which are RepastHPC and MASS, (the latter of which is our own simulator [6]); developed a benchmark test set based on the survey and identified challenges in current parallel ABM platforms from the viewpoint of both programmability and execution performance in Sect. 4; and clarified their challenges and sought for future solutions in Sect. 5.

2   Challenges in Agent-Based Modeling

This section surveys ABMs, examines potential parallelizations with conventional ABM platforms, and clarifies their challenges in parallelization.

2.1   ABM Applications

We are looking at ABMs in social, behavioral and economic (SBE) sciences as well as biological, ecological, and city-planning applications that are tightly coupled with SBE. Although our survey is still in progress, the following samples some ABM applications in each scientific discipline.

---

[4] https://sites.google.com/site/distributedmason/.
[5] http://www.flame.ac.uk.
[6] https://repast.github.io/repast_hpc.html.

1. **Social science**
   (a) *Social Network Modeling:* simulates activities among and event influence to online communities [1,9]. It can be modeled as a network of agents, each exchanging information along links with its neighbors.
2. **Behavioral science**
   (a) *Flows:* observe the dynamics of indoor and outdoor pedestrian crowd[7] and metropolitan emergency evacuation [20,21]. These simulations use cellular automata or observe agent movement over a 2D gird.
   (b) *Organizations:* forecast the team productivity for certain operations. For instance, Virtual Design Team (VDT) models a hierarchical software developer team that moves from one to another product phase [19].
3. **Economic science**
   (a) *Markets:* include bank bail-in/out [18] and Internet service provider (ISP) markets [3], both observing interactions among clusters of agents. The former distinguishes three clusters: firms, banks, and households, whereas the latter creates different ISP markets where customer agents move from one to another.
   (b) *Diffusions:* are quite closer to social network modeling where a product adoption is modeled as a word-of-mouth diffusion on social networks [3].
4. **Biological/Ecological sciences**
   (a) *Cell-level simulation:* simulates the growth of synapses [17], identifies control mechanism of granuloma formation by TB bacteria, macrophages and T-cells [25], and cell-level blood flow throughout the microvasculature network [27].
   (b) *Ecosystems:* simulate an emergent collective group behavior of artificial lives. The examples include Wa-Tor: an ecological war between sharks and fish [11] and Sugarscape: an artificial society [12], both based on agent migration over a 2D space. Conway's Game of Life, a well-known cellular automata game [14] could be considered as an artificial life.
   (c) *Epidemic simulation:* predicts a pandemic of a given disease such as dengue fever [16] and influenza [7]. They move agents from one to another community.
5. **Urban planning**
   (a) *Transport simulation:* predicts traffic flows under a given condition. The major simulators are TRANSIMS [2] and MATSim[8], each based on cellular automata and a queuing network respectively.
   (b) *Land use simulation:* simulates agent behaviors over households, businesses, and land areas[9]. The model is generally combined with transport simulation.

Apparently, some of these applications are based on a similar computing model in terms of how agents are spawned and interact with each other over their shared space. Therefore, we have categorized them from scientific disciplines into computing models from the viewpoints of static versus dynamic agents as well as based on the structure of their shared space:

---

[7] http://pedsim.silmaril.org/.

[8] http://www.matsim.org.

[9] http://www.urbansim.com.

1. **Static agents:** have no mobility over a simulation space.
   (a) *Clustered agents:* form one or more groups, each exchanging events with others and sharing them among its internal agents (Fig. 1(a)). Market simulation is this model.
   (b) *Cellular automata:* consider each cell as a static agent that communicates with its neighbors (Fig. 1(b)). This model includes Conway's Game of Life and TRANSIMS.
   (c) *Network of agents:* is a more generalized form of cellular automata by replacing a 2D/3D grid with a network (Fig. 1(c)). Social network modeling and economic diffusions belong to this category.
   (d) *Agents with dynamic communication:* stay static but extend its communication paths to further agents as seen in the growth of synapses (Fig. 1(d)).
2. **Dynamic agents:** have navigational autonomy over a space.
   (a) *Agent migration over grid:* moves agents over a 2D or a 3D space as shown in Fig. 2(a). Most ABM applications in biology and ecology can be categorized in this model.
   (b) *Agent migration over network:* walks or drives agents over a network (of roads or microvasculature) as illustrated in Fig. 2(b).
   (c) *Group migration over multi phases:* is a very special case in agent migration that corresponds to VDT. Figure 2(c) models a developer team's transition from one to another product phase.

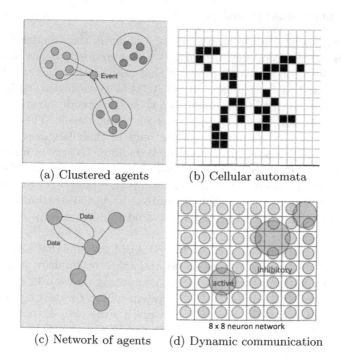

(a) Clustered agents   (b) Cellular automata

(c) Network of agents   (d) Dynamic communication

Fig. 1. Categorization for static agents

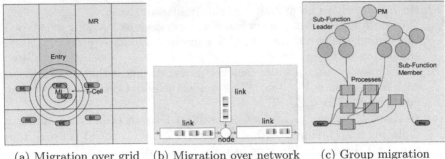

(a) Migration over grid   (b) Migration over network   (c) Group migration

Fig. 2. Categorization for dynamic agents

We understand that several more computing surveys on ABM research areas and applications have been already published[10] [3,4,13,24], and thus we need to cover all these surveyed models. However, our preliminary ABM categorization shown above can serve as a useful tool for our initial review on how efficiently conventional approaches have parallelized these computing models and what challenges still lie for ABM parallelization. Below we look into conventional approaches to ABM parallelization.

2.2 Conventional Approaches

As ABM scientists have confronted issues of scaling up their model size and calibrating their models from previous runs, (which were predicted as of 2002 [15]), they began to focus on parallel computing that is effective to increase both computation speed and space. The majority of ABM platforms based on interpretive languages such as Java and Logo suffer from their slower code interpretation than native mode execution, generally by one order of magnitude. Their parallelization is normally limited to multithreading built in their language, and is thus based on the shared-memory programming paradigm. To stay in minor changes for parallelization, D-MASON, (i.e., a distributed version of MASON) uses a centralized communication server that maintains the consistency of agent migration and communication, which contributes to only spatial scalability. Therefore, interpretive ABM platforms are generally bound to inherent slow execution and multithreading.

There are several parallel and distributed ABM systems that have addressed ABM computational needs in both speed and space by implementing a native-mode execution platform over a cluster of computing nodes [23]. Among them, RepastHPC is an MPI-supported C++ system where *Context* is an execution environment that populates agents over a given *Projection* instance such as a shared grid and space. However, one of RepastHPC's drawbacks is its heavy dependence on MPI, which results in a steep learning curve for users.

---

[10] http://www2.econ.iastate.edu/tesfatsi/ace.htm.

Another native-mode parallel platform is FLAME. Since FLAME users write their simulation in C, for object-based programming purposes, they need to declare all agents and environment variables in XML, in a similar way to C++ header files. Although the environment variables are used to shape a simulation space, FLAME does not instantiate any actual space in memory. Instead, agents are capable of broadcasting their messages among one another through message boards, each launched at a different MPI rank. Contrary to RepastHPC, FLAME is considered as a collection of communicating, state-transitting agents statically mapped over MPI ranks. From this viewpoint, FLAME would burden ABM designers with application-level manipulation of dynamic agents.

Some mobile agents were capable of creating trees or logical networks over a cluster system. Olden recursively created new tree branches, spawned and moved child threads along the branches, and let them execute a new function [22]. WAVE enabled its interpretive agents to create new network links/nodes and to dispatch their offsprings [5]. Their drawbacks are slow execution due to thread migration, interpretive execution, and overheads incurred by logical network creation.

These circumstances motivate us to examine common issues in parallelizing ABMs by developing a benchmark test set and to address them by proposing solutions to existing parallel platforms such as RepastHPC as well as enhancing our own MASS library as a general-purpose simulation environment.

3   Parallel ABM Simulators with Agent Mobility over Virtual Space

We focus on two parallel ABM platforms, MASS and RepastHPC, both of which facilitate agent mobility and thus cover execution of not only static but also dynamic agents.

3.1   MASS Library

We have developed and released to the public the MASS (Multi-Agent Spatial Simulation) library in Java and C++. The library has two key classes: *Places* and *Agents*. *Places* is a multi-dimensional array of elements that are dynamically allocated over a cluster of multi-core computing nodes. Each element is called a *place*, is pointed to by a set of network-independent array indices, and is capable of making a parallel function call with `Places.callAll(place.functionId)`, exchanging information with any other *places* through `exchangeAll()`, and facilitating visibility between neighboring *places* with `exchangeBoundary()`. *Agents* are a set of execution instances that can reside on a *place*, autonomously migrate to any other *places* with array indices through `Agent.migrate()` and `Agents.manageAll()`, and indirectly interact with other *agents* through variables local to the current *place*. Parallelization with the MASS library uses a set of multi-threaded communicating processes that are forked over a cluster of multi-core computing nodes with libssh2 in C++ and are connected to each other through TCP sockets. Multi-threads take charge of parallel method invocation and information exchange among *places* and *agents*.

3.2 RepastHPC

RepastHPC is an agent-based modeling and simulation framework that is implemented in C++ on top of MPI to facilitate high-performance parallel and distributed simulation. Agents are implemented as objects (C++ classes), each identified with a unique `repast::AgentId` and maintaining its state represented by the variables in the classes. The agent behavior is described by the functions in those classes. A *Context* is used to encompass the population of agents. Each context can only contain a single type of agents. When an agent is created, it is added to a Context with `addAgent()`. When they die, they are then removed from the Context with `removeAgent()`. *Context* also takes charge of moving agents over a shared space, using `move()` and `balance()`. RepastHPC distinguishes various simulation spaces called *Projections*, including `SharedNetwork`, `SharedDiscreteSpace`, `SharedContinuousSpace`, `DiffusionLayerND`, and `ValueLayerND`, each respectively modeling a different simulation space: a 2D/3D shared discrete space, a shard contiguous space, an N-dimensional layer of diffusing values over a space, and an N-dimensional array of values accessed by agents. These spaces provide agents with *Moore2DGridQuery* and *RepastEdgeContentManager* classes to find their neighbors within a closer distance or reachable through an agent network edge. RepastHPC utilizes a dynamic discrete-event scheduler with conservative synchronization. Events are scheduled to occur at a specific tick which is also used to determine order.

4 Comparisons

This section compares MASS and RepastHPC for agent and spatial descriptivity to identify what they lack for attracting attention from non-computing users. Thereafter, our benchmark test cases examine execution overheads incurred by their implementation when they run in parallel.

4.1 Analysis of Agent and Spatial Descriptivity

Six different types of applications have been chosen from Sect. 2.2, simplified as a general benchmark test, and coded in MASS C++ and RepastHPC[11]: Bank bail-in/out (*Bank*) as clustered agents, Game of Life (*Life*) as cellular automata, social network (*SocialNet*) as a network of agents, BrainGrid (*Brain*) as agents with dynamic communication, Tuberculosis simulation (*TB*) as agent migration over grid, and multi-agent transport simulation (*Transport*) as agent migration over network. Note that the seventh test case, (i.e., group migration) is still in progress.

Tables 1 and 2 summarize the model descriptivity of these six test cases in terms of simulation space and agent managements respectively. In space management, while RepastHPC facilitates both multi-dimensional spaces and any graph topologies as a simulation space, MASS must manage to emulate graphs using

---

[11] https://bitbucket.org/mass_application_developers/.

its *Places* array structure. On the other hand, RepastHPC supports only passive space for agents to store, retrieve, and share data, whereas *Places* in MASS can behave as a static collection of elements actively performing computation.

Table 1. Spatial management

Features	Appl.	MASS	RepastHPC
Creation			
Arrays	Life, TB Brain, Bank	+ Yes, with Places	+ Yes, with SharedDiscreteSpace
Graphs	SocialNet Transport	− Mimicked by Places, using neighbors in exchangeAll()	+ Yes, with successors in the agentNetwork class
Addressing			
Space	Life, TB Brain, Bank	− Only array indices allowed	+ Yes, with SharedDiscreteSpace and SharedContinuousSpace
Graphs	SocialNet	− Mimicked by neighbors in exchangeAll()	+ Yes, with successors in the agentNetwork class
Communication			
In array	Life, TB Brain	+ Yes, with exchangeBoundary()	+ Yes, with moor2Dspace()
Over graph	SocialNet	− Mimicked by neighbors in exchangeAll()	+ Yes, with agentNetwork and DiffusionLayerND.diffusion()
Space & agents	Transport TB, Bank	+ Yes, through Place.agents and Agent.place pointers	− From agent to space only with ValueLayerND.get/setValueAt()
Computation			
	All	+ Yes, with Places.callAll()	− Performed by agents only. No active space concepts

In agent management, RepastHPC needs user interventions to facilitate run-time agent creation and termination although it can populate agents over an entire space from the hawk's viewpoint, whose merits and demerits are opposite in MASS. Due to their different design concepts, MASS allows different classes of agents to behave on the same *Places*, whereas RepastHPC allows different *Contexts* to share the same *ValueLayerND* space. As MASS cannot create a network of agents, their direct communication is not supported. On the other hand, as RepastHPC supports read-only ghost space, agents may get collided onto the same logical location, which must be handled at a user level.

In entire simulation management as summarized in Table 3, MASS focuses on hiding the underlying parallel platforms from ABM applications much more than facilitating user-friendly event scheduling and data collection. On other hand, RepastHPC exposes users to underlying parallel platforms. They must understand MPI and handle agent/data packing, transfer, and unpacking. They must also maintain agent lists in Context and examine one after another agent, which is tedious and difficult to parallelize. None of both supports strong migration.

Table 4 compares MASS C++ and RepastHPC in lines of code (LoC) necessary to describe the test cases. In general, MASS C++ can describe these six

Table 2. Agent management

Features	Appl.	MASS	RepastHPC
Creation			
Population	All	− Individually with Agent.map	+ Entirely with Context.addAgent()
Multiclasses	Transport TB	+ Yes, with new Places()	− One class of agents per context but ValueLayerND shared among multiple contexts
Runtime	TB	+ Yes, with Agent.spawn() and Agent.kill()	− Marked as dead at a user level, then removed by agentRemove()
Communication			
Direct	Social	− No support	+ Yes, through the agentNetwork class
Indirect	Transport TB	+ Yes, through Place.agents or Place-local variables	+ Yes, through the moore2Dspace class
Broadcast	Bank	+ Yes, by sending a financial messenger to an agent cluster	− Emulated by having a firm/bank contact each of agents in their cluster
Computation			
	All	+ Yes, with Agents.callAll()	+ Yes, RepastHPCAgent.play()
Migration			
Autonomy	Transport TB	+ Yes, with Agent.migrate()	+ Yes, with RepastHPCAgent.move()
Strong migration		− No, weak migration only	− No, weak migration only
Collision		+ Yes, supported by system	− No, user emulation using the moore2Dspace class

test cases in 64% through 94% of the corresponding RepastHPC's code. However, this is because RepastHPC needs to add MPI-parallel and message pack/unpack code. In fact, RepastHPC can describe agent behavior in less LoC than MASS C++ when agents are static in space.

In summary, there is still some room for improvement in ABM parallelization before it attracts non-computing users: (1) underlying parallel platform should be masked as observed in MASS and initialization/data collection should be centralized as observed in RepastHPC; (2) ABM code can be further simplified with a plenty of simulation features including: discrete event scheduling, contiguous simulation space, graph construction, active computation in space, and more advanced agent mobility such as strong migration and agent collision avoidance.

Table 3. Entire simulation management

Features	MASS	RepastHPC
Scenario control	− main() describes an entire scenario	+ Context registers discrete events
Parallelization	+ Multi-processes spawned by libssh2	+ Multi-processes spawned by MPI
	+ Multithreading supported	− No multithreading for agent manipulation within each context
	+ System-supported agent/data transfer	− User-operated data pack/unpack
	− Synchronization required for agents to access the same place	+ Synchronization eased with sequential agent manipulation within context
Outputs	− MASS.log() collects data per process	+ repast::DataSet::record() collects data at rank 0
	− Both give users a burden to keep track of a specific agent	

4.2 Execution Performance

We evaluated the parallel performance of MASS and RepastHPC, using the University of Washington, Bothell's shared Linux cluster: 16 Dell Optiplex 710 desktops, each with an Intel i7-3770 Quad-Core CPU at 3.40 GHz and 16 GB RAM. Figure 3 shows the results of the six test cases. *Bank*, *Life*, *BrainGrid*, and *SocialNet* are static agents, while *Transport* and *TB* are dynamic agents. We adjusted their space size to 100×100–1000×1000 and # agents to 200–162000 so that all tests complete below 35 seconds for their sequential execution.

Table 4. Lines of code in MASS C++ and RepastHPC

Code	Bank		Life		BrainGrid		Social Net		Transport		TB	
	MASS	Repast	MASS	Repast	MASS	Repast	MASS	Repast	MASS	Repast	MASS	Repast
Env/space	302	400	107	386	120	386	114	409	344	398	424	407
Agents	227	194	223	131	467	240	332	161	185	307	143	200
Total	529	594	330	517	587	626	446	575	529	705	567	607
Ratio for entire code	0.89	1.00	0.64	1.00	0.94	1.00	0.78	1.00	0.75	1.00	0.93	1.00
Ratio for agent code	1.17	1.00	1.71	1.00	1.95	1.00	2.00	1.00	0.60	1.00	0.72	1.00

In static agents, *Bank* gathers agents in groups and thus showed less spatial parallelism. For better performance, agents must be handled with multithreading. *Life* demonstrated their super-linear performance due to more space made available with multiple nodes. *BrainGrid* did not perform better with 4+ nodes, because its computation completed quickly with the current random initialization of neurons. *SocialNet* was executed much faster, using RepastHPC's `agentNetwork` class that supports a graph of static agents. In dynamic agents, while *Transport* showed its clear CPU scalability, *TB* suffered from unbalanced load over 4+ computing nodes, because its agents tend to come together, which should be addressed with dynamic load balancing. It is inevitable that RepastHPC performs slower than MASS (except *SocialNet*) due to its MPI-based implementation and user-level agent serialization, whereas MASS directly uses sockets and automates all the serialization.

In summary, although a cluster system facilitates more computing resources in CPUs and memory that allow a simulation space and # agents to scale up, parallel simulators need to balance initial and dynamic distribution of a space and agents over cluster nodes, and should utilize CPU cores more efficiently.

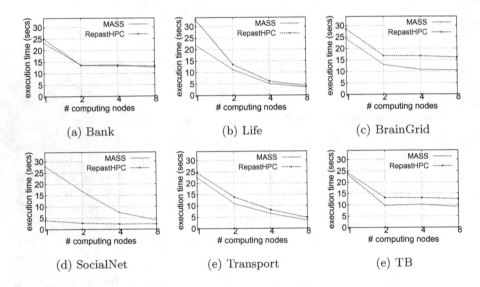

(a) Bank   (b) Life   (c) BrainGrid

(d) SocialNet   (e) Transport   (e) TB

Fig. 3. ABM execution performance

5   Conclusions

We surveyed ABM applications in SBE, biological and ecological sciences, and urban planning; categorized into seven models from the viewpoint of agent mobility; and analyzed MASS and RepastHPC for their agent and spatial descriptivity as well as measured performance overheads incurred by their implementation.

Based on our agent descriptivity analysis, we proposed that parallel ABM simulators should hide parallel-computing constructs from non-computing users, enrich simulation-space topological and computational features, and improve agent mobility as they can mimic human, animal, and moving objects. Our performance evaluation demonstrated substantial performance improvements with two cluster nodes but not always with 4+ nodes. For further scalable computation, ABM simulators should efficiently handle agents with CPU cores and to distribute a simulation space and agents uniformly over a cluster system, which balances computation and communication over computing nodes.

To pursue this research project, we will complete the VDT model as the seventh test case; fine-tune the complexity of all the seven test cases for covering more realistic agent behaviors; extend our performance evaluation to 32 ways, (i.e., 8 cluster nodes × 4 CPU cores per node); and develop agent annotations and sub-classes that predefine typical agent behavior at the system level.

References

1. Ang, C.S., Zaphiris, P.: Simulating social networks of online communities: simulation as a method for social design. In: IFIP Conference on Human-Computer Interaction - INTERACT 2009, Uppsala, Sweden, pp. 443–456, August 2009
2. Barrett, C.L., et al.: TRANSSIMS (TRansportation ANalysis SIMulation System) - Overview. La-ur-99-1658, Los Alamos National Laboratory, May 1999
3. Bohnabeau, E.: Agent-based modeling: methods and techniques for simulating human systems. In: Proceedings of the National Academy of Sciences of the United States of America, vol. 99, no. 3, pp. 7280–7287, May 2002
4. Borrill, P.L., Tesfatsion, L.: The Elgar companion to recent economic methodology. In: Agent-Based Modeling: The Right Mathematics for the Social Sciences?, pp. 228–258. Edward Elgar Publishers, February 2011
5. Borst, P.: The first implementation of the WAVE system for UNIX and TCP/IP computer networks. Technical report 18/92, University of Karlsruhe, December 1992
6. Bowzer, C., Phan, B., Cohen, K., Fukuda, M.: Collision-free agent migration in spatial simulation. In: Proceedings of 11th Joint Agent-oriented Workshops in Synergy (JAWS 2017), Prague, Czech, September 2017
7. Chao, D.L., Halloran, M.E., Obenchain, V.J., Longini Jr., I.M.: FluTE, a publicly available stochastic influenza epidemic simulation model. PLoS Comput. Biol. **6**(1), 517–527 (2010)
8. Chiacchio, F., Pennisi, M., Russo, G., Motta, S., Pappalardo, F.: Agent-based modeling of the immune system: NetLogo, a promising framework. BioMed Res. Int. (2014). https://doi.org/10.1155/2014/907171
9. Cicirelli, F., et al.: Edge computing and social internet of things for large-scale smart environments development. IEEE Internet of Things J. (2017). https://doi.org/10.1109/JIOT.2017.2775739
10. Deissenberg, C., van der Hoog, S., Dawid, H.: EURACE: a massively parallel agent-based model of the European economy. Appl. Math. Comput. **204**(2), 541–552 (2008)
11. Dewdney, A.K.: Computer recreations sharks and fish wage an ecological war on the toroidal planet Wa-Tor. Sci. Am. **6**, 14–22 (1984)
12. Epstein, J., Axtell, R.: Growing Artificial Societies: Social Science from the Bottom Up, p. 224. Brookings Institution Press, Washington, DC (1996)
13. Fortino, G., et al.: Modeling and simulating internet-of-things systems: a hybrid agent-oriented approach. Comput. Sci. Eng. **19**(5), 68–76 (2017)
14. Gardner, M.: The fantastic combinations of John Conway's new solitaire game "life". Sci. Am. **223**, 120–123 (1970)

15. Gilbert, N., Bankes, S.: Platforms and methods for agent-based modeling. In: Proceedings of the National Academy of Sciences of the United States of America, vol. 99, No. 3, pp. 7197–7198, May 2002

16. Jacintho, L.F.O., Batista, A.F.M., Ruas, T., Slive, F.A.: An agent-based model for the spread of the Dengue fever: a swarm platform simulation approach. In: Proceedings of the 2010 Spring Simulation Multiconference, SpringSim 2010. SCS, Orland, FL, April 2010, https://doi.org/10.1145/1878537.1878540

17. Kawasaki, F.: Accelerating large-scale simulations of coortical neuronal network development. Master's thesis, MSCSSE, University of Washington Bothell (2012)

18. Klimek, P., Poledna, S., Farmer, J.D., Thurner, S.: To bail-out or to bail-in? Answers from an agent-based model. J. Econ. Dyn. Control **50**, 144–154 (2015)

19. Levitt, R.E.: VDT computational emulation models of organizations: state of the art and practice. Technical report, Stanford University (2000). http://web.stanford.edugroup/VDT/VDT.pdf

20. Lu, W., Liu, C., Bhaduri, B.: Agent-based large-scale emergency evacuation using real-time open government data. In: Proceedings of Workshops on Big Data and Urban Informatics, Chicaco, IL, August 2014

21. Nuria, P., Allbeck, J.M., Badler, N.I.: Controlling individual agents in high-density crowd simulation. In: Proceedings of the 2007 ACM SIGGRAPH/Eurographics Symposium on Computer Animation. Eurographics Association (2017)

22. Rogers, A., et al.: Supporting dyanmic data structures on distributed-memory machines. TOPLAS **17**(2), 233–263 (1995)

23. Rousset, A., Herrmann, B., Lang, C., Philippe, L.: A survey on parallel and distributed multi-agent systems for high performance computing simulations. Comput. Sci. Rev. **22**, 27–46 (2016)

24. Savaglio, C., Fortino, G., Ganzha, M., Paprzycki, M., Bădică, C., Ivanović, M.: Agent-based computing in the internet of things: a survey. In: Ivanović, M., Bădică, C., Dix, J., Jovanović, Z., Malgeri, M., Savić, M. (eds.) IDC 2017. SCI, vol. 737, pp. 307–320. Springer, Cham (2018). https://doi.org/10.1007/978-3-319-66379-1_27

25. Segovia-Juarez, J.L., Ganguli, S., Kirschner, D.: Identifying control mechanisms of granuloma formation during M. tuberculosis infection using an agent-based model. J. Theor. Biol. **231**(3), 357–376 (2004)

26. Suresh, S., Gutmann, M.P.: Rebuilding the MOSAIC: fostering research in social, behavioral, and economic sciences at the national science foundation in the next decade. NSF 11–086, National Science Foundation, Directorate for Social, Behavioral and Economic Sciences, Arlington, VA USA (2011)

27. Thorne, B.C., Bailey, A.M.: Multi-cell agent-based simulation of the microvasculature to study the dynamics of circulating inflammatory cell trafficking. Ann. Biomed. Eng. **35**(6), 916–936 (2007)

Toward a Complete Agent-Based Model of a Honeybee Colony

Jérémy Rivière[1]([✉]), Cédric Alaux[2], Yves Le Conte[2], Yves Layec[3],
André Lozac'h[3], Vincent Rodin[1], and Frank Singhoff[1]

[1] Lab-STICC, Université de Bretagne Occidentale, CNRS UMR 6285, Brest, France
{jeremy.riviere,vincent.rodin,frank.singhoff}@univ-brest.fr
[2] INRA, UR 406 Abeilles et Environnement, Avignon, France
[3] GDSA29, Finistère, France

Abstract. The agent-based approach has been successfully used in the past years to model and simulate complex systems. We use this approach on a honeybee colony in a Dadant hive, where several tens of thousands of bees interact, in order to evaluate the impact of local actions at the bee-level (such as beekeeping practices) on the global system. In this article, we focus on the foraging activity, its recruitment mechanisms and the behaviour of foraging bees, and how these bees interact with the hive's environment, greatly different in scale. We present a customizable, agent-compliant module called the Ecosystem Module, that aims at modelling and simulating the foraging, according to the local weather and the surrounding nectar sources. First results back up our model, showing that these recruitment mechanisms lead to a self-organizing process of the best available sources' selection by the agents.

1 Introduction

Complex systems are commonly referred to "systems in which large networks of components with no central control and simple rules of operation give rise to complex collective behaviour" [10]. The agent-based approach, because it focuses on the individual to obtain the overall behaviour by emergence, is particularly suited to model and simulate complex systems (*e.g.* [3,8] in the past few years).

A honeybee colony, where several tens of thousands of honeybees interact and live together, is a great example of complex system. Indeed, one of the notable characteristics of *Apis mellifera L.*, used in beekeeping, and *Apis* bee species, is that they live in colonies based on eusocial behaviour patterns [20]. This social organisation depends on the multiple interactions (*e.g.* pheromones [18], nutrition, communication) occurring between specialized individuals (forager, nurse, builder, etc.) of different casts and ages. From these interactions, complex phenomena thus emerge at the system-level (the colony) allowing its self-regulation and self-adaptation, including but not limited to:

The authors would like to thank Antoine Gaget for his work.

- Changing roles depending on the needs of the colony [5];
- Thermoregulation and ventilation [17] and formation of the brood nest [6];
- **Selection of the best available nectar sources** [7, 16].

Our undertaking is to model these phenomena to simulate a honeybee colony. The objective is twofold. First, we aim at allowing direct interactions with bees *via* a 3D simulation, for two different uses: an educational use (*e.g.* to learn good beekeeping practices), and a scientific use, to evaluate ecological phenomena (parasites, virus) and anthropogenic factors. Second, investigating these phenomena may lead to identify the core mechanisms behind them, which, from an engineer's point of view, could help to resolve similar issues in other fields. For example, the bees' ability to detect high profitable sources and quickly exploit them before they fade is very efficient, and could inspire new organisation methods in (critic) resource allocation problems.

Some of these phenomena may be described at the colony-level by using differential equations and by not considering bees as individuals [1, 11, 12]. However, in order to investigate these phenomena and to allow interactions with bees, a bottom-up approach is required to deduce the effects of these micro actions in the short and long run on the colony. Discovering, formalizing and modelling the links between individuals (micro-level) and the behaviour of the system (macro-level) remain a major issue in complex systems. Population models, because they focus on the macro-level, do not take into account the micro-level and its existing links with the macro [4]. We thus choose to model the honeybee colony following an agent-based approach, where the honeybee is an agent, described by its biological cycle, behaviour, and its interactions with its environment.

We present in this article an agent-based model of foraging bees, and how their interactions and recruitment lead to the selection of the best nectar sources in the surroundings of the colony. Focusing on the hive to allow local actions, such as the removal of a frame, a beekeepers practice, makes the hive the obvious agents' environment, with the need to define a high-resolution behaviour for the bees within the hive. However, foraging bees go *outside the hive* to bring back resources (nectar, pollen, water), within a range of approximately 10 km [14], for an area of 314 km^2. There is thus great differences in granularity and scale between the hive (usually $38 \times 45 \times 31$ cm) and the outside environment, making the connection between the two environments difficult.

We tackle this issue by designing an **Ecosystem Module**. This customizable module is compliant with an agent-based simulation: Forager Agents, described in Sect. 4, interact with this module which rests upon the local weather, the days' length, and the surrounding pollen and nectar sources (see Sect. 3) to simulate the outside trip and bring back resources according to probabilities deduced, adapted or borrowed from previous models in literature.

In the next section, we take a look at some important related works on agent-based simulations of honeybee foraging and recruitment. Preliminary results of experiments conducted under the conditions (weather, sources) of the last three years in Brest (Bretagne, France) with our agent based-model and the Ecosystem

Module are presented and discussed in Sect. 5. Finally, we conclude and outline the perspectives of this work in Sect. 6.

2   Agent-Based Models of Foraging and Recruitment

As stated by previous works [13,15], recruitment is the cornerstone of a self-organization process that leads foraging bees to select the more profitable sources in the hive's surroundings. Among foraging bees, the scouts are basically explorers, going outside the hive to discover nectar and pollen sources, forage, and communicate their location and profitability (the waggle dance) to unemployed bees, waiting for to be recruited, when coming back at the hive. Surprisingly, the scouts represent a small proportion of the foraging force (around 10% [14]); and they can only convey the information to a small number of bees, recruiting 0.8 bees on average at each dance [7]. Seeley [14] also noticed that the colony's resources stock leads foraging bees to scout more often and to accept more easily a less profitable source when it is low. It is still unclear however how the stock's state is assessed by the bees, although local perceptions may play a role.

Most of agent-based models focusing on foraging are independent models built to investigate precise biological questions [7,19]. For example, Dornhaus et al. [7] conducted an experiment based on their model, aiming at quantifying the benefits of recruitment according to the size of the colony and the sources quality. This model introduces some interesting probabilities, adapted in our model, and a first line of approach for the forager agent's behaviour. However, in most cases, these models can hardly be integrated with a model of the colony in the hive because of the difference between the models' time and spatial scales.

On the other hand, a few agent-based models interact with other models in order to simulate the entire colony. In Beehave [1], the agent-based model, dedicated to the foraging activity, interacts with two other population-based modules simulating the life of the colony and the propagation of the parasite *Varroa destructor* in the colony. The agent-based model includes a spatially explicit landscape that the forager agents explore and on which they forage at flower patches. In this module, foragers are super-individuals representing 100 identical foragers. The model is executed once per day, and the time step of the simulation seems to be one minute. These last two parameters make difficult its adaptation to an agent-based model of the colony in the hive.

To conclude this section, we can draw one common characteristic from all these models: they mostly agree on the nature of the hive's environment, made up of nectar and pollen sources and the weather conditions.

3   The Ecosystem Module

The Ecosystem Module aims at simulating the foraging, at an agent's request, according to the outside environment of the hive. As seen in Sect. 2, two important factors are needed to take into account and evaluate the ecosystem's impact on the colony: a representation of the local climate, and the available pollen and nectar sources at the current time of the year. These two factors are each the target of a dedicated customizable module, the Weather and the Sources Modules.

The trip conditions of foraging bees are strongly influenced [14] by (1) the day's length: bees can forage only during daylight hours; and (2) the weather: foraging bees can go outside the hive only when the temperature is above approximately 11 °C, and when there is neither rain nor strong wind.

The *Weather Module* tackles these aspects by, firstly, approximating the time of sunrise and sunset, and secondly, providing real weather data. These aspects are customizable according to the current date and location. The weather data come from the Open Data service (Synop) of the French national meteorological service, Meteo France[1]. The Synop data are weather records for sixty-two stations in metropolitan France and Overseas territories of France, providing the current temperature, humidity, cloudiness etc. From these records and the time of the day, the Weather Module gives information on whether or not a foraging bee is able to go outside the hive.

The *Sources Module* allows to represent the surrounding nectar and pollen resources, their distance to the hive, their flowering duration and peak, and the sugar concentration of the available nectar, if present. When running a simulation, one can choose to generate a given number of random sources, and can also configure the main local sources. For example, some of the known sources around Brest, in France, and used in the experiment (see Sect. 5), are: the rape, that flowers from the 15th of April to the 15th of May, the bramble, from the 15th of June to the 15th of July, but also the sweet chestnut, etc.

Each source is ruled by a *source factor*, giving the accessibility of the nectar and/or pollen resources according to the date. The *source factor* (SF) is directly inspired by the season factor of the HoPoMo model [12], and is thus defined by the following normalized Gaussian function, where src is the source, nb is the day's number of the year, d is the flowering duration and p its peak:

$$SF(src, nb) = 1 - \left(\frac{1}{\frac{d}{4} \cdot \sqrt{2 \cdot \Pi}} \cdot \exp(-\frac{(nb - p)^2}{2 \cdot \frac{d}{4}^2}) \right)$$

Each source has also a **profitability**, computed from its distance to the hive, the nectar's sugar concentration and the quantity of accessible resources. As stated in [15], this profitability will impact the recruitment of bees, according to their perception of the colony's resources stocks (see Sect. 4.1).

The final component of the Ecosystem Module is the *Outside Agent*, which is the system's interface. We chose to design this interface as an agent to allow our agent-based model to communicate with the Ecosystem Module. The communication protocol lies on the FIPA-ACL standards: a Forager Agent first sends a *request* to the Outside Agent to forage at an aimed (ever by recruitment or from its memory) source or at a source it must first discover. According to the Weather and Sources Modules and the *p_death* and *p_full_return* probabilities (see Table 2), the Outside Agent then either *refuses* to answer the request

---

[1] https://donneespubliques.meteofrance.fr/.

(because the Forager Agent died, or it has found no source), or *accepts*. In this latter case, the Outside Agent communicates (1) the pollen and/or nectar quantity the Forager Agent can bring back to the hive, (2) the nectar quality of the source and (3), the travel time, in number of time steps of the simulation (see Sect. 4.4), the Forager Agent has to wait for to simulate its trip.

4   The Agent-Based Model of Foraging Bees

As we focus here on the foraging activity, we only consider the foragers, putting the other bees and the interactions with them aside, to be included in the future. From literature and data gathered by the biologist partners, we thus model the biological cycle of a *Forager Agent*, its behaviour, and the interactions with its environment. These inputs have also been used to verify and calibrate the model.

4.1   Recruitment and Self-organization Mechanisms

Recruitment and profitability are the prime notions on which an efficient source selection lays (as seen in Sect. 2). To reproduce this self-organizing process, we model the recruitment thanks to the following mechanisms:

- When coming back at the hive, the agent may communicate (*dance*) to unemployed agents the profitability and the location of the source they have found, according to:
  - this profitability value;
  - and their perception of the current state of the resources stock.
- The state of resources stock in the hive also weights the agent's decision to follow a recruiter or not, and also the probabilities to go scouting (*p_scout*) and to go on the dance floor (*p_dancefloor*).

As presented in the Sect. 5, the preliminary results show that these mechanisms seem sufficient to reproduce this self-organization in our model.

4.2   Environment

The Forager Agent's environment consists of the hive, the other agents and the Outside Agent (see Table 1). We chose here a minimalist representation of the hive, including only the values of the pollen and the nectar stock. We state that this representation is currently sufficient to reproduce the self-organizing process in the foraging activity, but, as said in the introduction, our objective includes a complete spatial representation of the hive.

This choice of conception has two consequences. First, the consumption of resources by the bees is simplified and simulated according to the number of bees (foragers, but also larva and other bees) in the hive. Secondly, in a real hive, the perception by the bees of the resources stock's state is a complex phenomena, only partially understood. In this model, this perception is thus simplified, computed by each bee from the stock quantities, with a random bias to simulate its imprecision.

Table 1. Interaction table of the forager agent with its environment.

Interactions	Forager agent	Hive	Outside agent
Forager agent	Recruitment	Drop resources	Send a request to go outside
Hive	Stock perception	Pollen and Nectar consumption	–
Outside agent	Accept/refuse the request to go outside	–	–

4.3   Forager Agent's Behaviour

Because of its simple graphical representation, the state chart presented in Fig. 1 has been the medium to enable an interdisciplinary discussion between biologists, beekeepers and computer scientists, in order to define the Forager Agent's behaviour. In addition to the interaction table and the table of probabilities and parameters (Table 2), it shows a dynamic view of the agent's behaviour.

In Fig. 1, transitions between states are probabilities and/or conditions verified at each time step by the agent. The Table 2 gives the values of the probabilities used by the Outside Agent (p_full_return and p_death) and by the Forager Agent. It also shows the values of the Forager Agent's parameters, which may have a random deviation, in order to introduce variability between the agents.

The Forager Agent thus follows the behaviour defined by this state chart, made of seven states. The most important states are:

- *OnTheDanceFloor*: this state is the crossroad of many transitions. The agent can come from the *Resting* state, in order to either wait for to be recruited by another agent or go outside as a scout (p_scout probability). The agent can also come from outside, bringing back resources or not (*FullReturn* and *EmptyReturn* states).
- *WaitingForToBeRecruited*: the agent is ready to receive a message from a recruiting agent (*Recruitment* state). In this case, it assesses the profitability of the conveyed source according to its biased perception of the colony's resources stock. If the source seems profitable enough, it will try to go outside to forage at this aimed source. In other cases, and if the agent has waited too long, it may also go scouting according to the p_scout probability.
- *TripOutside*: this state simulates the agent's trip outside the hive to bring back resources. It is in this state that it communicates with the Outside Agent and interacts with the Ecosystem Module.
- *Recruitment*: the agent, after a successful trip outside, goes back to the dance floor and may try to recruit (*dance*) other agents in the *WaitingForToBeRecruited* state according to the profitability of the source and its perception of the colony's resources stock. A source may be profitable (*found_source*) but not enough regarding the stocks. When recruiting, it sends a message to a

nbr_bees_listening with the name of the source and its profitability, then tries to go back outside to the same source if possible.

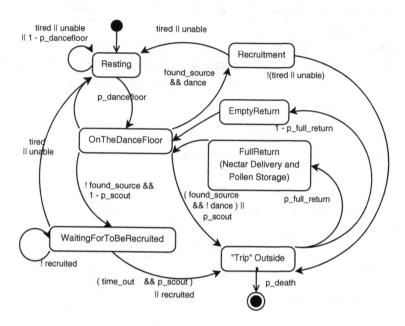

Fig. 1. State chart of the forager agent behaviour.

4.4 Implementation and Scheduling

The agent-based model and the Ecosystem Module have been implemented with JADE [2] in Java. JADE provides communication mechanisms and a well-suited architecture for our model: behaviours are independent of agents, and can be added or removed following the evolution of the agent's speciality. JADE also offers a *FSMBehavior* that allows to directly implement the state diagram and its transitions. Finally, this choice of platform also lies on the necessity to implement the model in a standard programming language to maximise code reliability and make it more easily extendible.

Bees being asynchronous entities, as all living beings, we selected a chaotic asynchronous scheduling, in which the agents are activated in a random manner to avoid a bias in the simulation [9]. As we deal with agents, though, this *activation* consists in receiving a message from a Scheduler Agent. However, nothing prevents the environment's scheduler (in our case, the Java Virtual Machine) to favour some agents to make more actions than others. The agents thus have to synchronize themselves at some point or another. This is done by introducing the following policy in the agents' behaviour:

Table 2. Probabilities and parameters used by the Outside and the Forager Agents. Each value is given according to the ratio $\frac{simulation\ time\ step}{real\ time} = \frac{1}{1000}$. Probabilities that can be weighted by the colony's resources stock are represented with a *.

Probability/Parameters	Value	Adapted from
Outside agent		
p_death	0.0108	[11]
p_full_return	0.43 when scouting	[16]
	0.93 when recruited	[16]
Foraging duration	[5.41; 11.37] min. for 650 m	[15]
Max. quantity in one trip:		
– of nectar	[14.6;16] mg	[7]
– of pollen	25 mg	[7]
Flight speed	1.29 m.s^{-1}	[15]
Nectar consumption in flight	0.0083 mg.m^{-1}	[14]
Forager agent		
p_scout *	0.00825	[7]
p_dancefloor *	0.001	Deduced from calibration
max_outing_on_a_row	[20; 30] trips in a row	[14]
min_go_out_temp	11 °C ± 1	[14]
max_go_out_temp	40 °C ± 1	[14]
nbr_bees_listening	[0; 3] agents per dance	[7]
wait_recruit_time	30 min	Deduced from calibration

1. The Forager Agent waits for the Scheduler Agent's activation message;
2. After reception, it makes *n actions*;
3. Then, it informs the Scheduler Agent that it has done, and waits again for an activation message.

For its part, the Scheduler Agent waits for all Forager Agents to be done before sending a new activation message, leading to a synchronization of all the agents. The smaller is the value of *n*, the greater will be the number of messages exchanged. On the other hand, a too great *n* value can lead to great differences between the number of *actions* done by the agents. These *actions* are defined within the states introduced above, as steps that take in reality approximately one second to be performed by the bee.

5   Experiments and Preliminary Results

We have conducted 3 experiments with our agent-based model and the Ecosystem Module, each conducted under the conditions (local weather and sources) of the last 3 years in Brest (Bretagne, France). The experiments run from the 1st of March to the 1st of September of each year. Each experiment consists in 10 runs with the same weather and location of sources, and the same initial state: 500 foraging bees, and rather low resources stock. As the agent-based model does not yet include the queen and the larva, the *p_death* probability is set to 0.

These first experiments aim at verify our model, by notably verifying the following hypothesis:

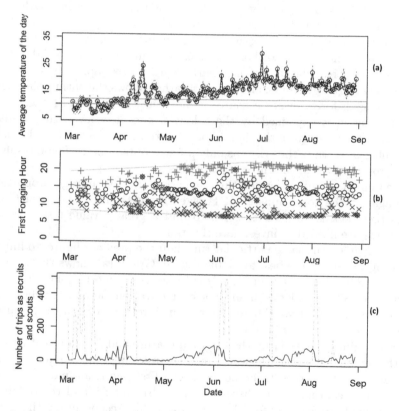

Fig. 2. Graph (a) on the top shows the average temperature per day of 2015 in Brest (circles) and the minimum (dash-dotted line) and maximum (dashed line) averages. Graph (b) shows the average first foraging hour per agent per day (circles), *i.e.* the time of the day at which the agents go forage for the first time. Minimum (+) and maximum (x) first foraging hour per day are also displayed. Graph (c) shows the number of trips done by scouting agents (solid line) and recruiting agents (dashed line) per day.

- H1: The weather influences the outing of Forager Agents, as stated in [14];
- H2: Agents select the best available sources in the surroundings of the hive;
- H3: Finally, Forager Agents scouting represent an average number of around 10% of the foraging force [14].

5.1 Preliminary Results

Figure 2 first gives an overview of the influence of weather on the outing of Forager Agents (H1). This is one run of the 2015 experiment. The first points on the left of the graph (b) mean that there are some agents going out around 10 a.m. (+), while the majority goes outside around 14 p.m. (circle), until 16 p.m. (x). In early March for example, there are some days where the agents cannot go outside at all because of the low temperature or the bad weather. Other days, the average first foraging hour can be very early in the day (*e.g.* in June).

As we take a look at the recruitment mechanism, graph (c) shows a correlation between the number of Forager Agents scouting outside (solid line) and the recruited agents (dashed line). In early April for example, a new profitable source is discovered by scouts, and, as the weather allows the outing, they recruit a great foraging force toward a source: almost 50% of the total foraging force. This phenomena is explained by the colony's stock low level, that leads the agents to go more easily on the dance floor and to accept less profitable sources. The number of recruits thus rises as only a few scouts remain. These results are found across all runs of the three experiments.

Based on the results over the three experiments, the average proportion of scouts against the total number of Forager Agents (H3) is between 6% and 7%. As the stock is low, we expected to find a greater value (10%), so more experiments are needed to investigate this point.

Figure 3 shows the same particular run than the previous figure, to illustrate how the agents select the best available source. Graph (a) shows that, from the 60th to the 80th days, the source S1 (solid line) is the most profitable. Then, a second source S2 (dash-dotted line), shorter in duration, becomes the best source for approximately 10 days. Finally, after a quick return of S1, a third source S3 (dashed line) takes over from the 95th day.

In the beginning of the run, the low temperature and the bad weather do not allow the agents to efficiently go forage, as we can see in graphs (b) and (c). Three points of interest are then to be noticed. The first one is around the 75th day (mid-March): scouting agents discover sources S1 and S2, and the recruitment leads the agents to leave S2 for S1 after 3 days. The second interesting point is about source S2, from the 81th to the 98th day, ignored by agents, whereas it is the best available source at this moment. This can partly be explained by the fact that scouting agents missed this source during this duration, maybe caused by a too great concentration of agents on S1 at this time.

Finally, around the 97th day (early April), we find again the great recruitment described earlier (see Fig. 2). At this point, agents foraging at sources S1 and S2 progressively leave these sources for the third one (S3), as scouting agents discover and communicate about this more profitable source.

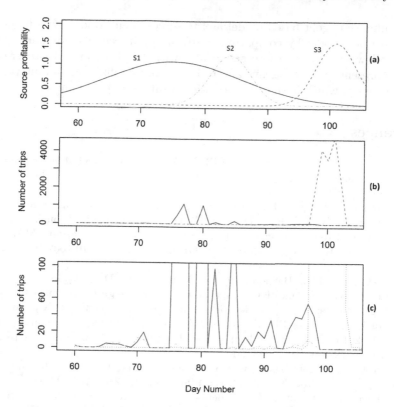

Fig. 3. Graph (a) shows the profitability evolution of three sources between early March and late April 2015. Graph (b) shows the number of trips per day outside the hive according to the same sources displayed on graph (a). The third graph (c) is an enlargement of (b).

6   Conclusion and Perspectives

We presented in this article an agent-based model of foraging bees, and the Ecosystem Module in relation with the Forager Agent's behaviour. This latter module aims at connecting two environments of different granularity and scales, in time and space, and allows agents to navigate between them.

Preliminary results of first experiments verify the influence of the environment on the model, and show that the Forager Agent's behaviour successfully reproduces recruitment, leading to a self-organizing process of the best available sources' selection by the agents. These results are a first step toward the verification of our model, that more experiments are planned to fulfil.

The building of the complete agent-based model is currently in progress and includes the definition of the behaviours of other roles and casts, such as the Queen, the larva, etc. In order to formalize and model more complex phenomena occurring within a colony, a spatially explicit hive and resources stock representation is also a work in progress. Ultimately, more experiments conducted on the enhanced agent-based model and the Ecosystem Module will be needed to validate our model by comparing the results with colonies dynamics data. Finally, allowing a user to interact locally with the bees involves to create a virtual representation of the hive and to integrate visualization and interactions with the colony, which have to be realistic, intuitive and ergonomic.

References

1. Becher, M.A., Grimm, V., et al.: BEEHAVE: a systems model of honeybee colony dynamics and foraging to explore multifactorial causes of colony failure. J. Appl. Ecol. **51**(2), 470–482 (2014)
2. Bellifemine, F., Bergenti, F., Caire, G., Poggi, A.: JADE – a java agent development framework. In: Bordini, R.H., Dastani, M., Dix, J., El Fallah Seghrouchni, A. (eds.) Multi-Agent Programming: Languages, Platforms and Applications. MASA, vol. 15, pp. 125–147. Springer, Boston (2005). https://doi.org/10.1007/0-387-26350-0_5
3. Bilbao-Castro, J.R., Barrionuevo, G., Ruiz-Lupión, D., Casado, L.G., Moya-Laraño, J.: Weaver: a multiagent, spatial-explicit and high-performance framework to study complex ecological networks. In: Bajo, J., Hallenborg, K., Pawlewski, P., Botti, V., Sánchez-Pi, N., Duque Méndez, N.D., Lopes, F., Julian, V. (eds.) PAAMS 2015. CCIS, vol. 524, pp. 139–150. Springer, Cham (2015). https://doi.org/10.1007/978-3-319-19033-4_12
4. Bonabeau, E.: Agent-based modeling: methods and techniques for simulating human systems. Proc. Nat. Acad. Sci. **99**(suppl. 3), 7280–7287 (2002)
5. Bonabeau, E., Theraulaz, G., Deneubourg, J.L., Aron, S., Camazine, S.: Self-organization in social insects. Trends Ecol. Evol. **12**(5), 188–193 (1997)
6. Camazine, S.: Self-organizing pattern formation on the combs of honey bee colonies. Behav. Ecol. Sociobiol. **28**(1), 61–76 (1991)
7. Dornhaus, A., Klügl, F., Oechslein, C., Puppe, F., Chittka, L.: Benefits of recruitment in honey bees: effects of ecology and colony size in an individual-based model. Behav. Ecol. **17**(3), 336–344 (2006)
8. Krichene, H., El-Aroui, M.-A.: Behavioral and informational agents-based modeling and simulation of emerging stock markets. In: Bajo, J., et al. (eds.) Trends in Practical Applications of Agents, Multi-Agent Systems and Sustainability: The PAAMS Collection. AISC, vol. 372, pp. 3–10. Springer, Cham (2015). https://doi.org/10.1007/978-3-319-19629-9_1
9. Kubera, Y., Mathieu, P., Picault, S.: How to avoid biases in reactive simulations. In: Demazeau, Y., Pavòn, J., Corchado, J.M., Bajo, J. (eds.) PAAMS 2009. AINSC, vol. 55, pp. 100–109. Springer, Heidelberg (2009). https://doi.org/10.1007/978-3-642-00487-2_11
10. Mitchell, M.: Complexity: A Guided Tour. Oxford University Press, Oxford (2009)
11. Russell, S., Barron, A.B., Harris, D.: Dynamic modelling of honey bee (Apis mellifera) colony growth and failure. Ecol. Model. **265**, 158–169 (2013)
12. Schmickl, T., Crailsheim, K.: HoPoMo: a model of honeybee intracolonial population dynamics and resource management. Ecol. Model. **204**(1), 219–245 (2007)
13. Seeley, T.D.: Division of labor between scouts and recruits in honeybee foraging. Behav. Ecol. Sociobiol. **12**(3), 253–259 (1983)
14. Seeley, T.D.: The Wisdom of the Hive. Harvard University Press, Cambridge (1995)

15. Seeley, T.D., Camazine, S., Sneyd, J.: Collective decision-making in honey bees: how colonies choose among nectar sources. Behav. Ecol. Sociobiol. **28**(4), 277–290 (1991)
16. Seeley, T.D., Visscher, P.K.: Assessing the benefits of cooperation in honeybee foraging: search costs, forage quality, and competitive ability. Behav. Ecol. Sociobiol. **22**(4), 229–237 (1988)
17. Sumpter, D.J., Broomhead, D.S.: Shape and dynamics of thermoregulating honey bee clusters. J. Theor. Biol. **204**(1), 1–14 (2000)
18. Traynor, K.S., LeConte, Y., Page, R.E.: Queen and young larval pheromones impact nursing and reproductive physiology of honey bee (Apis mellifera) workers. Behav. Ecol. Sociobiol. **68**(12), 2059–2073 (2014)
19. de Vries, H., Biesmeijer, J.C.: Modelling collective foraging by means of individual behaviour rules in honey-bees. Behav. Ecol. Sociobiol. **44**(2), 109–124 (1998)
20. Winston, M.L.: The Biology of the Honey Bee. Harvard University Press, Cambridge (1987)

PAAMS Workshop SIRS

A Swarm Based Algorithm
for a Healthcare Information System

Agostino Forestiero[(✉)]

CNR - ICAR, Institute for High Performance Computing and Networking,
National Research Council of Italy, Via Pietro Bucci,
7/11 C, 87036 Rende, CS, Italy
agostino.forestiero@icar.cnr.it

Abstract. This paper introduces H-finder, a bio-inspired algorithm
to build a decentralized and self-organized P2P information system in
healthcare environment. The algorithm takes advantage of the properties of *ant* systems, in which a number of entities perform simple operations at the local level and an advanced form of "intelligence" emerges
at global level. The work of ant-inspired agents is exploited to organize "metadata", that is, documents containing healthcare information,
like Electronic Health Records (EHR), in a network of clinical servers.
Agents travel the P2P interconnections among servers and spatially sort
metadata in order to organize similar metadata into neighbor hosts. Preliminary performance analysis proves that the proposed algorithm allows
the healthcare information to be useful reorganized thus improving the
data management.

Keywords: Electronic health records · Peer to Peer
Swarm intelligence

1 Introduction

Healthcare domain is composed of numerous and extremely dynamic information
sources over a heterogeneous infrastructure geographically distributed. Moreover, the increased adoption of electronic health records (EHRs) has led to an
unprecedented amount of healthcare information stored. The availability of a
large amount of data, however, has also raised concerns of information overload,
with potential negative consequences on clinical work, such as errors of omission,
delays, and overall patient safety [11]. Thus, the effective management of the huge
volumes of data that are produced daily, together with the effective management
of medical acts and processes are required as well. The main challenge today is
to build an appropriate Information System to support all the requirements of
the healthcare domain. Several solution for searching patient's EHR in shared
healthcare system were proposed, most of them based on a central index on the
documents' contents [13]. Limited size networks can be acceptably tackled with

© Springer International Publishing AG, part of Springer Nature 2018
J. Bajo et al. (Eds.): PAAMS 2018 Workshops, CCIS 887, pp. 509–516, 2018.
https://doi.org/10.1007/978-3-319-94779-2_43

a centralized approach, but in large and dynamic systems, centralized mechanisms show their limits and innovative distributed approaches are needed. Several P2P approaches have been proposed for organization and discovery resources in distributed systems, thanks to their inherent scalability and robustness [6,9]. The objective of these approaches is to allow users to locate resources or services, either hardware or software, with the required characteristics. Generally, resources are described through *metadata*, i.e. a syntactical/ontology description of resource/service capabilities, and therefore the aim is to locate the metadata with needed characteristics. In P2P systems, metadata are often indexed through bit vectors, which can have essentially two different meanings: (i) each bit represents the presence or absence of a given *topic* [3,12] (this method is particularly appropriate if the resource are text documents, because it is possible to define the different topics on which this document focuses); and (ii) metadata can be mapped by a locality sensitive hash function into a binary key. Locality sensitive hashing (LSH) is a commonly used technique to achieve efficient approximate nearest-neighbor search. By exploiting specially-designed LSH functions, all input similar high dimensional vectors can be hashed into the same bucket with high probability than distant ones [4]. In this way, similar index are assigned to resources having similar characteristics, i.e. with similar metadata [2,10]. In this paper, an algorithm, inspired by the behavior of some species of ants [1], to build an information system, is proposed. The algorithm, namely H-finder, is able to disseminate and reorganize metadata in order to facilitate discovery operations. The H-finder approach can be positioned along a well known research avenue whose objective is to devise possible applications of nature inspired algorithms [14], in particular of *ant algorithms*, i.e., algorithms inspired by the behavior of ants [5,7]. H-finder is specifically designed to address the case in which metadata representing health information are indexed through bit vectors obtained by LSH function – similar metadata are indexed with similar indexes – and then a similarity measure among resources, through the comparison of related indexes, can be defined. The approach is basically inspired by the work of Lumer and Faieta [8], who devised a method to spatially sort data items through the operations of simple robots. As in [8], the reorganization of metadata in H-finder is achieved by means of ant-inspired agents whose operations are driven by tailored probability functions. H-finder features a self-emerging organization and P2P *structured* properties emerge, since metadata are aggregated and spatially sorted on the basis of their indexes. Owing to these characteristics, H-finder shows important benefits that are typical of P2P structured systems. In particular, it enables the use of an *informed* discovery algorithm, through which a query message, issued to discover resources indexed by a specified *target* metadata, can efficiently explore the network and locate information about such resources. The rest of the paper is organized as follows: Sect. 2 describes the H-finder algorithm, Sect. 3 shows some encouraging experimental results and Sect. 4 concludes the paper.

2 *H-finder* Algorithm

H-finder algorithm exploits swam agents to build a P2P overlay network that allows healthcare information discovery operations faster. Information about health data, like the Electronic Health Records, are represented through metadata. Such metadata, are indexed through bit vectors with N_b bits obtained by exploiting a LSH function. In this way, similar metadata, therefore representing similar health data, are indexed with similar bit vectors. Metadata are moved by ant-inspired agents with the aim of accumulating similar health data in the same location. Based on its own state, indeed, each agent moves through the servers and performs local and simple operations. In particular, when a agent arrives in a new server: if it is unloaded, it decides whether to gather one or more metadata from the current server; while if it is loaded, it decides whether to release one or more metadata in the local server. Agents' decision are driven by two probability functions, P_g and P_d, both based on a similarity function introduced in [8]. Formula (1) reports the function that measures the similarity of a metadata d with all the metadata located in the region R.

$$S(\bar{d}, R) = \frac{1}{N_d} \sum_{d \in R} 1 - \frac{D_H(d, \bar{d})}{\alpha} \qquad (1)$$

The region R for the sever s is represented of all servers reachable from s with a given number of hops. Here the number of hops is set to 1. N_d is the overall number of metadata located in R, while $D_H(d, \bar{d})$ is the Hamming distance between d and $\bar{d}$. The similarity parameter α is set to 2. The value of S ranges from -1 to 1, but negative values are set to 0 [8].

Intuitively, the probability function of *gathering* metadata from a server has to be inversely proportional to the value of S, while, the probability function of depositing metadata has to be directly proportional to S. The probability functions to gather a metadata P_g and the probability function to deposit a metadata P_d, are reported in formulas (2) and (3), respectively.

$$P_g = \left(\frac{k_g}{k_g + S(\bar{d}, R)}\right)^2; \qquad (2)$$

$$P_d = \left(\frac{S(\bar{d}, R)}{k_d + S(\bar{d}, R)}\right)^2 \qquad (3)$$

The degree of similarity among metadata are tuned through the parameter k_g and k_d with values comprised between 0 and 1 [1]. Cyclically, the agents perform a given number of hops among servers, and when they get to a new server decide which probability function compute based on their condition (loaded or unloaded). In particular, if the agent does not carries metadata, it computes P_g, otherwise, if the agent carries metadata, P_d is computed. The processing load, Pl, that is the average number of agents per second that are processed by a server, is reported in formula (4). It does not depend neither on the network size nor on the churn rate. The value of the processing load only depends on the number of agents and the frequency of their movements.

$$Pl = \frac{N_a}{N_s \cdot T_m} = \frac{F_g}{T_m} \qquad (4)$$

where N_a and N_s represent the number of agents and the number of servers, respectively; T_m represents the average time between two successive movement of an agent and F_g represents the frequency with which agents are generated by a server.

To locate resources with given characteristics, generally, in distributed systems, each search operation collects a number of resources and the users can choose the resources that best fit their needs. In this system, a query message is issued by a server, on behalf of a user, to collect a set of metadata as similar as possible to the "target metadata". The target metadata is the metadata representing the content requested by the user. Thanks to the spatial sorting achieved by the agents, the discovery procedure can be simply performed by forwarding the request, at each step, towards the "best neighbor server". The selected neighbor server is the server that maximizes the similarity value between the target metadata and the *mean metadata* calculates by each server. The *mean metadata* is a bit vector composed of real numbers where the value of element is calculated by averaging the values of the each bits, in the same position, of all the metadata stored by the server. For example, the *mean metadata* of a server having the three metadata: $[0, 1, 1]$, $[1, 0, 1]$ and $[0, 1, 1]$ will be equal to $[0.33, 0.67, 1]$. The cosine measure, as reported in formula (5), is exploited to compute the similarity between the target metadata and the mean metadata. Here $\vec{u} \cdot \vec{v}$ indicates the *dot-product* between the vectors $\vec{u}$ and $\vec{v}$.

$$cos(\vec{u}, \vec{v}) = \frac{\vec{u} \cdot \vec{v}}{|\vec{u}|_2 \times |\vec{v}|_2} \qquad (5)$$

The search operation terminates whenever the best neighbor server is not better than the server where the query has arrived so far. A reply message with all metadata collected is forwarded to the server that has issued the request.

3   Experimental Results

A Java event-based simulator was implemented to evaluate the performance of the algorithm. In our very simple experiments, each server manages about 15 metadata representing the EHR and it is linked to 8 server on average. A graphical description of the logical reorganization is reported in Fig. 1. Each metadata is represented through a gray-scale and the server is represented with the color of the metadata managed with the maximum number of element. A portion of the network is photographed: (a) at $Time = 0$ time units, when the process is starting and the metadata are randomly distributed and (b) at $Time = 50,000$ time units, when the process is in steady situation. Notice that similar

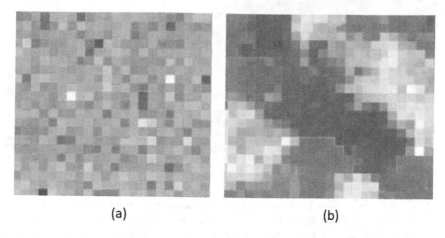

(a)   (b)

Fig. 1. Snapshots of a portion of the network when the process is starting (a), and when the process is in steady situation (b).

metadata are located in the same region and among near regions the color change gradually, which proves the spatial sorting.

The processing load, defined as the number of agents that go through a server per unit time, was calculated as in formula (4) and shown in Fig. 2(a). In the simulated scenario, T_m is equals to 60 s and F_g is equals to 0.5, so that each server processes about one agent every 120 s, which can be considered acceptable. Notice that the processing load does not depend on other system parameters such as the average number of metadata handled by a server or the number of server, that confirms the scalability properties of the algorithm. The value of processing load changes according to the maximum number of hops performed within a single agent movement. It was noted experimentally that the reorganization of metadata is accelerated if agent movements are longer, because they can explore the network more quickly. In order to select the right number of hops is necessary individuate a compromise between the processing load tolerable and the rapidity and efficiency of the reorganization process. In Fig. 2(b) the mean number of metadata maintained by a host when the length of the bit vector indexing the metadata ranges from 3 to 6.

The effectiveness of the algorithm was evaluated by defining of a similarity index, SI, as reported in formula 6. The similarity index over the whole network is obtained averaging the similarity indexes of all servers. The similarity index of a single server s, is obtained by averaging the Hamming distance between every couple of metadata contained in the region R related to the server s.

$$SI = N_b - \overline{D_H(d, \bar{d})}_{d, \bar{d} \epsilon R} \tag{6}$$

If similar metadata are collected in the same region, the value of the similarity index SI increases. Figure 3(a) shows the overall similarity index when N_b, i.e. the number of bit of the metadata describing each service, is varied.

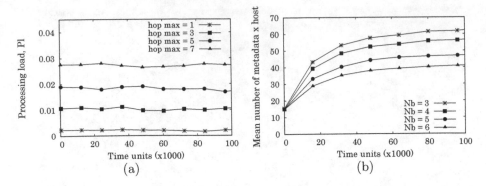

Fig. 2. (a) The processing load generated by the algorithm when the number of hops performed within a single agent movement ranges from 1 to 7; and (b) mean number of metadata handled by a host when N_b ranges from 3 to 6 bits.

Notice that the reorganization is obtained independently of the number of bits. The scalability nature of the algorithm is confirmed observing the behavior of the algorithm when number of involved servers changes from 1000 to 7000, as reported in Fig. 3(b). It is possible to note that the size of the network, N_s, has no detectable effect on the performance.

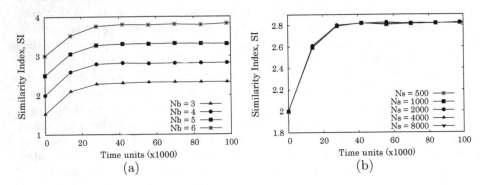

Fig. 3. (a) The similarity index of the network when N_b, i.e. the number of bit of the metadata, ranges from 3 to 6; and (b) the similarity index, vs. time, for different values of N_s, i.e. the number of servers.

The average number of results collected by a query, N_{res}, is reported in Fig. 4(a). We can note that, the number of results collected increases with time – the discovery operations become more efficient as metadata are organized – and it is inversely proportional to the length of the metadata N_d, because a large number of bit to represent the content causes a lower probability to locate a target metadata. The value of N_d has to be tuned for each application field taking into account that a wide classification can facilitate the discovery operations. A simple query is issued to find a given metadata, while, a range query is a query in which the target metadata contains one or more "star" bits. These bits can assume either the 0 or the 1 value.

If the target metadata contains b^* star bits, the range query can return 2^{b^*} possible metadata. The discovery algorithm was modified to handle the range queries. The neighbor selected to forward the query, is chosen by calculating the cosine similarity between the target metadata and the *mean metadata* of the neighbor server and omitting the star bits. As the simple queries, a range query terminates its discovery operation when none neighbor has a similarity value better than the current server. Figure 4(b) shows the effectiveness of the algorithm to execute the range queries. The value of N_d was fixed to 4 and and the number of the star bit was varied.

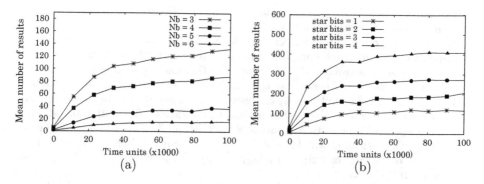

Fig. 4. (a) Average number of results for different values of the number of bits of the metadata, N_b; and (b) the average number of results of range queries with $N_d = 4$ and different numbers star bits.

A range query does not discover all possible target metadata that would be discovered with the corresponding number of simple queries, but, in one shot, discover much many results than a simple query.

4   Conclusions

In this paper a swarm based algorithm to build a Healthcare Information System, was proposed. Thanks to the features boasted by the swarm intelligence based systems, the proposed algorithm offers fully decentralization, adaptivity and self-organization. Swarm agents move and reorganize the metadata representing the Electronic Health Records and agent's operations are driven by simple probability functions evaluated when the agent gets to a new clinical server. Similar metadata, representing similar EHR, will be placed in neighbor servers an this global reorganization allows discovery operation faster and efficient. Moreover, the reorganization of metadata spontaneously adapts to the ever changing environment as the joins and departs of servers and the changing of the characteristics of the contents. The preliminary experimental results have proved the effectiveness of the algorithm.

References

1. Bonabeau, E., Dorigo, M., Theraulaz, G.: Swarm Intelligence: From Natural to Artificial Systems, vol. 4. Oxford University Press, New York (1999)
2. Cai, M., Frank, M., Chen, J., Szekely, P.: MAAN: a multi-attribute addressable network for grid information services. J. Grid Comput. **2**(1), 3–14 (2004)
3. Crespo, A., Garcia-Molina, H.: Routing indices for peer-to-peer systems. In: Proceedings of the 22nd International Conference on Distributed Computing Systems, ICDCS 2002, pp. 23–33 (2002)
4. Datar, M., Immorlica, N., Indyk, P., Mirrokni, V.S.: Locality-sensitive hashing scheme based on p-stable distributions. In: Proceedings of the Twentieth Annual Symposium on Computational Geometry, SCG 2004, pp. 253–262. ACM, New York (2004)
5. Dorigo, M., Bonabeau, E., Theraulaz, G.: Ant algorithms and stigmergy. Future Gener. Comput. Syst. **16**(8), 851–871 (2000)
6. Folino, G., Forestiero, A., Spezzano, G.: A JXTA based asynchronous peer-to-peer implementation of genetic programming. J. Softw. **1**(2), 12–23 (2006)
7. Forestiero, A., Mastroianni, C., Spezzano, G.: Building a peer-to-peer information system in grids via self-organizing agents. J. Grid Comput. **6**(2), 125–140 (2008)
8. Lumer, E.D., Faieta, B.: Diversity and adaptation in populations of clustering ants. In: Proceedings of the Third International Conference on Simulation of Adaptive Behavior: From Animals to Animats 3, SAB 1994, pp. 501–508. MIT Press (1994)
9. Nobre, J.C., Melchiors, C., Marquezan, C.C., Tarouco, L.M.R., Granville, L.Z.: A survey on the use of P2P technology for network management. J. Netw. Syst. Manag. **26**(1), 1–33 (2017)
10. Oppenheimer, D., Albrecht, J., Patterson, D., Vahdat, A.: Design and implementation tradeoffs for wide-area resource discovery. In: Proceedings of the 14th IEEE International Symposium on High Performance Distributed Computing, HPDC 2005. Research Triangle Park, NC, USA, July 2005
11. Pivovarov, R., Elhadad, N.: Automated methods for the summarization of electronic health records. J. Am. Med. Inf. Assoc. **22**(5), 938–947 (2015)
12. Platzer, C., Dustdar, S.: A vector space search engine for web services. In: Proceedigns of the Third European Conference on Web Services, ECOWS 2005, p. 62. IEEE Computer Society, Washington, DC (2005)
13. Pruski, C., Wisniewski, F.: Efficient medical information retrieval in encrypted electronic health records. In: Quality of Life Through Quality of Information: Proceedings of MIE2012, vol. 180, pp. 225–229 (2012)
14. Whitacre, J.M., Sarker, R.A., Pham, Q.T.: The self-organization of interaction networks for nature-inspired optimization. IEEE Trans. Evol. Comput. **12**(2), 220–230 (2007)

Bio-inspired Nest-Site Selection for Distributing Robots in Low-Communication Environments

Gregory Cooke[1](✉), Eric Squires[1], Laura Strickland[1], Kenneth Bowers[1], Charles Pippin[1], Theodore P. Pavlic[2], and Stephen C. Pratt[2]

[1] Georgia Tech Research Institute, Atlanta, GA 30332, USA
gregory.cooke@gtri.gatech.edu
[2] Arizona State University, Tempe, AZ 85287, USA

Abstract. We consider the problem of using only local communication to implement a distributed algorithm for large teams of mobile robots that searches space for locations of interest and distributes the robots across those locations according to quality. Toward this end, we take inspiration from insect societies that are able to coordinate without the use of pheromone trails. In particular, we focus on species that use only one-on-one local interactions to adaptively distribute scouts during nest-site selection tasks. Thus, there is a direct analogy between the insect communication mechanisms and peer-to-peer communication implementable in mobile, ad hoc networks of robots. Using chemical reaction networks as a conceptual bridge between behavioral descriptions from biology and event-triggered rules for robots, we develop a stochastic, biomimetic algorithm that achieves the desired goal. To validate our approach, we implement the algorithm on a large swarm of aerial, fixed-wing robots operating within the high-fidelity simulation package, SCRIMMAGE.

Keywords: Insect-inspired algorithms · Local communication
Mobile robots · UAVs · Swarms

1 Introduction

Methods of multi-robot coordination can vary in their communications range and bandwidth, the amount of reconfigurability they allow, and the necessary processing power on each agent [11]. Methods that make effective use of communication resources at some team sizes may scale poorly when applied to large teams. For example, recent demonstrations of large numbers of unmanned aerial vehicles (UAVs) that operate in close proximity have shown that UAV communication architectures can become saturated as the number of UAVs increases [6]. These practical challenges either require more sophisticated communication architectures [1] or a restructuring of the coordination methods so as to greatly reduce the dependence on communication. Toward this latter goal, we

© Springer International Publishing AG, part of Springer Nature 2018
J. Bajo et al. (Eds.): PAAMS 2018 Workshops, CCIS 887, pp. 517–524, 2018.
https://doi.org/10.1007/978-3-319-94779-2_44

seek direct inspiration from insect societies that naturally achieve sophisticated coordination in large, interacting groups despite having only a relatively weak communication architecture to directly coordinate across the group.

Social insects, such as ants and honeybees, are classic examples of natural systems whose many interacting parts self-organize into adaptive structures [5]. Some of the most successful examples of insect-inspired swarm intelligence are optimization metaheuristics that solve difficult problems, such as the traveling salesman problem, using a population of virtual ants that coordinate not through direct communication but instead by reacting to virtual pheromones "deposited" on potential solutions [10]. When considering algorithms that coordinate among unmanned aerial vehicles (UAVs), strategies that require modifying the physical environment are usually infeasible. Thus, instead of seeking inspiration from trail-laying ants in foraging problems, we focus on nest-site selection mechanisms in honeybees and ants of the genus *Temnothorax* [19]. These particular social insects are good models for UAV coordination because they communicate only locally and coordinate globally by using their own population demographics as opposed to modifications of the physical environment.

In this paper, we make use of chemical reaction networks (CRNs) as a framework for developing an insect-inspired algorithm for autonomous UAVs to detect relative quality differences between different sites and distribute themselves among those sites according to those quality differences. The CRN framework allows us to model spontaneous transitions of an agent from one state to another. In principle, formalizing these transitions as CRNs allows for the use of mathematical tools to aid in the analysis and control of reaction parameters [3], but our use of CRNs here is purely as a framework for translating descriptions of biological phenomena into implementable stochastic algorithms. The contribution we make beyond other insect-inspired, multi-robot allocation work is that we do not assume that robots have the ability to sense encounter rate directly [4,12], and we do not assume that the desired distributions are known *a priori* [2]. We develop an insect-inspired allocation heuristic, tested in simulation, that is *reactive* to quality differences in the environment.

This paper is organized as follows. Section 2 details the biological basis that motivates our approach, which is then translated to CRN form in Sect. 3. We then present results from our large-scale simulations in Sect. 4 and discuss implications of these results in Sect. 5. Section 6 contains our overall conclusions and proposed future work.

2   Biological Inspiration

We take inspiration from so-called *linear recruitment methods* observed in honeybees and in ants, such as those of the genus *Temnothorax* [17]. These societies build their nests in existing crevices (e.g., in trees, rocks, or hollow nuts), which means that colonies must engage in a highly decentralized house-hunting behavior if (as with honeybees) they reproduce by fission or (as with ants) their old, fragile nests are destroyed. There are ants that solve similar problems by depositing an ephemeral pheromone on the ground to recruit others, thereby communicating anonymously from one ant to possibly many ants later that can reinforce the signal. However, in social insects that use linear recruitment methods, one insect is limited to communicating with a finite number of other insects locally in time and in space. For example, with a probability that depends on the quality of the nest [13], a scout ant that randomly finds a nest can choose to lead a so-called "tandem run" that brings a single other ant to the nest for further assessment. Similarly, a honeybee may perform "waggle dances" for a period that varies with the quality of the nest, where each waggle dance is an instance of local communication of the location of a candidate nest. In both examples, nests of higher quality attract more recruits in the same amount of time, which has the effect of distributing recruits across the nests according to their relative qualities.

Because positive feedback is implemented not in the accumulation of chemicals on the environment but in the accumulation of nestmates within candidate nest sites [19], this feedback is implementable on UAVs that cannot modify their aerial environment but can detect the presence of other UAVs in the vicinity. Furthermore, the "waggle dancing" and "tandem running" can be easily converted into short-range communication of nest-candidate location. So in Sect. 3, we will describe a set of simple event-based rules that mimic nest discovery by scouts and the accumulation of scouts at nests in proportion to their quality. Although it has recently been shown theoretically that ant-like mobile agents can efficiently estimate the density of other agents around them using encounter information [15], our approach does not require individual robots to be sensitive to encounter rate. All "computations" are down at the level of the demographics of the robots as opposed to the robots themselves.

3   Bio-inspired Chemical Reaction Network Overview

Chemical Reaction Networks (CRNs) have become a commonly-used tool for constructing event-triggered, stochastic control policies for multi-agent systems [7,14,16,20]. In most of these cases, CRNs are used to generate dynamical systems that enable analysis or control. Here, we use a notation *inspired by* CRNs as a specification for an agent-based programming model that captures the salient features of nest-site selection. In particular, the notation $A \xrightarrow{r} B$ represents that an agent in state A spends an exponentially-distributed waiting time with average $1/r$ seconds before spontaneously transitioning to state B. Furthermore, the notation $A + B \xrightarrow{\text{w.p. } p} C + D$ represents that every time an entity of species A encounters an entity of species B, the resulting two entities will transition to entities of species C and D with probability p. Because we do not specify any rate information in the bimolecular interactions, this notation is essentially a kind of guarded command programming [9].

Here, we use the term "nest" to refer to each region that agents must allocate themselves to in proportion to quality. Each nest $i \in \{1, 2, \dots\}$ has an intrinsic quality $q_i \in [0, 1]$ that can be estimated by an individual agent visitor. In the

CRN framework, each nest i corresponds to a chemical species N_i that catalyzes state transitions in agents that encounter it. Initially, all agents start at a central location (their "home nest") in the *uncommitted* state, represented by chemical species U. Agents wait an average time $\tau_{UE} \triangleq 1000$ s in state U before spontaneously transitioning to *exploration* state E. In state E, an agent performs a random walk around the environment until it encounters nest i and transitions to state A_i, in which it acts as an *assessor of nest* i. These two transitions are represented by:

$$U \xrightarrow{1/\tau_{UE}} E \quad \text{and} \quad E + N_i \rightharpoonup A_i + N_i,$$

where the nest N_i acts as a catalyst for the transition of an agent in state E to an agent in state A_i, where the agents spend some amount of time forming an estimate $\hat{q}_i$ of the quality q_i of the nest i. For this work, we assume that quality can be detected perfectly and effectively instantly (i.e., within one simulation time step). Once the agent senses nest quality, it will either switch back to the uncommitted state or will escalate to a *recruitment* state R_i for nest i. These two transitions are represented by:

$$A_i + N_i \xrightarrow{\text{w.p. } [\hat{q}_i \leq 0.2]} U + N_i \quad \text{and} \quad A_i + N_i \xrightarrow{\text{w.p. } [\hat{q}_i > 0.2]} R_i + N_i,$$

where the Iverson bracket $[\cdot]$ maps the predicate in its argument to either 1 (for true) or 0 (for false). A recruiter in the recruitment state R_i will return to its home nest, then spontaneously decay into a *first quorum sensing* state $QS1_i$ after an average waiting time that depends on the quality estimate $\hat{q}_i$. However, while it is in the recruitment state R_i, it will cause any encountered uncommitted agents to transition into the assessor state A_i with a probability $\beta \triangleq 0.05$. These two transitions are represented by:

$$R_i \xrightarrow{1/\tau_{RQ}(\hat{q}_i)} QS1_i \quad \text{and} \quad R_i + U \xrightarrow{\text{w.p. } \beta} R_i + A_i$$

where $T_{RQ}(q) \triangleq [q \geq 0.2](375q + 25)$ s. Once in first quorum sensing state $QS1_i$ for nest i, the agent moves to nest i where it may escalate into *second quorum sensing* state $QS2_i$ when it encounters any other agent in the nest, which is represented by the reaction

$$QS1_i + X \rightharpoonup QS2_i + X$$

where X represents an agent in any other state. Alternatively, an agent in nest i in state $QS1_i$ will wait an average time of $\tau_{QR} \triangleq 200$ s before decaying either to the recruiting state R_i or the uncommitted state Q depending on whether the nest is high or low quality. If an agent is in the $QS1_i$ state for nest i and decays into recruiting state R_i, it will decrease its quality estimate $\hat{q}_i$ from its earlier value to $\hat{q}_i/2$, leading to a reduced recruiting time. These reactions are:

$$QS1_i \xrightarrow{[\hat{q}_i > 0.2]/\tau_{QR}} R_i \quad \text{and} \quad QS1_i \xrightarrow{[\hat{q}_i \leq 0.2]/\tau_{QR}} U$$

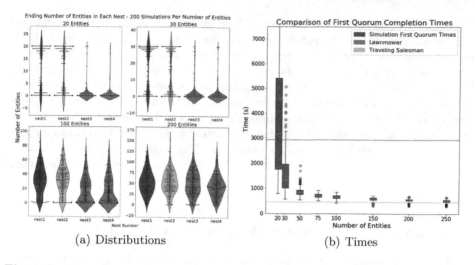

(a) Distributions   (b) Times

Fig. 1. Outcomes for a variety of different numbers of entities. In (a), ending distributions are shown for $n \in \{20, 30, 100, 200\}$ entities, with dots showing raw simulation outcomes and filled curves estimating a corresponding distribution. In (b), box-and-whisker plots characterize variability in completion times for 200 simulation runs at different numbers of entities. The two benchmark lines are described in Sect. 5.

Similarly, an agent in second quorum sensing state $QS2_i$ for nest i will escalate into *third quorum sensing* state $QS3_i$ after encountering another agent in the nest, or it will decay back into $QS1_i$ after mean waiting time $\tau_{Q2} \triangleq 2$ s. Those agents in state $QS3_i$ will transition to a final *done* state D on encountering another agent in nest i; otherwise, they will decay into $QS2_i$ after mean waiting time $\tau_{Q3} \triangleq 2$ s. So, using arbitrary agent X, we have:

$$QS2_i + X \rightharpoonup QS3_i + X \quad \text{and} \quad QS2_i \xrightarrow{1/\tau_{Q2}} QS1_i$$

$$QS3_i + X \rightharpoonup D + X \quad \text{and} \quad QS3_i \xrightarrow{1/\tau_{Q3}} QS2_i.$$

4 Simulation Results

In the following experiments, the CRN model was developed for fixed-wing UAVs modeled with a limited turning radius in the SCRIMMAGE simulator [8]. To focus on the effects of number of nest quality and number of agents, all simulations were run in an environment with a single home nest surrounded by four candidate nests equidistant from the center of the home nest. All agents started at random locations within the home base and utilized the same CRN model. Each simulation was run until every agent assessed that quorum had been reached at its current base, and the times at which the first and last agents sensed quorum were recorded. This process was performed for 200 simulations for each of 20, 30, 50, 75, 100, 150, 200, and 250 agents.

Figure 1(a) shows the distribution of final agent allocations for different numbers of entities. When the agent team sizes are relatively small, the final distribution of agents across nest sites matches the relative quality of the nest sites – nests 1 and 2 usually attract a large majority of the available agents. However, for large number of entities, the distribution across nests becomes less sensitive to nest quality, with nests 1–4 having similar distributions. Figure 1(b) shows the temporal performance of the simulations for a wide range of entity-number conditions. The box-and-whisker plots characterize the completion times for different runs at each entity-number condition. The other two lines are benchmarks that will be described in Sect. 5. With increasing numbers of entities, the completion time is greatly reduced and becomes far less variable across simulation runs.

5   Discussion: Number of Agents, Speed, and Accuracy

To better understand the shape of the decision-making latency distributions shown in Fig. 1(b), we also generated two benchmarks for comparison based on simple search strategies – a Lawnmower Search (LS) approach and a Traveling Salesman (TS) approach – that a single agent might use to discover the highest quality nest in its environment. In the LS approach, the agent is assumed to have no *a priori* knowledge of the positions or number of nests, so it exhaustively searches the entire environment for nests to discover their position and quality. The time required for this task is simply the time an agent takes to start in one corner of the environment and travel in straight lines and 180° turns until it covers the entire environment. In the TS approach, the agent is assumed to know the positions of every nest in the environment and must simply visit them to discover the highest quality nest. In that case, it first calculates the optimal tour starting from the home nest and traveling through each candidate nest. The time of the approach is then the time required to travel this tour.

The two benchmark times are shown as horizontal lines in Fig. 1(b). For very few numbers of agents, the time the distributed algorithm requires for the first CRN completion is comparable in the average to the LS method, but it can be much longer. As the number of agents increases, however, the completion time decays apparently exponentially to the theoretical lower limit set by the TS method. Thus, the benefit of larger team sizes seems to be a rapid decrease in completion time, with large teams of uninformed agents achieving the near-optimal time performance of a single, well-informed agent. A naive interpretation of this phenomenon is that it is an example of a kind of "wisdom of the crowd" [18]. However, when coupled with the distributional results in Fig. 1(a), it is clear that even distributed decision-making cannot avoid fundamental speed–accuracy tradeoffs in decision making; there is a significant accuracy cost that is concomitant with the increase in speed. As the number of entities approaches the theoretical decision-making speed limit found by the TS approach, the information about quality encoded in the distribution becomes minimally informative (i.e., it approaches a uniform distribution across nest sites – the theoretically least informative distribution).

The proximate mechanism explaining the decrease in accuracy for high numbers of agents appears to be the rapid escalation to the *Done* state for all recruits entering nests that are naturally crowded due to the large populations (i.e., a "madness of the crowd"). Thus, it may be adaptive to start such a distributed task with a limited number of available scouts and gradually increase that number the longer the team remains in an undecided state. Ultimately, this manifestation of the speed–accuracy tradeoff may explain why the scout team in real social-insect colonies is often much smaller than the total number of scouts in the colony. Moreover, when designing multi-agent systems, there may be intermediate team sizes that maximize task efficiency – more may not always be better.

6   Summary, Conclusions, and Future Work

We presented a bio-inspired nest-site selection algorithm and validated the approach via computer simulation of large numbers of UAVs. This approach can be used to distribute robots in an environment in proportion to the quality of notable locations in the environment, and it requires only local communications for the distribution to converge. Simulation results show a clear speed–accuracy tradeoff that has implications for the number of agents chosen to assist in a decentralized decision-making task. Naively, it might be expected that an increase in the number of agents will only benefit decision-making tasks by increasing discovery rate of nests. However, large numbers of agents may enhance early discovery artifacts that amplify the effect of spatial distribution over nest quality. Moreover, crowding associated with large number of scouts within candidate nests can hasten processes that would otherwise allow for differences in quality to lead to differences in nest-residence time. For a single-agent decision-making task, providing deliberation time is important to ensure accuracy; for multiple-agent, distributed decision making, adjusting the number of agents may be important for providing distributed deliberation time.

In future work, we will extend the CRN to address the distribution of agents in different environments and in the presence of dynamically changing numbers of adversaries. In addition, we plan to investigate extensions that will make the algorithm more accurate with larger numbers of agents. In other words, we will better characterize the Pareto frontier of speed and accuracy for distributed decision-making problems.

Acknowledgments. This work was supported by DARPA under the Bio-Inspired Swarming seedling project, contract FA8651-17-F-1013.

References

1. Bekmezci, İ., Sahingoz, O.K., Temel, Ş.: Flying ad-hoc networks (FANETs): a survey. Ad Hoc Netw. **11**(3), 1254–1270 (2013)
2. Berman, S., Halász, Á., Hsieh, M.A., Kumar, V.: Optimized stochastic policies for task allocation in swarms of robots. IEEE Trans. Robot. **25**(4), 927–937 (2009)

3. Berman, S., Halász, Á., Kumar, V., Pratt, S.: Algorithms for the analysis and synthesis of a bio-inspired swarm robotic system. In: Şahin, E., Spears, W.M., Winfield, A.F.T. (eds.) SR 2006. LNCS, vol. 4433, pp. 56–70. Springer, Heidelberg (2007). https://doi.org/10.1007/978-3-540-71541-2_5
4. Berman, S., Halász, A., Kumar, V., Pratt, S.: Bio-inspired group behaviors for the deployment of a swarm of robots to multiple destinations. In: 2007 IEEE International Conference on Robotics and Automation, pp. 2318–2323. IEEE (2007)
5. Camazine, S., Deneubourg, J.L., Franks, N.R., Sneyd, J., Theraulaz, G., Bonabeau, E.: Self-Organization in Biological Systems. Princeton University Press, Princeton (2001)
6. Chung, T.H., Clement, M., Day, M.A., Jones, K., Davis, D., Jones, M.: Live-fly, large-scale field experimentation for large numbers of fixed-wing UAVs. In: IEEE International Conference on Robotics and Automation (ICRA) (2016)
7. Correll, N., Martinoli, A.: Modeling and optimization of a swarm-intelligent inspection system. In: Proceedings of the Seventh International Symposium on Distributed Autonomous Robotics Systems, DARS 2004, pp. 369–378. Toulouse, France (2004)
8. DeMarco, K., Squires, E.: SCRIMMAGE (Simulating Collaborative Robots in Massive Multi-Agent Game Execution), August 2017. https://www.scrimmagesim.org/
9. Dijkstra, E.W.: Guarded commands, nondeterminacy and formal derivation of programs. Commun. ACM 18(8), 453–457 (1975)
10. Dorigo, M., Gambardella, L.M.: Ant colonies for the travelling salesman problem. Biosystems 43(2), 73–81 (1997)
11. Dudek, G., Jenkin, M.R.M., Milios, E., Wilkes, D.: A taxonomy for multi-agent robotics. Auton. Robots 3, 375–397 (1996)
12. Hsieh, M.A., Halász, Á., Berman, S., Kumar, V.: Biologically inspired redistribution of a swarm of robots among multiple sites. Swarm Int. 2(2), 121–141 (2008)
13. Mallon, E.B., Pratt, S.C., Franks, N.R.: Individual and collective decision-making during nest site selection by the ant Leptothorax albipennis. Behav. Ecol. Sociobiol. 50(4), 352–359 (2001). https://doi.org/10.1007/s002650100377
14. Matthey, L., Berman, S., Kumar, V.: Stochastic strategies for a swarm robotic assembly system. In: Proceedings of the 2009 IEEE International Conference on Robotics and Automation, pp. 1953–1958. Kobe, Japan, 12–17 May 2009
15. Musco, C., Su, H.H., Lynch, N.A.: Ant-inspired density estimation via random walks. PNAS USA, p. 201706439 (2017)
16. Napp, N., Klavins, E.: A compositional framework for programming stochastically interacting robots. Int. J. Rob. Res. 30(6), 713–729 (2011)
17. Shaffer, Z., Sasaki, T., Pratt, S.C.: Linear recruitment leads to allocation and flexibility in collective foraging by ants. Anim. Behav. 86(5), 967–975 (2013)
18. Surowiecki, J.: The Wisdom of Crowds: Why the Many Are Smarter Than the Few and How Collective Wisdom Shapes Business, Economies. Doubleday, Societies and Nations, New York (2004)
19. Visscher, P.K.: Group decision making in nest-site selection among social insects. Annu. Rev. Entomol. 52, 255–275 (2007)
20. Wilson, S., Pavlic, T.P., Kumar, G.P., Buffin, A., Pratt, S.C., Berman, S.: Design of ant-inspired stochastic control policies for collective transport by robotic swarms. Swarm Int. 8(4), 303–327 (2014)

Bacterial Colony Algorithms Applied to Association Rule Mining in Static Data and Streams

Danilo S. da Cunha$^{(\boxtimes)}$, Rafael S. Xavier, Daniel G. Ferrari, and Leandro N. de Castro

Natural Computing and Machine Learning Laboratory – LCoN,
Mackenzie Presbyterian University, São Paulo, Brazil
danilocunha85@gmail.com, rsixavier@gmail.com,
ferrari.dg@gmail.com, lnunes@mackenzie.br

Abstract. Bacterial colonies perform a cooperative and distributed exploration of the environmental resources. This paper describes how bacterial colony networks and their skills to search resources can be used as tools for mining association rules in static and stream data. The proposed algorithm is designed to maintain diverse solutions to the problems at hand, and its performance is compared to another well-known bacterial algorithm in both static and stream datasets.

Keywords: Bacterial colony algorithms · Association rules
Stream data mining

1 Introduction

Bacterial colonies can be seen as complex adaptive systems that use a collaborative system of chemical signals to explore the resources of a given environment and coordinate their social and behavioral tasks [1]. The collective and collaborative activities carried out by a colony are classified as a type of collective intelligence [2], where each bacterium is able to sense itself, the environment and maintain communication with other bacteria to perform coordinated tasks [3].

This paper provides a comparison between two algorithms inspired by bacterial colony, namely Bacterial Colony Association Rule Optimization-II (extended from [4]) and Bacterial Foraging Optimization [5], for mining association rules in transactional datasets and we introduce the necessary modifications so that they can be applied to data streams. The novel algorithm is able to avoid the genic *conversion problem* [6].

The paper is structured as follows. Section 2 gives a theoretical background about association rules, data streams and processing models. Section 3 presents bacterial algorithms for association rule mining to deal with static and stream data as well as the performance evaluation. The final remarks are shown in Sect. 5.

© Springer International Publishing AG, part of Springer Nature 2018
J. Bajo et al. (Eds.): PAAMS 2018 Workshops, CCIS 887, pp. 525–533, 2018.
https://doi.org/10.1007/978-3-319-94779-2_45

2   On Association Rule Mining and Data Streams

Association rules mining is a descriptive mining task, which uses unsupervised learning and focuses on the identification of associations between items in a dataset [7, 8]. A *transaction* is a set of items that occur together. In the market-basket analysis scenario, items in a transaction are those that are acquired together by an end user [9, 10]. An association rule is as follows:

$$A \to C \tag{1}$$

where A and C are itemsets of products selected by a consumer.

The first set A is called the *antecedent* and the other one C is the *consequent* of the rule. The intersection between these two sets is empty ($A \cap C = \emptyset$). The rule means the presence of (all items in) A in a transaction implies the presence of (all items in) C in the same transaction with some associated probability [9, 10].

2.1   Measures of Interest

The Confidence and Support [7, 8] are the most applied measures of interest in the literature. The support of a rule is a measure of its relative frequency in the set of all:

$$Support(A \to C) = Supp(A \to C) = P(A \cup C) \tag{2}$$

On the other hand, the confidence of a rule is a measure of its satisfiability when its antecedent is found in T; that is to say, from all the occurrences of A, how often C also occurs in the base:

$$Confidence(A \to C) = Conf(A \to C) = P(A|C) \tag{3}$$

Whilst confidence is a measure of the strength of a rule, the support corresponds to its statistical significance over the dataset. The interestingness of a rule, $I(A \to C)$, is calculated as follows [11]:

$$I(A \to C) = \left(\frac{|A \cup C|}{|A|} \right) * \left(\frac{|A \cup C|}{|C|} \right) * \left(1 - \left(\frac{|A \cup C|}{T} \right) \right) \tag{4}$$

where A and C are defined as previously, and T is the number of transactions in the dataset. This measure of interest, differently of support, looks for low frequency rules.

2.2   Data Streams

A sequence of objects that arrives in a timely order is named a *data stream* [12, 13]. Differently from traditional static data, data streams are continuous, unbounded, high speed and their data distribution changes with time [14].

There are three major stream data processing models for rule mining, *Landmark*, *Damped* and *Sliding-Windows* [15]: (1) **Landmark:** mines all frequent itemsets over the entire log of stream data from a limited point of time, named *landmark*, to the current one; (2) **Damped:** also named time-fading model, it finds frequent itemsets on streams in which each transaction has a weight decrease with time. Older transactions have a smaller weight toward itemset frequencies; and (3) **Sliding-window:** it finds and maintains frequent itemsets in sliding-windows. Only part of the data streams within the sliding-windows are stored and processed at the time while the data flows in. The sliding-window size is defined based on the application and system resources.

3   Bacterial Algorithms for Association Rule Mining

This section describes the proposed and adapted bacterial algorithms for mining association rules in static data and streams. We describe the candidate solution representation used for the association rules, the bacterial procedures and, finally, the implemented and evaluated bacteria-inspired tools.

3.1   Candidate Solution Representation

In the bio-inspired algorithms context for association rule mining each candidate solution encodes a single rule [16]. This approach was adapted to represent association rules in [17, 18], where each item in a rule is represented by two bits: 00 means items belonging to the antecedent; 11 means items belonging to the consequent; and 01 or 10 means items not belonging to the rule.

3.2   Fitness Function

The measures of interest often used to compute fitness values are modifications based on the ones employed for classification [19], with some slight adjustments. In the present paper we use: confidence and support. The fitness function used is:

$$fitness(A \to C) = w_1 * Supp(A \to C) + w_2 * Conf(A \to C) \qquad (5)$$

where, $w_1 = w_2 = 0.5$ and $w_1 + w_2 = 1$. Subject to: $A \cap C \neq \emptyset$ and $|C| > 0 < |A|$, where $|.|$ returns the cardinality of a set. The interestingness measure is used to compare the algorithms' performance from a different perspective, as in [20].

3.3   BFO for Association Rule Mining

The BFO, which stands for Bacterial Foraging Optimization algorithm, simulates the foraging strategy of Escherichia Coli. The algorithm was originally designed to solve optimization problems in continuous environments. It takes inspiration in the following mechanisms: chemotaxis, swarming, reproduction, elimination and dispersion [5]. The main mechanism is the chemotaxis (tumbling and swimming) and it is used bacterial mobility over the environment. Tumbling was implemented by randomly choosing a rule part to be shortened. Only parts longer than 1 element can be chosen. If after the tumble the bacterium adaptation is higher, it starts to run (still swimming) by removing more items from the same part until its size is equal to 1 or the number of swim steps is reached if else chemotactic behavior is finalized. It mimics an artificial bacteria avoiding an exploration inside a noxious region.

Another adaptation was applied in the chemotaxis mechanism to deal with association rule. The interaction parameters $d_{attract}$, $w_{attract}$, $h_{repellant}$ and $w_{repellant}$ are estimated from each bacterium instead of user-defined. These parameters were replaced by a vector with the following state transition: (1) **Attraction:** if there are 11 or 00 information representing an item in $bacterium_{i,i+1}$. A bacterium is able attract another binary pair to these positions if it has a higher fitness, and then another bacterium can be attracted by this bacterial information while in the same position $anotherBacterium_{i,i+1}$ has 01 or 10 information; (2) **Repulsion:** if there are 11 or 00 information representing an item in $bacterium_{i,i+1}$. A bacterium is able to repel another if it has a higher fitness and then another bacterium can be repelled by this bacterial information while in the same position $anotherBacterium_{i,i+1}$ there is 11 or 00.

The BFO algorithm is summarized in Pseudocode 1. It stars by initializing a colony P with $Cells_{num}$ artificial bacteria, and N_{ed} is the number of *elimination-and-dispersion* steps, N_{re} is the number of *reproduction steps*, N_c is the number of *chemotaxis steps*, N_s is the number of swim for each bacterium, $Step_{size}$ is a random vector with the same number of dimension of the problem, the `Problem` is the dataset or stream and P_{ed} is the probability of a bacterium being subjected to elimination-and-dispersal. The algorithm starts by initializing elimination-and-dispersion, reproduction and chemotaxis counters. After that, the chemotaxis step is performed. The next step is sort all bacteria according to their health (a measure that involves their fitness and amount of generation each bacteria is alive). Select half of bacteria according to their health. The reproduction step clones the survivals and the dispersion one relocates them in a random location.

```
procedure [P] = BFO(Cells_num, N_ed, N_re, N_c, N_s, Step_size, P_ed, Problem)
  initialize P(Cells_num)
  for l=0 to N_ed do
   for k=0 to N_re do
    for j=0 to N_c do
      Chemotaxis (P, Problem, Cells_num, N_s, Step_size)
      foreach Cell in Population do
       if Cost(Cell) ≥ Cost(Cell_best) then
          Cell_best ← Cell
      SortByCellHealth(Population)
      Selected ← ByHealth(Population, Cell_best/2)
      Population = Clone(Selected)
     for each Cell in Population do
      if Random() ≤ P_ed then
       Cell ← CellAtRandLocation()
  return Cell_best
```

Pseudocode 1: BFO Algorithm.

In a closer view inside the *Chemotaxis* procedure, we note that a bacterium interacts with the whole colony to compute its fitness. In other words, in BFO an agent is exposed to all bacterial elements and interacts directly with them.

3.4 BaCARO-II for Association Rule Mining

The algorithm named Bacterial Colony Association Rule Optimization-II (BaCARO-II) is inspired by the biological processes of intra and extracellular communication networks of bacterial colonies, as well as quorum-sensing, chemotaxis and bacterial dispersion [2, 21]. BaCARO-II steps and variables are detailed in Pseudocode 2. The probability of extracellular communication is accounted for in parameter ec and the probability of each cell being selected in the intracellular communication is represented by parameter ic, whilst P_{cha} is the probability of changing an element inside a rule, $Size_{net}$ is the size of bacterium chemical network is in and $\mathbf{D}$ is the dataset to be mined.

The intracellular communication can be seen as an individual effort where a bacterium tries to improve its own gene expression configuration based on local environmental sensing. In our approach we consider the extracellular communication network as an agent coordinating another agent mobility over the environment by exchanging chemical signals. In our proposal, the leader and follower agents are chosen based on their environmental adaptabilities, where the most adapted bacterium is followed by the least ones. If they have equivalent adaptabilities, some of them are randomly selected to be dispersed so as to explore other areas around them. The extracellular communication is naturally limited by a quorum-sensing threashold. The limited agents influence is a resource applied to avoid premature convergence, a reported issue from BFO [21].

```
procedure [P]=BaCARO-II(ec,ic,P_cha,D)
  initialize P
  t ← 1
    f ← evaluate(P,D)
  while not_stopping_criterion do
    rf ← inCellular(P,ic,P_cha,D)
    f ← update(f,rf)
    f ← exCellular(ec)
        % Conditional Quorum-sensing
        if(bacterialDensity(P)==true)
          P ← disperse(P) else
        For each P_bacterium in P
          1.  Link a chemical network with Size_net
          2.  Find the best bacteria
          3.  Change information
          4.  Move to the best position
    f ← evaluate(P,D)
    P ← select(P,f)
    t ← t+1
  end while
end procedure
```

Pseudocode 2: BaCARO-II Algorithm.

4   Performance Evaluation

All datasets used (*SPECT Heart, Mushroom, Balance Scale, Flare, Monks Problems*-1, *Nursery* [22]) were originally generated in static environments. We converted the static datasets into dynamic ones by applying a sliding-window approach over them, generating the *stream*SPECT, *stream*Mushroom, *stream*Balance, *stream*Flare, *stream*Monks and *stream*Nursery datasets. The parameters of BFO and sBFO were set as follows: $S = 100$, $N_{ed} = 10$, $N_{re} = 10$, $N_c = 10$, $N_s = 5$ and $P_{ed} = 0.4$. The parameters for BaCARO-II and sBaCARO-II were set as follows: $ic = 0.01$, $P_{cha} = 0.9$, $Size_{net} = 3$ and $ec = 0.6$. Populations were set as 100. In the static scenarios, we fixed the experiments in 100 iterations as stopping criterion.

All the results taken over ten simulations of BFO, sBFO, BaCARO-II and sBaCARO-II are summarized in Table 1. The values presented are the mean ± standard deviation values for the set of rules found in the final population of each algorithm, where S means support, C confidence, I interestingness, U unique rules found over the last set of candidate solutions, and P is the processing time. BaCARO-II and sBaCARO-II presented competitive results for all datasets. The average values of support, confidence and interestingness for BaCARO-II are higher than those obtained by BFO. However, the number of rules generated by BaCARO-II is not larger than that of BFO for most datasets. On the other hand, our approach produced association rules with higher values of support and confidence. Another favorable point for BaCARO-II is its average processing time, which is smaller than its competitors, though it performs worse than BFO for all datasets for the unique rules measure. The same parameter configuration adopted for the static environment were applied to the dynamical case. As datasets have different sizes, we fixed the sliding-window size at 100, changing 1 object per iteration.

5   Final Remarks

By nature, abrupt environmental changes are constants in microorganisms' life. Investigating how and when they act to survive in this kind of dynamical environment can give us more tools to solve stream data mining problems. We applied a new bacteria-inspired algorithm by taking a look at intra- and extracellular communication networks. The preliminary experiments performed by BaCARO-II here suggest a superior performance than the BFO algorithm in association rule mining in static data and streams.

Our bacterial approach showed a better performance than other bacteria-inspired approach, motivating more studies on recent advances in biological researches from sociology and microbiology to build more robust computational tools. As future investigation, sBaCARO-II should be applied to stream data mining tasks to prove its robustness as a search-heuristic with different kinds of stream data processing models.

Table 1. Results for static datasets in clear area were obtained by BFO and BaCARO-II; Results for stream datasets in shaded area were obtained by sBFO and sBaCARO-II. The values presented are the average ± standard deviation taken over ten simulations.

	BFO	BaCARO-II	sBFO	sBaCARO-II
	SPECT		*stream*SPECT	
S	0.402 ± 0.143	**0.432 ± 0.047**	**0.618 ± 0.004**	0.411 ± 0.052
C	**0.952 ± 0.019**	0.935 ± 0.016	**1.000 ± 0.000**	0.941 ± 0.035
I	**0.436 ± 0.076**	0.413 ± 0.088	0.636 ± 0.071	**0.823 ± 0.214**
U	**11.00 ± 4,760**	40 ± 2.403	**100 ± 0.000**	41.30 ± 4.448
P	18.5091 ± 2.383	**3.110 ± 0.167**	100.9 ± 1.852	**2.706 ± 0.106**
	Mushroom		*stream*Mushroom	
S	0.0001 ± 0.000	**0.010 ± 0.011**	**0.010 ± 0.000**	0.000 ± 0.000
C	**1.000 ± 0.000**	**1.000 ± 0.000**	**1.000 ± 0.000**	0.000 ± 0.000
I	0.029 ± 0.038	**0.132 ± 0.144**	**0.990 ± 0.000**	0.000 ± 0.000
U	**95.50 ± 1.840**	15.70 ± 3.860	**100 ± 0.000**	0.000 ± 0.000
P	2577 ± 58.84	**535.7 ± 13.81**	7662.3 ± 290.5	**866.5 ± 65.23**
	Balance		*stream*Balance	
S	0.001 ± 0.000	**0.007 ± 0.002**	0.010 ± 0.000	**0.098 ± 0.084**
C	**1.000 ± 0.000**	**1.000 ± 0.000**	**1.000 ± 0.000**	0.739 ± 0.347
I	0.022 ± 0.009	**0.051 ± 0.018**	0.137 ± 0.068	**0.146 ± 0.067**
U	**92.70 ± 2.830**	7.600 ± 1.712	**95.8 ± 2.898**	7.300 ± 3.020
P	29.84 ± 1.680	**5.731 ± 0.146**	117.2 ± 5.391	**6.519 ± 0.404**
	Flare		*stream*Flare	
S	0.064 ± 0.000	**0.707 ± 0.332**	0.160 ± 0.000	**0.969 ± 0.023**
C	**0.994 ± 0.009**	0.983 ± 0.020	**1.000 ± 0.000**	0.993 ± 0.022
I	0.2530 ± 0.173	**0.288 ± 0.196**	**0.990 ± 0.000**	0.215 ± 0.027
U	**95.40 ± 2.065**	22.20 ± 6.545	**100.0 ± 0.000**	17.60 ± 2.633
P	151.9 ± 7.249	**28.72 ± 1.056**	557.60 ± 20.764	**33.45 ± 0.706**
	Monks		*stream*Monks	
S	0.002 ± 0.000	**0.088 ± 0.091**	0.010 ± 0.000	**0.426 ± 0.144**
C	0.900 ± 0.210	**1.000 ± 0.000**	**1.000 ± 0.000**	**1.000 ± 0.000**
I	0.007 ± 0.001	**0.174 ± 0.117**	0.078 ± 0.022	0.347 ± 0.083
U	**94.40 ± 2.065**	10.70 ± 2.584	**97.700 ± 1.337**	12.10 ± 3.178
P	18.37 ± 0.572	**3.533 ± 0.119**	65.50 ± 1.779	**3.970 ± 0.149**
	Nursery		*stream*Nursery	
S	0.00007 ± 0.0	**0.171 ± 0.170**	0.010 ± 0.000	**0.934 ± 0.208**
C	0.464 ± 0.482	**1.000 ± 0.000**	**1.000 ± 0.000**	**1.000 ± 0.000**
I	$0.0001 ± 6.4e^{-5}$	**0.356 ± 0.327**	0.219 ± 0.228	**0.289 ± 0.130**
U	**95.70 ± 1.702**	15.20 ± 4.541	**100 ± 0.000**	11.80 ± 3.583
P	889.7 ± 34.70	**169.3 ± 4.735**	9740.4 ± 480,1	**409.2 ± 11.09**

Acknowledgments. The authors thank CAPES, CNPq, Fapesp, and Mackpesquisa for the financial support. The authors also acknowledge the support of Intel for the Natural Computing and Machine Learning Laboratory as an Intel Center of Excellence in Machine Learning.

References

1. Matsushita, M., Fujikawa, H.: Diffusion-limited growth in bacterial colony formation. Physica A **168**(1), 498–506 (1990)
2. Ben-Jacob, E.: Learning from bacteria about natural information processing. Ann. New York Acad. Sci. **1178**(1), 78–90 (2009)
3. Xavier, R.S., Omar, N., de Castro, L.N.: Bacterial colony: information processing and computational behavior. In: NaBIC 2011 (2011)
4. da Cunha, D.S., Xavier, R.S., Castro, L.N.: A bacterial colony algorithm for association rule mining. In: IDEAL 2015 (2015)
5. Passino, K.M.: Biomimicry of bacterial foraging for distributed optimization and control. IEEE Control Syst. **22**(3), 52–67 (2002)
6. da Cunha, D.S., de Castro, L.N.: The influence of selection and crossover in an evolutionary algorithm for association rule mining. In: AITAC 2012, vol. 1, pp. 170–174, November 2012
7. Agrawal, R., Imielinski, T., Swami, A.: Mining association rules between sets of items in large databases. ACM SIGMOD Rec. **22**(2), 207–216 (1993)
8. Agrawal, R., Srikant, R.: Fast algorithms for mining association rules. In: VLDB 1994 (1994)
9. Dehuri, S., Jagadev, A.K., Ghosh, A., Mall, R.: Multi-objective genetic algorithm for association rule mining using a homogeneous dedicated cluster of workstations. AJAS **3**(11), 2086–2095 (2006)
10. Cios, K.J., Pedrycz, W., Swiniarski, R.W., Kurgan, L.A.: Data Mining: A Knowledge Discovery Approach. Springer Science & Business Media, New York (2007). https://doi.org/10.1007/978-1-4615-5589-6
11. Jiang, N., Le Gruenwald, M.H.: Research issues in data stream association rule mining. ACM SIGMOD Rec. **35**(1), 14–19 (2006)
12. Gaber, M.M., Zaslavsky, A., Krishnaswamy, S.: Mining data streams: a review. ACM SIGMOD Rec. **34**(2), 18–26 (2005)
13. Aggarwal, C.C.: Data Streams: Models and Algorithms, vol. 31. Springer Science & Business Media, New York (2007). https://doi.org/10.1007/978-0-387-47534-9
14. Guha, S., Koudas, N., Shim, K.: Data-streams and histograms. In: Proceedings of the Thirty-Third Annual ACM Symposium on Theory of Computing, Hersonissos (2001)
15. Zhu, Y., Shasha, D.: StatStream: statistical monitoring of thousands of data streams in real time. In: VLDB 2002, Hong Kong (2002)
16. Booker, L.B., Goldberg, D.E., Holland, J.H.: Classifier systems and genetic algorithms. Artif. Intell. **40**(1–3), 235–282 (1989)
17. Mo, H., Xu, L.: Immune clone algorithm for mining association rules on dynamic databases. In: ICTAI 2005, Hong Kong (2005)
18. Su, Y., Gu, X., Li, Z.: Incremental updating algorithm based on artificial immune system for mining association rules. In: ICEBE 2006, Shanghai (2006)

19. Liu, T.: An immune based association rule algorithm. In: ICICIC 2007, Kumamoto (2007)
20. del Jesus, M.J., Gámez, J.A., González, P., Puerta, J.M.: On the discovery of association rules by means of evolutionary algorithms. Wiley Interdisc. Rev. Data Min. Knowl. Discovery 1(5), 397–415 (2011)
21. Agrawal, V., Sharma, H., Bansal, J.: Bacterial foraging optimization: a survey. In: Proceedings of the International Conference on Soft Computing for Problem Solving (SocProS 2011) (2012)
22. Lichman, M.: UCI Machine Learning Repository. University of California, School of Information and Computer Sciences, Irvine (2013)

Using Novelty Search in Differential Evolution

Iztok Fister[1,3](✉), Andres Iglesias[2,3], Akemi Galvez[2,3], Javier Del Ser[4,5,6],
Eneko Osaba[4], and Iztok Fister Jr.[1]

[1] Faculty of Electrical Engineering and Computer Science, University of Maribor,
Koroška cesta 46, Maribor, Slovenia
iztok.fister@um.si
[2] Toho University, 2-2-1 Miyama, Funabashi 274-8510, Japan
[3] University of Cantabria, Avenida de los Castros, s/n, 39005 Santander, Spain
[4] TECNALIA, Derio, Spain
[5] University of the Basque Country (UPV/EHU), Bilbao, Spain
[6] Basque Center for Applied Mathematics (BCAM), Bilbao, Spain

Abstract. Novelty search in evolutionary robotics measures a distance of potential novelty solutions to their k-nearest neighbors in the search space. This distance presents an additional objective to the fitness function, with which each individual in population is evaluated. In this study, the novelty search was applied within the differential evolution. The preliminary results on CEC-14 Benchmark function suite show its potential for using also in the future.

Keywords: Novelty search · Differential evolution
Swarm and evolutionary robotics · Artificial life

1 Introduction

Evolutionary Algorithms (EAs) and Swarm Intelligence (SI) based algorithms (also nature-inspired algorithms) have reached their maturity phase, characterized with their successful applications by solving the hardest problems in almost all domains of human activity. The new promising direction in further development of these algorithms is to embed them into hardware, where they play the role of autonomous artificial agent (also robot) embodied into an environment. Thus, a new era of Evolutionary Robotics (ER) and Swarm Robotics (SR) has been born [1]. In this new situation, the fitness function is not calculated from a phenotype of individuals, but from an evaluation of a nature-inspired robot's behavior. This evaluation is obtained after observing how the phenotype reacts on the conditions of the dynamic process governed by the environment. Actually, the traditional three-step evaluation chain in Evolutionary Computation (EC) consisting of genotype-phenotype-fitness, is replaced by a four-step evaluation chain in ER and SR, where behavior needs to be evaluated after evaluation of the phenotype before obtaining the fitness.

© Springer International Publishing AG, part of Springer Nature 2018
J. Bajo et al. (Eds.): PAAMS 2018 Workshops, CCIS 887, pp. 534–542, 2018.
https://doi.org/10.1007/978-3-319-94779-2_46

With moving the nature-inspired algorithms into the hardware, and rapid development of the ER and SR, however, new problems have arisen. One of the more serious is the selection pressure that directs the search process towards the best solutions at the expense of losing the population diversity. Consequently, the loss of population diversity directs the search process to get stuck into the local optima on the one hand, and to terminate the evolution process prematurely. Indeed, this is in contrast with the demands of an open-ended evolution [7] that are prerequisite for regular readiness of the nature-inspired robots. Actually, Artificial Life (ALife) discovers conditions under which the open-ended evolution can occur [2]. Two advances in nature-inspired algorithms enable the ER and SR community to tackle the selection pressure successfully [6]: (1) multi-Objective Evolutionary Algorithms (MOEAs) [8] and (2) Novelty Search (NS) [3]. The former are capable of evaluating each individual using more fitness values, while the latter does not guide the evolutionary search using only one fitness function. This paper is focused on the NS. For this reason, the MOEAs are not discussed in this paper.

NS was introduced by Lehman and Stanley [3], and it was developed on the basis of recognition that the natural selection does not always explain increases in evolutionary complexity [12]. Usually, fitness function does not reward the intermediate stepping stones leading the search process to the optimal solutions. Therefore, NS substitutes the fitness function with the novelty measure [5] that measures a distance of novelty solutions to k-th nearest neighbors in a search space. Indeed, many points in this space collapse to the same points in the behavior space. This means that the search for novelties can be performed in a search space independently of environment conditions [3]. As a result, NS prevents a deception of objective functions and premature convergence [4]. Thus, it is focused on direct search for novelty individuals, and not wait for the search process to discover them on the fly. Since 2008, the NS has been applied by solving a wide range of problems in different domains, like robot controllers [10], multirobot systems [9], machine learning [13], and games [11].

The Purpose of this Paper is to Verify that the NS can be Applied Successfully to Nature-Inspired Algorithms. To the knowledge of the authors, few effort are invested into using it for solving the global optimization problems (e.g., CEC-2014 benchmark suite). Although the NS could be applied to any nature-inspired algorithm, we select a Differential Evolution (DE) [14] due to its global search abilities. Moreover, the original DE, and its self-adaptive variant jDE [15], were hybridized with the NS to obtain NS in DE (nDE) and NS in jDE (njDE) algorithms, respectively. Indeed, the proposed algorithms are not embodied into hardware. Because searching for novelties in the behavior space is not possible, we assume that the points in this space are collapsed with points in the original search space. All algorithms used in our study were applied to the CEC-2014 benchmark suite. Thus, our motivation was to show that the new algorithms, with maintaining the higher population diversity, can improve the results of their original counterparts. Additionally, the results of the hybrid algorithms were compared with other state-of-the-art algorithms, like L-Shade [16] (the winner of the CEC-2014 Competition on Real-Parameter Single Objective) and MVMO [17], in order to show that they could be comparable also with these.

The structure of the remainder of the paper is as follows. Section 2 refers to highlighting the background information. A description of Novelty DEs are presented in Sect. 3. The results of experiments are illustrated in Sect. 4. Summarization of the performed work is the subject of the last section.

2   Background Information

2.1   Differential Evolution

DE belongs to the class of stochastic nature-inspired population-based algorithms and is appropriate for solving continuous as well as discrete optimization problems. DE was introduced by Storn and Price in 1995 [14] and since then many DE variants have been proposed. The original DE algorithm is represented by real-valued vectors and support operators, such as mutation, crossover, and selection.

In the basic mutation, two solutions are selected randomly and their scaled difference is added to the third solution, as follows:

$$\mathbf{u}_i^{(t)} = \mathbf{x}_{r0}^{(t)} + F \cdot (\mathbf{x}_{r1}^{(t)} - \mathbf{x}_{r2}^{(t)}), \text{ for } i = 1 \ldots NP, \tag{1}$$

where $F \in [0.1, 1.0]$ denotes the scaling factor that scales the rate of modification, while NP represents the population size and $r0$, $r1$, $r2$ are randomly selected values in the interval $1 \ldots NP$. Note that the proposed interval of values for parameter F was enforced in the DE community, although Price and Storn proposed the slightly different interval, i.e., $F \in [0.0, 2.0]$.

DE employs a binomial (denoted as 'bin') or exponential (denoted as 'exp') crossover. The trial vector is built from parameter values copied from either the mutant vector generated by Eq. (1) or parent at the same index position laid i-th vector. Mathematically, this crossover can be expressed as follows:

$$w_{i,j}^{(t)} = u_{i,j}^{(t)} x_{i,j}^{(t)} \tag{2}$$

where $CR \in [0.0, 1.0]$ controls the fraction of parameters that are copied to the trial solution. The condition $j = j_{rand}$ ensures that the trial vector differs from the original solution $\mathbf{x}_i^{(t)}$ in at least one element.

Mathematically, the selection can be expressed as follows:

$$\mathbf{x}_i^{(t+1)} = \begin{cases} \mathbf{w}_i^{(t)} & \text{if } f(\mathbf{w}_i^{(t)}) \leq f(\mathbf{x}_i^{(t)}), \\ \mathbf{x}_i^{(t)} & \text{otherwise.} \end{cases} \tag{3}$$

The selection is usually called 'one-to-one', because trial and corresponding vector laid on i-th position in the population compete for surviving in the next generation. However, the better according to the fitness function will survive.

Crossover and mutation can be performed in several ways in DE. Therefore, a specific notation was introduced to describe the varieties of these methods (also strategies), in general. For example, 'rand/1/bin' denotes that the base vector is randomly selected, 1 vector difference is added to it, and the number of modified parameters in the trial/offspring vector follows a binomial distribution.

2.2   jDE Algorithm

In 2006, Brest et al. [15] proposed an effective DE variant (jDE), where control parameters are self-adapted during the run. In this case, two parameters namely, scale factor F and crossover rate CR are added to the representation of every individual and undergo acting the variation operators. As a result, the individual in jDE is represented as follows:

$$\mathbf{x}_i^{(t)} = (x_{i,1}^{(t)}, x_{i,2}^{(t)}, ..., x_{i,D}^{(t)}, F_i^{(t)}, CR_i^{(t)}).$$

The jDE modifies parameters F and CR according to the following equations:

$$F_i^{(t+1)} = \begin{cases} F_l + \text{rand}_1 * (F_u - F_l) & \text{if } \text{rand}_2 < \tau_1, \\ F_i^{(t)} & \text{otherwise,} \end{cases} \tag{4}$$

$$CR_i^{(t+1)} = \begin{cases} \text{rand}_3 & \text{if } \text{rand}_4 < \tau_2, \\ CR_i^{(t)} & \text{otherwise,} \end{cases} \tag{5}$$

where: $\text{rand}_{i=1...4} \in [0,1]$ are randomly generated values drawn from uniform distribution in interval $[0,1]$, τ_1 and τ_2 are learning steps, F_l and F_u lower and upper bound for parameter F, respectively.

2.3   Novelty Search

NS measures the distance between each individual in a population and its k-th nearest neighbors in behavior space, in other words [3]:

$$\rho(\mathbf{x}) = \frac{1}{k} \sum_{i=1}^{k} dist(\mathbf{x}, \boldsymbol{\mu}_i), \tag{6}$$

where $\boldsymbol{\mu}_i$ is the i-th nearest neighbor of $\mathbf{x}$ with respect to the behavior distance metric $dist$.

Parameter k is a problem dependent, and must be determined by the developer experimentally. However, the same is also valid for selecting the distance metric. In general, the NS is weakly defined and leaves it to the developer's imagination as to how to tailor the search so that the results are as good as possible [5].

3   Novelty Differential Evolution

Novelty DE (nDE) is hybridization of the original DE with NS. Primarily, two main changes are demanded by the DE: (1) To implement the NS and (2) To adjust a DE population scheme suitably. The one-to-one selection evaluating trial solutions according to the problem-specific objective function is not suitable for evaluating the same solution also according to the second objective. Indeed, introducing the NS namely demands evaluation of solutions according to two conflicting objectives and, thus, changes the single-objective DE into the multi-objective.

The new population scheme acts as follows. Simultaneously to the traditional selection, a mating pool is created, into which trial vectors are archived in two ways. When the trial solution with higher fitness compared with the corresponding parent is found, then the parent is normally replaced, while the trial is stored on the first free position from top to bottom of the mating pool. In contrast, when a trial fitness is lower, the trial solution is not eliminated, but stored in the first free position from bottom to top of the mating pool. Finally, the mating pool is divided into two parts, i.e., the higher presents a set of survivors and the lower the set of novelties.

The NS in DE operates as follows. For each novelty solution, the k-th nearest neighbors are selected from the set of survivors. Then, the distance, $dist$, is calculated according to the following equation:

$$dist(\mathbf{x}_i, \mathbf{x}_j) = \begin{cases} \frac{d(\mathbf{x}_i, \mathbf{x}_j)}{\sigma_{sh}}, & d(\mathbf{x}_i, \mathbf{x}_j) > \sigma_{sh}, \\ 0, & \text{otherwise,} \end{cases} \tag{7}$$

where $d(\mathbf{x}_i, \mathbf{x}_j)$ denotes a Euclidean distance between vectors $\mathbf{x}_i$ and $\mathbf{x}_j)$ and, σ_{sh} determines the distance needed for recognizing the novelty solution. The pseudo-code of the NS algorithm is illustrated in Algorithm 1.

Algorithm 1. The NC within the DE algorithm

1: **procedure** NOVELTY SEARCH
2:     $A = \{\forall \mathbf{x}_i : f(\mathbf{x})_i < f(\mathbf{x}_j) \wedge i \neq j\}$;   // set of survivor solutions
3:     $B = \{\forall \mathbf{x}_i : f(\mathbf{x})_i \geq f(\mathbf{x}_j) \wedge i \neq j\}$;   // set of eliminated solutions
4:     **if** $|A| < k$ **then**   // number of survivor solutions less than the neighborhood?
5:         $A = A \cup B$;   // increases the neighborhood set to the whole population
6:     **end if**
7:     $\forall \mathbf{x}_i \in B : \exists \mathcal{N}(\mathbf{x}_i) : \mathbf{x}_j \in A \wedge i \neq j \wedge |\mathcal{N}(\mathbf{x}_i)| == k$; // select k-nearest neighbors
8:     $\forall \mathbf{x}_i \in B : \exists \rho(\mathbf{x}_i)$;   // calculate their novelty values
9:     $C = \{\forall \mathbf{x}_i, \mathbf{x}_j \in B : \rho(\mathbf{x}_i) > \rho(\mathbf{x}_j) \wedge i \neq j \wedge |C| \leq ReplSize\}$;
10: **end procedure**

Let us notice that the NS is launched as the last operator in the traditional DE evolution cycle and, thus, affects the complexity of the original DE substantially. Moreover, the nDE introduces two new parameters: (1) Learning rate parameter $\tau_3 \in [0, 1]$ that controls how often the NS is applied within DE, and (2) Replacement size $ReplSize \in [1, Np]$ that limits the number of novelty solutions. The same as for nDE is also valid for the njDE algorithm.

4   Results

The original DE is known as a good global optimizer insensitive to get stuck into a local optima. Therefore, the primary challenge of this study was to show that the behavior of this algorithm can be improved by using the NS. In line with this, wide analysis was performed of the results of various algorithms that were obtained on the CEC 14 Benchmark function suite. This consists of 30 shifted and rotated functions that are hard enough to represent troubles for the majority of the optimization algorithms. Due to the paper limit, we are focused only on representation of the results obtained by optimizing the functions of dimension $D = 10$.

The goals of our experimental work were two-fold: (1) To find the optimal parameter settings for NC in nDE and njDE, and (2) To show that both hybridized algorithms improve the results of their counterparts, and that these are also comparable with the other state-of-the-art algorithms, like L-Shade and MVMO. The parameter settings of algorithms as proposed in literature [14,15] are taken into consideration in our tests, while the population size was $NP = 100$, and 25 independent runs were launched per instance.

The results of the best run of the njDE as found during the experimental work are illustrated in Table 1. Finding the optimal parameter setting is a hard task that demands a lot of experimental work. In our case, four NC parameters were considered with their corresponding domain of values, as follows: $ReplSize \in \{1, 2, 5, 10, 20, 50\}$, $\sigma_{sh} \in \{40, 50, 60\}$, $k \in \{5, 10, 15, 20, 30, 50\}$, $\tau_3 \in \{.1, 2, .3, .4, .5\}$. In summary, we optimized $6 \times 3 \times 7 \times 5 = 630$ instances per hybrid algorithm or $630 \times 2 = 1,260$ per both algorithms. The optimal values of the parameter for nDE are as follows: $ReplSize = 20$, $\sigma_{sh} = 40$, and $k = 30$, while for njDE as follows: $ReplSize = 50$, $\sigma_{sh} = 40$, and $k = 10$. The learning rate τ_3 depends on the σ_{sh}, i.e.: when σ_{sh} is smaller, the learning rate is also lower

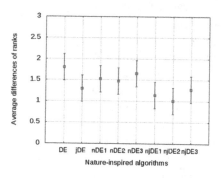

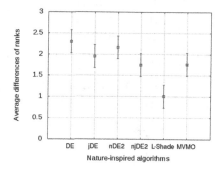

Fig. 1. Different DE-variants

Fig. 2. State-of-the-art comparison

(i.e., $\tau_3 = \{.1, .2\}$), while, when it is bigger, the learning rate can also be higher (i.e., $\tau_3 = \{.4, .5\}$). These results were obtained using the Friedman non-parametric tests. The best results obtained by hybrid DE algorithms are illustrated in Figs. 1 and 2. From the Fig. 1, it can be seen that our assumptions, set at the beginning of the section, are justified. This means, the best nDE variants, i.e., nDE1, nDE2, and nDE3 using $\sigma_{sh} = 40$, $\sigma_{sh} = 50$, and $\sigma_{sh} = 60$ outperformed the results of the original DE, while the best njDE variants are better than their original jDE counterpart. The Fig. 2 shows that the results of njDE2 are also comparable with the results of the state-of-the-art algorithms, like L-Shade and MVMO.

Table 1. Results of the njDE ($ReplSize = 50$, $\sigma_{sh} = 40$, $k = 25$, $\tau_3 = 0.1$).

Func.	Best	Worst	Mean	Median	Std
1	0	2.06E−11	9.61E−13	2.84E−14	4.10E−12
2	0	0	0	0	0
3	0	0	0	0	0
4	0	3.48E+01	2.82E+01	3.48E+01	1.35E+01
5	2.01E+01	2.03E+01	2.02E+01	2.02E+01	3.90E−02
6	0	5.20E−02	2.16E−03	0	1.04E−02
7	0	4.15E−02	1.35E−02	1.19E−02	1.12E−02
8	0	0	0	0	0
9	4.27E+00	9.79E+00	6.86E+00	6.79E+00	1.42E+00
10	0	1.54E+01	2.39E+00	6.25E−02	5.00E+00
11	1.57E+02	5.49E+02	3.77E+02	3.75E+02	1.01E+02
12	5.20E−01	9.27E−01	7.44E−01	7.68E−01	1.16E−01
13	6.77E−02	2.00E−01	1.41E−01	1.45E−01	2.99E−02
14	1.08E−01	3.03E−01	1.89E−01	1.86E−01	4.46E−02
15	7.47E−01	1.26E+00	9.73E−01	9.43E−01	1.38E−01
16	1.73E+00	2.66E+00	2.21E+00	2.22E+00	2.67E−01
17	4.45E−01	6.71E+01	1.60E+01	1.18E+01	1.47E+01
18	6.83E−02	2.81E+00	1.27E+00	8.72E−01	8.95E−01
19	1.62E−01	7.45E−01	3.84E−01	3.62E−01	1.22E−01
20	1.64E−02	3.99E−01	2.25E−01	2.29E−01	9.21E−02
21	3.51E−02	1.61E+00	4.89E−01	3.71E−01	4.09E−01
22	4.76E−02	5.94E+00	9.63E−01	3.05E−01	1.43E+00
23	3.29E+02	3.29E+02	3.29E+02	3.29E+02	2.32E−13
24	1.09E+02	1.17E+02	1.13E+02	1.12E+02	2.08E+00
25	1.00E+02	2.01E+02	1.51E+02	1.39E+02	3.49E+01
26	1.00E+02	1.00E+02	1.00E+02	1.00E+02	2.99E−02
27	1.61E+00	3.57E+02	8.79E+01	2.39E+00	1.41E+02
28	3.69E+02	3.81E+02	3.73E+02	3.69E+02	4.76E+00
29	2.22E+02	2.24E+02	2.23E+02	2.23E+02	7.33E−01
30	4.62E+02	5.13E+02	4.71E+02	4.63E+02	1.51E+01

5   Conclusion

Nature-inspired algorithms have gained a new momentum, with huge development of ER and SR. This so-called nature-inspired robotics demands embodying these algorithms into hardware, where they act as an autonomous artificial agents. New problems have arisen by moving them into the hardware, where the selection pressure is one of the topical issues. The higher selection pressure affects losing population diversity that is a prerequisite for the open-ended evolution and Alife. The NS presents one of the fundamental solutions for preserving the population diversity, because it introduces an additional measure for evaluating the individual's quality beside the fitness function.

In our study, the NS was applied within the DE to improve its behavior in the sense of getting stuck into local optima and fitness function deception. Thus, two versions of Novelty DE were developed, i.e., nDE and njDE. The results on the CEC-14 Benchmark function suite showed that both the hybridized DE algorithms improve the results of their original counterparts. Moreover, the results of these algorithms are comparable with the results of the other state-of-the-art algorithms.

As the future work, finishing experiments on the higher dimensional functions remains in first place. Additionally, the impact of the NS on the multi-agent systems based on DE could become a big challenge direction.

References

1. Eiben, A.E., Smith, J.E.: From evolutionary computation to the evolution of things. Nature **521**(7553), 476–482 (2015)
2. Nelson, A.L.: Embodied artificial life at an impasse can evolutionary robotics methods be scaled? In: 2014 IEEE Symposium on Evolving and Autonomous Learning Systems (EALS), Orlando, FL, pp. 25–34 (2014)
3. Lehman, J., Stanley, K.O.: Exploiting open-endedness to solve problems through the search for novelty. In: Proceedings of the Eleventh International Conference on Artificial Life (ALIFE XI), pp. 329–336. MIT Press, Cambridge (2008)
4. Gomes, J., Mariano, P., Christensen, A.L.: Devising effective novelty search algorithms: a comprehensive empirical study. In: Silva, S. (ed.) Proccedings of the 2015 Annual Conference on Genetic and Evolutionary Computation (GECCO 2015), pp. 943–950. ACM, New York (2015)
5. Doncieux, S., Mouret, J.B.: Behavioral diversity measures for evolutionary robotics. In: IEEE Congress on Evolutionary Computation, Barcelona, pp. 1–8 (2010)
6. Doncieux, S., Mouret, J.B.: Beyond black-box optimization: a review of selective pressures for evolutionary robotics. Evol. Intell. **7**(2), 71–93 (2014)
7. Lynch, M.: The evolution of genetic networks by non-adaptive processes. Nat. Rev. Genet. **8**, 803–813 (2007)
8. Deb, K.: Multi-Objective Optimization Using Evolutionary Algorithms. Wiley, New York (2001)
9. Gomes, J., Mariano, P., Christensen, A.L.: Avoiding convergence in cooperative coevolution with novelty search. In: Proceedings of the 2014 International Conference on Autonomous Agents and Multi-agent Systems (AAMAS 2014), pp. 1149–1156. International Foundation for Autonomous Agents and Multiagent Systems, Richland, SC (2014)

10. Lehman, J., Stanley, K.O.: Abandoning objectives: evolution through the search for novelty alone. Evol. Comput. **19**, 189–223 (2011)
11. Liapis, A., Yannakakis, G.N., Togelius, J.: Constrained novelty search: a study on game content generation. Evol. Comput. **23**, 101–129 (2015)
12. Standish, R.K.: Open-ended artificial evolution. Int. J. Comput. Intell. Appl. **3**(2), 167–175 (2003)
13. Naredo, E., Trujillo, L.: Searching for novel clustering programs. In: Blum, C. (ed.) Proceedings of the 15th Annual Conference on Genetic and Evolutionary Computation (GECCO 2013), pp. 1093–1100. ACM, New York (2013)
14. Storn, R., Price, K.: Differential evolution: a simple and efficient heuristic for global optimization over continuous spaces. J. Global Optim. **11**(4), 341–359 (1997)
15. Brest, J., Greiner, S., Bošković, B., Mernik, M., Žumer, V.: Self-adapting control parameters in differential evolution: a comparative study on numerical benchmark problems. IEEE Trans. Evol. Comput. **10**(6), 646–657 (2006)
16. Tanabe, R., Fukunaga, A.S.: Improving the search performance of SHADE using linear population size reduction. In: IEEE Congress on Evolutionary Computation (CEC), 2014, Beijing, pp. 1658–1665 (2014)
17. Erlich, I., Rueda, J.L., Wildenhues, S., Shewarega, F.: Evaluating the mean-variance mapping optimization on the IEEE-CEC 2014 test suite. In: 2014 IEEE Congress on Evolutionary Computation (CEC), Beijing, pp. 1625–1632 (2014)

Interplay of Two Bat Algorithm Robotic Swarms in Non-cooperative Target Point Search

Patricia Suárez[1], Akemi Gálvez[1,2], Iztok Fister[3], Iztok Fister Jr.[3],
Eneko Osaba[4], Javier Del Ser[4,5,6], and Andrés Iglesias[1,2(✉)]

[1] University of Cantabria, Avenida de los Castros s/n, 39005 Santander, Spain
iglesias@unican.es
[2] Toho University, 2-2-1 Miyama, Funabashi 274-8510, Japan
[3] University of Maribor, Smetanova, Maribor, Slovenia
[4] TECNALIA, Derio, Spain
[5] University of the Basque Country (UPV/EHU), Bilbao, Spain
[6] Basque Center for Applied Mathematics (BCAM), Bilbao, Spain
http://personales.unican.es/iglesias

Abstract. In this paper, we analyze the interplay of two robotic swarms applied to solve a target point search in a non-cooperative mode. In particular, we consider the case of two identical robotic swarms deployed within the same environment to perform dynamic exploration seeking for two different unknown target points. It is assumed that the environment is unknown and completely dark, so no vision sensors can be used. Our work is based on a robotic swarm approach recently reported in the literature. In that approach, the robotic units are driven by a popular swarm intelligence technique called bat algorithm. This technique is based on echolocation with ultrasounds, so it is particularly well suited for our problem. The paper discusses the main findings of our computational experiments through three illustrative videos of single executions.

Keywords: Swarm intelligence · Swarm robotics · Bat algorithm

1 Introduction

A recent trend in swarm robotics (SR) is the use of multiple robotic swarms operating simultaneously within the same environment [1]. The most common case in the literature and real-life applications is the *cooperative mode*, defined by the cooperation among swarms to achieve a common goal. In contrast, little attention has been given so far in the literature to the *non-cooperative case*, where each swarm tries to solve its own goals with little (or none at all) consideration to any other factor external to the swarm (e.g., other swarms' goals). Note however that this non-cooperative case also arises in some practical applications. Aimed at filling this gap, in this work we focus on the behavioral pattern of robotic swarms under this non-cooperative regime.

© Springer International Publishing AG, part of Springer Nature 2018
J. Bajo et al. (Eds.): PAAMS 2018 Workshops, CCIS 887, pp. 543–550, 2018.
https://doi.org/10.1007/978-3-319-94779-2_47

In particular, in this work we consider the case of two robotic swarms $\mathcal{S}_1$ and $\mathcal{S}_2$ comprised by a set of μ and ν robotic units $\mathcal{S}_1 = \{r_1^i\}_{i=1,\ldots,\mu}$, $\mathcal{S}_2 = \{r_2^j\}_{j=1,\ldots,\nu}$, respectively. For simplicity, we can assume that $\mu = \nu$ and that all robotic units are identical, i.e., $r_1^i = r_2^j$, $\forall i, j$. These robotic units are deployed within the same environment $\Omega \subset \mathbb{R}^3$ to perform dynamic exploration. We assume that the geometry of Ω is unknown to the robots and completely dark, so any vision sensor becomes useless to the robots. The goal of each swarm $\mathcal{S}_k$ is find a static target point $\mathbf{\Phi}_k$ $(k = 1, 2)$, placed in a certain (unknown) location of the environment. We assume that $||\mathbf{\Phi}_1 - \mathbf{\Phi}_2|| > \delta$ for a certain threshold value $\delta > 0$, meaning that both target points are not very close to each other so as to broaden the spectrum of possible interactions between the swarms. Although the environment is a 3D world, we consider the case of mobile walking robots moving on a two-dimensional map $\mathcal{M} = \Omega|_{z=0}$.

Regarding the artificial intelligence method, there are several possibilities to build a robotic swarm under these constraints [1]. In this paper, we focus on a powerful bio-inspired swarm intelligence approach called *bat algorithm*. This choice is very natural as this algorithm is based on the echolocation behavior of some species of microbats living in dark environments such as caves, thus meeting our previous assumptions. This algorithm has shown to be very effective to address difficult continuous optimization problems involving a large number of variables [2,3,7], including the efficient navigation in dynamic indoor environments [4,5]. A recent paper describes a physical and computational implementation of a swarm of bat algorithm-based robotic units. Such implementation is fully specialized in the sense that all components of the robots are designed and fully optimized to replicate the most relevant features of the real microbats and the bat algorithm as faithfully as possible [6]. This work is based on that approach. In fact, the physical robots, shown in Fig. 1, are already built according to the implementation described in [6]. However, since in this paper we are interested in the computational features, our description will be based on computer simulations exclusively. To this aim, the physical robots are replaced by their digital models, shown in Fig. 2.

The structure of this paper is as follows: in Sect. 2 we provide a gentle overview about the bat algorithm. Our SR approach for non-cooperative target point search is described in Sect. 3 and illustrated using two independent robotic swarms in Sect. 4. The paper closes with the conclusions and some plans for future work in the field.

2   The Bat Algorithm

The *bat algorithm* is a bio-inspired swarm intelligence algorithm originally proposed by Yang in 2010 to solve optimization problems [7–9]. The algorithm is based on the echolocation behavior of microbats, which use a type of sonar called *echolocation*, with varying pulse rates of emission and loudness, to detect prey, avoid obstacles, and locate their roosting crevices in the dark [10]. The idealization of the echolocation of microbats is as follows:

Fig. 1. Physical robots of the two robotic swarms in red and yellow, respectively. (Color figure online)

Fig. 2. Graphical models of the robots in Fig. 1.

1. Bats use echolocation to sense distance and distinguish between food, prey and background barriers.
2. Each virtual bat flies randomly with a velocity $\mathbf{v}_i$ at position (solution) $\mathbf{x}_i$ with a fixed frequency f_{min}, varying wavelength λ and loudness A_0 to search for prey. As it searches and finds its prey, it changes wavelength (or frequency) of their emitted pulses and adjust the rate of pulse emission r, depending on the proximity of the target.
3. It is assumed that the loudness will vary from an (initially large and positive) value A_0 to a minimum constant value A_{min}.

Some additional assumptions are advisable for further efficiency. For instance, we assume that the frequency f evolves on a bounded interval $[f_{min}, f_{max}]$. This means that the wavelength λ is also bounded, because f and λ are related to each other by the fact that the product $\lambda.f$ is constant. For practical reasons, it is also convenient that the largest wavelength is chosen such that it is comparable to the size of the domain of interest (the search space for optimization problems). For simplicity, we can assume that $f_{min} = 0$, so $f \in [0, f_{max}]$. The rate of pulse can simply be in the range $r \in [0, 1]$, where 0 means no pulses at all, and 1 means the maximum rate of pulse emission. With these idealized rules indicated above, the basic pseudo-code of the bat algorithm is shown in Algorithm 1. Basically, the algorithm considers an initial population of $\mathcal{P}$ individuals (bats). Each bat,

Require: (Initial Parameters)
    Population size: $\mathcal{P}$; Maximum number of generations: $\mathcal{G}_{max}$; Loudness: $\mathcal{A}$
    Pulse rate: r; Maximum frequency: f_{max}; Dimension of the problem: d
    Objective function: $\phi(\mathbf{x})$, with $\mathbf{x} = (x_1, \ldots, x_d)^T$; Random number: $\theta \in U(0,1)$
1:   $g \leftarrow 0$
2:   Initialize the bat population $\mathbf{x}_i$ and $\mathbf{v}_i$, $(i = 1, \ldots, n)$
3:   Define pulse frequency f_i at $\mathbf{x}_i$
4:   Initialize pulse rates r_i and loudness $\mathcal{A}_i$
5:   **while** $g < \mathcal{G}_{max}$ **do**
6:      **for** $i = 1$ **to** $\mathcal{P}$ **do**
7:         Generate new solutions by using Eqs. (1)–(3)
8:         **if** $\theta > r_i$ **then**
9:            $\mathbf{s}^{best} \leftarrow \mathbf{s}^g$ //select the best current solution
10:           $\mathbf{ls}^{best} \leftarrow \mathbf{ls}^g$ //generate a local solution around $\mathbf{s}^{best}$
11:         **end if**
12:         Generate a new solution by local random walk
13:         **if** $\theta < \mathcal{A}_i$ *and* $\phi(\mathbf{x_i}) < \phi(\mathbf{x}^*)$ **then**
14:            Accept new solutions, increase r_i and decrease $\mathcal{A}_i$
15:         **end if**
16:      **end for**
17:     $g \leftarrow g + 1$
18: **end while**
19: Rank the bats and find current best $\mathbf{x}^*$
20: **return** $\mathbf{x}^*$

Algorithm 1: Bat algorithm pseudocode

representing a potential solution of the optimization problem, has a location $\mathbf{x}_i$ and velocity $\mathbf{v}_i$. The algorithm initializes these variables with random values within the search space. Then, the pulse frequency, pulse rate, and loudness are computed for each individual bat. Then, the swarm evolves in a discrete way over generations, like time instances until the maximum number of generations, $\mathcal{G}_{max}$, is reached. For each generation g and each bat, new frequency, location and velocity are computed according to the following evolution equations:

$$f_i^g = f_{min}^g + \beta(f_{max}^g - f_{min}^g) \tag{1}$$

$$\mathbf{v}_i^g = \mathbf{v}_i^{g-1} + [\mathbf{x}_i^{g-1} - \mathbf{x}^*]\, f_i^g \tag{2}$$

$$\mathbf{x}_i^g = \mathbf{x}_i^{g-1} + \mathbf{v}_i^g \tag{3}$$

where $\beta \in [0,1]$ follows the random uniform distribution, and $\mathbf{x}^*$ represents the current global best location (solution), which is obtained through evaluation of the objective function at all bats and ranking of their fitness values. The superscript $(.)^g$ is used to denote the current generation g. The best current solution and a local solution around it are probabilistically selected according to some given criteria. Then, search is intensified by a local random walk. For this local search, once a solution is selected among the current best solutions,

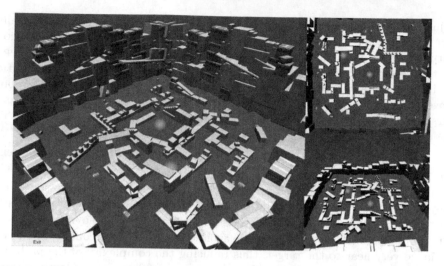

Fig. 3. Three different views of the graphical environment at initialization stage.

it is perturbed locally through a random walk of the form: $\mathbf{x}_{new} = \mathbf{x}_{old} + \epsilon \mathcal{A}^g$, where ϵ is a uniform random number on $[-1, 1]$ and $\mathcal{A}^g =< \mathcal{A}_i^g >$, is the average loudness of all the bats at generation g. If the new solution achieved is better than the previous best one, it is probabilistically accepted depending on the value of the loudness. In that case, the algorithm increases the pulse rate and decreases the loudness (lines 13–16). This process is repeated for the given number of generations. In general, the loudness decreases once a bat finds its prey (in our analogy, once a new best solution is found), while the rate of pulse emission decreases. For simplicity, the following values are commonly used: $\mathcal{A}_0 = 1$ and $\mathcal{A}_{min} = 0$, assuming that this latter value means that a bat has found the prey and temporarily stop emitting any sound. The evolution rules for loudness and pulse rate are as: $\mathcal{A}_i^{g+1} = \alpha \mathcal{A}_i^g$ and $r_i^{g+1} = r_i^0[1 - exp(-\gamma g)]$ where α and γ are constants. Note that for any $0 < \alpha < 1$ and any $\gamma > 0$ we have: $\mathcal{A}_i^g \to 0$, $r_i^g \to r_i^0$ as $g \to \infty$. Generally, each bat should have different values for loudness and pulse emission rate, which can be achieved by randomization. To this aim, we can take an initial loudness $\mathcal{A}_i^0 \in (0, 2)$ while the initial emission rate r_i^0 can be any value in the interval $[0, 1]$. Loudness and emission rates will be updated only if the new solutions are improved, an indication that the bats are moving towards the optimal solution.

3 Bat Algorithm Method for the Robotic Swarms

In this paper we consider the synthetic closed environment shown in Fig. 3. The figure is split into three parts for better visualization, corresponding to two side view cameras from different locations and a top view camera. The scene consists of a collection of cardboard boxes stacked in a messy way and forming challenging structures for the robots such as corridors, tunnels, dead ends, bifurcations,

T-junctions, and the like. Although the robots of the two swarms are functionally identical, they are depicted in red and yellow color respectively for visualization purposes. Two blue spherical-shaped points of light mark the target points Φ_k for the two robotic swarms. As explained above, the goal of each robotic swarm $\mathcal{S}_k$ is to find its corresponding target point Φ_k. In our approach, each robot moves autonomously, according to the current values of its fitness function and parameters, and communicates them to the other members of the swarm. To this aim, each virtual robot r_k^i is described at time instance j by a vector $\Xi_k^{i,j} = \left\{ f_k^{i,j}, \mathbf{x}_k^{i,j}, \mathbf{v}_k^{i,j} \right\}$, where $f_k^{i,j}$, $\mathbf{x}_k^{i,j} = (x_k^{i,j}, y_k^{i,j})$ and $\mathbf{v}_{i,j} = (v_{k,x}^{i,j}, v_{k,y}^{i,j})$ represent the fitness value, position, and velocity, respectively. The robots are deployed at initial random positions $\mathbf{x}_k^{i,0}$ and with random velocities $\mathbf{v}_k^{i,0}$ provided that they are restricted to move within the map $\mathcal{M}$. However, opposed to the usual procedure in swarm intelligence methods, we refrain from deploying the robots randomly within all the search space to avoid that some robots could accidentally initialize very near to the target, thus reducing the complexity of the problem. For instance, as shown in Fig. 3, the robots are initialized at random positions in the outermost parts of the map. For the robots motion, we assume that $\mathcal{M}$ is described by a tessellation of convex polygons $\mathcal{T}_\mathcal{M}$. Then, we consider the set $\mathcal{N}_\mathcal{M} \subset \mathcal{T}_\mathcal{M}$ (called the *navigation mesh*) comprised by all polygons that are fully traversable by the robots. At time j the fitness function $f_k^{i,j}$ can be defined as the distance between the current position $\mathbf{x}_k^{i,j}$ and the target point Φ_k, measured on $\mathcal{N}_\mathcal{M}$ as $f_k^{i,j} = ||\mathbf{x}_k^{i,j} - \Phi_k||_{\mathcal{N}_\mathcal{M}}$ so our problem consists of minimizing the value of $f_k^{i,j}$, $\forall i, j, k$. This minimization problem is solved through the bat algorithm described in Sect. 2.

A critical issue when working with swarm intelligence techniques is the parameter tuning, which is well-known to be problem-dependent. Our choice has been fully empirical. For computational efficiency, we set the population size to 9 robots for each swarm, as larger values increase the number of collisions among robots and, hence, the computational time. The initial and minimum loudness and parameter α are set to 0.5, 0, and 0.6, respectively. We also set the initial pulse rate and parameter γ to 0.5 and 0.4, respectively. However, our results do not change significantly when varying these values slightly. All executions are performed until all robots reach the target point, no matter the number of iterations needed for completion. Our method has been implemented in *Unity 5* on a 3.8 GHz quad-core Intel Core i5, with 16 GB of DDR3 memory, and a graphical card AMD RX580 with 8 GB VRAM. All programming code in this paper has been created in *JavaScript* using the *Visual Studio* programming framework.

4   Experimental Results

Our approach has been tested for many random initial locations of the robots in the scene. Only three of them is described here because of limitations of space, corresponding to three videos submitted as accompanying material. As above mentioned, the robots are initialized at the outermost parts of the scene, where the red and yellow swarms are randomly intertwined. Then, the bat algorithm starts and both swarms try to reach their corresponding target points, located in the middle of the central square of the scene for the yellow swarm and in a corner of the first ring around that square for the red swarm. The movement of the robots is driven by the bat algorithm but also affected by three factors: the complex and irregular geometry of the scene, the collisions with robots of the other swarm and their own, and the fact that the map is unknown to the robots. The later fact is clearly visible in *Video 1* (seconds 14–16), when a yellow robot crosses the central square on one side without realizing that is near to the target point. However, at seconds 20–22 two other yellow robots reach the central square just at the center, so they are actually very near to the target. At that point, one of them becomes the current best, attracting the other members of the swarm over the iterations. Note also that, owing to the echolocation, the robots can detect static obstacles and other robots before they collide, thus avoiding crashing. In those cases, the robots move rapidly wandering to the left and right, occasionally multiple times, trying to overcome the obstacle (see, for instance, the red robots in bottom corner of main window at seconds 5–9). This also explains why the robots are constantly moving, even after reaching the target point, as they are trying to avoid colliding with other members of the swarm. In some cases this leads to very crowded formations such as the contact-less scrummage-like in seconds 16–19, where several robots from both swarms gathering at a specific location try to avoid multiple collisions simultaneously.

We remark the ability of the robots to avoid the collisions and move forward towards the target, showing the good performance of the bat algorithm for this task. This fact becomes even more evident in *Video 2*, where all yellow robots get trapped by the red robots in a dead end in the neighborhood of the target point of the red swarm for seconds 28–45, until one of the yellow robots eventually finds a way to escape, dragging the rest of the swarm in its movement towards its own target point. The yellow robots are leaving the dead end one by one until the last yellow robot, still trapped by five red robots (seconds 68–79) is able to circumvent the red swarm and leaves the area. At their turn, these five red robots find troubles to reach the target point (even when the other four members are already there) due to their particular orientation facing each other, thus preventing them from moving forward for a while. Finally, *Video 3* shows one of the rare examples of the robotic swarms able to reach their target points with minimal interaction between the swarms.

5   Conclusions and Future Work

In this paper, we discuss some behavioral patterns found from the interplay of two robotic swarms coexisting in the same environment and following a non-cooperative approach when trying to reach their individual goals. To this aim, we consider two robotic swarms driven by the bat algorithm and moving in an unknown closed environment. As shown in the videos, the bat algorithm allows the robotic swarms that got trapped to move away while simultaneously avoiding to collide with the other robots, finding their targets in reasonable time.

In addition to the previous results, we found many other behavioral patterns for the robotic swarms. For instance, a qualitatively different behavioral pattern can be seen for the yellow robot nearest to the target point of the red swarm in seconds 21–31 of *Video 1*, when the robot stops moving while waiting for the red robots to gather around their target point and free the path to this robot to join its own swarm. Other patterns that we observed include moving in a formation (usually led by the global best of the swarm), aggregation patterns for intensive exploration near the optima, bifurcation moving patterns for simultaneous exploration and obstacle avoidance, cooperation among robots to force a robot of the other team to move away, and ability to escape from U and V configurations such as dead ends, among others. A full analysis of all these behavioral patterns and replicating these experiments with the physical robotic swarms in real life for comparison are part of our plans for future work in the field.

Acknowledgements. Research supported by: project PDE-GIR of the EU Horizon 2020 research and innovation program, Marie Sklodowska-Curie grant agreement No. 778035; project #TIN2017-89275-R of Agencia Estatal de Investigación and EU Funds FEDER (AEI/FEDER-UE); project #JU12, of SODERCAN and EU Funds FEDER (SODERCAN/FEDER-UE); project EMAITEK of Basque Government.

References

1. Brambilla, M., Ferrante, E., Birattari, M., Dorigo, M.: Swarm robotics: a review from the swarm engineering perspective. Swarm Intell. **7**(1), 1–41 (2013)
2. Iglesias, A., Gálvez, A., Collantes, M.: Multilayer embedded bat algorithm for B-spline curve reconstruction. Integr. Comput. Aided Eng. **24**(4), 385–399 (2017)
3. Iglesias, A., Gálvez, A., Collantes, M.: Iterative sequential bat algorithm for free-form rational Bézier surface reconstruction. Int. J. Bio-Inspired Comput. **11**(1), 1–15 (2018)
4. Suárez, P., Iglesias, A.: Bat algorithm for coordinated exploration in swarm robotics. Adv. Intell. Syst. Comput. **514**, 134–144 (2017)
5. Suárez, P., Gálvez, A., Iglesias, A.: Autonomous coordinated navigation of virtual swarm bots in dynamic indoor environments by bat algorithm. In: Tan, Y., Takagi, H., Shi, Y., Niu, B. (eds.) ICSI 2017. LNCS, vol. 10386, pp. 176–184. Springer, Cham (2017). https://doi.org/10.1007/978-3-319-61833-3_19
6. Suárez, P., Iglesias, A., Gálvez, A.: Make robots be bats: specializing robotic swarms to the bat algorithm. Swarm and Evolutionary Computation (in press). https://doi.org/10.1016/j.swevo.2018.01.005
7. Yang, X.S.: A new metaheuristic bat-inspired algorithm. In: González, J.R., Pelta, D.A., Cruz, C., Terrazas, G., Krasnogor, N. (eds.) NICSO 2010. SCI, vol. 284, pp. 65–74. Springer, Heidelberg (2010). https://doi.org/10.1007/978-3-642-12538-6_6
8. Yang, X.S.: Bat algorithm for multiobjective optimization. Int. J. Bio-Inspired Comput. **3**(5), 267–274 (2011)
9. Yang, X.S., Gandomi, A.H.: Bat algorithm: a novel approach for global engineering optimization. Eng. Comput. **29**(5), 464–483 (2012)
10. Yang, X.S.: Bat algorithm: literature review and applications. Int. J. Bio-Inspired Comput. **5**(3), 141–149 (2013)

Author Index

Printed in the United States
By Bookmasters